Human Rights in the Shadow
of Colonial Violence

PENNSYLVANIA STUDIES IN HUMAN RIGHTS

Bert B. Lockwood, Jr., Series Editor

A complete list of books in the series is available from the publisher.

Human Rights in the Shadow of Colonial Violence

The Wars of Independence in Kenya and Algeria

Fabian Klose

Translated by Dona Geyer

PENN

UNIVERSITY OF PENNSYLVANIA PRESS

PHILADELPHIA

The original edition was published under the title *Menschenrechte im Schatten kolonialer Gewalt. Die Dekolonisierungskriege in Kenia und Algerien 1945–1962* © 2009 by Oldenbourg Wissenschaftsverlag GmbH, Munich

English translation © 2013 University of Pennsylvania Press

The translation of this work was funded by Geisteswissenschaften International—Translation Funding for Humanities and Social Sciences from Germany, a joint initiative of the Fritz Thyssen Foundation, the German Federal Foreign Office, the collecting society VG WORT, and the Börsenverein des Deutschen Buchhandels (German Publishers & Booksellers Association).

Published by
University of Pennsylvania Press
Philadelphia, Pennsylvania 19104-4112
www.upenn.edu/pennpress

Printed in the United States of America on acid-free paper
10 9 8 7 6 5 4 3 2 1

Library of Congress Cataloging-in-Publication Data
Klose, Fabian.
  [Menschenrechte im Schatten kolonialer Gewalt. English]
  Human rights in the shadow of colonial violence : the wars of
independence in Kenya and Algeria / Fabian Klose ; translated by Dona
Geyer. — 1st ed.
    p. cm.— (Pennsylvania studies in human rights)
  English translation of Menschenrechte im Schatten kolonialer Gewalt:
die Dekolonisierungskriege in Kenia und Algerien 1945–1962, published in
2009 by Oldenbourg.
  Includes bibliographical references and index.
  ISBN 978-0-8122-4495-3
  1. Human rights—Kenya. 2. Human rights—Algeria. 3. Kenya—History—
Mau Mau Emergency, 1952-1960. 4. Algeria—History—Revolution,
1954-1962. 5. Great Britain—Colonies—Africa. 6. France—Colonies—
Africa. I. Title. II. Series: Pennsylvania studies in human rights.
  JC599.K4K5613 2013
  965'.046—dc23
                          2012045108

Contents

Abbreviations

ACICR	Archives du Comité International de la Croix-Rouge
AIR	Air Ministry
ALN	Armée de Libération Nationale
AMM	Affaires militaires musulmanes
ANC	African National Congress
ATOM	*The Conduct of Anti-Terrorist Operations in Malaya*
BBC	British Broadcasting Corporation
BRC	British Red Cross
BW	British Council
CAB	Cabinet Office
CAB	Cabinet civil des gouverneurs généraux
CAOM	Centre des archives d'outre-mer
CCE	Comité de Coordination et d'Exécution
CEF	Corps Expéditionnaire Français
CFLN	Comité Français de la Libération Nationale
CIPCG	Centre d'Instruction de Pacification et de Contre-Guérilla
CMI	Centre Militaire d'Internés
CNRA	Conseil National de la Révolution Algérienne
CO	Colonial Office
CRA	Croissant-Rouge Algérien
CRF	Croix-Rouge Française
CRUA	Comité Révolutionnaire d'Unité et d'Action
CSCE	Conference on Security and Co-operation in Europe
CTT	Centre de triage et de transit
DEFE	Ministry of Defence
DO	Dominions Office
DOM-TOM	Départements et Territoires d'Outre-Mer
DOP	Détachements Opérationnels de Protection

DPU   Dispositif de Protection Urbaine
ECHR   European Convention on Human Rights
ECOSOC   Economic and Social Council
ECOSOCOR   Economic and Social Council Official Records
EOKA   Ethniki Organosis Kyprion Agoniston
FIDES   Fonds d'investissement pour le développement économique
            et social
FLN   Front de Libération Nationale
FO   Foreign Office
FRELIMO   Frente de Libertação de Moçambique
FRUS   *Foreign Relations of the United States*
GAOR   General Assembly Official Records
GPRA   Gouvernement Provisoire de la République Algérienne
HMSO   Her Majesty's Stationery Office
ICRC   International Committee of the Red Cross
ILO   International Labor Organization
IMTs   International Military Tribunals
IWM   Imperial War Museum
KAR   King's African Rifles
KASU   Kenya African Study Union
KAU   Kenya African Union
KCA   Kikuyu Central Association
KNIL   Koninklijk Nederlands-Indisch Leger
LO   Law Office
MAE   Ministère des Affaires Étrangères
MLA   Mission de liaison pour les affaires algériennes
MNA   Mouvement National Algérien
MPLA   Movimento Popular de Libertação de Angola
MRLA   Malayan Races Liberation Army
NARA   National Archives and Records Administration, College
            Park, Maryland
NGO   Nongovernmental organization
NUOI   Nations Unies et Organisations Internationales
OAS   Organisation Armée Secrète
OPA   Organisation politico-administrative
OS   Organisation spéciale
PLO   Palestine Liberation Organization
PNI   Partai Nasional Indonesia

PPA	Parti du Peuple Algérien
PREM	Prime Minister's Office
RAF	Royal Air Force
RH	Rhodes House Library
SAS	Section Administrative Spécialisée
SCOR	Security Council Official Records
SHAT	Service Historique de l'Armée de Terre
SS	Schutzstaffel der NSDAP
TNA	The National Archives
UN ARMS	United Nations Archives and Records Management Section, New York
UNHCR	United Nations High Commissioner for Refugees
UNO	United Nations Organization
UNOG	United Nations Office at Geneva, Registry, Records and Archives Unit
WO	War Office
ZAA	Zone Autonome d'Alger

Preface

The focus of research in the area of decolonization—undoubtedly one of the most influential fields in twentieth-century international history—was centered for a long time on depicting the course of events and particularly on analyzing the causes for the end of colonial rule after World War II. This field of research produced only a small number of comprehensive surveys, as opposed to a vast number of individual studies on certain regions and various colonial empires.[1] Ever since the pioneering studies of the British historian John Darwin,[2] one explanatory model for the end of colonial empires has emerged to link together various existing theoretical approaches and has thus become the model generally accepted by most historians. According to this model, decolonization is the result of developments within the ruling metropoles (metropolitan theory), the growth of anticolonial national movements (peripheral theory), and decisive shifts in power relations within the international system (international theory).[3]

Although there is evidence of a growing trend in research that examines transnational factors of decolonization more intensively, the significance of international organizations is still given little attention. Very few studies emphasize the key role of the United Nations as an anticolonial forum where the colonial powers were diplomatically pilloried before the eyes of the world and foreign policy pressure exerted against them.[4] A similar development is observable with regard to the international discourse on human rights. Only the most recent literature on the historiography of the human rights idea has linked decolonization with the debates on universal fundamental rights.[5] Particular mention should be made here of the work by the American historian Paul Gordon Lauren. In his two books *Power and Prejudice: The Politics and Diplomacy of Racial Discrimination* and *The Evolution of International Human Rights: Visions Seen*, Lauren explicitly addresses for the first time the importance of the human rights discourse for the end of colonial rule.[6]

Recently, a still rather limited number of newer studies have appeared that do analyze the connection between the humans rights discourse and the collapse of European colonial empires, of which two deserve special mention, namely, Brian Simpson's *Human Rights and the End of Empire* and especially Roland Burke's *Decolonization and the Evolution of International Human Rights.*[7]

Another area that also played a subordinate role for a long time in academic debates was the history of the various decolonization wars, which not only became "white spots" in the national memory of the former colonial nations but also in the research landscape.[8] The publications in this area confined themselves primarily to providing strictly event and military histories of major individual conflicts, such as in Malaya, Indochina, and Algeria. The first studies to provide overarching and comparative analyses of "contested decolonization" include *The Process of Decolonisation, 1945–1975: The Military Experience in Comparative Perspective* by Jacques van Doorn and Willem J. Hendrix and *The Wars of French Decolonization* by Anthony Clayton.[9] The collected volume of essays resulting from a conference at the Institute for Commonwealth Studies in London and edited by Robert Holland, *Emergencies and Disorder in the European Empires After 1945*, contained not only articles on France's colonial rearguard battles but also a series of contributions on the British conflicts in Malaya, Cyprus, and Kenya, the military operations of the Netherlands in the Dutch East Indies, and Portugal's drawn-out wars against the national independence movements in its African colonial empire.[10] At the colloquium "Décolonisations comparées" in Aix-en-Provence in the fall of 1993, various contributions focused on the comparative aspects of decolonization wars, although the major emphasis was on the French conflict in Indochina.[11] Special mention should be made of the work *Colonial Wars and the Politics of Third World Nationalism*, in which the British sociologist Frank Füredi compares the three British "emergencies" in Malaya, Kenya, and Guyana in order to identify the special relevance of these conflict scenarios for the end of the empire and thereby reaches a conclusion that does more than merely question the British interpretation of "planned decolonization."[12]

With their book *Forgotten Wars: Freedom and Revolution in Southeast Asia*, Christopher Bayly and Tim Harper have produced an impressive study that systematically analyzes the various anticolonial conflicts in Southeast Asia during the immediate postwar period from 1945 to 1950.[13] What remains to be written is a comprehensive comparative study of decolonization wars in the various overseas territories of European powers.

In recent years, an evident trend in international research involving the study of "contested decolonization" has emerged to examine the various forms of unchecked colonial violence.[14] Subjects such as war crimes, the systematic use of torture, and colonial detention camps and relocation measures during the decolonization wars are being pushed more and more into the limelight of scientific interest, whereby a series of publications on the Algerian War have assumed a trailblazing role in this. For example, Rita Maran, an expert in international law, presented the first comprehensive analysis of the discourse on torture in Algeria in her book *Torture: The Role of Ideology in the French-Algerian War*,[15] which was followed by the republication of books on the same topic by the French historian and contemporary Pierre Vidal-Naquet.[16] Finally, in 2001, an excellent dissertation, based on new and extensive source material, was published by Raphaëlle Branche, *La torture et l'armée pendant la guerre d'Algérie*, in which she analyzes the torture system and the role of the French army.[17] Other violent phenomena in the Algerian War, such as the detainment and resettlement measures, also became the subjects of new publications.[18] Moreover, this new research trend has not simply narrowed its focus to French colonial history but expanded its view to include the decolonization wars of other European colonial powers.[19] In 2005, the above-mentioned historical studies on the British Mau Mau War appeared. Whereas Caroline Elkins concentrated primarily on the British detention camps and resettlement measures in her book *Britain's Gulag*, David Anderson examined British repression policy in general and the increased use of the death penalty in particular in his work *Histories of the Hanged*.[20]

Despite the increased scientific interest in this subject, no comprehensive comparative study has yet been written on the unchecked colonial violence in the various conflicts. Furthermore, a connection to the international human rights discourse has not yet been made except in a few places in Rita Maran's book. Therefore, the objective of this study is to close this gap in research at the interface between the history of the human rights idea and a comparative study on the wars of decolonization.

Sources

The constellation of case studies from two different colonial empires in combination with the international human rights discourse led to research both in Great Britain and France as well as at international organizations in Geneva and New York. Therefore, this study is based on a broad spectrum of source material from various international archives and research facilities,[21] whereby the perspective of the metropoles is given the greater emphasis. The political explosiveness of the topic, the unbridled use of violence in the colonies, and the grave human rights abuses linked to that violence were the central reasons why access differed considerably among the various archival inventories and was sometimes made very difficult.

In the case of the Mau Mau War in Kenya, almost no restrictions whatsoever were placed on access to the files of the relevant British ministries, foremost those of the Colonial Office (CO) and the War Office (WO) found in The National Archives (TNA) in Kew. On the basis of this vast resource of source material, the military and political debates among the decision makers both in London and in the colonial government in Nairobi could be reconstructed very well, thereby offering a broad view of the "emergency" from the perspective from the British colonial power. Files from the Foreign Office (FO) added detailed insight into the foreign policy issues involved in the conflict, especially with regard to the international debates on human rights and the position of Great Britain at the United Nations.

In addition to the official papers of the British government, the study also examines a series of publications by British settlers who witnessed the state of emergency and painted a vivid picture of the "colonial situation" and the "emergency mentality."[22] Particularly valuable with reference to such "settler literature" were the inventories at the British Library in London and the Schomburg Center for Research in Black Culture, a leading international research institute in the field of African culture and history located in Harlem, New York. In the Imperial War Museum (IWM) in London, a number of depictions, some previously published, were found in which individual British veterans described their military experiences in repressing the revolt. Subsequent research at the Rhodes House Library (RH) in Oxford also focused on certain individuals who played a key role during the emergency. Valuable facts were gleaned there from, among others, the documents of Arthur Young, who resigned from his post as Commissioner of Police in the East African crown colony in protest against the systematic war crimes committed by his own security forces.

Research on the Algerian War proved much more difficult, due primarily to the restrictive French archival policy in 2004. A law from 3 January 1979, which regulated access to all state archives in France, barred access for sixty years to all documents that involve either the private lives of individuals or the national security and defense interests of France.[23] This regulation and the extremely vague definition of these document groups meant that a series of inventories relating to the Algerian War were still closed to scientific research. Striking is the fact that the files affected by this regulation were particularly those believed to contain information on torture and war crimes, such as the entire inventory of the Commission de sauvegarde des droits et libertés individuels (Commission to Safeguard Individual Rights and Liberties), an official state commission. Although the French prime minister at the time, Lionel Jospin, announced in 2000 a greater opening of the archival inventories pertaining to the Algerian War, such access continued to be problematic. In order to gain the release of any classified dossier, one had to undertake a protracted "procedure de dérogation" with the respective ministry, which only culminated in a release—laden with restrictions—in certain cases.[24] Not until July 2008—following the conclusion of research for this book—was a new French archival law passed that significantly eased access to the inventories relevant to the Algerian War.[25]

Despite the difficult conditions during the research for this study, it nevertheless proved possible to use the main inventories of the various French archives extensively.[26] In the Centre des archives d'outre-mer (CAOM), the colonial archive in Aix-en-Provence, the Fonds territoriaux algérie, Gouvernement général de l'Algérie, Cabinet civil des gouverneurs généraux (CAB) provided an in-depth look at the files of the civilian colonial administration. At the same time, the État des fonds, fonds ministériels, deuxième empire colonial, Ministère d'État chargé des affaires algériennes (81 F 1- 2415) offered a comprehensive overall picture of the French Algerian policy through the papers of the various ministerial offices involved with North African affairs. Barred inventories, such as those of the Commission de sauvegarde, could be offset by the accessible Papiers Robert Delavignette (19 PA). The documents of Robert Delavignette, who was a member of the commission and resigned his post in September 1957 in protest against the passivity of the French government with regard to the systematic use of torture by security forces, provide highly interesting insights.

In Paris, research was concentrated on the inventories of the French military archive in the Château de Vincennes, on the one hand, and of the archives of the French foreign affairs ministry at Quai d'Orsay, on the other. Valuable information was found on various aspects of French warfare in the *Sous-série 1H: Algérie: La dixième région militaire et la guerre d'Algérie, 1945–1967 (1H 109–4881)* of the Service Historique de l'Armée de Terre (SHAT), in which the numerous military files of the Algerian War are bundled. However, it was particularly obvious that a great number of dossiers were closed because they were said to involve national security and defense interests. The inventories in the archive of the Ministry of Foreign Affairs (MAE), however, were available without any major restrictions. The key sources here were the papers from the series Nations Unies et Organisations Internationales (NUOI), which mirrored impressively France's foreign policy position at the United Nations and in the international human rights discourse against the backdrop of the Algerian War.

The research for this book concentrated on previously published source material when studying the two decolonization wars from the perspective of each of the respective anticolonial resistance movements. In the case of the Mau Mau movement, this primarily involves the autobiographies and memories of former Mau Mau fighters, which Marshall Clough collected and analyzed extensively in his source-critical study *Mau Mau Memoirs*.[27] Particularly noteworthy are publications like *Mau Mau from Within*, *Mau Mau General*, and *We Fought for Freedom*, works that provide good insight into the structure, warfare, and aims of the anticolonial resistance organization.[28] The main source of information used for the Algerian liberation movement was the comprehensive works *Les archives de la révolution algérienne* and *Le FLN: Documents et histoire, 1954–1962* by Mohammed Harbi, who was a member of the FLN from the very beginning and made important documents publicly accessible.[29]

With regard to the international discourse on human rights, the archival material from the United Nations and the International Committee of the Red Cross (ICRC) was invaluable. As neutral actors outside the propaganda of the conflicting parties, these international organizations provided a particularly valuable outside perspective in their files on the two decolonization wars, particularly on the topic of grave human rights abuse. In addition to a series of smaller inventories from the UN archives in New York, documents of the Human Rights Commission (UNOG, SO 215/1 UK and SO 215/1 FRA) from the UN archive at the Palais des Nations in Geneva proved to be especially important.[30] Due to their highly confidential nature, these papers had not been released previously and were only made available for the first time in conjunction with the research conducted for this book under the stipulation that no revealing facts about the persons and organizations involved would be published. Therefore, in order to uphold the principle of strict confidentiality, facts about organizations and private individuals are only described in very general and neutral terms in references to the corresponding documents.

Even greater evidence on the human rights violations occurring during the conflicts in Kenya and Algeria was provided by the inventories of Archives of the International Committee of the Red Cross (ACICR) in Geneva, inventories that were not released until April 2004 and therefore were also viewed for the first time during the research conducted for this book. The numerous documents and particularly the reports by various ICRC missions during the two wars facilitated a telling reconstruction of the dimension to which human rights were systematically violated from the perspective of the organization that played a key role in international humanitarian law. In light of the volume and quality of this material, the documents of the U.S. State Department (NARA RG 59) at the National Archives in College Park, Maryland, which also provide an outside view of the two conflicts, were only used to a minor degree in this book.

Chapter 1

Introduction

In the fall of 1959, a publication with the title *Gangrene* aroused tempers within British government circles.[1] While the first part of the book featured a detailed description of torture perpetrated on several Algerians at French police stations during the course of the Algerian War, it was the second part that deeply unsettled authorities in London. In it, the various authors described in detail the inhuman prison conditions and systematic mishandling in the British detention camps set up in Kenya during the Mau Mau War and highlighted in particular the murder of eleven African detainees in March 1959 at the Hola Camp. In his introduction to this book, Peter Benenson, who went on to found Amnesty International in 1961, justified this comparison of colonial force with a series of parallels said to exist between the two wars of decolonization in Kenya and Algeria.[2] In Benenson's opinion, the genesis of both conflicts lay in the respective colonial situation of white-settler rule over the indigenous population, which manifested itself especially in racism. Furthermore, it was striking that Great Britain and France basically disregarded and violated the humanitarian standards of international law in the fight against anticolonial resistance organizations. Despite numerous objections and protests by the international public, neither the French nor the British government had undertaken the necessary measures to prevent the assaults and abuse perpetrated by their security forces. Instead, Benenson came to the conclusion that both colonial powers deliberately stigmatized the indigenous population as "subhuman" in order to legitimize the use of massive force.

Whereas the Colonial Office (CO) in London demanded an immediate statement from the colonial government in Nairobi concerning the accusations, because the CO feared the consequences for the impending British parliamentary elections,[3] the British defense ministry labeled the publication "subversive." In a memorandum, Whitehall therefore recommended to other ministries to ban the book immediately, since the introduction by Benenson itself was tantamount to a justification of "Mau Mau terrorism."[4] By its own assessment, further dissemination would only provoke embitterment and unrest and therefore would not be in the public interest. With this suggestion, officials at the British defense ministry were following the example of the French government in Paris, where the French edition *La gangrène* had been placed on the list of banned publications immediately following its appearance in France.[5] The true dimension of the unchecked colonial violence used in Kenya and Algeria was under no circumstances to be revealed to the public.

The various attempted governmental cover-ups were replaced with a sort of national amnesia following the decolonization wars and the dissolution of the colonial empires. Both in Great Britain and in France, a culture of forgetting and repressing prevailed in the way the "contested decolonization" was treated, similar to the situation in the other former colonial nations.[6] The subject of human rights violations was simply not addressed and then became a taboo in public debate.[7] The political scientist Alfred Grosser speaks of the "white spots" on the map of collective French memory,[8] and the same can also be said of national memory in Great Britain concerning the Mau Mau War. In France, the state also actively abetted such general oblivion by way of an amnesty decree—issued on 22 March 1962 immediately after the cease-fire agreement was signed in the Algerian War—that guaranteed unlimited immunity for all actions linked to military operations.[9] Other amnesty laws followed and, in November 1982, French president François Mitterrand even accepted back into the ranks of the French army those generals of the Algerian army who had participated in a putsch against the republic in 1961: Raoul Salan, Maurice Challe, Edmond Jouhaud, and André Zeller.[10]

Signs that this national amnesia was beginning to lift and that the taboo surrounding "contested decolonization" and its phenomena of unchecked colonial violence was gradually being broken appeared not long ago and, at first, only in France. Fittingly, Mohammed Harbi and Benjamin Stora gave their new volume of collected essays on the Algerian War the subtitle *La fin de l'amnésie*.[11] On 18 October 1999, a law passed by the French national assembly went into effect in which the previous official reference to the conflict as "operations in North Africa" was replaced with the wording "Algerian War."[12] In doing so, Paris acknowledged for the first time in the thirty-seven years since France's forced retreat from Algeria that it had even conducted a war in North Africa, although it did not go as far as to admit the systematic violations of human rights and assume responsibility for them. Not until the publication of a newspaper article in 2000 on the torture during the war by French paratroopers of Louisette Ighilahriz, a veteran of the Algerian Front de Libération Nationale (FLN),[13] and the public confession of systematic torture by two leading officers of the Algerian army, General Jacques Massu and General Paul Aussaresses,[14] did a fundamental discussion begin in France about crimes committed during the Algerian War.[15] In the course of this wave of revelations, Aussaresses confessed in *Le Monde* to the murder of twenty-four prisoners by his own hand. In his published war memoirs, he justified the systematic abuse of prisoners without any sign of remorse by indicating that he had acted in the alleged interests of the country and to its benefit.[16] Moreover, the general advocated in a CBS interview on U.S. television in January 2002 that suspects should be tortured to obtain information in the war against al-Qaeda.[17] Owing to the French amnesty law, charges could not be brought against Aussaresses for his war crimes, and French president Jacques Chirac could only have him dishonorably discharged from the army and Legion of Honor. In addition, a court ordered the general to pay a fine of €7,500 for the offense of speaking out in defense of war crimes.[18]

In Great Britain, the Mau Mau War entered the public limelight at nearly the same time. As early as 1999, the first press reports appeared about a planned redemption lawsuit by a Mau Mau veteran organization against the British government.[19] This was underpinned by the charges of serious human rights violations leveled in the highly respected BBC documentary *Kenya: White Terror,* which was aired in November 2002 and thereby addressed the problem for the first time in British television.[20] The revelations of the BBC and the *Guardian* prompted Scotland Yard to start investigations in January 2003 of possible British war crimes in Kenya and the alleged violations of the Geneva Conventions by British citizens.[21] The public debate intensified in 2005 with the publication of *Histories of the Hanged: Britain's Dirty War in Kenya and the End of the Empire*[22] and *Britain's Gulag: The Brutal End of Empire in Kenya*[23] in which David Anderson and Caroline Elkins, respectively, analyze in great detail the systematic war crimes committed during the Mau Mau War.

The pinnacle of media and public interest in the British decolonization war in Kenya to date was reached in the spring of 2011. Four people formally imprisoned in British detention camps—Wambugu wa Nyingi, Paulo Muoka

Nzili, Ndiku Mutwiwa Mutua, and Jane Muthoni Mara—filed a lawsuit against Great Britain before the High Court for damages suffered through the serious abuse and torture to which they were subjected during their imprisonment.[24] These charges were supported by British government documents uncovered in the course of trial that had been stored for over fifty years in a special Foreign Office depository in Hanslope Park and thereby withheld from the public because of the explosive nature of their content.[25] For the most part, this new archival material corroborated the scholarly findings, based on documents from the Public Records Office, concerning the systematic abuse of human rights during the Mau Mau War and the direct involvement of the British government in it. Finally, in July 2011, the High Court ruled that the former Kenyan prisoners could indeed sue for damages and thereby set the stage for court proceedings starting in early 2012.[26] David Anderson sees this decision by the High Court as an important step toward an honest and long overdue reckoning with the "seamier side" of the British Empire.[27]

The public debate about the two decolonization wars gained a thoroughly different dimension and political explosiveness when comparisons began to be made with current developments in the so-called war on terror and the Iraq War. Direct analogies were drawn to the colonial past concerning the disregard for all principles of international humanitarian law, the creation of legal black holes by extensive emergency legislation, the creation of secret interrogation centers and detention camps such as in Guantánamo Bay in violation of international law, the systematic use of torture to extract information, as well as the use of certain military strategies in fighting terrorism. The *Guardian* commented on the alleged torture and execution of twenty-three Iraqi civilians by British troops by posing the question "Is This Our Hola Camp?"[28] while the *Observer* reacted to the revelations of the British detention camps in Kenya with the headline "Our Guantánamo."[29] Other commentators chose to point out the major parallels in the way war was conducted, and David Anderson went as far as to call the Kenyan decolonization war of the 1950s an "uncanny foretaste" of the Iraq War.[30] More and more, the decolonization wars were being viewed as a historic lesson for current conflict scenarios.[31]

In August 2003, the bureau for Special Operations and Low Intensity Conflict at the U.S. Defense Department provided an important clue in support of this interpretation by inviting its antiterrorist experts to an internal viewing of the award-winning film *La battaglia di Algeri* (*The Battle of Algiers*).[32] In this film from 1966, the Italian director Gillo Pontecorvo reconstructs extremely realistically one of the most gruesome chapters of the Algerian War: namely, the systematic use of torture by the French army in its fight against the urban guerrilla fighters of the Algerian Liberation Army. According to the testimony of a high Pentagon official, the film provided comprehensive insight into French military strategy in Algeria and at the same time was meant to prompt a discussion among experts about strategic challenges in the so-called war on terrorism.[33] However, the Algerian War was not the only conflict to serve repeatedly for years as an important point of reference for current developments in the battle against terrorism;[34] so did other decolonization wars like the British Mau Mau War in Kenya. In an influential newspaper article published in September 2003, John Arquilla, professor for defense analysis at the Naval Postgraduate School in Monterey, California, recommended that the U.S. armed services take a closer look at and even adopt successful British counterinsurgency measures used in East Africa, such as the formation of special commandos called "pseudo-gangs."[35]

Aside from the contexts of such highly topical debates, "contested decolonization" is primarily a subject for historical research, to which this book contributes a comparative study of the decolonization wars in both Kenya and Algeria. At the center of the analysis is the parallelism of two topical complexes that have rarely been linked together in a single context: the discourse on international human rights and unchecked colonial violence. Following World War II, transnational organizations like the United Nations in New York and the International Committee of the Red Cross (ICRC) in Geneva established the international regime of human rights,[36] which guaranteed universal rights to every individual. The colonial metropoles of both Great Britain and France contributed decisively to this development process and also championed the protection of human rights at the regional level by promoting the European Convention on Human Rights (ECHR) of 1950, an internationally binding treaty that far exceeded a mere declaration of intent. At the same time, however, the European colonial powers tried at all costs to prevent the spread of universal human rights to their overseas possessions out of fear that the basis of their colonial rule would be stripped of all legitimation. They thus sought to create a "divided world," one that featured a double standard with regard to human rights. Furthermore, the governments in London and Paris did not flinch from the use of massive force in fighting the growing anticolonial resistance in the periphery, even if this meant violating in a most elementary way the very principles of the new human rights regime that they championed in Europe.

Against this backdrop, the key question addressed here is how Great Britain and France, as European constitutional democracies, could contribute substantially to the international discourse on human rights, on the one hand, yet could resort to measures of unchecked violence in their overseas territories, on the other. The conflicts in both Kenya and Algeria serve here as case studies, not only because they were the largest wars of decolonization for each of these colonial powers but also because they involved serious war crimes, comprehensive measures of detention and resettlement, and the systematic use of torture. However, this book does not limit itself just to a comparative analysis of the phenomena of violence in the two colonial conflicts; first and foremost, it investigates the common pattern of legitimation with which the colonial metropoles attempted to justify the unchecked use of force and, in doing so, more closely examines the combined factors of colonial emergency rule, new military doctrines of antisubversive warfare, and the negation of the validity of international humanitarian law.

Great Britain and France resorted in both of the conflict scenarios to the constitutional instrument of declaring states of emergency and vested their security forces with extensive special powers. The Italian philosopher Giorgio Agamben refers to the state of emergency as a legal black hole created when a state suspends the legal order,[37] thereby severely curtailing an individual's fundamental rights, those codified as minimum standards in the international regime of human rights. In the colonial context, the question posed here is the degree to which the overall emergency situation led to a radicalization of the colonial situation and created the legal conditions for the unchecked use of force. At the same time, the military doctrines of antisubversive warfare have to be analyzed more closely in this context. As a reaction to the anticolonial challenge, British and French officers established new guidelines in combating guerrilla movements. The focus of the analysis here is to determine, in addition to the parallelism of developments, the impact of this on colonial warfare. In this context, the question thus emerges about the role of international humanitarian law. In both of the decolonization wars, the ICRC insisted on the validity of the humanitarian standards spelled out in the Geneva Conventions of 1949, while the colonial powers rejected this idea vehemently.

Unchecked colonial violence had consequences for the discussion of international human rights and decisively influenced the decolonization debates in the United Nations. Yet the case studies of Kenya and Algeria also clearly show how the two conflicts differed with regard to the way they were perceived and discussed by the global public. Whereas the Mau Mau War in Kenya took place almost completely under the radar of international attention, the Algerian War played out in full view of a global audience. The reasons for this thoroughly contrary international perception will be examined here, in terms of three main topics: the dissolution of European colonial empires, unchecked colonial violence, and the international debate on human rights.

Chapter 2

The New World Order, 1941–1948

A searching test of the ability of the postwar world
to give effect to the ideals and principles for which
World War II was fought to its victorious conclusion.

—Ralph Bunche, 1946

The Fight for Human Rights

Universal Fundamental Rights as a Response to the Danger
of Totalitarianism

In 1944, the Polish lawyer and legal scholar of Jewish descent Raphael Lemkin published what was, at the time, the most comprehensive analysis of Hitler's concept of a "New Order" in Europe.[1] In his book *Axis Rule in Occupied Europe*,[2] which he had begun in 1940 during his exile in Sweden, Lemkin described the murderous regime in occupied Europe based on his close study of the laws and ordinances of the Axis powers. Grounded in the National Socialist ideology of racism spelled out in detail by Hitler in his ideological manifesto *Mein Kampf* in 1925, the new order of the Continent was meant to benefit the self-proclaimed Aryan "master race." In describing German occupation policy, Lemkin felt the need to coin a new word: genocide. Combining the root words *genos* (Greek for "family, tribe, or race") and *caedere* (Latin, "to kill"), he gave the total physical and cultural destruction of nations and ethnic groups a specific label.[3] According to this Polish lawyer, the Axis powers were not only violating existing international law, they were conducting a war of annihilation in order to make their idea of a new order a reality. Therefore, he urged the nations united in the fight against the Axis powers to meet the greatest challenge to humankind by eradicating the theory of the "master race" and replacing it with "a theory of a master morality, international law and true peace."[4] Thus, Lemkin not only delivered a thorough depiction of the totalitarian threat to the democratic, liberal order, he also laid the cornerstone for the first UN human rights document of the postwar era, the 1948 Genocide Convention.[5]

Since the outbreak of World War II, the account published by Lemkin in 1944 had become cruel reality, and the demise of liberalism seemed to continue undeterred through "the collapse of values and institutions of liberal civilization," as the historian Eric Hobsbawm describes it in his book *The Age of Extremes*.[6] In Europe, the triumphal advances of the German Wehrmacht led to the German occupation of nearly the entire continent, and the defeat of the last bulwark of democracy, Great Britain, seemed only a matter of time. The British Empire was severely weakened by the loss of its East Asian colonies in 1942 within a short period after they were attacked by the army of the Japanese *tennō*. The totalitarian concepts of a new order envisioned for both the German and the Japanese empires, which Volker Berghahn thinks were compatible in their structure and ideology,[7] became an existential threat to the "Free World." Both regimes propagated racist ideological politics of violence, which they used to establish and expand their hegemonic position. The deadly consequences of the ideology claiming the alleged superiority of the "Yamato race" and the "Aryan master race" could not be overlooked. The war crimes committed by the Japanese in conquering large parts of East Asia, in which the most notorious example was the Nanking massacre in December 1937 that left about 250,000 people dead, were even surpassed by the German crimes in occupied Europe and the murder of millions of Jews. The totalitarian idea, which negated all individual rights to freedom and attempted to subordinate everything to such collective racial fanaticism, constituted not only a military challenge to the remaining democracies but also an ideological one. The historian Mark Mazower believes that it was not until the world was faced with the enemy's unbelievable brutality that a recommitment to the "virtues of democracy" and to the importance of individual liberty occurred.[8] The Allies saw themselves forced to confront totalitarian plans for a new order with their own concept of a new world order. This realization is evident from the files of the British War Aims Committee dated 4 October 1940: "There was a need for an alternative programme to that put out by Hitler."[9]

British historian Edward Hallett Carr maintained that the question should not be whether a new order was needed but how to establish one.[10] In his speech before the House of Commons on 3 September 1939, at the dawn of the war, Winston Churchill argued that the war had to be fought essentially to establish "on impregnable rocks, the rights of the individual."[11] The British foreign minister Lord Halifax concurred with this opinion in his radio address of 7 November 1939. He characterized the German challenge with the denial of basic human rights and came to the conclusion: "We are therefore fighting to maintain the rule of law . . . in the great society of civilized states."[12] It seemed absolutely necessary to defend the idea of democracy.[13] The British government committed itself in numerous public statements to these fundamental human rights, but references to the content of such rights remained very vague.

Not until the British writer H. G. Wells undertook a private initiative did the debate assume any form of specificity. Working with Ritchie Calder, the science correspondent of the *Daily Herald*, Wells drafted a "Declaration of Rights" containing eleven articles that was sent to prominent people throughout the world and appeared with commentary in the *Daily Herald* from 5 to 24 February 1940. This declaration, later known as the "Sankey Declaration,"[14] contained the demand for the universal guarantee of basic social and economic provision of people as well as the protection of life and property. In his book *The New World Order*, Wells reiterated these demands and expressed the view that the discussion about war aims should become a campaign for a new declaration of human rights.[15] As a consequence, the title of his next book posed the decisive question: *The Rights of Man, or What Are We Fighting For?* In it he emphasized the urgent necessity to enter the war with a clear aim. One was not fighting against the Germans, but against Hitler and all such regimes:[16] "We are fighting this war for human freedom . . . and a better way of living, or we are fighting for nothing worth fighting for."[17] Wells thus elevated human rights to the highest Allied war aim and considered it an urgent priority to collect as many countries as possible behind this idea. For this purpose, he published his "Rights of Man" in numerous newspapers and in many languages, including Swahili, Hindu, and Arabic. The defense ministry had copies dropped over occupied Europe. His contact with important individuals such as Chaim Weizmann, Mahatma Gandhi, and U.S. president Franklin Delano Roosevelt served—as did his lecture tour in the United States—to spread the idea of human rights.

Such ideas fell on particularly sympathetic ears on the far side of the Atlantic, where their most prominent supporter could be found in the White

House. In his State of the Union Address on 6 January 1941, Roosevelt had declared the Four Freedoms to be the maxim for action taken in U.S. foreign policy in light of the international threat to democracy and security.[18] The freedom of speech and expression, the freedom of religious worship, the freedom from want, and the freedom from fear were not to be part of a vision for some distant future but to be achieved by the generation alive then. "That kind of world is the very antithesis of the so-called 'new order' of tyranny which the dictators seek to create with the crash of a bomb." In conclusion, he added: "Freedom means the supremacy of human rights everywhere."[19] With this "new Magna Carta of democracy,"[20] Roosevelt had clearly placed himself against Hitler and on the side of Great Britain, although the United States was officially still maintaining neutrality at this point. The U.S. president did not shy away from taking clear positions, such as in the special message sent to Congress on 20 June 1941, in which he declared the freedom from cruelty and inhuman treatment to be a natural right.[21] British prime minister Winston Churchill was happy to receive this moral support but insisted on direct military support from the United States in light of the threatening German invasion of the British Isles. A first step in this direction was the bilateral treaty of 2 September 1940, in which it was agreed that fifty old American destroyers would be turned over to the Royal Navy. In exchange, U.S. forces would be permitted to have military bases on Newfoundland, on the Bermuda Islands, and in the Caribbean Sea for ninety-nine years.[22] With the Lend-Lease Act of 11 March 1941,[23] Washington authorized the provision of war supplies to friendly states. Still, Churchill's main aim was to have the United States enter the war.

The Atlantic Charter of 1941: From the Allied Declaration of Intent to the Basis of the New World Order

At their first secret meeting from 9 to 12 August 1941, in Little Placentia Sound off the coast of Newfoundland at Argentia, the two statesmen harbored different expectations. The hope of the British prime minister for a quick entry of the United States into the war was met with Roosevelt's intent to receive a guarantee from the United Kingdom that no territorial changes and agreements would be made before a general peace conference was held. To Churchill's great disappointment, the result of the conference was only an eight-point statement "to make known certain common principles in the national policies" of the two countries, "on which they base their hopes for a better future for the world."[24] The content of the so-called Atlantic Charter, on which the two leaders agreed on 12 August 1941, can be summarized as follows: no annexations or territorial adjustments against the wishes of the people concerned, self-determination for all peoples, equal access for all nations to world trade and raw materials, international economic cooperation to improve economic and social standards, the creation of a comprehensive peaceful world order guaranteeing freedom from fear and want, and freedom of the seas. The closing sentence stipulated a general disarmament and an extensive disarmament of the aggressor nations in order to create a comprehensive and lasting system of global security. Unmistakably, the charter contained the four basic freedoms that Roosevelt had announced only in January as guiding principles. The historian Warren Kimball calls the statement a classic New Deal document with which Roosevelt tried to superimpose the guidelines of his domestic policy onto the international level.[25] The Atlantic Charter was a bitter disappointment for the British government, because all Churchill brought home from the conference was a statement of principles that would be published by the press on 14 August, not a new war ally. For Roosevelt, who had to keep an eye on the isolationist currents within the United States, the charter was a success because it acted as a warning to the Axis powers while at the same time stipulated the principles for common cause with Great Britain.

At first, both sides agreed on the great symbolic value of the joint statement. In his speech on 24 August 1941, Churchill stressed the need for such a joint statement of principles to instill hope in the people who were suffering under the yoke of the Nazi regime and struggling for their freedom, to assure them that their efforts and suffering were not in vain.[26] In Washington, the State Department underlined the enormous strategic importance of the Atlantic Charter. On the basis of equality and national self-determination, the charter was to be a concept meant clearly to counter the National Socialist ideology of racist hierarchization and repression.[27] Washington referred to a universal validity of the charter, which was immediately refuted by Churchill. In the House of Commons, he announced on 9 September 1941, that the parties meant by the charter from Placentia Bay were chiefly those countries and peoples occupied by the German army and that there could be no talk of a universal application of the eight principles.[28] Admittedly, his deputy prime minister, Clement Attlee, had stated at an event with West African students just the month before, on 16 August, "The Atlantic Charter: It means dark races as well. Coloured peoples, as well as white, will share the benefits of the Churchill-Roosevelt Atlantic Charter."[29] However, for Churchill, a universal application was absolutely out of the question for the British Empire because it would be tantamount to the capitulation to nationalist demands in the colonies. In particular, London saw a great danger for the state of the empire in Article 3, which addressed the issue of self-determination. The overarching principle of the prime minister was and remained "hands off the British Empire,"[30] which he believed was the bedrock on which Great Britain's position as a world power was built. His speech on 10 November 1942, on the occasion of the successful Allied landing in North Africa, left no room for doubt: "Let me, however, make this clear, in case there should be any mistake about it in any quarter. We mean to hold our own. I have not become the King's First Minister in order to preside over the liquidation of the British Empire."[31]

The American ally, particularly Roosevelt, saw this completely differently. Already at their first meeting off the coast of Newfoundland, the president had made his views clear: "I can't believe that we can fight a war against fascist slavery, and at the same time not work to free people all over the world from a backward colonial policy. . . . The structure of the peace demands and will get equality of peoples."[32] For Roosevelt, the universal validity of the charter was undisputable. He emphasized that these principles and the Four Freedoms were valid not only for all countries on the Atlantic rim but for the entire world.[33] After the United States entered the war in December 1941, no one in Washington intended to conduct a war to reestablish the European colonial empires, and the principles of the Four Freedoms and the Atlantic Charter found bipartisan support. Roosevelt's Republican opponent in the presidential elections of 1940, Wendell Willkie, prophesized that the colonial empires would crumble as a result of World War II,[34] and Roosevelt's confidant and key adviser at the State Department, Undersecretary of State Sumner Welles, declared the end of the imperialistic age: "If this war is in fact a war for the liberation of peoples it must assure the sovereign equality of peoples throughout the world, as well as in the world of the Americas. Our victory must bring in its train the liberation of all peoples. Discrimination between peoples because of their race, creed or color must be abolished. The age of imperialism is ended. The right of a people to their freedom must be recognized, as the civilized world long since recognized the right of an individual to his personal freedom. The principles of the Atlantic Charter must be guaranteed to the world as a whole—in all oceans and in all continents."[35]

The anticolonial ideas of the State Department even went so far as to prompt the issuance of a "Declaration on National Independence"[36] on 9 March 1942 that called on the colonial powers to take steps as expediently as possible to lead dependent regions into independence. At the same time, co-lonial populations were encouraged to participate actively in the fight against the Axis powers in order to prove their willingness and ability to gain their own freedom. The chasm in the Anglo-American alliance over the colonial question grew at the Casablanca Conference in 1943, during which serious disgruntlement broke out between Churchill and Roosevelt, who made no secret of his anticolonial stance. According to the notes taken by Harold Macmillan, the remarks by the president on the end of imperialism equally embarrassed France and Great Britain.[37] Shocked over the conditions he dis-covered during a visit to the British colony Gambia, Roosevelt saw a potential threat to a peaceful postwar order in the existing colonial system: "The thing is, the colonial system means war. Exploit the resources of an India, a Burma, a Java; take all the wealth out of these countries, but never put anything back into them, things like education, decent standards of living, minimum health requirements—all you're doing is storing up the kind of trouble that leads to war."[38]

Despite the grave differences of opinion with the British allies regard-ing the future of the colonial territories, Roosevelt never wanted to seriously endanger the alliance and thereby the military victory. The struggle against the totalitarian danger held the greatest priority for him. However, the presi-dent had indeed recognized that the essential conflict in international rela-tions lay in the denial of elementary fundamental rights. State Department records document Roosevelt's deep concern over human rights abuse and his determination to make human rights the moral basis of the international order after the end of the war.[39] Undersecretary of State Welles underscored Roosevelt's intention: "This is in very truth a people's war. It is a war which cannot be won until the fundamental rights of the peoples of the earth are se-cured. In no other manner can a true peace be achieved."[40] As a consequence, the State Department soon began deliberations on the protection of human rights, which led to the drafting of a "bill of rights" by a legal subcommit-tee at the department in 1942. Furthermore, nongovernmental organizations (NGOs), such as the American Law Institute and the American League of Nations Associations, made numerous suggestions and recommendations in support of the government's work.[41] The report "International Safeguard of Human Rights" by the Commission to Study the Organization of Peace stated that universal human rights constituted the basic prerequisite for a new and lasting world order of peace and justice.[42] In order to realize this aim, a United Nations conference was to work on the development of the international protection of human rights and establish a permanent human rights commission. In this way, the United States was confident that universal fundamental rights would be entrenched inevitably as the foundation for a new world order.[43]

First, however, the war had to be won and an alliance as large as possible had to be gathered to support the common principles. On 1 January 1942, the Declaration by United Nations[44] was issued in support of the aims laid out in the Atlantic Charter. This declaration was signed by twenty-six countries; by 1 March 1943, the total number of signatory states had reached forty-seven. In Roosevelt's words, these nations had formed "a great union of humanity" dedicated to "world-wide victory over their common enemies" and in which they shared a "faith in life, liberty, independence and religious freedom, and in the preservation of human rights and justice in their own lands as well as in other lands."[45] Therefore, the principles of the Atlantic Charter did not merely pertain to the Anglo-American alliance but became the common basis of the entire alliance. Human rights had finally delivered the "ideological response" to the totalitarian challenge.[46] "The belief in the four freedoms of common humanity—the belief in man, created free, in the image of God—is the crucial difference between ourselves and the enemies we face today. In it lies the absolute unity of our alliance, opposed to the oneness of the evil we hate. Here is our strength, the source and promise of victory."[47]

With such an emphasis on their campaign to champion human rights, the question invariably arises about the extent to which the Allies felt committed in realpolitik to the principles of the Four Freedoms, the Atlantic Charter, and the Declaration by United Nations. Were these principles only an affirmation of an "informal alliance," or, as General George Marshall bitterly stated, "an effort to keep people entertained"?[48] Were they more than just a declaration of intent cloaked in morals and goodwill for the purpose of propaganda? As the handling of the war crimes committed by the Axis powers illustrates, these unquestionably represented the key Allied principles for both war and peace. The longer the war lasted, the more reports came in about the systematic perpetration of war crimes by German and Japanese troops in the occupied regions. Not only was the indigenous population affected, so were prisoners of war, as the examples of the mass murder of Soviet Red Army soldiers in German concentration camps and the inhuman treatment of Allied soldiers in Japanese prisoner-of-war camps showed. The Moscow Declaration of 1 November 1943 was the first united Allied step to prosecute war crimes.[49] The plans for a war criminal tribunal worked out by the United

Nations Commission for the Investigation of War Crimes was actually implemented by the London Charter of 8 August 1945, which represented the birth of the International Military Tribunals (IMTs) of Nuremberg and Tokyo.[50] Both series of procedures expressed the first direct reaction of the Allies to the grave human rights abuses that took place during the war. By creating the new statutory offense of "crimes against humanity" and adopting the Nuremberg principles,[51] the IMTs would also influence the human rights debate of the United Nations. All the declarations made during the war were to be followed by real action after it.

Although the Allied war coalition quarreled time and again over their universal applicability, the principles created the solid framework for both the war strategy and the postwar order.[52] Therefore, the Atlantic Charter and the 1942 Declaration by United Nations can be called the "germ cell of the UN."[53] Moreover, they became an important reference point for the human rights discourse, of which the crimes of World War II once again made the public more aware. The war had acted as a catalyst to develop international protection of human rights. By publicly championing the cause of equality and freedom, the Allies had set clear standards against which their actions could be measured after the war.

However, the moral basis of the war alliance had not only given hope to peoples living in the countries occupied by the Axis powers, it had also laid bare political inconsistence in the Allied camp.[54] By drafting a counterconcept to the totalitarian racial fanaticism and declaring "the enthronement of the rights of man"[55] as a major purpose of the war, one revealed one's own deficits on the issue of racial equality. In 1944, the American anthropologist Robert Redfield wrote about a type of self-scrutiny for democracies, which had been forced upon them by the National Socialist racial theory. "The ideal is now asserted as a program for an entire world—a free world. . . . And yet the leaders who announce this program are citizens of the countries in which racial inequality is most strongly apparent."[56] Indeed, the demands for racial equality became increasingly louder on the Allied side. In his 1944 study *An American Dilemma: The Negro Problem and Modern Democracy*, Gunnar Myrdal criticized the Allied double standard when it came to race, quoting a young black man about to be inducted: "Just carve on my tombstone, 'Here lies a black man killed fighting a yellow man for the protection of the white man.'"[57]

During the war to protect human rights, racial equality did not exist on the Allied side.[58] Racially segregated military units, housing, and medical services were the rule among the Allied armed forces. Representative John Rankin from Mississippi declared that the official practice of keeping blood reserves separate in the field hospital would prevent racial intermingling in the United States and that he would never permit the pumping of "Negro or Japanese blood into the veins of our wounded white boys."[59] The Allies now found themselves in the dilemma of being measured against their own standards for racial equality and freedom, standards that they themselves had declared in the war against the totalitarian racial ideology. The influential report by the Commission to Study the Organization of Peace viewed the situation of black people in the United States as fuel for enemy propaganda and stated: "The cancerous Negro situation in our county . . . makes our ideals stick like dry bread in the throat. In anti-Semitism we are a mirror of Nazi grimaces. These motes in our own eye are not to be passed over. . . .Through revulsion against Nazi doctrines, we may, however, hope to speed up the process of bringing our own practices in each nation more in conformity with our professed ideals."[60]

This struck especially hard at the core of the colonial rule by the European allies, who were well aware of the problem. Lord Moyne, the British colonial minister, expressed his deep concern: "We must avoid any reproach that, when we blamed Hitler for his poisonous doctrine of the *Herrenvolk*, we had a similar doctrine lurking in our own hearts."[61] Particularly among the colonial troops, resistance to discrimination within the Allied armed forces coalition began to grow. In addition, the promises and assurances made by the Allies during the war had raised the expectations of the colonial populations. No one in the colonies was willing to accept a return to the antebellum status quo. Moreover, in this war for human rights, the Allied powers relied heavily on the support of the colonies and, under all circumstances, had to prevent any support from drifting away into the enemy camp.

World War II as the Colonial Turning Point and Catalyst for Anticolonial Efforts

Allied Principles as Anticolonial Inspiration

In many parts of Asia and Africa, the politics of the Axis powers were not perceived as the greatest threat. Rather, the main enemies were imperialism and colonialism. The European colonial powers Great Britain, France, the Netherlands, and Belgium—all liberal democracies—were responsible in the eyes of the colonial populations for repression, exploitation, and the denial of fundamental human rights. According to Eric Hobsbawm, enemies of the imperialist powers became potential allies in colonial struggles for independence.[62] Therefore, grave danger existed that the colonies would denounce the loyalty to the "motherland" imposed upon them and defect to the side of the Axis powers. "Why fight against Japan?" South African prime minister Jan Smuts paraphrased the Africans, "We are oppressed by the whites and we shall not fare worse under the Japanese."[63] With this succinct statement, he expressed a view widely held throughout Africa and the Caribbean.

Colonialism was the best recruiting officer the Axis powers had. Therefore, they did not hesitate to pose as an anticolonial force and to promise the liberation of the colonies. Even in the prewar period, German propaganda flooded the French colonies in North Africa, championing the image of the German empire as a protector of the "Arabian race."[64] The topics of German propaganda efforts, which intensified during the war, were the repressive French regime, German-Arab friendship, and a shared anti-Semitism.[65] Through broadcasts via stations like Radio Berlin, Radio Libération, and Radio Voix Arabe Libre, the Germans attempted to induce the colonial population to openly resist France and later the Allies who had landed in North Africa.[66] The target audience of the anti-French propaganda was not only the Arab civilian population but particularly also the North African colonial troops. Although parts of the Arabian population did harbor sympathies for Hitler, this was never enough to pull people completely to the side of the German Reich, and the number of Arab volunteers in Wehrmacht units was negligible. Furthermore, the African colonies were never under the direct control of the Axis powers. The threat to British East Africa that Italy had posed was nullified by the quick retaking of Abyssinia in 1940. With the defeat of the German African Corps at El Alamein in October 1942 and the Allied landing in North Africa in November of that same year, the acute danger was eliminated for the African colonial territories.

The Asian theater of war was a completely different picture. In a very short span of time, European colonial rule in Southeast Asia had collapsed thoroughly under the onslaught of Japanese troops, and the gem of the British Empire, the Indian subcontinent, was directly threatened with invasion. Unlike Germany and Italy, Japan was a "colored" nation and therefore posed a far greater danger in this respect for European colonialism. In light of the passivity of the Western world during the Italian occupation of Abyssinia, W. E. B. Du Bois, a cofounder of the Pan-African movement, wrote in

October 1935: "Japan is regarded by all colored peoples as their logical leader, as the one non-white nation which has escaped for ever the dominance and exploitation of the white world."[67] In its campaign to conquer Southeast Asia, Japan claimed to be fighting under the banner of "Asia for the Asians"[68] as an anticolonial, anti-Western power and attempted to instrumentalize people's desire for national independence for its purposes.[69] Japan used its alleged anticolonialism for military purposes in forming non-Japanese units, such as the Burma Independence Army under Aung San and an Indian liberation army recruited from prisoners of war and under the command of Subhas Chandra Bose. In addition to the formal independence of the Philippines and Burma, the climax of these anticolonial propaganda efforts was the Greater East Asia Conference in 1943 in Tokyo, in which the Japanese puppet governments from China, Thailand, Burma, and Manchuria also participated.[70] However, the Greater East Asia Co-Prosperity Sphere was nothing more than a euphemism for the colonial exploitation of the occupied regions by Imperial Japan.[71]

Not only did the Japanese capture of Singapore on 15 February 1942 shake the very foundation of the British Empire, it caused a crisis concerning the legitimation of British foreign rule. In the aftermath of the disastrous defeat, people in Great Britain were shocked about the passivity of the indigenous population, who had not been willing to defend the British flag against the Japanese invasion. The British press placed the blame for the disaster on London's misguided politics, by calling into question "the whole spirit and basis" of British colonial policy.[72] The great vulnerability of the empire became exposed. Particularly the American allies thought the reason for the rapid Japanese conquest was the lack of moral legitimation of British colonialism. Hence, in the *Washington Post* on 21 February 1942 and thus after the fall of Singapore, the American journalist Walter Lippmann called for a radical change in Great Britain's stance. It was necessary to identify the war with the freedom and safety of the colonial populations and to overthrow, once and for all, the outdated idea of the "white man's burden."[73] The "deep patience of colored peoples" had come to an end, argued the American writer and Nobel laureate in literature Pearl S. Buck, and had been replaced by the inexorable will for liberation from white rule and exploitation.[74]

Americans proudly pointed to the heroic resistance by the Philippine people, their "colonial population," who fought alongside the U.S. Army against the Japanese invaders. The U.S. secretary of state Cordell Hull praised the participation of the Philippines in the fight for global freedom and confirmed its acceptance into the United Nations on the basis of the Atlantic Charter.[75] Roosevelt in particular recognized the urgent necessity to persuade colonial populations to cooperate with the Allied powers by giving them assurances regarding their independence. In the case of threatened India, he believed that the creation of a constitution and the declaration of independence would strengthen both the willingness of Indian troops to fight and the morale of the civilian population.[76] Mahatma Gandhi, the leader of the Indian independence movement, had pointed out in a letter to the American president "that the Allied declaration that the Allies are fighting to make the world safe for freedom of the individual and for democracy sounds hollow, so long as India and, for that matter, Africa are exploited by Great Britain, and America has the Negro problem in her own home,"[77] whereupon Roosevelt responded by asking him not "to make common cause against a common enemy," in light of the totalitarian danger.[78]

In the above-mentioned "Declaration on National Independence" produced by the State Department in 1942, the active participation of the colonies in the Allied war effort was said to test their capability for independence. In Roosevelt's eyes, the validity of the Atlantic Charter principles and the guarantee of fundamental rights for the colonial populations were not only morally justified but essential for the war effort. Even in the British parliament, this point began to be discussed. On 20 May 1942, the Earl of Listowel, a Labour MP, called for a British Colonial Charter, borrowing from the Atlantic Charter, wherein the British war aims and associated improvements for the colonial population were to be stipulated. The people in the colonies would thus understand what they were fighting for.[79] The English publicist William Arnold-Forster expressed this same idea: "If the Allies are to fight the war of ideas effectively, they must establish confidence, both by words and by deeds, that the 'new order' which they stand for is compatible—unlike Hitler's 'New Order' or Japan's 'Co-prosperity Sphere'—with expanding liberties for all people including those colonial in status. They should be in a position to convince the Burmese, for instance, that an Allied victory will mean for them more liberty, better living conditions, than they could expect under the regime of independence vouchsafed by an imperialist Japan."[80]

Since the start of the war, Great Britain had been forced to react to the anticolonial propaganda of the Axis powers and thereby stressed repeatedly the difference between German occupation and British colonial rule. As Anthony Eden, Britain's secretary of state for the dominions, put it, "The German conception of dominion and the modern British conception of imperialism present as sharp an antithesis as mankind has ever known. The German conception is based upon subjection and repression, ours upon equality and development."[81] In Eden's depiction, Great Britain fulfilled an honorable and responsible mission in its colonies to the benefit of the indigenous population. Another official statement concurred with this viewpoint, defending it all the more emphatically: "The British Empire is exactly the opposite [of Hitler's concept of empire]. There has been nothing like it in the world before; it is a commonwealth, a family of free nations—linked together by a loyalty to one king. It stands for progress; it is the hope of the future."[82] Still, one was aware of the contradiction in one's own camp and the Ministry of Information added: "We cannot afford to ride rough-shod over the peoples of the Colonies whilst maintaining to the World at large we were fighting for the freedom of mankind."[83] British propaganda tried to meet the challenge brought on by the "Singapore shock," particularly in light of American criticism, by introducing the new concept of colonial partnership.[84] It fell to the Ministry of Information to create an image of Great Britain as the leader of the free world and the protector of smaller and weaker countries.

Nevertheless, propaganda experts in the colonial administrations ran invariably into the problem of how to criticize the National Socialist politics without thereby undermining colonial rule. How could propaganda attack the Nazi ideology of racial superiority and not provoke the resistance of the colonial population with regard to colonial repression?[85] The British colonial ministry rejected the strategy of strongly attacking German racial doctrine for propaganda purposes, so as to avoid opening itself up to criticism of colonial racism. The words "freedom" and "war of liberation" were not to be used out of fear they would become an "inconvenient boomerang."[86] Despite reservations in London, passages from Hitler's *Mein Kampf* were used in the colonies,[87] since they had proved to be "good propaganda."[88] All told, the British propaganda efforts succeeded in depicting Hitler and his racism as an "evil thing."

Throughout World War II, the majority of the colonies remained loyal to their colonial rulers to a surprising degree. Too contradictory were the anti-colonial assertions and the realpolitik of the racist ideologies propagated by fascism, National Socialism, and Japanese imperialism that the leaders of the national independence movements in the colonies, men like Ferhat Abbas, Mahatma Gandhi, Kwame Nkrumah, and Habib Bourguiba, could have accorded them any credibility. In May 1943, Habib Bourguiba, the leader of the Tunisian national independence movement, declared his solidarity with

France and the Allied cause: "Today you must close ranks behind France. . . . I am convinced that the French nation, once freed from the Nazi yoke, will not forget her true friend, those who stood by her in her hour of trial. What matters most now is to win the war."[89] In the end, the anticolonial propaganda approach of Japan and Germany failed in the face of their own racial ideologies and the war crimes linked to them.

Much more attractive were the Allied avowals in the fight for human rights, which promised a real liberation from foreign rule and a better postwar world. The central argument of the Allies was that a victory of the United Nations would grant the colonial populations a better prospect for economic and political development according to the framework spelled out in the Atlantic Charter.[90] Consequently, the principles were received euphorically in the colonies.[91] For the young Nelson Mandela, the content of the charter affirmed the belief in the dignity of every individual and supported democratic principles: "Some in the West saw the charter as empty promises, but not those of us in Africa. Inspired by the Atlantic Charter and the Allied struggle against tyranny and oppression, the ANC created its own charter, called African Claims, which called for full citizenship for all Africans, the right to buy land, and the repeal of all discriminatory legislation. We hoped that the government and ordinary South Africans would see that the principles they were fighting for in Europe were the same ones we were advocating at home."[92]

Carlos Romulo, the Philippine general who later became president of the UN General Assembly, spoke of a "flame of hope" that began to spread throughout Asia with the announcement of the Atlantic Charter.[93] The principles of democracy and the right of national self-determination were embraced by Africans more than ever before, and the Nigerian Nnamdi Azikiwe described the electrifying effect of the Atlantic Charter on the African population.[94] For the later leader of the Ghanaian independence movement Kwame Nkrumah, the aim of the African youth movement was to make Africa's voice heard in the common global war again fascism and to help build "a post-war world based upon the principles of freedom as expressed in the Atlantic Charter."[95] William Phillips, Roosevelt's personal ambassador in India, corroborated the belief of his president concerning the great influence of the charter on the Indian national independence movement and "the new idea which is sweeping over the world, of freedom for oppressed peoples. The Atlantic Charter has given the movement great impetus."[96]

At the time, the global impact of the Allied principles was analyzed in numerous publications,[97] and most voices argued for the validity of the Atlantic

Charter in the colonies. In his book *The Atlantic Charter*, the Polish professor Stanislaw Stronski drew a connection between the people who were repressed by the Axis powers and those repressed by the colonial powers. By issuing the 1942 Declaration by United Nations, the signatory nations had declared the charter as their common program, in whose name they would fight for their own freedom and that of the entire world.[98] The Allied eight-point statement was to serve as the basis of civilization[99] and be applied to the dependent regions where the interests of the indigenous population should be given priority.[100]

On 8 September 1941, members of the Phelps Stokes Fund established the Committee on Africa, the War, and Peace Aims for the purpose of giving African ideas a voice in the creation of the postwar order and mobilizing broad public support for these ideas. Among the members were such well-known names as Ralph Bunche, W. E. B. Du Bois, and John Foster Dulles, all of whom had recognized the importance of the colonies for the Allied war effort and had thus made the application of the Atlantic Charter in Africa the focus of their study *The Atlantic Charter and Africa from an American Standpoint*.[101] The disastrous defeats of the colonial powers in Asia, such as the fall of Singapore and Rangoon, were said to have increased the importance of the colonial peoples in the fight for the survival of freedom. A voluntary cooperation of the colonies was therefore urgently necessary, and this point was underscored by the remarks of the British MP Arthur Creech Jones on 26 March 1942: "We talk of liberation. Let us secure the cooperation of the Colonial peoples identifying themselves freely with us because they are conscious that this war is not only a war of liberation for the great outer world, but also a war of liberation from the Imperialism we have in the past obliged them to experience."[102] The study emphasized the importance of an Allied victory for the future of civilization, yet pointed out that the credibility of the alliance would be measured against the realization of its promises. Only a fair solution to African problems would secure a basis for lasting freedom in the world, whereby the committee considered it elementary to guarantee economic, social, and political rights for the African population. Therefore, the final recommendation was that "the Eight Points of the Charter should all be applied to Africa in keeping with the broad humanitarian and democratic principles enunciated. That the goal of ultimate self-government should be definitely accepted in every colony."[103]

Pan-African organizations such as the Council on African Affairs worked on behalf of the colonial populations and called on the U.S. government to support all efforts to secure the independence and development of the African continent in accordance with the Atlantic Charter, efforts such as the main resolution of the Conference on Africa in April 1944, for example.[104] Black leaders like W. E. B. Du Bois, Kwame Nkrumah, Nnamdi Azikiwe, George Padmore, and Harold Moody demanded energetically that the Allies implement the promised principles of freedom and equality, as were again formulated by Moody in the Charter for Colored People at the conference of the League of Colored People in London in July 1944.[105]

The Allied principles for the worldwide fight for freedom were increasingly used as a point of reference for national movements in the colonies.[106] The leader of the moderate Algerian nationalist movement, Ferhat Abbas, published his *Manifeste du peuple algérien* on 10 February 1943, in which he referred directly to the Atlantic Charter.[107] Even immediately after the defeat of France in 1940, he had asked the new Vichy government to implement comprehensive reforms. In his report *L'Algérie de demain*,[108] addressed to Marshal Philippe Pétain, he described the catastrophic situation of the Muslim population and emphasized the necessity of a new order in Algerian relations within the new France. When the Vichy government simply ignored his demands, he placed all hope in the Allied invasion of North Africa in November 1942. As early as 7 November, Abbas met with Robert Murphy, Roosevelt's special envoy to North Africa, in order to get an impression of the U.S. stance toward Algerian wishes for independence. Although Murphy only talked in very general terms about such efforts in Africa and stressed that the military victory over Germany had greater priority,[109] the historian Amar Naroun thinks that this and further meetings greatly influenced Abbas's attitude toward the Atlantic Charter.[110] In response to the call on 11 December 1942 by Admiral François Darlan to all Muslim Algerians to actively participate in the fight against Hitler and for the liberation of their "Arabian brothers" in Tunisia, Abbas and his followers first issued the *Message des représentants des musulmans aux autorités responsables*.[111] If this war was indeed being fought for the liberation of people of all races and religions as proclaimed by the U.S. president, it stated, then the Muslim Algerians would be willing to commit themselves wholeheartedly to this endeavor. However, this had to result in a conference where elected Muslim representatives would negotiate political, economic, and social equality for the Muslim population. Participation in the war was linked to specific political demands.

After these demands had been rejected by the representatives of the Free French Forces, Abbas took the *Manifeste du peuple algérien* one step further and, referring to the Allied document, demanded the abolition of colonial repression, the right of self-determination for all peoples, and a constitution anchored in human rights for Algeria.[112] In *Additif du manifeste*,[113] he expanded the demands to include the recognition of the national sovereignty and independence of the Algerian people. In doing so, Abbas had derived the main points of the most important document of Algerian nationalism directly from the Allied principles.

According to Mohamed Khenouf and Michael Brett, the situation in North Africa and particularly in Algeria illustrates the entire dilemma of the Allied war strategy.[114] On the one hand, one had to use the promises implied in the Atlantic Charter to gain the support of the colonial populations for the Allied cause. On the other, one had to be careful not to encourage the national movements too much in their demands for equality and independence from the Allied colonial powers. Not only did the colonies need to be discouraged from drifting into the enemy's camp, it was even more important to mobilize them for the Allied war effort.

The Colonial Contribution to Victory and Raised Expectations

The colonies were very important for the Allied war effort as a source of raw materials and a transshipment point for supplies, as a reservoir of troops and manpower, and as a last refuge of retreat. In the fight for human rights, the Allies were dependent on colonial support for material and human resources. After the Asian colonies and the raw materials there fell into the hands of the Japanese, the African deposits of copper, bauxite, tin, uranium, cobalt, gold, and industrial diamonds became indispensable.[115] Because of its rich deposits of rare and precious metals, the Belgian Congo became the largest supplier of raw materials. In addition, the loss of Asia meant that Africa became increasingly important as a strategic transshipment point for supplies for both the North African and Asian theaters of war.

The Allies were interested in Africa not only for its mineral deposits, but also for agricultural use. Starting in 1941, the British colony of Kenya became the most important source of provisions to feed the British army in the Middle East and the leading supplier of agrarian products like sisal, which resulted in a significant increase in the area under cultivation. The Kenyan example also illustrates that the war and its increasing demand for vital war products could mean a phase of economic prosperity after the depression of the prewar period.[116] However, this held true to an overwhelming degree for white settlers only. The African population suffered under the rapid price increases and high costs of living as a result of the war. The heightened economic exploitation and strategic use of the colonies as a hub of Allied provision led to a considerable increase in construction with the building of airports, docks, supply centers, transportation routes, and military complexes.

The high demand for labor was filled by the indigenous population, in part through conscription.[117] The number of Africans who worked in the war industry, on plantations, and on the construction of public projects has been estimated by the historians David Killingray and Richard Rathbone to be several million. In their opinion, the mobilization of the colonies for the war effort acted as a catalyst for social and economic change in the overseas territories. Urbanization, rising costs of living, new expectations among Africans, the establishment of unions, and the high levels of unemployment once war production ceased after the war changed colonial society permanently.[118] Tensions rose enormously between the nonwhite population, who had borne the greatest burden of the war effort, and the white minority, who had profited from the increased importance of the colonies. The discontent of large parts of the African population grew in the face of the poor social and economic situation, and resistance began to form, such as among the dockworkers in Dar es Salaam: "From day to day we are being kicked and beaten just not like human beings . . . the treatment we receive from the African Wharfage is equal to the Nazi German, but we are being told that we are at war with Nazi German because the Nazi want to enslave the world, how is it that an English is making us a slave in the face of the capital of this country? You are also aware that our brethren are fighting up North and in other parts of the world all for freedom."[119]

One way to flee the social and economic misery was to enlist. Africans did not become soldiers for the idealistic reasons propagated by the Allies, such as the defense of democracy and freedom; they joined the army first and foremost in the hope of improving their personal plight. Why shouldn't a soldier of the King's African Rifles demand greater pay if he was to fight not only for King George but also for democracy?[120] Why should they, the nonwhite population in South Africa, commit themselves to fighting in North Africa or in Europe for the cause of freedom when freedom was being denied them at home?[121] In an oral history project with Ghanaian war veterans, 73 percent said that the main reason they enlisted in the British army was to get a regular wage, educational opportunities, and better provisions.[122] The army did indeed offer men a chance to learn to read and write, and to be trained and work as a mechanic, electrician, or driver. Warihiu Itote, who would later become a Mau Mau general, enlisted in order to flee unemployment in Nairobi.[123]

The need for fresh troops was enormous: a total of 525,000 Africans were enlisted in the service of Great Britain during the war either in labor companies or in combat units. At the start of the war, the British had attempted to assign Africans noncombatant jobs in pioneer services and provisions because the white settlers greatly feared that armed service could give Africans the wrong idea and turn them against their white rulers. However, as the war continued, the distinction between combatant and noncombatant blurred, and African soldiers, above all those in the King's African Rifles (KAR), played a decisive role in liberating Abyssinia, in occupying Vichy-loyal Madagascar, and in the British Burma campaign. In Kenya alone, 97,000 Africans participated in the war for worldwide freedom and equality. Yet even here they were confronted with racial discrimination in the form of separate living units and troop transports, lower pay, poorer provisions, and even an unequal allocation of beer.[124] Bildad Kaggia, a cofounder of the Mau Mau movement, was denied a promotion and pay raise because of his skin color. Moreover, his superior reprimanded him for rebuking a white subordinate and informed him that one was to judge a European not by his rank but by his level of civilization.[125] According to Kaggia himself, the experience of racial discrimination within the army opened his eyes, and he began to read political literature, such as the writing of Mahatma Gandhi and Abraham Lincoln.[126]

No one sensed more than General Charles de Gaulle and his followers that the French overseas territories were more than just an "appendage of the motherland"[127] in this war. They were critical for the survival of the cause and, after the disastrous defeat of 1940, served as the first territorial base for the Free French Forces. In his famous radio broadcast on 18 June 1940, de Gaulle underscored Africa's importance by emphasizing that France was not alone in this struggle, that it was being supported by its large colonial empire.[128] Although the greater part of the colonial empire remained true to Vichy, de Gaulle did succeed, with the help of the black governor of Chad Felix Eboué, to convince Cameroon and French Equatorial Africa to side with him. Brazzaville became the temporary capital of Free France.[129] It was from here and with the help of colonial troops that the liberation of the metropole could be undertaken. In line with this, General Jacques-Philippe Leclerc declared that the conquest of the Kufra Oasis in the Libyan Desert in 1941 was the first step in freeing France.[130] The French overseas territories served traditionally as a source for recruiting soldiers for the French army. They helped balance out the numerical inferiority compared to the German Reich and to buttress France's position as a leading power on the Continent. The Force Noire was considered the guarantee of national security. Like the British, the French had deployed their nonwhite troops in World War I and more than 80,000 West African soldiers had helped defend France in 1940.[131] The French defeat changed the situation fundamentally, because the indigenous soldiers no longer served the cause of the Free French as an auxiliary to the army, they now composed its core.

The Allied recapture of North Africa in November 1942 not only created a springboard from which to launch the invasion of occupied Europe from the south, but also provided the Free French Forces with a large new pool from which to recruit manpower. After the Comité Français de la Libération Nationale (CFLN) was founded in Algiers on 3 June 1943, as many as 250,000 North Africans were recruited for the liberation of the motherland.[132] In 1944, Algerians made up 23 percent of the French army, and, together with troops from Morocco, Tunisia, and 100,000 West African soldiers, they became the backbone of the French armed forces. In the Corps Expéditionnaire Français (CEF), the colonial troops distinguished themselves in the Allied Italy campaign through their combat strength. One such example of this was the battle of Monte Cassino, where Ahmed Ben Bella, a young Algerian *tirailleur*—as members of French colonial infantry were called—was awarded the Médaille Militaire for his deeds. Soldiers from the colonies also played a big role in the liberation of Elba and southern France. Thus, the historian Myron Echenberg has argued, with good reason, that the "French" victories under Generals Jean Joseph de Lattre de Tassigny, Marie-Pierre Kœnig, and Leclerc would not have been possible without the fighting power of the colonial troops.[133]

Although racial discrimination was not as pronounced in the French army as in the British armed forces, the feeling did spread among the indigenous troops that they were being exploited and sacrificed for the metropole.[134] Until then, nationalist propaganda from the colonies had shown little impact. The morale of the troops remained firm, emphasized General Pierre-Jean André, general of the division in Constantine, in a report.[135] This was certainly also a result of the strict military censorship exercised by the Affaires militaires musulmanes (AMM). Letters written by Algerian soldiers indicate that they usually knew nothing about the demands Abbas was making. More important, however, was their growing concern about the economic and social situation of their families in North Africa.[136] The discontent among the North African troops manifested itself more and more by the surfacing of symbols, such as the green flag of Islam and banners reading "À bas le colonialisme" and "Pour

la Charte de l'Atlantique."[137] However, the defining moment among the indigenous troops was the "whitening" order by de Gaulle,[138] who commanded
the exchange of soldiers of color for young white Frenchmen in order to let
the latter take part in the military victory and liberation of France. The Allied
command had limited the size of the French army to 250,000 men,[139] and
it was decided for political reasons to have as many Frenchmen as possible
participate in the liberation of the motherland. After having been the decisive factor in the Allied victories in North Africa, Italy, and southern France,
soldiers of color were now pulled from the front lines, forced to give up their
weapons and even their uniforms, and told, with victory so close at hand, that
their services were no longer needed and that they were to wait in southern
France for their transport back to Africa.[140]

The poor living conditions and the demoralizing way they were treated
led to many conflicts between demobilized soldiers and French security
forces. The most serious incident actually occurred in Senegal, where Senegalese veterans at the caserns in Thiaroye near Dakar rebelled when they were
refused pay and pensions. The reaction of the security forces cost thirty-five
Senegalese their lives and several hundred were severely wounded.[141] This
incident—like the Sétif unrest later in Algeria, which was sparked when Algerian veterans returned at the end of the war in search of their families in
villages destroyed by the French army—drastically demonstrated to African
soldiers how little their contribution to the Allied victory was valued and how
little had changed in the colonial situation.

The experience of the war influenced African veterans in various ways.
For many men, their enlistment in the army was their very first contact with
modern lifestyles and organization, which meant social and economic advancement through training, pay, better nourishment and medical care.[142]
New sources of information offered by Allied propaganda and the contact
with soldiers from throughout the colonial empire led to a broadening of
men's intellectual horizons, in the opinion of Waruhiu Itote.[143] Men had the
opportunity to compare the situation in the various colonies. For example,
meetings between Indian and Kenyan soldiers led to lively exchanges about
promises to grant independence once the war was won. One conservative
Kenyan tribal chief therefore noted with some irritation, "The Indian soldiers
seemed to talk about little else than self-government which tended to upset
the African askaris' ideas."[144] Contact with other Allied soldiers, especially
with black American GIs, was another source of exchange; therefore, the British army command attempted to prevent precisely such contacts.[145]

Yet even the shared experiences on the front with white soldiers had a large psychological impact on the nonwhite troops. For one, the myth of the superiority of the white race and civilization was obliterated by a war in which Europeans were fighting one another in a most brutal way;[146] for another, the war experiences shared by all soldiers blurred the existing racial lines within the army to a degree.[147] The consequence of this, combined with Allied propaganda about conducting a war for freedom and equality for the entire world, was that African soldiers began to reflect more about their own situation and how it was marked by social, economic, and racial discrimination. Except in a few individual cases, there is no well-founded evidence to substantiate the idea that masses of African veterans underwent a profound politicalization, as Imanuel Geiss and others argue.[148] The war experience influenced the political ideas of later militant leaders like Ahmed Ben Bella and Bildad Kaggia, but even Kaggia himself confirms in his autobiography how little the homeward-bound veterans were interested in nationalism.[149]

At the forefront of the minds of the great majority of returning veterans were the social and economic situations and not vague political ideas.[150] After spending years to save the world from the totalitarian threat, men were no longer willing to submit to the yoke of a repressive colonial regime. A report of the Post-War Employment Committee in Kenya evaluated the ideas of the average African veteran as follows: "His desires will be such that he will not generally be content with the low standard with which most Africans were content before the war."[151] The expectations to receive social and economic compensation for the sacrifice made to the war effort far exceeded those that the colonial powers were willing to fulfill. In the eyes of white settlers, the return of the African veterans was the personification of a threat to the colonial order.[152] The colonial authorities tried to resolve the problems of demobilization with a series of programs but ran up against the limitations of colonial realities. The colonial system was based on the discriminatory treatment of the indigenous population and did not lend itself to the restoration of domestic peace. The land distribution policy in the British colony of Kenya is a quintessential example of this. Whereas white veterans from South Africa and even former Italian prisoners of war were allotted land, the African veterans were left empty-handed and instructed to return to the reservations.[153]

An enhanced awareness of their own situation and a greater sense of expectation were evident not only among the veterans, but also within the entire colonial population. To an increasing degree, the colonial powers were concerned about the effects of their own propaganda. No longer did the demagoguery of the Axis powers cause them headaches, instead it was the American campaign championing the Atlantic Charter principles. Through propaganda efforts, World War II had led to an "information explosion"[154] and to the collapse of "imperial isolation."[155] It was nearly impossible for the colonial powers to control the content of the news, let alone prevent it from reaching the colonial population. Particularly the situation in North Africa was troubling. In a directive for the North African Arabic Service of the BBC, it was ordered that all reference to the Atlantic Charter be avoided, since this would lead to controversial questions in the French territories.[156] The work of the Centres interalliés de documentation, which distributed brochures like *Victory* and *La Charte de l'Atlantique* among U.S. troops, and the lively contact between the American liberators and the Muslim civilian population was evaluated by French authorities as a serious threat stimulating the nationalist forces.[157] The official report on the Sétif riots even claimed that anti-French propaganda by the United States and the misinterpretation of the Atlantic Charter were responsible for the severe unrest.[158]

The war aims had indeed made the colonial populations more aware of their own situation and raised their expectations for a better postwar order. The indigenous populations had resisted the seductive promises of the Axis powers, remained loyal to their colonial rulers, and supported the war against the totalitarian challenge at great sacrifice.[159] In return, they expected to be rewarded, along the lines of "equal sacrifice, equal rights," with an improvement of their social and economic situation. For the few active politicians of the nationalist movements like Abbas in Algeria and Jomo Kenyatta in Kenya, these expectations became the foundation on which they built their political argument. World War II had not politicized the masses in the colonies, but it had made them more receptive to the ideas of equality and freedom and thereby created a broad base of support for the leaders of the nationalist movements. Politicians like Abbas spoke not only to a small elite, but also to large sections of the population, whose changed attitude was being given a political direction.[160] These leaders used the vocabulary of Allied war propaganda and invoked the declared principles and promises. For example, with the end of the war in sight, the central committee of the party founded by Abbas, Amis du Manifeste et de la Liberté, declared: "Long live the victory of democracies over fascism, Hitlerism, colonialism, and imperialism."[161] In their eyes, the Allied victory was not simply a defeat of totalitarianism but also meant an end to colonial repression. As the British Colonial Ministry had feared, concepts like freedom, equality, independence, and self-government had become an "inconvenient boomerang,"[162] and the Atlantic Charter had spread like a bushfire across the vastness of the African continent.[163]

The moral armor of the Allies in the struggle against the totalitarian challengers was now donned by the nationalist movements in preparation for their attack on the colonial powers.[164] As African nationalist Ndabaningi Sithole put it, "During the war the Allied Powers taught the subject peoples (and millions of them!) that it was not right for Germany to dominate other nations. They taught the subjugated peoples to fight and die for freedom rather than live and be subjugated by Hitler. Here then is the paradox of history, that the Allied Powers, by effectively liquidating the threat of Nazi domination, set in motion those powerful forces which are now liquidating, with equal effectiveness European domination in Africa."[165]

From this standpoint, World War II would prove to be the decisive turning point in the collapse of the European colonial empires. The people of Africa and Asia now judged the new world order against the expectations evoked during the war.[166]

Divided World: Human Rights as a Moral Basis and a Colonial Burden

The Establishment of the International Human Rights Regime

The grave violations of human rights standards during World War II demonstrated dramatically the importance of universal basic rights.[167] The united fight against the threat of totalitarian regimes, aided by Allied propaganda, catapulted the debate on human rights into the limelight of public awareness.[168] The declarations of the Allies were now expected to be followed with specific steps to anchor human rights in the new postwar order as a legacy of the war. Even before the war had ended, Roosevelt had called human rights the necessary prerequisite for enduring peace and announced that the aim was not only to win the war but also to win the peace.[169] Basic human rights were not only to be protected within the framework of a new international organization, they were to be the foundation of nothing less than a new world order.

At the Dumbarton Oaks Conference from August to October 1944, at which the four big powers—the United States, the Soviet Union, Great Britain, and China—consulted on the form of a new world organization, there was no mention of human rights. The conference participants tried only with their concept of the "Four Policemen" to secure their positions of power and harvest the fruit of victory.[170] Essential aspects of the Atlantic Charter were ignored out of the fear of losing national sovereign rights. Only China incorporated a human rights aspect by demanding racial equality. The resulting Dumbarton Oaks Proposals sparked a veritable storm of protest from other members of the war alliance, such as Canada, New Zealand, and Australia, as well as from many NGOs. Above all, smaller countries and the colonial populations felt robbed of what they thought to be the due reward for their sacrifices, particularly in view of the repeated assurances by the big powers that the war was being fought to insure the establishment of human rights. As Professor Rayford Logan from Howard University pointed out at the time, the Dumbarton Oaks Proposals completely ignored the colonial problem.[171] For his part, W. E. B. Du Bois warned that the United Nations would not succeed in creating a lasting peace as long as people in the colonies were being denied their natural rights.[172] The prime minister of New Zealand, Peter Fraser, put it succinctly: "The principles of the Atlantic Charter are not platitudes. They are principles that must be honored, because thousands have died for them."[173]

As a reaction to the Dumbarton Oaks Conference, twenty nations attending the Inter-American Conference on Problems of War and Peace in Mexico City in March 1945 put forth their own proposals for the founding of an international organization. Invoking the principles of the Atlantic Charter, the final resolution stipulated that human rights be anchored in the United Nations Charter. In addition to the proposals advocated by these countries, NGOs made particularly great effort to influence the planning of the United Nations. It was to the credit of nongovernmental organizations such as the American Jewish Committee that the founding conference of the United Nations in San Francisco, at which human rights were incorporated into the UN Charter, did indeed become a marked turning point for the international protection of human rights.[174]

In his welcoming address, Harry S. Truman, the new U.S. president, claimed that the objective of the conference was to be the creation of a new world based on the respect of human dignity.[175] In the period that followed, however, the Western democracies were not the primary sponsors of this honorable objective; this role was assumed by human rights activists, humanitarian organizations, and delegations from countries of the "South."[176] For the countries of Latin America, Africa, and Asia, the calls for human rights and racial equality were an essential step on the path to equal standing in the new world order. Furthermore, the memory of being denied racial equality at the Versailles Peace Conference of 1919 was still all too fresh. Jan Burgers maintains that the push to strengthen the protection of human rights far beyond the originally proposed draft of the UN Charter was fueled not so much by the terrible human rights abuses of World War II but by the experiences of racial discrimination and colonial repression.[177] By advocating the inclusion of human rights in the UN Charter, the "nations of color" shook the foundations of an important pillar of the old order, namely European colonialism. How could countries like Great Britain and France, on the one hand, be members of a world organization that committed itself in its founding document to the promotion of racial equality and universal human rights and, on the other, remain colonial powers that denied great numbers of the world's population these same rights? The human rights discourse was thus linked to the question of the future of European colonies, and it is not surprising that the colonial rulers were not interested in prominently anchoring basic rights in the UN Charter. The failure of the initiative sponsored by Chile, Cuba, and Panama to include a "Declaration of Essential Human Rights" in the UN Charter[178] meant that human rights were not embedded in this document. The United Nations only acknowledged universal rights as a common objective.[179] Thus, the charter's preamble reaffirmed the faith of the international community "in fundamental human rights, in the dignity and worth of the human person, in the equal rights of men and women and of nations large and small."[180] This was supplemented in Article 1 of the UN Charter with the declared purpose of the United Nations "to achieve international co-operation . . . in promoting and encouraging respect for human rights and for fundamental freedoms for all without distinction as to race, sex, language, or religion."[181]

This objective was laid down both for the UN General Assembly in Article 13 and for the Economic and Social Council (ECOSOC) in Article 62 of the UN Charter. In addition, member states pledged themselves in Articles 55 and 56 to take joint action to promote human rights. Article 68 of the charter even went as far as to give the ECOSOC a mandate to set up its own commission for the purpose of promoting human rights. Furthermore, these same objectives were to be pursued in the territories placed in the newly created international trusteeship system of the UN, but were not applicable to colonial territories. An initiative to include a corresponding reference to human rights in the "Declaration Regarding Non-Self-Governing Territories" (Art. 73) was defeated by the resistance of the colonial powers. This fact and the euphemistic description of colonies as "territories without self-government" demonstrate the reticence of the United Nations to declare colonialism as incongruous with the new order of international law. The vocabulary used with regard to human rights also remained very vague and weak overall, because the text spoke only of "promoting" and "encouraging" instead of "protecting" and "guaranteeing" human rights. The member states also built in a defense mechanism in Article 2, paragraph 7, against the intervention of the world organization in their national sovereign rights.[182]

The resulting situation was paradoxical. On the one hand, nations pledged themselves to advance human rights on the international level, while, on the other, they violated these same rights domestically, as was evident in racial discrimination in the United States, the elimination of political opponents in the Soviet Union, and racial repression by the colonial powers. This paradox weakened whatever degree of authority the UN Charter attributed to universal rights. The willingness existed to preach but not to practice human rights. For this reason, several critics of the founding UN document called it "a charter for a world of power"[183] when compared to the idealistic promises of the war. Professor Logan called the result of San Francisco a "tragic joke" in which an organization had been created that was heavily armed with principles but without any practical means or power to implement these.[184]

Despite all these drawbacks and deficits, some people publicly praised the positive aspects of the charter, including the recognized international lawyer Hersch Lauterpacht: "It is in the Charter of the United Nations that the individual human being first appears as entitled to fundamental human rights and freedoms."[185] Others called the founding of the UN "a milestone in the evolution of human freedom" and the charter an "epoch-making document."[186] Even though Truman had to concede in his closing address in San Francisco that the Charter of the United Nations was not perfect, he reaffirmed his optimism that this document had created the framework for further development in human rights.[187] John P. Humphrey, the director of the human rights department at the UN General Secretariat, also emphasized repeatedly that human rights had been mentioned in various sections of the UN Charter that also were valid for the peoples living in areas without self-government. In his opinion, the prerequisite for solving the colonial problem meant that the responsible governments first had to firmly implant and implement human rights and fundamental freedoms there.[188]

Although the colonial populations were at first deeply disappointed with the results of the San Francisco conference, the founding of the United Nations renewed their hopes for a better future. They used the UN Charter as a point of reference in making their own demands for equality as well as for economic and social improvements.[189] The Fifth Pan-African Congress in October 1945 in Manchester, England, illustrates this impressively.[190] By demanding racial equality, self-determination, and human rights, the delegates affirmed their support of the principles spelled out by the United Nations. At the same time, they declared their readiness to resort to violence as a final means to secure these rights should the Western world continue to adhere to repression.[191] The second final resolution, "Declaration to the Colonial Workers, Farmers, and Intellectuals," underscored their determination to secure independence and fight against imperialism by issuing the appeal "Colonial and Subject People of the World— Unite!"[192] The Manchester conference thus became not only the high point of the Pan-African movement, but also an important event in the history of decolonization.[193]

The UN Charter did indeed create new opportunities to establish the international human rights regime. In the ECOSOC resolutions 5 (I) from 16 February 1946 and 9 (II) from 21 June 1946, the ECOSOC commissioned the newly founded Human Rights Commission, chaired by Eleanor Roosevelt, to draft an "International Bill of Rights."[194] With significant input by Charles Malik, Peng-chu Chang, John P. Humphrey, and René Cassin, the Drafting Committee produced various proposals. Initially, the starting point of the committee's work consisted of a 400-page paper by Humphrey, in which he collected various suggestions put forth by national governments, NGOs, and private individuals. According to Humphrey himself, he geared his work to the ideas of Hersch Lauterpacht, H. G. Wells, the Institute of International Law, and especially the American Law Institute.[195] Humphrey's paper was then reworked by René Cassin, who thereby became known erroneously as the sole "father of the human rights declaration."[196] After the commission approved the joint draft on 18 June 1948,[197] based on Cassin's version, the paper was submitted to the UN General Assembly to be voted on. On 10 December 1948, the General Assembly passed the Universal Declaration of Human Rights in Paris with forty-eight votes in favor and eight abstentions.[198]

The Universal Declaration[199] was conceived in the aftershock of the gruesome experiences of the war that had just ended. It was revolutionary in its content. For the first time in history, individuals were granted elementary rights by the international community of nations and thus evolved from a pure object to an acting subject of international law.[200] On the basis of human dignity, every person possessed inalienable and indivisible rights of a universal nature: "Everyone is entitled to all the rights and freedoms set forth in this Declaration, without distinction of any kind, such as race, color, sex, language, religion, political or other opinion, national or social origin, property, birth or other status."[201] This was an avowal of the fundamental principle of equality that excluded every form of discrimination. In Articles 3 to 19, the Universal Declaration guaranteed every person the right to life, to freedom from slavery and torture, and freedom of religion, conscience, and opinion, and in Articles 20 and 21, the political rights of a constitutional democracy, such as the freedom of peaceful assembly and association and the right to take part in the public affairs of the individual's country. The third group of rights, found in Articles 22 to 27, contained basic rights such as the right to social security, the right to work, and the right to rest and leisure. In addition to rights, Article 29 lists the duties of the individual toward the general welfare. The declaration was not a legally binding contract as recognized by international law, but a declaration of intent set forth by the international community of nations. Nevertheless, it represented an "international Magna Carta of all mankind"[202] with great moral authority, a "milestone in the long struggle for human rights,"[203] and it was considered to be "one of the most important achievements of the United Nations."[204] Not only did the declaration enter the canons of customary international law, it became a decisive reference for the further development of the international human rights regime, which experienced a brief flourishing in the immediate postwar period with the signing of with a series of important treaties.[205]

The Universal Declaration was not the first UN document issued to protect basic human rights. On 9 December 1948, the UN General Assembly passed the Convention on the Prevention and Punishment of the Crime of Genocide. As a legally binding treaty, the Genocide Convention went far beyond the mere declaration of rights from the standpoint of international law. In addition to defining the elements of genocide, it provided a legal basis to prosecute the worst crime against humanity, namely the planning and execution of the complete physical and cultural annihilation of ethnic, racial, religious, and national groups. However, soon after it was passed, the UN Genocide Convention disappeared in the archives for nearly forty-five years.[206]

Far more important was the role that the Universal Declaration played in further developing the international protection of human rights. It was very influential in the comeback of international humanitarian law as manifested by the 1949 Geneva Conventions. In a letter dated 15 February 1945 and addressed to the governments of the United States, Great Britain, the

Soviet Union, France, China, as well as to the national Red Cross committees, ICRC president Max Huber was already appealing for support to reaffirm if not even expand "Hague Law."[207] World War II had revealed the weaknesses of the existing conventions with brutal clarity. In the course of the ensuing human rights discourse, an improvement of international humanitarian law was achieved with the signing of the Geneva Conventions of 12 August 1949.[208] These conventions not only enhanced the status of prisoners of war, they introduced a new dimension by improving the protection of civilians during wartime and by extending the application of international humanitarian law to noninternational armed conflicts. Revolutionary was precisely this consensus on Article 3, which is included in all four conventions and hence referred to as the "convention in miniature."[209] It guaranteed minimum humanitarian standards in internal conflicts that could be ignored neither by governments nor by resistance movements without stepping outside the bounds of civilization.[210]

The Universal Declaration also became the central reference in the development of legally binding human rights conventions, the project on which the Human Rights Commission focused its work starting in 1948. However, the conflicts arising during the course of the Cold War and the resistance of the colonial powers impeded agreement on an acceptable draft until 1954, when one was indeed presented to the UN General Assembly. Yet another twelve years and many debates were necessary before both human rights covenants were finally adopted by the United Nations in 1966.[211] At the European level, success came considerably sooner with the creation of the European Convention on Human Rights (ECHR), signed in Rome on 4 November 1950.[212] The preamble of the ECHR referred directly to the Universal Declaration of Human Rights,[213] and the European Convention can be assessed as the first major success on the regional level for the protection of human rights.

"Source of Embarrassment"

The fact that the United Nations documents, the Geneva Conventions of 1949, and the European Convention on Human Rights established the international regime of human rights as the moral foundation of the new world order should not, however, be permitted to belie the occurrence of controversial debates over the protection of human rights, of resistance against it, and of its weaknesses.[214] Compared to the period prior to 1945, the international human rights regime had undoubtedly been revolutionized in just five years, and the newly created human rights documents formed the basis for all further development. However, debates on the protection of universal rights, be they in the United Nations or at the diplomatic conference of the International Red Cross in 1949, were overshadowed by the diplomatic trench-digging of the emerging Cold War. Each side tried to use human rights as a propaganda weapon in pursuit of its objectives.[215] At the same time, each side had to be careful—for its own protection—that nothing potentially dangerous to its own position be included in the human rights agreements.[216]

While the West attempted to portray itself as the guardian of human rights and demanded free elections in the Eastern Bloc, the Eastern European countries criticized race discrimination in the United States and in the territories under colonial rule.[217] These conflicts also reflected the efforts of both ideological camps to court the "nations of color" by publicly advocating universal rights. Therefore, Yugoslavia's attempt to name colonial populations explicitly in an article it proposed for the Universal Declaration was vehemently quashed by Great Britain in agreement with France. To specifically name certain groups of people, certain colonial populations, was argued to be prompted by propaganda motives and rather absurd, since all humans enjoyed the same rights according to Article 2.[218] In a 1949 circular to the British colonies, the colonial secretary Arthur Creech Jones called the Universal Declaration of Human Rights the best instrument "for purposes of Soviet propaganda and mischief making."[219]

The colonial powers were not only concerned about communist propaganda; far more disconcerting for them was anticolonial agitation worldwide. British foreign secretary Ernest Bevin maintained, "The repercussion of foreign opinion regarding Colonial policy cannot be ignored in our international relationship nor can governments carry on in the Colonies as in the earlier days because of the rapid growth of political consciousness among the Colonial people."[220] Members of the anticolonial movement used the United Nations as an international forum through which they could effectively publicize their demands. The nations of the "white world" still dominated the international organization when it was founded, but the acceptance to membership by new independent countries like India and Pakistan meant that former colonies were being internationally represented, and they also consistently used UN treaties and bodies for their own objectives.[221]

Already in June 1946, Indian diplomats accused South Africa of racial discrimination against its African and Indian populations, which prompted the UN General Assembly to pass Resolution 44 (I) from 8 December 1946, requesting that both countries conduct talks and submit a final report to the

General Assembly.[222] This decision did indeed mark the start of a new era; never before had an international organization so openly addressed the issue of race. South Africa's prime minister Jan Smuts reacted to this by noting that the United Nations was now dominated by the "coloured peoples."[223] Subsequently, the issue of racial discrimination became one of the most important human rights topics on the agenda of the United Nations, and with its help, UN member states from Africa and Asia successfully linked the discourse on human rights with the problem of colonial rule.

In their effort to enforce human rights, the former colonies relied primarily on the help and authority of the General Assembly, the Economic and Social Council, the Human Rights Commission, the Sub-Commission on Prevention of Discrimination and Protection of Minorities, and the Committee on Information from Non-Self-Governing Territories.[224] The legitimate basis for their demands was primarily the Universal Declaration of Human Rights, which had led a few UN delegations to find the "oppression of colonial peoples intolerable."[225] Without explicitly using the term "self-determination," the Universal Declaration had ventured beyond the UN Charter to declare the right to self-determination as a fundamental human right in Article 21.[226] According to this article, all people had the right to participate in the public matters of their country, whereby the will of the people was the foundation of legitimacy for public authority. A people's right to self-determination was thus transformed from a political principle as anchored in the UN Charter to a codified norm.

Against the strong resistance of the colonial powers, the African and Asian UN members fought to secure the human right to self-determination in legally binding UN documents.[227] From the standpoint of the British Colonial Ministry, any discussion on the right of self-determination in the non-self-governing territories was to be avoided as much as possible and the effort to include the right of self-determination in the human rights covenants was to be blocked because, it was said, this would lead to "disastrous confusion" in areas with mixed population groups, such as in the East African settler colonies.[228] Despite this resistance, the General Assembly adopted Resolution 421 (V) on 4 December 1950, in which the Human Rights Commission was directed "to study ways and means which would ensure the rights of peoples and nations to self-determination."[229] The resolutions of 1952 went even further in that they demanded the inclusion of the right to self-determination in the planned human rights covenants and the active promotion of this right.[230] With this de facto acknowledgement of the right to self-determination as a basic human right by the UN General Assembly, the discourse on decolonization became inseparably linked to the discourse on human rights.

At the Asian-African Conference in Bandung, Indonesia, in April 1955, the participating delegations referred to the Universal Declaration of Human Rights in their final communiqué and declared the independence of a people as a prerequisite needed to fully enjoy all fundamental rights. By denying fundamental human rights to subjugated peoples, colonialism was at the same time a threat to international security and freedom.[231] Moreover, the entire discussion on universal rights revealed the true face of colonialism, meaning the negation of natural rights for a vast majority of the world's peoples. In his introduction to Albert Memmi's famous book *The Colonizer and the Colonized*, Jean-Paul Sartre wrote: "Colonialism denies human rights to people . . . whom it keeps in poverty and ignorance by force."[232] Colonialism was being pilloried before the eyes of the world by the discourse on human rights, which offered African and Asian countries the opportunity to use human rights rhetoric to denounce the colonial powers and make them look foolish. Universal human rights had become the moral armor of the anticolonial movement, and therefore it lay in the interests of these countries to push for the expansion of the human rights regime and to embed the human rights discourse in the consciousness of the general public.[233]

This development enlarged the dilemma facing the colonial powers, who wished to appear as supporters of the international human rights regime, on the one hand, and vehemently defend their colonial ambitions, on the other.[234] It was in this vein that the British colonial governments for Gambia, the Gold Coast, and Sierra Leone commented on the Universal Declaration: "We can hardly expect to win the confidence of Africans by making statements of 'ultimate ideals' while in practice we take steps in precisely the opposite direction."[235]

As founding members of the United Nations, colonial powers like Great Britain and France had indeed strongly advocated the idea of human rights. At the San Francisco conference in 1945, the British secretary of state for dominion affairs Lord Cranborne had declared: "We are all in favor of freedom, but freedom for many of these territories [the colonies] means assistance and guidance and protection."[236] In light of its long liberal and democratic tradition, Great Britain was presented as a model in the international protection of human rights, and the treatment of the individual within the British Empire was praised as exemplary.[237] By presenting a series of its own proposals and drafts, the British Foreign Office tried to exert a definitive influence on the human rights documents if for no other reason than to prevent the "countries of the South" or the Eastern Bloc from taking the initiative. With regard to human rights, the second largest colonial power, France, even enjoyed a reputation as the "motherland of human rights," a reputation it intended to maintain by way of its commitment to human rights in the tradition of the French Revolution.[238] Yet the country, still reeling from the liberation from German occupation, could contribute little materially to the project of establishing the international human rights regime. Therefore, France's goal was to become the leading idea-giver, which was reflected in its proposals for the Universal Declaration of Human Rights, the European Convention on Human Rights, and the Geneva Conventions.

The colonial ministries of both countries were far less enthusiastic about the human rights commitment of their respective UN delegations. Particularly in Great Britain, developments in the area of human rights were watched with growing concern. In the secret section of the above-mentioned circular to the British colonies, dated 28 March 1949, the British colonial secretary at the time, Creech Jones, called the Universal Declaration a potential "source of embarrassment"[239] that would have undesirable effects on the colonies. Representing the stance of the British colonial administration, Kenya's governor Sir Philip Mitchell claimed that the international human rights declaration was extremely "dangerous to the security of the colony," and that he was being forced to implement it against his will.[240] His counterpart in Southern Rhodesia, Governor J. N. Kennedy, refused instructions to publish the Universal Declaration in the official law gazette and argued that such a step would make it look as if the document were legally binding, which in turn would be used as propaganda ammunition for agitators.[241] The Universal Declaration and the Human Rights Covenants were perceived as threats to colonial interests.

In the opinion of Creech Jones, Great Britain, as a member of the United Nations, had indeed committed itself to participate in the Human Rights Commission, where the British delegation was to ensure under all circumstances that the international agreements adopted a framework acceptable for the colonies: "In fact the requirements and the views of governors [of the colonies] are frequently the decisive factor in determining United Kingdom policy in regard to international agreements of a political character drawn up within the framework of the United Nations, e.g., the draft covenant on Human Rights."[242] British policy on human rights was thus geared toward colonial needs, and the British intervened each time that "too many" human rights disrupted "colonial security." For this reason, the British government rejected the idea of including internal armed conflicts of any sort in international humanitarian law, because it feared international intervention in connection with colonial unrest.[243] Above all, particular passages of the draft version of the Geneva Conventions, such as the ban on "collective punishment," caused the Colonial Office a great deal of headache because this was a common and efficient instrument used by the colonial government to suppress unrest. From the viewpoint of the Colonial Office, the practice of burning entire villages to the ground in Malaya and the punitive bombardments in the protectorate of Aden demonstrated the value of measures of collective punishment, and the ministerial authorities refused to let local security forces be robbed of such effective means. The Colonial Office informed the government that it was aware of the international complications, specifically the accusation of "imperialistic tyranny," but the importance of the measures for the colonies would more than justify any trouble in dealing with this.[244]

It was not until the French delegation at the 1949 conference submitted its proposal to apply only the minimum humanitarian standards of Article 3, instead of all humanitarian norms, to "internal conflicts" that the heated discussions ended and the decisive breakthrough occurred, which then led to the signing of the four Geneva Conventions.[245] In taking this step, the French had not been moved by their desire to see humanitarian protection applied to the colonial population during internal unrest. After all, the French had fought against including the phrase "colonial conflicts" in the conventions. Instead, the French had been motivated to play such a major role by their very recent experience with German occupation, in which resistance fighters had been denied the status of combatant,[246] and by France's objective to protect its own people in future wars.[247]

Far more problematic than the Universal Declaration, which was strictly a nonbinding declaration of commonly shared ideals, were the planned human rights covenants of the United Nations and the European Council. The legally binding nature of these two documents, if applied to the colonial territories, could cause colonial governments serious embarrassment and difficulties.[248] Besides the legal codification of fundamental rights like the freedoms of opinion, assembly, and association, the most problematic aspect was the means by which these rights were to be implemented, namely by a right to petition for individuals and NGOs. Such a means had to be prevented under all circumstances.[249] London's governor in Nairobi, Mitchell, even interpreted it as a threat to world peace to grant such a right to an organization "such as the United Nations, which has degenerated into nothing more than a means of international intrigue."[250] Hersch Lauterpacht had pointed out several times the enormous importance of the right to petition if human rights were to be effectively protected, for it was only through exercising this right that the proper bodies could be informed of human rights violations and mobilized to act.[251] Without an individual's right to petition, the international human rights regime was a paralyzed giant with out ears or eyes, a behemoth who was deaf and blind to reports of violations and unable to react to them.

A fierce debate had already occurred within the Human Rights Commission about the appropriateness of having the right to receive and react to petitions.[252] Yet the commission ended up being damned to passivity because the U.S. government feared grievances over racial discrimination, the colonial powers of Great Britain, France, Belgium, and Portugal shuttered over the possibility of grievances about the conditions and practices in their colonies, and the Soviet Union harbored concerns regarding Stalinist crimes perpetrated against its own people.[253] ECOSOC Resolution 75 (V) of 5 August 1947, in which the Commission recognized "that it has no power to take any action in regard to any complaints concerning human rights,"[254] was the equivalent of a legal incapacitation and led to a real inefficacy of the United Nations in monitoring and implementing human rights standards. In the words of John Humphrey, this process had just created what was "probably the most elaborate wastepaper basket ever invented."[255]

As far as the British Colonial Office was concerned, plans to include the right to petition in the human rights covenants needed to suffer the exact same fate. If this did not happen, London expected a flood of petitions to the United Nations from individuals and discontented political groups from the colonies, which "may land the United Kingdom in considerable embarrassment internationally."[256] Furthermore, such a right would give the United Nations an opportunity to intervene in the domestic affairs of the colonies, and the authorities feared a loss of loyalty among their colonial subjects, who might well come to think of the world organization as the final guarantor of their rights.[257] Once again, the views of the Colonial Office won out over those of the Foreign Office, and the British UN delegation adopted a staunch stance of resistance toward the proposed right to petition:[258] if, as a member of the United Nations, Great Britain was indeed committed to the protection of human rights, then at least such protection had to be made as ineffective as possible and the decisions of the Human Rights Commission as "harmless as possible."[259]

For this purpose, London needed a coalition of like-minded partners in the various UN bodies, and a search began among the other colonial powers. The British had been appalled to see Belgium and especially France strongly advocate the right to petition. So it became the intention of the British to encourage the two governments to increase their influence over their respective delegations in the Human Rights Commission and to compel the delegations to support a common line against the right to petition.[260] With this intent, the British Colonial Office sent a letter in April 1949 to the French and Belgium colonial ministers that referred to the agreement reached the previous January in which the three governments had vowed to work closely on matters regarding the human rights covenants. The right to petition, noted Lord Listowel, was a very dangerous weapon for discontented elements in the colonies, and the political backwardness of the colonial population would, with great probability, lead to a misinterpretation of the covenant and the right to petition included in it. In order to prevent intervention by the United Nations in the domestic affairs of the colonial powers and to hinder any instrumentalization for anticolonial propaganda, the colonial nations had to adopt a united front against the right of individual petition.[261] Particularly because it had the situation in the Congo in mind, Belgium fell into line behind the British.[262]

Only Paris hesitated. On the one hand, the French government, as a constitutional democracy, recognized the absolute necessity of the right to petition in order to implement human rights, while on the other, as a colonial power, it feared the danger of intervention.[263] This ambivalent stance was also caused by the awkward position in which the French UN delegation now found itself having to speak out against a principle that it had proposed itself in 1948 on the initiative of Cassin.[264] Moreover, the French republic was trying at the time to assert its tradition as the "nation of human rights" through the work on the human rights covenants by Cassin at the United Nations and by Pierre Henri Teitgen at the European Council. As an important pillar in the human rights discourse, France was able to enhance its reputation internationally and articulate its claims as a major power following its complete collapse in World War II. On the occasion of the rapid French ratification of the Genocide Convention, Lemkin congratulated the French foreign minister, Robert Schuman, on this exemplary step and praised "France as a major world leader, especially in humanitarian affairs."[265]

However, France's role as a leader suffered from growing anticolonial criticism and the heating up of the military situation in its overseas territories, such as Indochina. Even the French foreign ministry had to acknowledge that human rights were becoming a burden and a threat to colonial interests. Consequently, the ministerial authorities at Quai d'Orsay brought their position more in line with that of Great Britain in the period that followed. At a meeting on 31 March 1952 between the French colonial minister Pierre Pflimlin and his British counterpart Oliver Lyttelton, a close cooperation on all colonial matters was agreed upon.[266] In addition to regularly scheduled meetings at the ministerial level and mutual consultation, the two governments agreed on a joint position against every form of intervention by the United Nations in the domestic affairs of their overseas territories, namely the right to discuss political issues as well as to permit visiting missions and petitions.

Another instrument used by the French government to defend itself against the growing criticism of its human rights policies in the colonies was the drafting of the "Dossier de Défense contre les attaques anti-coloniales."[267] The French foreign ministry instructed its foreign missions in countries of the anticolonial bloc, like India, Saudi Arabia, Burma, Afghanistan, and Chile, to file extensive reports on the human rights situation on the ground there. For example, the French ambassador in Kabul reported that the principles of the Universal Declaration were embedded in the Afghanistan constitution, but were completely ignored in practice.[268] Likewise, Jacques Baeyens, France's representative in Santiago de Chile, reported on the discrimination of the indigenous people by the Chilean government.[269] With these dossiers, Paris sought to react to accusations at the United Nations by having the French UN delegation accuse the anticolonial states themselves of transgressions committed in implementing universal rights. In this manner, human rights also became an important tool of colonial propaganda to defend against anticolonialism. Especially during the course of the looming "contested decolonization," this strategy would become a crucial factor in the diplomatic defense of the colonial powers and, in the end, would make universal rights a diplomatic pawn in international debates.

Chapter 3

Contested Decolonization, 1945–1962

> In Africa, in the Middle East, throughout the Arab world, as well
> as in China and the whole Far East, freedom means the orderly but
> scheduled abolition of the colonial system. Whether we like it or
> not, this is true.
>
> —Wendell Willkie, 1943

Recolonization Instead of Decolonization

The "Second Colonial Invasion" and New Concepts of Securing
Colonial Rule

By 1957, all the talk about human rights had simply become too much for
Sir Robert Armitage, the British governor of Nyasaland. He outright refused
to include the Universal Declaration of Human Rights in the curriculum for
the colony's African schools,[1] despite the worldwide attention such a decision
could be expected to attract, especially in 1958 on the occasion of the tenth
anniversary of the Universal Declaration. In Armitage's opinion, the terminology of the UN document was inappropriate, and the task of differentiating
between ideal objectives and practical realities was too difficult for African
school children to grasp: "We are, of course, doing the exact opposite of that
which is set down in a number of the articles [of the Human Rights Declara-
tion], and no doubt will continue to do so for the next generation at least, if
not for ever."[2] The Colonial Office in London sympathized greatly with its
governor and concurred with his views.[3] Nine years after the international
community of nations had declared the existence of universal rights, nothing

substantial had changed in most of the colonial territories with regard to the human rights situation.

Neither the colonial governments nor the metropoles were interested in implementing democratic and human rights reform in the overseas territories in the near future, if at all. According to the historian Mark Mazower, this overall ambiguity was best symbolized by the fact that "most Europeans seemed scarcely aware that any inconsistency was involved in defending human liberties at home while acquiescing in imperial rule overseas."[4] One of the main reasons why the colonial metropoles vehemently resisted efforts to universalize fundamental human rights and ensure their international protection lay in the nature of colonial rule itself. The historian Jürgen Osterhammel believes that the "construction of inferior 'otherness,'" manifested in its most extreme form as colonial racism, and the European missionary belief connected with it constituted the basic element of colonial thinking,[5] in which colonial rule was seen as the moral duty to develop the "inferior" races, was "glorified as the gift and act of grace of civilization, and was respected as humanitarian intervention"[6] The universal recognition of natural, inalienable basic rights not only questioned such a moral legitimation of colonial rule and made the so-called "white man's burden" obsolete, it would inadvertently lead to the demise of the European empires.

Influential leaders and political masterminds of the anticolonial movement, such as the Vietnamese revolutionary leader Ho Chi Minh, the Tunisian Jew Albert Memmi, and the native of Martinique Frantz Fanon,[7] describe the colonial situation in their publications as a divided world[8] in which, against a racist backdrop, a majority of the global population[9] were being denied their most basic rights. Racism was, Memmi maintained, the quintessence of the relationship between the colonizers and the colonized,[10] the latter of whom were all but ignored as human beings but valued instead according to their assessed usefulness for the colonial rulers.[11] The indigenous population in the colonies was stereotyped as lazy, stupid, and brutal, and Memmi saw this constant humiliation as serving the purpose of self-aggrandizement for colonial rulers.[12] Ho Chi Minh also interpreted the situation this way but took it a step further: "If one has a white skin, one is automatically a civilizer. And when one is a civilizer, one can commit the acts of a savage while remaining the most civilized."[13] As a result, Ho Chi Minh, Fanon, and Memmi advocated armed resistance against colonial rule. In their view, violent colonization had to be ended through violent decolonization.[14] As Fanon stated in his "Manifesto of the Anticolonial Revolution," decolonization not only questioned the entire colonial situation, it included a plan for absolute upheaval.[15]

The European colonial powers harbored absolutely no interest in radically changing the existing power relations and reordering the colonial world. Decolonization "remained off the European political agenda."[16] On the contrary, the shared objective of the colonial powers was the reinstatement of the colonial status quo and a return to their colonial hegemonic position.[17] As previously mentioned, World War II had permanently shaken the political constellation, especially in the Asian territories, and increasingly threatening signals were being sent from the Far East to Europe that the region had come to a turning point in its colonial history.[18] On 17 August 1945, only three days after the Japanese surrender, the leader of the Partai Nasional Indonesia (PNI), Ahmed Sukarno, proclaimed the independent Republic of Indonesia and broke with the Netherlands.[19] Sukarno justified his desire for liberty with the words: "Is liberty and freedom only for certain favoured peoples of the world? . . . Indonesians will never understand why it is, for instance, wrong for the Germans to rule Holland if it is right for the Dutch to rule Indonesia. In either case the right to rule rests on pure force and not on the sanction of the populations."[20] Just a few weeks later in Hanoi, on 2 September 1945, Ho Chi Minh followed Sukarno's example and declared independence from France, with explicit reference to the American Declaration of Independence of 1776 and the French Declaration of the Rights of Man and of the Citizen of 1789.[21] A few weeks later, he justified the escalation to armed resistance in South Vietnam by arguing that France had betrayed the Allies already during the war by turning over the country to the Japanese. Now that the war had ended, Paris was again sabotaging the Allied promises of democracy and freedom. The Vietnamese people, however, clearly fought on the side of the Allies in the struggle against the Japanese occupiers and were acting according to Allied principles: "Not only is our act in line with the Atlantic and San Francisco Charters, etc., solemnly proclaimed by the Allies, but it entirely conforms with the glorious principles upheld by the French people: Liberty, Equality, and Fraternity."[22] In using this line of argumentation, the anticolonial nationalists held up a mirror to the European colonial powers that reflected with brutal clarity the betrayal of their own principles and the fundamentally antiliberal concept of their colonial rule.

The European powers thus had a common interest in regaining the initiative as quickly as possible, defusing the dangerous situation, and restoring colonial normalcy in the periphery. The historian John Springhall is absolutely right to speak of this as "the struggle for European recolonization" with the most prominent examples being the Dutch East Indies and Indochina.[23] To this end, the metropoles depended on their colonial solidarity, and Great Britain in particular came to the aid of France and the Netherlands in their efforts to regain the reins of power. After the Japanese surrender, the South-East Asia Command under Lord Louis Mountbatten attempted to fill the ensuing power vacuum as a colonial power.[24] The British interest in an orderly return of its colonial allies was rooted especially in the fear that uncontrolled anticolonial nationalism could spark a chain reaction also in British territories.

In order to prevent the spread of nationalism, the first British troops landed on Java and Sumatra on 28 September 1945, where they created a series of bridgeheads. The declared aim was the disarmament of Japanese soldiers, the liberation of Allied prisoners of war, and the reestablishment of colonial order in the Dutch East Indies.[25] As the irony of fate would have it, Indian troops composed the main contingent of this recolonizing military operation, which cleared the way for a return of the Netherlands to its colony. Under the protection of the British and Australian armies, an advance guard of the Royal Dutch Indies Army (KNIL)[26] arrived a few weeks later in Jakarta, and the army would grow to a force of 150,000 men by the spring of 1947. The immediate Dutch participation in the British expeditions against the Indonesian *pemuda* (nationalist rebel) militias only signaled the start of one of the bloodiest and most gruesome chapters of Dutch colonial history. The government in The Hague decided to resort to military force in order to protect the political and especially economic interests of the Netherlands.[27] In the operations carried out in 1947 and 1948—euphemistically called the first and second "police actions"—the KNIL availed itself of a horrific military strategy that would soon become the hallmark of all decolonization wars.[28] Only under pressure from the United Nations and the United States, which threatened to exclude its European allies from receiving Marshall Plan aid, did the Netherlands abandon its colonial ambitions.[29] The anachronistic attempt by the Netherlands to reconquer its colonial possession in the period from 1945 to 27 December 1949, when Indonesia finally gained its independence, cost 2,500 Dutch soldiers and an estimated 100,000 to 150,000 Indonesians their lives.[30]

In the French colony of Indochina, the British army occupied the southern part of the country up to the sixteenth parallel, as stipulated by the Potsdam Conference, and thereby also facilitated the return of the former colonial power.[31] On 24 September 1945, the French colonel Jean Cédile assumed the command over southern Vietnam, in order to prepare for the arrival of the expedition corps under General Leclerc and Admiral Georges Thierry d'Argenlieu. The establishment of a major military presence left no doubt that Paris intended to secure France's hold over all of Indochina and to make no concessions to the nationalistic demands of the Viet Minh. By the end of 1945, Laos, Cambodia, and South Vietnam had been successfully recaptured.[32] Only in the northern province of Tonkin had the Vietnamese government under the presidency of Ho Chi Minh been able to establish itself and political negotiations with the French ensued.

The diplomatic interlude, during which the Vietnam Republic was officially recognized and included in the French Union on 6 March 1946,[33] was still not enough to belie the growing tensions. Harmless customs disputes gave the French military command the pretext it needed to bombard the North Vietnamese port city of Haiphong from 23–28 November 1946, an operation believed to have killed six thousand people.[34] As it was, the die had long been cast in favor of a military solution to the Indochina question,[35] and the fires that nearly destroyed all of Haiphong also ignited France's first major decolonization war.

In light of the violence involved in recolonization, why did the colonial powers cling to their claims to the colonies and thereby run the risk of expensive colonial wars even though they themselves had been weakened by World War II? In short, both Great Britain and France linked their position as world powers primarily to their overseas possessions and saw this position threatened should the colonies be given up. The restructuring of the international system thus did not serve their interests, because their enormous empires enabled London and Paris to at least maintain their claim of global power parity with the new superpowers, the United States and the Soviet Union.[36] In January 1948, the British foreign secretary Ernest Bevin explained it this way: "We have the material resources in the Colonial Empire, if we develop them, and by giving a spiritual lead now we should be able to carry out our task in a way which will show clearly that we are not subservient to the United States of America or to the Soviet Union."[37] This view envisioned the colonies as being able to prevent what had actually already occurred, namely the decline of the country to a regional European power in the postwar period. Churchill's motto during the war, "Hands off the British Empire," was essentially adopted by the new Labour government under Prime Minister Clement Attlee, which was not at all willing to give up the empire, only to restructure it.[38]

During the war, de Gaulle had also left no doubt about the French willingness to maintain its colonial empire, the existence of which was both the key and guarantee of French *grandeur*.[39] In 1949, a poll showed that 81 percent of the French felt the colonies served the interests of France,[40] and French schoolbooks propagated this idea in sentences such as: "European France is a mid-sized power, together with Overseas France, it is a big power, the French Union."[41] Much like the case of the Netherlands, the colonies also served as a prestige object for France, with which the nation could obliterate the disgrace of occupation and defeat during World War II.[42] Thus, Gaston Monnerville declared on 25 May 1945 in the Assemblée consultative where he was serving as an elected delegate: "Without its colonial empire, France would only be a liberated country. Thanks to its colonies, France is a victorious nation."[43] The overseas territories proved to be an apt setting in which to erase the indignities suffered during the war and to demonstrate the new strength of the victor in military conflicts.[44]

By holding onto their colonies, the European colonial powers not only satisfied their ambitions for world power but also solved some very practical problems. The war had taken a great toll on Great Britain and even more so on France, and both colonial metropoles were in dire need of resources for their economic reconstruction.[45] During the war, the overseas territories had proven to be sources for raw materials and foodstuffs, and their full potential had not yet been realized. London and Paris sought to change this with large-scale investment programs and thereby strove to achieve a seminal improvement of the economic and infrastructural conditions in the colonies. Instead of an orderly retreat by the European rulers, the colonies experienced a "second colonial invasion,"[46] which focused increasingly on the African continent the more the two colonial powers found themselves on the defensive in Asia. As Jürgen Osterhammel notes, Africa had never been as important for the European powers prior to 1945 as it was in the decade and a half following the end of the war when they blanketed the continent in their developmental colonialism.[47] This new European attention meant that the overseas territories were overrun by an army of experts, colonial officials, and new settlers, all of whom aimed to implement successfully the ambitious plans for development. As a result, the colonial powers intervened more than ever in various social and economic structures in the colonies that had previously been unscathed by European intervention. Instead of the freedom they so longed for, colonial populations now experienced an intensification of colonial rule, which they perceived as being more severe and more threatening than ever before.[48]

Even during the war, Britain's Colonial Office had worked on plans for a new colonial development policy[49] in order to keep the colonies content and avoid colonial unrest, as Colonial Secretary Malcolm Macdonald expressed it at the outbreak of the war.[50] The Colonial Development and Welfare Act of 1940, which allotted five million pounds annually to development programs over a ten-year period, meant the beginning of a new era of state-run development policy in the colonies.[51] In September 1944, the Colonial Office was of the opinion that "the end of the fighting in Europe will . . . be the psychological moment at which to announce our intention to make fully adequate provision for the assistance from His Majesty's Government which will be necessary for a dynamic programme of Colonial development. It is the moment at which to demonstrate our faith and our ability to make proper use of our Colonial possessions."[52] The Colonial Development Act of 1945, which would be followed by four further pieces of legislation, underscored this demand with a budget allotment of 120 million pounds.[53]

At first, political reforms played a minor role in Colonial Office deliberations, even though, in his report in 1942, Lord Hailey had called for greater integration of Africans in the local councils and the colonial government.[54] A commission headed by Sydney Caine and Andrew Cohen adopted these ideas in May 1947 and spoke out in favor of African participation in political life.[55] In a gradual transfer of power, London strove to cooperate with the small African educated elite, whose help it wanted in guaranteeing British influence over the long run and in steering radical nationalist demands into more moderate directions.[56] The Commonwealth system lent itself as a means to do this for it represented an intermediate solution, as it were, between colonial status and complete independence. However, political reforms between 1948 and 1951 were limited to West Africa, where the colonial population was allowed to participate in elections and an Africanization of the administration took place. In other parts of the empire, such as in the East African settlement colonies, democratic reforms, like those proposed by Colonial Secretary Creech Jones in his circular directive to the African governors on 25 February 1947,[57] were vehemently rejected. London's officials in East Africa, particularly Sir Philip Mitchell in Kenya, were of the view that British rule was in the best interests and to the civilized benefit of the African population of their colonies.[58]

Reform and development became important pillars of British colonial policy and served several functions. The main objective of the announced reforms was to improve the economic and social situation in the colonies, in order to be able to better exploit existing resources for the reconstruction of

Great Britain.[59] The chronic lack of dollar reserves and raw materials motivated London to classify certain regions as essential for the British economy, like Malaya with its rubber plantations and tin mines.[60] The surrender of the empire's most valuable "dollar-earner" was never a topic of debate; instead, the British defended it doggedly in a protracted jungle war from 1948 to 1960 against the Malayan independence movement. At the same time, the reform policy served to renew and reshape the colonial empire in the aftermath of the upheaval caused by World War II. This policy was not to lead to the breakup of the empire; on the contrary, it was to carry out a measured and controlled transformation as stipulated only by the British themselves.[61] One consequence was that Great Britain retreated from regions like Burma and India in order to increase its involvement in the African colonies. Moreover, generous development programs were to help take the wind out of the sails of the unmistakable demands for freedom and independence voiced by national movements. However, authorities at the Colonial Office were not only attempting to impact the situation in the colonies. Economic and social reforms served also as a means to combat the growing international criticism of anachronistic colonialism, which was to receive a new humanitarian face and a new moral basis of legitimation by way of such "modernization."[62] In this way, outdated colonial ideas were to be translated into the democratic language of the twentieth century.[63]

Even supporters of Free France under de Gaulle were forced during the war to react to growing international pressure and to announce an expansive reform of colonial policy. In December 1943, the Comité Français de la Libération Nationale (CFLN) promised to implement a comprehensive reform policy affecting the peoples of Indochina, Algeria, and Madagascar. The high point of the announcements occurred at the end of January 1944 at the Conference of Brazzaville, where the guidelines for colonial policy in the postwar period were worked out in cooperation with the colonial governors.[64] The final communiqué of the conference recommended, among other things, the abolishment of both forced labor and the *code de l'indigénat*— the criminal code for indigenous peoples that was so hated by the colonial populations—and the creation of an investment fund for the "modernization" of the overseas territories.[65] The relationship between France and its colonies was to be reorganized into federal structures, whereby all tendencies toward self-determination outside the French Union were rejected unequivocally. Réne Pleven, the commissioner for the colonies of CFLN, made this point perfectly clear: "In colonial France, there are no peoples to liberate, no racial discrimination to abolish. . . . The overseas populations do not want any kind of independence other than the independence of France."[66] Therefore, Brazzaville was not the beginning of French decolonization, but the attempt to reinstate and reestablish French colonial rule completely.[67] At the same time, the reform announcements were also to act as "cover fire"[68] and as an appropriate answer to the liberal promises of the Atlantic Charter, in order to reduce the pressure being exerted by the international community, particularly by the United States.

Some of the promises of Brazzaville were indeed kept in the postwar period. A decree issued on 20 February 1946 abolished the *code de l'indigénat* and introduced French law in all colonies; forced labor was legally prohibited on 11 April 1946. The Lamine–Guèye Law of 7 May 1946 transformed all inhabitants in the French sphere of influence from subjects to citizens.[69] The introduction of these changes put France very close to the assimilation ideal of its traditional colonial philosophy, but at the same time would later make it enormously difficult to part with its overseas territories, as compared to Great Britain.[70] Once the Fonds d'investissement pour le développement économique et social des territoires d'outre-mer (FIDES) was established on 30 April 1946, Paris undertook the announced development and "modernization," which marked the departure from the old French colonial doctrine of *mise en valeur*. Just in the years from 1947 to 1952, Paris invested 326 billion francs in its overseas territories, followed by another 348 billion francs through the Deuxième plan de la modernisation introduced in 1954.[71] Thus, in the twelve years from 1947 to 1958, France invested more public funds in its colonial empire than it had during the entire period from 1880 to the outbreak of World War II.

The French government did not limit its reform only to economic reorganization but also redefined the relations between metropole and periphery. With the adoption of the new French constitution in October 1946, Paris struck the term "colonial empire" from the political vocabulary and replaced it with "French Union."[72] On the basis of equality and civil rights, a new national unit was created that combined France with its former colonies, which were renamed Départements et Territoires d'Outre-Mer (DOM-TOM). The new name actually changed little about the situation of the colonial populations, who were given no opportunity to vote on the new constitution. The dominant position of France remained untouched in the new constitution, and the government in Paris retained the all authority.[73] France's head of state was simultaneously the president of the new union, decisions were made in the French National Assembly, whereby the role of the regional colonial parliaments was only an advisory one, and, with the help of separate electoral colleges, France ensured a white majority in parliament. Like the federal structures, the reforms were reduced to a cosmetic minimum and made apparent the irresolvable contradiction between the equality principle and France's hegemonic position.[74] The constitution of the Fourth Republic was the attempt to proclaim the end of colonialism without really losing the overseas territories and to implement reforms without forfeiting any power.

The Use of Force to Maintain Colonial Power

By introducing reform and investment measures, France and Great Britain were pursuing the same aim, namely to recolonize their overseas territories and secure a long-term position of power. Yet this happened at a point when resistance in the colonies was becoming increasingly stronger. The British sociologist Frank Füredi refers to the years from 1944 to 1952 as "the radical moment of anticolonial politics."[75] During this period, the anticolonial movement would undergo the decisive development and radicalization that would leave its mark on the next two decades. From the anticolonial perspective, the nationalists needed to take advantage of the defensive position in which the colonial powers found themselves before the prewar status quo could be reestablished. The interaction between weakened imperial control, social discontent, and an enormously raised level of expectations with regard to the postwar order offered the national movements ideal conditions to address the colonial populations and produce "a basic anticolonial consensus."[76] Measured against the new expectations of people in the colonies, the proposed reforms were too little too late to stem the tide of anticolonial nationalism. Promises to better the social and economic situation in the colonies could not cancel out the desire for political codetermination and individual liberty.[77] The ever-growing dissatisfaction over the colonial situation and the perceived threat posed by the "second colonial invasion" was new grist for the mill of nationalist agitation. From the perspective of the colonial powers, the demands for self-reliance and independence tellingly disrupted their plans to recolonize these territories and needed to be repressed under all circumstances. Where peaceful announcements of reform could not pacify colonial protest, the colonial powers resorted to recolonization by force.

On the day World War II ended in Europe, 8 May 1945, the French army demonstrated in a bloody show of force that Paris would not tolerate any form of colonial resistance.[78] The victory celebrations in the Algerian towns of Sétif, Guelma, and Kherrata escalated to violent protests by Arab demonstrators against French colonial rule, including some subsequent attacks against the region's European population.[79] The French army did not hesitate to answer this provocation by launching concentrated air force and naval artillery attacks that arbitrarily destroyed entire Arab villages. The official statistics listed 3,000 Algerian victims as a result of these "measures to restore order" over a period of a month, whereas the number is today estimated to be between 15,000 and 45,000.[80] Not only did Sétif become one of the worst cases of repressive force in French colonial history, it also destroyed the entire basis for liberal reform in Algeria and heralded the beginning of the bloody recolonization of France's colonial empire. In the years that followed, Paris chose time and again to follow the old colonial recipe of demonstrating military strength and brutally putting down any form of resistance. This is also what happened in September 1945 in the Cameroon port of Douala, where French troops opened fire on stone-throwing demonstrators and killed over a hundred Africans. In the opinion of the historian Yves Benot, the cases of Sétif and Douala were excellent illustrations of the typical French reaction to use more or less violent colonial protest as an opportunity to "shoot into the crowd" and to resort to unhampered repressive measures.[81]

Worse was yet to come. The preliminary climax of violent recolonization was the repression of the uprisings in Madagascar in 1947 and 1948. On 29 March 1947, the first post-1945 national independence war in Africa began with attacks against military garrisons and gendarme posts and the participation of an estimated 15,000 to 20,000 rebels, the majority of whom were World War II veterans of the French colonial army.[82] Not until the French garrison was increased to 18,000 troops—chiefly Senegalese, Moroccan, and Algerian *tirailleurs*—did France succeed in restoring its control over the island by the end of the year. In doing so, the army under the command of General Pierre Garbay conducted a brutal war, at the time unprecedented in French colonial history. Places like Moramanga, the "Oradour of Madagascar,"[83] became synonymous for torture, mass executions, and the systematic destruction of entire areas in the wake of the French "cleansing operations." These measures, along with the gruesome mutilation of victims, were meant to act as a deterrent on the Madagascan population, who then fled in large numbers into the mountains and forests of the central province. This mass escape resulted in many of the 89,000 Madagascan deaths, not because those fleeing were killed in the fighting but because they died of hunger and sickness in the remote areas of the jungle.[84]

While the government in Paris presented new reforms and declared the colonial populations to be full-fledged citizens of France, the French army overseas used force against these new citizens. Diplomatic approaches were sacrificed with increasing frequency to military responses, as the example of Indochina demonstrates impressively. Although a peaceful solution had been signed by treaty with the government of Ho Chi Minh on 6 March 1946, France was still willing to risk an expensive eight-year colonial war to retain its Asian territories.[85] The military option, which was not abandoned until the disastrous defeat of Dien Bien Phu in 1954,[86] cost the lives of 75,000 soldiers of the French colonial army and of somewhere between 500,000 and 800,000 Vietnamese.[87]

Parallel to the war in Southeast Asia, the French army continued its "pacification mission" in other parts of the newly founded French Union, such as the Ivory Coast and Cameroon.[88] Particularly starting in 1947 in the North African areas of Morocco and Tunisia, the growing nationalism escalated into a series of armed incidents. Among the worst were the killing of more than one hundred Moroccans during the unrest in Casablanca on 8 December 1952,[89] and the French military operation in the Tunisian province of Cap Bon between 28 January and 1 February 1952, with over two hundred Tunisian deaths.[90] Once again, the troops under General Garbay, who had led operations in Madagascar, demonstrated their particular brand of ruthlessness in "pacifying" the Cap Bon region. Garbay justified the actions of his troops by maintaining that looting, raping, and the often ensuing abortions belonged to traditional local practices: "Rapes and abortions are a part of Tunisian customs and traditions."[91] Yet all of this was overshadowed by the events that would begin on 1 November 1954, in the Algerian Aurès Mountains, which marked the start of the Algerian War and the death blow to the contradictory double strategy to restore control over the colonial population using cosmetic reform, on the one hand, and radicalized force, on the other.

Compared to this, the manner in which Great Britain dealt with colonial resistance seems moderate at first. Unlike the government in Paris, London declined to use force to hold onto its entire empire. Instead, the British government—under pressure from the anticolonial national movements—withdrew in 1947 from areas like India and Burma, which would only have been retainable at great military and financial cost.[92] Even in the Mandate of Palestine, of great strategic importance for the British position in the Near East, it was decided to bend to Arab and Jewish resistance and transfer custody of the area to the United Nations.[93] However, as noted earlier, the British retreat was only a strategic move to prevent the weakened forces from becoming overburdened and to concentrate on certain other regions. Although Great Britain experienced colonial protest to an increasing degree, as are shown by the general strike in Nigeria and the unrest in Buganda in 1945, London initially reacted prudently. Force was only to be used in emergency situations and with great care, in order to avoid endangering the recently initiated reform measures.

This changed fundamentally in 1948 when two incidents caused panic at Whitehall and permanently shifted the British reaction to anticolonial resistance.[94] In February 1948, police forcefully stopped a protest march by African war veterans in front of Christiansborg Castle, the seat of the British governor in Accra, and in the ensuing unrest, 29 Africans were killed and 237 were wounded.[95] The Colonial Office was shocked by this incident because the Gold Coast had been seen as a model colony until then. In addition, the events fanned the fear of further attacks by "subversive" movements in other parts of the British realm. The murder of European planters in the Malayan town of Sungei Siput a few months later seemed to confirm these fears. With the declaration of a state of emergency in Malaya on 16 June 1948, the Colonial Office now switched to a policy of special laws and military force. For the next twelve years, what was called a "state of emergency" became an integral element of British colonial policy, as is proven by the cases of Nigeria and Uganda in 1949, the Gold Coast in 1950, and the Central African Federation in 1959.[96] Even smaller conflicts, such as the 1948 strike by sugar workers in British Guyana, were enough to deploy military troops. Following the "panic of 1948" and the incidents in Accra and Malaya, the Colonial Office had come to the conclusion that the growing nationalist danger in the colonies not only had to be countered with reform measures but also had to be fought increasingly with force.

The basis of this new policy was a paper written in January 1949 by the British high commissioner for Malaya, Sir Henry Gurney, about his experiences with the state of emergency in his territory.[97] In this paper, Gurney argued for the early use of emergency laws as a preventive measure. He believed that the deployment of police and military troops would wipe out colonial resistance in its early phase and thus prevent a large-scale conflict. Gurney's recommendations, which were highly influenced by the experiences in Palestine, became the Colonial Office guidelines for handling colonial unrest.[98] Governor Arden Clarke of the Gold Coast stated that he had followed Gurney's recommendations exactly by declaring a state of emergency on the occasion of the general strike in January 1950.[99] The deployment of security forces as the ultimate guarantee of colonial rule was meant to give London the pause it needed to restore control and implement its own ideas of development in the colonies.[100]

The state of emergency in Malaya lasted from 1948 to 1960 and became the first major decolonization war for Great Britain.[101] By deploying 35,000 British soldiers, London tried to stop the guerrilla attacks of the Malayan Races Liberation Army (MRLA), which had emerged from the communist partisan units of World War II. British troops destroyed entire villages and conducted the same type of warfare—meaning torture and mass executions—as their French counterparts had already done in Madagascar and Indochina. The Chinese population in particular was under universal suspicion of conspiring with the enemy and consequently suffered from repressive military operations. The excessive use of force, such as the practice by Gurkha troops of beheading the bodies of enemies killed, did not result at first in any notable military success.[102] Not until counterinsurgency warfare under generals Sir Harold Briggs and Sir Gerald Templer was used from 1952 to 1954 did the British succeed in combating the rebels; thus a good measure of the resistance had been broken by 1955.

When a state of emergency was declared in the crown colony of Cyprus on 25 January 1955,[103] due to the increasing number of attacks by the Cypriot liberation organization Ethniki Organosis Kyprion Agoniston (EOKA),[104] British security forces consequently fell back on the example set by General Templer in Malaya.[105] In defending the strategically vital Mediterranean island, which had become the headquarters of British troops in the Near East after the withdrawal from Palestine and the Suez Canal Zone, the British moved with great brutality against the Cypriot resistance in the years from 1955 to 1959. Bombings and attacks by the EOKA on British soldiers were answered with the collective punishment of the civilian population in the areas involved. The inhuman conditions and systematic torture of prisoners in the detention camps and the arbitrary execution of Cypriots even brought the case of Cyprus before the United Nations and prompted the Greek government to begin proceedings against the United Kingdom at the Council of Europe for violating the European Convention on Human Rights.[106] Although the human rights abuse that occurred during the major British "emergencies" in both Malaya and Cyprus was serious, it would be surpassed by the abusive force used in the biggest British war of decolonization: the repression of the Mau Mau movement in Kenya.

The Mau Mau War in Kenya, 1952–1956

"White Man's Country"

The beginning of British colonization and the forceful occupation of Kenya were closely connected to the building of a railway between the port city of Mombasa and Lake Victoria at the end of the nineteenth century.[107] Once the construction of the so-called Uganda Railway was completed in December 1901, the outposts of the empire reached farther into the interior and thereby manifested the British claim to the East African regions. The push for expansion soon met with bitter resistance by native African ethnic groups, like the Kikuyu who lived in the fertile Kenyan highlands. Through a series of "punitive expeditions" the British troops had managed by 1905 to "pacify" the new protectorate of British East Africa using great force. Voices could even be heard, like that of Francis Hall, a representative of the Imperial British East Africa Company, calling for the complete extermination of the Kikuyu as a pacification solution.[108] The military operations known as "nigger hunts"[109] increasingly came to resemble campaigns of destruction against the African population. In September 1902, as Colonel Richard Meinertzhagen stated himself: "I gave orders that every living thing except children should be killed without mercy. . . . Every soul was either shot or bayoneted."[110] The British officer described the modus operandi used by his troops as the typical policy of "scorched earth," which included the complete destruction of fields and villages and the random killing of people. According to him, the number of African victims was so high that the losses had to be falsified in the official reports out of fear of negative reactions from London.[111]

These destructive expeditions, coupled with the outbreak of imported epidemics of smallpox and the flight of the surviving Kikuyu, led to the depopulation of the Kikuyu tribal lands. The fertile highlands were now almost completely uninhabited and therefore soon attracted the increased interest of the British colonial government, which began to press for the settlement of this attractive region by a white population. Under the supposedly humanistic banner of a civilizing mission, this part of Africa was now to be transformed into a "white man's country."[112] The prospects of huge areas of cheap fertile land at first attracted mainly settlers from the English aristocracy to Kenya, who, like Lord Delamere, took possession of immense latifundios in the highlands. In this way, what had once been the tribal lands of the Kikuyu became the "White Highlands."[113]

Several waves of settlement turned Kenya, next to Southern Rhodesia, into the main settlement colony of Great Britain on the African continent.[114] British army veterans and aristocrats in particular made up the largest percentage of the new immigrants and created Kenya's image as a "gentleman's colony." Due to their extremely reactionary and racist mind-set, these groups of settlers felt they were destined to turn Kenya into a bastion of white supremacy forever. They were aware of being in a minority position compared to the African population and saw themselves as "an island of white in a sea of black."[115] Such a self-perception caused the settler society to flee in near paranoia from the "black danger" that they felt threatened their white supremacy with uprisings and murder plots. By developing a racist societal order, the white colonial rulers strove to gain complete control over the African majority and to guarantee their privileged position of power. Thus, settlers confronted Africans with a deep-seated racism and stripped them of humanity, as the words of Captain Chauncey Stigand in 1913 illustrate: "For the proper understanding of the savage African, one must not look on him as a human being, but as a rather superior kind of animal."[116]

Skin color became the decisive classification criterion of the economic, social, and political hierarchies in Kenya, at the lower end of which the African population was placed.[117] Tribal reservations were established and a series of regulations passed, such as those prohibiting Africans from even entering hospitals, hotels, restaurants, and schools, in an effort to set up racial segregation.[118] However, this soon became a dilemma for the white colonial rulers[119] because economic prosperity and thus the wealth of white farmers in the highlands was dependent primarily on the cheap labor of the African populations,[120] who were classified according to the criterion of "economically useful" or "economically useless."[121] Therefore, it could not lie in the interests of the white settlers to segregate the races completely and to push them off onto reservations. Instead, the aim had to be the controlled exploitation of African labor.

For this purpose, the semifeudal system of squatters was set up to provide white farmers with cheap African labor over a long period of time.[122] By introducing a "head and hut" tax, confiscating further African lands, and prohibiting the cultivation of profitable crops like sisal, tea, and coffee, the colonial government forced large segments of the African populations to leave the reservations and get wage-paying jobs in order to pay the overburdening taxes.[123] European settlers now made small parcels of their land available to these segments of the African population for their own agricultural use. In turn, the African squatters had to work for the white farmers without pay for a certain number of days. Without political rights and their own rights to land, African squatters thus found themselves completely dependent on their white masters, who could drive them from the farms at any time and thereby rob them of their basis of existence.[124]

The system of *kipande*, a passport with fingerprints, work permits, and personal data, which Africans had to have on their person at all times once they left the reservation, was yet another humiliating instrument of colonial control. In addition, the squatters were defenseless against the arbitrariness of their white masters, who eagerly took the law into their own hands and subjected their African workers to corporal punishment for even the slightest of wrongs.[125] Whipping with the *kiboko*, a whip made of rhinoceros skin, was something generally experienced among Africans working on European farms. Between 1917 and 1923, a series of serious abuse occurred in which African workers were beaten to death.[126] This type of physical violence was an integral element in upholding white rule and characteristic for racial relations in the colony. The exploitative feudal domination of the settlers over their African workers was representative for the repressive colonial regime in Kenya. Therefore, it is not surprising that the later Mau Mau movement recruited a large number of its members from the ranks of the squatters.

African resistance against the racial discrimination in all areas of life, experienced first and foremost by the Kikuyu, began to form in 1921 when the East African Association under the leadership of Harry Thuku was founded. Following his arrest and deportation, a group of his supporters formed the Kikuyu Central Association (KCA) in 1924, which became the main political body of the African population because it called for the abolishment of the *kipande* system and the introduction of comprehensive land reform, as well as social and political equality.[127] However, protest was limited to the political level. By establishing independent Kikuyu schools and churches in the years from 1921 to 1935, this ethnic group attempted to challenge the colonial state in the areas of education and religion.[128] Yet it was the acute problem of land reform that was the greatest source for the popularity of the KCA. Even though the Crown Land Ordinance of 1915 had recognized property rights of Africans, and the Devonshire Declaration of 1923 referred to the priority of African interests in Kenya,[129] nothing changed with regard to the unfair social and economic distribution of goods. On the contrary, the Kenya Land Commission of 1934 appalled the moderate African nationalists by confirming the validity of existing property relations and corroborating the rights of white landowners to monopolize the fertile highlands.[130]

As the historian Wunyabari Maloba notes, the development of African nationalism in Kenya was thus the result of social frustration and protest over racist colonial policy.[131] Not even the outlawing of the KCA in 1940 by the colonial government could break the growing resistance. In October 1944, the Kenya African Study Union (KASU) was founded, and under the new name of Kenya African Union (KAU) and the leadership of Jomo Kenyatta, it became the first national party in Kenya and began to campaign for the independence of the country. The far-reaching upheaval brought about by the war not only fundamentally changed the situation in Kenya, but it opened new doors to the African nationalist movement to recruit supporters.

The outbreak of World War II at first meant a major economic boom for the colony because of the increased demand for foodstuffs and vegetal raw materials essential for the war, like sisal. Thanks to this leap in economic grown, the white settlers enjoyed greater importance and tried to translate their stronger position into political power and to seal themselves off from the influence exerted by the Colonial Office.[132] To this end, they founded the Electors' Union in 1944, with the declared aim of guaranteeing white supremacy even in the restless postwar years. The period from 1940 to 1946 marked the high point of the influence of the settlers in the history of the colony. Their new self-confidence manifested itself in, among other things, the attempt to further increase the dependence of African workers by passing ever more restrictive measures and to eliminate Africans completely as economic competitors.[133]

Even the squatters had shortly enjoyed the prosperity of rising crop yields and income caused by the increased war demand. This development was to be abruptly ended by the restrictions on farming rights, the ban on keeping livestock, and far more disadvantageous work contracts.[134] The aim of such measures was to eliminate squatters as economic competition. As a means to fight African protest and the refusal to accept the new work conditions, the white colonials threatened to drive Africans from the white farms and send them back to the reservation. The forceful expulsion of 100,000 Kikuyu in the years between 1946 and 1952 brought the problems of the squatter system to a dramatic climax and led to a radicalization of African resistance.[135]

The Colonial Office was finding it increasingly burdensome to deal with the actions taken autonomously by the settlers, because the aggravation of domestic tensions undermined Britain's postwar colonial strategy. Therefore, London attempted to rein in the influence of the settler lobby in order to be able to implement its own ideas. Like other parts of the empire, Kenya was to benefit from the new British development policy as laid out in the Colonial Development Act.[136] To this end, the Development Committee, founded by Governor Mitchell, drafted a ten-year development plan in January 1945, whereby it recommended an intensification of the use of the highlands based on the economic success experienced during the war.[137] The result was the implementation of a series of agricultural improvement programs, such as terracing hillsides to protect the ground against erosion, whereby most of the work was performed by African forced labor.

Political reforms, combined with the gradual transfer of power as had been done in the West African colonies, were not a viable option in East Africa because white settlers held such a dominant position. Further, these reforms did not correspond with the ideas of the East African governors, who vehemently resisted any such plans put forth by Colonial Secretary Creech Jones.[138] In the mind of Kenya's governor Sir Philip Mitchell, the solution to the societal challenges lay instead in the development of a "multiracial" system. Starting from the imperialistic theory of "equal rights for all civilized men," his vision of multiracialism made it necessary first to educate the African population to become a civilized people.[139] Once they had fulfilled the British requirements of what it meant to be civilized, they would be allowed to participate fully in social, economic, and political life. This paternalistic transformation process was proposed as a long-term goal, which never once questioned the dominant position of the white population. The terms "multiracialism" and "racial partnership" were East African euphemisms with which one attempted to guarantee white supremacy at the cost of the African majority population.[140]

Instead of the anticipated improvement of their living standards following the war, the African population, especially the Kikuyu, experienced deterioration. Particularly on the reservations, the population explosion and the palpable shortage of farmland linked to it exasperated the social and economic problems.[141] This already tense situation was then worsened when the reservations had to incorporate the squatters who had been driven off the white farms. Many landless Kikuyu tried to escape the hopelessness of the reservations by moving to the outskirts of Nairobi,[142] which resulted in the dramatic growth of the slums—known as the "African Locations"—an increase in crime, and the proletarianization of large segments of the Kikuyu people. Furthermore, a large number of new white settlers immigrated to the colony after the war and were offered fertile farmland. This prompted the Kikuyu chief Koinange to remark in frustration that the Kenyans had suffered a heavy death toll to support the British in the fight against the Axis powers in World War II, but "now there are Italians and Germans in Kenya and they can live and own land in the highlands from which we are banned, because they are white and we are black. What are we to think? I have known this country for eighty-four years. I have worked on it. I have never been able to find a piece of white land."[143]

The land problem became the key issue for the Kikuyu because the land ownership not only enabled the Kikuyu to provide for themselves, it was also an elementary cornerstone of their traditional culture.[144] Without land, no Kikuyu could hope to achieve a respectable position within Kikuyu society and was thus forced to remain at the bottom of the social hierarchy. At the same time, the conflict between Africans and the colonial government was intensified all the more by the implementation of further compulsory measures connected with the new British development policy, which chiefly benefited white farmers. Instead of freedom, the "second colonial invasion" meant that the colonial state was making inroads into all facets of life and strengthening colonial rule.[145] The hopes born during the war for political participation and social and economic equality were bitterly dashed in this manner. The discontent was best embodied by the group of African veterans who had enjoyed training and social advancement in the army but were now returning home to find no opportunity in colonial Kenya to realize their new dreams and fulfill their expectations.[146]

The fuel that fed the fires for the African protest movement was a mixture of all these components: the deterioration of African living standards, the disappointment over unfulfilled expectations raised during the war, the worsening of the squatter problem, and especially the consequences of the "second colonial invasion." The strike in Mombasa in January 1947 and the unrest in Olenguruone and Murang'a were clear signals that the conflict was heating up. With its "development policy," the British colonial government had antagonized the majority of the African population more than ever and pushed them unwittingly into the arms of the KAU.[147] The hopes of the African populace concentrated above all on Jomo Kenyatta, who had returned to Kenya from London in 1946 and been elected president of the KAU the next year.[148] Kenyatta, who had argued the case for autonomy of the Kikuyu culture and African emancipation back in 1938 in his book *Facing Mount Kenya*,[149] became the symbolic figure of the protest against white supremacy. At the Pan-African Congress in Manchester in 1945, he clearly defined his political aims: "What we do demand is a fundamental change in the present political, economic and social relationship between Europeans and Africans . . . the Africans make their claim for justice now, in order that a bloodier and more destructive justice may not be inevitable in time to come."[150]

At first, Kenyatta's objective was to turn the KAU, which was primarily supported by Kikuyu, into a truly national movement for all Kenyan ethnicities and to mobilize the population on a massive scale.[151] In order to secure the loyalty and cohesion of as large a base as possible, political events included the holding of oath ceremonies, which were deeply engrained in the tradition of East African societies. The rising discontent offered Kenyatta a chance to sensitize the African population to his political demands and mobilize their support for the lifting of racial barriers, for more social and economic equality, and for the guarantee of political rights. Despite a large political campaign, the KAU could not move the colonial government to initiate serious political reforms. Five million Africans still lived in Kenya with no political representation and no guarantee of their individual liberties under a racist regime dominated by a white population totaling twenty-nine thousand. Too great was the resistance of the settlers' lobby, which unabashedly announced the continuation of their authoritarian rule in the 1949 publication of the *Kenya Plan* by the Electors' Union.[152] The authorities in Nairobi thus passed up an opportunity to democratize the country in cooperation with moderate nationalists and obviously underestimated the looming danger of a radicalization among the African populace.

Kenyatta's failure to change the colonial situation by political means meant that many young Kikuyu turned their backs on the KAU in disappointment and joined radical forces:[153] "Normal political methods through KAU seemed to be getting nowhere. The young men of the tribe saw that a time of crisis was approaching when great suffering might be necessary to achieve what they believed in."[154] In their eyes, white domination had to be ended by force, since the politics of the moderate nationalists had not led to any tangible results. It was particularly the squatter protest movement that was turning more and more into a militant wing of Kenyan nationalism.[155] Nairobi became the stronghold of the radicals, who began to organize themselves into various groups.

One of these, the Forty Group—whose members had been recruited mainly from among the ranks of disillusioned war veterans—soon assumed a leading position in the slums of the capital city.[156] Militant leaders like Fred Kubai, who would become the head of the Mau Mau, and Eluid Mutonyi finally succeeded in recruiting members from the Forty Group to form the secret organization Muhimu, which means about the same as "important." The first aim of the militant cell, also called the Central Committee, was to create an extensive organizational structure and to procure weapons, ammunition, and money.[157] On the political level, these men tried to weaken the influence of moderate politicians within the KAU and to infiltrate the party with their own people, which succeeded with the election of Kubai as chair of the Nairobi section of the KAU on 10 June 1951. Starting in 1950, the Muhimu also greatly expanded the use of oath ceremonies to recruit new members.[158] The aim of the oath was to strengthen solidarity within the movement and to commit the new members to common goals.[159] Over time, the ceremonies and oaths took on ever more aggressive forms, including the call for the banishment and killing of white people. Forced oaths under the threat of violence were certainly not uncommon. Deeply engrained in the cultural tradition of the Kikuyu, the oath constituted a strong instrument of power, the betrayal of which was life-threatening. By mid-1952, over 90 percent of the Kikuyu had sworn the "oath of unity."[160]

Increasingly concerned about these developments, the authorities in Nairobi began to show interest in the secret organization and eventually banned the Mau Mau Society in August 1950, following a rise in the number of violent incidents. The origins of the term "Mau Mau" has yet to be determined conclusively, so that a number of explanations still circulate.[161] During one police raid of an oath ceremony, a participant is said to have yelled out "uma uma," which roughly means "get out, get out." Another version is based on the police interrogation of a Masai about his participation at one such secret meeting, in which the man said that he had indeed been at the "mumau," the incorrectly pronounced Kikuyu word *muma*, or "oath." Regardless of its origins, "Mau Mau" became for both the British authorities and the white population at large the established term for the militant movement and a synonym for a sectarian group of Kikuyu who performed "barbaric" tribal rituals.[162]

Determined to prevent the revolt from spreading to other Kenyan ethnicities, the colonial government covered up the legitimate political demands of the Mau Mau and described them as a criminal organization that "intentionally and deliberately" sought "to lead the Africans of Kenya back to bush and savagery, not forward into progress."[163] According to Governor Mitchell, no one could characterize such disgusting evilness as a resistance movement, unless what was meant was a movement against God, morality, and everything that distinguished humans from scavenger reptiles.[164] Yet the British completely overlooked the economic, social, and racial causes for the outbreak of

violence. As the Mau Mau fighter Mohamed Mathu put it, "By paying the African slave wages for his labour, denying him access to secondary and higher
education, removing from him the best land in Kenya and treating him with
less respect than a dog, the white man of Kenya had created over the years a
resentment and hatred amongst Africans which had to explode into violence.
The European created the very thing he now condemns."[165]

The historians Carl Rosberg and John Nottingham are correct to assert
that the failure of the colonial authorities to make decisive reforms is responsible for the emergence of the Mau Mau, whom the historians consider a radical national movement, regardless of the view propagated by the British.[166]
Although the resistance movement recruited members mainly from the Kikuyu, a smaller number of Meru, Embu, and Masai attest to the fact that the
movement was indeed pursuing national aims that affected all Kenyan ethnic
groups.[167] By calling themselves the Land Freedom Army, the organization
emphasized this claim to be a national movement and made clear its priority
was to end colonial rule through the use of force. Eluid Mutonyi, a cofounder
of the movement, described the intention of the Mau Mau: "Our main objective was to demonstrate by action that Africans were fed-up with European
imperialism. We had noted that the demands made firstly by KCA and later
KAU as constitutional political organizations had fallen on deaf imperialist
ears. . . . We wanted to force the issue of independence."[168]

The lack of an intellectual leadership and a revolutionary party organization did, however, lead to the fact that no far-reaching politicalization of the
movement occurred and thus that there was no political strategy at all.[169] The
leaders concentrated mainly on the armed struggle and the development of a
military organization.[170] The Central Committee, headed by Kubai, Mutonyi,
and Bildad Kaggia, founded the War Council in early 1952, which was given
the job of procuring weapons and building military camps in the jungle. Because the Mau Mau, unlike other independence movements, had to survive
without any foreign support and logistic provisions, they were dependent
on the theft of weapons and ammunition. In addition, they concentrated on
violent actions to eliminate Kikuyu collaborators. The aim was to unify the
entire ethnic group and eventually the whole African population of Kenya by
eliminating the hated accomplices of the colonial regime within their own
ranks.

The main targets were the African chiefs who remained loyal to the British, as well as police informants and other Kikuyu who sided with the government. Over the course of the year 1952, the number of political assassinations

and murders increased dramatically. However, the Central Committee did not have a strong hand over the individual commandos, which sometimes acted on their own initiative and thereby provoked an escalation of the violence. David Anderson has correctly described the situation on the eve of the emergency as a mixture of planned political action and aimless criminal violence.[171] Though presented as a well-planned and carefully organized uprising against the colonial state by F. D. Corfield in his official report commissioned by the British government,[172] it was nothing of the sort. Rather, the declaration of the state of emergency occurred at least a year too soon for the Mau Mau leadership. The movement did not yet have a sufficiently powerful fighting corps nor was it equipped organizationally or logistically for a large-scale confrontation.[173]

The State of Emergency as a Means to Restore Colonial Order

The assassination of Chief Waruhiu on 7 October 1952 by a Mau Mau commando was the immediate cause for Governor Evelyn Baring to declare a state of emergency in his colony on 20 October 1952. As the paramount chief for Central Province and a declared opponent of the Mau Mau movement, Waruhiu, whom the *Daily Mail* bestowed the epithet "Africa's Churchill" post-mortem,[174] was the perfect figure to symbolize African collaboration with the hated colonial regime in the minds of the Mau Mau. His murder was a painful loss for the British authorities in Nairobi because he had been an important pillar in upholding British power, yet at the same time it gave them the opportunity to enact more severe measures. Vested with the far-reaching powers provided by the emergency regulations, the authorities in Nairobi now had a much greater arsenal at their disposal, such as the arbitrary internment of suspects without court order and the suspension of civil rights.[175] Moreover, security forces could count on the support of the military, which was beefed up by five regiments of the King's African Rifles (KAR) and the Lancashire Fusiliers.

The target of the initial military operation, given the code name "Jock Scott," was the arrest of 180 leading African politicians and suspected Mau Mau commanders, including Kenyatta, Kubai, and Kaggia. By decapitating the national movement in one swift police raid, the colonial government hoped to eliminate the small conspiratorial group believed to have been responsible for all the problems. The Kenya Emergency, planned as a preventive strike, opened the door to a military offensive against the growing wave of African nationalism as a whole and to the elimination of the national project in Kenya with one stroke.[176] As Gurney recommended in his guidelines, London intended to prevent the widespread growth of resistance by declaring a state of emergency early in the game. However, British authorities overlooked the fact that, by arresting and placing in detention moderate Kenyan nationalists, they had robbed themselves of the negotiation partners they needed. Kenyatta, whom the British altogether wrongfully accused in a political trial of being the organizer of the Mau Mau movement and hence sentenced to seven years of forced labor, thus became a martyr of the movement.

The British operation to decapitate the movement did not produce the desired result of weakening African nationalism; instead it led to radicalization.[177] Militant leaders like Dedan Kimathi and Stanley Mathenge assumed the vacated leadership positions and began, after their flight into the jungle, to create cohesive combat units. At the same time, the enhanced measures of repression used by security forces and the vigilante actions of white settlers drove an ever-increasing number of new recruits into the forest regions. Many white settlers apparently interpreted the declaration of the state of emergency to be like the "opening of the hunting season" on all Kikuyu, Embu, and Meru, who were universally suspected of conspiracy with the Mau Mau.[178] In addition to the forceful expulsion of 100,000 Kikuyu from white farms back to the overflowing reservations, the dramatic increase in the number of attacks against them led many Kikuyu to believe "that the Europeans were trying to exterminate the whole Kikuyu."[179] The flight of many young Kikuyu into the jungle was thus motivated by the will to fight and the aim to reach a place where they would be safe from settlers. Carl Rosberg and John Nottingham are correct to note that the violence perpetrated by the Mau Mau was itself derived from the conditions created by the state of emergency.[180] The planned preventive strike of the emergency thus achieved the exact opposite of its intended purpose: it transformed African resistance into open revolt.[181]

The densely forested and almost inaccessible regions of the Aberdare Mountains and Mount Kenya provided the Mau Mau with an ideal retreat. Here the rebels found a naturally protected location in which they could begin to develop a guerrilla organization militarily and logistically without being disturbed. To this end, a group of jungle camps was set up as a base for operations. Modeled on the British military camp, these facilities included troop accommodations, kitchens, mess halls, infirmaries, weapon production facilities, and provisional storehouses.[182] Camp life followed a strict regimen of military discipline according to a comprehensive code of conduct, which was upheld by a self-established military court.[183] In creating a military hierarchy, the Mau Mau also used the model of the British army insofar as they introduced military ranks and troop designations. This reflects the inevitable influence of the veterans, who brought their military experience from World War II to the armed resistance.[184] To train the new recruits, the former members of the British army applied what they had learned while fighting in the jungles of Burma. Over the course of the war, the rebel fighters developed a remarkable ability to adapt to difficult environmental conditions and to use these for their aims.[185] Therefore, the Mau Mau forces were not the marauding band of gangsters depicted by British propaganda, but a well-structured military unit. By developing its own rules, flags, identification cards, and military hierarchy, the resistance organization placed the authority of the British colonial state into question and documented its own claim to sovereignty.[186]

Despite its military organization, the Land Freedom Army never possessed a centralized high command and a commonly coordinated strategy throughout the duration of the emergency. The units on Mount Kenya were under the command of Waruhiu Itote, who called himself "General China," while Stanley Mathenge and Dedan Kimathi competed for the command of the troops in the Aberdare Mountains. In August 1953, the attempt was made at the Mwathe meeting to correct these basic shortcomings by establishing the Kenya Defense Council, which formally recognized the eight armies of the movement, their leaders, and regions of operation. Poor communications, the lack of a clear hierarchy of command, and the personal rivalry among the various commanders, particularly between Mathenge and Kimathi, made it impossible to turn the Defense Council into a high command; instead, the various troop leaders retained their independence.[187]

Efforts also failed to develop a political strategy parallel to military operations. In February 1954, the Kenya Parliament[188] was established under the leadership of Kimathi, who was appointed prime minister, and claimed to represent a type of African transition government, but one without its own political program.[189] Instead, the Mau Mau adopted the central demands of the KAU and subordinated themselves under the party's claim to political leadership: "Our demands are independence and land . . . and if the Government wishes for peace, our leaders, now in detention, must be released. They are the politicians and can argue for our national independence. If this is done, the Forest Fighters will stop war."[190] The imprisoned Kenyatta was honored as a national hero and accorded the position of an undisputed political leader. The Mau Mau saw themselves as a national liberation movement that used violent means to lend weight to political demands and thereby force Great Britain to relent to these demands.[191]

In this struggle, the forest fighters were completely dependent on the support of their "passive wing," which secured supplies from the reservations and particularly from Nairobi. The city slums continued to be the stronghold of resistance even after the emergency was declared and developed into the lifeline of the Land Freedom Army. "Nairobi was the main source of arms, recruits and other supplies for the fighters in the Aberdares and Mount Kenya."[192] The city guerrillas had established in Nairobi an autonomous region run by their rules, in which they assassinated collaborators, recruited new fighters through oath ceremonies, and stole urgently needed weapons and ammunition on a daily basis. Despite their efforts at thievery, the chronic lack of modern firearms could not be remedied; the Mau Mau did not even possess one thousand precision arms. Without foreign support, they saw themselves forced to battle the modern army of the British Empire with self-built guns and antiquated weapons such as bows and arrows, spears, and the machetes known as "pangas."[193] Despite these structural deficits and the utter technological inferiority of their arms, the Mau Mau mutated into an able fighting force of twelve thousand men between October 1952 and June 1953, a force that would grow to as many as thirty thousand forest fighters at the high point of recruitment. With these forces at their back, the movement could dare to go on the offensive. At the end of 1952, panic broke out among the white population when a series of attacks on settlers ended in the killing of Eric Bowker and Ian Meiklejohn.[194] More shocking was the murder of the entire Ruck family on 24 January 1953. This led to a protest march by an excited crowd culminating at the governor's palace in Nairobi, where protesters demanded the extermination of the Kikuyu. The remote farms in the White Highlands were almost in a state of siege. The aim of the attacks by the Mau Mau was to create a climate of fear and thereby make life unbearable for the white population in Kenya.[195] Even though the British propaganda used the attacks for its own purposes and suggested that Kenya was strewn with dead settlers, these attacks remained sporadic in nature. During the entire emergency, no more than thirty-two white settlers died, which was a number significantly lower than that of the traffic deaths in Nairobi during the same period of time.[196]

The attacks by the forest fighters were far more often directed against loyal Kikuyu, posts of the Home Guard—a militia consisting of Africans—and police facilities. Due to their geographic proximity to the forests and their insufficient defenses, these were predestined to be the targets of the night-time guerrilla attacks by the Mau Mau, who adopted a "hit-and-run" tactic in which they slipped quickly back into the natural protection of the jungle following an attack.[197] Using this tactic, they dealt severe blows to the security forces and achieved their greatest successes, such as the raid on a police station in Naivasha on 26 March 1953.[198] In this coordinated operation, a commando not only freed 170 prisoners, it also captured fifty guns with ammunition. At almost the same time, several hundred Mau Mau fighters assaulted the loyal-ist village Lari.[199] The attack was directed at Chief Luka and his supporters, who were to be punished as traitors for their collaboration with the British. The raid illustrates in a gruesome way the civil-war dimension of the conflict, a fight between loyal Kikuyu and the Mau Mau that lasted the duration of the emergency and led to the deaths of 1,819 loyalists.[200] In the end, far more Africans fell victim to the Mau Mau than white settlers, who were actually the main enemy. The Lari massacre was the largest bloodbath of the entire con-flict because 120 villagers lost their lives in the Mau Mau attack and another 400 Kikuyu were arbitrarily killed in the ensuing retaliatory measures.[201] Brit-ish propaganda stylized the massacre as the symbol of the bestial savagery of the Mau Mau while failing to mention the war crimes committed by its own side. The mutilated corpses of the Lari massacre were to become the most important British propaganda weapon in the fight for public opinion. What is more, the attacks on Naivasha and Lari demonstrated, to the horror of British armed forces, that up to that point they had thoroughly underestimated the ability of the Mau Mau to successfully attack military targets and important pillars of support for the colonial regime.

Shocked by the events in Kenya, authorities in London began to take the Mau Mau seriously and to rethink their own military operations. The inabil-ity of General W. R. N. Hinde to cope with the problems in Kenya cost him the high command in Nairobi in May 1953, when he was replaced by Gen-eral George Erskine. Erskine, a personal friend of Churchill, was given the command of all security forces, including police and reserve units, and thus vested with unlimited military authority.[202] In the War Council, founded in March 1954, he could better coordinate and effectively deploy each of the various military units. First the general decided to increase troop strength by bringing in three additional British battalions and six battalions of the KAR as well as by expanding the units of the Kenya Police Reserve, the Kenya Regi-ments, and the Home Guard.[203] This troop buildup was rounded off with a squadron of Harvard and Lincoln bombers from the Royal Air Force (RAF), whose job it would be to bombard the jungle camps. With such an impressive, well-equipped force of more than fifty thousand men, Erskine ventured to undertake an offensive.[204] For this purpose, more bases received better facilities and roads were built for rapid troop deployment in the inaccessible mountain regions. Entire stretches of land were declared "forbidden zones" in which anyone could be shot without warning. Although confrontations with the enemy became more frequent toward the end of 1953, the British troop advance into the jungle regions did not bring about the expected results. The enemy, who better adjusted to the natural conditions of the jungle war, could almost never be flushed out for a direct and decisive battle. Nor did the fifty thousand tons of bombs dropped in RAF air raids over the Kenyan jungle and the two million rounds of ammunition fired[205] bring about the desired results. Erskine realized that this war could not be won with conventional means.[206]

To win, in his opinion, it was crucial to gather detailed information on the location of this seemingly invisible enemy, which led to a massive escalation in the intelligence-gathering activity of the Special Branch.[207] In addition to setting up a system of informants, special screening teams began to interrogate interned Kikuyu. At the same time, Erskine believed it was also important to destroy the vital nerve of the Mau Mau, namely the broad base of support within the population. To this end, twenty-five thousand soldiers completely cordoned off Nairobi, the stronghold of the Mau Mau, on 24 April 1954, and began a systematic search of the various quarters of the city.[208] During "Operation Anvil," which lasted until 26 May, a total of fifty thousand people were interrogated and twenty-four thousand Kikuyu were sent to detention camps.[209] This meant that nearly half of the entire Kikuyu population of the city was interned, while the other half, primarily women and children, were forcefully sent back to the reservations. The destruction of the Mau Mau's urban networks made "Operation Anvil" the "turning point in the Emergency."[210] Erskine had broken the back of the movement by disrupting the supply lines so vital to the rebels' survival in the forests.

British security forces then commenced efforts against supporters in the reservations by interning a massive number of people suspected of sympathizing with the Mau Mau and forcing a million Kikuyu to resettle in "new villages."[211] Officially the purpose of these fortified villages was to protect inhabitants from Mau Mau attacks. In reality, the "villagization program" aimed to exert extensive control over the population.[212] At the same time, the troop strength of the Home Guard was increased to twenty-five thousand men, thus making the Home Guard indispensable in monitoring the population on the reservations and preventing contact with the Mau Mau.[213] Guarded barriers made up of trenches, traps, and barbed wire were set up around the jungle areas to prevent the Mau Mau from leaving the forests.

These measures did not fail to have the desired effect, because the lack of food, weapons, and ammunition put the Mau Mau completely on the defensive.[214] Particularly the constant hunger transformed their situation more and more into a struggle simply to survive. After the Mau Mau networks in the city and on the reservations had been almost completely destroyed, the British high command then began to increase the military pressure in the jungle regions. In a coordinated effort between ground troops and the air force, the forests were to be combed sector by sector and the Land Freedom Army put through the wringer. The large-scale purging actions "Operation Hammer" in the Abedare Mountains and "Operation First Flute" on Mount Kenya, carried out in early 1955, meant the beginning of the end of the Mau Mau, whose units were being chopped up into small scattered groups.[215] Exposed to unceasing attack by the British armed forces, the rebels were forced to retreat deeper and deeper into the mountainous forest regions, where the raw climate and gnawing hunger took their deathly toll.

When Erskine turned over his command in late April 1955 to his successor, General Gerald Lathbury, the Land Freedom Army was largely destroyed. It remained Lathbury's task to flush out and eliminate the remaining rebels. In doing so, he decided against undertaking further expensive military operations and concentrated on hunting down the rebels in the jungle by deploying small special commandos, the pseudo-gangs.[216] Eventually one of these special units, under the command of the white settler Ian Henderson, succeeded in catching the last remaining Mau Mau leader, Field Marshal Kimathi.[217] With his arrest on 21 October 1956 and subsequent execution, the last resistance was broken and the war in the forests ended. The estimated five hundred half-starved and wounded Mau Mau fighters who still held out in the jungle no longer posed any danger, so the majority of the British troops were shipped out of Kenya in November 1956. Although the military operations had ended, the state of emergency remained in effect until 1960.

The Kenya Emergency, which had been planned as a small police operation to arrest the African leadership of the nationalist movement, turned out to be the largest British war of decolonization. The armed conflict lasted more than four years and cost the lives of 167 British soldiers—63 of whom were white—and 1,819 loyal Africans. The number of Mau Mau fighters killed was listed as 11,503 in the official statistics,[218] but this figure may lie well under the actual number of deaths. Current estimates assume that 20,000 to 100,000 people died because the British figures do not include either the fighters in the forests who starved or succumbed to their wounds or those who were tortured to death or killed in the detention camps.[219] The military intervention did result in the complete annihilation of the Mau Mau movement, but not before the rebels had succeeded in dealing a few painful blows against British armed forces and in challenging the empire despite the serious technical inferiority of their weapons.

Ultimately, the Land Freedom Army could be destroyed because it did not have the support from abroad that helped other independence movements succeed. The fight for independence by the Mau Mau ended without the achievement of either of their political goals, land and freedom. Kenya remained a British colony and white rule seemed more firmly entrenched than ever. However, in light of the revolt, the colonial government in Nairobi did find it necessary to make a series of concessions to undermine support for the rebels and to pull the African population to their side.[220] The Swynnerton Plan included land reforms benefiting the African loyalists,[221] while at the same time the regulations restricting lucrative agricultural products like coffee and tea were relaxed. The Carpenter Committee Report argued for the introduction of a minimum wage for African workers and the Lindbury Commission on the Civil Service applied the principle of equal pay for equal work, regardless of ethnicity. The high point of these reform efforts was the proposal by the Lyttelton Constitution that all population groups participate in political life in Kenya.

The emergency had made it clear to the British government in particular that the rule of the white settlers could not be sustained without its extensive military and financial intervention.[222] Yet Great Britain was no longer willing to do this in the future, considering the enormous cost of £55,585,424[223] and the uncontrollable excesses of violence that had occurred during the state of emergency. The murder of eleven prisoners by guards at the Hola Detention Camp in March 1959 was a decisive turning point and accelerated the reorientation of the British government under Prime Minister Harold Macmillan and his new colonial minister, Iain Macleod.[224] The objective was no longer to hold blindly onto colonial rule in East Africa, but to cooperate with moderate African politicians with the intent to secure the controlled transfer of power.[225] The "wind of change," as Macmillan characterized the decolonization process on the African continent in his famous speech of 3 February 1960 before the South African parliament,[226] was acknowledged to be an irreversible political given and led finally to Kenya's independence on 12 December 1963.[227]

The Algerian War, 1954–1962

The Myth of the Three North African Departments

Algeria had belonged to the French sphere of influence since the military expedition conducted by General Thomas-Robert Bugeaud in 1830.[228] An expedition corps of thirty-seven thousand men had landed on the coast near Sidi-Ferruch to occupy first the important seaports of Algiers, Oran, and Bône. From these military bases, further conquest of Algerian territory was to be undertaken—as Bugeaud noted—to give Algerians the opportunity to enjoy French civilization, reason, and the European way of doing things.[229] However, the mission to civilize the Algerians only camouflaged far more self-serving motives such as the financial interests of the merchant bourgeoisie in Marseille and an urgently needed foreign-policy success to buck up the shaky Bourbon throne. The French push into Algeria soon met with bitter resistance from the Arab population in a series of uprisings.[230] In his guerrilla attacks from 1835 to 1847, the Emir of Mascara, Abdel Kader, was particularly successful in handing French troops a series of humiliating defeats.

France's reaction was to conduct an increasingly cruel conquest that came to resemble a campaign of destruction against the Arab population.[231] In this regard, the French colonel Lucien-François de Montagnac described the aim of the "pacification" by noting that "everything is to be destroyed that does not crouch at our feet like dogs."[232] Following the "scorched earth" military tactic, General Bugeaud had villages destroyed systematically and rewarded his soldiers after a victory by allowing them to plunder and rape arbitrarily. The gruesome climax of this policy was the suffocation of five hundred Arabs in 1845 in the grotto at Dahra, where they had fled and were then "smoked out" by the French army.[233] In his notes about his Algeria trip, Alexis de Tocqueville wrote about the French warfare: "I returned from Africa with the distressing notion that we are now fighting far more barbarously than the Arabs themselves. For the present, it is on their side that one meets with civilization."[234] All told, France needed more than forty years to finally subdue the last resistance, which was an uprising led by Sheik El-Haddad in 1871. During this period, the size of the indigenous population shrank from an estimated three million to two million inhabitants.[235] Despite the "pacification,"

Algeria continued to be a potential center of conflict within the French colonial empire.

In order to consolidate the subjugation of the populace and strengthen French rule, a systematic and intensive settlement policy was introduced. Bugeaud was convinced that the increased immigration of Europeans would marginalize the Arab population and thereby reinforce the military conquest.[236] In the period from 1833 to 1848 alone, the number of European settlers rose from 7,813 to 109,400.[237] In addition to the French, particularly poor immigrants from Malta, Italy, and Spain flocked to the country.[238] Although they never succeeded in challenging the numerical majority of the Arab population, the new immigrants did drive the indigenous population from all positions of leadership and from their lands. Algeria's colonial history was, as Jean-Paul Sartre noted, "the progressive concentration of European land ownership at the expense of Algerian ownership."[239] Several million hectares of fertile soil were confiscated and made available to the new European settlers, while the original owners were relegated to more inferior lands.[240] This wave of confiscation and displacement had a big impact on the consciousness of the Arabian population and bred "agrarian patriotism."[241]

At the same time, a colonial society developed in which the white-settler minority, known as the *colons* or *pieds noirs*,[242] dominated all facets of life, and racial discrimination was a key feature: "Racial affiliation was the line of demarcation among people. The privileged were, regardless of all class differences, the Europeans, even the workers among them. They all understood themselves as French, as the occupiers of Algeria, and as victorious conquerors. The vanquished were to pay tribute to them in one way or another."[243] This meant that the Arabs suffered extreme discrimination in all societal realms, be it the legal and tax system, income distribution, occupational distribution, education and training, or medical care.[244] The per capita income of the *colons* was, on average, five and a half times as high as that of an Arab worker.[245]

The Algerian two-class society was mirrored not only in economic and social issues, but especially in everyday racism. For the majority of Europeans, the Arabs were a "dirty people," unable to manage their own country effectively. Jules Roy, a journalist born in Algeria and a friend of Albert Camus, described the attitude of the *pieds noirs*: "It is what every European in Algeria thinks, without exception: the Arabs are a filthy breed and our mistake has been to treat them as human beings. They are good for nothing, the minute you trust them they rob you, they are opposed to any form of social progress, and the education we give them only makes us ridiculous."[246] There could be no talk of treating them as human beings, because white people permanently humiliated the Arabs with derogatory slang like *bicot*, *melon*, and *raton* that collectively denied them human qualities.

In October 1871 Algeria was turned into three *départements* and thus became an integral part of France. Albert Grévy, the French governor general in Algiers, stated that Algeria was now no longer a colony but a *prolongement*, a prolongation of France.[247] Consequently, the ministry for the interior became responsible for the country, and, as French citizens, the inhabitants of the new departments could send elected representatives to the National Assembly in Paris. For the Arabs, however, nothing changed, because they continued to be French subjects without civil rights or political representation and participation.[248] Citizenship remained dependent on service in the military, knowledge of the French language, and the rejection of the Islamic religion and lifestyle habits, which the great majority of Muslims refused to do. Furthermore, the Arabs were not subject to French law but to the regulations of the *code de l'indigénat*, the arbitrary criminal law for the indigenous population that included, among other things, corporal punishment, forced labor, collective punishment, and the confiscation of property. The code was an important instrument of colonial control and therefore came to symbolize unjust foreign rule to the indigenous population.[249]

Assimilation among the two sectors of the population also did not occur in the economic and social realms. Contrary to the grandiose promises to lead the overseas territories from backwardness into modernity as part of France's mission to bring civilization, Algeria remained an underdeveloped land. Periods of famine, during which children were forced to compete with wild dogs for scraps of discarded food, were a common phenomenon, according to Albert Camus's description.[250] With regard to France's achievements in developing the country, Jean-Paul Sartre asked pointedly: "Will we ask the Algerians to thank our country for allowing their children to be born into poverty, to live as slaves and to die of hunger?"[251] He also criticized the mission to introduce French civilization while denying the indigenous population access to education: "As for our famous culture, who knows whether the Algerians were very keen to acquire it? But what is certain is that we denied it to them. . . . But we did want to make our 'Muslim brothers' a population of illiterates. Still today 80 per cent of Algerians are illiterate."[252] Colonial reality debunked both the French ideal of assimilation and the transformation of Algeria into a *prolongement* as no more than a myth. As a result of this complete failure of France's assimilation policy, Algeria remained in a type of limbo that left it "more than a colony but less than a part of the motherland."[253]

Arab discontent over the extreme repression and racial discrimination manifested itself not only in a series of uprisings and strikes in 1916 and 1936, but especially in the emergence of Algerian nationalism in all of its various forms.[254] The religious organization Ulema d'Algérie, which grew out of the Koran schools, strove to restore an Islamic society and thus became bitterly opposed to assimilation, promoting instead the idea that "Islam is our religion, Algeria is our country, Arabic our language."[255] Even Ahmed Messali Hadj, who had founded the Étoile Nord-Africaine as the first Algerian party in 1926, rejected any rapprochement with France. As a radical representative of Algerian nationalism and chair of the Parti du Peuple Algérien (PPA), founded in 1937, he demanded immediate independence from French colonial rule. Moderate nationalists like Ferhat Abbas disagreed with this and called first for reforms to bring about social, economic, and political equality for the Arab population. Abbas appeared to have found a receptive ear for his demands in the newly elected Popular Front government under Léon Blum in France. The Blum-Violette Plan of 1937 intended to improve the situation of the Arab Algerians[256] but failed because of the resistance put up by the *colons*, who felt the plan endangered their privileged position.[257] Still, Abbas remained an advocate of assimilation policy and founded for this purpose the Parti de l'Union Populaire Algérienne pour la conquête des droits de l'homme et du citoyen in 1938.[258] He continued to reject the idea of Algeria as a fatherland and envisioned a future on the side of France.

The outbreak of World War II changed everything because the situation of the Arab population in Algeria rapidly deteriorated.[259] Failed crops in the years from 1940 to 1942, austerity in the overall food supply, the outbreak of a typhus epidemic, and the reactionary stance of the Pétain regime radicalized the Algerian nationalist movement. The Allied invasion at Sidi-Ferruch in November 1942 raised the hopes of Algerian nationalists that the end of colonial repression was near. Abbas, who had come to realize that equality and codetermination could not be achieved under French rule, now advocated independence for his country.[260] Inspired by the principles of the Atlantic Charter and discussions with Robert Murphy, Roosevelt's special envoy to North Africa, Abbas drew up the *Manifeste du peuple algérien*, published on 10 February 1943.[261] In it he called on the Free French, the United States, and the United Nations to ensure political self-determination and the end of colonialism, as was stipulated in the Atlantic Charter principles.[262] He specified these aims in the *Additif du manifeste*,[263] which appeared on 26 May 1943 and documented Algeria's claim to national self-determination and the independence. On 7 March 1944, the association Amis du manifeste et de la liberté was founded,[264] through which Abbas pursued his aim to form a coalition of all Algerian nationalists for the common cause of independence.

Although the French transition government officially declared its willingness to institute reforms, in reality it intended to fight the Algerian nationalist movement and reestablish France's rule in North Africa. The French high commander in Algeria, General Henry Martin, received the following instructions from de Gaulle on 14 August 1944: "We must prevent North Africa from slipping through our fingers while we are liberating France."[265] The tragic consequence of these instructions was the bloody suppression of the Sétif unrest in May 1945. The Algerian poet Kateb Yacine described this key Algerian experience: "My sense of humanity was affronted for the first time by the most atrocious sights. . . . The shock that I felt at the pitiless butchery that caused the deaths of thousands of Moslems I have never forgotten. From that moment my nationalism took definite form."[266] The events of Sétif were deeply seared into the collective memory of the Arab populace and led to the break with France. In particular, the horror of the colonial massacre convinced the many Muslim soldiers returning home, like Ahmed Ben Bella, of the necessity of an "Algeria for the Algerians."[267]

In France, the developments in its North African departments were evaluated from a thoroughly different perspective. In 1945, the socialist representative Raymond Blanc depicted the common future in the most glowing colors in the Assemblée consultative: "In its recovered grandeur, [France] will tomorrow spark a social revolution, shatter the power of money, eliminate feudalism, bestow true freedom to people, place the free press in the service of free people, and finally create a truly united and fraternal republic. In this republic, the people of Algeria will be included and no more problems will exist."[268]

In the course of reforming its colonial policy, Paris also intended to redefine its relationship to Algeria. To achieve this, it issued the Statut de l'Algérie[269] on 20 September 1947 in which, among other things, Arabic was introduced as the second official language, the Arab population was guaranteed political codetermination, and the Assemblée Algérienne was established.

The primary competencies of the Algerian regional parliament lay in the areas of financial, economic, and social policy, where the central government in Paris guaranteed a certain degree of regional autonomy. However, promises for political equality remained empty because eight million Muslims were represented by only sixty parliamentarians, while one million white settlers were represented by the very same number of parliamentarians. In place of a simple majority vote in parliament, French interests were also protected by a two-thirds quorum, so that nothing could be undertaken against the will of the *colons* in the end. At the same time, electoral fraud in Algeria, as witnessed in the 1948 elections, became a state arrangement that was viewed as a legitimate means to defend French sovereignty.[270] Instead of a comprehensive reorganization, the Statut de l'Algérie only brought about small cosmetic reforms.[271]

Parallel to the political situation, the social and economic development of the country also stagnated. Above all, the living conditions of the Arab population deteriorated so dramatically at the end of World War II that the journalist André Mandouze characterized the relations between France and Algeria in July 1947 as "Le mythe des trois départements" (the myth of the three departments).[272] The rapid growth of the Arab population from five million in 1926 to more than eight million in 1954 led to a shortage of farmland, major problems in the food supply, and an increased exodus from rural areas.[273] The outskirts of Algiers developed more and more into Arab slums. Large sectors of the Arab population found themselves in a process of immiseration that the French ethnologist Germaine Tillion calls *clochardisation*.[274] Particularly the people in rural areas suffered from chronic food shortages, which forced them to eat roots and grass to keep from starving. The French officer J. Florentin described the degree of underdevelopment in rural Algeria as such: "It only takes a few minutes to fly with the helicopter into Neolithic age."[275] His assessment was confirmed by the official Maspétiol Report, which pointed out, among other things, that over a million Muslim Algerians had no work and income.[276]

Such conditions, coupled with the political stagnation, caused many Algerian nationalists to turn away in frustration from the parliamentarian path and to attempt instead to achieve their aims by military means. In doing so, they could count on the broad support of the Arab population, who had noticed no improvement in their lives thanks to the new "fraternal republic" promised by the French. For them, Algeria remained rather a land lacking hope and rights.[277] Under the leadership of Hocine Ait Ahmed and Ben Bella, the former followers of Messali Hadj formed the paramilitary Organisation spéciale (OS) in 1947.[278] The group began to prepare for a violent confrontation with France by setting up weapon depots and conducting raids, such as the one on the Oran Post Office in 1949. In 1951, French security forces succeeded in arresting important leaders like Ben Bella and smashing the organization for a while, but the number of OS members had already grown to 4,500 men, who then went underground and formed the core of what later became the FLN, the National Liberation Front in Algeria.[279]

After Ben Bella escaped from a French prison, he began to plan a new resistance movement with fellow comrades. In April 1954, the "Historic Nine"[280] formed the Comité Révolutionnaire d'Unité et d'Action (CRUA), from which the FLN subsequently evolved on 10 October of that same year. The declared aim of the Liberation Front was to force France to leave Algeria through violent revolution. The war in Indochina served as their model, a war in which many Algerians had fought on the side of France yet had been influenced by the anticolonial propaganda directed deliberately at them by the Viet Minh.[281] The victory of the Vietnamese independence movement in the battle of Dien Bien Phu, in which the reputedly undefeatable French colonial army was devastatingly crushed, was seen by the FLN leaders as the beacon of hope for ending French colonial rule in Algeria. The task was to seize the opportunity and to deal a weakened France yet another blow, a "North African Dien Bien Phu." Following the Vietnamese victory, the hope for success grew stronger than ever before.[282]

The "Pacification" of French Algeria

The Algerian War started in the night of 31 October 1954 with the FLN attacks on the remote gendarme station T'Kout and the bus line Biskara–Batna.[283] An all-out offensive took place at various locations, mainly in the region of the Aurès Mountains, in which a series of raids and bombings killed a total of eight people. Compared with the relatively minor loss of property and lives, the psychological impact was enormous. In a broadcast over Radio Cairo, the FLN addressed the Algerian people for the first time, urging them to join the fight for national liberation.[284] The goal was nothing less than the complete independence of Algeria, to be achieved by abolishing the colonial system at home and by internationalizing the Algeria issue abroad. In keeping with this goal, the armed wing of the FLN, the Armèe de Libération Nationale (ALN), began to form six command regions within Algeria, the so-called *wilayas*.[285] Organized as cells, these units, whose total strength at first was about 1,500 men, attacked facilities of the French state, Muslim collaborators, and white *colons*. In these aimed attacks, the ALN deliberately followed the military tactic used by the French resistance and the Viet Minh, in which they struck a surprising blow, then quickly retreated into hiding to avoid direct confrontation with the superior security forces.[286] A decisive military victory was not within the realm of possibility for the Liberation Army, which was armed in the beginning with primitive weapons formerly belonging to the German Africa Corps and the arms and equipment left behind by the Allied expedition forces during World War II. As the conflict continued, the ALN could improve its weaponry because it received strong support from Arab and socialist countries. Using their guerrilla tactics, the Liberation Army created a climate of insecurity and fear in order to demonstrate to the populace that the French colonial power was unable to guarantee order and security in Algeria.[287] The Aurès mountain region was a good place to initiate the war because the rebels profited from the natural terrain, which seemed predestined for guerrilla war with its inaccessible gorges and valleys and its maze of caves. In addition to the military action, the FLN created the Organisation politico-administrative (OPA), responsible for propaganda, administration, and supplies.[288] The stated objective of the OPA was to set up parallel structures to the French governmental administration and thereby also challenge the colonial state in this area.

The French government and military high command, both of which had been thoroughly surprised by the attacks, assumed at first that this was a regional uprising of no consequence for the entire country.[289] Since Algeria was an integral part of the French republic, stated Prime Minister Pierre Mendès-France in his address to the National Assembly on 12 November 1954, criminal efforts to cut this connection would never be tolerated.[290] His minister of the interior, François Mitterrand, underscored this point: "Algeria—that is, France, because the departments of Algeria are actually departments of the French republic."[291] In his opinion, the only law, the only parliament, the only nation that existed from Flanders to the Congo was the French one. These attacks, referred to only as *événements*, thus constituted a domestic matter that would be quickly handled in police operations.[292] Since the unrest in Morocco and Tunisia had already weakened France's position in North Africa, the French government could not afford another trouble spot. For Paris, Algeria was highly important for strategic reasons as the geopolitical axis connecting the Central African colonies and as the headquarters of the French Mediterranean fleet in Mers-el-Kebir.[293] The iron will to defend French Algeria may well have been strengthened by the discovery of oil in the Sahara Desert and the desire to hold onto the testing grounds for the French atomic weapons program in the Algerian desert.[294] From France's perspective, the loss of this country was unacceptable. Therefore, Paris increased the number of troops sent to combat the rebels. Although a state of emergency was declared for the Aurès and Kabylie Mountains on 3 April 1955, the French security forces did not at first succeed in repressing the revolt.

On the contrary, the FLN strengthened its position and successfully recruited new fighters for the Liberation Army. The bombarding and destruction of entire villages in the "cleansing operations" called *ratissages*, carried out by the French army, were the best recruiting officer for the movement, according to Mostafa Ben Boulaid, the commander of the ALN in the Aurès Mountains.[295] Even the French governor general Jacques Soustelle remarked on the procedure of French troops in 1955: "To send in tank units, to destroy villages, to bombard certain zones, this is no longer the fine comb; it is using a sledgehammer to kill fleas. And what is much more serious, it is to encourage the young—and sometimes the less young—to go into the maquis."[296] Strengthened by new fighters, the ALN gradually expanded its area of military operations to all of Algeria and went on the offensive with larger troop units. On 20 August 1955, the anniversary of the exile of Moroccan sultan Mohammed V, ALN units assaulted the cities of Constantine and Philippeville and a number of smaller European settlements,[297] during the course of which European civilians were massacred, thus prompting the retributive murders of several thousand Muslims by the French army and militia units.[298]

These incidents not only meant a dramatic escalation of the violence, they also led to the final break between Arabs and Europeans. On the French side, the authorities reacted to the intensification of the conflict by extending the state of emergency to all of Algeria and, with a number of special powers, gave the army a completely free hand in fighting the rebels. Paris then felt compelled to increase the troop strength enormously, so that the number of troops stationed in Algeria at the high point of the war far exceeded 400,000 men,[299] the majority of whom were French conscripts.[300] Contrary to the war in Indochina, which had been fought primarily by professional soldiers and the Foreign Legion, the Algerian War touched the lives of French society through these conscripts and would thus have direct consequences at home.[301] Next to the evident military buildup, the French government attempted to pull the Muslim population to their side once again by passing reform packages like the Soustelle Plan.

For its part, the FLN could expand its rule over large parts of the country quite unfazed by the French countermeasures. By mid-1956, the movement supported a force of 8,500 soldiers, which would grow to a number between

35,000 and 50,000 over the course of the war.[302] During its Cairo exile, the external FLN leadership centered around Ben Bella had succeeded in getting Arab states, especially Egypt, to support the war of independence financially and logistically. Following their independence in 1956, the neighboring states of Tunisia and Morocco became crucial bases of support for the Liberation Army, which could set up infirmaries, training camps, and supply depots in these countries that remained fairly safe from attacks by the French army.[303] In August 1956, the FLN even undertook the risk of hosting a conference in the Soummam Valley on Algerian territory in order to institutionalize its legitimacy further. A type of revolutionary parliament was established in the Conseil National de la Révolution Algérienne (CNRA), while the Comité de Coordination et d'Exécution (CCE) assumed the duties of the executive. Not only was the FLN able to give internal structure to the organization,[304] it also managed to clarify objectives and draw up guidelines for its future strategy, as stipulated in the platform "Programme de la Soummam."[305] The armed struggle was to be intensified in order to weaken colonial rule, while the Liberation Front tried at the political level to isolate France worldwide and to internationalize the conflict in this way.

After secret negotiations between the independence movement and the government in Paris were sabotaged by the kidnapping of top FLN leaders by the French military on 22 October 1956, the FLN moved its activities more and more to Algiers, where it hoped to attract greater international attention.[306] By bombing many civilian targets like European cafés and movie theaters, Algerian rebels spread fear and terror throughout the city. Just in the months from July to December 1956, the number of attacks rose from 50 to more than 120 a month.[307] The casbah, the old city of Algiers with its maze of winding narrow streets, soon found itself under the control of the FLN and became, as the Zone Autonome d'Alger (ZAA), the base for further operations.

Since the security situation in the city was threatening more and more to spin out of control, Governor General Robert Lacoste decided to turn to the army for help. On 7 January 1957, General Jacques Massu assumed total command over the city, enforced by eight thousand troops from the Tenth Paratrooper Division. Massu's soldiers, who were just returning from the humiliating Suez debacle, were eager to prove themselves militarily in the fight against the Algerian "terrorists." The top priority of the army was to force the end of the general strike that the FLN had announced for 28 January to coincide with a UN session on Algeria in New York. According to the Soummam platform, the purpose of the strike was to help the independence movement attract greater international attention that would then give greater weight to the demands of the FLN delegates in New York.[308] However, the French army decided to do more than break the strike; it sought to destroy the entire FLN structure in the city.

To that end, Massu superimposed a *quadrillage*, a grid of military posts, over Algiers that, coupled with permanent search-and-seizure operations, was designed to police the population and ferret out the enemy. For the first time, the army put its doctrine of antisubversive warfare into practice against the *guerre révolutionnaire*,[309] thus making the "Battle of Algiers" the most gruesome chapter of the entire war.[310] More than 24,000 people were arrested and "questioned" on a systematic basis, of whom far more than 3,000 died as a result of the torture they endured.[311] The military action ended in the utter defeat of the FLN by late September 1957, when the organization left the city. The *pieds noirs* celebrated this victory excessively and honored Massu's paratroopers as heroes. However, in its euphoria, the French side overlooked the political price it had to pay for this military success. The army's systematic use of torture and other excesses made it impossible to cover up the manner in which the French had conducted the war.[312] The ever-increasing number of reports of French crimes began to convince public opinion that this was a *sale guerre* (dirty war) and to transform the military victory into a political defeat.[313] Massu's success became a Pyrrhic victory, as Paul Teitgen, the secretary-general of the police in Algiers, noted: "Massu won the Battle of Algiers; but that meant losing the war."[314]

Although the FLN had been soundly defeated in Algiers, it continued to hold a strong position in the rural areas. So the French army command decided to apply the successful model used in Algiers with the *quadrillage* and the antisubversive countermeasures to all of Algeria. Under General Raoul Salan, the military extended a system of fortified posts and declared entire regions as "forbidden zones" after the populations had been forced to resettle elsewhere.[315] At the same time, the high command decided to cut off the independence movement from its supply bases in Morocco and Tunisia by installing border fortifications. It created the so-called Morice Line, a 360-kilometer-long and 20-kilometer-wide zone full of minefields, electrical fences, and bunker installations on the border to Tunisia, and a counterpart on the Moroccan border, thus cutting the supply lines so vital for the survival of the rebels.[316] The ALN's efforts to break through these lines led to a growing number of border incidents with Tunisia, which climaxed on 8 February 1958, in the bombardment by the French air force of the Tunisian border town Sakhiet-Sidi-Youssef. This internationally illegal attack on sovereign

Tunisian soil cost seventy-nine civilians their lives, caused a "diplomatic Dien Bien Phu"[317] for the French government, and brought about yet another unwanted internationalization of the conflict.[318]

France was tarnished internationally, and domestically the Algerian War was growing into a threatening state crisis. On 13 May 1958, a group of right-wing extremist *pieds noirs* occupied the residence of the governor general in Algiers with support from army circles and founded a Committee of Public Safety to be chaired by General Massu. The putschists gave Paris the ultimatum to create a national government of public safety under the leadership of General de Gaulle and thus to secure the existence of French Algeria.[319] The looming danger of a coup d'état and civil war finally led to the return of de Gaulle as the head of state of France on 29 May 1958. One week later, on 4 June, he traveled to Algeria, where he attempted to stabilize the situation in his famous speech with the ambiguous statement "Je vous ai compris" (I have understood you).[320] De Gaulle, who would become president with enormous power under the new constitution of the Fifth Republic, intended first to restore the government's authority in the North African departments. With the "Plan de Constantine" of 3 October 1958, he promised to improve the economic and social situation in Algeria drastically within five years by giving 250,000 hectares of land to the Muslim population, building new housing for one million people, and creating 400,000 new jobs.[321] Paris once again attempted to calm the situation in its overseas territories using development policy and thereby to bind them to France. At the same time, de Gaulle signaled his willingness to talk with the FLN and called for the "Paix des Braves" (peace of braves) on 23 October 1958.[322]

The Algerian Liberation Front rejected both de Gaulle's peace offer and his Constantine Plan as a new form of colonialism. While de Gaulle was making his overtures of reconciliation, the FLN founded a provisional government, the Gouvernement Provisoire de la République Algérienne (GPRA),[323] in Cairo on 19 September 1958, thereby making up lost ground on the road to an independent Algeria. At about the same time, the Liberation Front tried to bomb the Algerian War into the consciousness of the French nation.[324] In August and September of 1958, the FLN blanketed all of France with a series of attacks aimed at military, economic, and political targets in order to export the conflict to the "colonial motherland" and remind the French public, in the words of an FLN bulletin, "that there is a dirty war underway in Algeria."[325] While the independence movement proved successful in diplomatic reception rooms and was in a position in France to go on the offensive, it found itself on the brink of total military defeat in Algeria.

Besides the difficulties in getting supplies through the French border fortifications, the reason for the movement's dire straits was the new French offensive in 1959 and 1960 under General Maurice Challe.[326] On the initiative of the general, more resettlements took place and the size of the "forbidden zones" was expanded enormously. Then the army sealed off these areas and *commandos de chasse* began, sector by sector, to hunt down and kill the ALN soldiers.[327] These operations relied heavily on the deployment of *harki* units, recruited exclusively from Algerians, so the size of this force was increased from 26,000 to 60,000 men. In the strategic planning of General Challe, these indigenous units played a major role because they not only took some of the burden off the French army but also were of great political significance since they were Algerians fighting against the Algerian Liberation Front.[328] Highly mobile due to the deployment of helicopters, these fighter commandos attacked the enemy unrelentingly—following Challe's call to leave neither the mountains nor the night to the FLN[329]—and dealt it severe blows. The result of the military operations of the "Challe Plan" was the nearly complete destruction of the independence movement on Algerian soil, so that the general could proudly claim upon his farewell in 1960 that "the rebel is no longer the king of the *djebel*;[330] he is trapped there. . . . The military phase of the rebellion is terminated in the interior."[331] In the eyes of the army command, the three North African departments had been successfully pacified.

The *pieds noirs* and many generals of the Algerian army therefore appeared all the more perplexed by the change of direction in de Gaulle's policy, which began to head toward Algerian independence. On 16 September 1959, in his address on Algerian policy, the French president conceded, for the first time, to give the Algerian people the chance to freely decide their own fate.[332] The man who had been hailed by the white settlers as the guarantor that French Algeria would prevail was turning into the man of French decolonization. Unlike his generals Salan and Challe, who were convinced that total military victory in Algeria was possible, de Gaulle considered the Algerian War to be an impediment to the further development of France.[333] Three years earlier, in 1956, the editor in chief of *Paris Match*, Raymond Cartier, had argued that the colonies were financially exploiting the metropole, an argument that turned the idea of *mise en valeur* completely on its head. In Cartier's opinion, the billions in French tax revenue would be better invested in modernizing France instead of subsidizing an obsolete colonial empire.[334] In 1960 alone, the Algerian War devoured ten billion francs, which equaled 60 percent of the military budget and 15 percent of the entire national budget.[335] Above all, the conflict often tied the government's hands politically and contributed significantly to the international isolation of the republic. In de Gaulle's eyes, the solution to the problem was his concept of an *Algérie algérienne*.[336] Therefore, in a press conference held on 11 April 1961, the general announced: "Decolonization is in our interest and is therefore our policy."[337]

This radical shift in policy met with bitter resistance from the *colons*. The Algeria issue led to an increasing radicalization in French domestic politics and to the brink of civil war.[338] The "barricade revolt" in Algiers in January 1960 was followed in April 1961 by a military putsch of Generals Challe, Salan, Jouhaud, and Zeller, who intended to overthrow the government in Paris from Algeria. Even after the overthrow attempt failed, the Organisation Armée Secrète (OAS),[339] a secret paramilitary organization founded by putschists, continued their fight against an independent Algeria and instigated a bloody wave of terror in an effort to sabotage the peace negotiations between the French government and the GPRA. Despite these efforts, a ceasefire was reached between France and the provisional Algerian government in the Évian Accords, signed 18 March 1962,[340] which certified the end of French colonial rule in North Africa.

The Algerian War, which began as a small "pacification operation" against rebels in the Aurès Mountains, developed into France's largest decolonization war. The seven-year conflict cost 2,788 European *pieds noirs* and 24,000 French soldiers their lives.[341] On the Algerian side, official statistics listed the ALN losses at 143,000 soldiers,[342] while various figures circulate with regard to the number of civilians killed. The Algerian allegation of a million victims[343] is an exaggerated figure, and the actual number probably lies between 250,000 and 500,000.[344] Added to this must be the 70,000 to 150,000 *harkis* who were murdered after the war out of revenge by the victorious ALN.[345] Even though the Évian Accords stipulated protection for the European population, nearly 1.5 million *colons* left the country and headed to France in a mass exodus prompted by the fear of retaliation.[346] On the basis of a referendum agreed upon in the accords, Algeria finally won its complete independence on 3 July 1962. Still, neither the creation of the new Algerian state nor the independence of Kenya a year later could belie how bloody the end of European colonialism had been for both countries. France and Great Britain had fought long and brutally against the decolonization of their overseas territories and, in doing so, justified the deployment of force in the colonies in very similar ways.

Chapter 4

The Legitimation of Colonial Violence

> The colonial regime owes its legitimacy to force and at no times
> tries to hide this aspect of things.
>
> —Frantz Fanon, 1961

Colonial Emergency as the Radicalization of the Colonial Situation

The Colonial Situation and the "Normality of Violence"

The excessive use of violence was a basic element of colonial expansion and rule.[1] In a letter addressed to the U.S. secretary of state at the end of the nineteenth century, the African American journalist and historian George Washington Williams protested against the rule of the Belgian king Leopold II in the Congo, calling it a "crime against humanity."[2] Williams thus used this term long before it made its way into international law during the course of the Nuremberg War Criminal Trials. The regime of Leopold II, which Joseph Conrad fittingly rendered with the words "the horror! the horror!"[3] in his book *Heart of Darkness*, transformed the Congo into "one of the major killing grounds of modern times"[4] and became a synonym for the excessive use of force in the colonies. Yet all of the other colonial regimes also exhibited a great potential and strong propensity for violence.[5] For this reason, the historian Michael Mann characterizes colonial rule as "reign of terror for the subjugated population."[6]

Kenya and Algeria can be cited as characteristic examples of British and French colonial rule, respectively. Both Colonel Meinertzhagen and General

Bugeaud availed themselves of a radical policy in using force for their colonial military conquests, euphemistically referred to as "pacification," in which the extremely racist attitude toward Africans led not only to the submission and subjugation of these peoples but also to the annihilation of large segments of the population.[7] The comment of one European settler in East Africa succinctly reflects this mentality: "I look upon the natives as merely superior baboons and the sooner they are exterminated the better."[8] Even after the military conquest was over, the threat and use of violence remained key elements in securing power.

In the words of Aimé Césaire, the Afro-Caribbean poet and founding member of the Négritude movement, the relationship between colonizer and the colonized was characterized by the brutal link between domination and subjugation, "which turn the colonizing man into a classroom monitor, an army sergeant, a prison guard, a slave driver."[9] Albert Memmi attributed the privileged position of Europeans over that of the native populations to the protection provided by the police, army, and air force, which were willing to defend the interests of the colonial rulers at all times.[10] For Frantz Fanon, colonial coexistence was also based on the power of bayonets and canons,[11] although he added: "This reign of violence will be the more terrible in proportion to the size of the implementation from the mother country."[12] He proved to be right, for settlement colonies like Kenya and Algeria were indeed the places where the bloodiest confrontations of decolonization occurred.[13]

One reason for this lay in the sense of besiegement felt by the white settlers, who as a minority perceived the superior numbers of the indigenous population as a constant threat and permanent danger. The almost paranoid fear of an African revolt influenced the colonial settlement society in a lasting way and brought about a type of militarism in the behavior of the white population.[14] Thus, the colonial state found itself on permanent alert to defend its own position of power the only way it was believed could guarantee success, namely through the use of draconian measures.[15] In the view of an East African settler, the African only understood the language of force: "His primitive mind regards argument as a sign of weakness . . . superior force is the only law he recognizes. I applied the law, with fist and boot."[16]

The use of physical force on the indigenous population was viewed by the colonial rulers as something thoroughly "normal," simply part of the everyday reality of colonial life. As a result, the majority of the French saw nothing unusual in beating a North African,[17] and the white settlers in Kenya considered the whipping of Africans to be "a salutary and uncostly method of preserving law and order."[18] This "normality of violence" was legitimized by the racist argument that Africans were less sensitive to pain than Europeans and therefore also more resistant to corporal punishment.[19] From the perspective of the colonial rulers, the position of strength enjoyed by white people and the prestige derived from it had to be maintained at all costs, meaning that every anticolonial provocation was to be answered with retaliation.

For the indigenous population, who received little protection from the established legal norms because of colonial racial justice such as the *code de l'indigénat*, the colonial situation meant that they were at the mercy of their colonial masters at all times.[20] The marked differences in the legal standards made colonial justice a mirror image of the relations in colonial society.[21] This is well illustrated in the disproportion of the punishment handed down in the case of the white settler Richard Gerrish on the eve of the Mau Mau War. On 6 June 1952, Gerrish was ordered to pay a five-pound fine for the unauthorized beating of an African. Because he beat the victim in the face with a pistol for which he had no legal permit, the court ordered him at the same time to pay a twenty-pound fine for the illegal possession of a weapon.[22]

This type of terror regime intensified as soon as the colonial state was challenged by indigenous resistance. "Colonial war," said Fanon, "represents the radicalization of colonial policy."[23] In his opinion, increasingly radical forms of repression were used in the armed conflicts in the colonies, such as detention camps, the principle of collective punishment, the scorched earth policy, and torture, whereby racism and the dehumanization of the colonial population were the essential features of the conflicts. The colonial state of emergency unleashed additional potential for violence, and the more critical the dangerous situation appeared, the greater was the readiness to use force.[24]

The Colonial Emergency as a Legal Vacuum

Originally, it was not strictly a colonial phenomenon to declare a state of emergency; this constitutional instrument had been developed and deployed in the metropoles to enable the state to respond to extraordinary external and internal threats to public safety and order, which it believed could not be mastered with the usual means.[25] The original types of emergency rule, from which several other types later developed,[26] were the wartime state of siege and the imposition of martial law,[27] in which all competence of civil authorities was transferred to military authorities, individual basic rights were greatly limited, and the jurisdiction of military courts was expanded to civilians. Because of this far-reaching shift in legal authority, the governments in the metropoles decided to resort to such procedures only in extreme emergencies and with great caution. However, in the overseas territories, the concentration of state power in the hands of the military was a well-established element in the way colonial powers responded to crises in the periphery.[28] Great Britain imposed martial law very often in its fight against numerous colonial uprisings[29] and saw this as an important instrument to secure imperial rule, as Major General Charles Gwynn explained in his pioneering work *Imperial Policing*, published in 1934.[30] In the course of the many uprisings, Ireland in particular developed into a testing ground of British emergency law.[31]

A special variation of the state of emergency was implemented to counter an internal threat to the existence of a state, without imposing martial law.[32] Unlike the state of siege, the powers of civilian authorities were officially untouched. However, the emergency measures included a series of special powers, which shifted a broad range of legal authority from the legislative to the executive and at the same time suspended fundamental individual rights.[33] For this reason, the Italian philosopher Giorgio Agamben sees this lack of a separation of powers as a characteristic element of the state of emergency. However, he identifies the disjunction of enforcement and the law itself as a decisive feature of the emergency state: the state of emergency is "a 'state of the law' in which, on the one hand, the norm is in force but is not applied (it has no 'force') and, on the other, acts that do not have the value of law acquire its 'force.'"[34] For Agamben, the state of emergency is a legal vacuum, an anomic zone resulting from the suspension of lawful order with a massive impact on the fundamental rights of the individual.[35]

In developing the international regime of human rights, it was recognized that human rights are under a particularly great threat during a state of emergency. By pointing to the extraordinary danger present, the state could legally limit or completely suspend basic rights such as the right to liberty, the right to the security of person, the right to freedom of movement, the right to freedom of speech and peaceful assembly, and the protection of privacy. The result was that security forces were no longer bound to legal norms in their operations and could thus resort to measures like detention and torture.[36] The protection and guarantee of fundamental rights in times of emergency therefore became an important issue in the international protection of human rights.[37] With the help of the emergency clauses, the attempt was made to establish fundamental rights as minimum standards even in times of emergency.

The Geneva Conventions of 1949 assumed a pioneering role in this issue by addressing armed conflict, the most direct form of states of emergency, with respect to international law.[38] In addition to the provisions stipulated for international wars, the Geneva Conventions especially spelled out in Article 3 the minimum provisions for humanitarian protection in internal armed conflicts. In the classic emergency scenario, acts against the physical integrity of a person, such as murder, torture, and cruel treatment, as well as injury to personal dignity and the curtailment of guaranteed rights were prohibited at all times and in all places; furthermore, the prohibition of such acts could not even be lifted by exceptional regulations.[39] During the course of the consultations on the United Nations covenants on international human rights, the Human Rights Commission also worked intensively on this issue from 1947 to 1952.[40] The draft of an international human rights convention submitted by Great Britain in 1947 contained a special clause in Article 4 that referred, for the very first time, to states of emergency.[41] However, this did permit member states to suspend the treaty provisions in a state of emergency. Instead of making basic rights "emergency proof," the draft merely required the compulsory reporting to the United Nations of any implemented measures suspending rights. The British delegate Geoffrey Wilson justified the draft article by pointing out that "Article 4 represents a loophole for not enforcing the Bill in the cases of national emergency or some similar reason."[42] This unfortunate choice of words betrayed a great deal about London's actual motives and appeared to be logical in light of the frequency with which states of emergency were declared in the colonies.[43] In the end, the draft failed because of opposition by other commission members, who began in 1949 to promote the proposal put forth by the World Jewish Congress, which prohibited any suspension or limitation of fundamental basic rights.[44]

Consequently, Great Britain proposed an additional paragraph to Article 4 that was meant to guarantee limited rights even in a state of emergency.[45] However, this proposal did not go far enough to satisfy the French delegation, so it drafted its own, more comprehensive list of "emergency-proof" basic rights,[46] on which the commission voted individually—right for right—in 1950. Yet even before the vote was taken, France itself removed particularly controversial rights from its proposed list, such as the right to personal freedom and security, the right to due process of law, and the right of freedom of movement. Despite this, the French proposal became the core of the catalog of basic rights for Article 4, which was eventually included as the emergency clause in the UN human rights covenants in 1966.[47]

Although Great Britain's version—limited to only four basic rights—was being rejected by the United Nations, it proved far more successful on the European level. Originally, no emergency clause had been planned for the ECHR, but the British delegation submitted the same draft to the responsible expert council of the European Council in 1949.[48] The result was that the right to life,[49] freedom from torture and from slavery, and the prohibition of retroactive penal legislation were included as the public emergency clause (Article 15) of the ECHR in 1950.[50] This meant that the invariable minimum standards of the European Council corresponded to a great extent with those of the Geneva Conventions and can therefore be called the "irreducible core of human rights."[51] Ironically, the original idea to introduce the public emergency clause in order to have a backdoor through which to circumvent human rights commitments led instead to the establishment of a minimum standard of emergency-proof basic rights in the international human rights documents. The colonial powers Great Britain and France both had participated significantly to this development.

In overseas territories like Kenya and Algeria, however, each minimum standard securing basic rights for the indigenous population was perceived as a factor confounding efforts to secure colonial rule. Particularly during periods of colonial unrest and uprisings, the besiegement mentality of the white settler population radicalized to the point that all concessions toward the natives were viewed as intolerable weaknesses and unacceptable dangers. In the fight against "anticolonial terrorism," it was argued that one's own position should not be recklessly weakened by democratic and legal norms. Instead, the principles of a state governed by rule of law should be suspended in order to give security forces a completely free hand in their operations against "subversive" forces.

In light of the escalation of tensions in Kenya in 1952, Michael Blundell, the representative of the white settlers, declared that law and order first needed to be completely restored: "Above all, it will mean the removal of many privileges which we have come to regard wrongly as rights. For many years the privileges of freedom of movement of the individual and of assembly, the freedom of the press, the right to manage independent [African] schools, will need to be strictly and firmly controlled."[52] In Blundell's opinion, the freedoms to which he referred were not inalienable human rights, but privileges that needed to be deprived to the African population in order to restore order.

For the majority of white settlers, however, it was not enough to simply restrict basic rights, which they considered anyway to be thoroughly out of place in Kenya. Equal rights and constitutional law were to be reserved only for "civilized" people, in their opinion.[53] Further, they criticized the humanitarian and liberal forces in Westminster, who—by curtailing draconian punishments—deprived them, in their view, of a valuable disciplinary instrument and encouraged the natives to rise up against the colonial government.[54] The stronger the threat posed by the Mau Mau was perceived as being, the louder became the voices calling for harsher intervention and collective punishment of all Kikuyu. In the opinion of the settler Ione Leigh, a "primitive" enemy like the Mau Mau should not enjoy the protection of British law: "Though British justice may be the finest in the world for civilized persons, it has proved entirely unsuited to a primitive population. Its slow, ponderous tread impedes the Army, the Police and the Administration generally."[55] Therefore, Leigh advocated a rigorous policy of force, pointing out how the French and Germans handled similar situations in their colonies. Women and children were to be removed from villages under suspicion, after which the entire male population was to be shot and the village razed to the ground.[56] Had such collective measures been implemented, he was convinced that the Mau Mau problem would have been solved by then, long before the rusty machinery of British justice was set into motion.

The rising number of raided white farms and murdered settlers provided the necessary acceptance of this radical attitude among the European population of Kenya. Under the leadership of Colonel Ewart Grogan, a prominent pioneer from the era of the white settlement in Kenya, the Kenya Empire Party was founded in 1953, which openly campaigned for the principle of collective punishment, "justice by the whip," the expansion of the death penalty, and the abolition of constitutional order.[57] In the wake of the gruesome murder of the Ruck family, this settler extremism escalated on 24 January 1953 when an excited crowd attempted to storm the gubernatorial palace in Nairobi, demanding the annihilation of fifty thousand Kikuyu to set a deterring example for the African population.[58] Following consultations with the governor, white-settler leader Blundell appeared before the crowd saying, "I am glad to tell you that I now, at long last, bring you your shooting orders."[59] With this, he then announced the creation of forbidden zones in which settlers could shoot any African found there without warning. Many whites interpreted this as a general "license to kill." In connection with this settler extremism, even the Colonial Office spoke of an "emergency mentality,"[60] whereby the radical settlers were dubbed the "white Mau Mau"[61] because of their demands and actions.

In the Algerian departments, the crisis also radicalized the colonial situation. The racist delusion of supremacy and the indifference of the *pieds noirs* to the fate of the Arabs were replaced with an animosity of almost hysterical dimension.[62] Especially after the ALN raids on the cities of Constantine and Philippeville and a series of smaller settlements in August 1955, the Europeans viewed every Muslim as a "terrorist," according to Governor General Jacques Soustelle.[63] The consequence was that ten Arabs were killed for every dead Frenchman in the subsequent retaliatory raids carried out by the army and the settler militias.[64] Soustelle's adviser Vincent Monteil described the situation accurately: "Both population groups are now incited against one another; a race war, irresponsible and merciless, is at our doorstep."[65] Tensions between the European and Arab populations heated up quickly as the fighting spread. Serious clashes ensued once the FLN started in 1956 to target localities popular with the *pieds noirs* in Algiers, like cafés and bars, for bombing attacks. Enraged Europeans countered the bombing terror of the FLN with the infamous *ratonnades* against the Arab population, in which a number of Arabs were lynched in the course of the riots.[66]

The consequences resulting from this tense atmosphere were demands by the *colons* for a more drastic crackdown by government forces, demands that found widespread support in army leadership circles. In particular, the advocates of the *guerre révolutionnaire* theory, like General Massu, considered liberal and constitutional principles to be vulnerabilities, since these could be exploited by the rebels to their advantage and would hinder security forces in their mission.[67] One of the many who supported this position was General Jacques Allard, who complained in a letter to their common superior that there was no legislation adapted to the Algerian conditions.[68] Democracy and legality were extremely negatively valued, since they could not sufficiently protect the victims from the perpetrators.[69] In the opinion of Commandant Emile Mairal-Bernard, the nation should not tolerate a situation in which the "generosity" and liberalism of its laws were being instrumentalized by subversive forces for antinational aims.[70] For this reason, Commandant Jacques Hogard concluded, "The time has come to realize that the democratic ideology has become powerless in today's world."[71]

Many officers believed that the solution to the problem would be a reverse in orientation whereby the army would no longer be forced to adapt its strategy to comply with the constitutional principles of the French republic, but instead, the state would have to adapt to the needs of counterinsurgency. A military study from August 1957 warned of a lack of adaptability within both the French judiciary and the legislature and recommended to state institutions that they adapt the law as quickly as possible to the new challenge.[72] In order to fulfill its mission, the military should rigorously deploy all the weaponry of modern warfare and only be answerable to its own judicial system.[73] According to General Massu, French soldiers should act within the framework of biblical law: an eye for an eye, a tooth for a tooth.[74] At a lecture in a training center for counterinsurgency, Colonel Charles Lacheroy translated this standpoint into a secular motto: "One does not fight a revolutionary war with the Code Napoléon."[75]

State of Emergency, *État d'urgence, Pouvoirs spéciaux*: The Omnipotence of Emergency Law

The British and French governments did not wait long to react to the growing pressure being exerted by the settlers and the military. At an early stage in both conflicts, London and Paris officially resorted to the tool of declaring a state of emergency. By investing their security forces with a wide range of special powers, the governments greatly expanded the colonial repression apparatus. For the indigenous population, the already violent colonial situation was radicalized further because even the very minimum existence of a rule of law was thereby abolished.

In his letter to Colonial Secretary Lyttelton on 13 September 1952, the outspoken Labour MP Fenner Brockway condemned the constraints on basic rights planned in Kenya as an elementary violation of the Universal Declaration of Human Rights.[76] This legislative bill reminded him more of totalitarian regimes on the other side of the Iron Curtain than of a democratic society. The solution to the problems in Kenya did not lie in strengthening repressive measures, but in eliminating social and political injustice and racial discrimination. In the incited clamor ringing through the crown colony, Brockway's sharp criticism was not heard. Instead, the administration in Nairobi restricted the freedom of the press, of association, and of movement in the first legislative package, passed on 25 September 1952.[77]

The growing number of attacks and finally the assassination of Chief Waruhiu handed Governor Baring an immediate justification to impose a state of emergency in the colony on 20 October 1952, with the express approval of the colonial ministry.[78] The legality of this was based on the Emergency Powers Order in Council of 1939,[79] which empowered Baring to enact far-reaching emergency regulations in the months that followed. Among other things, these emergency regulations[80] contained a ban on meeting and assembling, a ban of all African political organizations, tighter controls on obligatory identification, a stricter censure of the press, a ban on the publication of "subversive" writings, the limitation of the freedom of movement and of travel through curfews, a complete control of means of transportation, as well as collective punishment by way of special taxes and the confiscation of land and other property. At the same time, security forces were granted unlimited authority to conduct searches and police checks and to declare certain regions as "forbidden zones," in which it could be deadly for Africans to enter and stay. Detention orders enabled every British representative of law and order to arbitrarily arrest those people considered suspicious and a public danger, even without a judicial warrant. With this step, the colonial government created the legal basis for the arrest and detention of thousands of Kikuyu.

Thanks to these emergency regulations, London was able to avoid the imposition of martial law and could maintain the veneer of civil normality.[81] Although many aspects of the state of emergency in Malaya served as a model, in the Kenyan case the military high command was not amalgamated with the civilian leadership. Kenya's commander in chief, General Erskine, did not officially enjoy the proconsular authority of his Malayan counterpart, General Templer, who not only held the military post of commander in chief, but was also the high commissioner of the colony.[82] In Kenya, the army was officially separated from civilian authorities, and, in cooperation with the police, this triumvirate was to maintain domestic order. However, this ideal of a harmonious separation of powers was distorted by a secret letter from Prime Minister Churchill to his personal friend Erskine. This document, which hung like the sword of Damocles over the heads of the civilian colonial administration, empowered the military commander to impose martial law at any time as he saw fit and to assume civil control of the colony. It took no more than the small gesture of opening and closing his eyeglasses case, where Erskine kept this ultimate trump card, to silence troublesome representatives from both the colonial administration and the settlers.[83]

Even though the enacted measures were already quite far-reaching, the emergency regulations were once again strengthened during the course of the state of emergency. While the active participation in "terrorist" Mau Mau attacks had been ruled a capital offense and punishable by death, in December 1952 authorities in Nairobi called for extending the use of the death penalty to other crimes. In their minds, merely holding a Mau Mau oath ceremony should have been punishable by death. In London, the Colonial Office at first rejected the proposal with the argument that no concessions should be made to the demands of European settlers to impose harsh measures that, in the end, would prove counterproductive.[84] Yet only four months later, in April 1953, such arguments no longer played a role. The raid on the police station in Naivasha and the Lari massacre led to yet another expansion of the colonial repression apparatus, whereby the emergency regulations gradually became the mirror image of the radicalization of the colonial situation.

The new emergency regulations imposed the death penalty for any form of direct and indirect support of the rebels, including sabotage, leading an oath ceremony, collecting provisions and supplies, and possessing weapons and ammunition.[85] The possession of a single cartridge alone was enough to be hanged. As Hugh Holmes, an officer of the Royal Northumberland Fusiliers, described in his memoirs, one of the common practices among the security forces was thus to slip a cartridge into the possession of suspects and wounded individuals in order to "convict" them of a capital crime and turn them over to the executioner.[86] Transportable gallows, which were mounted on trucks and driven from place to place,[87] and public executions dramatically underscored the new British approach and were meant to deter the African population from supporting the Mau Mau movement in any way.[88]

The rapidly growing number of court trials prompted the colonial government in Nairobi to set up special emergency assize courts exclusively for holding trials involving infractions of the emergency regulations.[89] Between April 1953 and December 1956 alone, these special courts sentenced 1,574 people to death by hanging. British authorities had a total of 1,090 Kikuyu hanged, whereby the great majority of them were not convicted of murder but of far less serious crimes such as holding oath ceremonies and possessing weapons.[90] In all, the number of executions surpassed several times over the total number of executions in the other emergencies of the British Empire taken together since World War II and was more than twice as high as the number of French executions during the entire Algerian War.

David Anderson correctly points out that state execution has never been used to such an intensive degree in any other place or at any other time in the history of British imperialism as it was in Kenya.[91] Faced with this fact, even British veterans like the police officer Peter Hewitt had to admit the dictatorial nature of the emergency regulations, yet not without simultaneously legitimizing the measures by pointing to their necessity to ensure security.[92] Even though the resistance of the Mau Mau movement had been completely put down by the end of 1956, the state of emergency remained officially in force until 12 January 1960.[93] Great Britain's East African crown colony was thus governing by the emergency regulations for nearly eight years.

As the situation in Algeria began to heat up, the government in Paris also reacted in April 1955 by declaring a state of emergency there. Since the constitution of the Fourth Republic did not contain emergency regulations,[94] and the authorities did not want to declare martial law under a state of siege—the *état de siège*—considering the "domestic problems" in the North African departments,[95] it was necessary to create a new legal entity. Subsequently, a legislative bill was put forth by the Faure government on the *état d'urgence* and passed by the French National Assembly with an overwhelming majority on 3 April 1955.[96] Originating from an initiative by the French military, the *état d'urgence* was to be a compromise between a normal state of affairs and a state of siege that Paris believed would enable it to adequately react to the new security challenges.[97] In keeping with French republican tradition and the appearance of civil order, the civil authorities were to be invested formally with new powers, under which the military continued to be subordinate.[98]

However, the declaration of a state of emergency, which was at first limited to six months and only extended to all of Algeria on 28 August 1955 following the bloody incidents in Philippeville, actually gave the executive nearly absolute dictatorial power to limit, if not suspend, constitutionally guaranteed civil rights. The Algerian governor general now had the right to limit the freedom of movement, to declare certain areas as security zones in which people were prohibited from entering, to ban gatherings, to close venues, and to subject the press to severe censorship.[99] Security forces were delegated unlimited powers to search houses and conduct raids at any time of day or night without a special court order. The expanded competence of the military jurisdiction to certain crimes connected with the state of emergency brought about a marked militarization of criminal justice.[100] Article 6 of the emergency legislation had a particularly decisive impact on the situation in Algeria. With the *assignation à résidence*, authorities had the right to assign people to a place to live if they where thought to present a threat to public order and security. Although the wording of the law expressly forbade the establishment of detention camps, this measure evoked memories of the Vichy period in several socialist and communist legislators,[101] and in practice the *assignation à résidence* did indeed lay the legal groundwork for the extensive resettlement and detention measures implemented during the Algerian War.[102]

As a result of the dissolution of the National Assembly on 1 December

1955, the *état d'urgence* became invalid, and the new government under Guy Mollet declined to declare a new a state of emergency.[103] Instead, on 16 March 1956, the French parliament passed a law that would be known as the *pouvoirs spéciaux*,[104] in which Paris first announced an extensive program for the economic and social development of Algeria as well as comprehensive administrative reform. However, Article 5 also authorized the government "in Algeria . . . to undertake all extraordinary measures necessary under the circumstances to restore order, protect persons and goods, and to preserve the territorial sovereignty of the state." The issuance of decrees was to define more specifically the content of these "extraordinary measures" and enabled the government to reinstate the *assignation à résidence* and to legalize detention camps.[105] In this way, the *pouvoirs spéciaux* actually surpassed the provisions of the *état d'urgence* and not only meant an escalation of the colonial emergency situation but also gave the French security forces carte blanche to fight insurrection. Although the new special powers did not legalize torture, as the historian Pierre Vidal-Naquet notes in his attention-getting book *La torture dans la république*, they did set up the parameters to do everything in the name of France and to protect the republic.[106] The Algerian departments were increasingly subject to a "regime by decrees"[107] that allowed the colonial power to repress any form of indigenous resistance by "legal" means.

Astonishingly, voices were being raised from army circles claiming that even these broad powers were inadequate in the fight against the subversive enemy. A military working group had studied the existing emergency regulations and come to the conclusion in a secret internal report that neither the *état de siège*, the *état d'urgence*, nor the *pouvoirs spéciaux* sufficiently provided the security forces the means they needed.[108] Although many measures did indeed meet the expectations of the military, the report found too many restrictions and barriers in the existing laws. Since revolutionary war required an all-encompassing strategy, security forces should be invested with complete power, which is why newer, more radical laws on counterinsurgency were being demanded.[109] At the same time, the study recommended that civil offices turn over all their competence to the military.[110] Only by way of this concentration of power and complete independence from civil supervision could the army effectively battle the subversive threat single-handedly.

The consequence was that the French military leadership not only demanded more and more power from the civil administration, but actually took over and transformed Algeria into a type of military province.[111] Formally, the civil agencies retained their authority, which in practice, however, they relinquished to their military counterparts.[112] Particularly evident was this capitulation of the constitutional state in the Battle of Algiers, in which the city prefect Serge Baret authorized General Massu to take all measures necessary to restore order.[113] This creeping disempowerment of civil authority and the chaos it caused in exercising authority were strongly criticized in a letter written in 1957 to Robert Lacoste, then resident minister in Algeria, by the secretary-general of the prefecture, Paul Teitgen, who had refused to approve the use of torture despite great pressure. In Teitgen's opinion, the problem was not of getting tangled up in illegality in this fight, but in an anonymity and lack of responsibility that would inevitably lead to war crimes: "Through such improvised and uncontrolled methods, despotism finds every sort of conceivable justification. What is more, France runs the risk of losing her soul to ambiguity."[114]

One particularly critical manifestation of the continuing militarization of all civil spheres was the intervention of the army in judicial matters.[115] The military hindered and threatened the defense lawyers of arrested FLN supporters, while at the same time it abolished guarantees of due process in the code of criminal procedure.[116] In the eyes of the officers in charge, the efficiency of court trials had to be enhanced, which meant nothing else but increasing the level of repression.[117] The judiciary was to be subjugated to the logic of war and mutate into an effective weapon of the *guerre contre-révolutionnaire*.[118] On the basis of a decree issued on 17 March 1956, the jurisdiction of the military judiciary was expanded, prompting military courts to intervene with increasing frequency in areas of civil jurisdiction.[119] The consequence was a dramatic increase in the number of death sentences and executions of alleged "terrorists," especially after the series of FLN bombings began in Algiers.[120] Much like the case in Kenya, the judiciary transformed itself into an instrument of colonial repression at the cost of constitutional norms, whereby the insistence on judicial procedure served to preserve the appearance of legality.

The aspect so exceptional about the emergency in Algeria was that the radicalization of the colonial situation unleashed forces that would not remain contained within the borders of the North African departments but would eventually threaten even the colonial metropole. The suspension of constitutional norms and the growing militarization of all facets of the government in Algeria were also expressions of an increasing politicization of the French army[121] directed against the political system. The severe breach of trust between the government and the high command, which had first appeared during the Indochina campaign, led to the absolute alienation of the military from civil authority.[122] Particularly the elite units of the Foreign Legion and the paratroopers cultivated their own martial esprit de corps, the "esprit para,"[123] highly reminiscent of the republic-hostile, antidemocratic attitude of the German Freikorps.[124] At the same time, the comprehensive powers of the emergency laws enabled high officers and leading proponents of the *guerre révolutionnaire* theory to intervene more and more in French domestic policy. Prominent high points of this *malaise de l'armée*[125] were the support given to the incited *pieds noirs* in occupying the residence of the governor general in Algiers on 13 May 1958, with the subsequent establishment of the Committee of Public Safety headed by General Massu, and the putsch by the leading Algerian generals Challe, Salan, Jouhaud, and Zeller on 22–25 April 1961.[126] In both cases, the Algerian army, armed with the special powers to protect the state, now threatened the existence of the French republic. The government in Paris felt compelled to declare an *état d'urgence* in France itself in 1958 for the first time and then again in 1961.[127] The state of emergency had been legally introduced by the metropole because of events in the periphery, but now it boomeranged. Above all, it had created the legal prerequisites to implement the new military doctrines of counterinsurgency with almost no constitutional barriers.

Antisubversive War: The Military Response to the Anticolonial Challenge

Revolutionary Guerrilla Warfare as an Anticolonial Danger

Guerrilla warfare was not a phenomenon that the colonial powers faced in their overseas territories only after 1945. The term "guerrilla" is originally derived from an early nineteenth-century European theater of war, namely the Spanish resistance to Napoleonic occupation.[128] In the colonies, the "small war" was the dominant form of military confrontation.[129] Contrary to the "big wars" of regular armies in Europe, these were asymmetric conflict scenarios in which the African and Asian resistance movements attempted to compensate for their technical inferiority to the colonial occupation power by fighting a war of attrition.[130] Colonial expansion meant that the colonial powers faced with increasing frequency what appeared in their view as the unconventional methods of the insurgents. On the part of the European metropoles, the military soon began to search for an adequate response to this strategic challenge in the overseas territories, because the countermeasures customary in classic warfare had not produced any noteworthy success in many cases.

General Thomas-Robert Bugeaud played a leading role in the French "pacification" of Algeria in the mid-nineteenth century. By disbanding the large, cumbersome army units and replacing these with small mobile task forces known as "flying columns," Bugeaud was copying the fighting methods of his Algerian opponent Abdel Kader. The enhanced mobility enabled French troops to attack the rebels constantly and to cut them off from civilian support in raids against Arab villages.[131] Not only did the French general change military strategy, at the same time he also recognized the importance of guerrilla warfare on the political-administrative level. The purpose of creating the *bureaux arabes* was to politically penetrate and monitor the Arab population in order to nip any future uprisings in the bud. Bugeaud's combination of military force and political measures served as a model for the French military in the fight against colonial uprisings.[132] The lessons learned by the military in the Algerian campaign lay the groundwork for the pacification strategy of the *tache d'huile* of General Joseph-Simon Galliéni in Indochina and Madagascar at the end of the nineteenth century and of General Louis-Hubert-Gonslave Lyautey in Morocco in the 1920s.[133] With the help of a vast colonial administration and a specific indigenous policy, the authorities sought to strengthen their control over the colonial population and simultaneously to win over their hearts for the French republic by introducing economic and social improvements.

Great Britain was also always being challenged by rebels using guerrilla tactics throughout its empire.[134] However, British military leadership decided to forego the establishment of uniform doctrines for guerrilla warfare and reacted flexibly to each situation.[135] The groundwork for British strategy was laid by the experiences and lessons from numerous operations in the colonies, which Charles Callwell summarized in his handbook *Small Wars: Their Principle and Practice* for the army in 1896 at the request of the British war ministry. Callwell argued that all means were necessary and justified for a successful campaign in "small wars," including, for example, the complete destruction of food supplies and villages.[136] At the same time, he recommended the study of other means of counterinsurgency in order to improve one's own capabilities.[137] So it happened that men like the young Winston Churchill were sent to observe the repression of the Cuban revolt by the Spanish and thus became acquainted with the program of civilian reconcentration.[138] A few years later, the British deployed this very same strategy in the Second Boer War from 1899 to 1902. Their tactic consisted of interning the Boer population in concentration camps and destroying homesteads and farms, crops and livestock as potential supply sources.[139] The European colonial areas evolved more and more into experiments in counterinsurgency. At the same time, certain procedures such as purges, detention, and resettlement were used by various colonial powers and created the basis for the development of doctrines of counterinsurgency after 1945.[140]

After Great Britain and France used partisan tactics to combat the National Socialist occupation of Europe during World War II,[141] they themselves became the victims of such strategies in their overseas territories once the war ended. In the phase of incipient decolonization, national movements in the colonies relied on "small war" methods in their struggle for independence against the seemingly superior enemy.[142] In doing so, they often followed the example of a refined variation of guerrilla war, namely the revolutionary war of Mao Zedong.[143] The leader of the Chinese communists had developed his concept from the practical experiences gathered during the Chinese civil war and the resistance to Japanese occupation in World War II.[144] Mao's teachings on warfare provided, in the words of the publicist Sebastian Haffner, a "recipe for the war of social and national liberation and independence."[145] In addition to the reliance on classic guerrilla tactics, a key aspect was to mobilize broad masses of the population and thus create enormous waters in which, on one hand, the guerrilla could swim about like fish and, on the other, the enemy would drown.[146] It was Mao's idea that the people create a protective shield and support base for the army with which they would conflate into an undefeatable entity.[147] Having this advantage over a regular army, the revolutionaries could strike unexpectedly at any time and then retreat into the anonymity of the civilian population. The decisive prerequisite for the amalgamation of combatants and civilians was the creation of a comprehensive political organization that worked underground to indoctrinate the population ideologically, gain the allegiance of the people to common political aims, and organize them as needed.[148] Only after such widespread support was established could revolutionary armed forces dare to engage in a long guerrilla war against a seemingly overpowering enemy. The time factor also played a decisive role in Mao's view. By prolonging the war, the impact of attrition would bear out fully on the enemy, while at the same time the strength of the revolutionaries would grow and eventually lead to the victory of the weaker side over the supposedly stronger one.[149]

The first Western power to suffer from the efficiency of this theory was France. The French attempt to recolonize Indochina was met with bitter resistance from the Viet Minh, who used tactics modeled closely on Mao's guidelines.[150] Under the leadership of Ho Chi Minh and General Vo Nguyen Giap, the Vietnamese liberation organization succeeded to mobilize large sections of the population for its struggle for independence and to deal the French expeditionary forces several painful blows.[151] In this "war without fronts,"[152] the Viet Minh impressively demonstrated the efficiency and power of revolutionary guerrilla warfare and ended French colonial rule in Southeast Asia with its victory at Dien Bien Phu. To the shock of the French military leadership, not only had their own troops failed to defend the Asian overseas territories against an enemy that was militarily far inferior, they had actually suffered a terribly humiliating defeat. Yet, many officers of the Indochina army blamed not chiefly themselves for the disgraceful defeat but politics. The indignity France suffered did not stem from Dien Bien Phu, maintained General Henri Navarre, but from the peace talks in Geneva, thus France should hold the politicians accountable instead of his soldiers.[153] As a consequence of this, certain elements within the French officer corps became increasingly politicized, if not radicalized, and viewed the civil government in Paris with great mistrust.[154] In addition to the idea of political betrayal, the military also reasoned away the debacle in Southeast Asia by pointing to the new form of enemy warfare, for which the French soldiers had been fully unprepared to combat.[155]

Great Britain's Successful Model of Antisubversive Warfare

Upon its return to its Southeast Asian possessions, Great Britain was also confronted with the revolutionary tactics of a communist guerrilla movement. The MRLA, which began armed conflict in 1948, endangered British rule in the economically important colony of Malaya. Borrowing from Mao's concept of revolutionary war, the Malayan rebels achieved notable success from the start of their campaign against the British troops, who could not get the enemy to confront them head-on in a decisive battle.[156] Since the British had already gained some experience in countering guerrilla tactics during the Greek civil war and in the Palestine Mandate, the army leadership slowly adapted to the new military challenge, unlike their French counterparts, and succeeded in fighting the Malayan guerrillas.[157]

The key to their success was a military strategy of counterinsurgency based on isolating the rebels from the civilian population and undertaking a well-aimed propaganda campaign.[158] According to the plans of General Harold Briggs, the army cut off the rebels from their lifeline of support by resettling five hundred thousand Chinese into five hundred "new villages" and subjecting the inhabitants of the new settlements to rigid control.[159] The resettlement measures, known as the Briggs Plan, were continued and expanded under General Templer, who assumed the high command of the colony in February 1952.[160] Templer was of the opinion that 75 percent of the work was to win the support of the population and only 25 percent was of it was to hunt down the rebels.[161] For this reason, the high command started a comprehensive propaganda campaign aimed at winning the "hearts and minds" of the Malayan people.[162] However, this campaign did not stop the British army from pursuing its repressive policy of imposing curfews, denying food, and inflicting collective punishment, which prompted a comparison by the British *Daily Herald* to National Socialist means of terror.[163] The military did not even shy away from the use of chemical weapons, such as the poisonous chemical trichlorophenoxyacetic acid (2,4,5-T), which it used to destroy crops that might have been a food source for the rebels and to defoliate the jungle that provided them with protective camouflage.[164] Later, the British army freely offered the results of their chemical-weapon missions in the Malayan jungle to American scientists, who used this information to further develop the chemical arsenal of the U.S. armed forces. This research eventually brought about the deployment of the notorious herbicide Agent Orange, among other substances, in the Vietnam War.[165]

The "Malayan experience" of revolutionary warfare left a lasting mark on the British army leadership. Contrary to Indochina, the colonial power in Malaya triumphed over the anticolonial resistance movement and maintained its position. This success meant that the military operations against the MRLA became the model for effective counterinsurgency and received a great deal of attention in military circles.[166] Under the supervision of General Templer, Walter Walker subsequently compiled the most important findings in the handbook *The Conduct of Anti-Terrorist Operations in Malaya (ATOM)*,[167] which became a type of manual on military counterinsurgency for the British armed forces. In Malayan Kota Tinngi, a special school for jungle warfare was also established in which the new military methods became the core training curriculum.[168] With this knowledge, the British army had a promising strategy to fight subversive movements and uprisings, one that could be applied throughout the entire empire.

The very next opportunity to arise was in Kenya, where initially the

security forces were not being effective in countering the Mau Mau movement. For this reason, Kenya's governor Evelyn Baring contacted General
Templer in January 1953 to learn about Templer's formula for success.[169]
Convinced by what he learned from the general, Baring decided to adopt the
methods of antisubversive warfare and established emergency committees,
thereby reorganizing the command structure along the lines of the Malayan
model.[170] In addition, Baring sent the head of the Community Development
Department, Thomas G. Askwith, to Southeast Asia in the summer of 1953 to
study closely the "rehabilitation measures" of the colonial administration.[171]
During the inspections of the "new villages" and detention camps, the local
authorities explained to the visitor from East Africa that the resettlement and
"reeducation" of the rebels and their supporters were aimed at establishing
a long-term peace in the colony and that the propaganda campaign to win
the "hearts and minds" of the indigenous population was very important in
this effort.[172] Askwith's trip achieved its purpose because his observations and
experiences were decisive in implementing a similar policy in Kenya.[173] At the
same time that the civil colonial administration began to look more closely
at Malaya, the military high command in Nairobi did so as well. In August
1953, General Erskine ordered a copy of the *ATOM* manual from the headquarters in Kuala Lumpur, noting that he intended to use it as the basis to
train the military for anti-Mau Mau operations.[174] Indeed, the *Handbook on
Anti-Mau-Mau Operations*,[175] which the army issued a year later as a manual
for training and warfare in Kenya, was modeled to a great extent on its Malayan predecessor.

The extent to which the Malayan model for counterinsurgency served as
a model in East Africa[176] and the degree of similarity between the British
methods in the two emergencies is shown in a 1957 study by the Operational
Research Unit Far East. In an extensive strategy paper entitled *A Comparative Study of the Emergencies in Malaya and Kenya*,[177] Colonel J. M. Forster
analyzed and compared the two military operations. The aim of the study
was to identify the necessary lessons from the experiences in order to better
prepare the armed forces for such conflict scenarios in the future.[178] Forster
first determined that, in both cases, the army had used nearly identical propaganda methods to undermine the enemy's morale and at the same to gain
the favor of the people.[179] He also found major parallels in the organization
and structure of the intelligence services, which took on a key role in fighting
the rebels.[180] However, the most conspicuous similarities were in dealing with
the civilian population. Since both resistance movements were completely

dependent on the help of their indigenous sympathizers due to a lack of foreign support, one of the major aims of the security forces was to establish total control over the populace. Through the resettlement and detention of the Chinese in Malaya and the Kikuyu in Kenya, this goal was effectively achieved and thus became the basis for success.[181]

For Forster, an extremely interesting development in the Kenya war theater was the deployment of special commandos, the pseudo-gangs.[182] As planned by the originator of this concept, British military intelligence officer Frank Kitson, these small groups, recruited from imprisoned Mau Mau fighters, were sent off to hunt down their former comrades under the command of a white officer.[183] Optimally informed on the details of the resistance organization, the pseudos imitated the fighting methods of their enemies. Not only did they create great chaos and generate fear of betrayal in rebel circles, they became the most effective British weapon in the fight against the Mau Mau. In this context, Forster also emphasized the importance of British settlers who were predestined to head such operations because of their knowledge of the local conditions. Therefore, he recommended that, in future operations, the army command rely on such loyal groups in the populace, should they exist in the respective colony, and take them into account in military planning.[184]

Except for the military innovation of pseudo-gangs, the British methods in Southeast Asia and East Africa were nearly identical, which led Forster to identify the determinants of counterinsurgency. Since this was primarily a struggle for control of the population, two basic factors were crucial: psychological warfare and a well-organized intelligence service.[185] At the same time, the population had to be managed to ensure security and controllability. The dictatorial nature of such measures apparently did not bother Forster much, since he advocated the implementation of the strategy in future military operations. However, to advance the further development of a uniform doctrine, he did recommend that similar studies be done on the cases of Cyprus and, in cooperation with French authorities, especially on the wars in Indochina and North Africa.[186]

The French Theory of *Guerre révolutionnaire*

Actually, such cooperation between the two colonial powers had already occurred on the subject of experiences with antisubversive warfare. In the context of the NATO Inter-Allied Training Program, the British high command in Nairobi had invited a French officer from Madagascar in June 1954 to accompany, for study purposes, a battalion operating against the Mau Mau.[187]

In March of 1956, the British ambassador in Paris Gladwyn Jebb strongly supported Anglo-French bilateral staff consultations on guerrilla warfare, at which France was able to profit from the British experience with this new type of warfare in Malaya and Kenya, thus enabling the French military to adapt as quickly as possible to this new challenge.[188]

Thanks to an invitation of the French army, the British officer A. J. Wilson had the opportunity to see for himself the situation in Algeria on the eve of the Battle of Algiers. During his week-long trip through the country in January 1957, Wilson experienced a lively exchange of opinions in numerous discussions between himself and his French hosts.[189] Wilson repeatedly pointed to the British methods in Kenya and recommended their implementation in Algeria. He argued that the "terrorism" in Algiers could only be effectively eliminated by using measures modeled on those in "Operation Anvil," the comprehensive "purge operation" in Nairobi in April 1954.[190] The deployment of special small commandos resembling the Kenyan pseudo-gangs[191] and the "villagization"[192] of the Arab population would also be very important for the success of French troops. Wilson also stated that the Indochina veterans, who had greater theoretical knowledge than the British army, would have adapted much better to the requirements of counterinsurgency than the officers from France and from the French garrison in Germany who were sent directly to Algeria.[193]

Wilson's report provided valuable information to his superiors on the military operations in the Algerian departments.[194] At first, the British army command considered sending other officers on observation missions to Algeria, particularly to study closely the French military innovation of helicopter warfare.[195] However, these plans were abandoned in March 1957 under pressure from the Foreign Office, because it was feared that any conceivable link between the British army and the French war in Algeria could seriously harm the standing of Great Britain in the Arab world and especially in Libya, where the British maintained important military bases.[196] In particular, the growing brutality of the war in the wake of the Battle of Algiers so shocked the British allies that London distanced itself from the French military.[197] Great Britain's actions are surprising insofar as the French army command at this point was "only" being consequent in applying the methods of counterinsurgency that had already been used in Kenya in a similar fashion. The great expertise of Indochina veterans in antisubversive warfare, which Wilson had so praised during his trip, now became bloody reality.

Contrary to Great Britain, the French army command could not simply resort to a "Malayan model for success" to combat guerrilla warfare in the conflict in North Africa. Instead, it first had to deal with the humiliating defeats and the loss of colonies in Southeast Asia. High-ranking officers of the defeated expedition forces were primarily the ones to see the looming danger of a "second Indochina," should the army fail to start adapting to the new military challenges. In their view, the most urgent task was to draw the necessary conclusions from the military debacle.[198] In comprehensive studies, Indochina veterans like Colonel Jean Nemo and the former commander in chief General Paul Ely dissected the Southeast Asian military operations in the firm conviction that an adequate counterstrategy would prevent a second debacle.[199] Thus, the Indochina trauma became the catalyst for the development of the French doctrines of antisubversive warfare that would soon decisively influence military operations in the Algerian War.[200]

The analysis resulted in the theory of the *guerre révolutionnaire*, which was identified as a new communist combat strategy based on Mao's concept of revolution.[201] The new military challenge was discussed extensively in relevant military publications.[202] In their respective articles, both Colonel Charles Lacheroy and Commandant Jacques Hogard described revolutionary war as a phenomenon that took place in five stages.[203] The suddenly incipient terror of the guerrilla movement was countered with unpopular measures by the security forces, whereupon the revolutionaries stepped up their efforts to lay a political groundwork for the revolution. Guerrilla warfare and political agitation complemented each other symbiotically in the shared aim to unify the broad masses behind the insurgents. By creating parallel political structures in liberated zones and gradually transforming guerrilla troops into regular army units, the rebels intended to weaken the established political order, which would then be toppled in the final phase by an all-out military offensive. The two authors emphasized in their analysis the fatal impact of psychological warfare. As the experiences of the *pourrissement* in Indochina showed, the enemy won the backing of the population and decisively weakened the morale of the security forces with the help of an ideological propaganda campaign. The systematic attempts to indoctrinate French prisoners in the camps of the Viet Minh awakened painful memories for many Indochina veterans.[204] For Lacheroy, Hogard, and many other officers, it was clear at the end of 1956 that the decisive advantage of the revolutionary enemy consisted of a strong ideological conviction and the successful courting for the broad support of the masses.[205]

Thus it was maintained that the *guerre révolutionnaire* was a new type of war requiring a thoroughly new strategic approach.[206] The main focus was no longer on combating enemy troops; instead greater effort had to be invested in the fight for popular support.[207] As early as October 1954, General Lionel-Martin Chassin had warned that the free world would die a violent death if it did not adopt certain enemy methods.[208] At the start of 1957, Hogard and Massu therefore advocated that their own military operations be more strongly adapted to the strategy of the enemy.[209] Subversive revolutionary war could not be won with the means of classic warfare but required special counterrevolutionary measures, argued Massu.[210]

These calls to adapt to the new circumstances of war were reflected in the doctrines of the *guerre contre-révolutionnaire*. It was clear to the proponents of the new military concept that success in this war scenario was dependent not solely on military means but especially on a specific political counter-campaign.[211] Captain André Souyris attributed greater priority to means of warding off the danger of revolution than to military retaliation. With the aid of a substantially enlarged intelligence service, comprehensive social and economic reforms, and a special propaganda campaign, it would be possible to protect the population effectively from enemy indoctrination and thereby pull the people to the side of France.[212] Hogard incorporated this view into his strategic concept.[213] Besides isolating the rebel territories and completely destroying the rebel organization, Hogard also made psychological warfare a top priority in his ten guidelines for counterinsurgency. The central focus of French military doctrine was the "conquest of the people,"[214] who, at the same time, were to be shielded from enemy infiltration.

Officers like Lacheroy and Colonel Roger Trinquier did not shy away from deploying totalitarian measures to achieve these aims and advocated a comprehensive control of the population.[215] "Call me a fascist, if you want," said Trinquier, "but we have to bring the population to heel. Each step a person takes has to be controlled."[216] This was to be brought about by weaving a tight network of intelligence operations and establishing a central monitoring organization, the Bureau de l'Organisation et du Contrôle des Populations.[217] The intelligence service was given the key role in this system because it was to monitor each individual, gather information, and track down and eliminate subversive elements. Trinquier was completely aware how radical his ideas were and even acknowledged the analogy to totalitarian organizations.[218] For him, the fundamental difference was that his measures served solely to protect the population from the "terrorist" danger.

When the Algerian conflict broke out only months after the end of the war in Southeast Asia in November 1954, many French officers viewed this as the continuation of their defensive campaign against the worldwide expansion of communism. Although no communist backdrop existed in Algeria and the uprising was clearly the manifestation of an anticolonial national movement, parallels were drawn to Indochina, and the Indochina veterans at first referred to the Algerian rebels as *les viets*.[219] In their view, only the geographical location of the war had changed, not the type of conflict. The *guerre révolutionnaire* was now taking place in North Africa and offered them the unique opportunity to redeem themselves after the humiliation of Dien Bien Phu. The preservation of French Algeria became an inextricable part of the "sentimental geography of the French army,"[220] for which they would rather die than once again face disgrace.[221] At a 1957 military conference, high-ranking officers drew an imaginary map to show the advance of "world communism" over North Africa. Therefore, it was said that the essence of the French army's mission in Algeria was to defend the "free world and Western civilization."[222]

In order to do this, the first important step was to educate their own troops in the new military doctrines and thus prepare them for this type of war. For this purpose, the army established the Centre d'Instruction de Pacification et de Contre-Guérilla (CIPCG) in June 1956. Located in the Algerian city of Arzew, the CIPCG trained a total of ten thousand officers in the tactics and techniques of antisubversive warfare.[223] Particularly under the direction of Colonel André Bruge, the training began in July 1957 to focus more on the teachings of *guerre contre-révolutionnaire*.[224] Bruge, who had survived five years' imprisonment in Viet Minh camps, seemed predestined to explain the new military imperative of the French army to his students in weeks of course work.[225] This form of training for newly recruited troops was considered essential by both the high command in Algiers and the defense ministry in Paris, which led to the establishment of other facilities, such as the Centre d'Entrainement à la Guerre Subversive Jeanne d'Arc near Philippeville.[226] Training was not restricted to high-ranking officers. Starting in 1958, training centers for noncommissioned officers and other enlisted ranks were set up in Oran, Dellys, and Bougie.[227]

By extending the ranks involved and constantly trying to increase the number of seminar participants, the high command intended to indoctrinate as many of its own troops as possible. This objective became even more crucial because the public criticism of the way the war was being conducted increasingly threatened to undermine the morale of the French soldiers, especially the conscripts. A confidential report by Colonel Buchod on a pre-paratory seminar for reserve officers at the training center Jeanne d'Arc shows that the curriculum aimed not only to teach the techniques of counterinsur-gency but also to strengthen military morale.[228] The training participants, full of optimism, confirmed after their twenty-day seminar that they had received an excellent picture of the military's important role in developing Algeria,[229] and that the *mission humaine* was a newly discovered side of the French army that was being criticized too strongly and put in a bad light back in France. The only exception to this overall very positive opinion held by officers was the evaluation of three priests who spoke out against the methods of antisub-versive warfare and broke a taboo by addressing the issue of torture.[230] Colo-nel Buchod attributed this "subversive" behavior to the lack of both patriotic sentiments and intellect of the persons involved. However, his conclusion was that the overwhelming majority of seminar graduates had developed a great appreciation of the pacification mission. The manner in which the French were conducting the war in Algeria placed such special demands on its own troops that they needed to receive a thorough indoctrination and thereby an immunization against public criticism before their deployment.

Still, it took until early 1957 before Algeria could finally become the testing grounds of this new French military strategy.[231] When the wave of FLN attacks rolled over Algiers and the situation in the city threatened to spin out of control, the opportunity finally arose for General Massu and his Tenth Paratrooper Division to put the theoretical principles of *guerre contre-révolutionnaire* into practice. By destroying the urban underground network of the Liberation Front, Massu thoroughly convinced his superiors of the effi-ciency of the new military doctrines, which then became the highest maxims of the army command. The Battle of Algiers was used almost as a model for further French warfare in Algeria.[232]

The immediate consequence was an expansion of psychological warfare, for which a special division was created.[233] The Cinquième Bureau, headed by Colonel Lacheroy, was responsible not only for ideologically defending Al-geria in the propaganda campaign against the enemy but also for completely smashing the entire FLN political network.[234] As a result, the propaganda division held a highly influential position in all war efforts and rapidly de-veloped into a powerful autonomous organization quite independent of the government in Paris. The "battle for the hearts" of the Arab people was to be won in the meantime by the Section Administrative Spécialisée (SAS), which had been set up already in 1955 and whose activities were now expanded.[235]

Following the example of the Bureaux Arabes initiated by General Bugeaud and the old French pacification strategy of *tache d'huile* from General Galliéni, SAS officers were to use their work in the areas of infrastructure, education, and health services to convince the Arabs of the humanity of the French republic and to immunize them against any temptation posed by the FLN. However, from the standpoint of the military leaders, psychological warfare was not enough if France was to "conquer the people." Instead, extensive control had to be guaranteed through physical seizure. To this end, the military extended the scope of its previously limited detention and resettlement measures to cover all of Algeria.[236] All contact between the rebels and the general population was to be thus prevented, while at the same time the camp prisoners underwent a radical "reeducation."[237] The experiences of Algiers had also shown how important the intelligence service was in monitoring the populace and in fighting the secret network of the FLN. The *officier de renseignement* therefore began to assume a key role.

As in the previous British military operations in Malaya and Kenya, the Algerian War developed into a textbook example of antisubversive warfare as of 1957. Military staffs from other countries wanted to profit from the expertise of their British and French allies. As developments unfolded in Vietnam, the United States became particularly interested in the antisubversive methods of France and Great Britain.[238] So the Pentagon had the abovementioned study by General Ely translated into English with the title "Lessons from the War in Indochina,"[239] and the RAND Corporation, a think tank with close connections to the U.S. military, produced its research memorandum "Doctrine and Tactics of Revolutionary Warefare: The Viet Minh in Indochina,"[240] which included a comprehensive analysis of the organizational structure, strategy, and warfare of the Vietnamese liberation movement. In this strategy paper, the author George K. Tanham explicitly emphasized: "Most of the research for this project was carried out in Paris, where the French government, chiefly through General Paul Ely, was most co-operative in giving the author access to war records and special studies of Indochina. . . . In addition to his extensive study of the documents, the author had the privilege of numerous and detailed discussions with French officers who had served in Indochina."[241]

In April 1962, only a few weeks after the ceasefire in Algeria, the RAND Corporation held its own symposium on counterinsurgency in Washington, D.C. Instead of featuring a strictly academic and theoretical discussion on the problem of guerrilla warfare, the five-day event pursued a far more pragmatic approach "to draw on the knowledge of men of recent and direct experience in counterinsurgency, with a view to assembling a large body of detailed information and judgment on the multifarious aspects of this inadequately explored form of conflict. . . . Such a pragmatic approach would not only provide fruitful insights into earlier struggles but would, above all, yield valuable lessons for the future."[242] The main criterion for selecting the symposium participants was practical experience with successful counterinsurgency, by which Malaya, Kenya, and Algeria were designated as "key areas," in addition to the Philippines and South Vietnam. Therefore, half of those participating were British and French officers with relevant experience in combat operations in Southeast Asia or North Africa, including such prominent men as the British military intelligence officer Frank Kitson and the French colonel David Galula, both of whom had further advanced the military doctrines in their respective countries. In several discussion rounds, this circle of experts debated all of the various aspects of antisubversive warfare in great detail, whereby the experiences from the wars of decolonization served as the dominant point of reference.

A study of the biographies of these colonial fighters reveals that their lives were closely interlocked with the U.S. military beyond the scope of this symposium.[243] These officers transferred their strategic knowledge and experience concerning decolonization wars directly to the U.S. military through various teaching and advisory positions at U.S. military universities and think tanks, so that the military could profit from this knowledge in postcolonial conflict scenarios. The RAND Corporation even recruited a high-ranking member from French government circles to analyze the Algerian War. In his memorandum "The French Campaign Against the FLN," Constantin Melnik, who had been an adviser to French prime minister Michel Debré in matters of secret intelligence between 1959 and 1962, analyzed France's own approach to the Algerian War for the benefit of the Americans.[244] In his analysis, Melnik particularly emphasized the great success of French strategy in the Battle of Algiers, in which the army succeeded within just a few weeks to destroy the urban FLN network and to stop terrorist attacks against the European population. In this context, Melnik frankly acknowledged that torture had been mutated into a "principle weapon" to procure necessary information, while at the same time noting: "It is not appropriate for us to discuss here the moral question of the means used to get information. Its defenders asserted that it was not practiced in a sadistic manner, but with purely utilitarian spirit; that it permitted them to save human lives; that it constituted a form of risk appropriate to the type of combat conducted by the terrorist, etc. Indeed, it must be understood that it permitted the attainment of impressive results in dismantling the insurrectionary networks."[245] According to such military logic, the alleged success in the fight against antisubversive forces justified any means.

The colonial powers of Belgium and Portugal also showed increased interest in the British and French strategic concepts. Troubled by the African raids on white settlers in Kenya, the Belgian Congo sent the man second in command of its security forces to Nairobi in November 1952.[246] The reason for his ten-day trip was to observe the British police methods closely in order to be prepared for and to react appropriately to the emergency of an African uprising should one occur in the Belgian colony. The Portuguese government sent delegations of high-ranking officers, among them army chief of staff General Lopez da Silva, to Algeria to study the new French military doctrines and the deployment of paratroopers.[247] The "success" of these study trips became clear in the Portuguese decolonization wars from 1961 to 1974, in which the last remaining European colonial power closely followed the French principles.[248]

The doctrines that had been developed in response to the anticolonial challenge greatly influenced the further strategic development of counterinsurgency.[249] In the case of Great Britain, this even prompted officers like General Kitson to use a slightly refined adaptation of what they had learned about guerrilla warfare[250] in Kenya, Malaya, and Cyprus in British military operations in Northern Ireland.[251] In this way, key strategic aspects of warfare were imported from the colonies back to Europe. For the decolonization wars in Kenya and Algeria, the new military doctrines had the fatal consequence that the implementation of unrestricted repressive measures was justified by underscoring military necessities and special colonial challenges. From the standpoint of the colonial powers, the provisions of international humanitarian law did not pose a hindrance for such methods.

War Without Rules: The Conflicts in Kenya and Algeria, the Geneva Conventions, and the International Committee of the Red Cross

"Savage Wars of Peace": Colonial Wars and International Humanitarian Law

Traditionally, the colonial powers justified the unchecked use of force by arguing that colonial conflicts[252] differed fundamentally from wars between "civilized" states. "Small wars" in the overseas possessions, maintained the British military theoretician Charles Callwell, were "expeditions against savages and semi-civilized races by disciplined soldiers."[253] In the opinion of U.S. president Theodore Roosevelt, such a conflict was a relentless race war that could not abide by the rules of international morality.[254] From a Western military viewpoint, international treaties on warfare were not valid in such war scenarios.[255] The rules of "civilized" warfare did not pertain to armed conflict against an opponent who, as "uncivilized barbarians," would not understand them. British General Sir John Ardagh offered an explanation: "It is very different with a savage. Even though pierced two or three times, he does not cease to march forward, does not call upon the hospital attendants, but continues on, and before anyone has time to explain to him that he is flagrantly violating the decisions of the Hague Conference, he cuts off your head."[256]

While the nations participating in the Hague Peace Conferences of 1899 attempted to regulate and "humanize"[257] war between "civilized" nations by banning certain weapons like poisonous gases and dumdum bullets,[258] the colonial powers were doing everything possible at the same time to exclude these protective measures from colonial wars. At first it was agreed that the Hague Convention was not universally binding, but only valid between the signatory states, thereby excluding the populations in the colonies. For example, the ban on using dumdum bullets included in Declaration 3 of the Hague Convention applied to "civilized" warfare, but not in the fight against wild animals and "wild peoples."[259] This was particularly in the interests of Great Britain, which had designed this type of ammunition specifically for deployment in its overseas territories.[260] Thus the colonial powers succeeded in keeping the protective provisions of international humanitarian law out of their own colonies. The colonial conflicts, glorified by the British writer and poet Rudyard Kipling to "savage wars of peace,"[261] were in reality wars conducted without rules and norms, in which all military measures that were considered necessary also appeared to be permissible.

The decolonization wars in Kenya and Algeria were also conducted along the lines of this "colonial tradition." However, after 1945, the British and French governments faced the problem that the political framework had changed decisively with the development of the human rights regime. In an international atmosphere in which colonialism was coming under increasingly strong criticism from various directions, the metropoles were put on the moral defensive by the anticolonial resistance. To an ever greater degree, the use of force in the colonies was attracting national and international attention, thus forcing London and Paris to take public opinion into account.[262]

In his influential paper "The Problem of Nationalism in the Colonies," Harold Ingrams, an adviser to the Colonial Office, summarized this situation: "Provided that we have the force necessary, it is well arguable that there are circumstances in which we should use them, but it is an indispensable condition of that use that it should not be for the preservation of any advantage which can be reasonably presented as imperialistic."[263]

In addition to growing public pressure, Great Britain and France became further bound to the norms of international law as "Hague Law" was expanded and developed.[264] Although the colonial powers had succeeded in blocking any mention of "colonial conflicts" in the 1949 Geneva Conventions, the revised international humanitarian law obliged countries to maintain certain minimum standards, even in the case of armed conflicts of a noninternational character.[265] Ironically, a French initiative[266] was to be credited for extending the validity of the Geneva Conventions to internal conflicts, thereby granting protection to civilians, members of the armed forces, and combatants who were no longer fighting due to illness, wounds, detention, or any other cause. According to Article 3, which is included in all four conventions and is therefore dubbed the "convention in miniature," this group of people were to be treated humanely and equally in all circumstances. For this reason, "violence to life and person, in particular, murder of all kinds, mutilations, cruel treatment and torture, taking of hostages, outrages upon personal dignity, in particular humiliating and degrading treatment, the passing of sentences and carrying out of executions without previous judgment pronounced by a regularly constituted court, affording all the judicial guarantees which are recognized as indispensable by civilized people,"[267] were prohibited everywhere and at all times. Moreover, paragraph 2 of the article stipulated that humanitarian organizations like the ICRC could offer their services to the warring parties. This provision was meant to protect the relief efforts of humanitarian organizations from being seen as hostile acts of intervention in the internal affairs of a sovereign state.

On the one hand, the recognition of these minimum humanitarian protections in internal conflicts meant a radical breakthrough for humanitarian law; yet on the other, it did not completely clarify the question with regard to the applicability of Article 3.[268] The phrase "armed conflict" did not clearly stipulate whether civilian unrest and especially colonial rebellion fell into this category. The ICRC adopted the standpoint that the areas of applicability had to be considered as large as possible, because the Article 3 provisions were only minimum standards of protection that had been anchored in national law long before the signing of the Geneva Conventions.[269] By contrast, the colonial powers of Great Britain and France refused to give their colonial confrontations in Kenya and Algeria the official status of "armed conflict." In order to block the applicability of humanitarian law and the intervention of international actors, they believed it was necessary to avoid any designation that could be interpreted as meaning armed confrontation, or even war, no matter what the circumstances. How did the colonial powers go about achieving this in practice? The war without rules became a war without a name. By using the neutral terms "emergency" and "civil disturbance," London attempted to belie the true nature of events in East Africa.[270] In July 1954, the Colonial Office stated in an internal paper that it would be extremely undesirable to have the "emergency" in Kenya treated as a war.[271] The British government even shied away from the loaded term "rebellion" and chose instead to call the events a "civil disturbance."[272]

Officially, the French government also acted as if no war was taking place in Algeria, only that it was dealing with several *événements*.[273] During his trip to Algeria in late November 1954, the French minister of the interior, François Mitterrand, explained such official language, which continued to be used until 1999:[274] "We will avoid everything that could be interpreted as a state of war of any sort; we don't want that."[275] Subsequently, Paris belittled the Algerian War as a series of "opérations de police" (police operations), "actions de maintien de l'ordre" (actions to preserve order) and "entreprises de pacification" (pacification measures).[276] From the perspective of the French government, it was not fighting a war in Algeria, which was an integral part of France, but was "solving" a domestic problem.

By describing the situation with euphemisms like "civil unrest" and "events," the governments in London and Paris attempted not only to cover up the true nature of the conflicts, but also to criminalize their opponents.[277] Accordingly, the occurrences were the deeds of "subversive elements" endangering the legitimate order in the overseas possessions. Thus, colonial security forces were obliged to take police action against these troublemakers and guarantee domestic security. In the eyes of the British, the Mau Mau movement was a criminal band of "terrorists" and "primitive savages" who plundered indiscriminately and murdered defenseless people.[278] For this reason, captured Mau Mau fighters were not treated as prisoners of war, but as common criminals, as was reported by the British command in Kenya to the Colonial Office.[279] The conflict in Kenya was increasingly depicted as a confrontation between the "civilized" British authority and the dark forces of "African barbarism."[280]

From the French standpoint, the struggle in Algeria was also a fight against "terrorists" and "bandits" who posed a threat to the unity of the nation and its North African departments.[281] As *hors-la-loi* (outlaws), the FLN fell outside the jurisdiction of French law and therefore had no legitimate claim to legal protection for its members.[282] In both cases, the colonial powers viewed the members of the liberation movements as criminals, not soldiers. Because the insurgents lacked the status of combatant, they could not assert a claim to the protection accorded by humanitarian law. One French sergeant justified the execution of captured FLN fighters by stating: "We don't take prisoners. . . . These men aren't soldiers."[283]

The colonial powers went further than simply criminalizing the enemy. During the course of the conflicts, colonial racism became radicalized to such a degree that the rebels were eventually stripped of any affiliation to the human species.[284] For the majority of white settlers and colonial officials in Kenya, Mau Mau fighters were "wild beasts of the forest"[285] and were given racist labels like "monkey," "mickey," and "mouse" to equate them to wild animals and vermin.[286] The American mercenary William Baldwin, who fought in a British police unit during the emergency in Kenya, justified the execution of prisoners with the argument that they had lost their right to be treated as humans by participating in the uprising: "I looked upon them as diseased animals, which, if left alive, were a constant menace to the community."[287]

In Algeria, this form of racism was also expressed in a radicalization of the language. The racist terms traditionally used for the Arab population, namely, "fig stumps" and "billy goats," were now replaced by the expression *ratons*,[288] whereby the term *ratonnade*, rat hunt, became synonymous with riots against the Arabian population.[289] As representative of a view common within the French army, the French paratrooper Pierre Leulliette describes the attitude of a sergeant who was in charge of torturing prisoners: "He was bored. It was always the same. All the vermin screamed the same way: you got fed up crushing the loathsome creatures under your heel."[290]

According to the psychologist Sam Keen, the use of archetypical enemy images, like those of criminals, barbarians, and wild animals, served to dehumanize the enemy, which was the decisive prerequisite in order to fight and destroy the enemy with all possible means and with no moral qualms.[291] By deliberately negating the status of an armed conflict and by degrading the members of the Kenyan and Algerian liberation movements with labels like "terrorist," "wild beasts," and "vermin," the colonial powers released their own troops from the normative code of conduct dictated by humanitarian law.

The Attitude of the Independence Movements Toward the Geneva Conventions

Contrary to the way the colonial powers depicted them, the independence movements were in no way a marauding, murdering band of criminals, but militarily organized units with a command hierarchy and insignia. In their attacks, the Mau Mau fighters and members of the FLN undoubtedly resorted to cruel methods, which often led to the murder and mutilation of the victim. The use and spread of terror was a key element in their guerrilla tactics, but it was one directed specifically at representatives of the hated colonial regime and not arbitrarily against the entire population. In fact, the independence movements attempted to compel their troops to uphold certain rules of war.

The story propagated by the British that the Mau Mau mainly butchered women, children, and the elderly mercilessly and slowly tortured their victims to death was at odds with the truth.[292] The British doctor J. Wilkinson refuted this idea in his report on the victims at Tumutumu Hospital, in which he concluded that the rebels largely spared women, children, and the elderly and that the majority of victims did not show any evidence of torture but of being killed by a well-aimed blow with a panga.[293] One particularly bloody exception was the Lari massacre in March 1953. As a reaction to this excessive use of violence, the Mau Mau did indeed pass a resolution at a meeting in July 1953 under the direction of the leading generals Dedan Kimathi and Waruhiu Itote in which the killing of women and children by their soldiers was strictly forbidden.[294] Unlike the British colonial power, the Mau Mau leadership began to establish rules of war, which were followed by the vast majority of their troops.[295] The "Rules of Conduct," passed 4 January 1954, prohibited the killing of persons under the age of eighteen, the mishandling of civilians, the rape of women, and attacks on civilian facilities such as hospitals and schools.[296] With the passage of these rules, the Mau Mau movement committed itself to enforcing certain minimum humanitarian standards. Yet, no reference was made here to the provisions of "Geneva Law" because the vast majority of Africans were not even aware of their existence. Only later, on rare occasions, did internees, like the prisoner spokesman Josiah Mwangi Kariuki, refer in their protests to the Geneva Conventions and demand treatment according to these standards.[297] The prisoners in Kenyan detention camps first came into direct contact with representatives of international humanitarian

law through the ICRC missions there, which prompted Kariuki to write a letter to the committee in Geneva expressing his particular interest in the work
of the International Red Cross.[298]

The FLN, however, was very well informed about the provisions and
particularly the political importance of the Geneva Conventions. As early as
February 1956, the representatives of the Algerian delegation in Cairo, Mohamed Khider and Ahmed Ben Bella, wrote a letter to the ICRC in which
they accused France of having fundamentally violated the provisions protecting prisoners of war by executing Algerian freedom fighters.[299] It was the
declared objective of the Algerian Liberation Front to have the validity of
all four Geneva Conventions applied to the conflict in North Africa.[300] In
order to achieve this, one basic prerequisite was that its own troops respect
the provisions of "Geneva Law." Therefore, the Algerian executive committee instructed the commanders of the various *wilayas*, as well as the officers
and noncommissioned officers of the ALN, to strictly observe the provisions
of the Geneva Conventions and to treat captured troops according to the
humanitarian standards stipulated for prisoners of war.[301] A report by the
French chief of staff confirmed the existence of this order, but also noted that
the various troop units of the ALN did not see themselves uniformly bound
to these instructions.[302]

At the same time, the FLN decided to establish the Croissant-Rouge Algérien (CRA) and incorporate it into the strategy of the national struggle for
liberation.[303] In its statutes of 8 January 1957, the Algerian Red Crescent, with
a temporary seat in Moroccan Tangier, committed itself to help implement
humanitarian law and to support the work of the missions sent by the Red
Cross and other relief organizations during the war.[304] Further, a delegation
from the CRA, headed by Dr. Djilali Bentami, was to intensify contact with
the ICRC, even though the international umbrella organization in Geneva
refused to recognize the organization as a national Red Crescent society.[305]
The government in Paris observed the entire development with great concern, since it feared that the Algerian relief organization, under the cloak of
humanitarianism, would be able to serve the international propaganda objectives of the FLN and would make all of the collected relief supplies directly
available to the ALN.[306]

In official communiqués, the FLN repeatedly professed its commitment to the principles of international humanitarian law. In his first statement as president of the provisional Algerian government on 26 September
1958, Ferhat Abbas emphasized that the GPRA would highly welcome every

international initiative to ensure the application of the Geneva Conventions to the Algerian War.[307] In addition, Abbas pointed out in a memorandum to the ICRC, dated 24 November 1958, that the Algerian leadership had always championed the observance of the Geneva Conventions in this conflict, unlike France, which continually and seriously violated its legal international commitments.[308] Algerian efforts on behalf of the recognition of the Geneva Conventions reached a high point in 1960 when the GPRA officially decided to ratify the conventions[309] and signed them in Bern on 20 June of that same year.[310]

This development was accompanied by a well-directed propaganda campaign, which included the publication of the *White Paper on the Application of the Geneva Conventions of 1949 to the French-Algerian Conflict*[311] by the FLN office in New York. In this white paper, the FLN explained extensively its reasons for the unilateral recognition of the entire "Geneva Law" to the war in Algeria. According to the provisions of the Hague Regulations of Land Warfare, the ALN was to be treated as a regular army, subordinate to the provisional Algerian government and embroiled in an international war against the French occupational power.[312] At the same time, the paper documented French torture practices, cases of "missing" people, retaliation measures by the French army against the civilian population, as well as the policy of internment and resettlement as evidence of France's humanitarian violations, whereby reference was made expressly to the findings of the neutral inquiry reports of the ICRC, the French Commission de sauvegard des droits et libertés individuels and the Commission internationale contre le régime concentrationnaire.[313] The purposes of the white paper were, first, to urge other signatories of the Geneva Conventions to exert pressure on France and get Paris to recognize all four conventions as applicable to the war in North Africa, and, second, to document the efforts of the FLN to "humanize the conflict."[314] However, the Liberation Front did not undertake this initiative solely for humanitarian reasons, but actually used it to cloak a far more calculated realpolitik.[315] By professing its full recognition of the principles of "Geneva Law" and permanently pointing out the grave violations perpetrated by France, the FLN managed to pillory its enemy in full view of the international public and at the same time to enhance its own international standing.[316] Another effective means was the unilateral and unconditional release of French prisoners as a sign of goodwill.[317] While the French military treated Algerian resistance fighters as common criminals and "terrorists" and sent them to the guillotine, the ALN simply released certain individual prisoners[318] or turned them over to ICRC delegates.[319] From October 1958 to December 1961, six such releases took place.[320] In doing so, the FLN aimed to achieve the greatest publicity effect and media presence possible,[321] and the statements by the freed soldiers and civilians about the good treatment they received at the hands of the ALN could be instrumentalized very well for propaganda purposes.[322] Still, this policy did not prevent the Liberation Front from also killing prisoners and having them put to death as retaliation for the execution of their own supporters, with the clarification that, in such cases, the people involved were not prisoners of war but war criminals.[323]

With the help of this "humanitarian strategy"[324] and a well-functioning propaganda apparatus, the FLN did succeed overall in convincing the international public of its unconditional commitment to international humanitarian law and in using this for its political objectives. All efforts to have the Geneva Conventions applied to the war were given great priority by the Algerian independence movement, not only as a way to protect its own troops and to exploit any resulting propaganda advantages, but also because it represented an important step in achieving international recognition for the GPRA.[325]

Too Little, Too Late: The Role of the ICRC in the Kenyan War of Decolonization

In both of these wars of decolonization, the ICRC in Geneva attempted to fulfill its role as the most important institution to safeguard and promote international humanitarian law. Therefore, in a letter dated 13 December 1954, Pierre Gaillard, the head of the ICRC's executive body, expressed his opinion that, in light of the situations in Kenya and North Africa, the organization needed to find modalities for intervening in these internal conflicts. In his view, it was already clear that the ICRC could not remain uninvolved in situations of this kind.[326] As a result, the International Committee finally decided late in December of 1954 on certain guidelines in handling "internal unrest."[327] According to these guidelines, each intervention was to pursue strictly humanitarian objectives and was neither to interfere with nor to evaluate government measures on restoring order. The International Committee in Geneva stressed not only its own neutrality and nonpartisanship as a humanitarian organization but also the highly confidential character of its missions, the results of which were not meant for the public but for the responsible government authorities exclusively. Moreover, the guidelines underscored that a humanitarian intervention on the part of the ICRC was not to be interpreted as any form of legal or de facto recognition of the parties involved. Support by the national Red Cross organization in the countries involved was welcome, but at the same time one was aware of the fact that national Red Cross societies tended to act in the interest of their governments and not as nonpartisan organizations. In conclusion, the ICRC officials emphasized that certain humanitarian standards, such as the humane treatment of the detained and the wounded and the prohibition of torture, were to be upheld under all circumstances, including a state of emergency.

Thus, the job of assisting victims of "internal unrest" became one of the most important tasks of the ICRC and, at the same time, one of its most difficult.[328] For this reason, in October 1955, the committee appointed for the second time since 1953[329] another independent international commission of experts to work out the organization's own scope of action in this type of conflict. The final report by this commission came to the conclusion that international humanitarian law should be given great weight also in internal conflicts and that the ICRC could be active in its function as a humanitarian organization on the basis of Article 3, paragraph 2, of the Geneva Conventions.[330] In the eyes of the authorities in Geneva, this opened new doors to the Red Cross to be active in internal conflicts,[331] while the colonial powers viewed the final report with growing concern.

Particularly at the British Foreign and Colonial Offices, officials worried that the ICRC, much like the United Nations, would subsequently be instrumentalized as an international organization to exert pressure on the colonial governments and serve the propaganda intentions of the anticolonial bloc.[332] Therefore, with regard to the situations in Malaya and Kenya, London instructed the delegates of the British Red Cross (BRC) to vehemently oppose the new intervention policy at the Nineteenth International Conference of the Red Cross that was to be held in New Delhi in January 1957.[333] In spite of the fact that a few national Red Cross societies did take this stance at the conference, the International Committee in Geneva, backed by the findings of the expert commission, began to become more intensively involved in the colonial wars in North and East Africa.[334]

The ICRC had been following the conflict in Kenya with growing interest since October 1952,[335] receiving valuable information from the ICRC delegate for British Central Africa, G. C. Senn, as well as from reports issued by nongovernmental organizations like the Kenya Committee.[336] Senn not only reported on the catastrophic humanitarian situation in the British colony but also strongly criticized the role of the BRC. Instead of supporting the intervention efforts of the International Committee and impartially offering

humanitarian aid, as stipulated by the principles of the Red Cross, the organization in Kenya, Senn reported, acted according to the racial discriminatory regulations established in the colony and served above all the interests of
the white colonial rulers.[337] Therefore, the devastating evaluation of the ICRC
delegate was that "this is sufficient evidence that the British Red Cross does
NOT do its duty in the whole matter, has never done it and does not show any
intention to change its attitude."[338]

In Geneva, ICRC officials were also forced to concede that there was no
hope they would receive support from the British Red Cross representatives
for their efforts in East Africa. In addition to the fact that the aid supplied by
the BRC concentrated exclusively on the victims of Mau Mau violence,[339] the
leadership in London opposed any form of intervention by the ICRC. The
situation in the British crown colony was said by the vice chair of the BRC,
Lady Limerick, not to be comparable to the situation in North Africa, where
the International Committee had already commenced with its activities.[340]
In Kenya, the problem was not civil war but only "barbarian" tribal unrest,
which was now under the control of security forces. Therefore, one saw no
reason for the International Committee to be active, especially since several
colleagues had already provided extensive humanitarian aid. The Red Cross
society in London also agreed with the official position of the British government that Article 3 of the Geneva Conventions could not be applied in the
Kenyan emergency.[341]

Despite the adverse British stance, the officials at the ICRC in Geneva still
continued their efforts to gain both the support of the BRC[342] and permission
from British authorities to send a mission to inspect the conditions in the
Kenya detention camps.[343] Finally their efforts paid off, and at the beginning
of 1957, at a point when military operations had nearly ceased, the government in London granted the ICRC delegates L. A. Gailland and H. P. Junod
access to various camps and prisons.[344] During their two-month-long mission
in March and April 1957, the two men visited a total of fifty-two detention
sites and eighteen "new villages," where they were able to inspect conditions
and talk to detainees without the presence of guards or other detention officials.[345] The findings from this mission were summarized in a confidential
report,[346] which was submitted to the British government with a few recommendations.[347] Overall, the ICRC delegates assessed the prison conditions in
the British detention camps positively; they confirmed finding an excellent
state of hygiene, decent housing options, a sufficient diet and adequate medical care for the prisoners, and camp locations with good climate conditions.[348]

They only criticized the use of whipping as a form of punishment and demanded that it be ceased immediately.

Remarkably, the ICRC report neither brought up the issue concerning the widespread use of torture and the mishandling of prisoners in the camps by British interrogation teams nor did it mention the "rehabilitation measures" of the "dilution technique." This method consisted of the deliberate use of brute force against hard-core supporters of the Mau Mau movement with the aim of breaking their resistance in order to be able to release them to general detention upon completion of the "rehabilitation process." The colonial government in Nairobi made no effort to conceal this procedure from the ICRC mission; on the contrary, officials discussed the topic extensively with the ICRC delegate Junod. In a highly confidential letter dated 25 June 1957 and addressed to the colonial secretary, Governor Baring wrote: "I have privately discussed this question with Dr. Junod of the International Red Cross, who I knew well in South Africa and who has spent his whole life working with Africans and most of it with African prisoners. He has no doubt in his own mind that if the violent shock was the price to be paid for pushing detainees out . . . we should pay it."[349] In this way, Junod condoned, as an ICRC representative, the mishandling of detainees and, after having witnessed himself the dilution technique, noted to his British escort Terence Gavaghan: "Do not distress yourself. Compared with the French in Algeria, you are angels of mercy."[350] Therefore, it is not astonishing that the British considered Junod a man to trust;[351] he was even consulted thereafter by authorities in Nairobi on issues concerning the use of physical force on prisoners. Moreover, Governor Baring asked him in a letter, dated 9 July 1957, to suggest alternatives for the dilution technique, which Baring considered extremely necessary but could also cause serious "political difficulties."[352]

Eventually, it was these feared "consequences" of British practices that led the ICRC to send a second mission to Kenya in 1959. The excessive use of force in the British detention camps became the focus of public interest following an incident on 3 March 1959, in which eleven prisoners were slain in Hola Camp as a result of a "shock treatment."[353] The government in London resorted to cover-up tactics in an effort to reduce the public pressure growing from the incident. To this effect, it considered publishing the confidential report of the first ICRC mission, in order to convince the public of the good conditions in the camps. The Red Cross in Geneva raised no objections to the resulting government request to publish the report but pointed out that the findings were by then two years old and recommended a new mission in light of recent events.[354] This proposal was well received by the Colonial Office since, in the eyes of Colonial Secretary Alan Lennox-Boyd, a renewed involvement on the part of the ICRC would be seen as a positive signal after the Hola incident.[355] Governor Baring shared this opinion and supported the idea of a Red Cross mission, "particularly if Monsieur Junod could again be associated with this work, since he has great experiences of prisons and detainee camps and a wide knowledge of Africans."[356]

Under these circumstances, the ICRC delegates Dr. J. M. Rubli and H. P. Junod visited a total of eight different Kenyan detention sites in June and July 1959.[357] However this time, unlike in 1957, the delegates discovered such grievous offenses during their inspections that the ICRC in Geneva felt compelled to send Dr. Rubli and ICRC vice president Dr. Marcel Junod[358] to London in early August, even before the final report was submitted, in order to consult personally with the British government.[359] In addition to a series of recommendations to improve prison conditions, the ICRC representatives addressed in particular the mishandling of prisoners and expressed their shock at the extent of the use of force in the detention camps.[360] According to Dr. Rubli, several witnesses had reported severe torture by British Special Branch officers in order to force confessions and break prisoners' will to resist.[361] Contrary to 1957, when the ICRC delegates did not even mention the dilution technique in their report, let alone protest against it, Dr. Rubli and Dr. Junod now vehemently demanded the immediate halt to torture and corporal punishment. The recommendations of the ICRC were widely supported within the Colonial Office, and officials promised to implement them without delay.[362] Surprisingly and completely contrary to the behavior of the Foreign Office and the BRC, the ministry was even of the opinion that the immediate application of Article 3 of the Geneva Conventions to the "problems in Kenya" could have prevented a series of serious unpleasantries.[363]

In the end, the ICRC did manage to finally fulfill its mission and get Great Britain to maintain humanitarian standards in the Kenyan detention camps. However, this occurred at a point when the British had already decided to release those being detained. Following the murders in the Hola Camp, the detention practices could no longer be justified, and the new British colonial secretary Iain Macleod ordered the closure of all existing camps as soon as possible.[364] Hence, the International Red Cross had not been able to influence the "hot" phase of the Mau Mau War from 1952 to 1956 in any way and had carelessly wasted a valuable opportunity to do so during its 1957 mission.

A Losing Battle: The ICRC and the Algerian War

The ICRC acted differently in the Algerian War, a conflict taking place before the eyes of the entire world. Immediately after hostilities started in November 1954, the ICRC began to consider a possible intervention there.[365] For this reason, ICRC delegate William H. Michel met with French Prime Minister Pierre Mendès-France on 31 January 1955. At this meeting, the International Committee offered its humanitarian aid and proposed to send a mission to visit the detention sites in North Africa.[366] Mendès-France accepted this offer under the condition that the activities of the Red Cross would be restricted solely to the detention camps and that the final report would be treated as highly confidential.[367] By granting the ICRC this permission, the French prime minister made possible the first mission to Algeria from February to March 1955.[368] It was the first of many extensive activities by the International Committee throughout the entire war.[369]

By July 1962, a total of nine subsequent missions had been sent, resulting in the inspection of more than five hundred different detention sites. However, the scope of activity of the ICRC during this period did not remain limited to the inspection of prison conditions but expanded as the war progressed. In addition to the mediation role it played in the exchange of French prisoners by the FLN, the International Red Cross also tried from 1957 on to mitigate the needs of the Algerian civilian population with large-scale relief supplies in the refugee camps in Tunisia and Morocco, as well as in the resettlement camps.[370] The humanitarian work benefiting the displaced Algerian civilian population was supported by the Croix-Rouge Français (CRF) starting in the summer of 1959, but only after Geneva had vehemently demanded the participation of the national Red Cross society.[371] The CRF supplied only limited amounts of aid and concentrated on helping children, since little sympathy could be mustered for the Muslim population and particularly for potential rebels.[372]

Still, the central task of the ICRC continued to be the inspection of prison facilities and detention camps. Although the delegates were denied access to several camps during their first visit to Algeria in 1955,[373] they were allowed in subsequent missions to talk to prisoners without supervision and summarize all of their findings in a final report.[374] The basis of legitimation for the work of the International Committee was not the Geneva Conventions as a whole but only the limited mandate spelled out in Article 3. This led to the paradoxical situation that the French government silently accepted the validity of Article 3 in the Algerian War by permitting the ICRC missions,[375] while adamantly refusing to officially recognize international humanitarian law in the "domestic affairs" in North Africa. Officials in Geneva repeatedly tried to commit both warring parties to compliance with the minimum standards of international law.[376] On 28 May 1958, the ICRC sent a letter addressed to both the FLN and the French government in which it demanded that both sides unconditionally uphold Article 3 and that the captured members of each of the armed forces be treated humanely and viewed not as common criminals but as prisoners of war as stipulated by the standards of the conventions.[377]

As mentioned above, this appeal was received with open arms on the part of the FLN leadership. For the French government, the Geneva initiative made it difficult to maintain its contradictory position, which it therefore gradually abandoned.[378] In a letter dated 30 July 1958, the French foreign ministry expressed great surprise at the criticism leveled by the ICRC, since France, as one of the first signatories of the Geneva Conventions, already fully respected all Article 3 provisions and any violation was punished severely and immediately.[379] The extensive support given to the Red Cross missions was said to prove this, and Paris in turn demanded that the International Committee should concentrate its efforts instead on making the rebels uphold the rules of war.

Even within the French army command in Algeria, the unceasing efforts of the International Red Cross led to a change of heart, particularly with regard to captured ALN members.[380] As early as 24 November 1957, the supreme commander of French forces in Algeria, General Raoul Salan, issued a secret order that rebels who openly bore arms and were captured in battle were to be treated, as best as possible, as prisoners of war according to the provisions of the Geneva Conventions.[381] This order was broadened on 19 March 1958 with the establishment of special military internment camps, the *centres Militaires d'Internés* (CMIs), in which prisoners, *pris les armes à la main*, were to be treated as liberally as possible.[382]

This new attitude of the French high command was due less to humanitarian concerns than to military necessity. The military had discovered that, even in the most hopeless situations, ALN fighters preferred to fight to the death rather than be taken prisoner because of the reports circulating about the horrific torture and subsequent executions of their captured comrades by French troops. By pursing the most liberal prisoner policy possible, the high command intended to eliminate the fears of the enemy, "with the aim thereby of reducing one's own casualties."[383] At the same time, however, Salan once again underscored in his order that the internees were not to be viewed as prisoners of war and that the Geneva Conventions were not applicable to them. Not until November 1959, after Salan was succeeded by General Challe, were the prisoners of the military internment camp referred to as "assimilés aux membres d'une armée ennemie."[384] Yet it was not until 1961, at a point when the French government was already conducting talks with the GPRA, that the validity of Article 3 of the Geneva Conventions was officially recognized and its implementation became mandatory in the CMIs.[385]

Especially by way of the mission reports, the ICRC attempted to influence the situation of the detainees in the camps and prisons. In order to do so, the International Committee kept in close contact with the French government and, in private talks, presented the French with a series of suggested improvements. In 1956, French prime minister Guy Mollet proved very open to these recommendations from Geneva and promised to undertake the necessary measures.[386] In Paris, the government was glad that the second mission report of the ICRC had evaluated the handling of prisoners on the whole as being humane.[387] As a result, the French even considered publishing the findings, despite the confidential status of the report.[388] In the period that followed, the Red Cross reports also spoke of progress in the state of the facilities at the camps, the housing options, and the hygienic conditions. Yet at the same time, the ICRC expressly warned France to stay the course.[389]

In his secret report to the International Committee in Geneva on 17 April 1960, even Paul-Albert Fevrier, the former commandant of Camp Colbert, confirmed the positive influence of the ICRC missions, which he said were absolutely necessary.[390] Fevrier reported that the visit by Red Cross representatives at a camp was immediately followed by the permission to distribute packages, letters, and blankets, while funds for construction projects in the camp became available faster and in greater amounts. However, Fevrier also stated that the missions had no impact on the treatment of prisoners, who continued to be "routinely" mishandled and tortured. The numerous improvements implemented by French authorities were not strongly motivated by a sense of humanity but served the purpose of maintaining the "humanitarian" façade of the camps.

A letter by General Dominique Hubert written in October 1958 proves this point quite poignantly. Huber notes that a recent inspection of the facilities at Camp Beni Messou had revealed serious defects. Since the Red Cross was due to visit the camp again, these had to be fixed without delay.[391] In the eyes of the French military staff in Algiers, the ICRC in general was not to be given any reason to file an unfavorable report, "which, should it be published, would demoralize the army and put the government on the spot in future negotiations."[392]

Contrary to the positive development of the physical conditions at the camps, the ICRC delegates registered a growing number of complaints about serious abuse in the course of interrogation by security forces.[393] In October and November 1956, the medical expert in the third mission, Dr. Gailland, discovered that a large number of detainees had serious injuries caused by beatings and suffered from severe burns caused by cigarettes extinguished on the skin and by electric shocks applied particularly to the genital area.[394] The vehement protest of the ICRC to the French government against these "interrogation methods" had no impact. Especially during the Battle of Algiers in the spring of 1957, the number of torture cases increased dramatically.[395] Numerous prisoners reported to the ICRC representatives that they had been severely tortured during their interrogation by police and special military units, particularly the paratroopers. Consequently, in the report on the fifth mission, the authorities in Geneva once again sent an insistent message to Paris: "The International Committee of the Red Cross, which has pointed out this grave problem to the French government repeatedly (in its reports from July 1956, November 1956, July 1957) is compelled once again to direct the urgent attention [of the French government] to facts that are in complete violation of the spirit of Article 3 of the Geneva Conventions."[396]

Later, ICRC reports confirmed that none of the protests from Geneva against the systematic mishandling of detainees led to any appreciable results.[397] On the contrary, an internal paper by the International Committee in December 1959 verified that the use of torture was again dramatically on the rise in Algeria, as a consequence both of the concentration of state power in the hands of the French army and of military operations connected to the Challe Plan, in which intelligence gathering played a key role.[398] In addition to these reports of torture, the International Committee in Geneva received information time and again from its delegates about serious war crimes perpetrated by the French army, such as the bombardment of villages with napalm and the mass executions of prisoners.[399]

On 5 January 1960, the French newspaper *Le Monde* published the confidential report of the seventh ICRC mission, which had landed inexplicably in the hands of the paper's journalists.[400] The published findings on systematic torture in Algeria shocked the international public and unleashed a storm of protest.[401] However, the newspaper article also documented the powerlessness of the ICRC, which had not succeeded in effectively stopping major human rights violations despite its intensive efforts over the years. One reason for this was certainly the fact that the mandate of the ICRC delegates was limited to Article 3 of the Geneva Conventions and that the French government only permitted visits to detention sites,[402] which meant that they could have no influence on the general conduct of war. At the same time, it was impossible for the International Red Cross to monitor effectively the enormous number of Algerian camps, especially because the organization was denied entrance to the secret "interrogation centers" run by the army and the police, the places where most of the torture took place.[403] Therefore, in a circular memorandum to the national Red Cross societies, the International Committee acknowledged with resignation that—despite the improvements in camps conditions—it had not been able in Algeria "to 'humanize' a conflict which was so savage and ferocious, nor . . . to ensure respect for the provisions of Article 3."[404] Hence, the Red Cross officials from Geneva had proved powerless against the unchecked colonial violence that occurred in Algeria and Kenya and against the related phenomena of war crimes, detention, resettlement, and the systematic use of torture.

Chapter 5

The Unleashing of Colonial Violence

> We are witnessing the awful death throes of colonialism.
>
> —Jean-Paul Sartre, 1957

Collective Punishment and Arbitrary Execution as Key Elements of Colonial Warfare

War Crimes as Colonial Deterrence

In general, war crimes are understood to be grave breaches of international humanitarian law. In reaction to the atrocities committed during World War II, the term underwent a great deal of specification in the course of the expansion of "Hague Law" and the international war criminal trials of Nuremberg and Tokyo.[1] For the first time, the 1949 Geneva Conventions actually codified the legal definition of the term "war crimes" by specifying which acts against the wounded, war prisoners, civilians, and even protected goods— the so-called "grave breaches" of the conventions—were outlawed.[2] Among these were willful killing, torture, inhumane treatment, the willful causing of great suffering or serious injury to body or health, illegal and arbitrary destruction and appropriation of property not justified by military necessity, forced service in enemy armed forces, deliberate denial of the right to due process of law and an impartial trial, illegal persecution and imprisonment, and hostage-taking.[3] Article 33 of the Fourth Geneva Convention explicitly stated that "no protected person may be punished for an offence he or she has not personally committed. Collective penalties and likewise all measures of intimidation or of terrorism are prohibited."[4] The Nuremberg principles, codified by the United Nations and derived directly from the Charter and Judgment of the International Military Tribunal, adopted this definition.[5] However the principles linked an additional area of international law to war crimes: murder, extermination, enslavement, deportation, and other inhumane acts done against a civilian population or persecutions on political, racial or religious grounds were now classified as "crimes against humanity."[6]

As prosecuting parties in the Nuremberg Trials and as signatory states of the 1949 Geneva Conventions, Great Britain and France had significantly contributed to this development of international criminal law. However, as mentioned above, both countries rejected the validity of international humanitarian law in their colonial conflicts and thereby relieved their troops from the responsibility of upholding the principles that they had just agreed upon. In short, war crimes were nothing less than an essential characteristic of their colonial warfare.[7] Such crimes did not usually occur as spontaneous attacks and revengeful acts by security forces losing discipline in the heat of the fight but as the deliberate policy of using excessive force by the colonial powers. Grave breaches of the Geneva Conventions were an essential element of colonial warfare and had a strategic function in the military's calculation.[8] By conducting a war that violated all principles of international humanitarian law, Great Britain and France wanted to deliver a "demonstration of strength" meant to once again secure their colonial domination. The indigenous population was to be intimidated by a "climate of counterterror" and deterred from offering the rebels any means of support.[9] Loyalty to the colonial state was to be coerced. Therefore, Mark Mazower is completely correct to argue that the basic principle of answering terror with terror, as used by German forces in combating partisans during World War II, served as a model for European colonial powers after 1945 in their own antiguerrilla campaigns.[10] Collective punishment, expulsion, forced resettlement, detention, torture, and mass executions created an outright "system of war crimes" in Kenya and Algeria.

Collective Punishment and Shoot-to-Kill Policy in Kenya

In April 1953, Richard A. Frost, a representative of the British Council for East Africa, submitted to his superiors a report of his experiences during a trip through Kenya's Central Province. In it, he described the common procedure carried out by security forces of indiscriminately mistreating innocent Africans for as long as was necessary to make these people fear Europeans more than the Mau Mau.[11] The consequence was, he continued, that many Africans were joining the rebels out of fear of whites. The practices described by Frost were those of the counterterror phenomenon. In the colony, the general attitude of settlers and security forces was to answer the terror of the Mau Mau with a far greater degree of counterterror.[12] In the eyes of the British colonial rulers, the aim was to reinstill the "necessary respect" and to deter people from any form of participation in the anticolonial resistance. Targeted measures of terror perpetrated against the African civilian population therefore became an established tactic of British warfare, whereby the settler D. H. Rawcliffe noted that such measures were "often reminiscent of Nazi methods."[13]

This type of warfare was particularly evident in the principle of collective responsibility, introduced by the emergency regulations in October 1952. In a special directive, Governor Baring ordered the collective punishment of all inhabitants of regions where the rebels were active.[14] Even apart from raids and attacks, lesser infractions such as holding an oath ceremony were already enough to warrant the confiscation of all livestock and crops, as well as all motor vehicles in the region in question. Further punishment included the forced closing of all shops and markets, while at the same time the population was to be driven out of their homes and prevented from returning later. Whether guilty or not, each person, without exception, was made responsible for the deeds of the Mau Mau. Besides pointing out the direct support for the rebels, Baring justified this procedure by arguing that the population in the areas affected had not acted responsibly enough to stop rebel attacks or to prevent the guilty parties from escaping.

The policy of collective punishment was rigorously implemented during the emergency and was primarily directed against the Kikuyu.[15] In September 1953 alone, sixty orders of collective punishment were issued, in which a total of 7,962 cattle and donkeys and 33,686 sheep and goats were confiscated.[16] The declared aim of the colonial government was to discipline the Kikuyu.[17] By depriving the people in villages of their livelihood and increasing economic pressure on them, the solidarity of the civilian population with the rebels was to be broken. According to the estimates of police commissioner Michael S. O'Rorke, the first successes of the strategy became evident as early as December 1952. In a secret report, he maintained that the Kikuyu population was beginning to divide into two opposing camps due to the growing pressure of the collective punishments.[18] One group sought to avoid further punitive measures and to return to a safe existence, whereas the other continued to support violent resistance. Therefore, O'Rorke recommended the massive expansion in implementing measures of collective punishment to bring about conflict between the two groups to the point of violent attacks. This evaluation of the situation was confirmed in an intelligence report by a Captain Waring in February 1953.[19] The economic pressure of recent months had led to signs of growing discontent among the Kikuyu with the Mau Mau, who were now being held responsible for the current desperate situation in the reservations. The time had come, maintained Captain Waring, for every possible facilitation and support of the Kikuyu Home Guard.

Contrary to the police and army, John Whyatt, the justice minister of the crown colony, assessed the "success" completely differently: "Punishing the innocent as well as the guilty only breeds resentments and achieves no useful result. This is particularly true where the population is subject to terrorist intimidation."[20] Whyatt categorically rejected the practice of demonstrating colonial strength regardless of the injustice it caused and openly criticized the counterterror methods. Despite these objections by a high-ranking member of the colonial government, the security forces continued to pursue their strategy. In fact, the principle of collective responsibility became a type of leitmotif for all of their actions. Whether driving African squatters off white farmlands and back to the reservations or implementing extensive detention and resettlement measures, the primary orientation was on ethnicity. The entire Kikuyu population, with the exception of the loyalist forces of the Home Guard, were considered potential supporters of the Mau Mau movement and were therefore held accountable for the actions of the rebels.

The implementation of these repressive measures also helped radicalize the attitude of many white settlers, who now felt empowered to take the law into their own hands. For example, a group of polo players formed a private cavalry unit in order to hunt "Mau Mau gangs" together on horseback in the Aberdare Mountains.[21] For a large number of Europeans, this marked the opening of "hunting season," as the historian Don Barnett notes: "Guilty or innocent it made little difference to many who, operating on the premise of collective punishment for collective guilt, believed the only good 'Kyuk' was a dead one."[22] This development was abetted especially by the creation of special "death zones." As part of the emergency regulations, Governor Baring declared certain regions from which a danger to public order loomed to be prohibited areas.[23] It was strictly forbidden to enter or linger in these prohibited areas, which were primarily the rebel regions around Mount Kenya and the Aberdare Mountains. Army and police units were permitted to shoot anyone found there on sight and without warning.[24] In the adjacent areas, the so-called "special areas," security forces could also open fire on anyone who did not halt when ordered to do so. The order was thus handed down to the British troops, whereby officers of the Thirty-ninth Infantry Brigade were explicitly instructed by headquarters not to use the wording "shoot to wound" in their orders. This method was said to be unknown in military circles, and, in the case of army intervention, soldiers always acted according to the principle of "shoot to kill."[25] Commander W. R. N. Hinde also emphasized that officers and soldiers should not feel constrained by fear of any legal consequences for their actions.[26] Practices would not be punished as long as a soldier, in his own judgment, acted within reason, in good faith, and in performance of his duties.

The shooting order thus became a type of free pass for the arbitrary killing of Africans, as was evident in the many shootings that occurred outside the prohibited areas on the slightest pretense.[27] Prompted by a series of disconcerting letters from Kenya, Labour MP Brockway contacted Colonial Secretary Lyttelton several times. He informed the secretary about various cases in which security forces showed up at the huts of Africans at night, called them to come out, and then simply shot them as they emerged.[28] "Shot while resisting arrest" and "shot while attempting to escape" became almost standard pat phrases to give arbitrary shootings an official justification.[29] In one case, even the Colonial Office found it highly unlikely that all five prisoners would have been killed and not a single one simply wounded during an alleged attempt to escape. Therefore, London expressed to Kenya's deputy governor Sir Frederick Crawford its particular concern about a certain "trigger-happy attitude."[30] However, in the opinion of many a white settler, the British troops were not hitting hard enough, because they occasionally first called out to suspects before they fired at them. One Boer from the region of Thompson Falls, who proudly reported the execution of twenty-six suspects in a single night on the farm of a friend, expressed the attitude of the settlers: "We just take out our Sten guns and, vee-vee-vee, vee-vee-vee, we let the bloody vermin have it."[31]

Ground-troop operations in the prohibited areas were supported by missions carried out by the RAF. The aim of such air raids was to force the rebels out of their retreats and into the arms of the hunting parties, to inflict the greatest possible casualties on them, and thereby break their morale.[32] In the heavily wooded, inaccessible forest regions, the British military could rarely rely on accurate target coordinates, so the RAF systematically carpet-bombed entire regions, also deploying the four-engine Lincoln bombers.[33] Such "indiscriminate attacks,"[34] as defined and banned by international law, were justified by the colonial secretary on the grounds that people were prohibited to be in these areas. Thus, the victims were, without exception, "terrorists" and legitimate military targets. The risk of collateral damage to innocents was therefore minor.[35] Still, the effectiveness of the air attacks remained controversial and, following the completion of the larger military operations, the army command decided to withdraw the bomber squadron, primarily because the cost of the mission was enormously high. In a confidential telegram sent by the U.S. embassy in London to the State Department, it was reported "that the RAF, which has found this mission useful training for bomber crews, is the only official agency not entirely happy about the withdrawal."[36] In other words, the British air force had merely viewed the decolonization war in Kenya as valuable "target practice."

At the same time, the ground-troop operations also left the impression that the declared aim was not to wound or capture but to kill the enemy.[37] Within several units, this deliberate shoot-to-kill policy led to "killing contests" in which success was measured by the number of enemy dead.[38] For example, in its November 1953 issue, the newspaper of the Devonshire Regiment reported openly on the major rivalry between the deployed companies for the greatest number of enemy dead.[39] The motivation of the soldiers was spurred on all the more by the bonus offered by the commanding officers of five pounds for each company's first "kill."[40] In the case of the D Company, a certain Sergeant Channing even presented his company commander a "human Gyppo trophy"[41] as proof that he had fulfilled his promise not to return from the jungle without a "kill." In addition to the collection of human "war trophies," it was common practice to hack off the hands of killed Mau Mau warriors.[42] Instead of transporting the entire corpse from the jungle to the next police post for identification, it sufficed the British security forces to get the chopped-off hands, from which fingerprints could be taken. In the opinion of the police officer Peter Hewitt, this method, which was secretly and discreetly continued after the high command expressly banned it, helped a great deal to facilitate the identification process and was not merely a form of "trophy collecting."[43] Yet even Hewitt had to condemn the callous behavior of some of his comrades who liked to place their "evidence of kill" on the canteen tables.[44]

Security forces kept "scoreboards" on the number of enemy killed, which were proudly presented as proof of their success to other units and the public. However, in July 1953, General Erskine prohibited the daily publication of these statistics. In doing so, the commander in chief intended to prevent competition among the units, in which each attempted to achieve the highest score as if in "a sort of football league."[45] In a circular to the troops, the high command also stated that the system of reporting Mau Mau losses was unsatisfactory.[46] The death totals clearly outnumbered the number of prisoners taken, which was argued to be unavoidable considering the special nature of the current operations but still led to very annoying political consequences. In order to throw a better light on the number of those killed and captured in the future, the authorities ordered the implementation of a new reporting system in which the number of arrested persons, British losses, and civilian victims were also to be listed, among other things.[47] By implementing this revised statistical compilation, the British high command did not end the arbitrary shoot-to-kill policy of its troops but simply tried to mask the true face of its military operations.

This same objective was fulfilled by an internal commission under General Kenneth McLean, which the War Office created in December 1953 to study the various practices of its soldiers. The commission's final report repudiated as thoroughly unfounded, except in a few isolated cases, the accusations of a bonus for killed "terrorists," the keeping and publishing of "scoreboards," the encouragement of a competitive atmosphere between units, and other inhuman methods.[48] On the issue of chopped-off hands, the investigative commission even expressed its satisfaction with the fact that such dismemberment of killed Mau Mau fighters served the exclusive purpose of identifying the dead and had only been done in cases where the entire corpse could not have been transported back to camp.[49] Even though this report exonerated his units almost completely, it is astonishing that General Erskine still felt the need to offer an official reaction. After he had ordered the distribution of ink pads to his troops for the continued purpose of taking fingerprints, albeit in another manner than had been done up to that point,[50] the commander in chief once again issued a special order explicitly forbidding all the abovementioned practices.[51] Yet, overall, Erskine was satisfied with the findings of the McLean Commission, which had confirmed that the units under his command, with only a few isolated exceptions, had "carried out their difficult and complex duties in accordance with the highest traditions of the British army."[52]

Irrespective of this evaluation of their commander in chief and his instructions, the British security forces continued their type of warfare in which soldiers distinguished themselves through their brutality. The operations against the Mau Mau marked, for example, the beginning of the military career of a young African sergeant of the KAR named Idi Amin,[53] who was even described by his superiors as being unmercifully cruel.[54] The operations in the Kenyan jungle were developing more and more into a "manhunt." American William Baldwin, in his war memoirs published under the telling title *Mau Mau Man-Hunt*, offers disturbing proof of this. Baldwin, who had joined the Kenya Police in April 1954 for reasons of financial need and a desire for adventure, describes with a certain amount of boasting several cases in which wounded and captured Africans were murdered in cold blood, often by him.[55] The bodily remains of the victims, Baldwin contends, were left to be eaten by hyenas and jackals.[56] In his account, the police officer Peter Hewitt attests the existence of "impetuous trigger activity"[57] among British security forces and reports on the constant efforts of the British commanders to improve the "contact/kill efficiency" in the jungle.[58] However, efforts were also made to take prisoners, since a living "terrorist" was an unmatched source of information.[59] According to Hewitt's account, the public display of dead or dying Mau Mau fighters was also a daily occurrence.[60] In the case of the Mau Mau general Kago, who was gravely wounded when taken prisoner, the security forces even brought him back to the reservation, where they publicly executed him by burning him alive.[61] The suffering of the severely wounded and the view of disembodied corpses were intended to have a deterrent effect on the African population and were therefore deliberately integrated into the strategy of counterterror.[62]

The French *Ratissages* in the Algerian War

There are a number of parallels between the British operations in Kenya and the French warfare in Algeria. In May 1955, Paul Cherrière, commander in chief in Algeria, delegated troops the authority to deploy heavy weaponry ruthlessly in the new rebellion zones and added: "Collective responsibility to be vigorously applied. There will be no written instructions given by the Governor."[63] However, after receiving reports on the destruction of entire Algerian villages during the course of French punitive expeditions, General Henri Lorillot rescinded the instructions of his predecessor in late 1955, because he was of the opinion that innocent victims and unnecessary destruction only played into the hands of the enemy.[64] Only villages that served to protect the rebels were allowed to be attacked as legitimate military targets. Raids against uninvolved persons and any form of repressive action were strictly forbidden.[65] In a circular to military commanders, Governor General Soustelle even called it a major mistake to place the Muslim population under general suspicion and thus to drive people into the arms of the rebels.[66] The "police operations" were to be conducted in a respectful manner without brutality and race discrimination: "In summary, it is our mission to restore peace and order, not against the Muslim population, but for them and with them."[67]

These official instructions and depictions did not have even the slightest to do with the reality of the Algerian War. The principle of collective responsibility was indeed a leitmotif for the actions of the French troops, in which they made no distinction between combatant and noncombatant.[68] Every Arab was considered a potential rebel and was treated accordingly. This attitude was not even influenced by the serious accusation[69] that collective responsibility followed the same repressive principle used by German occupying forces during World War II in destroying the French village Oradour-sur-Glane.[70] Instead, one conscript asserted that they created a new Oradour every day in Algeria.[71] The French military answered every ambush and attack against its soldiers with a retaliatory strike, which usually meant that the nearest village was punished collectively. In a private conversation with a representative of the British consulate general in Algiers, a corporal of the 1er Régiment d'Infanterie de l'Air claimed that the Arab population feared his unit deeply because they knew that anytime a shelling occurred from a village, it meant that—fifteen minutes and a warning later—the village would be razed by French troops. Although only the elderly, women, and children were living there, his unit reacted to the brutality of the rebels with their own cruelty, maintained the corporal.[72] In another unit, the commanding lieutenant followed the motto that "should one of my men be killed some day in an ambush, then I will go into the nearest village, gather up all the inhabitants and shoot every second one on the spot. . . . The reason: they did not warn the French that they were about to be ambushed."[73]

Yet even without alleged "grounds for retaliation" the military was ruthless in its treatment of the Arab civilian population. In searching for FLN depots of weapons and supplies, French troops arbitrarily destroyed entire Arab settlements and terrorized the inhabitants. In addition to plundering and serious mishandling, rape was a common occurrence.[74] Algerian women were often sexually abused collectively by French soldiers before the eyes of their relatives. Apart from the horrendous individual suffering of the victims, this also represented a heavy blow to one of the major pillars of Algerian society, namely the inviolableness of women.[75] Such actions were also meant to humiliate and abase Muslim men who were not in a position to protect their women. Although rape was strictly forbidden officially and punishable by a military court, many in command refrained from doing anything against it.

On the contrary, they encouraged their soldiers to commit such offenses but with caution: "You can rape, but do it discreetly!"[76]

More and more, the infamous *ratissages* of the French army pursued a "scorched earth" strategy.[77] While searching villages, army units often followed the logic that the discovery of weapons could be equated to support for the FLN on the part of all inhabitants. If, however, no suspicious provisions were found, the troops simply assumed that the alleged storage place was too well hidden. In both cases, the security forces drove the inhabitants out of the village and set it on fire, on the basis of discovered evidence or no more than vague suspicion.[78] The aim of such operations was to depopulate regions that were difficult to control and turn them into wastelands in which the rebels found neither shelter nor supplies. This development was accelerated all the more by the creation of *zones interdites*. Starting in spring 1956, the French military began to declare rebel regions as "prohibited zones" in which no one was permitted to remain under any circumstance.[79] Like the prohibited areas in Kenya, anyone found in the *zones interdites* could be shot on sight. Air force and artillery units were authorized to use these areas as free firing zones subject to the "systematic deployment of all firepower" and indiscriminate attack.[80]

In addition to this unrestricted firing, French forces had also been granted extremely "generous" shooting orders outside the prohibited zones. The military guidelines for treating rebels and suspects in Algeria contained a common order by the French ministries for the interior and defense, issued 1 July 1955, with the following instructions: "Every rebel who uses his weapon or has a weapon in his hands or is seen committing a crime is to be shot on the spot. . . . Every suspect who attempts to flee is to be fired upon."[81] With this order, the French government created the legal prerequisite for the summary execution of the enemy.[82] In a war scenario in which every Arab was considered a potential enemy, this meant that during their *ratissages* the French troops used their guns ruthlessly also against the Arab civilian population. In their eyes, fleeing civilians were considered collectively to be "suspicious" and therefore declared legitimate targets. A soldier named Noel Favrelière reported, for example, that his captain offered the sharpshooter of his unit five hundred francs to shoot a seven-year-old Arab girl who was running away during the search of the village.[83] Based on the casualty lists, Denise and Robert Barrat, a married French couple who were both journalists, documented in their book *Livre blanc sur la répression*, which would be presented as proof for French war crimes to the UN General Assembly, how numerous such outright executions of Arab civilians were just in the period from 1955 to 1956.[84] Summary executions became a characteristic phenomenon of the war. In March 1960, three Paris lawyers, Jacques Vergès, Maurice Courrégé, and Michel Zavrian, submitted a report to the president of the ICRC in which they listed a series of executions as proof for the grave breach of Article 3 of the Geneva Conventions.[85] The lawyers calculated that a total of several thousand people had been killed in this way. They were of the opinion that French security forces performed such outright executions in Algeria on a daily basis. What made this particularly obvious, it was argued, was the fact that the victims usually were killed during a so-called attempted escape. In the official lingo of security forces, the term *fuyards abattus* became the standard justification for an execution and gave it the touch of legality.[86]

Another well-established phrase used by French soldiers was the *corvée de bois*.[87] What was meant by this seemingly harmless term was in reality the common practice of sending prisoners out to "gather wood" and then shooting them for "trying to escape." Not only could the soldiers rid themselves of the burdensome problems of taking prisoners, but they also "solved" another problem, according to the testimony of one French soldier:

> They called for volunteers to shoot down the boys who had been tortured (so that no traces would remain and one avoided the risk of any stories). I didn't like this. . . . So I never spoke up, and finally I was the only one who had not yet killed "his" guy. They called me a little girl. One day the captain called me and said: "I can't stand little girls. . . . Better get ready because the next one is yours!" Then, a few days later, there were eight tortured prisoners who had to be shot. I was called and in front of all the comrades I was told: "Now it's your turn, little girl! Forward, march!" I went up to the guy: he looked straight at me. I still see his eyes. . . . I felt sick. . . . I fired. . . . After that, it didn't bother me much, but I tell you, that first time really messed me up.[88]

A view widely held among the troops was that half of all prisoners taken died during torture, while the rest were sent out for *corvée de bois*.[89] In light of this, it is not at all astonishing to learn of the assertion made by General Salan, the French commander in chief in Algeria, in 1958 that ALN soldiers preferred to die fighting in a hopeless situation than to be taken prisoner.[90]

Meanwhile, the ICRC was receiving a constantly growing number of unsettling reports from Algeria, so that the authorities in Geneva even spoke in June 1960 of a "systematization of the ordered execution of prisoners."[91] This was particularly obvious in a report by the ICRC delegate Laurent Vust on his experiences in the department of Titeri.[92] In it he reported on the systematic executions of prisoners and suspects, among which was the case of a French intelligence officer who had liquidated at least 250 people himself. As representative of the general attitude within the French army, Vust also described a conversation with an artillery commander, in which Vust deliberately withheld the information that he was a Red Cross representative: "He told me that it wasn't any more inhumane to execute several *fellaghas* [armed nationalist militants] than to bombard villages full of women and children with napalm . . . and, that it would be far more humane, by the way, to shoot three of them today instead of twenty-five in three months."[93]

Napalm, Gas, Atomic Waste: Special Aspects of French Warfare in Algeria

Despite all the parallels between the British operations in Kenya and France's conduct of the war in Algeria, one significant difference was the systematic deployment by the French of internationally outlawed chemical weapons. In 1925, following the precedent set by the 1899 Second Hague Declaration (Declaration on the Use of Projectiles the Object of Which Is the Diffusion of Asphyxiating or Deleterious Gases),[94] the Geneva Protocol (Protocol for the Prohibition of the Use in War of Asphyxiating, Poisonous, or Other Gases, and of Bacteriological Methods of Warfare)[95] renewed and expanded the international ban on the use of chemical weapons.[96] However, various colonial powers ignored this treaty and used poisonous gas as a welcome addition to the arsenal of weapons deployed in the colonial wars.[97] As early as 1920, the RAF dropped gas grenades on the rebelling Afghans at the northwest Indian border,[98] and between 1922 and 1927 Spain asphyxiated the Rif revolt led by Abdel Krim in its Moroccan protectorate in a cloud of mustard gas.[99] Italy also initially used this poisonous gas in the colonial "pacification" in Libya in 1928, and deployed it once again in the invasion of Abyssinia from 1935 to 1936 on a massive scale and with disastrous consequences for the Abyssinian population.[100] The international ban of certain weapons was not respected in the overseas territories, and France upheld this "colonial tradition"[101] during its military operations in Algeria. Right after the outbreak of the Algerian War, the French governor general Leonard stipulated unequivocally in a letter dated 4 November 1954 that the use of napalm was prohibited by the French government.[102] Although napalm, as an incendiary weapon, did not fall clearly under the stipulations of the Geneva Protocol, the authorities in Paris officially held the position that it was also to be considered an internationally outlawed combat agent.[103] Surprisingly, however, reports on the use of napalm by the French army began to surface the longer the war continued. The Algerian Red Crescent leveled several charges against the French in this regard and tried to provide proof by submitting the medical records of Algerian napalm victims to the ICRC, among other things.[104] To this end, the organization also presented to the local ICRC delegate Camille Vautier in Morocco four FLN fighters whose burn wounds were so serious they had to be treated in a hospital in Rabat.[105] Yet even without this evidence, the International Committee in Geneva gradually became thoroughly convinced on the basis of the findings of its own missions to Algeria that the French air force often used the feared incendiary weapons in the bombing raids.[106]

Each time, the French government reacted to these charges with emphatic denials. In a private conversation with the ICRC delegate William Michel on 24 November 1958, the representative from the French foreign ministry, Henri Langlais, refuted the leveled accusations as thoroughly unfounded. The French army, argued Langlais, had never used napalm, and orders from the French high command in Algeria strictly prohibited such weapons.[107] However, documents from the French military archives in Vincennes prove precisely the opposite. From orders outlining the mission "Débroussaillage de terrain par incendie," it becomes clear through the notation of precise target coordinates that the military did indeed set entire regions afire as part of its "scorched earth" strategy.[108] By destroying all vegetation, the French sought to strip the rebels of any type of camouflage. The term "napalm" is very rarely mentioned in the instructions; as a rule, more neutral terms were used instead, such as *incendiaires*[109] and *bidons spéciaux*. For example, an evaluation written in June 1960 on bombing raids using the content of these "special canisters" underscored the great psychological impact of the attacks on the inhabitants of the nearby villages—referred to as "onlookers"—and summarized: "excellent results with napalm."[110] In addition to using napalm systematically as incendiary bombs, the army performed a series of experiments in an attempt to improve the efficiency of the combat agent and used it, among other things, in the form of mines planted in the prohibited areas in the region bordering on Tunisia.[111]

The use of the so-called *armes chimiques* (chemical weapons) began to take on a steadily greater role in military planning in the Algerian war zone. This led to the creation in December 1956 of the task force Armes Spéciales,[112] which was expanded in November 1958 into the Groupe Armes Spéciales pour les expérimentations nucléaires.[113] Efforts were made as early as August 1956 to destroy the harvest in rebel regions by spraying crops with growth hormones[114] or by setting them on fire using phosphorus compounds.[115] The military leadership even went as far as to consider the ideas of chemically contaminating water holes and deploying mustard gas. These ideas were subsequently scrapped out of concerns both for the unforeseeable consequences for the general supply of drinking water and for the diplomatic complications that could arise over the issue of poisonous gas.[116] However, the "special weapons" were important in combating the underground hideouts of the FLN. The many cave systems in the Algerian mountains offered the resistance fighters ideal conditions for setting up operational and supply bases and thus posed a serious problem for the French army.[117] The sole mission of the Sections Grottes was to destroy all such secret camps and to make the caves unusable for rebels for a long time.[118] For this purpose, these units were equipped with a specially designed weapons arsenal.[119] With the help of incendiary weapons such as aluminum and phosphorous bombs, they tried to "smoke out" the rebels in their hideouts. The carbon monoxide created by these efforts had such a disastrous effect and was so dangerous that the French high command drastically tightened the safety measures for its own soldiers following cases of poisoning in its own ranks.[120] This procedure was not new: the French army had done the same thing back in 1845 in the Dahra grotto during the "pacification" of Algeria. Only now it conducted its operations more systematically and with modern means, which consisted primarily of several tens of thousands of gas grenades to gas entire cave systems. These were not poisonous gases but various irritant gases. However, depending on the combination and dosage, even these had a lethal effect in the closed-off, oxygen-poor caves and, as a rule, led to the suffocation of those trapped inside.[121]

Special units thus launched a systematic campaign against the suspected hideouts of the FLN.[122] Yet often these missions produced casualties among the Algerian civilian population because people used the caves as protection against the French air raids and as refuge from the feared *ratissages*. According to the accounts of both the Algerian Red Crescent and the provisional Algerian government, one particularly tragic incident occurred in March 1959 when 112 people, primarily women and children, were gassed in a cave near Douar Terchioui.[123] In a telegram protesting the attack, GPRA president Abbas called on the ICRC to intervene immediately in Paris and to insist vehemently that international humanitarian law be upheld.[124] The reaction of the French government consisted of no more than a complete rebuttal of the accusations by its foreign ministry.[125] Citing the French high command and the defense ministry, it stated that the operation had been undertaken to free forty Muslim prisoners from the hands of the rebels, during which the only ones killed were thirty-two rebels.[126]

The extensive use of gas served the Sections Grottes as a means not only to combat the resistance fighters in the underground hideouts but also to prevent them from returning to these locations. Therefore, as a prophylactic measure, the special units systematically contaminated entire cave systems with gas to make them unusable as shelters for months if not years.[127] In particularly difficult cases in which "conventional" methods proved ineffective, the military resorted to other means to "neutralize" the caves. When one cave in his mission area survived several attacks, Colonel Pinsard issued a disturbing request in a letter dated 3 January 1957: "The use of atomic waste, which is tried out in other regions of the tenth military district [Algeria], could bar, on the threat of death, every rebel access to these places of refuge. Therefore, it is my honor to request the distribution of radioactive waste to neutralize this cave."[128] Besides systematically deploying internationally outlawed chemical weapons like napalm and gas, the French army did not even recoil from deliberate radioactive contamination in its operations in Algeria.

Camps and Forced Resettlement: Instruments for Extensive Colonial Control

Camps as a Colonial Tradition and the Spatialization of the State of Emergency

The historic origins of camps created to concentrate great numbers of civilians lie in European colonial history.[129] In 1896, the Spanish captain general Valeriano Weyler y Nicolau gave orders during the Cuban war of independence to "reconcentrate" the rural population of the island into enclosed spaces in the vicinity of fortified locations and cities.[130] With this forced deportation, the Spanish commander intended to subject the population to comprehensive control, in order to cut off the rebelling guerrillas from their supply lines and circle of supporters. Weyler's order meant that somewhere between 400,000 and 600,000 people were herded into thoroughly overfilled reconcentration zones under disastrous hygienic conditions with insufficient housing and food. Next to starvation, a main cause of the estimated 60,000 to 170,000 deaths of these *concentrados* between 1896 and 1898 was the outbreak of epidemics of typhoid, dysentery, and yellow fever. This pacification policy prompted much international criticism, especially on the part of the United States, where Weyler was given the epithet of "the Butcher" and where the desperate situation of the Cuban population was effectively stylized into publicity good for giving the U.S. military intervention on the Caribbean island a humanitarian aim.[131] However, this criticism and publicity campaign did not stop Washington from imitating Weyler's methods in the ensuing Philippine–American War, where the civilian population was also relocated in concentration zones as part of the struggle against the Philippine guerrilla movement led by Emilio Aguinaldo.[132]

Yet it was Great Britain that modeled its strategy on that of Captain General Weyler and implemented the "Spanish methods," as called for by part of the British press, on a grand scale during the Second Boer War from 1899 to 1902.[133] In reaction to what was seen as the "uncivilized" guerrilla warfare of the enemy, British commander Lord Robert Kitchener ordered the deportation of 116,000 Boer civilians to fifty-eight "concentration camps" starting in 1900.[134] There the detainees, primarily women, children, and the elderly, had to live under horrible conditions in which starvation and disease claimed the lives of 20,000 to 28,000 of them. Only after a public cry of indignation about these "barbaric methods" echoed throughout Britain and the world did the situation of the Boer prisoners improve permanently and the death rate declined significantly. Yet the wave of protest changed nothing about the fate of the 115,000 Africans who were interned separately in sixty-six camps. The standards of "civilized warfare" and international norms were only applied to the interned white population, in a way that caused the African civilian population to suffer far more under the British conduct of the war.[135]

In the first case of twentieth-century genocide, namely the suppression of the Herero and Nama uprising from 1904 to 1908 by imperial troops in German Southwest Africa,[136] concentration camps also were part of the face of war. After the majority of both ethnic groups had fallen victim to a deliberate German extermination policy, the scattered survivors of the genocide were detained in a series of camps.[137] As part of this effort, German colonial powers also expanded the function of such camps for the first time in history by introducing the aspect of the work camp to the original purpose of simply concentrating rebellious groups of indigenous peoples. The prisoners became slave labor for colonial projects such as the construction of the Lüderitzbuch–Keetmanshoop railroad line or were profitably leased as laborers to private companies. The combination of forced labor, chronic undernourishment, and epidemics caused by the catastrophic living conditions in the camps led to the deaths of half of the prisoners. As the place in which 3,000 of the overall total of 7,682 victims died,[138] the camp on Shark Island in Lüderitz Bay became the most notorious concentration camp of the German colony.[139]

For all the colonial powers, the common motive for conducting war in this way lay in the nature of guerrilla warfare. In a war scenario in which it was not possible to clearly distinguish between combatant and noncombatant, the solution to the problem in the eyes of the colonial metropolis was in the establishment of camps and in large-scale relocation operations. During these operations, the security forces could subject the indigenous population to comprehensive colonial control, prevent any kind of support for the revolt, and isolate the rebels in a decisive fashion. Even after 1945, nothing changed about this basic constellation except that the military focused primarily on the struggle for control over the general population.[140] As mentioned above, British and French strategists made this the central aim of their doctrine of counterinsurgent warfare. To deprive the rebels of access to the population was like draining the water from the pond in which a fish lived.[141]

In addition to facilitating military strategy, the emergency laws laid the groundwork for this policy of absolute control over the population. The political philosopher Giorgio Agamben considers it to be a definitive development when what he calls a "state of exception" is expanded to include the entire civilian population in the context of colonial war. Quite rightly, he underscores the close nexus between states of exception and the creation of concentration camps.[142] The camp is the space that is created to make the otherwise temporary state of exception permanent—to make it the rule. In the form of a camp, the state of exception, for Agamben, receives a permanent spatial facility and becomes a location that exists permanently and completely outside any normal legal order.[143] His thesis is strikingly proven by the "detention order" in Kenya and the *assignation à résidence* in Algeria that were included in the respective emergency laws for the two colonies. In both cases, these laws gave the colonial powers the legal right to detain people in the detention camps without a court order or without leveling charges for an unlimited period. In these camps, the prisoners found themselves stripped of legal guarantees and the protection of their basic rights and at the mercy of the arbitrariness of the camp personnel.

Such detention was in clear violation of Article 9 of the UN Universal Declaration of Human Rights[144] and particularly of Article 5 of the legally binding European Convention on Human Rights.[145] The colonial powers justified their practices by claiming to be in an emergency state and therefore, according to Article 15 of the European Convention, not obligated to uphold the human rights convention.[146] Great Britain in particular set great store on this point, because it—unlike France—had already ratified the convention and was therefore obligated to uphold it as international law. In a memorandum to the cabinet members from 8 February 1954, British colonial secretary Lyttelton recommended that the practice of interning Mau Mau supporters be expanded on a massive scale and that the detained camp prisoners also be subjected to forced labor.[147] Concerns that Great Britain could thus be violating the ECHR and the convention on forced labor were brushed aside by the colonial secretary based on the stipulation about states of emergency. In response to parliamentary and international criticism, he argued, the government could justify the practice as emergency measures that would be lifted once normal order had been restored. Therefore, the declaration of a formal state of emergency served as an alibi for the British colonial administration and explains why the emergency in Kenya lasted for such a long time, until 12 January 1960. During World War II, British prime minister Winston Churchill had declared the arbitrary imprisonment of people without court order to be extremely abhorrent and the foundation for all totalitarian regimes, whether fascist or communist.[148] The international human rights regime of the postwar order attempted to do more to rectify this through protective provisions. However, these did not stop Great Britain and France from availing themselves of such practices during the decolonization wars to a degree unprecedented to that point in each of their colonial histories.

"Kenyan Gulag" and New Villages

In Kenya, Britain's first moves against the Mau Mau movement consisted of the detention of suspicious persons.[149] On 21 October 1952, as part of the operation "Jock Scott" that marked the official beginning of the emergency, security forces imprisoned 180 leading African politicians suspected of being ringleaders of the rebellion movement. Yet this move to decapitate the national movement never produced the success its planners promised; on the contrary, it led to the radicalization of the African resistance. Therefore, the colonial administration in Nairobi felt compelled to treat all Kikuyu as potential supporters of the Mau Mau. For this purpose, the Kikuyu who, as squatters, worked the farmland of white settlers were driven into hastily erected transit camps starting in December 1952, from which they were then deported to the reservations in the Central Province.[150] At the same time in early 1953, specially created screening teams operating in the transit camps and in specially built screening camps began to "question" with brutal inter-rogation methods all of the deportees about their involvement in the rebel movement. With the help of such mass interrogations, security forces hoped not only to get important information about the enemy but also to be able to classify prisoners into different groups.[151] To be color-classified "white" (in-nocent) meant that an African could be deported to the reservation, while people classified as "grey" (some Mau Mau activity) and "black" (Mau Mau "hardcore") were sent to the detention camps.[152]

This detention program was carried out on a major scale starting in April 1954 when 24,000 Kikuyu were deported from Nairobi to camps in the course of the purge "Operation Anvil."[153] Pivotal to this program were the views of Commander in Chief Erskine, who considered the increased imprisonment of suspicious Kikuyu to be a "prophylactic measure" lead-ing to a successful pacification.[154] To this end, he demanded the marked expansion of the camp system and an increase of the entire intake capacity to 100,000 persons. The Colonial Office in London had absolutely no objec-tions and gave this military plan its unqualified approval,[155] thus clearing the way for massive and arbitrary detentions in the East African crown col-ony. In December 1954 alone, 71,346 people found themselves imprisoned in camps, whereby the number of prisoners for the entire duration of the emergency reached 77,000 persons, according to official British statistics.[156] The actual number of those detained may have been far higher. Estima-tions today assume that at least every fourth male Kikuyu was imprisoned by the British for some length of time between 1952 and 1958,[157] whereas the historian Caroline Elkins says the overall number of prisoners reached somewhere between 160,000 and 320,000.[158]

By conducting this gigantic detention campaign, the British aimed, on the one hand, to pluck members of the resistance movement off the streets and, on the other, to again put the African population fully under the yoke of their control. In accordance with their classification system, the so-called "Mau Mau hardcores" were locked up in special camps because they were "in-corrigible,"[159] and at one point the colonial government even considered the idea of deporting this group of prisoners to "exile camps" outside of Kenya.[160] Those Africans classified as "tainted" were sent to labor camps that, accord-ing to the authorities in Nairobi, not only served as a prison but were also meant primarily to facilitate the reformation and reintegration of prisoners considered necessary in the colonial society.[161] Under the aegis of Thomas G. Askwith, the head of the Community Development Department, a comprehensive "rehabilitation plan" was drawn up, inspired greatly by the Malayan experiences.

With the help of a series of "education programs" and intensive propaganda efforts, internees were to be freed from the throes of "barbaric" Mau Mau ideology and brought back into the fold of civilization. One critical prerequisite for a successful "rehabilitation" was to break the will of the prisoners and to extract from them a full confession of their "crimes."[162] The key aspect of the "reeducation measures" was "rehabilitation" through work. For the internees, this meant that they were forced to work on colonial development projects such as landscape terracing, reforestation, and road building. This process, called the "pipeline,"[163] led until 1957 to the release of the majority of the camp internees.[164] Only 4,668 "hardcore prisoners" who represented a threat to domestic order and safety remained imprisoned.

The vast majority of the white population thoroughly rejected the idea of "rehabilitation" and "reintegration." In their opinion, Africans were not to be integrated again but were to receive a painful lesson for having challenged white rule. The camp was to be a place of punishment, which meant, as the settler Sir Richard Woodley saw it, "slavery from dawn to dusk, on a ration sufficient to keep him alive and working but no more." Furthermore, prison officials in charge were to have the power "to cut rations and inflict corporal punishment of a severe nature for misdemeanour."[165] In the widely held view shared by Ione Leigh, the detention camps had not been a place of punishment for Africans up to that point because there they were provided sanitary facilities, kitchens, hospitals, and even their own sports fields to keep themselves physically fit.[166] Good and regular meals even meant that the prisoners were gaining weight, which is why Africans had given the prison the nickname "Hoteli King Georgi."[167] Leigh's cynical and racist description had nothing in the least to do with the reality of camp life. Rather, the public was faced with headlines like "Kenya Prison Like Hell" and "From the Gates of Hell Jail."[168] Daily life in Kenyan camps corresponded exactly with the way Woodley argued it should be and made Askwith's "rehabilitation concept" a complete farce. In their memoirs, former internees recorded the appalling conditions under which people in the camps were forced to live and how this traumatic experience remained seared into their consciousness.[169] In his extensive analysis of several Mau Mau memoirs, the historian Marshall Clough points out the parallels between the more than fifty British camps and those of the Stalin era in the Soviet Union; in this connection he uses the term "Kenyan Gulag."[170]

At first, the difficult prison conditions were caused by the thoroughly insufficient infrastructure of the camps, which had been set up as makeshift facilities often in particularly unfavorable desert climates and malaria-invested regions. The otherwise poor hygienic conditions were aggravated all the more by the vast overcrowding of the camps,[171] especially during and after "Operation Anvil," when thousands of new arrivals pushed facilities far beyond their occupancy capacity. At Manyani Camp, for example, 16,000 people were kept in a place designed to hold 6,000 prisoners, which is why it was also called the largest detention camp outside of the Iron Curtain.[172] The combination of a lack of hygiene, overcrowding, and thoroughly insufficient medical care led inevitably to the outbreak of infectious diseases like typhus, dysentery, and tuberculosis. Reports urgently warning that such camp conditions would lead to epidemics, such as those written by H. G. Waters, the deputy director of the Kenyan Medical Service, were simply ignored.[173] The consequence of this negligent behavior was the outbreak of a typhus epidemic in September 1954 at Manyani Camp, in which one prisoner died each day in October and several hundred had succumbed before it was over.[174] Other camps were also hit, such as Langata and Mackinnon Road, making contagious disease a part of the daily life in the Kenyan detention camps. As the number of cases rose dramatically, the colonial administration decided to send the infected prisoners back to the reservations and thus ease the situation in the camps. However, the decision was made without taking into consideration the consequences of this action for the African civilian population.[175]

Another factor contributing significantly to the very poor state of health in the camps was mal- and undernutrition.[176] Both the quantity and quality of food rations were inadequate to feed the internees and caused a high death rate, particularly among the children in the women's camp Kamiti.[177] Starvation was an everyday phenomenon in Kenyan camps. One reason was that the denial of food proved to be one of the most common means used by camp guards to punish prisoners and break their wills.[178] At the smallest sign of resistance or the most insignificant violation of the strict camp rules, camp personnel punished prisoners by reducing or even completely denying them their food rations. Hunger became an effective weapon against prisoners, who often had to survive for days without food and water and were left to feed themselves from rainwater alone.[179] In Showground Camp in Nyeri

District, the camp commander used this punishment so intensively that the prisoners gave him the epithet "Famine."[180]

"Starvation punishment" was used particularly often when the internee refused to work. Work duty was considered the central aspect of the "rehabilitation measures," yet in reality it was no more that slave labor. Even the colonial ministry in London was aware of this fact and therefore feared criticism from the International Labor Organization (ILO)[181] and the United Nations Ad Hoc Committee on Forced Labor.[182] Not only was the denial of food used to force prisoners to work, often they were coerced by brute force, whereby any "misconduct" was also punished by blows from rifle butts and whips: "Work in the quarry was a terrible punishment. When one got too tired to work, one was beaten up until one became unconscious. One was then dumped into cold water to regain consciousness."[183] Forced labor in the camps and the mistreatment associated with it meant that many prisoners died from exposure and exhaustion.[184] The commanders of Embakasi Camp, a place widely known as "Satan's Paradise," were notorious for working their prisoners to death.[185]

In addition to disease, hunger, and forced labor, the camp was for prisoners first and foremost a place of systematic violence. The use of corporal punishment by white colonialists against the African population had been one the most common, legally recognized forms of punishment in Kenya even before the emergency. Therefore, Governor Baring recommended its use in the camps for the purpose of ensuring discipline and order.[186] Even the most minor infraction of camp rules and any type of disobedience was penalized by corporal punishment.[187] For example, Kariuki, a spokesman for his fellow prisoners, was often the victim of floggings during his imprisonment because he had written letters of protest that had been smuggled out of the camp,[188] while Gakaara wa Wanjau was beaten for simply speaking without permission.[189]

This state-legitimized violence was applied routinely and systematically by the camp guards. In May 1956, Eileen Fletcher, who had worked as a "rehabilitation officer" in Kenya, was the first to publicize the terrible conditions in her eyewitness account *Truth About Kenya*.[190] Further criticism of the brutality in the Kenyan camps then followed, particularly in reports by former prison officers. In his letter of protest to Colonial Secretary Lennox-Boyd in February 1959, Major Philip Meldon listed the types of prisoner abuse as being total physical exhaustion from overwork, assault, floggings, beatings, and torture.[191] In a series of other letters and publications, Meldon emphasized his criticism of camp conditions, which he felt represented a public scandal and a complete disregard of all of the principles incorporated into the Univeral Declaration of Human Rights.[192] The affidavit of Victor Charles Shuter concerning his experiences in the camps Manyani, Mariira, Kamaguta, and Fort Hall gave the impression that abuse in the camps was ubiquitous and an actual part of a camp policy.[193] In his testimony, Shuter reported that prison guards beat prisoners indiscriminately with self-made clubs and very often with the *kiboko*, a whip made out of rhinoceros hide, whereby the precaution was made to remove severely abused prisoners from the camp shortly before the visit of an ICRC delegation.[194] Statements like those of Captain Ernest Law[195] and white criminal convicts[196] corroborated testimony on the "regime of the whip" in the Kenyan prisons and camps.

The consequence of this abuse was that many prisoners were permanently crippled or even died from the beatings.[197] Despite the pervasive violence, there was nothing camp inmates feared more than the arrival of a screening team. These "interrogation experts" tried to force information and confessions out of prisoners using methods of torture and thereby spread fear and terror.[198] Brutality in the camps was taken to another level when the colonial government decided that the dilution technique could be used starting in 1957. With the help of this combination of physical and psychological terror, the resistance of the remaining "hardcore" prisoners was to be broken, and they were to be forced to renounce the Mau Mau ideology as the prerequisite for their "rehabilitation" and subsequent release.[199] The use of such state-encouraged and legitimized excesses of violence eventually led to an incident on 3 March 1959 in which eleven prisoners were beaten to death by guards at Hola Camp.[200] At first, British authorities tried to cover up the incident by announcing that the eleven victims had died from contaminated drinking water; but this effort failed.[201] Instead, the Fairn Committee, set up by the government to submit recommendations on the future of detention camps, confirmed the systematic abuse during "shock treatment" and advocated the immediate cessation of such methods.[202] In the end, the deaths of the eleven Hola prisoners created more public and political pressure than had the seven years of suffering of hundreds of thousands of Kenyan internees, and the colonial government had the last four detention camps closed.

During the emergency in Kenya, camps were not the only places to find comprehensive control and systematic violence. After more than 100,000 African squatters had been forcefully returned to the reservations in several deportation waves, the British War Council decided in June 1954 to initiate a comprehensive resettlement campaign. Under the catchword "villagization," a total of 1,077,500 Kikuyu were forced out of their settlements, scattered widely across reservation territory, and concentrated into 854 so-called "new villages" between June 1954 and October 1955.[203] Modeled after the operation conducted by General Templer in Malaya, this measure was intended to sever contact completely between the general population and the rebels. In his secret planning of the operation in 1955, Commander in Chief Erskine thus placed the highest priority on intensified villagization in order to control the indigenous population as comprehensively as possible.[204] The historian Maurice Sorrenson believes that this was the decisive blow dealt by the British military against the Mau Mau movement, which now had to endure complete isolation in the forest, cut off from its supply base.[205] Another "advantage" of concentrating the civilian population into designated areas was that more precise demarcations could be drawn up for the "prohibited zones" in which it was permitted to shoot on sight any person found there.

The colonial government in Nairobi presented these measures in a very positive light as part of their "rehabilitation and development program."[206] By establishing these new villages, not only could the infrastructure be modernized in the underdeveloped reservations and the standard of living of the Kikuyu noticeably improved, but the civilian population could also be protected from the attacks by the Mau Mau. Dr. Mary Shannon, a missionary for the Church of Scotland, spoke of a new social revolution emerging in Kikuyuland in connection with the villagization program.[207] Based on her own experience, she was confident that the "new way of life" would give people justified hope for a better future in the areas of education, health, and general welfare. However, this description had very little in common with the reality of the new villages and belied the true nature of the measure. Villagization was actually another form of detention in which the entire Kikuyu ethnic group was taken hostage in a way. The obvious aim of the resettlement campaign was the absolute control, discipline, and punishment of the African population. This had already been made perfectly clear by the forced relocation. Ruth Ndegwa, a woman from the Nyeri district, described how people were driven from their homes without warning by the British security forces: "The police just came one day, and drove everybody out of their homes, while the Home Guards burned the houses right behind us. Our household goods were burned down, including the foodstuffs like maize, potatoes, and beans, which were in our stores. Everything, even our clothes were burned down. One only saved what one was wearing at the time!"[208] Nothing was to be left behind that could have been used in any way by the Mau Mau fighters. Like thousands of other Kikuyu women, Ruth Ndegwa lost her children, whom she would never see again, in the chaos of the displacement and was finally deported to a "new village."

The outward appearance of the new villages revealed their function clearly.[209] Built with watchtowers and surrounded by high palisades and a moat filled with sharpened rods of bamboo, these "protected" villages were set up in the immediate vicinity of fortified Home Guard posts and designed to keep the population in and the Mau Mau out.[210] This form of concentrating the general population enabled British security forces to closely monitor every movement of the Kikuyu and, by declaring curfews, bring all life outdoors to a halt.[211] All contact between village inhabitants and the rebels for the purpose of providing supplies was to be made impossible. At the same time, all foodstuffs were subject to strict control in which unauthorized transports of food were forbidden and the sale of goods on the market was heavily regulated.[212] Facilities built specifically as fortified and protected enclosures for cattle and goat herds completed this surveillance system.

For the resettled population, the new villages meant that people were subject not only to extensive control but also to systematic violence. Here they were at the mercy of the arbitrary rule of the Home Guard, which created a regime of terror and whose fortified posts became "epicenters of torture."[213] The numerous incidents of excess violence aimed to punish villagers for being potential supporters of the Mau Mau and to deter them from any further support. Individuals suspected of helping the rebels were often publicly tortured and executed, and their corpses were placed on display in the village square as a warning. The mass rape of women in the villages by the security forces was a widespread phenomenon of this reign of terror.[214]

After the relocated people were forced to build their own prison-villages, forced labor also subsequently remained a permanent feature of the new daily routine and part of British strategy.[215] Villagers were deployed primarily to build a fifty-mile-long trench along the forest region of Mount Kenya and the Aberdare Mountains meant to isolate the Mau Mau fighters.[216] Since most of the men were already interned in camps, the women carried the brunt of the work. From morning to evening they were forced like slaves to work to the point of exhaustion under the careful watch of the Home Guard, leaving them with no time to care for their own fields and families.[217] Consequently, the supply situation worsened dramatically. Eileen Fletcher reported in her eyewitness account that in 1955 starvation was widespread and that an espe-cially enormous number of children were the victims.[218]

For the villagers, the acute lack of food became the greatest problem, as a woman named Wandia wa Muriithi explained: "Hunger was the worst prob-lem; that was killing most of the people. They were starving us on purpose, hoping we would give in."[219] As in the detention camps, the colonial rulers used hunger in the prison-villages as a way to discipline and pressure the people.[220] Food rations were dependent on their willingness to cooperate and their loyalty to the British colonial power and could be reduced or ceased altogether at any time and for no reason at all. The permanent undernour-ishment and the epidemics of disease linked to this caused the death rate to soar, particularly among children and the elderly.[221] Those who survived re-member the Kenyan Central Province as becoming one huge unmarked mass grave.[222] The brutality of the Home Guard, forced labor, and the starvation of several thousands of people illustrate how little villagization had to do with a "rehabilitation and development program." Instead, it was an instrument of colonial control and punishment.

Centres d'Hébergement, Camps de Regroupement, and Nouveaux Villages

With the outbreak of the war in Algeria, French security forces also began to detain, without court orders, people considered suspicious and danger-ous. The authorities were acting first and foremost on earlier experiences with political unrest and concentrated their efforts on those individuals who had already drawn attention to themselves for their anticolonial or nationalist agi-tation. In addition to former members of the militant OS and supporters of Messali Hadj, this affected particularly the small Muslim middle class, the majority of whom supported the moderate nationalism of Ferhat Abbas. The arrest of this particular political group robbed Algerian nationalism of its countervailing influences and thus definitely pushed a peaceful solution to the conflict into the distant future.[223] The legal basis for the internment was provided by Article 6 of the emergency law of 3 April 1955, the *assignation à résidence*, although the creation of detention camps was expressly forbid-den in it.[224] Yet this ban proved to be a complete farce in light of the Algerian reality. As becomes clear from an ICRC internal report and an article in the French newspaper *France Observateur*, several hundreds of individuals were imprisoned in four so-called *centres d'hébergement* already in May 1955.[225] These detention camps, baptized with the euphemism "accommodation centers" to conceal their true nature, became the hubs for a dense network of camps that soon began to expand across the three Algerian departments.[226]

At first, civilian authorities only made moderate use of the internment practice. In the period between 17 April 1956 and 7 January 1957, there were only about 1,500 known cases of interned individuals.[227] This changed radically after the military took power. General Massu captured control over Algiers with the Tenth Paratrooper Division on 7 January 1957, and 950 suspects were arrested the very next day. The general considered the solution of the military problem to be the systematic internment of thousands of supporters and members of the rebel organization.[228] For this purpose, Governor General Robert Lacoste delegated his internment power to the prefects and particularly to the military, which began to set up special *centres de triage et de transit* (CTTs), or "screening centers," in the various military sectors and subsectors.[229] In these centers, army specialists interrogated the arrested persons and decided on their future fates. Depending on the findings of the "questioning," the internees were either released, should their "innocence" have been proven, or transferred to the *centres d'hébergement* for reasons of political security, as was the case for most individuals. The French army used this procedure to such excess that the authorities had great difficulties during the Battle of Algiers guarding and housing all the new arrivals in the camps.[230] Just in the months from January to September 1957, the military interned 24,000 people, a number representing 15 percent of the city's adult Muslim population.[231]

In Algeria, the camp first functioned as a place to isolate and directly control those people who represented "subversive elements" in the eyes of the colonial rulers. By way of internment, representatives and supporters of the anticolonial resistance were to be prevented from continuing their *guerre révolutionnaire* and spreading their revolutionary ideology. At the same time, French authorities, like their British counterparts in Kenya, intended to use the camp as a place of "reeducation." As early as August 1956, Governor General Lacoste thus sent a circular to all prefects in which he emphasized the importance of *rééducation* and imposed "reeducation measures."[232] Since the camp prisoners would one day be set free again, the enemy propaganda had to be effectively neutralized. Therefore, argued Lacoste, physical force would be completely counterproductive and could lead to serious political complications. With the help of multistep "reeducation programs" and increased propaganda efforts, the time in internment was to be used instead to transform the prisoners into committed supporters of an *Algérie nouvelle française*.[233] As the champion of the republican ideals of *liberté*, *égalité*, and *fraternité*, France was presented as a strong and just motherland, which would fight against a criminal rebellion and for an Algeria of development, emancipation, and reform.

The realities of camp life did nothing, however, to convince the internees of the merits of a "new Algeria" under French rule. For the thousands of people incarcerated behind the barbed wire, the French national motto of freedom, equality, and fraternity was but empty words. The detention camps lacked adequate sanitation and housing facilities, so prisoners were forced to sleep in tents or in hastily erected wooden barracks. Even the responsible governmental agency, the Service Central des Centres d'Hébergement, had to admit in a report in August 1956 that the living conditions in the camps were extremely primitive.[234] The overall conditions were exasperated by the hostile desert climate, in which it was very difficult to ensure a sufficient supply of water. Not only the acute lack of water, but also the lack of sanitation facilities led to catastrophic hygienic conditions. Fleas, lice, rats, scorpions, and snakes were a constant plague and threat for the internees. Combined with a thoroughly insufficient diet—which often consisted only of a bowl of soup, some bread, and date porridge[235]—these conditions led to the outbreak of epidemics. In a letter written in 1956 to the governor general in Algiers, the commander of Djorf Camp reported the following: "Dysentery prevails in this camp permanently, and a great number of people suffer from chronic tuberculosis and various other infectious diseases."[236] Five years later, the regional association of physicians from the Algerian city of Bône protested against these terrible conditions in a letter addressed to the ICRC president. The doctors emphasized the direct link between diseases like typhus and dysentery and poor hygiene.[237] Furthermore, a French governmental commission was able to see for itself in October 1961 just how deficient conditions were in Djorf Camp and, based on its devastating findings, recommended the closure of the camp.[238]

Yet Djorf was not a unique case. On the contrary, it was quintessential for the generally difficult conditions under which the prisoners were forced to live. In its mission reports, the ICRC repeatedly listed serious deficiencies in the various camps and permanently advised the French government to correct these.[239] As has been shown earlier, the criticism from Geneva led in several cases to the improvement of the physical infrastructure and the hygienic standards, but had almost no influence on the treatment of the internees. The camp remained an isolated place and a legal black hole in which the internees could not rely on any constitutional guarantees and protection of their rights. Numerous attempts to draw the attention of the outside world to their desperate situation, such as the petition filed on 2 April 1957 by prisoners in Arcole Camp to the Algerian governor general and the French prime minister,[240] were just as unsuccessful as were the efforts of lawyers attempting to influence the fate of their interned clients.[241] In this legal vacuum, the internees were defenseless against their guards, who exercised their power in the camps with draconic measures. The prisoner Nadji Abbas Turqui described the abuse in Paul-Cazelles Camp, where beatings and whipping were an everyday occurrence, as were solitary confinement and the practice of *mise au tombeau*, in which prisoners were buried up to their chins in sand and left for a period of up to forty-eight hours.[242]

The Algerian camps were notorious not only for brutal tyranny over the internees but especially also for systematic torture. This was less true for the *centres d'hébergement* than for the *centres de triage et de transit*, the army's screening camps where "questioning" was conducted by interrogation specialists. Camps like Souk el Had and Ferme Améziane developed into outright torture chambers.[243] In addition to these places, there were also *camps noirs*, the army's secret torture sites, the existence of which was not officially acknowledged.[244] In its third mission report of November 1956, the ICRC noted a growing number of cases where torture marks were evident on prisoners, a number that increased constantly and reached a dramatic high point during the Battle of Algiers.[245] These findings were substantiated by numerous petitions to the Committee in Geneva. For example, in their letter to the ICRC president on 28 October 1959, the lawyers Maurice Courrégé, Jacques Vergès, and Michel Zavrian demanded that an international inquiry commission be sent to a number of torture sites and backed their accusations with a detailed report on the torture of prisoners in the Améziane camp.[246] In the years that followed, lawyers repeatedly drew the attention of the ICRC to the various torture chambers strewn across Algeria, in which, according to their knowledge, people were routinely and systematically tortured.[247]

For his part, General André Boyer-Vidal, the French general inspector for the detention centers, did not find any disconcerting abnormalities during this inspection trip to various CTTs. The methods used by interrogation specialists were said to be completely "normal" and indicated no irregularities. Even in his conversations with a number of internees, he had found no indication of physical abuse during interrogation.[248] However, the general's depiction of violence-free questioning in the camps was refuted by the secret report of Paul-Albert Fevrier, submitted to the ICRC in April 1960. The former commander of the screening camp Colbert provided extensive documentation about the brutal methods of the intelligence officers and the murder of prisoners based on notes he had taken over a period of months.[249] Fevrier came to the conclusion that torture and serious abuse were daily occurrences in the camps and were viewed as completely "normal." Nearly every person who was sent to a CTT had been forced to learn that there existed "no legal guarantees anymore. . . . Every time an internee arrived at the camps, he became a toy in the hands of those who held him prisoner."[250]

Another type of camp found in the Algerian theater of war was the *camp de regroupement*. Such camps sprang up as a result of the army's relocation policy. Like the British in Malaya and Kenya, the French military leadership intended to cut off the FLN completely from its supply of information, provisions, and recruits by subjecting the rural population to extensive control through forced mass resettlement.[251] Instead of sending troops to each of the widely scattered settlements across the country, the villagers were to be concentrated in certain areas as benefited military strategy.[252] These measures also enabled the army to depopulate entire regions and declare them *zones interdites*. In these prohibited zones, everything that could be of any possible use to the FLN was destroyed, as stipulated by the "scorched earth" principle, and every individual was treated as a rebel. This was carried out particularly in the regions bordering on Morocco and Tunisia, parts of the Sahara, and the inaccessible mountain regions of Kabylei, Aurès, and Atlas Blidéen that were known to be strongholds of resistance.[253] According to the statistics cited by the French sociologist Michel Cornaton, there were 3,740 resettlement camps in all, and at least 2.3 million people were resettled over the course of the war, a figure representing 26.1 percent of the entire Muslim population in Algeria.[254]

Immediately after the war began in November 1954, a "wild resettlement" took place without direct instructions from the responsible authorities in Algiers. This occurred solely on the assessment of individual commanders who declared certain regions as cleared for military operations and had the population driven away and suspected rebel-friendly villages destroyed during the course of their *ratissages*. In 1955, General Gaston Parlange founded the first relocation camp for the inhabitants of mountain villages in his command region of Aurès-Nementchas.[255] Starting in 1957 when the fighting was extended to all of Algeria and the doctrine of antisubversive war became the basis of French military operations, resettlement measures developed into an important cornerstone of that strategy.[256] Especially as the operations of the Challe Plan got underway, the "prohibited zones" were expanded and relocation measures enhanced.[257] The number of people forcefully relocated took on dramatic proportions, which evoked strong criticism by the French media in light of the poor supply situation of the *regroupés*.[258] This wave of protest followed an official government report on the situation in the resettlement camps, which General Inspector Michel Rocard submitted to Governor General Paul Delouvrier on 17 February 1959.[259] Even the French governor general in Algiers had to acknowledge that the army measures threatened to get completely out of hand and to lead to a serious destabilization of the situation in his departments. Therefore, on 31 March 1959, Delouvrier decided to take the matter of resettlement into his own hands and to subordinate it to his direct control.[260] Further, he appointed a commission of experts who were to present a comprehensive "development program" for the relocated population upon its evaluation of the situation.[261]

The result was the concept of *mille villages* ("thousand villages") in which the temporary relocation camps were to be transformed into "centers of human progress and upward social mobility."[262] With the introduction of this catchphrase, the phase of official resettlement policy began under the direction of civilian authorities in Algiers. In addition to de Gaulle's "modernizing plan" for Algeria, announced in a speech at Constantine, Algeria, in 1958, the construction of new model settlements, featuring schools, hospitals, and a modern infrastructure, was to advance measurably the social and economic development of rural Algeria.[263] In the instructions issued on 25 May 1960, Governor General Delouvrier therefore ordered that relocation measures be implemented according to these new guidelines, that civilian and military offices work in close cooperation, and that the resettlement camps be referred to as *nouveaux villages* from that point on.[264] In order to better coordinate these "modernizing efforts," battalion commander Florentin from the newly established Inspection Générale des Regroupements even recommended in a confidential report the founding of an entity modeled after the Organisation Todt in Nazi Germany.[265] Apart from the somewhat different terminology that was now highly reminiscent of the Kenyan "new villages," Delouvrier's instructions meant, above all, that the army was no longer able to act completely on its own and according to its assessment of security needs with regard to resettlement operations; instead, it also had to take into consideration the new political dimension and actively support it.[266]

What had been originally an operation designed to pacify and heavily control the population was developing more and more into a propaganda project of the civilian colonial authorities. In one report, General Parlange, who had become general inspector of the Inspection Générale des Regroupements, did point out the military origins of the measures but emphasized particularly the crucial importance of the "new villages" in the process of "modernizing" rural Algeria. In his words, the relocation was the beginning of the "transformation into modern people" for the rural Algerian population.[267] Contrary to Great Britain's villagization in Kenya, the French policy of *regroupement* was subject to far greater public awareness and criticism, which prompted General Parlange to order a comprehensive "Campaigne d'information sur les regroupements et nouveaux villages" in July 1960.[268] By way of strategically placed articles in the media, information brochures, and feature spots in cinemas, television, and radio, this public relations campaign aimed to convince not only the Muslim population but especially the United Nations and the rest of the world of the positive aspects of the French policy before the next UN General Assembly convened.

Another part of this propaganda campaign, for example, was to have the association of French expatriates living in Portugal, a fellow colonial power, assume the sponsorship for the new Algerian village Qued el Haad, at the invitation of the French foreign minister, and organize a donation campaign as a sign of their solidarity with the national cause.[269] Publications like *Algérie: Naissance de mille villages*[270] tried, with cleverly made photo documentation, to effectively publicize the immense progress made in the "new villages." Photos of poverty-stricken Algerian settlements were contrasted with those of the *nouveaux villages*, featuring schools, sports facilities, and apartment buildings with a water supply, as well as photographs of children who were happily splashing about in the village's own swimming pool. The concluding summation of the achievements proudly claimed that 1,024 "new villages" had been built by December 1960 and now housed a million people in all.[271] In his book *Nouveaux villages algérois*,[272] published in 1961, even the author Xavier de Planhol praised the achievements of the French development, which he claimed had enormously raised the overall quality of life for the Algerian rural population and represented a motor for the economic and social development of Algeria. Therefore, Planhol concluded unequivocally that the overwhelming majority of the Muslim population wished to live in the "new villages" with modern infrastructure and to enjoy the benefits of this rapid progress.[273]

This intensively conducted propaganda campaign was but an indication that the French were trying everything to deflect attention from the actual realities of the *regroupement*, which had little resemblance to the idyllic world depicted in the "new villages." In fact, the concept of the *mille villages* remained no more than a utopia.[274] The manner in which the army conducted its operations makes it impossible to speak of a voluntary and peaceful resettlement of the population for the people's own benefit. Instead, during the "purges," the French military drove village inhabitants forcefully from their settlements, which were subsequently leveled. People who refused to leave the area were executed or died in French bombings.[275] Once the inhabitants had lost everything they owned through these measures, they were then "evacuated" and concentrated in temporary camps. Usually, these *centres provisoires* did not have sufficient housing, so the people either lived outdoors or were packed tightly together in makeshift housing.[276] For example, in the camp Ighzer Amokrane six hundred women and children had to share a floor of a single granary under insufferable conditions.[277]

In his sensational report, Michel Rocard called the situation of the *regroupés* tragic. The hygienic conditions in the camps were generally deplorable and child mortality was so high that, statistically speaking, a child died every second day.[278] As a consequence of these pacification measures, nearly a million men, women, and children were threatened with starvation.[279] Rocard's assessment of the situation was confirmed by Jean Rodhain, the secretary-general of the French Catholic relief organization, who also underscored in his report to Governor General Delouvrier the extremely threatening food situation facing the relocated population.[280] In several camps, the food supply worsened so dramatically that people began to eat grass, and their physical well-being deteriorated to the point that even medication no longer had any effect.[281] In addition to starvation, the outbreak of tuberculosis and malaria epidemics also decimated the number of refugees. In the camp Merdji, for example, 30 percent of the inhabitants were infected with tuberculosis, and 250 people died within a month.[282]

With the construction of the "new villages," at least the food and housing situation improved for the people sent there. However, in light of the gigantic number of refugees (more than two million), the building of 1,024 model settlements was clearly not enough to house them all. Moreover, the concept of *mille villages* completely neglected to consider the serious long-term consequences of relocation policy, namely the destruction of Algerian society.[283] In the wake of the relocation, Algerian farmers had lost their fields and livestock, their sole source of food and income. As a result, they either became cheap labor on the landed estates of the *colons* or were condemned to a life of unemployment.[284] In several cases, the commanders of the resettlement camps permitted the fellahin to return to their fields, yet at the risk of being shot as rebels by airplanes or hunting commandos while doing fieldwork.[285] The loss of the *matmora*, the traditional grain reserve, also undermined the social prestige of the head of the family as the chief breadwinner and led to a change in the Algerian social structure.[286] In their 1960 sociological study, Pierre Bourdieu and Abdelmalek Sayad labeled the entire process as *déracinement*, as the complete uprooting of the indigenous population. The relocation policy was an attempt to homogenize the Algerian society according to colonial ideas without any consideration for its social, economic, and cultural peculiarities.[287]

Most important, the relocation measures meant the loss of personal freedom for the indigenous population.[288] Fenced in resettlement camps surrounded with barbed wire, they found themselves totally dependent on the French army, which exerted massive pressure by stopping the delivery of food supplies and thereby coerced loyalty to France.[289] Camps were the ideal place to limit freedom of movement and prohibit any contact with the rebels. Thus, the true nature of *regroupement* had very little to do with a "modernizing campaign"; instead it more closely resembled a strategic weapon in counterinsurgent warfare.[290] Established exclusively on military criteria, the resettlement camps were designed to subject the indigenous population to such comprehensive control that it amounted to taking the Algerian people hostage.[291] In order to escape the dreaded fate of relocation and "imprisonment," many Algerians elected to cross the borders to Morocco or Tunisia. These streams of refugees exported the humanitarian catastrophe of the Algerian population to the two neighboring countries, where international relief organizations like the ICRC and the UN refugee agency (UNHCR) attempted to ease the suffering of the displaced masses with extensive deliveries of aid.[292]

Systematic Torture and the "Battle for Information" in Antisubversive Warfare

International Bans and New Dimensions of Torture

In 1874, Victor Hugo expressed his conviction that torture had ceased to exist.[293] The reason for this bold statement was the fact that, in the course of the Enlightenment, the instrument of forceful "questioning" had been legally abolished in one European country after another at the end of the eighteenth century and the beginning of the nineteenth.[294] Banned in England since 1689, torture was prohibited in France by two decrees issued by Louis XVI in 1780 and 1788,[295] and Article 9 of the Declaration of the Rights of Man and of the Citizen of 1789 explicitly included protection from torture.[296] To the degree that Hugo's claim appeared correct when talking about Europe, it was all the more incorrect for the European colonies, where torture had never ceased to exist. On the contrary, it was one of the instruments used in the colonial empires to secure power.[297] The prohibition of torture proclaimed in the European metropoles was meaningless under the special conditions of the colonial situation in which the indigenous populations were guaranteed absolutely no individual liberty or legal protection out of racist motives. A British report from 1855, for example, documents the brutal interrogation methods used to break prisoners' wills at Indian police stations.[298] Eighty years later, the French journalist Andrée Viollis produced a disturbing document about torture in French Indochina in her book *Indochine SOS*.[299] Hence, in the European colonies, physically abusive "questioning" had a long, gruesome tradition and was an integral part of the colonial apparatus of repression.

Particularly in the years between 1917 and 1945, Europe experienced a revival of torture.[300] One crucial reason for this renaissance of torture was thought by experts to be the rise of totalitarian regimes, as is argued by the French legal scholar Alec Mellor in his highly respected book *La torture: Son histoire, son abolition, sa réapparition au XXe siècle*.[301] The systematic application of brutal interrogation methods did indeed surface first with the Soviet secret police Cheka, then reappeared in fascist Italy and Spain as well as in Nazi Germany.[302] As a consequence of this development, the international community of nations tried at the end of World War II to establish an absolute ban of torture in the new human rights documents. The Universal Declaration of Human Rights of 1948 stipulates in Article 5: "No one shall be subjected to torture or to cruel, inhuman or degrading treatment or punishment."[303] This same absolute and irrepealable prohibition of torture was included almost verbatim in Article 3 of the legally binding European Convention on Human Rights.[304] For its part, the ICRC worked to make this same stipulation applicable in wartime and in armed conflicts as part of the 1949 Geneva Conventions.[305] In addition to the general ban stipulated in Article 3, a separate article in each of the four conventions also explicitly prohibits the use of torture.[306] The treaty on the handling of war prisoners dictates that they may not be subjected to either physical or psychological torture in order to extract information from them.[307]

Despite these protective provisions of the international human rights regime, torture remained a permanent problem and again entered the spotlight of public awareness in the mid-1950s. This time, however, the source was not a totalitarian regime but the behavior of Western democracies in their colonies. From the British colonies Cyprus and Kenya and particularly from the Algerian warfront, a growing number of reports on torture came to light. They made it clear that torture was not strictly a problem of totalitarian systems like Nazi Germany and the Soviet Union under Stalin.[308] The democratic West was also infected by this twentieth-century pest, as Jean-Paul Sartre wrote: "Today it is Cyprus and it is Algeria; all in all, Hitler was just a forerunner. Disavowed—at times very feebly—but systematically applied behind the façade of democratic legality, torture may be defined as a semi-clandestine institution."[309] This assessment was corroborated in an ICRC memorandum that verified the dramatic spread of torture.[310] Authorities in Geneva were particularly concerned about the tendency to present torture in connection with the "war on terrorism" as allegedly being in the interest of society and in accordance with existing laws. Cloaked in special laws on combating terrorism, methods of torture now returned that had been universally outlawed by civilized humankind. The ICRC condemned the strategy to fight terrorism with its own weapons as a "devastating abdication of humanity" and thereby blatantly criticized the new military doctrine. Contrary to earlier reports on torture in the overseas territories, reports now indicated a thoroughly new dimension of torture. In the course of counterinsurgency, British and French security forces resorted to systematic mass torture to extract information about the covert operations of the enemy.[311] In the eyes of the British and French colonial powers, all means were legitimized by the military necessity of the "battle for information" in antisubversive warfare.[312]

Screening and the Dilution Technique

Based on the experience of earlier colonial conflicts in Palestine and especially later in Malaya, Great Britain had come to realize the crucial importance of a well-functioning intelligence service.[313] In the previously mentioned and influential strategy paper *A Comparative Study of the Emergencies in Malaya and Kenya*, Colonel J. M. Forster maintained that the identification of "terrorists" and early information on their methods were absolutely essential to ensure the effectiveness of one's own operations.[314] In a letter written after the

emergency was declared in Kenya, Governor Baring had immediately noti-
fied Colonial Secretary Lyttelton of the necessity to undertake an extensive
improvement of the entire secret intelligence system.[315] Therefore, in February 1953, the first step was taken by creating the Kenya Intelligence Committee to better coordinate the work between the police and the military. In
the period that followed, the activity of the intelligence service was broadened and upgraded, especially under the new commander in chief, George
Erskine.[316]

The rapid and targeted gathering of information held the highest priority
in the eyes of those responsible for a successful conduct of the war.[317] The intensive interrogation of suspects and prisoners was supposed to expose Mau
Mau members and provide information that was as comprehensive as possible about the secret resistance movement. Detailed instructions emphasizing the informational "value" of prisoners stipulated the rules for conducting
such "interrogations."[318] Individuals were to be interrogated intensively immediately upon their capture, in order to be able to use the extracted knowledge as promptly as possible for one's own operational aims. The instructions
did not specify the type of interrogation methods to be used but merely
pointed out that in the past the use of physical force had rarely produced
exact information.[319]

One exceptional case was that of rebels who surrendered and voluntarily
gave themselves up. In the view of the British military, experience in Malaya
showed that this group of people was a very valuable source if not abused by
security forces.[320] In such cases, the psychological strategy of "softening up"
through good treatment was said to be far more effective than brute force.
Therefore, the high command in Nairobi ordered that Mau Mau fighters
who voluntarily surrendered were not to be mistreated but used instead as
a weapon of propaganda to encourage their former comrades to give up the
fight. These guidelines were compiled in the War Council instruction "The
Treatment of Captured and Surrendered Terrorists" issued in November
1955, in which the importance of intensive interrogation and the "immediate operational use" of the prisoners was emphasized explicitly once again.[321]

As a rule, interrogations were conducted by members of the so-called
screening teams recruited from the ranks of the army and police forces in
early 1953. In order to get the desired information, these "interrogation specialists" did not flinch in their choice of means. Hence, for African suspects,
screening usually meant hours if not days of torture.[322] In a letter to his former
London colleague, police inspector Tony Cross described the interrogation

methods at his new post, the Gekondi Police Station in Nyeri, as "Gestapo stuff."[323] In the pursuit of useful information, Cross reported, it was not at all unusual that prisoners would die in the cells or be shot for no reason. Cross's letter, which accidently fell into the hands of the press and from which excerpts were published,[324] revealed exemplarily the full extent of the brutality exhibited by British security forces. In addition to the ceaseless beatings, the most common torture practices were the extinguishing of cigarettes on bare skin, burning torture, mutilation, electroshocks, as well as anal and vaginal penetration using bottles, knives, snakes, and vermin.[325] Hence, the truth content of the extracted information was, as Muthoni Likimani emphasized, more than doubtful: "In this condition, you said whatever you thought would make your interrogators happy, whether it was true or not. The most important thing was to get away."[326]

This physically abusive treatment to the "third degree"—as it was called— was so commonplace, noted the settler D. H. Rawcliffe, that every member of the security forces knew about it, talked about it, or participated in it.[327] Several white settlers even traveled around the reservations as mobile interrogation teams and established their own torture chambers. One man in the Rift Valley gained such a reputation for his particularly gruesome methods of torture in his private screening camp that he became known as the "Joseph Mengele of Kenya."[328] Among other things, he had the skin burned off living suspects and forced other prisoners to eat their own testicles.

The cleric T. F. C. Bewes from the Church Missionary Society was one of the first to inform the British public of the systematic torture of prisoners in the East African crown colony. At a press conference held on 9 February 1953, he reported the shocking findings of his official trip through Kenya and described the torture methods of security forces that had led to the death of Elijah Gideon Njeru, a former teacher at a mission station.[329] During his stay in Kenya, Bewes had sent Governor Baring a confidential letter informing him of a series of grave abuses.[330] Among other things, the missionary reported having learned from various reliable sources that some policemen had cut off the fingertips of suspects who had refused to disclose information. In other cases, prisoners had been castrated, whereby two men had died. Bewes repeated his accusations in a private meeting with Colonial Secretary Lyttelton, which had been arranged at the intervention of the head of the Anglican Church, the archbishop of Canterbury.[331] The Colonial Office and the colonial government in Nairobi then vowed to investigate the incidents extensively and to undertake the necessary disciplinary steps.[332]

In the case of the murdered teacher Njeru, the official investigation report by the magistrate R. A. Wilkinson confirmed that the victim had been severely beaten and had died from the subsequent shock resulting from this abuse.[333] However, Wilkinson refuted the medical autopsy report in which an old tuberculosis infection of the teacher was said to have had no impact on his death. In Wilkinson's opinion, Njeru's overall poor state of health and his weakened resilience were to be linked directly to this previous illness, because the blows themselves would never have been sufficient to kill him. The magistrate showed great sympathy for the practices of the security forces and rejected the idea of punishing them. The colonial government concurred with the evaluation presented in this report.[334] Physical force was used in interrogations to gain information of vital importance for the public interest. The fact that this case involved an active Mau Mau supporter was but further provocation for such a reaction. The interrogation team could not have known, however, that a previous illness had weakened the suspect and that the blows could thus have deadly consequences for him. Although the colonial government had stood behind the security forces, the two European officers responsible in this case, Jack Ruben and Richard Keates, were brought to trial in September 1953, because the incident had attracted the attention of the public. In the end, the men were acquitted of manslaughter and only fined fifty and one hundred pounds, respectively, for battery.[335] To the benefit of the defendants, the jury had weighed the difficult conditions of the colonial emergency as particularly mitigating circumstances.[336]

The number of cases in which members of the British security forces were tried and convicted for mistreating prisoners remained miniscule and represented no more than the tip of the iceberg.[337] Granted, the colonial government in Nairobi was forced to admit that some torture and abuse had occurred since the beginning of the emergency, but it maintained that these cases had been investigated immediately upon becoming known and that those responsible had been held accountable.[338] Although Nairobi officials depicted these as regrettable isolated incidents, General Erskine still felt it necessary to intervene. The brutality had since reached such a magnitude that the commander in chief began to be concerned generally about the disciplinary state of his troops. In his circular of 23 June 1953 to all police and army unit officers, he thus made his point absolutely clear.

> I will not tolerate breaches of discipline leading to unfair treatment
> of anybody. . . . I am practical soldier enough to know that mistakes

can be made and nobody need fear my lack of support if the mistake is committed in good faith. But I most strongly disapprove of "beating up" the inhabitants of this country just because they are the inhabitants. I hope this has not happened in the past and will not happen in the future. Any indiscipline of this kind would do great damage to the reputation of the Security Forces and make our task of settling MAU MAU much more difficult. I therefore order that every officer in the Police and the Army should stamp at once on any conduct which he would be ashamed to see used against his own people. I want to stand up for the Honour of the Security Forces with a clear conscience—I can only do that if I have absolutely loyal support and I rely on you to provide it.[339]

Furthermore, Erskine announced that he would have each and every complaint against the security forces immediately investigated and criminally prosecuted.

Contrary to official accounts[340] and Erskine's later claims that the army and police had largely followed his order,[341] brutal interrogation practices continued. In December 1953, for example, Governor Baring had to inform the Colonial Office that three European police officers stationed at a post near Naivasha, together with their askaris, had regularly and arbitrarily whipped Africans in the area to get information from them.[342] In one interrogation, an elderly suspect who vehemently denied having taken the Mau Mau oath had been held headfirst over a fire for so long that his clothes had started to burn, severely injuring him.

Instead of coming to an end, the torture practices were exported to the northern provinces of the neighboring British colony Tanganyika. Fearing the spread of unrest, the colonial government in Dar es Salaam requested a screening team from Kenya, which Governor Baring sent to Arusha in October 1953.[343] The task of the interrogation team headed by Brian Hayward was to gather information on the links between Kikuyu in the neighboring colony to the Mau Mau movement. The responsible provincial commissioner explicitly emphasized "the importance of proper and discreet behavior" to his colleagues from Kenya upon their arrival.[344] However, Hayward and his team chose to act in accordance with standard Kenyan practices. In at least thirty-two cases, the team seriously injured suspects by whipping the bare soles of their feet, burning their skin with lit cigarettes, and strangling them with leather straps, with which the victims were tied and dragged over the ground. Horrified by the degree of brutality, the authorities in Tanganyika stopped all "questioning" and, following an inquiry, had those responsible for the brutality tried in court. Hayward and his team were convicted of battery and received a sentence of three months of hard labor. Moreover, Hayward was fined one hundred pounds, a sum that was actually paid by local white settlers on his behalf.[345]

In Kenya, the announced disciplinary measures were instead limited primarily to members of the military. Erskine sought to lend weight to the threat of criminal prosecution in his issued order and made an example out of the case of Captain G. S. L. Griffith.[346] Griffith, a KAR officer, had offered a bonus for every Mau Mau killed and had verifiably tortured and then executed prisoners. Following an extensive investigation of the events, he was consequently given a dishonorable discharge from the army and sentenced by a military court to five years of imprisonment, which he had to serve as a common criminal in a London prison.[347] Contrary to this, units of the Kenya Police, the Kenya Police Reserve, and the Kenya Regiment,[348] which recruited their members chiefly from white settlers who were thus fighting in their own interests, as well as the African Home Guard were spared such punishments for the most part. These branches of security enforcement continued to torture suspects routinely with such brutality that some British soldiers preferred to turn their prisoners loose than to hand them over to police units as the regulations stipulated.[349]

Police behavior was not concealed from the colonial government; on the contrary, Nairobi was fully aware of what was happening.[350] In January 1954, a parliamentary delegation sent to the colony discovered that police abuse was so widespread that it represented a serious threat to public trust in the forces of law and order.[351] In the subsequent report, the delegation members recommended a thorough reorganization of the entire Kenyan police apparatus in order to restore proper discipline. To fulfill this precarious mission, the London government appointed Colonel Arthur Young, who had successfully solved similar problems during the emergency in Malaya and was therefore thought to be predestined for this mission.[352] In March 1954, Young assumed his new office as Kenyan police chief and in his first decree ordered the reduction of physical force to a minimum.[353] In the course of his tenure, the new police chief was forced to see just how disastrous the situation truly was. Young felt obligated to make Governor Baring aware that "members of the Civilian security forces were uncontrolled and were committing crimes of violence and brutality upon their alleged enemies, which were unjustified and abhorrent."[354] Young informed the governor of these anarchic conditions and vehemently called on the colonial government—as in his letter of 22 November 1954, for example—to investigate the situation immediately:

> The other lamentable aspect of this case is the horror of some of the so-called Screening Camps which, in my judgment, now present a state of affairs so deplorable that they should be investigated without delay so that the ever increasing allegations of inhumanity and disregard of the rights of the African citizen are dealt with and so that Government will have no reason either to be embarrassed or ashamed of the acts which are done in its name by its own servants. . . . I do not consider that in the present circumstances Government have taken all the necessary steps to ensure that in its Screening Camps the elementary principles of justice and humanity are observed.[355]

Even the highest judicial authority of the crown colony, the Court of Appeal for Eastern Africa, criticized the colonial government for tolerating police methods that did not differ from those of the Gestapo and warned it of the serious danger that police authority itself could become law.[356] These grave accusations were buttressed by a chronological report from Duncan MacPherson, Young's assistant, in which he cataloged the crimes of the African Home Guard that had gone unpunished by colonial authorities.[357]

Young waited in vain for a written reply from Governor Baring. The colonial government showed no reaction whatsoever to the emphatic call of its police chief and admitted complete failure by declaring clearly that it would not criminally prosecute its own security forces. This was particularly evident in the government's stance in the case of Home Guard Chief Mundia, who was suspected of having tortured internees to death. In the pending police investigation, Governor Baring intervened personally. During a joint visit with the colonial secretary in South Nyeri, Baring talked with K. P. Hadingham, the civil authority in charge of the investigation, not without first explicitly noting the unofficial nature of their conversation. The governor emphasized that "he considered that it would be politically most inexpedient to prosecute a loyal Chief who had taken a leading part in the fight against Mau Mau. He said that a loyal Kikuyu would find it difficult to differentiate between killing Mau Mau in the heat of battle and killing the Government's enemies out of battle."[358] Therefore, he urgently recommended that the investigation not be continued, for political reasons, should there be no clear evidence proving

Mundia's direct guilt. The morale and fighting power of their own troops should not be weakened by "unnecessary" criminal trials, but should take priority over constitutional norms.[359]

Young drew the consequences from Baring's position and resigned only nine months after being appointed to the post of police chief. He cited the colonial government's unwillingness to cooperate as the reason that made it impossible, in his estimation, for him to do his job. Young said another major reason was his apprehension that the role of an impartial judiciary would continue to be filled instead by the "rule of fear."[360] The resignation was meant as open protest against the crimes perpetrated by security forces and against the complete passivity of the responsible authorities in Nairobi. The colonial government reacted with surprise over Young's reasons for resigning and claimed that the Kenyan government was thoroughly determined to fight against any form of irregularity.[361] It would never accept a "rule of fear" and counterterror and argued that Young was giving a completely false impression of the situation in Kenya by justifying his resignation as he did. Instead of deliberating the serious accusations leveled by the departing police chief and undertaking something to correct the situation, the authorities in Nairobi and London spent their energy only on steeling themselves against the possible consequences of public and parliamentary criticism. In a later account of the events, Young maintained that subsequent cases of brutal abuse like the Hola Camp incident could have been prevented had the colonial government taken the necessary steps at that time.[362]

In the years that followed, torture continued to be a daily and widespread phenomenon of the Kenyan emergency. For example, in a highly confidential telegram sent to the colonial secretary in January 1955, Governor Baring was again forced to report a series of deaths resulting from "questioning," including one case in which a district officer had killed an African by "roasting [him] alive."[363] In September of that same year, the provincial court in Nyeri was compelled to impose fines and several months of hard labor on four police officers because that had tortured to death the suspect Kamau s/o Gichina in the most brutal of ways for a period of six days.[364] In his sentence, Judge A. C. Harrison said it was particularly regrettable that the victim had been completely innocent, both de facto and de jure. At the same time, Harrison stated with satisfaction that the defendants had not acted out of egoistic motives but only for reasons related to the performance of their official duties.

Torture in the name of the British state again reached a new dimension at the start of 1957. In seeking for a way with which the remaining thirty thousand internees could be moved to confess and then be eligible for release from the camps as "rehabilitated" people, the colonial government discovered the methods of the camp commander John Cowan. Under the motto that evil had to be beaten out of a person,[365] Cowan had the so-called dilution technique used in Gathigiriri Camp. Prisoners would be divided into small groups and mishandled until their resistance had been broken and they had agreed to cooperate with the camp authorities. In one visit to the camp with other high-ranking colonial officials, Eric Griffith-Jones, Kenya's attorney general, observed this new way of treating prisoners and described it in a secret memorandum: "In some cases, however, defiance was more obstinate, and on the first indication of such obstinacy three or four of the European officers immediately converged on the man and 'rough-housed' him, stripping his clothes off him, hitting him, on occasion kicking him, and, if necessary, putting him on the ground. Blows struck were solid, hard ones, mostly with closed fists and about the head, stomach, sides and back. There was no attempt to strike at the testicles or any other manifestations of sadistic brutality."[366] For the colonial attorney general, this was the only possible way to handle "hardcore" prisoners, and he added a number of practical pointers in his memorandum.[367] Because the use of this form of physical force was not performed as punishment but only to ensure discipline, severe injury by blows to sensitive parts of the body were to be avoided. This treatment was only to be carried out by conscientious European officers, who had been selected for their strong character qualities. In addition to giving dilution prisoners a medical examination, camp authorities were also to determine first that the use of force was necessary, appropriate, and in no manner excessive or resulting in serious injury. If these safeguards were implemented, Griffith-Jones concluded, the camps could continue to use "shock treatment".[368]

In a BBC interview decades later, Terence Gavaghan, an officer responsible for this type of "rehabilitation" described the procedure as a "kind of rape,"[369] and it was inherent in the nature of things that prisoners were beaten to death.[370] Such calculated risk did not daunt Governor Baring; he argued in favor of the systematic use of the dilution technique. In his view, the suspension of this method would only have negative consequences for what was now a successfully progressing way of "bringing down a 'pipeline' towards release of many Mau Mau detainees."[371] With this argument, the governor even managed, as mentioned earlier, to convince the ICRC delegate Junod of the necessity of violent shock.[372] Since a majority of the internees eventually broke down under this treatment and gave up their resistance, Baring was

always able to report to London about the government's success in reducing the number of internees.[373] At first, Colonial Secretary Lennox-Boyd had
reservations about the new methods, because he greatly feared that this could
be used as a political weapon against him in public.[374] In the end, he gave the
colonial government a free hand in this matter.[375]

The dilution technique was used systematically in Kenya until the murder
of the eleven prisoners in the Hola Detention Camp in March 1959. Only
on the recommendation of the Fairn Committee, created to investigate the
incident, was the continuation of this torture method prohibited.[376] Instead
of adequately reacting to the vast amount of information gathered on the
systematic torture done by screening teams, the authorities in London and
Nairobi had not only covered up the practices of the security forces during
the entire duration of the emergency but had even organized state torture
themselves in the case of the dilution technique.

"La Question"

The use of physical force during interrogations in Algeria was already well
established in the repertoire of police investigative methods even before
1 November 1954,[377] but the outbreak of the war meant an increase in the use
of torture. Proof of this was found in two newspaper articles reporting on the
serious mishandling of people in police custody in early 1955: "Votre Gestapo
d'Algérie"[378] by Claude Bourdet and "La question"[379] by François Mauriac.
Thereafter, French interior minister François Mitterrand assigned General
Inspector Roger Wuillaume the job of investigating the serious accusations.
Wuillaume came to the conclusion in his investigation that the content of
the press reports was basically true[380] and that these interrogation methods
had already been used in peacetime, particularly in difficult cases.[381] In this
internal report, he confirmed the torture of prisoners by beatings and by subjecting them to water and electric shocks, although he did not fail to note that
water and electric torture did not leave any visible traces.[382] However, in order
to avoid any unnecessary interference in successful police investigative work,
Wuillaume endorsed the continuation of the *procédés spéciaux*, but with less
gruesome methods and under the strict supervision of the officers' respective
superior.[383] At the end of his report, the general inspector also recommended
that letters of gratitude and praise be sent to the officers assigned with this
sensitive work in order to protect them from possible feelings of guilt.[384]

The head of the French police, Jean Mairey, was horrified about the use
of torture by French security forces, which Wuillaume had tried to legitimize

with his recommendations. After having already informed the prime minister of his opinion in March 1955, Mairey again presented evidence of severe mishandlings in his December report and demanded the immediate end of such practices.[385] As the director of the Sûreté Nationale, he found it intolerable that the practices of French police officers were "reminiscent of Gestapo methods."[386] At the same time, Mairey warned of anarchic conditions among French security forces and urgently called on the national leadership to take countermeasures. Despite this alarming message from its national police chief, the French government did not react accordingly and continued its silent toleration of the conditions in Algeria. By failing to take decisive steps against the severe abuse early on, the authorities in Paris also created the prerequisites for the systematic use of torture later.[387] This did not occur until the beginning of 1957 when the army took full control in the Algerian departments and the doctrines of *guerre contre-révolutionnaire* went into effect.[388]

According to this new strategic dogma, another high-priority objective, in addition to the extensive control of the population, was the gathering of reliable intelligence.[389] Only with the help of such information was it possible, in the eyes of the military, to fight an enemy operating underground successfully. The Algerian War thus rapidly became a *guerre de renseignement*,[390] in which information gathering was the "nerf de la guerre."[391] In his statement of 30 April 1957 on the fight against rebellion and terrorism, General Salan explicitly ordered the army to take over police and intelligence activities in addition to its classic military missions.[392] In these operations, the army was allowed to enter private homes to chase down and arrest suspects. In addition, Salan permitted military units to interrogate the people arrested during such police operations for military purposes and then transfer them to the nearest *centre de triage et de transit*.[393] Vested with these extensive powers, the army could combat the rebellion forcefully and effectively, concluded Salan.[394] In instructions issued 10 March 1959, General Massu also emphasized, among other things, the fundamental importance of this "police technique" in combating the political-administrative arm of the rebel movement.[395] In Massu's view, interrogation played a key role. Without going into any detail about special interrogation techniques, the general spelled out several basic rules. The interrogation had to be conducted under the direction of an officer, whereby the following was to be taken into account: "For reasons of efficiency, the maximal force of conviction has to be applied. If this proves insufficient, then it is appropriate to use forceful measures, the purpose and limitations of which have been exactly explained in a special directive."[396] When the general referred to "forceful measures," he meant nothing else but torture. Yet just like Salan, Massu also avoided the word *torture*, for in military circles one only spoke officially of *interrogatoire*.[397]

In his deliberations on the "modern war," Colonel Roger Trinquier expounded the nature of these interrogations. A lawyer was not allowed to be present there at all. Should the suspect disclose the information demanded from him without any difficulty, the interrogation was to be ended quickly. Otherwise, specialists had to wrest his secrets from him, whereby he would then be confronted with pain and perhaps even death.[398] Trinquier justified this procedure by underscoring the urgent necessity of gaining information on planned "terrorist" attacks in time to protect the lives of innocent people.[399] The violence of "terrorism" was to be answered with the extreme force of the state as a means to protect the majority of its citizens. General Massu adopted this viewpoint and explained in the book he published later that there had been a gruesome necessity for the torture that occurred during the Algerian War, for it had prevented hundreds of innocent victims.[400] In the account presented by both officers, torture was a legitimate weapon in anti-subversive warfare and viewed as an "acte élémentaire de guerre."[401] The result was that the Algerian people were neither considered nor treated as people any longer but, as a former French intelligence officer maintained, only as a potential *source de renseignement*: "Among ourselves we speak about a prisoner like we do about first-class material from which we are to make the best use. These technical discussions fascinate the specialists, and they continue to talk sometimes for hours. In such moments we completely forget the nature of our first-class material: the human being."[402]

In early 1957, the military began to turn its concepts into reality within the framework of the Battle of Algiers and to establish a specialized apparatus of intelligence gathering by creating the Dispositif de Protection Urbaine (DPU) and the Détachements Opérationnels de Protection (DOP).[403] The work of the DPU was limited to Algiers, where the entire Muslim population was to be monitored with the help of a block warden system and the intelligence needed to combat the FLN urban guerrillas was to be gathered.[404] At the same time, the creation of the DOP meant that every army unit now could rely on a special independent branch for intelligence gathering.[405]

Starting in October 1957, the criminal investigation police, the gendarmerie, and the riot police were placed under the DOP, thereby enhancing its clout.[406] During the war, somewhere between 10,000 and 15,000 soldiers worked for these "operational protection units," which expanded their networks across all of Algeria and mutated to an independent army within the French armed services because of the broad powers given to the DOP.[407] The work of the various intelligence services was coordinated under the authoritative leadership of Trinquier by way of the *centre de coordination interarmée*. Within this system, the *officiers de renseignement* developed into "key figures"[408] of the war and were specially trained for their work in schools for antisubversive warfare. From the transcript of a trainee who attended the Jeanne d'Arc training center, we find that the five criteria of "torture humaine" were included in the curriculum.[409] According to these criteria, torture was to be clean, was allowed under no circumstance to be carried out in the presence of youth and sadists, and was the responsibility of the officer in charge. Above all, it was to be humane, meaning that the use of physical force was to be ended as soon as the prisoner began to talk. The recommended methods were water and electroshock torture, since these did not leave any visible marks.

The operation "Champagne," carried out by the Tenth Paratrooper Division under the command of General Massu in the casbah of Algiers, marked the beginning of systematic torture.[410] In their security checks and nightly raids, soldiers arbitrarily arrested people on the streets, broke into private homes, and carried off the inhabitants in order to subject them to intensive "questioning."[411] In a private conversation with R. F. G. Sarell, British consul general in Algiers, Captain Robert Frequelin, an intelligence officer in the notorious paratrooper regiment of Colonel Marcel Bigeard, described this procedure in great detail and reported unashamedly that they had tortured each of their prisoners.[412] The sole exception was Mohamed Larbi Ben M'hidi, the head of the FLN in Algiers, who was spared such treatment upon his capture on the express orders of Bigeard. The gesture was meant by the colonel as an expression of his respect for this opponent, said Frequelin. However, this did not stop Bigeard from subsequently having Larbi killed and officially announcing his death as "suicide."[413]

Characteristic of this military operation was the phenomenon of *disparus*. After their arrest, people simply disappeared without a trace and without their relatives ever learning anything about their fate. For the nine-month duration of the Battle of Algiers, the secretary-general of the prefecture, Paul Teitgen, officially listed the number of those who had "vanished" at 3,024 people,[414] however, the number of unknown cases certainly makes this figure much larger in reality. Three Parisian lawyers—Jacques Vergès, Michel Zavrian, and Maurice Courrégé—submitted their *Cahier vert* to the ICRC as an extensive documentation on various cases of "vanished" individuals and thus tried to draw attention to the fate of these people.[415] The reason for the "disappearance" was that the prisoners either did not survive the "interrogation" or were executed by the army afterward.[416] As the French paratrooper Pierre Leulliette reported in his account, this was done to save the cost of holding prisoners and at the same time to get rid of troublesome witnesses:[417] "A huge common ditch, large enough to swallow up a whole company, had been dug just after we arrived by the prisoners themselves, in the farthest corner of the park, under the dark shadows of the orange trees. There would always be enough room."[418] The combination of torture and systematic "disappearing" was meant to create a climate of fear in the Arab population, which the army considered to be a weapon of *contre-terreur*.[419]

Papers recording the arrival and release of prisoners did not usually exist, so the official version of what happened to these people often simply was that the temporarily detained persons had been released after a few days and thus there was no information concerning their whereabouts.[420] In the case of Maurice Audin, a mathematic lecturer at the University of Algiers and a member of the Algerian Communist Party, the officer in charge maintained that the suspect had managed to flee custody during his transportation to another facility and had not been recaptured by security forces.[421] In actuality, Audin had been severely tortured in El-Biar Prison after his arrest by paratroopers on 11 June 1957, and subsequently strangled by Lieutenant André Charbonnier. Josette Audin tried frantically to learn the whereabouts of her husband and mobilized public support for his cause, refusing to let herself be deterred by the efforts of the military to intimidate her.[422] The result of her publicity campaign was the creation in late 1957 of the Comité Maurice Audin on the initiative of Professor Laurent Schwartz, Audin's doctoral adviser, and the historian Pierre Vidal-Naquet. The announced aim of this committee was the complete clarification of Audin's fate.[423] Further, publications like *L'affaire Audin*[424] and *Un homme a disparu*[425] intended to inform the public of the systematic torture in Algeria,[426] because Professor Schwartz was convinced that Audin was not an isolated case like the French national affair involving Alfred Dreyfus but symbolic of the torture of thousands.[427]

Unlike his friend Audin, Henri Alleg, the editor of the communist newspaper *Alger Républicain*, survived the "interrogation" by paratroopers. His journalistic activities led to his arrest on 12 June 1957, and he was also taken to the torture center at El-Biar. He succeeded in smuggling a report out of prison on the terrible torture taking place there. This was published with the title *La question* and described the common interrogation practices. Shortly after his arrival, Alleg was placed naked and bound on "a black plank, sweating with humidity, polluted and sticky with vomit left, no doubt, by previous 'customers'"[428] and then tortured with electroshocks: "Suddenly, I felt as if a savage beast had torn the flesh from my body. Still smiling above me, Ja—— had attached the pincer to my penis. The shocks going through me were so strong that the straps holding me to the board came loose. . . . They had thrown cold water over me in order to increase the intensity of the current, and between every two spasms I trembled with cold."[429] These torture sessions were repeated daily in several variations by the "interrogation specialists," who suggested suicide to Alleg as a way to spare himself from further torment. After suffering this ordeal for a month, Alleg was finally transported to the detention camp Lodi and eventually to the civil prison Barberousse, where he could secretly write his report: "For whole nights during the course of a month I heard the screams of men being tortured, and their cries will resound for ever in my memory. I have seen prisoners thrown down from one floor to another who, stupefied by torture and beatings, could only manage to utter in Arabic the first words of an ancient prayer."[430]

With numerous petitions to the UN Human Rights Commission, the international press, trade union organizations, and especially to the ICRC in Geneva, Alleg's wife Gilberte also tried to attract attention to her husband's fate and thereby protect him from "disappearing."[431] Immediately following the appearance of *La question,* Alleg's report on torture, in March 1958, the publication was banned and confiscated by police. Yet this report, above all else, made it impossible for the French government to cover up the systematic torture taking place in Algeria.[432] Even as the Battle of Algiers was being fought, the number of critical voices increased dramatically, and a "virtual explosion of information on torture" occurred.[433] In February 1957, the Catholic newspaper *Témoignage Chrétien* published the "Dossier Jean Muller," in which French war crimes and torture were reconstructed from letters written by the fallen military conscript Muller.[434] In March, on the occasion of the publication of the book *Contre la torture* by Pierre-Henri Simon, *Le Monde* ran the incredulous question "Sommes-nous les 'vaincus de Hitler'?" as a front-page headline.[435] Simon, a French army captain who had survived five years in German prisoner-of-war camps, compared torture practices in Algeria with the methods of the National Socialists[436] in the hope of "waking up France" with his book.[437]

Even high-ranking representatives of the French colonial power such as Paul Teitgen,[438] secretary-general of the police prefecture of Algiers, and General Jacques Pâris de Bollardière, grand officer of the Legion of Honor and the commander of two brigades in the eastern sector of the Atlas Mountains, vehemently protested against the state use of torture and therefore resigned their posts. General Bollardière even ventured to criticize the army's methods in an open letter published in the magazine *L'Express*,[439] for which he was sentenced to two months of fortress detention, the greatest penalty for an officer during the Fourth Republic in connection with the Algerian War. In his later book *Bataille d'Alger, bataille de l'homme*, the general justified his position as follows: "In the battle for Algiers, the government cowardly shirked its responsibility, the army abnegated its tradition and its honor, the country suffered its most appalling defeat. The defeat of a people with an old humanistic and Christian culture, who, full of indifference and hypocrisy, repudiated the hallowed principle of its civilization: namely to see a fellow man in every human being."[440]

The evidence of severe torture in Algeria was so overwhelming that the French government finally felt forced to react to the growing public pressure. On 10 May 1957, Prime Minister Guy Mollet officially announced the formation of the Commission de sauvegarde des droits et libertés individuels.[441] France was the nation of human rights, said Mollet in his announcement, and was morally obliged due to this tradition to fight vigorously against any infringement of individual liberty and human dignity.[442] Under the direction of Paul Béteille, the twelve independent members making up the commission were to investigate the accusations that had arisen in Algeria.[443] Despite the difficulty of its job, the Commission de sauvegarde was not vested with any measure of real power. The body had neither its own legal power nor the authority to issue directives; instead it was completely dependent on the cooperation of the local civilian and military offices.[444] Under these conditions, it was impossible to conduct an independent investigation, and the efforts of the delegates to throw light on the matter proved just as difficult. The final report, presented to the French government on 14 September 1957, thus came to the conclusion that there had been isolated but not systematic abuse.[445] However, in its summary, the report did mention once again that the commission had not been given the authority necessary to conduct its investigation and could do no more than offer an opinion.[446]

In protest over the lack of support and complete passivity on the part of the government in Paris, Robert Delavignette declared his resignation from the Commission de sauvegarde on 22 September 1957, followed by Maurice Garçon and Émile Pierret-Gérard.[447] Delavignette, a former governor general of Cameroon, had documented and criticized fatal abuse in the report he authored on his own in July 1957.[448] In his letter of resignation, he emphasized the absurdity of the situation in which the commission distinctly condemned torture, while at the same time this practice continued unabated.[449] By resigning from the commission, Delavignette wanted the government to understand his move as a clear signal of his criticism, which is also why he sent a copy of his letter of resignation to be printed in *Le Monde*. *Le Monde* founder Hubert Beuve-Méry was also the one who eventually published the commission's final report on 14 December 1957.[450] Although the French government had rejected the idea of publishing the report to that point, when it appeared, the government acted unruffled. In fact, the Algerian governor general Lacoste used the passage in which isolated cases of abuse were said to have occurred as an important argument with which to counter allegations of systematic torture.[451] In the same issue of *Le Monde*, Lacoste had a summation of atrocities committed by Algerian rebels printed as a way to rebut further allegations and put them into perspective.[452] The instrumentalization of the report illustrates clearly the full failure of the Commission de sauvegarde, which could never fulfill its actual task and served only to provide an alibi for the authorities in Paris.[453]

Irrespective of this debate in the colonial metropole, French security forces continued the use of systematic torture even after the Battle of Algiers ended in September 1957. The victory over an obliterated urban FLN network served as a model and a catalyst for further developments.[454] The task of soldiers charged with interrogation consisted mainly of "torturing the bound and naked prisoners, one after another, from morning till night, under the guise of interrogation."[455] A former member of the DOP estimated in his later account that he himself had tortured 250 people during his tour of duty in Algeria.[456] The special units tortured on such a regular basis that it became something completely "normal" if not "routine."[457] In addition to beatings and the burning of sensitive parts of the body, torture with electroshocks—referred to as *gégène*—was one of the most common "methods of intelligence gathering." Electrodes were placed on the nipples, tongues, ears, and genitals of the victims, who were doused with water to increase the effect of the electricity.[458] For General Massu, who described systematic torture in hindsight as "part of a certain ambiance,"[459] there was nothing objectionable about this type of "interrogation." Out of curiosity he once even applied a small dose of electricity to himself, which led him to note: "If electroshocks are used in a precise dosage, the personality of the enemy is not degraded in any way. Naturally it shakes one up and is understandably very unpleasant, but one survives it without serious damage afterward. There are many examples of people who had complained about the so-called torture that they were subject to and, when we later met again, were in full health. They do not appear to have truly suffered very much."[460]

The halfhearted efforts from Paris under the new national leadership of the Fifth Republic to end this "normality of torture" remained largely inconclusive.[461] For example, during a visit to the troops in August 1959, President de Gaulle personally ordered Colonel Bigeard, the commander of the sector Saida, to cease torture practices immediately. Bigeard then passed on the message in a meeting with his officers by saying: "No more torture. Gentlemen, I say to you: no more torture, but continue to torture them as before."[462] By vesting the army with unbounded authority to solve the "Algerian problem" and by silently condoning, if not covering up, the "pacification methods" of the military for a long time, the French government became responsible for a situation gone completely out of control. The task of once again imposing state authority over the soldiers who tortured in the name of the French republic proved to be a nearly hopeless endeavor.

As it was, torture was used in Algeria until the war ended. Moreover, reports of torture from 1959 prove that Algerians were severely abused in various French prisons and police stations.[463] The "Algerian methods" thus returned to the French mainland and spread, as the historian Vidal-Naquet noted, like a cancerous tumor throughout French democracy.[464]

Furthermore, on the orders of the police prefect Maurice Papon, French police also used brute force against peaceful demonstrators while disbanding a pro-Algerian rally on 17 October 1961. They brutally bludgeoned people on the streets of Paris, thereby killing over two hundred demonstrators, and some of the bodies were then simply thrown into the river Seine.[465] The blatant disregard for all principles of constitutional law and natural basic rights inherent in the antiliberal policies first used in the periphery landed like a boomerang at the point of origin, the European metropole. There it began to undermine the liberal order. As Jean-Paul Sartre very strikingly described it later: "In order to avoid the famous selling-off of our Empire, we have sold off France: in order to forge arms, we have cast our institutions into fire, our freedoms and our guarantees, Democracy and Justice, everything has burnt, nothing remains. Simply ending the fighting is not enough to reclaim our wasted wealth: we too, I am afraid, in a different area, will have to start from scratch."[466] Above all, the numerous reports on unchecked colonial violence triggered debates that began to play a role in the international discourse on human rights, each in a different way.

Chapter 6

The International Discourse on Human Rights as Marked by the Wars of Decolonization

What Africans are fighting for is nothing revolutionary, it is found in the Charter of the United Nations.

—Tom Mboya, 1958

Kenya on the Sidelines of the International Human Rights Discourse

Desperate Efforts to Attract International Attention

In his thoughts on partisan warfare, Carl Schmitt underscores the decisive role of a "third party" for the success of a guerrilla movement: "The powerful third party supplies not only weapons and ammunition, money, material aid, and medicine of all sorts, it also provides a type of political recognition, which the irregular partisan fighters need to keep from sinking, like the bandit and the pirate, into the realm of the unpolitical, which here means the criminal realm."[1] In Schmitt's view, the ally is not only the logistical lifeline in armed conflict but also fulfills an important political function. Particularly in asymmetrical conflict scenarios like decolonization wars, in which the military victory of poorly equipped guerrilla troops seemed a nearly futile endeavor against a highly armed colonial power, it was vital for the independence movement to combine armed conflict with a political strategy.[2] Backed by a "powerful third party," a movement had to try to convince the global public that its anticolonial endeavor was justified and to mobilize support.[3] In a favorable international climate, dominated by the two anticolonial superpowers, the Soviet Union and the United States, the enemy was to be put under political pressure and moved to relent in the face of its growing international isolation. The United Nations was the ideal forum for this purpose, and the topic of human rights served as the moral armor for anticolonial independence movements in their quest to pillory the colonial powers before the international community.[4]

In the case of Kenya, however, this "strategy of internationalization" was never pursued. This was due primarily to the basic organizational and strategic weakness of the Land Freedom Army, which had neither a revolutionary party organization nor an intellectual leadership. After the arrest of the entire political elite at the beginning of the emergency, the new military leaders like Kimathi and Mathenge concentrated solely on armed conflict, without combining this with a political concept.[5] Very sporadically efforts were made to contact political sympathizers abroad, as a letter confiscated by British security forces and a few other documents prove.[6] Unlike other anticolonial independence movements, such as the Algerian FLN and later the Movimento Popular de Libertação de Angola (MPLA) and the Frente de Libertação de Moçambique (FRELIMO), the Mau Mau had no organization operating in exile that conducted a targeted propaganda campaign and sought to win allies.[7] Therefore, the uprising was completely isolated not only from all logistical support but especially from all political support from abroad.[8] Without the intervention of a "powerful third party," the necessary internationalization of the Kenyan conflict did not occur.

Clear evidence of this is the fact that the largest British war of decolonization never appeared as a serious topic on the agenda of the United Nations. Only in May 1953 did the United African Nationalist Movement, a leftist Afro-American organization, attempt to convince the group of Arab-Asian UN member states to intervene on the Mau Mau's behalf before the Security Council. In its petition to the Pakistani UN delegate Bokhari, a representative of the anticolonial bloc, this NGO justified its demand by arguing that the serious human rights abuses taking place in Kenya represented a clear threat to peace and security.[9] In London, authorities reacted to this earnest diplomatic threat immediately. The British high commissioner for Pakistan was instructed to use the full weight of his influence on the Pakistani government to kill this petition.[10] Instead of bringing the situation in Kenya before the UN Security Council as requested, the Arab-Asian group eventually decided, on the initiative of Egypt, India, and Iraq, only to discuss the matter in the UN Committee on Information from Non-Self-Governing Territories.[11] British UN diplomats were then calmer in their reaction to this clearly far more politically moderate undertaking but continued to threaten to pull out their delegates immediately should the Kenya question appear on the agenda of the Committee on Information.[12] Experience had shown that, in the past, this diplomatic threat "had a most salutary effect."[13] In general, even the Foreign Office in London considered it highly unlikely that the Arab-Asian group would actually pursue their plans in the committee. Still, British diplomats in New York were told to follow very closely all developments at the United Nations regarding Kenya.[14]

The initiative of the anticolonial bloc did indeed come to nothing, and only one other time was there an effort to raise the issue of Kenya by addressing directly the UN secretary-general. On the occasion of Jomo Kenyatta Day, the African-Asian member states called on UN General-Secretary Dag Hammarskjöld to act on behalf of the immediate release of Kenyatta. Further demands were to end the emergency, to normalize basic political and civil rights, and to acknowledge the inalienable right of African independence.[15] However, this petition was issued in September 1959, at a point when the military conflict in Kenya had been over for three years and the first clear signs of a change in British policy toward Kenya were becoming evident. Moreover, UN Human Rights Commission documents prove that there had been next to no international interest in the situation in the East African crown colony during the entire duration of the emergency. In light of the dimension of human rights abuse in Kenya, the UN body registered an infinitesimally small number of petitions from individuals[16] and a very few NGOs.[17] For example, only the League of Human Rights from Zanzibar wrote to Hammarskjöld in December 1957 to inform him about the racial discrimination, the killing competition among British security forces, and the catastrophic conditions in the detention camps.[18] The complete lack of so-called mass communications, petitions from internationally important organizations, and entreaties by states with anticolonial sympathies tellingly demonstrates how meaningless the Kenya issue was for the United Nations and how sidelined it was in the international discourse on human rights.

Since no international public relations campaign was being conducted by an organized Kenyan independence movement, such efforts were limited to the initiatives of a few individuals. One such person was Joseph Murumbi, the secretary-general of the KAU who had fled abroad even before his party was banned by the colonial government in Nairobi in March 1953.[19] During numerous trips, for example, to India, Murumbi tried at press conferences to inform the public about the real reasons for the Mau Mau uprising and the brutal reality of British repression.[20] During his stay in India, he even succeeded in conducting talks with Prime Minister Jawaharlal Nehru. From India, Murumbi traveled in August 1953 to Egypt, where he was received by the president, General Mohamed Naguib. Officials at the British foreign ministry who were closely watching Murumbi's performances on the international stage were on edge. In a diplomatic protest note, the British ambassador Robert Hankey officially complained to the government in Cairo that a man connected to an anti-British terror organization was granted an audience with the head of state, while a representative of His Royal Majesty had been waiting in vain for such an audience.[21] Contrary to the reports in the Egyptian and British press, Murumbi was not at all a "Mau Mau delegate," let alone their "vice president."[22] He represented the positions of Kenyatta's party. Therefore, he sharply condemned such labels and threatened to sue the *Times* of London for libel.[23] As secretary-general of the KAU, he used his stay on the Nile as a platform to extensively criticize the repressive colonial policies in his East African homeland.[24]

British diplomats were primarily concerned with a rumor that began to circulate during Murumbi's trip. According to the British High Commission for India in New Delhi, a Middle Eastern country was intending to bring the Kenya issue before the United Nations.[25] These concerns were fueled further by the announcement of the Egyptian UN delegation head, Dr. Abdel Hamid Badawi, in the newspaper *Al Misri* that his delegation would be giving top priority at the United Nations to the struggle against British imperialism in Kenya.[26] In face-to-face talks with Dr. Mahmoud Fawzi, the Egyptian foreign minister, Ambassador Hankey responded to this by maintaining that under no circumstances did internal affairs such as those of the East African crown colony fall under the jurisdiction of the world organization.[27] Moreover, continued the British ambassador, the Mau Mau movement was a wild band of murderers fighting against the progress of civilization while killing the large majority of Africans in a horrible manner. If that was the case, Fawzi countered, Great Britain could use the United Nations as the ideal forum to present its view of the affairs. This suggestion was rejected adamantly by the British side. Instead, Great Britain's ambassador sternly warned the foreign minister that any direct or indirect intervention by the Egyptian delegation with regard to Kenya at the United Nations would immediately lead to a very serious crisis in the relations of the two countries. Hankey's unrelenting manner and his unambiguous warning to the Cairo government were explicitly approved and supported by the British foreign ministry.[28]

Irrespective of these diplomatic developments caused by his trip, Murumbi continued his public relations work, only now he tried to attract the attention of the British public by working directly in Great Britain itself,[29] together with other exiled Kenyans like Mbiyu Koinange, who had formed the Kenya Committee, and in close cooperation with the Movement for Colonial Freedom,[30] which had been founded on the initiative of Labour MP Brockway,[31] among others, in May 1954.[32] At the same time, the political opposition in the House of Commons was to be supplied with the information necessary to act against the Kenya policy of the Conservative government. Murumbi viewed the Kenyan problem in the broader context of worldwide developments and with a strong link to the topic of human rights. Therefore, in his article "Human Rights: Let's Make Them Real," appearing on 8 June 1956, he wrote:

> The Universal Declaration of Human Rights of which Britain and other colonial powers were signatories is a righteous document, but cases could be cited of flagrant breaches of these rights in almost all colonial territories. There are, for instance, 43,512 persons detained in Kenya without trial, while 301 are detained under similar circumstances in Cyprus. Free speech and the right to travel are denied to the people in Kenya and British Guyana. Freedom of association and the right to form political organisations of their own choice is denied to the people of Kenya. Forced evictions and concentration camps are the order of the day in Kenya, Cyprus and Malaya. . . . The Bandung Conference brought the people of Asia and Africa together for the first time. If the people of Britain are not going to stand with them in the fight for Human Rights, the peoples of these two great continents, representing nearly two-third[s] of [the] human race, would have to depend on their own efforts to gain their Rights.[33]

Another person whose activities attracted attention was Tom Mboya,[34] the young secretary-general of the Kenya Federation of Labour whose political rise to trade union leader was closely linked with the successful organization of the dockworkers' strike in Mombasa in 1955. Thanks to a scholarship, Mboya was able to enroll that very same year for a year-long study at Ruskin College in Oxford. He used his study time not only to make close contacts with British trade union leaders and Labour MPs but also to stress the enormous problems in Kenya to the British public.[35] Mboya published proposed solutions in his book *The Kenya Question: An African Answer*, in which he demanded the unconditional implementation of racial equality and the realization of individual rights: "For these reasons I accept the political philosophy of democracy, in which each individual has an equal voice in the choice of his government and an equal opportunity freely to express his opinions on its actions. I accept the principle of the rule of law and the equality of all citizens before the law. . . . These are ideals and very far from practice in Kenya today."[36]

He described the situation in his homeland as socially and politically unjust in light of the pressing problem of land distribution, open racial discrimination, and the total hegemony of Europeans. Although the young trade union leader clearly distanced himself from the violent actions of the Mau Mau, he stated that the emergence of this movement was the direct consequence of years of frustration and bitterness among the African population.[37] Mboya sharply criticized the practices of collective punishment, arbitrary arrest, and brutal screening methods used by the colonial government and condemned the tyranny of the security forces where constitutional democracy should prevail. In his opinion, the African answer to the "Kenya question" was not brute military force, but solely the realization of universally valid human rights and the introduction of a true democracy aiming toward Kenyan self-determination.[38]

In addition to his public relations work in Great Britain, Mboya also accepted in the fall of 1956 an invitation by the American Committee on Africa, an American NGO, to give a lecture tour in the United States, much to the consternation of the British government.[39] The British embassy in Washington, D.C., thus asked for precise instructions on how to handle the unwanted guest from Britain's own empire and, above all, how to prevent a planned press conference of the trade union leader in connection with the United Nations. Douglas Williams, the British colonial attaché in Washington, was convinced that a man of Mboya's stature could cause great damage in the current political climate.[40] Therefore, the instructions from London strictly forbade all support and all public contact with him by both the embassy and the British UN delegation in New York.[41] Undeterred by this stance, Mboya went on with his travel plans, held numerous lectures, spoke with the American press, and tried to gain support in influential circles in the United States. In an interview on 5 September 1956, he explained that the objective of his trip was to inform the American public about the real problems of Africa.[42] Asked about the situation in his Kenyan homeland, Mboya repeated his argument that the emergence of the Mau Mau movement was rooted in economic, social, and political frustration among the African population and that the solution to the problem lay in the guarantee of basic universal rights. Yet he had no compelling way to explain why, as compared with the independence movements in Tunisia and Morocco, the Kenyan liberation struggle was not being successful in effectively mobilizing public opinion and thereby subjecting the British colonial power to international pressure.

In truth, the struggle for independence in Kenya did not come anywhere close to garnering the attention and support in either the colonial metropole or on the international level that the French conflicts in North Africa did. In Great Britain, an organized public protest movement against military operations in Kenya never formed. Not even the elements within the Labour opposition in the House of Commons who sharply criticized the practices of their own security forces in Kenya were able to bring this about.[43] Members of Parliament like Leslie Hale, Anthony Wedgwood Benn, and particularly Fenner Brockway[44] and Barbara Castle[45] were the ones who raised the issues of colonial injustice and human rights abuses.[46] In a newspaper article that appeared in September 1955, Castle said that a police state existed at the heart of the British Empire against which Labour had now declared war.[47] In November 1955, she even undertook a trip to Kenya on her own in order to see the situation for herself.[48] In articles like "The Truth About the Secret Police"[49] and "Justice in Kenya,"[50] she published afterward her shocking travel reports and thus tried to start a public debate. The credible reports of a British member of Parliament, together with the previously mentioned published statements of contemporaries Tony Cross, Eileen Fletcher, and Richard Meldon, provided the British public sufficient information that London was conducting a "dirty war" in East Africa. Still, the expected wave of protest never materialized, and until the end of the emergency, Great Britain wrapped itself in a cloak of nearly silent apathy with regard to the human rights situation in Kenya, with the exception of the Hola Camp incident in 1959.[51]

On the international level, the press in countries holding a clear anticolonial position reported on the British repression. For example, the Irish lawyer Peter Evans, who had been expelled from the crown colony by the Kenyan colonial government because his reporting had been considered far too critical, subsequently published his articles on the Kenyan concentration camps and trigger-happy white settlers in the *Times of India*.[52] At the same time, reports in Caribbean daily newspapers[53] aroused an annoying amount of attention among the African-born population, at least from the standpoint of the British colonial power, which is why the Colonial Office in London immediately and emphatically increased its propaganda activities in its West Indian colonies.[54] The Eastern Bloc countries, spearheaded by the Soviet Union, also reported on the uprising in East Africa and used it as a welcome opportunity to attack British colonialism sharply.[55] Despite it all, the international public was never truly mobilized on this issue. On the whole, the reports in the international press more closely resembled an anticolonial reflex than a campaign to support the Kenyan fight for independence. Furthermore, as more and more information on the Mau Mau movement became known in countries with a clear anticolonial agenda, a growing hesitancy to openly declare sympathy and solidarity with the fight of the Land Freedom Army became evident.[56]

"The Horned Shadow of the Devil Himself":
The Successful Demonization of the Mau Mau

The reason for the failure to mobilize support and consequently for the complete international isolation lay in part in the previously mentioned organizational weakness of the Kenyan independence movement, which at no point appeared as a cohesive group. Yet another major reason for this was British propaganda, which succeeded quite impressively in manipulating public opinion in favor of the colonial power despite adverse international conditions.[57] In the political climate of the postwar period, in which the struggle of an anticolonial movement for self-determination and independence was basically viewed in a positive light, Great Britain had to avoid at all costs its military operations being seen as the colonial repression of legitimate demands. For this reason, the British defense strategy focused on negating the political and national legitimation of the Land Freedom Army. With the term "Mau Mau," London portrayed its enemy instead as a criminal association of cruel murderers and "terrorists," against whom the security forces were legally justified to combat.[58] According to such a depiction, Great Britain was not acting as a repressor of a national independence movement but as the guarantor of order, development, and security in Kenya. Colonial propaganda was also assigned the vital task of transmitting precisely this image as effectively as possible to the world and thereby to draw public opinion to its side. The result was a campaign against the Mau Mau, which the Kenyan historian Wunyabari Maloba has correctly called one of the most intensive propaganda attacks on an African national movement.[59]

The Colonial Office pointed out the major importance of effective public relations work in Kenya in a memorandum dated 23 October 1952, issued immediately following the declaration of the state of emergency.[60] With the warning that the total failure of public relations efforts in 1948 was also greatly responsible for the unrest in the Gold Coast colony, authorities in London recommended the immediate creation of an efficient information machine. The military leadership emphatically supported this endeavor. In his Emergency Directive No. 1 issued in April 1953, General W. R. N. Hinde, the commander in chief, attributed very high priority to propaganda efforts and was explicit in his orders that every conceivable support be given the information services.[61] The strategy of British propaganda was twofold, to reach people both within and outside the crown colony. The task of informing and manipulating the opinion of the African population in the interest of the colonial government was assigned to the African Information Service.[62] For this purpose, a large number of newspapers, brochures, and flyers were published in the various African languages of the country in which the brutality of the Mau Mau was described extensively and the merits of British rule were praised. However, due to the high rate of illiteracy, radio developed into the most effective instrument of propaganda. With the help of mobile "information vans" and thousands of radios spread across the colony, the colonial government transmitted its messages directly to the African population in special programs translated into Kikuyu, Swahili, and each of the other national languages.

The Kenya Government Press Office[63] was given the task of providing adequately filtered information on the situation in the crown colony to the national and international media.[64] According to its own sources, international press work was particularly important. Since Kenya found itself making headlines worldwide because of the emergency, the Press Office had to ensure that the government's policy was not presented falsely or even twisted about unfairly.[65] To avoid such "misinterpretations," the Kenya Government Public Relations Office was also created in London under the direction of the journalist Granville Roberts. It was chiefly responsible for the international public image of the Kenya question.[66] In countries having a special importance with regard to colonial issues, like the United States and India, the press office in Nairobi was linked directly to the offices of the British Information Service[67] operating in those respective locations. It was hoped that such direct contact would facilitate effective public relations work and enable the information services to react as quickly as possible to relevant international developments.

The effectiveness of British propaganda did not depend solely on its organizational structure; the right selection of topics to publicize played the most decisive role. For example, in an operations review in December 1952, the Kenyan commissioner of police Michael S. O'Rorke called it very regrettable and imprudent to report on French defeats against the Viet Minh rebels in radio broadcasts that were transmitted specifically in Kikuyu.[68] The average African, maintained O'Rorke, knew nothing about international affairs; therefore, this type of information only served African agitators as welcome material to help incite unrest. Even Colonial Secretary Lyttelton himself participated in the discussion on the right selection of topics. In a letter to Governor Baring, he pointed out what he saw, with an eye on international public opinion, as the weaknesses in the way the British themselves were depicting the situation. There was too much emphasis, the colonial secretary argued, on publicizing military news like the statistics on the number of Mau Mau fighters killed and of people arrested,[69] but far too little was reported on the positive things regarding peace and development in the crown colony.

The discussion about the most effective form of self-propaganda went deep into detail, including questions concerning the suitable selection of words. The BBC, for example, informed the Colonial Office of the protest by one of its listeners, who sharply criticized the use of the phrase "rounded up for questioning" in a story on a Mau Mau screening operation.[70] The term "rounding up" is suitable in references to cattle, but not people. To the ears of Africans and Indians, this could be insulting, and it could also serve the Soviet Union as welcome propaganda ammunition in its fight against the "imperialistic powers." The BBC responded to the angered listener that this phrase did not originate in its own vocabulary but was the official wording of British military authorities. So, the BBC forwarded the entire matter to the Colonial Office, where reports of criticism on news reporting had been received already from other parts of the empire. According to its own findings, people in West Africa were harboring growing resentment over the wording of the BBC Overseas Service in stories on military operations against the Mau Mau.[71] Used far too often were phrases like "bag of terrorists" and "gangs being flushed," wording reminiscent of hunting jargon more than police operations. Therefore, the Colonial Office instructed Brigadier General William Gibson, who headed the information department in Nairobi, to dissuade BBC special correspondents from using these expressions as much as possible and, at the same time, to refrain from such terminology in all of its own stories.[72] Following an extensive review, Gibson repudiated the accusations as exaggerated but assured the authorities in London that more care would be taken in the choice of words.[73]

The British information services began to follow more closely the ideas of Colonial Secretary Lyttelton in the selection of topics. Immediately following the declaration of the emergency, Lyttelton had boasted in a Commons debate: "Let everyone know that in Kenya we are not to be turned aside by a band of terrorists. We are in the country to develop it and not to exploit it."[74] Thus a press campaign was launched that aimed to present British rule in a particularly positive light and especially to place the supposed developmental achievements in the foreground.[75] Great Britain's presence in East Africa was to be presented to the public as a guarantee for the social and economic development of Kenya to the benefit of the African population. The content of press articles to be published was spelled out in detail by the Colonial Office. For example, a list of topics from June 1953 included typical core themes like "The Committee on African Advancement in Kenya—designed to improve the social and economic advancement of Kenya," "Round-up on education and technical training for Africans," "Assistance to African farmers," "Social and welfare schemes in Kenya," "Health service for Africans," and "Development of housing schemes for Africans in East Africa (special reference to Kenya)."[76] At the same time, British propaganda efforts sought to reach India and the Muslim world with special topics like "The growth and development of Asian communities in East Africa,"[77] "The Asian citizen in Kenya," and "The Moslem community in Kenya"[78] in order to convince even leading representatives of the anticolonial bloc of the prospering coexistence of various ethnicities in the British crown colony. The government's public relations work was also accompanied by an intensive campaign aimed at white settlers that followed the same strategy. In its publications, the government presented the precolonial period as an era of primitivity and ignorance, epidemics of disease, hunger, and horrible tribal wars. Only upon the arrival of the white settlers did the fate of Kenya take a turn for the better, and the African population was given the unique opportunity to emerge from barbarism and enter civilization.[79]

British propaganda did not only emphasize the colonial developments achieved by the colonial rulers; it aimed primarily to demonize the enemy. The Mau Mau were stylized into the "horror story of Britain's empire,"[80] in which all sides were to be deterred effectively from supporting the uprising. At the same time, Great Britain's actions were to be idealized as a struggle to defend human civilization. At the heart of the propaganda was "Mau Mau bestiality,"[81] which the British interpreted as being evident in the Mau Mau oath ceremony, among other things. Therefore, the news agencies attempted to disseminate as much chilling information as possible on the rituals,[82] including some reports that were strictly fictitious and others that were at least highly exaggerated.[83]

Yet it was intelligence reports that served as the basis for a special memorandum by a parliamentary delegation that traveled on an inquiry mission to Kenya in January 1954.[84] In the opinion of the parliamentarians, this memorandum contained such repulsive and obscene details that the British public could not be confronted with it. Therefore, it was decided not to publish the entire memorandum and to allow the members of Parliament to view the report in its entirety in the parliamentary library.[85] At the same time, government offices supplied government-friendly press representatives with select information on the oath rituals, pieces of which were then fed to readers, allowing enough room for the reader's own horrifying interpretations.[86] This thoroughly contradictory information policy—in which information on the Mau Mau oath was held in strict secrecy, on the one hand, while select insinuations were leaked, on the other—achieved the desired effect of permanently capturing both the curiosity and attention of the public. The comments of Michael Blundell, a leader of the settlers, provide a particularly graphic example of this ambivalent behavior. Blundell refused to give details of the "horror of the Mau Mau oaths" but at the same time added: "Suffice it to say that masturbation in public, the drinking of menstrual blood, unnatural acts with animals, and even the penis of dead men all played a part in this terrible destruction of the Kikuyu mind."[87] Precisely such statements were the fertile soil from which sprang the wildest speculations and fantasies in the public mind about the "demonic" character of the Mau Mau.[88]

British propaganda provided further proof for its claim about the "bestiality" of the enemy particularly by citing the atrocities committed by the rebels and thereby using and manipulating horrifying images of the war.[89] Photos showing mutilated animals and machete-slashed human bodies in the aftermath of Mau Mau raids were meant to make the conflict appear as a fight between civilization and barbarism.[90] At first, the Colonial Office hesitated to publish these photos because of the appalling scenes and recommended that they be shown only to the appropriate people for the purposes of discussion.[91] The Foreign Office felt it would be valuable to send this photographic material to information officers in various select posts abroad to be shown to the local influential opinion makers.[92] The declared aim was to make a lasting impression on the public and "to silence misinformed expressions of sympathy for the Mau Mau."[93] Starting in January 1953, entire collections of photo documentation were sent to certain people to convince them of the "true nature of the Mau Mau."[94] In the case of India, the Colonial Office even made the following suggestion to the colonial government in Nairobi: "In view of Indian preaching of pacifist methods, you might consider sending some photographs of the brutalities committed by Mau Mau not only against Africans but also against cattle."[95]

The Lari massacre per se developed into "the war's iconographic moment."[96] The Mau Mau raid of 26 March 1953 on the village of the loyalist chief Luka and the murder of 120 villagers provided the colonial power a sufficient amount of particularly awful photos. The numerous close-up shots of children hacked to pieces and inhabitants mutilated beyond recognition were meant to finally dispel any doubt about the limitless bestiality of the enemy.[97] Therefore, the commentary by the information services on the back of one of these horror photos read: "This is Mau Mau—this is not some highly principled group of men fighting for a just cause."[98] In the struggle to sway public opinion, Lari became the number one topic on the British side, whereby the "full propaganda value of the horror was squeezed out to the last drop."[99] The day after the attack, the colonial government held an international press conference directly from the site of the atrocity to mark the start of an intensive media campaign.[100] In numerous reports in the print media, radio, and film, the public was "informed" about the incident in the Kenyan village, while news about the retaliation strike by British security forces, in which nearly four times as many people were killed arbitrarily, was prudently swept under the rug.[101] The authorities in London gave up their initial reluctance to publish horror photographs, which now were to have an impact on the largest public possible.[102] Edmund J. Dorsz, the U.S. consul general in Nairobi, sent to the State Department a copy of the Swahili weekly newspaper *Tazama*, in which an entire series of photos of the massacre were published.[103] In his cover letter, Dorsz reported that the Europeans in Kenya were being urged to circulate this issue among their African workers "in order to bring home to them the barbaric brutality of Mau Mau."[104] One of the ways the shocking photos were presented to the national and international public was the publication in 1954 in London of the brochure *The Mau Mau in Kenya* in close collaboration with the Kenya Public Relations Office.[105] This brochure would cement the myth of "Mau Mau bestiality."

For the Land Freedom Army, the Lari massacre turned out to be a crushing political defeat, as settler leader Blundell noted: "The news of this atrocity . . . had a profound effect in Great Britain and on the international scene. It largely eliminated sympathy for the Mau Mau movement, and it brought public opinion face to face with the savagery and brutality of what was happening in our country. The concept of the noble African fighting for his legitimate rights against the wicked imperialists was difficult to sustain when the bodies of the Kikuyu women hacked to death and battered skulls of their children cried out to the contrary."[106] Had support for the Kenyan independence movement been only rather tenuous since the start of the war, the photos of Africans gruesomely mutilated and slaughtered at the hands of other Africans thoroughly destroyed any last remnants of sympathy and solidarity for the cause. The perception of an anti-imperialist struggle between black and white was effectively replaced by the image of "Mau Mau horror." Even representatives and fellow travelers in the anticolonial movement distanced themselves from the "Kenyan horror scenario" with which they did not want to be associated under any circumstances.

For the British government, however, the Lari massacre was a first-class propaganda victory. One benefit was that, for their own public relations campaign, the information services were able to exploit, for example, a resolution of the Kenya Indian Congress[107] and a statement by the Nigerian politician Abubakar,[108] both of which unequivocally condemned the bloodbath. In light of the news out of Kenya, individual voices once expressing support for the movement went completely silent, like that of Canadian prime minister Louis St. Laurent, who had called the Mau Mau a legitimate national movement at the start of the emergency much to the consternation of London.[109] In the attempt to rattle the Afro-Asian solidarity emerging in Asia, British propaganda countered every criticism of the operations of its own security forces in Kenya by vehemently pointing out the cruelty of the Mau Mau.[110] In answer to the critical reporting by the Ceylonese newspaper *Samasamjist*, the Kenya Public Relations Office did not shy away from alleging cannibalistic actions by the Mau Mau, like the sucking of blood from freshly killed babies.[111]

In its attempts to publicly stigmatize "Mau Mau terror," the colonial government in Nairobi came up with a particularly bizarre idea in December 1953,[112] in which Ralph Bunche,[113] the head of the UN Trusteeship Council, would be invited to the crown colony to condemn publicly the violent methods of the Mau Mau. The symbolism in an appearance by the well-known American civil rights leader, United Nations diplomat, and first black Nobel Peace Prize laureate[114] would have been hard to top as a demonstration to the world that the violence and terror of the Mau Mau was being sharply condemned from all sides. Aside from the assumption that Bunche never would have performed this propaganda service for the British, the entire plan was finally squashed by the adamant veto of a seriously concerned commander in chief, General Erskine. At that point, the general was preoccupied with attempts to get his trigger-happy troops under control again and, understandably, had no interest whatsoever in having a black UN diplomat and Nobel Peace Prize laureate present in his power domain, where people were being interned, tortured, and shot in droves based on their ethnicity.

Besides, British propaganda about the atrocities was very successful and effectively demonized the enemy even without an appearance by Bunche. In Great Britain, the name "Mau Mau" epitomized horror. Parents warned their disobedient children that the Mau Mau would come and get them if they didn't behave, while MPs in the House of Commons denounced ruckus by their political opponents as "Mau Mau terror."[115] Even Colonial Secretary Lyttelton seemed to be susceptible to the effect of his own propaganda. In his memoirs, he reported how the Mau Mau would appear before him while he worked on governmental documents pertaining to Kenya: "I can recall no instance when I have felt the forces of evil to be so near and so strong. As I wrote memoranda or instructions, I would suddenly see a shadow fall across the page—the horned shadow of the Devil himself."[116]

The Algerian War and the Competition for World Public Opinion

Human Rights as an Effective Instrument in Mobilizing the International Public

During his 1962 trip to various countries on the African continent, the leader of the armed wing of the African National Congress (ANC), Nelson Mandela, also visited Rabat. During the days of his stay in the Moroccan headquarters of the Algerian revolutionary army, Mandela learned a great deal about the independence struggle of the FLN and was invited, among other things, to visit the combat lines on the Algerian border front and to watch a military parade in honor of Ahmed Ben Bella, who had just been released from French imprisonment. The head of the Algerian mission in Morocco, Dr. Mustafa, not only explained their guerrilla strategy in detail to his South African guest but also strongly advised Mandela, when planning his own military endeavor, "not to neglect the political side of war while planning the military effort. International public opinion, he said, is sometimes worth more than a fleet of jet fighters."[117]

This advice given to Mandela contained the "recipe for success" of the Algerian Liberation Front, namely the effective combination of military and political strategy. The Algerians compensated for their absolute inferiority in combat strength against the highly armed French army with a diplomatic offensive, which would indeed turn out to be the decisive factor for victory. In addition to winning the war for independence, the FLN declared in its very first proclamation to the Algerian people on 31 October 1954, that its paramount goals were to internationalize the conflict, to bring about North African–Arab unity, and to gain support within the framework of the United Nations.[118] With the help of a targeted political strategy abroad and the support of all allies, the Algerian problem was to become a "reality for the entire world."[119] This international strategy was endorsed at the internal FLN conference in Soummam in August 1956, where "the political isolation of France in Algeria and in the world"[120] was included in the catalog of official war aims and emphatically expressed the determination of the Liberation Front to force France to its knees, politically and diplomatically. In this context, the American historian Matthew Connelly speaks of a "diplomatic revolution," because the decisive factor in the success of the FLN was not the achievement of conventional military aims but the fight for public opinion on the international stage.[121] The Algerian War served as a valuable model for liberation movements to follow, such as the ANC or the Palestine Liberation Organization (PLO) under Yasser Arafat.[122] However, above all, Connelly's thesis offers a plausible explanation for the paradoxical situation in which the Algerian Liberation Front achieved its greatest political victory on the road to independence at the point when its troops had been almost completely defeated by the French army. Independent of the military developments in Algeria, the FLN managed to mobilize public opinion on its behalf at the international level and thereby put France under massive pressure.[123]

The first basic requirement to successfully internationalize the conflict was to develop an effective organization abroad that would find allies and represent the cause of Algerian independence internationally.[124] The external wing of the FLN consisted of Mohamed Boudiaf, Hocine Ait Ahmed, Ahmed Ben Bella, and Mohamed Khider. Even before the war started, they set up their headquarters in the Egyptian capital, where the struggle for Algerian liberation was proclaimed in a Radio Cairo broadcast on the evening of

1 November 1954. It became the responsibility of the Algerian delegation on the Nile to establish diplomatic contacts,[125] to requisition provisions for the ALN, and especially to motivate the fellow Arab states to support the cause. Contrary to the Kenyan Land Freedom Army, the FLN had in Nasser's Egypt a "powerful third party" to give the cause critical support materially and politically.[126] Other Arab League countries also began to act on behalf of the Algerian revolution and to back it on an ongoing basis.[127] Following their own independence, Morocco and Tunisia became particularly close allies and served the ALN as safe logistic havens from which to advance into and retreat from Algeria.

An important juncture for the further organizational development of the Liberation Front occurred at the Soummam Conference, at which—as mentioned earlier—the executive body CCE and the revolutionary parliament CNRA were created.[128] With regard to international strategy, the session also led to the creation of eight permanent offices abroad, including one in New York, and to increased activity by mobile FLN delegations in various capitals throughout the world.[129] The high point of this development of parallel governmental structures was finally the founding of the provisional Algerian government on 19 September 1958, with seats in Cairo and Tunis.[130] In his first official statement, Ferhat Abbas, the president of the GPRA, pledged to uphold the principles of the UN Charter and the Universal Declaration of Human Rights, which he declared as the sacrosanct basis of Algerian politics.[131] The declared aim of the new government in exile was to make the international public even more aware of the Algerian cause.[132] Therefore, the greatest diplomatic success proved to be the fact that the GPRA was officially recognized shortly after its founding by fifteen governments, including all Arab states except Lebanon, the communist regimes of Asia, and Indonesia.[133] At the same time, the provisional government expanded its diplomatic network particularly in Europe and the Near East.[134] All told, forty-five envoys represented the interests of the FLN in twenty different countries, including the United States, the Soviet Union, and Great Britain.[135] Thanks to this well-structured organization, the Algerian Liberation Front was able to launch an effective propaganda campaign aimed at winning the battle for public opinion worldwide.

The main location for their diplomatic efforts and attempts to internationalize the conflict was New York, where an outright "battle for the UN"[136] broke out. The world organization was used by the FLN as a forum to force the international public to focus on the fight for independence.[137] France was to stand in the international dock as it had in the cases of Tunisia and Morocco.[138] To achieve this, the Liberation Front was very dependent on the help of its Arab allies, since only member states could make the Algerian question a topic of discussion in the various UN bodies.[139]

Saudi Arabia undertook the first initiative by calling for action from the UN Security Council on 5 January 1955, on the grounds that the serious situation in Algeria represented a threat to international peace and security.[140] Further, the Saudi embassy in Washington presented a letter from the Committee for the Freedom of North Africa to President Dwight D. Eisenhower in which the committee asked the United States to give its support to the Algerian struggle in the Security Council.[141] In July, a petition signed by thirteen Afro-Asian countries was submitted to put the Algerian question on the agenda of the tenth session of the UN General Assembly.[142] The petitioners explained that the colonial occupation of Algeria presented a threat to peace and meant that the indigenous population was being denied its right to self-determination as a people and to fundamental human rights.

For the entire duration of the Algeria debate at the UN in the years that followed, Paris maintained a strategy of defending itself by arguing, first and foremost, that the three North African departments had long been an integral part of France and, according to Article 2, paragraph 7, of the UN Charter,[143] the United Nations therefore had no authority to intervene in the internal matters of a member state.[144] Still, the anticolonial bloc succeeded in winning a paper-thin majority vote to place the topic of Algeria on the agenda, which prompted Paris to boycott the General Assembly and related committees altogether.[145] The members of the French delegation did not return to their seats until the topic was removed from the agenda at India's proposal.[146]

However, the initiatives of 1955 were only the prelude to a symphony of similar initiatives pertaining to the Algerian question that would appear continually on the agenda of the UN General Assembly until 1961.[147] The anticolonial bloc justified its intervention primarily on the looming threat to peace and international security as well as on the principle of self-determination of peoples as guaranteed in the UN Charter.[148] Likewise, the issue of human rights was also placed at the heart of the various petitions.[149] For example, a number of Afro-Asian member states called on the UN Security Council twice in 1956 and demanded in their common communiqué of 13 June an immediate reaction by the world organization to the grave human rights abuse in Algeria.[150] A few months later, the anticolonial bloc justified its petition to discuss the Algeria question again in the General Assembly with several arguments including the point that, in combating the FLN, the French government had since adopted a policy of annihilation against the Algerian population that was tantamount to a clear violation of the UN Genocide Convention.[151]

In a memorandum addressed directly to UN Secretary-General Hammarskjöld in June 1957, the UN ambassadors of the Arab states reported the widespread destruction of Algerian villages, massacres of the civilian population, systematic torture, and the use of poisonous gases by the French army and therefore accused France of having become guilty of crimes against humanity.[152] In July 1959, the anticolonial bloc again called on the Security Council and once again pointed out the continuing excesses.[153] Moreover, French armed forces were disregarding all of the stipulations for handling prisoners of war in the Geneva Conventions. This appeal to the Security Council urgently tried to draw attention to the fate of a million Algerians who had been forcefully relocated and whose situation was worsening dramatically. Even in the UN Human Rights Commission an unprecedented event occurred. In the name of nineteen African and Asian UN member states, Ceylon petitioned in April 1957 to have the current human rights situation in Algeria added to the work schedule and daily agenda of the commission.[154] France, Great Britain, and Italy rejected this on the basis that the human rights body lacked the necessary competence. Yet it was not until the Soviet delegation made a surprising proposal to table the issue that Ceylon's petition was postponed for an indefinite period. Pivotal for this unusually reserved behavior of the anticolonial superpower USSR was an announcement by the Italian delegation: should Algeria become a topic in the Human Rights Commission, the Italians threatened to counter it by bringing up the situation in Hungary.[155]

The diplomatic efforts of the anticolonial bloc produced very meager results. These were at first limited to the 1956 UN resolution,[156] which was confirmed once again at the very next session of the UN General Assembly.[157] In it, the United Nations merely expressed its hope that a peaceful, democratic, and just solution to the Algeria question could be found in the spirit of cooperation and in concordance with the principles of the UN Charter. Such a harmless, nearly meaningless statement did not make a serious impression on anyone in Paris and consequently did not at all influence French politics, specifically on the war in North Africa. Still, the activities of the Afro-Asian UN member states did achieve one of the major objectives of the Algerian Liberation Front. By way of their numerous petitions, they were permanently pushing the Algeria issue onto the center stage of the world organization and forcing France into some sort of diplomatic reaction, be it the attention-getting departure of the French delegation from the UN General Assembly or the numerous attempts to justify its policies in the various UN bodies. Such activities sustained public awareness and internationalized the conflict in Algeria.

While the UN members sympathetic to the Algerian cause fulfilled their tasks from within the world organization, the FLN tried to influence the situation from the outside. For this purpose, the Liberation Front sent a standing representative to New York starting in September 1955 and, in the wake of the decisions made at the Soummam Conference, set up a permanent office, the Algerian Office, on the East Side. The mission of the office, under the direction of Abdelkader Chanderli and Mohamed Yazid, was to coordinate the cooperation among the anticolonial bloc countries and to conduct well-aimed public relations work in the United States and especially in the general environment of the United Nations.[158] In addition to disseminating its own press releases and propaganda brochures, the FLN created a constant public presence by making numerous contributions to print media, radio, and television, participating in various conferences, and giving lectures at American universities.

The Liberation Front also presented its cause directly to the United Nations by submitting petitions and memorandums. For example, in its white paper on the Franco-Algerian conflict, presented to the UN Secretariat on 12 April 1956, the FLN accused France of conducting a colonial war to reconquer Algeria, a war that seriously endangered peace and international security.[159] By declaring a state of emergency and granting the accompanying *pouvoirs spéciaux*, the colonial power had installed an outright terror regime in Algeria, and the French army was implementing repressive measures of "genocidal proportions"[160] in its extensive military operations against the Algerian civilian population. As proof of these serious accusations, reference was made to torture, collective punishment measures, and arbitrary mass executions. In conclusion, the FLN urged the United Nations to intervene immediately "in order to prevent perpetuation of genocide and aggravation of the situation in North Africa."[161]

The Algerian Office intensified its activities in early 1957.[162] The immediate cause for this was the eight-day general strike declared by the FLN in Algiers. This strike had been timed to begin precisely with the start of the Algeria debate in the United Nations and was to offer impressive proof to the global public of the validity of the FLN's claim to represent the Algerian people. While the paratroopers of General Massu were forcefully thwarting this plan, Ferhat Abbas and Mohamed Yazid submitted a letter to the president of the UN General Assembly in the name of the FLN protesting the lynching, plundering, and terror committed by the French security forces in the casbah of Algiers. The letter closed with an appeal for help in which the world organization was asked to use the full force of its influence against the French government and to stop this "new act of genocide" against the Algerian people.[163] The serious human rights abuses committed by France as a colonial power were included more and more in the arguments of the FLN and became a focal point of its public relations work following the Battle of Algiers.[164] In numerous publications and memorandums, the topic was the brutal "pacification" of the Algerian people, which was repeatedly characterized as "genocide."[165] The Liberation Front was supplied with ample ammunition to support its public relations assaults in the form of the French "scorched earth" policy, the systematic destruction in the "forbidden zones," the extensive measures of internment and resettlement, and the stream of refugees to Morocco and Tunisia.[166] In his memorandum to UN Secretary-General Hammarskjöld in April 1959, the Algerian Office head Chanderli criticized not only the torture and military executions, but above all the forced displacement and relocation of more than a million Algerians who were now crowded together in camps under catastrophic conditions. In light of this humanitarian catastrophe that was also underscored by the 300,000 Algerian refugees in the neighboring countries of Tunisia and Morocco, Chanderli appealed to the United Nations to interfere immediately.[167]

The FLN's great success in mobilizing international opinion about the serious human rights abuse is clearly evident in the documents of the UN Human Rights Commission. Completely contrary to the British war of decolonization in Kenya, the body received innumerable petitions on the Algeria case from Arab groups, humanitarian organizations, trade union associations, and international student associations, as well as letters from prominent artists, writers, and journalists, in which the French war was sharply attacked and the United Nations called upon to react immediately.[168] In addition to the Battle of Algiers,[169] the protests focused on well-known cases of torture, such as that of the journalist Henri Alleg[170] and the Algerian trade union leader Aissat Idir.[171] Another issue was the fate of the twenty-two-year-old Djamila Bouhired, a woman who was wounded in a gun battle in April 1957 and fell into the hands of French security forces, only to then be severely tortured for days in a military hospital.[172] After a military court sentenced the FLN fighter to death for her participation in bombing attacks in Algiers, a great wave of international protest arose. Particularly in Arab countries, innumerable lists of signatures and preprinted petitions protesting against her execution arrived on her behalf at the UN Human Rights Commission as one of the very first incidents of such a mass communication phenomenon.[173] Djamila Bouhired became an icon of the Algerian struggle for liberation and was depicted on propaganda posters, among other poses, as the French Marianne waving the Algerian flag in front of charging ALN troops.[174] In March 1958, the French government commuted the death sentence for Bouhired and two of her women comrades into a prison sentence. In doing so, the French UN delegation explicitly emphasized in a letter to UN Secretary-General Hammarskjöld, who had also intervened on behalf of the imprisoned women in private talks with various delegations,[175] that this act of clemency was to be attributed to the leniency of the French president.[176] Actually, France had been forced to bow to the immense international pressure although it never conceded this publicly.

The United Nations was not the only platform for protest against the serious human rights abuses in Algeria. The ICRC in Geneva was also the recipient of numerous petitions and appeals for help,[177] whereby the Algerian Red Crescent (CRA), established by the FLN, also played a crucial role. Using its own envoy in Geneva, the CRA not only turned directly to the International Committee for help[178] but mobilized support worldwide from other national Red Cross societies.[179] France's numerous violations of the Geneva Conventions, such as the execution of prisoners, was strongly condemned by the Red Crescent societies in various Arab states as well as by the Red Cross in countries like Hungary, East Germany, and Venezuela.[180] At the same time, the FLN pursued the aforementioned "humanitarian strategy"[181] of unconditionally releasing individual prisoners of war. While France was having Algerian rebels executed as "terrorists," the CRA was releasing French soldiers to the ICRC in a very effective public relations move. The Algerians were attempting to document their unconditional commitment to the principles of international humanitarian law and win the sympathy of the international public.

On the whole, the efforts directed at the United Nations and the ICRC were supported in a decisive way by the globally operating network of the Liberation Front. In addition to articles in the main propaganda organ, the revolutionary newspaper *El Moujahid*,[182] FLN envoys published memorandums and brochures in their assigned countries in which the topic was human rights abuse in Algeria. For example, the foreign delegation in Tokyo published reports on the fate of Algerian refugees and the conditions in the resettlement camps,[183] while in Germany numerous FLN publications appeared in German,[184] including the brochure *Kolonialistische Unterdrückung und Kriegsverbrechen*,[185] in which the Liberation Front documented many testimonies of those who witnessed torture, military executions, and the destruction of Algerian villages. In the cover letter accompanying this publication, the FLN stated that the purpose of this modest publication was to pierce the seemingly impenetrable French news shroud in order to "direct the eyes of the world to the gruesome and horrifying incidents occurring day after day in Algeria."[186] All of these international efforts—be it in New York, Geneva, or any other city—shared the same objective of confronting France with a moral front that would exert foreign-policy pressure on Paris and completely isolate the French government.

France's Counteroffensive and Diplomatic Defeat

These various activities by the anticolonial bloc and the FLN forced France to act. Especially at the United Nations, France's position weakened appreciably.[187] Paris continued to refer to Article 2, paragraph 7, of the UN Charter in its argument that the world organization was prohibited from intervening in domestic affairs,[188] but gradually it became necessary to adopt a more nuanced defense strategy. After the French navy seized the ship *Athos*, where it found a significant stash of weapons and ammunition purchased and shipped out of Egypt and destined for the ALN,[189] France again took the initiative in October 1956 and brought charges before the UN Security Council against the Egyptian government for its military support of the Algerian rebels.[190] The government in Paris certainly had no intention of leaving the international stage of the world organization to the allies of the FLN without a fight. On the contrary, it sought to use the United Nations for its diplomatic counteroffensive.

For this reason, French diplomatic missions in the countries of the anticolonial bloc were once again given the task, as in 1952,[191] of submitting detailed reports on the economic, social, and human rights situations in their assigned countries.[192] The information gathered through these reports was presented by the French foreign ministry as a statistical handbook in which data on health, education, and social areas in Algeria were compared to those of the anticolonial bloc countries, in order to document the latter's backwardness against its own achievements in developing North Africa.[193] At the same time, the dossier listed numerous violations of the Universal Declaration of Human Rights in various countries. For example, Islamic countries were criticized for their complete lack of religious freedom and the cruelty involved in applying the sharia, while Ceylon and India were condemned for the discrimination of their caste systems. By pointing out the major deficits in development and the human rights violations of its enemies, the government in Paris sought to counter successfully the anticolonial attacks at the United Nations. Moreover, it also began to compile detailed dossiers on various topics in Algeria.[194] Therefore, even before the first UN debate on the Algerian question took place in 1955, the French interior ministry was able to provide its own UN delegation with extensive information on the positive social and political developments in the three North African departments[195] and added special photographic documentation of the atrocities committed by the rebels.[196] In April 1956, the foreign ministry again underscored the urgent necessity to take steps against the growing propaganda activity of the Algerian nationalists operating abroad and especially in the United States.[197] The international public needed to be better informed about the true nature of the "subversive movement" in North Africa and France's own positions on the Algeria issue. This prompted the project of compiling extensive dossiers that would provide the armor necessary for the "battle for New York" when diplomatic confrontations also occurred at the United Nations in the years to follow.[198] A newly established department at the foreign ministry, the Mission de liaison pour les affaires algériennes (MLA), headed by Henri Langlais, guaranteed the easy exchange of information among the responsible governmental offices and the various diplomatic missions.[199] This clearly defines the cornerstones of the French line of argumentation: France's own achievements in developing Algeria were to be emphasized while the destructive force of "FLN terrorism" was to be condemned. A memorandum from November 1956 points out, for example, that the rebels were systematically destroying the schools and hospitals that France had built. Nothing could justify such an unleashing of barbarism in light of the principles of Western civilization and the ideal of the United Nations.[200]

Authorities in Paris eventually compiled these various studies and reports into the *Dossier Algérie*, which provided the French UN delegation with guidelines and comprehensive back-up material for its argumentation in the many debates.[201] Divided into different rubrics, the handbook was designed to counter opponent criticism and provided suitable answers to all questions concerning the Algerian issue. Among other things, the dossier contained a detailed list of rebel acts of violence, such as the destruction of public buildings[202] and the murder and mutilation of civilians, which was illustrated at length in graphic photographs.[203] Another major accent in the handbook was placed on France's own economic and social achievements in developing Algeria, a point increasingly emphasized, particularly after de Gaulle announced the "Constantine Plan" in October 1958. The five-year reform package costing millions served as a particularly valuable argument for the UN delegation in New York to support their point about the comprehensive French development policy in Algeria.[204] The resettlement measures and the creation of *mille villages* could be presented in this context as part of the "modernization campaign" through which the living standard of the rural population was being markedly improved.[205] However, in order to do this, terms like *zone de terre brûlée* and *zone interdite* had to be stricken from the official vocabulary because these evoked strong associations with forceful displacement and could be used by opponents for propaganda purposes.[206]

The diplomatic efforts of the French delegation at the United Nations were backed by a comprehensive propaganda campaign directed at the public at large. Algerian Governor General Lacoste complained to the press in December 1956 that a truly diabolical campaign was being started in New York by the Arab side, in which France was to be discredited in the eyes of the American public.[207] For this reason, Paris stepped up the activity of the Service de Presse et d'Information connected to its diplomatic mission in Manhattan. Provided with a remarkable budget, the information office, under the direction of Roger Vaurs, could send numerous propaganda films[208] to the various American broadcast companies and produce hugh editions of publications in various languages. At the start of the Battle of Algiers, the office published 1.65 million pages of propaganda material in January and February alone, thus far exceeding the efforts of the Algerian Office.[209] This gigantic campaign was meant to marginalize the impact of FLN propaganda in American public opinion, especially in United Nation circles, and replace it with the positive image of a prospering *Algérie française*. The work of the New York office also served as a model for other public relations work abroad.[210] With the help of all French diplomatic missions, the activities of the Liberation Front were to be combated throughout the world and France's own positions energetically put forth, particularly in countries whose voting behavior at the United Nations was uncertain from the French point of view.[211] On the diplomatic and propagandistic level, the Algerian War was developing into a conflict of global dimensions.[212]

In selecting topics, French propaganda was closely aligned with the defense strategy used at the United Nations. Publications such as *L'Algérie d'aujourd'hui*[213] and *Notions essentielles sur l'Algérie*,[214] which were distributed in the millions nationally and internationally, stressed the enormous French development achievements. Thanks to the presence of France, Algeria had transformed since 1830 into a modern country, in which the living standard of the entire population had increased significantly and over nine million French lived together in fraternal peace.[215] Special brochures on various topics like agriculture, trade, and industry were to illustrate in an impressive way the progress made in all sectors.[216] Therefore, the French focused on the reform efforts that would continue to help advance this positive development in the future.[217] In this context, Prime Minister Guy Mollet spoke in November 1956 of a "true social and economic liberation" of all inhabitants in the three North African departments,[218] while four years later de Gaulle's Constantine Plan was portrayed as the "battle for the full development of Algeria."[219] In publicizing this message on development, French propaganda relied on the impact of highly symbolic imagery. One example is found in the propaganda brochure *Algérie—quelques aspects des problèmes économiques et sociaux*, which featured in its conclusion a photo with the title *Le vrai visage de la pacification*.[220] This photo showed a young Arab girl with a little school chalkboard in her hands sitting happily in the lap of a smiling French soldier.

According to the French interpretation, the picture of peaceful coexistence and thriving progress in Algeria was endangered only by "FLN terror." Paris juxtaposed its own development achievements with the destruction and acts of violence committed by the rebels, who were characterized as a band of brutal "terrorists."[221] At the same time, colonial propaganda also blamed the Liberation Front for the suffering of the civilian population and accused it of having forced Algerian peasants to leave their villages and flee to Tunisia, thereby artificially creating a refugee problem.[222] Particularly with regard to the international charges of grave human rights abuse by their own security forces, the French side began to document the atrocities committed by the enemy[223] and publish these in "horror books." The publication *Documents sur les crimes et attentats commis en Algérie par les terroristes*[224] claimed it would open the eyes of the international public, which had been deceived by false allegations, to the reality in Algeria. The actions of the self-named Algerian Liberation Army were said to be actually nothing more than one continuous crime against humanity, civilization, and progress.[225] Evidence of these serious accusations was offered in the form of shocking photos of rebel raids in which only the horribly mutilated bodies of civilian victims were to be seen.

The publication *Aspects véritables de la rébellion algérienne*[226] also availed itself of this ghastly imagery of severed heads and limbs and slashed corpses. FLN slogans like "we are fighting for a just cause, a humanitarian cause" were placed next to photos of the faces of victims mutilated beyond recognition.[227] The inclusion of many shocking photos of children, women, the elderly, religious representatives, and doctors killed during attacks was to prove that the rebels' supposed struggle for liberation was actually a struggle against all forms of humanity. This publication, claimed the author, would enable the reader to evaluate better the fantastical fairy tales of enemy propaganda and recognize "the true face of the Algerian rebellion" behind the mask it wore.[228]

According to the French interpretation, this "true face" consisted primarily of the enemy's unchecked brutality, which could be effectively depicted particularly by publicizing the gruesome mutilations. Therefore, thousands of copies of the article "Les mutilations faciales au cours du terrorisme en Algérie et leur réparation,"[229] originally published in a medical journal and containing photos of people whose noses, ears, and lips had been cut off, were distributed worldwide to health organizations and medical associations.[230] The same thing was done with a special issue of the journal *Algérie Médicale* entitled "Les mutilations criminelles en Algérie" and dealt exclusively with this topic.[231] One of the articles in it documented the work of the special surgical children's clinic in Algiers with photographs of the young victims of FLN bombings.[232] Another article put forth the argument, supported by particularly horrifying photographs, that mutilation was an almost "characteristic aspect of Algerian criminality" from which neither women nor children were spared.[233]

The Melouza massacre also suited the purposes of French atrocity propaganda particularly well.[234] In a raid by an FLN commando in May 1957 against suspected supporters of the rival organization Mouvement National Algérien (MNA)[235] led by Messali Hadj, the Liberation Army flattened the Algerian village and killed the majority of the Arab inhabitants. The French government tried to exploit the incident to its benefit and depict it as a symbol of the enemy's barbaric cruelty, much as Great Britain had handled the Lari massacre. Propaganda posters declared Melouza to be the "new Oradour" and claimed that the rebels were in no way less horrific than the Nazi SS.[236] One highly illustrated publication distributed worldwide put the Algerian village in the same category as places of Nazi crimes like Lidice and called the massacre an act of genocide.[237] Voices from the international press were printed in it as proof that public opinion throughout the entire world sharply condemned the terror of the Liberation Front. Yet France flatly refused the proposal that the FLN submitted to the United Nations to establish an international inquiry commission on the Melouza massacre.[238] Apparently the concerns in Paris were too great that unwanted details of French warfare would thereby come to light.

Despite all its diplomatic efforts and the intensively conducted propaganda campaign, France did not succeed in winning any ground in the battle against the FLN for international public opinion.[239] The French international position worsened steadily because there were clear indications that its Algeria policy was failing completely and overwhelming evidence that its own troops had committed war crimes systematically. With increasing frequency, France was finding itself under accusation, especially at the United Nations, and diplomatically isolated. The situation was also exacerbated by de Gaulle's generally dismissive attitude toward the world organization, which he derogatorily called a *machin* (gimmick), and particularly by his extremely tense relationship with UN Secretary-General Hammarskjöld.[240] The result was a permanent boycott of the UN debates on Algeria by the French delegation starting in 1958 and a growing reluctance to cooperate with bodies at the United Nations.[241] At the same time, the admittance of new African member states strengthened the position of the anticolonial bloc, which now had the necessary majority of the vote in the UN General Assembly.[242] This new majority led to the passage of Resolution 1573[243] on 19 December 1960, in which the United Nations recognized the right of the Algerian people to self-determination and independence. The UN document also underscored the urgent necessity and responsibility of the world organization for the just implementation of this right. The Algeria resolution of 1960, which was confirmed once again a year later,[244] manifested the complete diplomatic defeat of France and the overwhelming success of the FLN strategy to internationalize the Algeria question.

Human Rights as an Anticolonial Threat

From a "Source of Embarrassment" to an "Anticolonial Weapon"

The concern of the British colonial secretary Creech-Jones in March 1949 that human rights could become a serious "source of embarrassment"[245] for the colonial powers was never as clear as it was during the course of the decolonization wars. France was being subjected to strong criticism by the anticolonial bloc at the United Nations for serious violations of the Universal Declaration of Human Rights and the UN Convention on Genocide, and Great Britain was not immune from such diplomatic attacks. Although the British had succeeded in manipulating public opinion in the Kenya case and had kept the war off the United Nations agenda, London was less successful in the case of another military conflict in its empire. In combating the Cypriot liberation organization EOKA, which fought between 1955 and 1959 against British rule over the Mediterranean island and for its annexation to Greece, British security forces had also used the well-known repression measures of collective punishment, detention camps, systematic torture, and arbitrary executions. Although the extent of human rights abuse on Cyprus never even came close to that of the Kenyan decolonization war, the issue attracted far greater international attention. As the "powerful third party" of Cypriot resistance, Greece was prompted to file an interstate complaint, the very first to be filed within the ECHR framework, and to accuse Great Britain twice, in 1956 and 1957, before the European Council of violating the convention.[246] In addition, the government in Athens put the issue of Cyprus on the agenda of the United Nations and justified this step in July 1957 by arguing the point, among others, that the British colonial administration had committed grave human rights violations against the Cypriot people.[247] In its petition, the Greek UN delegation referred to the numerous cases of systematic torture, which they called "crimes against humanity."[248]

The attempt to forcefully uphold their colonial rule and the intensification of the human rights problem linked to this in the overseas territories were the main reasons why Great Britain and, to a greater degree, France were being increasingly brought before the United Nations. The appearance of the Cyprus issue and especially the Algeria question on the agenda of the world organization time and again offered the anticolonial bloc the welcome opportunity to attack the politics of the colonial powers in general and to exert diplomatic pressure on them. In this way, the wars of decolonization acted as a catalyst that noticeably increased the intensity of the debate on colonialism and forced the United Nations to focus its attention more and more on this debate.

In reaction to the shared scenario threatening their colonial interests, Great Britain and France found themselves corroborating closely.[249] As early as October 1955, London promised the French government its maximum diplomatic support regarding the issue of Algeria.[250] In addition to greater military cooperation, the British ambassador in Paris, Sir Gladwyn Jebb, recommended to the Foreign Office that it issue public statements clearly supporting the French position and to instruct its own diplomatic missions in anticolonial-leaning countries to place France's Algeria policy in the best light possible.[251] In September 1956, the French government even requested that London use its full influence among the Commonwealth countries to get them to veto or at least abstain in the vote on including the Algeria question on the agenda of the next session of the UN General Assembly.[252] In return, France promised its British allies full support in the Cyprus issue, which Paris gladly did in light of the aggressive behavior of Greece during the debates on Algeria.[253]

This British–French cooperation continued even after a political solution was found for Cyprus, thus eliminating that issue as a matter of diplomatic confrontation starting in 1959. The two colonial powers still shared the common interest of preventing UN intervention in their internal colonial affairs and ensuring the strict adherence to the ban on intervention, as stipulated by Article 2, paragraph 7, of the UN Charter. The Algeria debate also played another very special role for Great Britain. In a secret letter written to the Foreign Office in July 1959, Harold Beeley, a member of the British UN delegation in New York, pointed out the major parallels between the situations in Algeria and in Britain's own settler colonies of Kenya and Rhodesia.[254] It was to be feared that Britain itself would soon be placed on the defensive at the United Nations, and it was highly likely that the debate on Algeria would be used as a precedent. For this reason, Beeley urgently recommended that Britain consider the future development in its own African territories when taking a position on the Algeria question. Moreover, he warned that the greatest possible restraint should be used in drawing any parallels to the French situation in North Africa, so as to avoid provoking an unwelcome UN discussion on Britain's own problems in East and Central Africa.

The close cooperation between Great Britain and France was not limited just to the two cases of Cyprus and Algeria. Starting in March 1952, when the French colonial minister Pflimlin and his British colleague Lyttelton first met, the two countries regularly conducted close mutual consultations on colonial issues being addressed at the United Nations.[255] As the importance of the anticolonial movement grew over the years, London and Paris expanded the circle of participants at these talks to include the colonial powers of Belgium and Portugal.[256] The declared purpose of these yearly meetings, which took place just prior to the start of each session of the UN General Assembly, was to coordinate their diplomatic positions on various colonial problems.

By agreeing on a common strategy, each country sought to defend its own colonial interests against the increasing number of anticolonial attacks at the United Nations.[257]

The continued development of the human rights regime became the cause of increasing headache for the colonial powers. Since 1948, the United Nations had devoted a great deal of effort in developing the two human rights conventions that, unlike the Universal Declaration, were to be legally binding.[258] Although the Human Rights Commission submitted drafts for both covenants by 1954, the ensuing consultations lasted yet another twelve years. Not until 16 December 1966 did the UN General Assembly adopt the International Covenant on Economic, Social, and Cultural Rights and the International Covenant on Civil and Political Rights.[259] Besides the diplomatic confrontation caused by the Cold War, another reason for the unusually long period of consultation and the controversial discussion on the content of these pacts lay in the objections raised by the colonial powers, who vigorously opposed any potential grounds for intervention in their colonial affairs.

In an internal cabinet paper of March 1952, the Foreign Office in London warned, for example, that the Eastern Bloc countries as well as Latin American and Arab states were instrumentalizing the human rights debate for their diplomatic attacks at the United Nations and thereby attempting to transform the human rights covenants into an "anticolonial weapon."[260] An incisive example of this development, it was argued, was the resolution passed by a large majority to include an article on self-determination in the covenants. The Foreign Office was referring to UN Resolution 545 (VI), "Inclusion in the International Covenant or Covenants on Human Rights of an Article Relating to the Right of People to Self-Determination," from 5 December 1952.[261] With regard to its empire, the British government considered such a step to be a "dangerous doctrine" and thoroughly unacceptable. The British did not consider self-determination a human right but merely a political principle.[262] In a confidential strategy paper dated October 1955, the British UN delegation explained why this position was so fundamentally important. Should self-determination be recognized as a right, the anticolonial bloc would be able to demand that the United Nations intervene in Great Britain's colonial policy on the basis of international law. Protection from any intervention in internal affairs as stipulated by Article 2, paragraph 7, of the UN Charter would thus be obliterated.[263] Therefore, London categorically rejected all concessions on this point and announced that it would not sign the human rights covenants should they include the article on self-determination.[264]

The dispute over the inclusion of articles on self-determination developed into one of the most controversial topics in the entire debate on the two UN covenants.[265] Like all of the other colonial allies, France shared Britain's oppositional stance.[266] The French government was also aware of the great danger that an international codification of self-determination as a human right would pose for the retention of colonial territories.[267] In a report on its own position in the Human Rights Commission from 1955, the foreign ministry at Quai d'Orsay referred to the major role that France had played until then in the development of the international human rights regime and again emphasized the French claim of being the leading inspiration in the realm of human rights. Yet at the same time, efforts by the anticolonial UN members to incorporate an article on self-determination in the human rights covenants were blamed for that fact that France now saw itself forced to adopt a reserved stance with regard to the pacts.[268] Because of its colonial interests, the "nation of human rights" distanced itself from the further development of the international human rights regime and, like the UN founding member Great Britain, proceeded to stonewall more and more.

For the colonial powers, the discourse on universal rights was increasingly becoming a serious diplomatic burden. For example, at the 1958 colonial talks in Lisbon with Great Britain, France, and Belgium, the Portuguese delegation expressed grave concern that the African and Asian UN members might exploit the tenth anniversary of the Universal Declaration to introduce a disagreeable debate on human rights and to launch once more some strong anticolonial attacks.[269] In London, the government was already particularly aware of this embarrassing prospect because, in addition to international actors, there were also members of the House of Commons who strove to instrumentalize the 10 December 1958 date effectively. Already in 1957 the Labour MP and declared colonialism opponent Anthony (Tony) Wedgwood Benn had submitted a legislative bill to establish a special human rights commission in the British colonies to promote dynamically the idea of universal rights throughout the empire.[270] After this bill failed miserably to garner support in Parliament, Benn wrote a personal letter to UN Secretary-General Hammarskjöld describing his initiative and announcing that he planned to distribute printed copies of his bill throughout the British colonies and Great Britain in order to campaign on its behalf.[271] Officials at the United Nations were thrilled at the idea, and UN diplomat Martin Hill offered Benn advice and encouraged him to continue his project.[272] In another letter to the world organization, Benn also announced that he would submit the bill to

Parliament yet again, including the reactions he had received from New York, on the occasion of the tenth anniversary of the Universal Declaration. He closed this letter by noting: "Even if success doesn't come immediately, the discussion the Bill stimulates is well worthwhile."[273]

UN Resolution 1514: The End of Colonialism and the Beginning of a New Human Rights Policy

Although the stonewalling of the colonial powers postponed the passage of the two human rights covenants by the UN General Assembly, it could not stop another important development. Starting in 1955, the ongoing process of decolonization meant that an increasing number of former colonies were now joining the United Nations as new member states. This wave of new members crested in 1960,[274] which became known as the "year of Africa"[275] in light of the independence of seventeen African colonies that year. The influx of new member states changed the composition of the world organization decisively and meant an enormous increase in backing for the anticolonial bloc.[276] The Colonial Office recognized that an immediate consequence of this development would be the increasing domination of African and Asian countries in colonial matters facing the United Nations. The new entries also meant that the voting ratio in the General Assembly had finally shifted unfavorably for the West, which could therefore no longer prevent a two-thirds majority by the anticolonial opponents on important issues.[277] The fear expressed back in 1946 by South Africa's prime minister Smuts that "coloured peoples" would dominate the UN had now finally become the political reality.[278]

The African and Asian countries took advantage of the favorable turn of events and began, during the memorable session of the UN General Assembly in 1960, to throw around the impressive weight of their new diplomatic power. The participation of nearly all leading statesmen, including Eisenhower, Khrushchev, Macmillan, Nehru, Nasser, Sukarno, and Tito, transformed this fifteenth session of all UN members into a summit of the highest level and made it in many respects one of the most unique events in the history of United Nations.[279] In the shadow of the downing of an American U2 spy plane over the Soviet Union, the debates in the General Assembly were first dominated by fierce Cold War confrontations, in which tumultuous scenes broke out. During the speech of one delegate, for example, the Soviet leader Nikita Khrushchev thought nothing of taking off one of his shoes and banging it on the table in order to emphatically emphasize his view of things. The Eastern Bloc leader was determined to use his three-week stay in New

York to attack the Western camp as much as possible. To this end, he brought up the topic of colonialism often and initiated a proposal to have the UN declare the granting of independence to colonial territories.[280] In this proposal aimed firmly against the West, the Soviet delegation demanded the immediate end of any form of colonial rule and the independence of all colonial territories. According to the way Khrushchev perceived the outcome of such a power play, this proposal would force the Western colonial powers further into the defensive and at the same time earn the Soviet Union the sympathies of the new independent states.[281]

Although the African and Asian UN member states welcomed the Soviet advance in general, they refused to back the draft declaration. The propaganda aims of the Soviet Union were so obvious that even Guinea's president Sekou Touré, who maintained close friendly relations to the communist countries, appealed to the Eastern Bloc not to instrumentalize the decolonization debate for its own political aims.[282] Under no circumstances did the anticolonial movement want to risk becoming grist in the mill of the East–West confrontation and thereby pulverized by the rivalry between the blocs. Therefore, forty-three countries of the Afro-Asian group under the direction of Cambodia decided to submit their own draft resolution to a vote by the General Assembly.[283] Unlike the failure of the Soviet proposal, this one passed by an overwhelming majority on 14 December 1960 as Resolution 1514 (XV) with the title "Declaration on the Granting of Independence to Colonial Countries and Peoples."[284] Without a single vote cast against the resolution, eighty-nine members supported it and only the colonial powers of Great Britain, France, Belgium, Portugal, and Spain and their allies Australia, the Dominican Republic, South Africa, and the United States abstained.

As a resolution, this declaration was only of a recommendatory nature and not legally binding. In reality, however, Resolution 1514 proved to be an epochal document, one that became the major point of reference in the struggle of the anticolonial movement and heralded the end of colonialism. In this context, the historian Evan Luard even calls it "the Bible of the anticolonial religion."[285] By passing this resolution, the global community finally had its say on colonialism. Based on the overwhelming vote by UN members in support of it, the resolution was endowed with a high moral authority. In the preamble, the UN document immediately made the continuation of colonial rule responsible for the increasing number of armed conflicts and called it a serious threat to world peace. Therefore it was necessary to end colonialism in all its forms quickly and unconditionally. To achieve this aim, the resolution declared that "the subjection of peoples to alien subjugation, domination, and exploitation constitutes a denial of fundamental human rights, is contrary to the Charter of the United Nations, and is an impediment to the promotion of world peace and co-operation."[286] At the same time, all peoples were expressly granted the right to self-determination, and the pretext of inadequate political, economic, social, and educational preparedness was never permitted to delay independence. Moreover, every form of armed action and repressive measures against dependent peoples was to be ceased immediately in order to enable them to exercise freely their right to complete independence. In all dependent territories, steps were to be taken promptly to transfer all power to the population there without conditions and reservations. In its conclusion, the declaration noted explicitly that the principles of the UN Charter and the Universal Declaration of Human Rights were to be observed faithfully.

Despite its far-reaching demands, the resolution did not contain any specific measures for implementation, nor did it provide for the creation of a monitoring body. Therefore, it was once again left to the Soviet Union to take the initiative a year later by strongly criticizing at the United Nations the sluggish pace of decolonization and urging a rapid implementation of the 1960 declaration.[287] In a draft resolution, the Soviet delegation called for the complete elimination of colonialism by the end of 1962 and proposed the creation of a special committee to oversee the process.[288] Once again, the African-Asian groups refused to support this proposal for the same reasons they had a year earlier. Thirty-eight of the members again produced their own proposal calling for the rapid granting of independence. It was adopted on 27 November 1961, by a large majority of the General Assembly, despite strong opposition by the colonial powers, and led to the creation of a special committee for decolonization.[289] This body, which grew from its original seventeen members in 1962 to twenty-four and consisted chiefly of anticolonial states like India, received the tasks of reviewing and supporting the implementation of Resolution 1514.[290] By way of direct hearings on petitions from non-self-governing territories, the compilation of detailed country studies, and visiting missions to the territories, the committee would gather the information necessary to be able to make the respective recommendations to the General Assembly and the Security Council.

For the colonial powers, particularly France and Great Britain, this development at the United Nations meant diplomatic catastrophe, because the central concerns of the anticolonial movement, against which the metropoles had successfully defended themselves for such a long time, were now officially being recognized by the international community of nations as irrefutable facts. Resolution 1514 denounced colonialism in general as a serious abuse of human rights and a danger to international peace, while at the same time it endowed the self-determination principle of peoples with a legally binding character. In establishing the special twenty-four-member committee on decolonization, the United Nations created an institution that could conduct independent inquiries on the state of decolonization and thus enhanced the importance of the declaration's stipulations. Furthermore, Resolution 1514 gave crucial new impetus to another key concern of the anticolonial movement, the fight against racism.[291] The International Convention on the Elimination of All Forms of Racial Discrimination, which the UN General Assembly passed by an overwhelming majority on 21 December 1965, referred directly in its preamble not only to the UN Universal Declaration of Human Rights from 1948 but especially to the 1960 decolonization charter.[292]

From France's perspective, anticolonialism developed in this period into the "Gospel of the United Nations,"[293] and dominated all international debates. The relationship between France and the world organization, which was already tense due to the Algeria question, worsened even further over this. The French government viewed the Declaration on the Granting of Independence as the base from which fierce anticolonial attacks were launched and attempted justifications were made to violate the UN Charter by intervening into the internal affairs of the colonial powers.[294] Consequently, Paris refused to support the UN declaration of 1960 and categorically refused to cooperate with the special committee for decolonization in any way.[295] The policy of complete noncooperation adopted by France in 1958 under de Gaulle in light of the debates on Algeria was thus being continued in a more adamant form.

In early 1961, the British delegation to the United Nations also came to the sober realization that, in the future, it would become definitely more difficult to control the situation in New York with regard to colonial problems.[296] At the moment, the focus of interest was still on Algeria, the Portuguese overseas territories, and South Africa, but international attention could soon shift to their own problems in Kenya and those of the Central African Federation, especially if security forces were once again deployed. Therefore, British envoys recommended to their government that London adapt immediately to the new situation and adopt a corresponding strategy to deal with the United Nations. Unlike France, the British understood such adaptation not as rigid noncooperation but as a flexible policy of cooperation.[297] It would continue to defend its own colonial position, but not at the price of open conflict with the United Nations, which could seriously damage Great Britain's international standing and ability to act. Through its presence in the various UN bodies and its active participation in the debates, Britain sought to exert the greatest influence possible on the decisions of the world organization, in order to help modify these and lessen their impact on the British Empire.

Therefore, Great Britain was also the only colonial power to be represented on the UN special committee for decolonization. Although the British had been against the creation of this body, they still participated with the objective "to influence its actions, to disarm criticism, and to hit back strongly at the Soviets."[298] Moreover, London began to distance itself from the colonial policy of its former close colonial allies because of the growing opposition within the United Nations toward Portugal.[299] In a strategy paper from December 1961, the British again reiterated their intent to cooperate fully with the United Nations and especially with the new states, but simultaneously made the point that this willingness to cooperate was not limitless.[300] Attempts from the outside to intervene directly in the internal affairs of their colonies would force the British to withdraw their participation and adopt a policy of "noncooperation." With this threat, which was only seen as a last resort, the British government was giving itself a back door should the situation in New York spin completely out of control.

UN relations with Great Britain and especially with France did not normalize until both countries had granted independence to most of their colonial possessions by the mid-1960s. The decolonization allowed both London and Paris to shed the international stigma of being colonial powers, which in turn enabled them to develop new foreign policy capabilities and influence. Among other things, this was expressed in a new attitude toward the international human rights regime.[301] For example, the French government began in 1962—immediately after the Algerian War ended—seriously to consider ratifying the ECHR. This human rights document, which France had helped significantly to draft and signed in Rome on 4 November 1950, had still not been ratified by the French National Assembly, primarily because of the war in North Africa and the associated concern that France would be held responsible on the international level.[302] The cases brought before the European Council against Great Britain by Greece for serious human rights violations on Cyprus served as a warning for the French.[303] Once the war in Algeria had ended, this central hindrance fell away, and Paris discovered the diplomatic advantages of ratification.[304] France could finally correct the difficult position in which it had found itself in the European Council as the only founding member to have not yet ratified the convention. At the same time, France sought to appease public opinion and effectively declare its unwavering commitment to the principles of human rights. The French now perceived the ECHR, which they had rejected during the war, as a certain guarantee to protect the basic rights of the European minority still living in Algeria. Although the ratification of the convention did not occur until 1974, this debate after the Algerian War ended was meant to demonstrate the will of the French government to participate actively again in the international human rights discourse and to distinguish itself once more in its traditional pioneering role as the "nation of human rights."[305]

For its part, Great Britain, which had already ratified the ECHR with reservations and had even extended its application to its overseas colonial territories in October 1953,[306] put great emphasis on getting the human rights article included in the new constitutions of the countries being granted independence. What was pivotal here, among other things, was the wish to long protect the interests of the remaining European minority, like those people living in Kenya.[307] Since British decolonization was not yet complete in 1962, unlike French decolonization, and London therefore had to take colonial sensitivities into consideration longer, the great shift in its position on the international human rights regime took somewhat longer, but then it was all the more substantial. Starting in 1965 and on the initiative of the Foreign Office, serious consultations began on a completely new direction for the entire British human rights policy and a more active role in this area of foreign policy.[308] Even the colonially oriented Commonwealth Office had to admit that Great Britain had demonstrated a very backward attitude until then with regard to the international human rights discourse.[309] This would change fundamentally by way of its own initiatives, such as the establishment of an international UN human rights seminar and its planned support for Costa Rica's proposal to create the office of High Commissioner for Human Rights at the United Nations. Britain wished to make a clear commitment to its new human rights policy.[310]

In the context of this new direction, London also gave up its reservations concerning the ECHR in early 1966. The objection to the individual's right to petition was dropped and the compulsory jurisdiction of the European Court of Human Rights was recognized.[311] At the same time, the British government also corrected its former position at the United Nations that accusations of human rights abuse leveled against governments on the basis of the intervention ban of Article 2, paragraph 7, of the UN Charter were not allowed to be discussed. In its new interpretation, the international community of states was indeed justified to scrutinize a UN member who violated its human rights commitments to the UN Charter and to make corresponding recommendations.[312] The British were thereby setting their sights not only on the communist countries but especially on the apartheid regime of South Africa. Because of its stance on the intervention ban, Great Britain had repeatedly found itself in the past in the diplomatic predicament of having to vote against UN action against the South African policy of apartheid.[313] Once it had politically repositioned itself, this hindrance fell away, and the British delegation in New York could take a clear stance against the racist regime in Pretoria.

The striking climax of this policy shift by the two former colonial powers France and Great Britain regarding the international human rights regime was their vote in favor of the International Covenants on Human Rights in the UN General Assembly on 16 December 1966.[314] After both states, with an eye on their colonial empires, had viewed the project with suspicion for years and blocked it at times, they now no longer saw any compelling reason to oppose the legally binding international treaties. Without colonial commitments, Great Britain and France did not have to hesitate to enter the two conventions, which both declared in the identically worded Article 1 the following to be an elementary human right: "All peoples have the right of self-determination. By virtue of the right, they freely determine their political status and freely pursue their economic, social, and cultural development."[315]

Chapter 7

Conclusion

You who are so liberal, so humane, who take the love of culture to
the point of affection, you pretend to forget that you have colonies
where massacres are committed in your name.
—Jean-Paul Sartre, September 1961

Today the colonial past has a notable place in the public and political discourse of the former colonial nations.[1] Particularly noticeable are revisionist
trends that attempt to glorify the role of the metropoles and place their colonial era in a positive light. Following an official visit to Kenya as chancellor
of the exchequer in February 2005, Gordon Brown said, for example, that
Great Britain finally had to stop apologizing for colonialism and should instead look back with pride at its major colonial achievements in Africa.[2] At
about the same time, on 23 February 2005, the French National Assembly
passed a law meant to regulate the way its own colonial history was handled. It stipulated that the curriculum in French schools present "above all
the positive role of the French presence on other continents, particularly in
North Africa"[3] and duly honor the sacrifice made by the French army there.
The law made absolutely no mention of the dark chapter of French colonial
history but exhibited instead the symptoms of national amnesia, as the British
finance minister had.[4]

For this reason, the historical analysis of the interrelated topics of colonialism and violence seems more important than ever. Contrary to other
studies in the field of "violent decolonization," this book does not look merely
at the historical events of the decolonization wars[5] or just provide a depiction

of colonial force.[6] The various violent phenomena of war crimes, detention and resettlement, and systematic torture are compared extensively for the first time using two case studies from different colonial territories.[7] In addition to this comparative aspect, the study especially pursues a new approach in which it concentrates on the link between colonial violence and the international discourse on universal human rights. These two topical areas have rarely been considered in connection with one another in scholarly study to date, even though both developments exhibit a great degree of parallelism and mutually influence one another.

During World War II, the Allies fought for human rights under the banner of the principles they shared, whereby universal basic rights served as the ideological answer to the totalitarian challenge in Europe and Asia. With time, the Atlantic Charter of 1941 developed from merely a declaration of intent to the foundation for the new postwar world order. By arguing that they were fighting for freedom and equality worldwide, the European metropoles mobilized their resources in the colonies. This mobilization led to decisive changes in the colonial structure and aroused expectation among the colonial populations that they would be correspondingly compensated for their major contribution to the Allied victory. In this way, World War II became the crucial turning point in the history of colonialism. When the war ended, the colonial powers discovered that an anticolonial movement was beginning to form, a movement that used the Allied wartime rhetoric of freedom. Leading anticolonial politicians like Ferhat Abbas in Algeria and Jomo Kenyatta in Kenya succeeded in giving the aroused expectations of the colonial populace a political dimension and thereby mobilized the indigenous population. Thus, the moral armor for the anticolonial independence movement was hammered out of the ideological answer that the Allies had used against the totalitarian threat.

As universal human rights were being established in international documents and within the context of organizations like the United Nations and the ICRC, the colonial possessions increasingly became a burden for the colonial powers. Universal rights were now, as this book clearly shows, in many ways a "source of embarrassment" and proved incompatible with the system of colonial rule. Therefore, Great Britain and France noticeably distanced themselves from the project of establishing a strong, legally binding human rights regime that was armed with tough measures of implementation. Instead of manifesting the declared principles, the colonial powers did all they could to shield their colonies from human rights debate and to protect themselves from any intervention in their internal affairs without losing face at the international level.

This undertaking proved to be all the more difficult the more critical the situation in the overseas territories became. Finally the colonial situation blew open into full military conflict. Inspired by the new international context, the anticolonial movements went on the offensive and demanded a rapid implementation of the newly codified universal basic rights. However, the European powers were not willing to let go of their overseas possessions. Instead, national interests motivated the governments in London and Paris to cling to their rule in the periphery and to attempt to recolonize and reorder colonial relations within the context of a "second colonial invasion."[8] The European refusal to make serious political reforms and concessions prompted the anticolonial independence movements to announce at the Fifth Pan-African Congress in Manchester in 1945 their intent to resort to armed resistance against colonial oppression. A number of decolonization wars resulted, during which Great Britain and France did not shy away from the use of massive military force, while at the same time playing a dominant role in the international human rights discourse on the diplomatic level.

The fiercest confrontations took place in Kenya and Algeria, both of which were settler colonies and, as such, presented a special colonial situation.[9] In these places, a system based on daily racism and exploitation of the indigenous population ensured white settlers a privileged position. Every form of concession to the African majority was seen as a threat to the ruling white minority. Thus, the white settlers fought bitterly against liberal reform proposals meant to accommodate the colonial national movements and thereby provoked a radicalization of colonial resistance to the point of open warfare. The Algerian War and the Mau Mau War in Kenya represent two extreme examples in which the two leading colonial powers attempted to ward off the process of decolonization and to defend by force their claim to power. Without a doubt, the two conflicts differ considerably with regard to the organization of the independence movement, the scope of military engagement, the duration of the armed conflict, and the number of victims. Likewise, there is a great discrepancy in their national and international import. Whereas the emergency in East Africa received very little public attention in Great Britain, the war in North Africa directly affected French society and deeply rattled the domestic policy of France.[10] The British metropole was also spared any direct attacks like the bombings by the FLN in France, and the military operations had only a very limited impact on British domestic policy. The same can also be said for the international consequences: the struggle for national independence in the Kenyan forest took place without any form of foreign support or international attention, while the Algerian War unfolded before the eyes of the entire world.

Despite these differences between the two decolonization wars, they also had some major things in common with regard to the use of colonial violence. While in Europe, Great Britain and France cultivated their democratic tradition and attached great importance to the principles of constitutional democracy, in Africa they resorted to measures that violated the norms of international law and the newly formed international human rights regime. The key findings of this book show that both colonial powers reacted in an identical way to legitimize the force being used. The combination of measures introduced by declaring a state of emergency in the colonies, the emphasis on the new military doctrine of antisubversive warfare, and the refusal to recognize the validity of international humanitarian law within their colonial possessions created the conditions that proved decisive for the unleashing of colonial violence.

In both of the overseas possessions, the state of emergency radicalized the situation in the colonies. The existential threat to the colonial system of rule increased the sense of besiegement among Europeans and became a catalyst to unleash more violence. The governments in London and Paris reacted to these dangerous situations by declaring an official state of emergency in the territories involved. The radicalization taking place in the colonies was clearly mirrored in the legislation accompanying the state of emergency and the *état d'urgence*, which was strengthened time and again during the conflicts. By abolishing all constitutional norms, each European metropole formalized and legalized the expansion of the colonial apparatus of repression by vesting its security forces with special unlimited powers for dealing with the indigenous population. For France and Great Britain, the incompatibility of being democratic constitutional states in Europe and at the same time authoritarian colonial powers overseas became particularly obvious in the colonial emergencies. On the international level, both countries campaigned to establish emergency-resistant basic rights in the human rights documents, while in their overseas colonies they resorted to emergency measures that meant a complete capitulation of elementary human rights standards.

Against this backdrop, European democracies such as France and Great Britain were not the stronghold and defender of liberal values but the source for the negation of basic universal rights. With a note of sarcasm regarding the pretentious self-depiction of Europe as the incarnation of respect for human dignity, Aimé Césaire addressed this paradoxical situation: "But let us move on, and quickly, lest our thoughts wander to Algiers, Morocco, and other places where, as I write these very words, so many valiant sons of the West, in the semi-darkness of dungeons, are lavishing upon their inferior African brothers, with such tireless attention, those authentic marks of respect for human dignity which are called, in technical terms, 'electricity,' 'the bathtub,' and 'the bottleneck.'"[11] At the precise moment that the West found itself intoxicated with the word "humanism," it was farther than ever before from being able to live true humanism.[12] Moreover, as Césaire went on to point out, the colonial policy of violence would eventually bring about the ruin of Europe itself: "They thought they were only slaughtering Indians, or Hindus, or South Sea Islanders, or Africans. They have in fact overthrown, one after another, the ramparts behind which European civilization could have developed freely."[13]

The military leadership of both colonial powers played a major role insofar as they developed new strategic concepts of antisubversive warfare in reaction to the anticolonial resistance. The British army leadership profited from the success of its military operations in Southeast Asia. Thanks to the "Malayan experience," Great Britain had a promising model for combating guerrilla warfare that could be pragmatically applied and further developed throughout the entire empire, as it was in Kenya. French officers, however, had suffered a humiliating defeat in Indochina, and the lessons learned from this were reflected in the ensuing theory of *guerre révolutionnaire*. Despite the divergent experiences, the highest maxim of both counterinsurgent strategies was to control the population. Likewise, both military strategies advocated and outlined the implementation of radical measures like detention, forced resettlement, and total surveillance by intelligence services.

It becomes particularly evident that the principles of international humanitarian law did not hinder the colonial powers in pursuing this strategy. Great Britain and France simply refused unconditionally to recognize the validity of the Geneva Conventions in their wars of decolonization. The conflicts in Kenya and Algeria remained, despite the expansion of international humanitarian law to internal conflicts, colonial wars without rules. In what the colonial powers saw as a legal fight against terrorism and subversive elements, all measures to restore order appeared justified. The governments in London and Paris did not consider any serious concessions to the Geneva Conventions until the military option had taken the back burner in favor of a political solution. The internationally illegal conduct of the wars in the Kenyan forest and the Algerian *djebel* could not be prevented by the International Red Cross, whose involvement remained limited primarily to missions to the detention camps. Yet even there, the ICRC delegates were helpless in the face of the systematic torture of prisoners or, as the case of Kenya shows, wasted what opportunities they had.

According to the official depiction of Great Britain and France, each country's troops fulfilled their mission "honorably" in what was called the "pacification" operations in Kenya and Algeria.[14] According to the articles of the Geneva Conventions, however, they were guilty of war crimes that clearly met the criteria defined by the Nuremberg principles for "crimes against humanity." In implementing their maxim of "collective responsibility," the two colonial powers created an atmosphere of fear and "counterterror" meant to deter the indigenous population from supporting the resistance movement in any way and thus to subject the people again to colonial rule. Therefore, systematic war crimes became a characteristic feature of colonial warfare and fulfilled the military objectives laid out by military doctrines of antisubversive warfare.

This was clearly demonstrated by the scope of the detention and resettlement measures. In pursuing the military objectives of counterinsurgency, the colonial rulers imprisoned hundreds of thousands of Africans in camps quite arbitrarily and at the same time drove over three million people from their communities, forcing them to resettle in "new villages." Granted, the aim of this action was not the annihilation perpetrated in the National Socialist concentration camps;[15] it was to discipline and monitor the African population. The detention camps and resettlement camps constituted the spatialization of the colonial state of emergency, used by the colonial state in its attempt to break anticolonial resistance and to restore the old colonial order. The massive number of deaths resulting from the forced labor, disease, starvation, and severe abuse linked to such detention and relocation did not deter either British or French authorities. Instead, it was simply accepted.

Torture was also a characteristic feature of the wars of decolonization in Kenya and Algeria. The old colonial tradition of "coercive questioning" developed there into a full-fledged system. Officials in London and Paris created the necessary framework for it by vesting their security forces with nearly unlimited authority. In this context, definitions of "state crimes" appear to apply here. Despite their international obligations arising from the international human rights regime, including the strictly prescribed prohibition of torture, both governments failed not only to prevent torture but also to take any decisive action against it when it occurred. Instead, the governments gave security forces a free rein to solve the "colonial problem" in their own way and then protected them against the emerging criticism. According to the strategic dogma of antisubversive warfare, intelligence gathering was an essential pillar of warfare. The military justified torture as a "legitimate" weapon and a lesser evil of the war. Such steps had to be taken because of the necessity to win the "battle of information" against the seemingly invisible enemy. For Jean-Paul Sartre, this attempt to legitimize the practice was nothing more than hypocrisy: "We were fascinated by the abyss of the inhuman. . . . The 'question' is not inhuman; it is quite simply a vile, revolting crime, committed by men against men, and to which other men can and must put an end."[16]

In the discourse on universal basic rights, the grave human rights abuses during the two decolonization wars played a completely different role in each of the conflicts. This was dependent primarily on the existence of a "powerful third party." Despite the efforts of various individuals, the Mau Mau never succeeded in effectively directing international attention to the enormous dimension of human rights abuse in the East African conflict. Thus they remained incapable of mobilizing public opinion worldwide and of exerting international pressure against Great Britain. In fact, the paradox of the Kenyan case was how successful the colonial power was in using the moral armor of the anticolonial movement and instrumentalizing the human rights issue for its own aims. Thanks to a near monopoly on information and a sophisticated propaganda apparatus, London was able to present itself to the world as the guarantor of economic and social rights benefiting the African population. At the same time, it used a well-aimed propaganda campaign about Mau Mau atrocities to stigmatize its enemy as the epitome of "bestiality," if not even the "devil incarnate." It was not the British security forces but the Mau Mau who trampled and hacked to pieces with their machetes the most basic human rights of Africans. The more horrifying the images and reports of "Mau Mau cruelties" were, the more successful British propaganda became in pushing the war crimes of its own troops into the shadows, in quelling the criticism of military operations in the crown colony, and in winning the backing of public opinion.

Whereas the decolonization war in Kenya took place completely on the sidelines of the international human rights discourse, its counterpart in Algeria experienced the exact opposite. During the course of the Algerian War, the competition for international public opinion became decisive for the outcome of the conflict.[17] Both sides used the human rights topic extensively to gain international public opinion in favor of their aims. France pursued a propaganda strategy similar to that used by Great Britain in Kenya. On the one hand, Paris emphasized its self-proclaimed achievements in developing the three North African departments, while on the other, a targeted propaganda campaign on enemy atrocities conjured up the danger that the "barbaric terror" of the FLN posed to the progress of civilization. Contrary to the Mau Mau movement, the Algerian nationalists did have a "powerful third party" in the form of their brother Arab countries, who effectively spearheaded efforts to introduce and thus internationalize the Algeria question on the diplomatic battlefield of public opinion at the United Nations. With its serious human rights abuses, France unwittingly provided the FLN and its allies with sufficient ammunition for the fight for public opinion worldwide, which was carried out very efficiently thanks to the worldwide network of the liberation front. Hence, during the Algerian War, human rights became a key topic of diplomatic contention, which was eventually decided in the FLN's favor.

The decolonization wars thus influenced the human rights discourse in various ways. On the one hand, they obstructed significant expansion of the international human rights regime in the 1950s and 1960s. Together with their Western allies, colonial powers like Great Britain and France were not at all interested in effectively protecting universal human rights and codifying them in binding international law because they were specifically pursuing a radicalized policy of violence in overseas territories like Kenya and Algeria. The governments in London and Paris saw universal human rights as a threat to their colonial interests and as a growing diplomatic burden. The right of individual petition and in particular the planned international codification of self-determination in the two UN human rights covenants were viewed as an "anticolonial weapon" against which the colonial metropoles defended themselves by a tactic of noncooperation at the United Nations.

On the other hand, the period of contested decolonization was also a type of testing ground and a catalyst for the new human rights regime after 1945; it was a period during which vast shortcomings were being relentlessly exposed, while at the same time crucial lessons were being learned for the future. This became particularly obvious in the advancement of international humanitarian law. As was shown, the provisions of the Geneva Conventions of 1949 were far too insufficient to offer adequate protection.[18] As the expert commission of 1955 revealed, this realization had already occurred during the course of the decolonization wars and had propelled the issue of addressing internal conflicts to the top of the agenda for the ICRC in Geneva.[19] In its Resolution 2444 (XXIII), "Respect for Human Rights in Armed Conflicts,"[20] of 1968, the United Nations General Assembly demanded that international humanitarian law be revised in cooperation with the ICRC. The result of the protracted process that followed[21] were two additional protocols to the Geneva Conventions, passed on 8 June 1977.[22] Reflecting the lessons learned, so to speak, from the wars of decolonization of the 1950s and 1960s, the first protocol expanded the protection of international humanitarian law explicitly to include "armed conflicts in which peoples are fighting against colonial domination and alien occupation and against racist regimes in the exercise of the right of self-determination,"[23] while the second additional protocol focused completely on the protection of victims of noninternational armed conflict. As this document expressly emphasized, these protocols were meant to develop and supplement Article 3 of the provisions from 1949. The loopholes in international humanitarian law that had become so sorely evident in the wars of decolonization were thus closed.

All in all, the bloody conflicts to dissolve the European colonial empires fueled the debate on fundamental human rights for a long time. The topic of serious human rights abuse in the conflicts in Cyprus and especially in Algeria became an integral part of diplomatic debates at the United Nations. For the first time, key instruments to protect human rights were used, such as the right of member states to file complaints and the allowance of mass petitions as guaranteed in the ECHR. The Algerian War serves as the most illuminating example. The systematic torture and summary executions by the French army greatly intensified the public awareness of massive human rights abuses in Algeria and prompted the first mass petitions to the UN Human Rights Commission in Geneva. Therefore, human rights did not simply become enormously important overnight in the 1970s.[24] Rather, this development also evolved out of the fierce anticolonial conflicts of the two preceding decades and climaxed in the passage of the UN Resolution 1514 in 1960, which explicitly condemned colonialism as a violation of human rights.

Only after the wars of decolonization ended and a surge of newly independent states joined the international community did the stagnation in the further evolution of the human rights regime, which had lasted more than fifteen years, come to a close and the former colonial powers like France and Great Britain normalized their relationship with the United Nations. Without the burden of colonial wars, these European states could now fulfill their self-declared advocacy for human rights. Without the burden of their empires, they could, for instance, decide not to vote in the UN General Assembly to support South Africa's apartheid system. At the same time, they were now in a position to attack the Soviet Union and the Eastern Bloc for civil rights abuses without running the danger of being harshly criticized for similar shortcomings in their colonies. The former colonial powers could increasingly deploy against the Soviet Union the same "anticolonial weapon" of human rights once aimed against them—a development that would achieve its ultimate impact with the Helsinki Final Act of the Conference on Security and Co-operation in Europe (CSCE) in August 1975.[25]

Notes

Preface

1. An excellent review of the literature, if no longer the most up-to-date, is found in Osterhammel, "Spätkolonialismus und Dekolonisation." Of the existing comprehensive studies, the following publications deserve mention: Albertini, *Dekolonisation*; Grimal, *Decolonization*; Ansprenger, *Auflösung der Kolonialreiche*; Holland, *European Decolonization*; Betts, *Decolonization*; Springhall, *Decolonization*; Thomas, Moore, Butler, *Crises of Empire*. For specific regions, see especially Gifford and Louis, *Transfer of Power*; Hargreaves, *Decolonization*; Birmingham, *Decolonization of Africa*. On decolonization in Southeast Asia and with an emphasis on the role of the United States, see Frey, *Dekolonisierung in Südostasien*. From the abundance of individual studies on the various European colonial empires, the following books represent work done on British and French decolonization: Lapping, *End of Empire*; McIntyre, *British Decolonization*; Betts, *France and Decolonization*; Ageron, *Les chemins de la décolonisation*; Ageron, *La décolonisation française*. Other case studies are found in Mommsen, *Das Ende der Kolonialreiche*.

2. On this point, see Darwin, *Britain and Decolonization*. Darwin reinforces the arguments he makes in his book *The End of Empire*, in which he extensively analyzes and contrasts the various theoretical approaches with one another.

3. Based on the central focus of their work, certain historians can be associated with specific theoretical approaches. For the "metropolitan theory," see, for example, Gallagher, *Decline, Revival and Fall*; Kahler, *Decolonization in Britain and France*; and Holland, *European Decolonization*. Representatives of the "peripheral theory" include Easton, *Rise and Fall of Western Colonialism*; Low, *Eclipse of Empire*; and Grimal, *Decolonization*. Examples of names connected with the "international theory" are McIntyre, *Commonwealth of Nations*; and Lapping, *End of Empire*.

4. The following are the exceptions: Schümperli, *Die Vereinten Nationen und Dekolonisation*; El-Ayouty, *United Nations and Decolonization*; Luard, *History of the United Nations*, vol. 2; Normand and Zaidi, *Human Rights at the UN*; Mazower, *No Enchanted Palace*, 149–89.

5. For a good review of the state of historical research and new perspectives in the area of human rights, see Cmiel, "Recent History of Human Rights"; Eckel, "Utopie der Moral"; Moyn, *Last Utopia*, 311–21; Hoffmann, "Introduction: Genealogies of Human Rights."

6. Lauren, *Power and Prejudice*; Lauren, *Evolution of International Human Rights*.

7. Simpson, *Human Rights*; Burke, *Decolonization*; Maul, *Human Rights, Development and Decolonization*; Cmiel, "Human Rights, Freedom of Information"; Madsen, "France, the UK, and the 'Boomerang'"; Moyn, *Last Utopia*, 84–119; Eckel, "Human Rights and Decolonization";

Ibhawoh, *Imperialism and Human Rights*, 141–72. The influence of fundamental rights on post-colonial constitutions in independent states is the main topic of the work by Parkinson, *Bills of Rights and Decolonization*.

8. One exception is certainly the work by Jacques van Doorn and Willem J. Hendrix on the Dutch decolonization war in the Dutch East Indies, in which the authors explicitly address the unrestrained used of violence. See van Doorn and Hendrix, *Ontsporing van geweld*.

9. Van Doorn and Hendrix, *Process of Decolonisation*; Clayton, *Wars of French Decolonization*. On the French decolonization wars, see also Ruscio, *Décolonisation tragique*. In their book of collected essays *Policing and Decolonization*, David Anderson and David Killingray also emphasize the special role of the colonial security forces in the process of decolonization in eight different conflicts. Bührer, Stachelbeck, and Walter, *Imperialkriege*, a 2011 German collected volume on colonial wars, analyzes and compares various war scenarios; the Algerian War is the topic of several of its contributions.

10. Holland, *Emergencies*.

11. On this point, see the section "Guerres de décolonisations comparées" in the edited volume by Ageron and Michel, *L'ère des décolonisations*, 9–204.

12. Füredi, *Colonial Wars*. See also his earlier contribution on the topic, Füredi, "Decolonization Through Counterinsurgency."

13. Bayly and Harper, *Forgotten Wars*.

14. The following publications could be seen as representative for this general trend in research: Benot, *Massacres coloniaux*; Ferro, *Livre noir*; Liauzu, *Violence et colonisation*; Le Cour Grandmaison, *Coloniser, exterminer*. For this development in research, see also Howe, "Colonising and Exterminating?"

15. Maran, *Torture*. For a more recent English-language publication on the topic of torture in the Algerian War, see Lazreg, *Torture and the Twilight of Empire*. Unfortunately, Lazreg does not include the findings presented in Maran's book in her publication.

16. On this, see Vidal-Naquet, *La torture dans la république*; Vidal-Naquet, *Les crimes de l'armée française*.

17. Branche, *La torture*.

18. See the republication of the book originally published in 1967 by Cornaton, *Camps de regroupement*, as well as Rocard, *Rapport sur les camps de regroupement*. In their book on the history of camps, Joel Kotek and Pierre Rigoulot also include a chapter on the internment and resettlement practices of the Algerian War: Kotek and Rigoulot, *Jahrhundert der Lager*, 546–54.

19. For Dutch decolonization, see the essay by Hirschfeld, "Kriegsverbrechen in der niederländischen Kolonialzeit."

20. For a critical review of both books, see Ogot, "Britain's Gulag."

21. The translation of all French quotes has been provided by the author, German quotes by the translator.

22. Special mention should be made here of Carey, *Crisis in Kenya*; Leigh, *Shadow of the Mau Mau*; Stoneham, *Mau Mau*; Stoneham, *Out of Barbarism*.

23. Law no. 79-18 of 3 January 1979, *Journal Officiel, Lois et Décrets*, 5 January 1979, 43. See also decree no. 79-1038 of 3 December 1979, *Journal Officiel, Lois et Décrets*, 5 December 1979, 3058.

24. For a detailed account of the archival problems pertaining to research on the Algerian War, see especially Branche, *La guerre d'Algérie*, 147–74, and Stora, *La gangrène et l'oubli*, 269–74.

25. Law no. 2008-696 of 15 July 2008, *Journal Officiel, Lois et Décrets*, 16 July 2008, 11322. I am grateful to Raphaëlle Branche for pointing out this law to me.

26. For an extensive presentation of French inventories pertaining to the Algerian War, see Goudail, "Les sources françaises." Abdelkrim Badjadja reviews in detail the entire spectrum of

the various national and international archival inventories on the Algerian War; see Badjadja, "Panorama des archives de l'Algérie."

27. Clough, *Mau Mau Memoirs*.

28. Barnett and Njama, *Mau Mau from Within*; Itote, *Mau Mau General*; Gikoyo, *We Fought for Freedom*. For a new source-critical evaluation of "Mau Mau literature," see also Alam, *Rethinking Mau Mau*.

29. Harbi, *Archives de la révolution algérienne*; Harbi and Meynier, *Le FLN*.

30. I wish to express my special gratitude for the support given me by Carla Edelenbos and Maria Ize-Charrin from the UN Human Rights Commission at the Palais Wilson in Geneva.

Chapter 1. Introduction

1. Calder, *Gangrene*.

2. Benenson, "Introduction," in ibid.

3. CO to the colonial government in Nairobi, telegram, 29 September 1959, TNA, CO 822/1777.

4. Memorandum, "Subversive Publications, 'Gangrene' published by Calder Books London," by the Ministry of Defence for the Council of Ministers, n.d., TNA, CO 822/1777.

5. See Belhadj et al., *La gangrène*.

6. On the handling of the violent colonial past and the related current debates, see Stora, *La gangrène et l'oubli*; Prost, "Algerian War in French Collective Memory"; Dard and Lefeuvre, *L'Europe*; Raben, "Koloniale Vergangenheit"; for a comparative perspective, see especially Howe, "Colonising and Exterminating?"; Eckert, "Colonialism in the European Memory." But even in the independent countries of Kenya and Algeria, the memory of the each land's war of independence was difficult and politically laden. In addition to the civil-war dimension between the various indigenous groups during the conflicts, this was due particularly to the prerogative of interpretation claimed exclusively by the postcolonial governments and the corresponding instrumentalization of the decolonization wars. On this point, see, e.g., Speitkamp, "Spätkolonialer Krieg"; Stora, *La gangrène et l'oubli*, 227–37, 302–16; Stora, "Algerienkrieg im Gedächtnis Frankreichs," 84–86.

7. With regard to the Algerian War, see, e.g., Sigg, *Le silence et la honte*, 21–28.

8. Grosser, *Ermordung der Menschheit*, 206.

9. Decree no. 62-328 of 22 March 1962, *Journal Officiel, Lois et Décrets*, 23 March 1962, 3144.

10. On this point, see Stora, *La gangrène et l'oubli*, 281–83. On the problem of amnesty and the role of history, see Branche, *La guerre d'Algérie*, 111–39. For the way in which the French state handled the official memory of the Algerian War, see especially Cohen, "Algerian War."

11. See Harbi and Stora, *La guerre d'Algérie*; Aldrich, "Colonial Past and the Postcolonial Present", 334–56. The first signs of a growing interest in the French public for the topic "Algerian War" were evident during the trial of Maurice Papon in 1997–98. In the course of the trial, in which Papon was sentenced to a ten-year imprisonment for crimes against humanity because he organized the deportation of French Jews during the Vichy period of 1942–44, his involvement in crimes during the Algerian War was revealed. The topic of particular interest was his role in the murder of two hundred Algerian demonstrators in October 1961, while he was the chief of police in Paris. On this subject, see Einaudi, "Le Papon des ratonnades"; "Bordeaux 1942–Paris 1961: Massacres à répétition," *L'Humanité*, 6 February 1999; Le Cour Grandmaison, *Le 17 octobre 1961*; House and MacMaster, *Paris 1961*.

12. Law no. 99-882 of 18 October 1999, *Journal Officiel, Lois et Décrets*, 20 October 1999, 15647.

13. In 1957, Louisette Ighilahriz was tortured for three months by "specialists" of the Tenth Paratrooper Division. She survived only because a French military physician was able to smuggle her into a hospital. See Beaugé, "Torturée par l'armée française en Algérie"; Durmelat, "Revisiting Ghosts."

14. Beaugé, "Général Jacques Massu"; Bernard, "Torture en Algérie."

15. On this point, see especially MacMaster, "Torture Controversy"; Cole, "Intimate Acts."

16. Beaugé, "Général Paul Aussaresses"; Aussaresses, *Services spéciaux*.

17. "Le tortionnaire et le terroriste," *Le Monde*, 27 January 2002.

18. Johannès, "Le général Aussaresses."

19. Gough, "Mau Mau Will Sue Britain"; Cook, "Whitehall Put in the Dock."

20. McGhie, "British Brutality." The BBC documentary *Kenya: White Terror* was broadcast for the first time on 17 November 2002 on BBC2.

21. McGhie, "Police Investigate."

22. David Anderson, *Histories of the Hanged*.

23. Elkins, *Britain's Gulag*. The book also appeared under the title *Imperial Reckoning: The Untold Story of Britain's Gulag in Kenya*.

24. For example, see David Anderson, "Britain's Dark Secrets"; McGreal, "Torture and Killing in Kenya"; Cobain and Walker, "Secret Memo."

25. Macintyre, "50 Years Later"; Kenber, "Colonial Files"; Casciani, "British Mau Mau Abuse Papers"; Macintyre and Kenber, "Brutal Beatings." On this, see especially David Anderson, "Mau Mau in the High Court;" Howe, "Flakking the Mau Mau Catchers," 695–97; Elkins, "Alchemy of Evidence," 731–48; Bennett, "Soldiers in the Court Room," 717–30.

26. Bowcott, "Mau Mau Torture"; Casciani, "Mau Mau Kenyans Allowed to Sue."

27. David Anderson, "It's Not Just Kenya."

28. Bunting, "Is This Our Hola Camp?"

29. Preston, "Our Guantánamo."

30. David Anderson, "Uncanny Foretaste." For references to the great parallelism in the waging of these wars, see also Curtis, "Colonial Precedent"; Younge, "Cruel and Usual."

31. Stewart, "Lessons for the U.S."; Whitaker, "History Lessons."

32. The film is considered to be the trend-setting masterpiece of director Gillo Pontecorvo. It was awarded the Golden Lion at the 1966 Venice Film Festival and was nominated for three Oscars, although prohibited that year in France. It was not shown in French movie theaters until 1971, and even then it was soon pulled from movie programs as the result of political pressure and several bomb threats. Not until May 2004 was the film shown again in France when it ran at the Cannes Film Festival.

33. Hunter, "Pentagon's Lessons"; Kaufmann, "What Does Pentagon See"; Gourevitch, "Winning and Losing."

34. On this point, see above all the published study by Major Gregory D. Peterson from the U.S. Army Command and General Staff College at Fort Leavenworth, Kansas, in which he recommends the French war strategy in Algeria as a model for U.S. operations in the Iraq War. Peterson, *French Experience in Algeria*, 50.

35. Arquilla, "9/11: Yesterday and Tomorrow."

36. The term "international regime," as used in this context, originates in political science and defines complexes of principles, norms, rules, and institutionalized arrangements for solving problems that lie in the interests of several countries simultaneously. For a more specific definition of the term, see Woyke, *Handwörterbuch*, 429–31.

37. Agamben, *State of Exception*, 50.

Chapter 2. The New World Order

Note to epigraph: Excerpt from a speech by Ralph Bunche in 1946, one of the architects of the UN Charter, on the way to handle non-self-governing areas within the new world order, quoted in Urquhart, *Decolonization and World Peace*, 12.

1. On Hitler's concept of a "New Order" in Europe, see especially Mazower, *Hitler's Empire*.

2. Lemkin, *Axis Rule in Occupied Europe*.

3. Ibid., 79.

4. Ibid., xiv.

5. The Convention on the Prevention and Punishment of the Crime of Genocide was passed on 9 December 1948, one day before the General Assembly of the United Nations passed the Universal Declaration of Human Rights in Paris. On the importance of Lemkin for the UN Genocide Convention, see also Mazower, *No Enchanted Palace*, 124-33; and John Cooper, *Raphael Lemkin*.

6. Hobsbawm, *Age of Extremes*, 109.

7. Berghahn, *Europa im Zeitalter der Weltkriege*, 158.

8. Mazower, *Dark Continent*, 140.

9. Report of the War Aims Committee, 4 October 1940, TNA, CAB 87/90 WA.

10. Edward Hallett Carr quoted in Acland, *Forward March*, 9.

11. Holborn, *War and Peace Aims*, 1:158.

12. Ibid., 165.

13. MacKay, *Peace Aims and the New Order*, 7.

14. For the "Sankey Declaration," see Opitz, *Menschenrechte*, 252-54. On the human rights campaign organized by Wells, see Whelan, *Indivisible Human Rights*, 42-47; Normand and Zaidi, *Human Rights at the UN*, 76-78.

15. Wells, *New World Order*, 127.

16. Wells, *Rights of Man*, 103.

17. Ibid., 37.

18. Roosevelt's State of the Union Address, 6 January 1941, in Rosenman, *Public Papers*, 9:663-72.

19. Ibid., 672.

20. The American newspaper publisher William Allen White quoted in Hoopes and Brinkley, *FDR and the Creation of the UN*, 27.

21. Rosenman, *Public Papers*, 10:228.

22. Notter, *Postwar Foreign Policy*, 36.

23. Lend-Lease Act in Holborn, *War and Peace Aims*, 1:34-38.

24. Text of the Atlantic Charter as a State Department press release, 14 August 1941, NARA, RG 59.3, Records of Harley Notter, 1939-45, Lot File 60-D-224, Box 13.

25. Kimball, "Atlantic Charter," 104. For more, see also Borgwardt, *New Deal for the World*.

26. Speech by Churchill, 24 August 1941, in James, *Churchill*, 6475-76.

27. See "Comment on the Atlantic Joint Declaration of President Roosevelt and Prime Minister Churchill" by Harley Notter, 11 September 1941, NARA, RG 59.3, Records of Harley Notter, Lot File 60-D-224, 1939-45, Box 13, 39-40.

28. Speech by Churchill, 9 September 1941, in James, *Churchill*, 6481-82.

29. Speech by Attlee, 16 August 1941, quoted in Louis, *Imperialism at Bay*, 125.

30. Memorandum, Churchill to Eden, 31 December 1944, quoted in Woodward, *British Foreign Policy*, 5:314.

31. Speech by Churchill, 10 November 1942, in James, *Churchill*, 6695.

32. Quote by Franklin D. Roosevelt, in his son Elliott Roosevelt's book *As He Saw It*, 37.

33. See the speech by Roosevelt, 23 February 1942, on the occasion of George Washington's birthday, in Rosenman, *Public Papers*, 11:115.

34. Willkie quoted in Louis, *Imperialism at Bay*, 199.

35. Welles, Memorial Day address, 1942, in Holborn, *War and Peace Aims*, 1:90.

36. Declaration by the United Nations on National Independence, 9 March 1942, NARA, RG 59.3, Records of Harley Notter, 1939–45, Lot File 60-D-224, Box 13, 3.

37. Macmillan, *Blast of War*, 75.

38. Quote by Franklin D. Roosevelt, in Roosevelt, *As He Saw It*, 74.

39. An excellent source for this is the State Department report "Official Statements of the United States Relating to the Promotion of the Observance of Basic Human Rights," NARA, RG 59.3, Alger Hiss Files, 1940–46, Lot File 61-D-146, Box 2. On this point, see also Whelan, *Indivisible Human Rights*, 24–30.

40. Welles quoted in Lauren, *Evolution of International Human Rights*, 139.

41. See the State Department report "Proposals for an International Bill of Rights," August 1944, NARA, RG 59.3, Alger Hiss Files, 1940–46, Lot File 61-D-146, Box 2.

42. Commission to Study the Organization of Peace, "International Safeguard of Human Rights." See also Whelan, *Indivisible Human Rights*, 36–40.

43. Tony Evans, *U.S. Hegemony*, 48–56; Mazower, "Strange Triumph," 385–87.

44. Declaration by United Nations, 1 January 1942, in Holborn, *War and Peace Aims*, 1:1.

45. Roosevelt to Churchill on the first anniversary of the signing of the Atlantic Charter, NARA, RG 59.3, Alger Hiss Files, 1940–46, Lot File 61-D-146, Box 2.

46. Simpson, *Human Rights*, 157. On the importance of human rights as an ideological answer on the part of the Allies, see also Normand and Zaidi, *Human Rights at the UN*, 81–106.

47. Address by Roosevelt, 14 June 1942, NARA, RG 59.3, Alger Hiss Files, 1940–46, Lot File 61-D-146, Box 2.

48. General George Marshall quoted in Kimball, "Atlantic Charter," 86.

49. Schabas, *Genocide in International Law*, 30–33.

50. Ball, *Prosecuting War Crimes and Genocide*, 49–53.

51. For the development and content of the codified Nuremberg principles, see United Nations, *Yearbook of the International Law Commission, 1950*, 2:182–95.

52. Crockatt, *Fifty Years War*, 41–42.

53. Gietz, *Neue Alte Welt*, 86.

54. See the excellent chapter "The Second World War as Race War" in Füredi, *Silent War*, 160–92.

55. Lauterpacht, *International Law*, 281–82.

56. Redfield, "Ethnological Problem," 81.

57. Myrdal, *American Dilemma*, 1006.

58. Tinker, *Race*, 46–47.

59. John Rankin in January 1943, quoted in Lauren, *Evolution of International Human Rights*, 150.

60. Commission to Study the Organization of Peace, "International Safeguard of Human Rights," 21.

61. Lord Moyne quoted in Tabili, *We Ask for British Justice*, 161.

62. Hobsbawm, *Age of Extremes*, 171–72.

63. Smuts quoted in Füredi, *Colonial Wars*, 28.

64. "Note du Directeur de l'Administration Générale et Communale à M. l'Ambassadeur, Résident Général de France à Tunis," 4 August 1939, CAOM, 81 F998.

65. Metzger, *L'empire colonial français*, 180–81.

66. Préfecture de Constantine, Renseignements, Propagande Radiophonique Ennemie, 30 October 1943, SHAT, 1H 2816; and Division de Constantine, Rapport sur le moral, mois de février 1944, 26 February 1944, SHAT, 1H 2812.

67. Du Bois quoted in Füredi, *Colonial Wars*, 27.

68. Von Albertini, *Dekolonisation*, 234.

69. Ansprenger, *Auflösung der Kolonialreiche*, 149.

70. Hobsbawm, *Age of Extremes*, 216–17.

71. Berghahn, *Europa im Zeitalter der Weltkriege*, 158; Reinhard, *Europäische Expansion*, 3:175.

72. Noel Sabine, memorandum, "Future of Public Relations," 18 March 1942, TNA, CO 875/14/9.

73. Lippmann, "Post-Singapore War in the East."

74. Buck, *American Unity and Asia*, 25.

75. U.S. Secretary of State Hull to the President of the Philippine Commonwealth, 13 June 1942, *FRUS, 1942*, 1:908.

76. Roosevelt to Churchill, 25 January 1942, cited in Gietz, *Neue Alte Welt*, 108.

77. Gandhi to Roosevelt, 1 July 1942, *FRUS, 1942*, 1:678.

78. Roosevelt to Gandhi, 1 August 1942, *FRUS, 1942*, 1:703.

79. Louis, *Imperialism at Bay*, 140.

80. Arnold-Forster, *Charters of the Peace*, 39–40.

81. Anthony Eden quoted in Füredi, *Colonial Wars*, 60.

82. McLaine, *Ministry of Morale*, 224.

83. Ministry of Information, note on propaganda to the colonies, 25 July 1941, TNA, CO 875/5/6281.

84. Smyth, "British Propaganda," 69.

85. See the discussions taking place within the Colonial Office TNA, CO 875/5/6; and Füredi, *Silent War*, 184.

86. Minutes by Dawe, 22 September 1939, TNA, CO 323/1660/6281.

87. Holbrook, "British Propaganda," 353.

88. MacDonald, note on telegram from British Guyana, 13 September 1939, TNA, CO 323/1660/6281.

89. Bourguiba quoted in Grimal, *Decolonization*, 117.

90. On this point, see the letter from U.S. Secretary of State Hull to the U.S. Ambassador in Great Britain, 27 August 1942, *FRUS, 1942*, 4:26–29.

91. Borgwardt, *New Deal for the World*, 34–35; Ibhawoh, *Imperialism and Human Rights*, 142.

92. Mandela, *Long Walk to Freedom*, 83–84.

93. Romulo quoted in Lauren, *Evolution of International Human Rights*, 191.

94. Azikiwe, *Atlantic Charter and British West Africa*. See also Ibhawoh, *Imperialism and Human Rights*, 152–55; Eckert, "African Nationalists."

95. Nkrumah, "Education and Nationalism in Africa," 39.

96. William Phillips to Roosevelt, 3 March 1943, *FRUS, 1943*, 4:205.

97. The following make up a small selection of contemporary publications dealing with this subject: Holcombe, *Dependent Areas in the Post-War World*; Julian S. Huxley, "Colonies in a Changing World"; Hinden, "A Colonial Charter."

98. Stronski, *Atlantic Charter*, 26.

99. Johnsen, *"Eight Points" of Post-War World Reorganization*, 3.

100. Stone, *Atlantic Charter*, 139.

101. Committee on Africa, the War, and Peace Aims, *Atlantic Charter and Africa*.

102. Ibid., 3, quoting MP Creech Jones in the debate over labor laws, 26 March 1942.

103. Ibid., 105.

104. Geiss, *Panafrikanismus*, 296–97.

105. Lauren, *Power and Prejudice*, 155–56.

106. On the international origins of anticolonial nationalism right after World War I, see especially Manela, *Wilsonian Moment*; Adas, "Contested Hegemony."

107. Ferhat Abbas, *Manifeste du peuple algérien*, 10 February 1943, in Jauffret, *La guerre d'Algérie*, 31–38.

108. Ferhat Abbas, "L'Algérie de demain: Rapport présenté à Monsieur le Maréchal Pétain," 10 April 1941, CAOM, 4 CAB 17.

109. Murphy, *Diplomat unter Kriegern*, 153–54.

110. Naroun, *Ferhat Abbas*, 93.

111. *Message des représentants des musulmans aux autorités responsables*, 20 December 1942, CAOM, 81 F768.

112. *Manifeste du peuple algérien*, in Jauffret, *La guerre d'Algérie*, 38.

113. *Additif du manifeste*, 26 May 1943, in Jauffret, *La guerre d'Algérie*, 40.

114. Khenouf and Brett, "Algerian Nationalism," 263.

115. See Dumett, "Africa's Strategic Minerals."

116. Anderson and Throup, "Africans and Agricultural Production," 345; Lonsdale, "Depression and the Second World War," 121.

117. See Killingray, "Labour Mobilisation," 68–96.

118. Killingray and Rathbone, *Africa and the Second World War*, 14–15.

119. Dockworkers of the African Wharfage Co. to General Manager Smith Mackenzie, 1 January 1943, quoted in Westcott, "Impact of the Second World War," 155.

120. Sabben-Clare, "African Troops in Asia," 157.

121. Grundlingh, "Recruitment of South African Blacks," 190.

122. See Holbrook, "Oral History," 149–66.

123. Itote, *Mau Mau General*, 16.

124. See ibid., 23; Parsons, *African Rank-and-File*, 193–94.

125. Kaggia, *Roots of Freedom*, 32.

126. Ibid., 28.

127. Albertini, *Dekolonisation*, 412.

128. Radio address by de Gaulle cited in Betts, *Decolonization*, 25.

129. For the French Empire during World War II see Thomas, *French Empire at War*.

130. Clayton, *France, Soldiers, and Africa*, 135.

131. See on this topic: Alexander, "Colonial Minds Confounded," 248–82.

132. Recham, *Les musulmans algériens*, 236.

133. Echenberg, "Morts pour la France," 379.

134. De Lattre, *Reconquérir*, 74–75, 131–32.

135. Général Pierre-Jean André, Commandant la Division Territoriale de Constantine, Rapport sur le moral de l'armée, mois d'octobre 1944, 6 November 1944, in Jauffret, *La guerre d'Algérie*, 143.

136. Les rapports des officiers des AMM, 3e Division d'infanterie algérienne, février 1944 à avril 1945, 1ère Division blindée, janvier 1944 à janvier 1945, SHAT, 11P 61 and 186.

137. De Lattre, *Reconquérir*, 74–75, 131–32.

138. De Gaulle, *Mémoires de guerre*, 3:32.

139. De Lattre, *First French Army*, 173–75.

140. Echenberg, "Morts pour la France," 374–75; Thomas, *French Empire at War*, 253–254.

141. See Echenberg, "Tragedy at Thiaroye," 109–28; on the topic of West African veterans, see particularly Gregory Mann, *Native Sons*.

142. Gary, *Case for African Freedom*, 152–53; Clayton and Savage, *Government and Labour in Kenya*, 234.

143. Itote, *Mau Mau General*, 12–15, 30.

144. Carson, *Life-Story of a Kenya Chief*, 30.

145. Shiroya, "Impact of World War II on Kenya," 97–99.

146. Sithole, *African Nationalism*, 19; Clayton and Savage, *Government and Labour in Kenya*, 233.

147. Dudley Thompson, *From Kingston to Kenya*, 31–32.

148. Geiss, *Panafrikanismus*, 283.

149. Kaggia, *Roots of Freedom*, 65.

150. Killingray, "Soldiers, Ex-Servicemen, and Politics," 527; Headrick, *African Soldiers*, 31–32.

151. Colony and Protectorate of Kenya, *Post-War Employment Committee Report*, 5–6.

152. Füredi, "Demobilized African Soldier"; Füredi, *Colonial Wars*, 83; Parsons, *African Rank-and-File*, 235.

153. Headrick, *African Soldiers*, 27.

154. Smyth, "British Propaganda," 78.

155. Füredi, *Colonial Wars*, 76.

156. Directive for BBC North African Arabic Service, 27 August 1943, TNA, FO 371/36249.

157. Note sur les activités américaines, 9 April 1945, and Note au sujet de la propagande américaine effectuée en Algérie par les Centres interalliés de documentation, CAOM, 81 F1006.

158. Gouvernement Général de l'Algérie, Rapport de la Commission chargée de procéder à une enquête administrative, sur les événements qui se sont déroulés dans le département de Constantine, 8 May 1945 and subsequent days, CAOM, 81 F768, 22–24.

159. Hashem, *United Nations*, 200.

160. Ageron, "Ferhat Abbas et l'évolution politique," 144.

161. Comité central des Amis du Manifeste et de la Liberté, Manifestation à l'occasion de l'armistice, 4 May 1945, CAOM, 81 F768.

162. Minutes by Dawe, 22 September 1939, TNA, CO 323/1660/6281.

163. Smyth, "British Propaganda," 78.

164. Ibhawoh, *Imperialism and Human Rights*, 157–60.

165. Sithole, *African Nationalism*, 20.

166. Padmore, *Pan-Africanism*, 154–58.

167. Michael Barnett, *Empire of Humanity*, 102–3.

168. Humphrey, *Great Adventure*, 10. For a long-term perspective on the human rights discourse, see especially Mazower, "End of Civilization."

169. Roosevelt's radio address, 9 December 1941, cited in Notter, *Postwar Foreign Policy*, 61.

170. Hilderbrand, *Dumbarton Oaks*, 246; Mazower, "Strange Triumph," 391–92; Moyn, *Last Utopia*, 46; Waltz, "Universalizing Human Rights," 51–52; Normand and Zaidi, *Human Rights at the UN*, 107–12.

171. Logan, "Dumbarton Oaks Proposals Ignore Colonial Problem," *Chicago Defender*, 9 December 1944.

172. Du Bois cited in Plummer, *Rising Wind*, 120. On the overall important role of Afro-American civil rights advocates in the fight for human rights, see especially Carol Anderson, *Eyes Off the Prize*.

173. Peter Fraser quoted in Lauren, *Evolution of International Human Rights*, 173–74.

174. On the role of nongovernmental organizations in creating the United Nations Charter, see Korey, *NGOs*, 29–50; Iriye, *Global Community*, 42–44.

175. Truman's radio address welcoming the conference participants in San Francisco is found in Truman, *Memoirs*, 1:94–95.

176. Hunt, *Inventing Human Rights*, 202–3. See also Glendon, "The Forgotten Crucible."

177. Burgers, "Road to San Francisco," 474–77; on this point, see also Waltz, "Reclaiming and Rebuilding," 438–40.

178. Johnson and Symonides, *Universal Declaration*, 30; on the significant role played by smaller states in drafting the UN Universal Declaration of Human Rights, see especially Waltz. "Universalizing Human Rights."

179. For more on the development of the UN protection of human rights, see especially Paul Kennedy, *Parliament of Man*, chap. 6, "Advancing International Human Rights," 177–205.

180. Preamble of the Charter of the United Nations, in Ishay, *Human Rights Reader*, 491.

181. Article 1 of Charter of the United Nations, in ibid.

182. Mazower, "Strange Triumph," 393; Normand and Zaidi, *Human Rights at the UN*, 132–33.

183. This was the opinion of *Time* magazine, as quoted in Divine, *Second Chance*, 297.

184. Logan as quoted in Plummer, *Rising Wind*, 149.

185. Lauterpacht, *International Law*, 33.

186. Lauren, *Evolution of International Human Rights*, 200.

187. Truman, *Memoirs*, 292.

188. Humphrey to Eleanor Roosevelt, 1 April 1947, UN ARMS, DAG-18/1.1.0 Box 4.

189. Benson, "International Organization," 302, 309.

190. Esedebe, *Pan-Africanism*, 164.

191. Final resolution "The Challenge to the Colonial Powers," in Padmore, *Pan-Africanism*, 170.

192. Final resolution "Declaration to the Colonial Workers, Farmers, and Intellectuals," in Nkrumah, *Towards Colonial Freedom*, 44–45.

193. Geiss, *Panafrikanismus*, 317.

194. ECOSOC Resolutions 5 (I) and 9 (II), in Tolley, *Commission on Human Rights*, 225–26. On the role of Eleanor Roosevelt, see above all Glendon, *A World Made New*. On the drafting process, see Normand and Zaidi, *Human Rights at the UN*, 177–96.

195. Humphrey, *Great Adventure*, 31–32.

196. Agi, *René Cassin*; Sluga, "René Cassin"; Waltz, "Reclaiming and Rebuilding," 441–42.

197. Tolley, *Commission on Human Rights*, 20.

198. Since then, 10 December is celebrated annually throughout the world as Human Rights Day.

199. Text of the Universal Declaration of Human Rights, in Ishay, *Human Rights Reader*, 493–97.

200. Lauterpacht, *International Law*, 61; Ignatieff, "Human Rights as Politics," 5–6.

201. Article 2 of the Universal Declaration of Human Rights, in Ishay, *Human Rights Reader*, 494.

202. Quote taken from the speech by Eleanor Roosevelt before the UN General Assembly on 10 December 1948, as quoted in Humphrey, *Great Adventure*, 73.

203. Cassin, *La pensée et l'action*, 118.

204. Humphrey, *No Distant Millennium*, 97.

205. Lauren, *Evolution of International Human Rights*, 244.

206. The UN Genocide Convention was not applied until 1993 when the ad hoc courts of the UN, the International Criminal Tribunals, were established for Rwanda and the former Yugoslavia. Mark Mazower points out how the two UN documents diverged, because the Genocide Convention focused on the interwar idea of minority rights while the UN Declaration of Human Rights clearly stood up for the fundamental rights of the individual; see Mazower, *No Enchanted Palace*, 129–30.

207. Best, *War and Law*, 80–81.

208. Forsythe, "Human Rights." On the process of drafting the Geneva Conventions of 1949, see especially Pictet, "New Geneva Conventions"; Bugnion, "Geneva Convention."

209. Pictet, *Geneva Convention*, 34.

210. Bugnion, *Protection of War Victims*, 336.

211. Tolley, *Commission on Human Rights*, 24. For a detailed account of this drafting process over the years, see Whelan, *Indivisible Human Rights*, chaps. 4–6.

212. Vasak, "Council of Europe," 458; Madsen, "'Legal Diplomacy'"; Buchanan, "Human Rights, Memory of War."

213. "Considering the Universal Declaration of Human Rights proclaimed by the General Assembly of the United Nations on 10th December 1948 . . . ," preamble of the European Convention on Human Rights, in Ishay, *Human Rights Reader*, 500.

214. Samuel Moyn even goes as far as to speak of a complete failure in the development of human rights in the postwar period. For him, the breakthough did not occur until the 1970s. See Moyn, *Last Utopia*, 68–83.

215. "Human Rights," FO report, 16 September 1948, TNA, FO 1110/116; "Communism and the Importance of Colonial Propaganda in the Cold War," Colonial Policy Discussions, U.S. State Department, 22 June 1950, NARA, RG 59.3, Subject Files of Durward V. Sandifer, Lot File 55-D-429, 1944–54, Box 7, 2; Evans, *U.S. Hegemony*, 79–83; Cmiel, "Recent History of Human Rights," 129; Normand and Zaidi, *Human Rights at the UN*, 197–200.

216. Lauren, *Evolution of International Human Rights*, 245–46.

217. Lauren, *Power and Prejudice*, 199.

218. CO to the FO, 31 November 1948, TNA, CO 537/3411.

219. Secret circular 25102/2/49, 28 March 1949, TNA, DO 35/3776.

220. "Publicity About the British Commonwealth and Empire," FO memorandum, 13 February 1946, TNA, FO 930/514.

221. See El-Ayouty, *United Nations and Decolonization*; and especially, on this development, Mazower, *No Enchanted Palace*, 149–89.

222. UN GAOR Resolution A/RES/44 (I), "Treatment of Indians in the Union of South Africa," 8 December 1946.

223. Smuts quoted in Tinker, *Race*, 111; for Smut's role and position as an adviser to the United Nations, see especially Mazower, *No Enchanted Palace*, 29–65; Dubow, "Smuts."

224. See particularly the new study by Burke, *Decolonization*.

225. New Zealand UN delegate Newlands, quoted in Morsink, *Universal Declaration*, 99.

226. El-Ayouty, *United Nations and Decolonization*, 56.

227. For the debates on the right of self-determination, see above all Burke, *Decolonization*, 35–50; Normand and Zaidi, *Human Rights at the UN*, 212–21; Evans, *U.S. Hegemony*, 132–38.

228. CO to the FO, 3 January 1951, TNA, FO 371/101435.

229. UN GAOR Resolution A/RES/421 (V), "Draft International Covenant on Human Rights and Measures of Implementation: Future Work of the Commission on Human Rights," 4 December 1950; see also Whelan, *Indivisible Human Rights*, 77–86.

230. UN GAOR Resolution A/RES/545 (VI), "Inclusion in the International Covenant or Covenants on Human Rights of an Article Relating to the Right of People to Self-Determination," 5 February 1952; UN GAOR Resolution A/RES/637 (VII), "The Right of Peoples and Nations to Self-Determination," 16 December 1952.

231. Final communiqué of the Asian-African Conference, Bandung, 24 April 1955, in Kahin, *Asian-African Conference*, 76–85; on the importance of the Bandung Conference in the discourse on human rights, see especially Burke, *Decolonization*, 13–34; also on the Bandung Conference, see Ampiah, *Political and Moral Imperatives*; Tan and Acharya, *Bandung Revisited*; Christopher Lee, *Making a World After Empire*.

232. Jean-Paul Sartre, "Albert Memmi's *The Colonizer*," in Sartre, *Colonialism and Neocolonialism*, 50.

233. Samuel Moyn argues that anticolonialism was not a human rights movement because it more greatly invoked the idea of self-determination and less that of human rights; Moyn, *Last Utopia*, 84–119. Making a similar argument is Afshari, "On Historiography of Human Rights," 51–59; Eckel, "Human Rights and Decolonization." However, in his book *Decolonization and the Evolution of International Human Rights*, Roland Burke convincingly reveals the very active role played by the anticolonial movement in the discourse on human rights within the framework of the United Nations. For more on the debate, see also http://www.humanityjournal.org/blog/2011/01/response-jan-eckel, as well as http://www.humanityjournal.org/blog/2011/01/another-response-jan-eckel. As is shown, leading figures of the anticolonial movement also explicitly referred to human rights in their arguments; on this, see also Lauren, *Evolution of International Human Rights*, 154–55, 214–15; Bush, *Imperialism, Race, and Resistance*, 225, 271–72; Von Eschen, *Race Against Empire*, 79–83; Cmiel, "Human Rights, Freedom of Information," 107–30; Waltz, "Reclaiming and Rebuilding," 445; Cmiel, "Recent History of Human Rights," 123–24.

234. Madsen, "France, the UK, and the 'Boomerang,'" 60–61.

235. Joint statement from the three British colonies of Gambia, the Gold Coast, and Sierra Leone, quoted in Simpson, *Human Rights*, 458.

236. Lord Cranborne on 20 June 1945 at the San Francisco conference, quoted in Holborn, *War and Peace Aims*, 2:576.

237. Schwarzenberger, "Protection of Human Rights," 187; on Great Britain's position in the emergence of the human rights documents, specifically in the preparation of the ECHR, see Geoffrey Marston, "United Kingdom's Part."

238. Hessel, "Un rôle essentiel," 254.

239. Secret circular 25102/2/49, 28 March 1949, TNA, DO 35/3776.

240. Secret letter from Governor Mitchell to Colonial Secretary Creech Jones, 29 July 1949, TNA, CO 537/4581.

241. Governor Kennedy to the FO, 7 June 1949, TNA, FO 371/78949.

242. Colonial Secretary Creech Jones to Governor Mitchell, 26 November 1949, TNA, CO 537/4581.

243. "Revision of Geneva Conventions," FO memorandum, 25 January 1949, TNA, FO 369/4143; "Civil War Articles," letter of the United Kingdom Delegation to the Diplomatic Conference for the Protection of War Victims to the FO, 19 July 1949, TNA, FO 369/4158. On the overall position of the British government, see also Best, "Making the Geneva Conventions" and Bennett, "Other Side of the COIN," 641–44.

244. CO to the FO, 25 June 1949, TNA, FO 369/4155.

245. Best, *War and Law*, 174.

246. See "Rapport sur l'activité du Comité international de la Croix-Rouge en faveur des 'partisans' tombés aux mains de l'ennemi," *Revue Internationale de la Croix-Rouge* 28, no. 334 (October 1946): 797–806; Durand, *History of the International Committee of the Red Cross*, 551.

247. Best, *War and Law*, 88.

248. CO to the Department of the Lord Chancellor, 29 September 1950, TNA, CO 537/5686.

249. Secret circular no. 37 of the CO to all colonies, 17 March 1948, TNA, CO 537/3413; CO to the FO, 5 June 1950, TNA, FO 371/88753; see also Marston, "United Kingdom's Part," 815–20.

250. Response of Governor Mitchell to secret circular no. 37 of the CO, TNA, CO 537/3422.

251. Lauterpacht, "State Sovereignty," 421–23; and Lauterpacht, *International Law*, 236.

252. For a detailed account of the years of debates on the right to petition, see Burke, *Decolonization*, 59–69.

253. Alston, "Commission on Human Rights," 141.

254. UN ECOSOCOR Resolution E/RES/75 (V), "Economic and Social Council Resolution on Communication Concerning Human Rights," 5 August 1947; on this, see also Normand and Zaidi, *Human Rights at the UN*, 157–62.

255. Humphrey, *Great Adventure*, 28.

256. "Enforcement of the International Covenant of Human Rights," memorandum, 1948, TNA, CO 537/3406.

257. "Human Rights: Petition to the United Nations," secret draft cabinet paper, April 1948, TNA, CO 537/3413.

258. "Human Rights," secret circular from CO to the colonies, 28 July 1948, TNA, FO 371/72810.

259. FO to the British delegation of the UN Human Rights Commission, confidential telegram no. 206, 20 January 1947, TNA, FO 371/67486.

260. FO letter, 22 April 1949, TNA, CO 537/4579.

261. CO to the colonial ministers of France and Belgium, April 1949, MAE, NUOI Carton 385.

262. Belgian Colonial Ministry to the CO, 20 May 1949, TNA, CO 537/4579.

263. MAE memorandum "Droit de Pétition," 15 October 1949, MAE, NUOI Carton 385.

264. Ministère de la France d'Outre Mer to MAE, 19 May 1949, MAE, NUOI Carton 385.

265. Lemkin to French Foreign Minister Schuman, 25 August 1950, MAE, NUOI Carton 595.

266. CO secret circular "Anglo-French Colonial Relations," 15 May 1952, TNA, DO 35/3842. On Anglo-French relations in regard to the situation in North Africa see: Thomas, *French North African Crisis*.

267. "Dossier de Défense contre les attaques anti-coloniales," MAE, NUOI Carton 537.

268. French Ambassador Bouffandeau to MAE, 8 July 1952, MAE, NUOI Carton 537.

269. "Minorités indiennes au Chile," French Ambassador Baeyens's report to MAE, 15 May 1952, MAE, NUOI Carton 537.

Chapter 3. Contested Decolonization

Note to epigraph: From the 1940 Republican presidential candidate as included in the report on his 1942 trip around the world; Willkie, *One World*, 184–85.

1. Confidential paper of the CO, 1 July 1957, TNA, CO 1015/1819.

2. Governor Armitage to the CO, 9 August 1957, TNA, CO 1015/1819.

3. CO to Governor Armitage, 10 September 1957, TNA, CO 1015/1819.

4. Mazower, *Dark Continent*, 195–96.

5. Osterhammel, *Colonialism*, 108.

6. Ibid., 110. For more about the justifications of colonial expansion on the glorified grounds of humanitarianism and the advancement of civilization, see also Conklin, *Mission to Civilize*; and Conklin, "Colonialism and Human Rights."

7. For the biographies and careers of several important leaders of the anticolonial movement, see Tinker, *Men Who Overturned Empires*. Criticism of Europe's colonial expansion has a long tradition reaching back to the eighteenth century; see especially Stuchtey, *Europäische Expansion und ihre Feinde*; with regard to Memmi and Fanon, see 387–90.

8. Fanon, *Wretched of the Earth*, 29 ("The colonial world is a world cut in two. The dividing line, the frontiers are shown by barracks and police stations"). Currently Fanon's ideas are again being discussed in research on contemporary history; see, among others, Eckert, "Predigt der Gewalt?" For a biography of Frantz Fanon, see Macey, *Fanon*.

9. At the height of colonial expansion, immediately after World War I, more than 600 million people, representing two-fifths of the world population, were under colonial rule; see Girault, *Principes de colonisation*, 17.

10. Memmi, *Colonizer and the Colonized*, 70, 74. Memmi's major essay and Fanon's book *Wretched of the Earth* were significant contributions to the canon of the anticolonial movement.

11. Memmi, *Colonizer and the Colonized*, 83: "At the basis of the entire construction, one finally finds a common motive; the colonizer's economic and basic needs, which he substitutes for logic, and which shape and explain each of the traits he assigns to the colonized. In the last analysis, these traits are all advantageous to the colonizer."

12. Ibid., 81–82: "Whenever the colonizer adds, in order not to fall prey to anxiety, that the colonized is a wicked, backward person with evil, thievish, somewhat sadistic instincts, he thus justified his police and his legitimate severity."

13. Excerpt from "French Colonization on Trial," in Ho Chi Minh, *On Revolution*, 82.

14. On this, see also Tibi, "Nationsbildung in den Kolonien."

15. Fanon, *Wretched of the Earth*, 27 ("Decolonization, which sets out to change the order of the world, is, obviously, a programme of complete disorder"). On the topic of colonialism and resistance, see also Frederick Cooper, "Conflict and Connection."

16. Mazower, *Dark Continent*, 210.

17. Grimal, *Decolonization*, 135.

18. Devillers, "Indochine, Indonésie"; on the situation in Southeast Asia, see especially Bayly and Harper, *Forgotten Wars*.

19. Rothermund, *Das Ende kolonialer Herrschaft*, 55.

20. Sukarno quoted in McMahon, *Colonialism and Cold War*, 95.

21. "Declaration of Independence of the Democratic Republic of Vietnam," 2 September 1945, in Ho Chi Minh, *On Revolution*, 143.

22. "Speech Delivered in the First Days of the Resistance War in South Vietnam," November 1945, in Ho Chi Minh, *On Revolution*, 158.

23. Springhall, *Decolonization*, 31.

24. See Dennis, *Troubled Days of Peace*; Bayly and Harper, *Forgotten Wars*, 137–89.

25. On Allied recolonization and the subsequent Indonesian war of independence, see Reid, *Indonesian National Revolution*.

26. KNIL stands for Koninklijk Nederlands Indisch Leger.

27. Groen, "Militant Response," 30; see especially the chapter "Justifying Military Action" in Van Doorn, *Soldier and Social Change*, 111–32.

28. On the way the KNIL conducted war, see Hirschfeld, "Kriegsverbrechen in der niederländischen Kolonialzeit"; Van Doorn, "Use of Violence"; Groen, "Militant Response," 35–41.

29. See Dahm, "Dekolonisationsprozeß Indonesiens," 86–87; Kersten, "International Intervention"; Luard, *History of the United Nations*, 1:132–59.

30. Beauflis, "Colonialisme aux Indes néerlandaises," 259.

31. Bayly and Harper, *Forgotten Wars*, 140–58.

32. Ruscio, *Décolonisation tragique*, 42–43.

33. "Accords Sainteny–Ho Chi Minh," 6 March 1946, in Dalloz, *Textes*, 31–32; Brötel, "Dekolonisierung," 104.

34. Benot, *Massacres coloniaux*, 98–103.

35. Shipway, "Creating an Emergency."

36. See Betts, *Decolonization*, 16; Osterhammel, *Colonialism*, 116; Holland, *European Decolonization*, 95.

37. Memorandum, "The First Aim of British Foreign Policy," 4 January 1948, TNA, CAB 129/23.

38. Darwin, *Britain and Decolonization*, 126; Darwin, *End of Empire*, 29; Hargreaves, *Decolonization*, 86; Füredi, *Colonial Wars*, 87. For a more detailed analysis of the policy of each British government on decolonization, see especially Heinlein, *British Government Policy and Decolonisation*.

39. Marshall, "Free France in Africa," 717, 748; Betts, *France and Decolonization*, 49–50; Ageron, "La survivance d'un mythe."

40. Ageron, *La décolonisation française*, 109.

41. Girardet, *L'idée coloniale*, 288.

42. Frey, "Drei Wege zur Unabhängigkeit," 401, 432.

43. Gaston Monnerville quoted in Girardet, *L'idée coloniale*, 195–96.

44. Diner, *Das Jahrhundert verstehen*, 257; Springhall, *Decolonization*, 63.

45. Ageron, *La décolonisation française*, 105; Birmingham, *Decolonization of Africa*, 89; Holland, *European Decolonization*, 74.

46. Hargreaves, *Decolonization*, 107–8; Crowder, "Prelude to Decolonisation," 28; Darwin, *Britain and Decolonization*, 139; Darwin, *End of Empire*, 117; Low, *Eclipse of Empire*, 173–76; Reinhard, *Europäische Expansion*, 4:136; Bayly and Harper, *Forgotten Wars*, 95.

47. Osterhammel, *Colonialism*, 37–38; see also Young, *African Colonial State*, 208–13.

48. Darwin, *End of Empire*, 89.

49. J. M. Lee, "Forward Thinking and the War," 64–79.

50. Malcolm Macdonald quoted in Constantine, *Colonial Development Policy*, 246.

51. On this point, see Fieldhouse, "Decolonization, Development and Dependence," 486; on the various colonial reform initiatives, see especially Frederick Cooper, *Decolonization and African Society*, 110–70.

52. CO, 21 September 1944, TNA, CO 852/588/19275.

53. See Morgan, *Official History of Colonial Development*.

54. Gordon, *Decolonization*, 37–39.

55. Cohen–Caine Committee Report, May 1947, TNA, CO 847/46.

56. Louis and Robinson, "United States and the Liquidation of British Empire," 51, 55.

57. Circular dispatch from Creech Jones to the African governors, 25 February 1947, in Hyam, *End of Empire*, 1:119–29.

58. Dispatch from Mitchell to Creech Jones, commenting on the circular dispatch, 30 May 1947, in Hyam, *End of Empire*, 1:129–41; Pratt, "Transfer of Power in East Africa," 259–60.

59. McIntyre, *British Decolonization*, 34; Darwin, *Britain and Decolonization*, 138.

60. Stockwell, "British Imperial Policy," 78.

61. Constantine, *Colonial Development Policy*, 303–4; Betts, *Decolonization*, 29.

62. Hargreaves, *Decolonization*, 59–61.

63. On this point, see Füredi, *New Ideology of Imperialism*.

64. On this point, see *La conférence africaine française, Brazzaville, 30 janvier 1944–8 février 1944*; Lemesle, *Conférence de Brazzaville de 1944*.

65. "Recommendations de la Conférence de Brazzaville, 6 février 1944," in Dalloz, *Textes*, 20–22.

66. René Pleven quoted in Grimal, *Decolonization*, 125.

67. Person, *French West Africa and Decolonization*, 144; Betts, *France and Decolonization*, 59; Pervillé, *Empire français*, 101.

68. Bessis, "L'opposition France–États-Unis," 344; Ageron, *La décolonisation française*, 134.

69. Aldrich, *Greater France*, 281.

70. Tony Smith, "Patterns in the Transfer of Power," 91; Springhall, *Decolonization*, 25.

71. Ageron, *La décolonisation française*, 118–19; Suret-Canale, "From Colonization to Independence," 449–52.

72. See "L'Union française dans la Constitution de 1946," in Dalloz, *Textes*, 36–39.

73. Aldrich, *Greater France*, 282; Betts, *France and Decolonization*, 71.

74. Pervillé, *Empire français*, 112.

75. Füredi, *Colonial Wars*, 36–37.

76. Ibid., 52.

77. "Kenya To-day, Equality Is Our Slogan," *Pan-Africa*, June 1947, 7–8.

78. On the French wars of decolonization, see Clayton, *Wars of French Decolonization*.

79. On the unrest, see Jauffret, "Origins of the Algerian War," 19–22; Planche, "La répression civile"; Benot, *Massacres coloniaux*, 9–19; Tabet, *Le 8 mai 1945 en Algérie*; Thomas, "Colonial Minds and Colonial Violence," 140–73.

80. Benot, *Massacres coloniaux*, 14; Baier, "Gefangen in Algier."

81. Benot, *Massacres coloniaux*, 79.

82. On the uprising in Madagascar, see Tronchon, *L'insurrection malgache*; Koerner, *Madagascar*, 329–55; Benot, *Massacres coloniaux*, 114–23; Clayton, *Wars of French Decolonization*, 79–87.

83. Boiteau, "Moramanga, l'Oradour malgache." Oradour-sur-Glane is a town in west-central France. The original village was destroyed on 10 June 1944 by German Waffen-SS, who massacred 642 villagers reportedly in retaliation for local partisan activity.

84. Weigert, *Traditional Religion and Guerrilla Warfare*, 19.

85. On the French war in Indochina, see Dalloz, *War in Indo-China*; Clayton, *Wars of French Decolonization*, 39–78.

86. On the battle of Dien Bien Phu, see Frey, "Dien Bien Phu," 358–73; Windrow, *Last Valley*.

87. Ruscio, *Décolonisation tragique*, 223.

88. Benot, *Massacres coloniaux*, 146–58; Benot, "La décolonisation de l'Afrique française," 532–34.

89. Clayton, "Emergency in Morocco," 135.

90. Ruscio, *Décolonisation tragique*, 93.

91. General Garbay quoted in Julien, *Tunisie devint indépendante*, 51.

92. McIntyre, *British Decolonization*, 33; Holland, *European Decolonization*, 81.

93. Darwin, *End of Empire*, 21; Reinhard, *Europäische Expansion*, 3:189; Rothermund, *Das Ende kolonialer Herrschaft*, 101–2; Charles Smith, "Communal Conflict and Insurrection," 62.

94. Füredi, *Colonial Wars*, 88–89, 143.

95. David Anderson and David Killingray, "An Orderly Retreat? Policing the End of Empire," in Anderson and Killingray, *Policing and Decolonization*, 1.

96. Füredi, "Britain's Colonial Emergencies," 253; Darwin, "Central African Emergency," 217.

97. Gurney to Secretary of State, 30 May 1949, TNA, DEFE 11/33.

98. Füredi, *Colonial Wars*, 191.

99. Arden Clarke, General Strike, January 1950, Gold Coast, TNA, CO 537/5812.

100. Füredi, "Creating a Breathing Space," 93–94; Füredi, "Britain's Colonial Emergencies," 261.

101. On the decolonization war in Malaya, see Coates, *Suppressing Insurgency*; Short, *Communist Insurrection in Malaya*; Lawrence James, *Imperial Rearguard*, 137–57; Bayly and Harper, *Forgotten Wars*, 407–56.

102. Springhall, *Decolonization*, 55.

103. On the decolonization war in Cyprus, see Holland, "Never, Never Land," 148–76; Holland, *Britain and the Revolt in Cyprus*; Crawshaw, *Cyprus Revolt*.

104. Ethniki Organosis Kyprion Agoniston (EOKA), in English, is the National Organization of Cypriot Fighters.

105. David Anderson, "Cyprus Emergency," 187.

106. See also the detailed account "The First Cyprus Case," in Simpson, *Human Rights*, 924–89.

107. On the British conquest of Kenya, see Lonsdale, "Conquest State of Kenya."

108. Muriuki, *History of the Kikuyu*, 15.

109. Hindlip, *British East Africa*, 48.

110. Meinertzhagen, *Kenya Diary*, 51.

111. Ibid., 158.

112. Elspeth Huxley, *White Man's Country.*

113. See Sorrenson, *Land Reform in the Kikuyu Country*, 15–33.

114. Osterhammel, *Colonialism*, 7; on the history of white settlement in Kenya, see especially Sorrenson, *Origins of European Settlement in Kenya.*

115. Statement by Rhodesia's prime minister Godfrey Huggins, 1938, quoted in Dane Kennedy, *Islands of White*, 2.

116. Quoted in Edgerton, *Mau Mau*, 21.

117. Ochieng' and Atieno-Odhiambo, "On Decolonization," xv.

118. Frost, *Race Against Time*, 103–4.

119. Kennedy, *Islands of White*, 148–49.

120. For more about the dependence of white settlers on the African labor force, see Mosley, *Settler Economies*, 5–8.

121. Lord Cranworth considers the Kikuyu to be "economically useful," although he labels the Masai as "economically useless"; see Cranworth, *Colony in the Making*, 25.

122. Füredi, *Mau Mau War*, 10; on the development of the squatter system, see also Frederick Cooper, *From Slaves to Squatters.*

123. Kanogo, *Squatters*, 9.

124. Füredi, *Mau Mau War*, 29.

125. David Anderson, *Histories of the Hanged*, 77–78.

126. David Anderson, "Master and Servant," 472.

127. Edgerton, *Mau Mau*, 45.

128. Buijtenhuijs, *Le mouvement "Mau Mau,"* 130.

129. Government of the U.K., *Memorandum Relating to Indians in Kenya.*

130. Government of the U.K., *Report of the Kenya Land Commission.*

131. Maloba, *Mau Mau and Kenya*, 49.

132. Holland, *European Decolonization*, 144; Springhall, *Decolonization*, 157.

133. Füredi, *Mau Mau War*, 31.

134. Kanogo, *Squatters*, 105.

135. Throup, *Economic and Social Origins*, 110.

136. On this point, see Lewis, *Empire State-Building.*

137. Gordon, *Decolonization*, 86.

138. Hargreaves, *Decolonization*, 129; Darwin, *Britain and Decolonization*, 184.

139. Berman, *Control and Crisis*, 286–87.

140. Pratt, "Transfer of Power in East Africa," 261.

141. Berman, *Control and Crisis*, 274.

142. Berman, "Bureaucracy & Incumbent Violence," 228.

143. Chief Koinange quoted in Dudley Thompson, *From Kingston to Kenya*, 61.

144. Kershaw, *Mau Mau*, 213.

145. Throup, *Economic and Social Origins*, 25.

146. On this see Easterbrook, "Kenyan Askari in World War II"; Kershaw, *Mau Mau*, 221; Kaggia, *Roots of Freedom*, 66.

147. Berman, *Control and Crisis*, 300; Throup, *Economic and Social Origins*, 239–40.

148. Kershaw, *Mau Mau*, 216.

149. Kenyatta, *Facing Mount Kenya.*

150. Kenyatta, *Kenya: Land of Conflict*, 22.

151. Ogot, "Mau Mau and Nationhood," 18.

152. Electors' Union, *Kenya Plan*.

153. Kanogo, *Squatters*, 130; Ogot, "Mau Mau and Nationhood," 19; Kaggia, *Roots of Freedom*, 112.

154. Kariuki, *Mau Mau Detainee*, 22.

155. Füredi, *Mau Mau War*, 41.

156. On this point, see Füredi, "African Crowd in Nairobi."

157. Anderson, *Histories of the Hanged*, 36–37.

158. Rosberg and Nottingham, *Myth of Mau Mau*, 268; Buijtenhuijs, *Essays on Mau Mau*, 12–13.

159. Itote, *Mau Mau General*, 273.

160. Edgerton, *Mau Mau*, 61.

161. Ibid., 56.

162. Particularly in the white settler literature, the Mau Mau were described as the brutal return to "African barbarism"; see Leakey, *Defeating Mau Mau*; Carey, *Crisis in Kenya*; Leigh, *Shadow of the Mau Mau*; Stoneham, *Mau Mau*.

163. Government of the U.K., *Report to the Secretary of State for the Colonies by the Parliamentary Delegation to Kenya*, 4.

164. Mitchell, *African Afterthoughts*, xvii–xviii.

165. Mohamed Mathu quoted in Don Barnett, *Urban Guerrilla*, 15.

166. Rosberg and Nottingham, *Myth of Mau Mau*, xvii. A number of scientists have adopted this viewpoint and emphasize the national character of the Mau Mau movement; see Clayton, *Counter-Insurgency*, 1; Maloba, *Mau Mau and Kenya*, 171; Füredi, *Mau Mau War*, 142.

167. Barnett and Njama, *Mau Mau from Within*, 199–200; Buijtenhuijs, *Essays on Mau Mau*, 149, 154.

168. Mau Mau cofounder Eluid Mutonyi quoted in Buijtenhuijs, *Essays on Mau Mau*, 143.

169. Barnett, *Urban Guerrilla*, 8.

170. For an organizational diagram of the various Mau Mau councils, see Buijtenhuijs, *Le mouvement "Mau Mau,"* 186.

171. Anderson, *Histories of the Hanged*, 43.

172. Corfield, *Historical Survey*.

173. Newsinger, "Revolt and Repression in Kenya," 168–69.

174. "Mau Mau Shoot Africa's Churchill," *Daily Mail*, 8 October 1952.

175. Clayton, *Counter-Insurgency*, 13–15; Anderson, *Histories of the Hanged*, 62.

176. Buijtenhuijs, *Essays on Mau Mau*, 43; Ogot, "Mau Mau and Nationhood," 20–21.

177. Füredi, "Decolonization Through Counterinsurgency," 144.

178. Barnett and Njama, *Mau Mau from Within*, 71.

179. Barnett, *Urban Guerrilla*, 17.

180. Rosberg and Nottingham, *Myth of Mau Mau*, 277.

181. Füredi, *Colonial Wars*, 154; Maloba, *Mau Mau and Kenya*, 114.

182. A detailed description of a Mau Mau camp is found in Barnett and Njama, *Mau Mau from Within*, 159–68.

183. On camp rules, see ibid., 164–66; Gikoyo, *We Fought for Freedom*, 62; Kinyatti, *Kenya's Freedom Struggle*, 21–22.

184. Itote, *Mau Mau General*, 27; Weigert, *Traditional Religion and Guerrilla Warfare*, 29.

185. See Jackson, "Survival Craft in the Mau Mau Forest Movement."

186. Derek Peterson, "Writing in Revolution," 91–93.

187. Edgerton, *Mau Mau*, 122–23.

188. On the Kenyan Parliament, see Barnett and Njama, *Mau Mau from Within*, 329–74.

189. Maloba, *Mau Mau and Kenya*, 129–30.

190. Quote from the Mau Mau general Kareba in 1954 in answer to a British demand that the Mau Mau surrender, in Itote, *Mau Mau General*, 189.

191. Kaggia, *Roots of Freedom*, 194; Barnett, *Urban Guerrilla*, 37. The national goals and national character of the Land Freedom Army are emphasized especially by the Kenyan historian Maina wa Kinyatti in his book *Kenya's Freedom Struggle: The Dedan Kimathi Papers*, in which he publishes the various documents of the independence movement; see, above all, the Kenya Land Freedom Army Charter, at 16–17.

192. Barnett, *Urban Guerrilla*, 26.

193. James, *Imperial Rearguard*, 182; Clayton, *Warfare in Africa*, 12.

194. A detailed account of these attacks is found in Anderson, *Histories of the Hanged*, 86–95.

195. Buijtenhuijs, *Le mouvement "Mau Mau,"* 203.

196. Edgerton, *Mau Mau*, 106.

197. On the tactics of the Mau Mau, see Itote, *Mau Mau in Action*.

198. Itote, *Mau Mau General*, 83.

199. On the Lari massacre, see Anderson, *Histories of the Hanged*, 119–80; Edgerton, *Mau Mau*, 79.

200. Buijtenhuijs, *Essays on Mau Mau*, 171; Buijtenhuijs, *Le mouvement "Mau Mau,"* 343–64. For the civil-war dimension of the conflict, see especially Branch, *Defeating Mau Mau*.

201. The Irish lawyer Peter Evans describes the ensuing retaliatory measures in his book *Law and Disorder*, 170–71, 187–88.

202. Directive to C-in-C East Africa, Top Secret, 27 May 1953, TNA, PREM 11/472.

203. Edgerton, *Mau Mau*, 85.

204. Buijtenhuijs, *Le mouvement "Mau Mau,"* 214.

205. Weigert, *Traditional Religion and Guerrilla Warfare*, 33.

206. Füredi, "Decolonization Through Counterinsurgency," 151.

207. Maloba, *Mau Mau and Kenya*, 83–84.

208. "Operation Anvil, Outline Plan by Joint Commanders, Top Secret," TNA, WO 276/448.

209. Governor of Kenya to Secretary of State for the Colonies, secret telegram, 13 May 1954, TNA, DO 35/5352.

210. General Erskine, "The Kenya Emergency, June 1953–May 1955," TNA, WO 276/511.

211. Edgerton, *Mau Mau*, 93; Anderson, *Histories of the Hanged*, 268.

212. Füredi, "Decolonization Through Counterinsurgency," 155.

213. Maloba, *Mau Mau and Kenya*, 88–90; Branch, *Defeating Mau Mau*, 66–88.

214. Barnett and Njama, *Mau Mau from Within*, 375; Gikoyo, *We Fought for Freedom*, 179.

215. Edgerton, *Mau Mau*, 99–100.

216. Clayton, *Counter-Insurgency*, 30; Mockaitis, *British Counterinsurgency*, 132.

217. See Henderson, *Hunt for Kimathi*.

218. For statistics on the death toll, see Corfield, *Historical Survey*, 316.

219. David Anderson assumes the number of dead to be over 20,000, while Caroline Elkins speaks of more than 100,000 victims; see Anderson, *Histories of the Hanged*, 4; Elkins, *Britain's Gulag*, xiv. John Blacker considers Elkins's estimations on the number of casualties to be exaggerated and comes to the conclusion in his own study that the maximum figure was 50,000 dead; see Blacker, "Demography of Mau Mau."

220. Ogot, "Decisive Years, 1956–63," 48–49.

221. Branch, *Defeating Mau Mau*, 120–25.

222. Newsinger, "Revolt and Repression in Kenya," 181.

223. Corfield, *Historical Survey*, 316.

224. Hargreaves, *Decolonization*, 167; Springhall, *Decolonization*, 165; Maloba, *Mau Mau and Kenya*, 155; Edgerton, *Mau Mau*, 237.

225. Austin, "British Point of No Return," 237.

226. Ovendale, "Macmillan and the Wind of Change."

227. Darwin, *Britain and Decolonization*, 261–69.

228. On the French conquest of Algeria, see Ferro, "La conquête"; Frémeaux, *La France et l'Algérie*; Abou-Khamseen, "First French-Algerian War." For a new study on the French conquest of the Algerian Sahara, see Brower, *A Desert Named Peace*.

229. Bugeaud, *L'Algérie*, 62.

230. Aldrich, *Greater France*, 26–27.

231. Frémeaux, "Conquête de l'Algérie"; on the French conquest strategy and occupation policy in Algeria, see especially Le Cour Grandmaison, *Coloniser, exterminer*.

232. Colonel de Montagnac quoted in Ferro, "La conquête," 492.

233. Clayton, *France, Soldiers, and Africa*, 21; Le Cour Grandmaison, *Coloniser, exterminer*, 138–46; Gallois, "Dahra and the History of Violence," 3–25.

234. Tocqueville quoted in Cheryl B. Welch, "Colonial Violence," 248.

235. Harbi, "L'Algérie en perspectives," 35; Le Cour Grandmaison, *Coloniser, exterminer*, 188.

236. Pervillé, *Pour une histoire*, 18.

237. Ferro, "La conquête," 495.

238. On the history of the white settlers, see Lefeuvre, "Les pieds-noirs," 267–86; Baussant, *Les pieds-noirs*; Stora, "'Southern' World of the Pieds Noirs."

239. Jean-Paul Sartre, "Colonialism Is a System," in *Colonialism and Neocolonialism*, 34–35.

240. See Ruedy, *Land Policy in Colonial Algeria*; Aldrich, *Greater France*, 217–18.

241. Lacheraf, *Algérie: Nation et société*, 69; see also Lacheraf, "Le patriotisme rural."

242. The origin of the term *pieds noirs* has not been definitively explained to date. Raymond Betts and Alistair Horne derive the name from the black shoes worn by settlers and the military. However, Daniel Lefeuvre thinks the origin lies in the name of a gang of young European settlers in Casablanca, the pieds noirs, which the press picked up and used to refer to French settlers in Algeria. See Betts, *France and Decolonization*, 102; Horne, *Savage War*, 30; Lefeuvre, "Les pieds-noirs," 267.

243. Harbi, "Bauern und Revolution," 127–28: "Die Zugehörigkeit zu einer Rasse markiert die Trennungslinie zwischen den Menschen. Die Privilegierten waren, ungeachtet aller klassenmäßigen Differenzen, die Europäer, selbst die Arbeiter unter ihnen. Sie alle verstanden sich als Franzosen, als Okkupanten Algeriens und als siegreiche Eroberer. Die Besiegten sollten ihnen auf diese oder jene Weise Tribut zollen."

244. See Ageron, *Histoire de l'Algérie contemporaine*, 55–69.

245. Münchhausen, *Kolonialismus und Demokratie*, 57.

246. Roy, *War in Algeria*, 27.

247. Albert Grévy quoted in Blet, *France d'outre mer*, 63.

248. Pervillé, *Empire français*, 159; Aldrich, *Greater France*, 212; see also Blévis, "Droit colonial algérien de la citoyenneté."

249. Aldrich, *Greater France*, 213–14. For more about the *code de l'indigénat*, see especially Le Cour Grandmaison, *De l'indigénat*.

250. See the essay "Misère de la Kabylie" in Camus, *Actuelles III*, 38.

251. Jean-Paul Sartre, "Colonialism Is a System," in *Colonialism and Neocolonialism*, 37–38.

252. Ibid., 41.

253. Münchhausen, *Kolonialismus und Demokratie*, 31.

254. Stora, *Les sources du nationalisme algérien*, 39–41; Harbi, *La guerre commence en Algérie*, 12–15.

255. Grimal, *Decolonization*, 74.

256. On the reform initiatives of the Popular Front government, see Tostain, "Popular Front and the Blum-Violette Plan."

257. Pervillé, *Empire français*, 160; Hargreaves, *Decolonization*, 46–47; Aldrich, *Greater France*, 118–19.

258. See Ferhat Abbas, "L'Union Populaire Algérienne pour la conquête des droits de l'homme et du citoyen," 1938, CAOM, 3 CAB 86.

259. See Koerner, "Le mouvement nationaliste algérien."

260. Ibid., 55; Ageron, "Ferhat Abbas et l'évolution politique," 125.

261. Le Tourneau, *Évolution politique de l'Afrique du Nord musulmane*, 338.

262. *Manifeste du peuple algérien*, in Jauffret, *La guerre d'Algérie*, 38.

263. *Additif du manifeste*, 26 May 1943, in Jauffret, *La guerre d'Algérie*, 40.

264. Les Amis du Manifeste et de la Liberté, Statuts, CAOM, 81 F768.

265. Texte du rapport du Général Henry Martin, SHAT, 1H 1726.

266. Kateb Yacine quoted in Prochaska, *Making Algeria French*, 238.

267. Horne, *Savage War*, 28; Koerner, "Le mouvement nationaliste algérien," 62; Jauffret, "Origins of the Algerian War," 22.

268. Raymond Blanc, quoted in *Journal Officiel, Assemblée Consultative Provisoire, Débats*, 1945–1946, 1372.

269. "Statut de l'Algérie," *Journal Officiel, Lois et Décrets*, 21 September 1947, 9470–74.

270. Oppermann, *Algerische Frage*, 63.

271. Clayton, *Wars of French Decolonization*, 110.

272. Mandouze, "Le mythe des trois départements."

273. Clayton, *Wars of French Decolonization*, 108.

274. Tillion, *L'Algérie en 1957*, 7–8.

275. Commandant J. Florentin quoted in Cornaton, *Camps de regroupement*, 59.

276. Münchhausen, *Kolonialismus und Demokratie*, 137.

277. Sarrazin (pseudonym for the government adviser Vincent Monteil), "L'Algérie, pays sans loi."

278. Heggoy, *Insurgency and Counterinsurgency*, 32–41; Tibi, "Dekolonisationsprozeß Algeriens," 24–25; Harbi, *La guerre commence en Algérie*, 52–56; Frémeaux, *La France et l'Algérie*, 122–23.

279. Horne, *Savage War*, 75.

280. The "Historic Nine" were understood to be the nine founding members of the FLN: Hocine Ait Ahmed, Ahmed Ben Bella, Mostafa Ben Boulaid, Mohamed Larbi Ben M'hidi, Rabah Bitat, Mohamed Boudiaf, Mourad Didouche, Mohamed Khider, and Belkacem Krim. On the origins of the FLN, see Harbi, *Aux origines du FLN*.

281. Clayton, *France, Soldiers, and Africa*, 259–60.

282. Fanon, *Wretched of the Earth*, 55: "Not a single colonized individual could ever again doubt the possibility of a Dien Bien Phu."

283. Alleg, *La guerre d'Algérie*, 1:429–32.

284. "Proclamation au peuple algérien, aux militants de la cause nationale," 31 October 1954, in Harbi and Meynier, *Le FLN*, 36–38.

285. On the organization and structure of the various individual *wilayas*, see Pervillé, *Atlas de la guerre d'Algérie*, 22–25.

286. Talbott, *War Without a Name*, 49; Clayton, *Wars of French Decolonization*, 113.

287. Elsenhans, *Frankreichs Algerienkrieg*, 376.

288. Münchhausen, *Kolonialismus und Demokratie*, 149.

289. Martel, "Le calme est revenu dans l'Algérois et en Oranie."

290. *Journal Officiel, Assemblée Nationale, Débats,* 12 November 1954, 4961.

291. Speech of François Mitterrand to the National Assembly on 12 November 1954, in Dalloz, *Textes,* 66–67.

292. Jauffret, "Origins of the Algerian War," 27.

293. Elsenhans, *Frankreichs Algerienkrieg,* 300.

294. See Frémeaux, "Sahara and the Algerian War."

295. Ben Boulaid quoted in Horne, *Savage War,* 110.

296. Jacques Soustelle quoted in Horne, *Savage War,* 107.

297. See Ageron, "L'insurrection du 20 août 1955."

298. Schoen, "Bulletin politique mensuel," on the events of 20 August 1955 and the ensuing retaliatory measures, contains a detailed listing of the casualties on both sides.

299. Clayton, *Wars of French Decolonization,* 126.

300. In the years from 1954 to 1962, 2.7 million young Frenchmen did their military service in Algeria; see Lemalet, *Lettres d'Algérie,* 7.

301. See Jauffret, "Mouvement des rappelés."

302. George Armstrong Kelly, *Lost Soldiers,* 172.

303. Elsenhans, *Frankreichs Algerienkrieg,* 23.

304. See "Procès-verbal du Congrès de la Soummam," in Harbi and Meynier, *Le FLN,* 241–45.

305. "Programme de la Soummam," in Dalloz, *Textes,* 74–75.

306. Hutchinson, *Revolutionary Terrorism,* 88–90.

307. Talbott, *War Without a Name,* 82.

308. Connelly, *Diplomatic Revolution,* 125; Hutchinson, *Revolutionary Terrorism,* 89.

309. Münchhausen, *Kolonialismus und Demokratie,* 197.

310. On the Battle of Algiers, see especially Pellissier, *Bataille d'Alger;* in addition, the above-mentioned film *La battaglia di Algeri* from 1966 by the Italian director Gillo Pontecorvo gives a very realistic view of this chapter in the Algerian War, despite the fact that it is a feature film.

311. Clayton, *Wars of French Decolonization,* 132.

312. Connelly, *Diplomatic Revolution,* 132.

313. Heggoy, *Insurgency and Counterinsurgency,* 235.

314. Paul Teitgen quoted in Horne, *Savage War,* 207.

315. Elsenhans, *Frankreichs Algerienkrieg,* 522.

316. See Vernet, "Barrages pendant la guerre d'Algérie."

317. Governor General Lacoste quoted in Ageron, *La décolonisation française,* 157.

318. Wall, *France,* 111; Connelly, *Diplomatic Revolution,* 160.

319. On the putsch from 13 May 1958, see especially Münchhausen, *Kolonialismus und Demokratie,* 278–303.

320. De Gaulle quoted in Daniel, *De Gaulle et l'Algérie,* 62.

321. Münchhausen, *Kolonialismus und Demokratie,* 328.

322. Horne, *Savage War,* 306.

323. "Composition du Premier GPRA," in Harbi and Meynier, *Le FLN,* 358–59.

324. Hutchinson, *Revolutionary Terrorism,* 93–100; on the spreading of the war to France, see especially Amiri, *Bataille de France,* 69–74.

325. "La Nouvelle Forme de la Lutte Inaugurée le 25 août 1958—ses effets," September–October 1958, in Harbi, *Archives de la révolution algérienne,* 228–29.

326. On the various military operations during the Challe offensive, see SHAT, 1H 1933/3.

327. Elsenhans, *Frankreichs Algerienkrieg,* 528; Clayton, *Warfare in Africa,* 30–31.

328. Martin Evans, "Harkis," 122; Hamoumou, "Harkis," 322; Faivre, *Combattants musulmans,* 55.

329. Horne, *Savage War*, 332.

330. *Djebel* is the Arab word for mountain range.

331. General Challe quoted in Horne, *Savage War*, 338.

332. De Gaulle's address on Algerian policy in Cointet, *De Gaulle*, 57.

333. Hargreaves, *Decolonization*, 169; Holland, *European Decolonization*, 173; Springhall, *Decolonization*, 111.

334. Betts, *France and Decolonization*, 123; Pervillé, *Empire français*, 240.

335. Elsenhans, *Frankreichs Algerienkrieg*, 837–38. For a list of French governmental expenditures, see Elsenhans, *Materialien zum Algerienkrieg*, 155–57; Lefeuvre, "Coût de la guerre d'Algérie."

336. See Cointet, *De Gaulle*, 119.

337. "Les raisons positives de la décolonisation, vues par le général de Gaulle," in Pervillé, *Empire français*, 245–46.

338. See especially Shepard, *Invention of Decolonization*, 82–100.

339. On the history of OAS and its terrorism, see Déroulède, *OAS*; Kauffer, *OAS*.

340. "Accords d'Evian," in Dalloz, *Textes*, 94–110; see also Scholze, "In Evian beginnt Algeriens Unabhängigkeit."

341. Pervillé, "Combien de morts," 483–84; Ageron, *La décolonisation française*, 160.

342. "Pertes forces de l'ordre et pertes rebelles," SHAT, 1H 1937/2.

343. Pervillé, "Combien de morts," 477.

344. Ibid., 491; Stora, *La gangrène et l'oubli*, 184.

345. Roux, *Harkis*, 199–203; Evans, "Harkis," 127; Hamoumou, "Harkis," 330–32.

346. Shepard, *Invention of Decolonization*, 207–28.

Chapter 4. Legitimation of Colonial Violence

Note to epigraph: Fanon, *Wretched of the Earth*, 66.

1. On this point, see especially Ferro, *Livre noir*; Liauzu and Liauzu, "Violence coloniale et guerre d'Algérie," 119–29; Eckert, *Kolonialismus*, 4, 68–72; For the major role of violence in colonial conquest and control see especially the recent study: Martin Thomas, *French Colonial Mind*, Vol. 2.

2. Williams to U.S. Secretary of State Blaine, 15 September 1890, in Bontinck, *Aux origines de l'État indépendant du Congo*, 449.

3. Conrad, *Heart of Darkness*, 100.

4. Hochschild, *King Leopold's Ghost*, 3.

5. For example, see Taithe, *Killer Trail*.

6. Mann, "Gewaltdispositiv," 118: "Schreckenherrschaft gegenüber der beherrschten Bevölkerung."

7. Van Walraven and Abbink, "Rethinking Resistance," 24–25; Aldrich, *Greater France*, 200; Berghahn, *Europa im Zeitalter der Weltkriege*, 38; Le Cour Grandmaison, *Coloniser, exterminer*, 137–61.

8. Thomson, *Rhodesia and Its Government*, 115.

9. Césaire, *Discourse on Colonialism*, 42.

10. Memmi, *Colonizer and the Colonized*, 11 ("But during the peak of the colonial process, protected by the police, the army, and an air force always ready to step in"). For the role of police forces in protecting violently the colonial interests and order in the European Colonial Empires between 1918 and 1940 see especially the recent study Martin Thomas, *Violence and Colonial Disorder*.

11. Fanon, *Wretched of the Earth*, 28.

12. Ibid., 69.

13. On the term "settlement colony," see the introduction to the volume by Elkins and Pedersen, *Settler Colonialism*, 1–20; Veracini, *Settler Colonialism*. On the issue of decolonization of settler colonies and the close connection to "contested decolonization," see Pervillé, "Décolonisation"; Elkins, "Race, Citizenship, and Governance."

14. Dane Kennedy, *Islands of White*, 136; Eckert, *Kolonialismus*, 81–82.

15. Mann, "Gewaltdispositiv," 116, 120.

16. Alfred Mussow quoted in Kennedy, *Islands of White*, 64.

17. Branche, *La torture*, 27.

18. Stoneham, *Mau Mau*, 31.

19. Edgerton, *Mau Mau*, 20; Branche, *La torture*, 27.

20. Osterhammel, *Colonialism*, 59–60.

21. On this point, see Thénault, *Drôle de justice*, 15–22.

22. Peter Evans, *Law and Disorder*, 3.

23. Lecture about the Algerian war given by Fanon in Accra in August 1960, in Report of the French ambassador to Ghana to the MAE, 26 August 1960, MAE, MLA 28.

24. Mann, "Gewaltdispositiv," 119. On the colonial state of emergency, the radicalization of violence and human rights violations see also my article: Klose, "Source of Embarrassment."

25. Folz, *Staatsnotstand*, 23; Gerth, *Staatsnotstand im französischen Recht*, 1; Chowdhury, *Rule of Law*, 11, 14.

26. For the historical development of the state of siege, see Schmitt, *Die Diktatur*, 171–205.

27. Ballreich, "Staatsnotrecht in Frankreich," 33–39; Jaenicke, "Staatsnotrecht in Großbritannien," 91–97; Folz, *Staatsnotstand*, 36–38; Gerth, *Staatsnotstand im französischen Recht*, 62–63.

28. Schmitt, *Theorie des Partisanen*, 18; on the various applications, see especially Townshend, "Martial Law."

29. Several examples from a plethora of cases are 1798, 1916, 1920–21 in Ireland, 1848 in Ceylon, 1865 in Jamaica, 1899–1902 in South Africa; see Simpson, *Human Rights*, 67–68; Jaenicke, "Staatsnotrecht in Großbritannien," 92. For a legal study of the colonial emergency and its impact in India, see Hussain, *Jurisprudence of Emergency*.

30. Gwynn, *Imperial Policing*; Gwynn describes the importance of martial law and the army in maintaining order within the empire by citing a series of British military operations, such as the repression of the Egyptian unrest of 1919, the Moplah Rebellion of 1921, and the uprising in Burma in 1930–32.

31. See Campbell, *Emergency Law in Ireland*; Townshend, *British Campaign in Ireland*, 104–55; Simpson, *Human Rights*, 78–80.

32. Folz, *Staatsnotstand*, 61.

33. Marks, "Principles and Norms," 175; Fitzpatrick, *Human Rights in Crisis*, 29.

34. Agamben, *State of Exception*, 38.

35. With his thesis of the state of emergency as a legal vacuum, Agamben is also challenging the theory of Carl Schmitt, who tries in his "political theology" to place the emergency in a legal context; ibid., 50.

36. Fitzpatrick, *Human Rights in Crisis*, 35–38.

37. Oráa, *Human Rights in States of Emergency*, 1.

38. Fitzpatrick, *Human Rights in Crisis*, 51–52.

39. Marks, "Principles and Norms," 193; Chowdhury, *Rule of Law*, 145.

40. See Svensson-McCarthy, *Human Rights and States of Exception*, 200–216, 380–92; Oráa, *Human Rights in States of Emergency*, 87–91; Fitzpatrick, *Human Rights in Crisis*, 53–54; Chowdhury, *Rule of Law*, 144.

41. UN ECOSOCOR Document E/CN.4/AC.1/4, Annex 1, draft of an "International Bill of Rights" by the British UN delegation, 5 June 1947.

42. UN ECOSOCOR Document E/CN.4/AC.1/SR.11, Commission on Human Rights, Drafting Committee, International Bill of Rights, First Session, Summary Record of the Eleventh Meeting, 19 June 1947.

43. Svensson-McCarthy, *Human Rights and States of Exception*, 213.

44. UN ECOSOCOR Document E/C.2/194, Memorandum of the World Jewish Congress, 11 May 1949.

45. UN ECOSOCOR Document E/CN.4/188, "Proposals on Certain Articles" of the British UN delegation, 16 May 1949.

46. UN ECOSOCOR Document E/CN.4/324, "Amendment to the United Kingdom Amendment" of the French UN delegation, 13 June 1949.

47. Article 4 of the International Covenant on Civil and Political Rights, in Ishay, *Human Rights Reader*, 508.

48. Kitz, *Notstandsklausel*, 11; Svensson-McCarthy, *Human Rights and States of Exception*, 286; Oráa, *Human Rights in States of Emergency*, 91.

49. However, the right to life is limited in the case of lawful acts of war.

50. Article 15 of the ECHR, in Ishay, *Human Rights Reader*, 503.

51. Oráa, *Human Rights in States of Emergency*, 96. The four designated basic rights constitute the common denominator found in the emergency clause of the ECHR, the International Covenant on Civil and Political Rights, the American Convention on Human Rights, and the Geneva Conventions. In 1984, the International Law Association included them, among others, in "The Paris Minimum Standards of Human Rights Norms in a State of Emergency."

52. Blundell quoted in Evans, *Law and Disorder*, 78–79.

53. Carey, *Crisis in Kenya*, 8; Stoneham, *Out of Barbarism*, 106–7.

54. Stoneham, *Mau Mau*, 88; Stoneham, *Out of Barbarism*, 96–97.

55. Leigh, *Shadow of the Mau Mau*, 175.

56. Ibid.

57. Edgerton, *Mau Mau*, 150; Evans, *Law and Disorder*, 89.

58. Blundell, *So Rough a Wind*, 137; Berman, *Control and Crisis*, 356.

59. Blundell quoted in Evans, *Law and Disorder*, 90.

60. For an example of references to "emergency mentality," see "Colonial Policy Committee, Kenya, Proposed Amnesty," CO memorandum, November 1959, TNA, CO 822/1337/10.

61. For an example of the reference to "white Mau Mau," see Lieutenant Colonel MacKay to General Hide, 27 September 1953, Papers of General Robert Hide, RH, Mss.Afr.s.1580.

62. Münchhausen, *Kolonialismus und Demokratie*, 156.

63. Soustelle quoted in Horne, *Savage War*, 123; see also Savarèse, *Invention des Pieds-Noirs*, 212.

64. Chikh, *L'Algérie en armes*, 95.

65. Quote taken from an article that Monteil published under the pseudonym François Sarrazin, "L'Afrique du Nord et notre destin," 1664.

66. Delpard, *Histoire des Pieds-Noirs*, 211–17.

67. Massu, *Vraie bataille*, 48; Heymann, *Libertés publiques*, 2; Maran, *Torture*, 103–5.

68. General Allard to the High Command in Algeria (Commandant Supérieur Interarmées, Commandant la Xe Région militaire), 15 September 1957, quoted in Massu, *Vraie bataille*, 376–78.

69. Ambler, *French Army in Politics*, 170–73.

70. Commandant Mairal-Bernard quoted in George Armstrong Kelly, *Lost Soldiers*, 110.

71. Hogard, "Cette guerre de notre temps," 1317.

72. Étude du 2ᵉ bureau, 5 August 1957, SHAT, 1H 1927/1.

73. Trinquier, *Guerre moderne*, 81, 190.

74. Massu, *Vraie bataille*, 168.

75. Talk by Colonel Lacheroy in Arzew, May 1958, SHAT, 1H 1942.

76. Brockway to Colonial Minister Lyttelton, 13 September 1952, TNA, CO 822/437.

77. Colonial Office Information Department, Law and Order in Kenya, Texts of Eight Bills Published, September 1952, TNA, CO 822/437.

78. Colonial Minister Lyttelton to Governor Baring, telegram, 21 October 1952, TNA, CO 822/438; "Proclamation of the State of Emergency," TNA, CO 822/443. The first general account of the state of emergency was provided by Fred Majdalany in 1962 with his book *State of Emergency*; in it, the rightist author describes the emergency exclusively from the perspective of the white settlers and the security forces and expressly tries to legitimize the emergency measures and particularly the massive use of force.

79. The 1939 Emergency Powers Order in Council also served also as a legal basis for other colonial emergencies in the British Empire. See Roberts-Wray, *Commonwealth and Colonial Law*, 642; Simpson, *Human Rights*, 89; Jaenicke, "Staatsnotrecht in Großbritannien," 104–5; French, *British Way in Counter-Insurgency*, 76-79.

80. On the individual emergency laws, see Colony and Protectorate of Kenya, *Official Gazette Extraordinary*, Nairobi, 30 October 1952; Colony and Protectorate of Kenya, *Emergency Regulations Made Under the Emergency Powers Order in Council 1939*, Nairobi 1954; "The Emergency Powers Order in Council, 1939; the Emergency Regulations, 1952," government notice, TNA, CO 822/728.

81. Townshend, *Britain's Civil Wars*, 200.

82. Beckett, *Modern Insurgencies*, 124.

83. See Elkins, *Britain's Gulag*, 53; Edgerton, *Mau Mau*, 85; David Anderson, *Histories of the Hanged*, 180; Clayton, *Counter-Insurgency*, 8.

84. Colonial Minister Lyttelton to Governor Baring, telegram, 4 December 1952, TNA, CO 822/439; on this issue, see also the ministerial meeting on 15 December 1952, TNA, CO 822/464.

85. Baring to Lyttelton, telegram, 20 April 1953, TNA, CO 822/728.

86. Holmes, *One Man in His Time*, 179; see also Edgerton, *Mau Mau*, 70–71; Clayton, *Counter-Insurgency*, 15.

87. Edgerton, *Mau Mau*, 154; Newsinger, *British Counterinsurgency*, 80.

88. Clayton, *Counter-Insurgency*, 15; Evans, *Law and Disorder*, 83.

89. For more on the emergency assize courts and the trials, see above all the excellent work by Anderson, *Histories of the Hanged*, 151–77.

90. Ibid., 291, 353–54.

91. Ibid., 7.

92. Hewitt, *Kenya Cowboy*, 196, 198.

93. Governor Renison to Colonial Minister Macleod, telegram, 11 January 1960, TNA, CO 822/1900.

94. Ballreich, "Staatsnotrecht in Frankreich," 30.

95. Heymann, *Libertés publiques*, 15.

96. Law no. 55-385 of 3 April 1955, *Journal Officiel, Lois et Décrets*, 7 April 1955, 3479–80.

97. Heymann, *Libertés publiques*, 16.

98. Gerth, *Staatsnotstand im französischen Recht*, 110; Elsenhans, *Materialien zum Algerienkrieg*, 420; Ballreich, "Staatsnotrecht in Frankreich," 41; Heymann, *Libertés publiques*, 18; Münchhausen, *Kolonialismus und Demokratie*, 128.

99. On each individual provision of the emergency law, see law no. 55-385 of 3 April 1955, *Journal Officiel, Lois et Décrets*, 7 April 1955, 3479–80.

100. Folz, *Staatsnotstand*, 63.

101. Thénault, *Drôle de justice*, 35.

102. C. Pilloud, dossier note, "Exercise des pleins pouvoirs en Algérie," n.d., ACICR, B AG 200 008-001.

103. Gerth, *Staatsnotstand im französischen Recht*, 111.

104. Law no. 56-258 of 16 March 1956, *Journal Officiel, Lois et Décrets*, 17 March 1956, 2591.

105. Decree no. 56-274 of 17 March 1956, *Journal Officiel, Lois et Décrets*, 19 March 1956, 2665–66.

106. Vidal-Naquet, *La torture dans la république*, 61.

107. Münchhausen, *Kolonialismus und Demokratie*, 184.

108. Groupe de Travail, "Les insuffisances des textes concernant la lutte antisubversive," n.d., SHAT, 1H 1943/D1, 20–21.

109. Ibid., 25.

110. Ibid., 2, 5.

111. Girardet, *Crise militaire française*, 186; Pahlavi, *Guerre révolutionnaire*, 44.

112. Heymann, *Libertés publiques*, 69; Kelly, *Lost Soldiers*, 179; Ambler, *French Army in Politics*, 164; Münchhausen, *Kolonialismus und Demokratie*, 130.

113. Heymann, *Libertés publiques*, 74.

114. Paul Teitgen quoted in Münchhausen, *Kolonialismus und Demokratie*, 200.

115. Above all, see the extensive work by Thénault, *Drôle de justice*.

116. Elsenhans, *Materialien zum Algerienkrieg*, 429–31. For a comprehensive documentation of the obstruction of lawyers, see Vergès, Zavrian, and Courrégé, *Le droit et la colère*, 80.

117. See the confidential study "La justice face à la rébellion en Algérie," 8 December 1958, CAOM, 81 F76.

118. Thénault, *Drôle de justice*, 68–71, 89–97.

119. Decree no. 56-269 of 17 March 1956, *Journal Officiel, Lois et Décrets*, 19 March 1956, 2656; and decree no. 56-474 of 12 May 1956, *Journal Officiel, Lois et Décrets*, 13 May 1956, 4462; on the expansion of the jurisdiction of military justice, see also Heymann, *Libertés publiques*, 81–92.

120. Thénault, *Drôle de justice*, 53–59.

121. Pahlavi, *Guerre révolutionnaire*, 95–98.

122. Stora, *La gangrène et l'oubli*, 83–85.

123. On the "esprit para" and its specific rituals and prayers, see Vittori, *Nous, les appelés d'Algérie*, 81.

124. Talbott, *War Without a Name*, 67; Münchhausen, *Kolonialismus und Demokratie*, 219; on the republic-hostile attitude of the paratroopers, see also Alleg, *The Question*, 47.

125. On this point, see Planchais, *Malaise de l'armée*.

126. Girardet, *Crise militaire française*, 200; Pahlavi, *Guerre révolutionnaire*, 99–108.

127. Law no. 58-487 of 17 May 1958, *Journal Officiel, Lois et Décrets*, 17 May 1958, 4734; decree no. 61-395 of 22 April 1961, *Journal Officiel, Lois et Décrets*, 23 April 1961, 3843.

128. Schmitt, *Theorie des Partisanen*, 11–12; Schulz, "Irregulären," 11; on the term "small war," see Beaumont, "Small Wars."

129. Osterhammel, *Colonialism*, 43–44; Laqueur, *Guerrilla Warfare*, 51; for an overview on this topic, see also Polk, *Violent Politics*.

130. Beaufre, *Revolutionierung des Kriegsbildes*, 25, 86; Münkler, *Imperien*, 182–83; Daase, *Kleine Kriege*, 96–97; Frémeaux, *La France et l'Algérie*, 81.

131. Frémeaux, *La France et l'Algérie*, 196–98; Laqueur, *Guerrilla Warfare*, 70–71; Vandervort, *Wars of Imperial Conquest*, 62–70.

132. Michel Martin, "From Algiers to N'Djamena," 81; Toase, "French Experience," 42–43.

133. Beckett, *Modern Insurgencies*, 40–41; Beckett and Pimlott, introduction to *Armed Forces*, 4.

134. See Featherstone, *Colonial Small Wars*.

135. Pimlott, "British Army," 16; Beckett, *Modern Insurgencies*, 32; Laqueur, *Guerrilla Warfare*, 121.

136. Callwell, *Small Wars*, 40–41, 148.

137. Ibid., 24.

138. Beckett, introduction to *Roots of Counter-Insurgency*, 9.

139. Mockaitis, *British Counterinsurgency*, 19, 147.

140. Particularly Ian Beckett makes this argument; see Beckett, introduction to *Roots of Counter-Insurgency*, 9, 15.

141. On the connection between Allied warfare and partisan tactics, see Schulz, "Zur englischen Planung," 322–58; Knipping, "Militärische Konzeptionen der französischen Résistance"; Heideking, "Amerikanische Geheimdienste und Widerstandsbewegungen."

142. Münkler, *Die neuen Kriege*, 53; Clayton, *Warfare in Africa*, 5.

143. See Kraemer, "Revolutionary Guerrilla Warfare."

144. Beckett, *Modern Insurgencies*, 70–78.

145. Haffner, "Der neue Krieg," 6: "Rezept für den sozialen und nationalen Befreiungs- und Unabhängigkeitskrieg."

146. See specifically "Über den verlängerten Krieg" in Mao, *Theorie des Guerillakrieges*, 169–70.

147. Ibid., 198–99.

148. Ibid., 180.

149. Ibid., 151–61; Beaufre, *Revolutionierung des Kriegsbildes*, 53.

150. On the way the Viet Minh conducted war, see also Giap, *People's War, People's Army*.

151. Beaufre, *Revolutionierung des Kriegsbildes*, 181.

152. Fall, *Dschungelkrieg*, 7.

153. Navarre, *Agonie de l'Indochine*, 315.

154. Ambler, *French Army in Politics*, 160–61; Beckett, *Modern Insurgencies*, 117.

155. "La stratégie révolutionnaire du Viêt-Minh," *Le Monde*, 3 August 1954; Thénault, "D'Indochine en Algérie," 236.

156. On the MRLA conduct of war, see Malayan Communist Party, "Strategic Problems of the Malayan Revolutionary War, December 1948," and "Supplementary Views of the Central Political Bureau of the Malayan Communist Party on Strategic Problems of the Malayan Revolutionary War, 12 November 1949," both in Hanrahan, *Communist Struggle in Malaya*, 170–200; Coates, *Suppressing Insurgency*, 59–62; Laqueur, *Guerrilla Warfare*, 287–90; Beaufre, *Revolutionierung des Kriegsbildes*, 192.

157. See Timothy Llewellyn Jones, *Development of British Counterinsurgency Policies*. For British counter-insurgency between 1945 to 1967 see the recent study: French, *British Way in Counter-Insurgency*.

158. Beaufre, *Revolutionierung des Kriegsbildes*, 193.

159. For more on the Briggs Plan, see Clutterbuck, *Long War*, 55–64; Harry Miller, *Jungle War in Malaya*, 69–82; Coates, *Suppressing Insurgency*, 82–99; Newsinger, *British Counterinsurgency*, 45–51; Paget, *Counter-Insurgency*, 56–61; French, *British Way in Counter-Insurgency*, 96-100 and 178-182.

160. On the counterinsurgency measures undertaken by General Templer, see Clutterbuck, *Long War*, 79–86; Paget, *Counter-Insurgency*, 64–74; Newsinger, *British Counterinsurgency*, 52–55; Coates, *Suppressing Insurgency*, 114–36.

161. Beckett, *Modern Insurgencies*, 102.

162. See Stubbs, *Hearts and Minds*; Carruthers, *Winning Hearts and Minds*, 72–127; Paget, *Counter-Insurgency*, 76–77.

163. "Hitler's Way Is Not Our Way, Templer," *Daily Herald*, 20 April 1952. Huw Bennett

argues convincingly that British counterinsurgency did not follow the often self-proclaimed principle of "minimum force," but relied on the use of massive violence in colonial conflicts such as Kenya. See Bennett, "Mau Mau Emergency," 143–63; Bennett, "Other Side of the COIN," 638–64; Bennett, "Minimum Force," 459–75.

164. On the British deployment of chemical weapons in Malaya, see Harris and Paxman, *Higher Form of Killing*, 101, 194; Lawrence James, *Imperial Rearguard*, 155; Clutterbuck, *Long War*, 160; Newsinger, *British Counterinsurgency*, 55–56.

165. The deployed defoliant Agent Orange consisted in part of the highly toxic chemical 2,4,5-T used by the British in Malaya; see Harris and Paxman, *Higher Form of Killing*, 195; James, *Imperial Rearguard*, 155; Cecil, *Herbicidal Warfare*, 17; Gartz, *Chemische Kampfstoffe*, 102–4.

166. Charters, "From Palestine to Northern Ireland," 193; Beaufre, *Revolutionierung des Kriegsbildes*, 194; Mockaitis, *British Counterinsurgency*, 192; Stockwell, "Origins of the Malayan Emergency," 67; Clutterbuck, *Long War*, 10; Paget, *Counter-Insurgency*, 78; French, *British Way in Counter-Insurgency*, 201-204.

167. British Army Director of Operations, Malaya, *The Conduct of Anti-Terrorist Operations in Malaya*. For the importance and impact of ATOM-handbook see: French, *British Way in Counter-Insurgency*, 203-208.

168. Coates, *Suppressing Insurgency*, 32; Mockaitis, *British Counterinsurgency*, 8–9; Kiernan, *From Conquest to Collapse*, 212; Newsinger, *British Counterinsurgency*, 53.

169. Secretariat circular no. 5, 21 January 1953, TNA, CO 822/439.

170. Baring to the CO, telegram, 10 April 1953, TNA, CO 822/440; Chenevix Trench, *Men Who Ruled Kenya*, 239; Charters, "From Palestine to Northern Ireland," 198–99; French, *British Way in Counter-Insurgency*, 100-102.

171. Baring to the CO, telegram, 1 August 1953, TNA, CO 822/703; on Askwith's trip to Malaya, see Edgerton, *Mau Mau*, 179; Elkins, "Detention," 197–98; Elkins, *Britain's Gulag*, 103–6.

172. Thomas G. Askwith, "Memoirs of Kenya, 1936–61," 49. Papers of Thomas Askwith, RH, Mss.Afr.s.1770.

173. "Templer Rehabilitation Plan in Use in Kenya," *Manchester Guardian*, 25 July 1953; Elkins, *Britain's Gulag*, 103, 235; Beckett, *Modern Insurgencies*, 125; Newsinger, *British Counterinsurgency*, 74; Paget, *Counter-Insurgency*, 99–100.

174. Erskine to General Headquarters Far Eastern Land Forces, 11 August 1953, TNA, WO 276/159.

175. East Africa Command, *Handbook on Anti-Mau Mau Operations*.

176. Füredi, "Decolonization Through Counterinsurgency," 155; Buijtenhuijs, *Le mouvement "Mau Mau,"* 399; Beckett, *Modern Insurgencies*, 121; Mockaitis, *British Counterinsurgency*, 167.

177. J. M. Forster, Operational Research Unit Far East, *A Comparative Study of the Emergencies in Malaya and Kenya*, Report No. 1/1957, TNA, WO 291/1670.

178. Ibid., 2.

179. Ibid., 27–28.

180. Ibid., 29–30.

181. Ibid., 35–36.

182. Ibid., 30.

183. Chief of Police Richard Catling, secret information "Special Force," 4 July 1955, TNA, WO 276/460; on the pseudo-gang tactic, see especially Kitson, *Gangs and Counter-Gangs*.

184. Forster, *Comparative Study*, Report No. 1/1957, TNA, WO 291/1670, 30.

185. Ibid., 73–74.

186. Ibid., 2.

187. WO to the FO, 9 June 1954, TNA, FO 371/108150.

188. Jebb to Eden, 7 March 1956, TNA, FO 371/119394; see also Alexander, "Les évaluations militaires britanniques," 51.

189. See A. J. Wilson, confidential report on visit to operations in Algeria, 8–16 January 1957, TNA, FO 371/125945. On additional visits of Wilson to observe French operations in Algeria see: Martin Thomas, *French North African Crisis*, 94–96.

190. Wilson, Confidential report, TNA, FO 371/125945, 2.

191. Ibid., 6, 11.

192. Ibid., 12.

193. Ibid., 10.

194. British embassy in Paris to the FO, 27 February 1957, TNA, FO 371/125945.

195. WO to the FO, 20 February 1957, TNA, FO 371/125945.

196. FO to the WO, 12 March 1957, and FO to the British embassy in Paris, 22 March 1957, TNA, FO 371/125945.

197. "Visits by British Officers to the French Army in Algeria," FO paper, 15 March 1957, TNA, FO 371/125945.

198. See Conférence du Colonel Lacheroy, "Leçons de l'action Viêt-Minh et communiste en Indochine," SHAT, 1H 2524bis/1; Zervoudakis, "From Indochina to Algeria"; Paret, *French Revolutionary Warfare*, 6–7; Thénault, "D'Indochine en Algérie," 235.

199. The studies under the direction of Colonel Jean Nemo and commander in chief General Paul Ely from 1955 were highly influential; see "Enseignements des Opérations," SHAT, 10H 985; "Guerre en Surface au Tonkin de 1946 à 1954," SHAT, 10H 2509; "Enseignements de la Guerre d'Indochine," SHAT, 10H 983.

200. On the formative influence that the Indochina experience had on the development of French doctrines on antisubversive warfare, see Kelly, *Lost Soldiers*, 9; Paret, *French Revolutionary Warfare*, 100; Ambler, *French Army in Politics*, 160, 170, 308; Münchhausen, *Kolonialismus und Demokratie*, 209; Pimlott, "French Army," 58–59; Schmitt, *Theorie des Partisanen*, 65; Marill, "Héritage Indochinois"; Heggoy, *Insurgency and Counterinsurgency*, 262.

201. On the theory of *guerre révolutionnaire*, see Delmas, *Guerre révolutionnaire*; Arnold, *Guerre révolutionnaire*; Robert Thompson, *Revolutionary War*; Fairbairn, *Revolutionary Warfare and Communist Strategy*; Paret, *French Revolutionary Warfare*, 9–19; Kelly, *Lost Soldiers*, 111–19; Beaufre, *Revolutionierung des Kriegsbildes*, 48–71; Ambler, *French Army in Politics*, 308–36; Pahlavi, *Guerre révolutionnaire*.

202. The *Revue Militaire d'Information* even published a special issue on the topic in the spring of 1957: "La guerre révolutionnaire," *Revue Militaire d'Information*, February–March 1957.

203. Lacheroy, "Scenario-type de guerre révolutionnaire"; Hogard, "Guerre révolutionnaire et pacification."

204. Thénault, "D'Indochine en Algérie," 236; Zervoudakis, "From Indochina to Algeria," 56; on the French prisoners in the Viet Minh camps, see Bonnafous, *Prisonniers français dans les camps Viêt-Minh*.

205. Paret, *French Revolutionary Warfare*, 19; Beaufre, *Revolutionierung des Kriegsbildes*, 59.

206. Trinquier, *Guerre moderne*, 15–19.

207. Louis Pichon, "Caractères généraux de la guerre insurrectionnelle," July 1957, SHAT, 1H 2577, 1–2; Ambler, *French Army in Politics*, 193; Frémeaux, *La France et l'Algérie*, 84.

208. Chassin, "Le rôle idéologique de l'armée," 13.

209. Hogard, "L'armée française," 88.

210. General Massu, memorandum, 29 March 1957, SHAT, 1R 339/3.

211. Paret, *French Revolutionary Warfare*, 20; Ambler, *French Army in Politics*, 170.

212. Souyris, "Les conditions de la parade et de la riposte," 91–109.

213. Hogard, "Stratégie et tactique."

214. Trinquier, *Guerre moderne*, 49.

215. See "Les principes de l'action psychologique et de la 'guerre subversive,'" *Le Monde*, 10 July 1958; Ambler, *French Army in Politics*, 171.

216. Trinquier quoted in Kelly, *Lost Soldiers*, 138.

217. Trinquier, *Guerre moderne*, 51–55.

218. Ibid., 57.

219. Ageron, "Guerres d'Indochine et d'Algérie," 57–58; Jauffret, "War Culture of French Combatants," 103; Ambler, *French Army in Politics*, 311; Paret, *French Revolutionary Warfare*, 25. On the question of the Algerian War as a Cold war front line see: Thomas, *French North African Crisis*, 158–178.

220. Girardet, *L'idée coloniale*, 146; Kiernan, *From Conquest to Collapse*, 217.

221. Ambler, *French Army in Politics*, 365; Paret, *French Revolutionary Warfare*, 29; Clayton, *Wars of French Decolonization*, 76.

222. General Allard, Colonel Godard, Colonel Goussault, "Les missions de l'armée française dans la guerre révolutionnaire d'Algérie," paper presented at the military conference, 15 November 1957, SHAT, 1H 1943/D1.

223. Guelton, "French Army 'Centre,'" 37; Heggoy, *Insurgency and Counterinsurgency*, 176–81.

224. On the training program, see Programme d'étude, Fall 1957, SHAT, 1H 2523/1.

225. Guelton, "French Army 'Centre,'" 41–43.

226. Defense Minister to the State Secretary for Ground Forces, secret letter "Création d'un Centre d'Entrainement à la guerre subversive," 21 March 1958, SHAT, 1H 2577; State Secretary for Ground Forces to the High Command in Algiers, "Création d'un Centre d'Entrainement à la guerre subversive," 11 April 1958, SHAT, 1H 2577/D1.

227. Brigade General Marguet to the Defense Ministry, "Formation des Sous-Officiers d'Infanterie," 2 October 1958, SHAT, 1H 1369/D4.

228. "Rapport du Colonel Buchod Commandant le Centre d'Entrainement à la guerre subversive en fin de cycle d'instruction des Officiers de Reserve Rappelés" to the High Command in Algiers, 18 November 1958, SHAT, 1H 2759/D4.

229. See "Évolution des Officiers de Reserve en cours de stage et état d'ésprit en fin de stage," SHAT, 1H 2759/D4.

230. On this point, see "Cas particulier des prêtres," SHAT, 1H 2759/D4.

231. Pimlott, "French Army," 60.

232. Branche, "Lutte contre le terrorisme urbain," 475–77; Pahlavi, *Guerre révolutionnaire*, 67–70.

233. Aggoun, "Psychological Propaganda"; Paret, *French Revolutionary Warfare*, 55–62; Kelly, *Lost Soldiers*, 129.

234. For more on the Cinquième Bureau, see Descombin, *Cinquième Bureau*; Pahlavi, *Guerre révolutionnaire*, 81–90.

235. On this point, see Mathias, *SAS*; Omouri, "Sections administratives spécialisées"; Horne, *Savage War*, 108; Elsenhans, *Materialen zum Algerienkrieg*, 497; Heggoy, *Insurgency and Counterinsurgency*, 188–211; Paret, *French Revolutionary Warfare*, 46–52; Ambler, *French Army in Politics*, 179–81.

236. Kelly, *Lost Soldiers*, 188; Heggoy, *Insurgency and Counterinsurgency*, 214.

237. Paret, *French Revolutionary Warfare*, 62–66; Thénault, "D'Indochine en Algérie," 242.

238. The case studies produced by the Special Operations Research Office of American University in Washington, D.C., provide a good example of this growing interest; see Jureidini, *Case Studies*.

239. General Paul Ely, "Lessons from the War in Indochina," 31 May 1955, NARA, RG 472 A1 474 Box 107.

240. Tanham, "Doctrine and Tactics."

241. Ibid., 9.

242. Hosmer and Crane, *Counterinsurgency*, iii.

243. See ibid., xv–xix, for biographies of the participants.

244. Melnik. "The French Campaign Against the FLN."

245. Ibid., 72.

246. British General Consulate in Leopoldville to the FO, confidential, 6 November 1952, TNA, CO 822/448.

247. "Visites en Algérie d'Officiers Portugais" from French Defense Ministry to the MAE, 13 December 1957, CAOM, 81 F1004.

248. Beckett, *Modern Insurgencies*, 121.

249. On colonial antiguerrilla warfare as a model and basis of instruction, see McCuen, *Art of Counter-Revolutionary War*, 315–23; Paget, *Counter-Insurgency*, 155–79.

250. On Kitson's ideas about strategy, see Kitson, *Im Vorfeld des Krieges*.

251. Newsinger, *British Counterinsurgency*, 170; Elkins, *Britain's Gulag*, 306; this argument is made especially by Roger Faligot in *Britain's Military Strategy in Ireland*.

252. On characterizing colonial wars, see the introduction by Henk L. Wesseling in Wesseling and de Moor, *Colonial Wars*, 1–11; Le Cour Grandmaison, *Coloniser, exterminer*, 173–87; Walter, "Warum Kolonialkrieg?"

253. Callwell, *Small Wars*, 21.

254. Theodore Roosevelt quoted in Lauren, *Power and Prejudice*, 68.

255. Brehl, "Koloniale Gewalt in kollektiver Rede," 210; Köppen, "Krieg mit dem Fremden," 267.

256. General Ardagh quoted in Dülffer, "Chances and Limits of Armament Control," 103.

257. See "Declaration (IV, 2) Concerning Asphyxiating Gases" and "Declaration (IV, 3) Concerning Expanding Bullets" in Roberts and Guelff, *Documents on the Laws of War*, 60–61, 64–65.

258. These are expanding bullets, the name of which is derived from the arsenal located in the Indian town of Dum Dum near Calcutta where this type of ammunition was produced for British colonial troops at the end of the nineteenth century. Dumdum bullets caused severe injury with a great loss of blood and were deployed for their "stopping power."

259. Brehl, "Koloniale Gewalt in kollektiver Rede," 211; Kiernan, *From Conquest to Collapse*, 157.

260. See Spiers, "Use of the Dum Dum Bullet."

261. Quoted from Rudyard Kipling's famous poem "The White Man's Burden" from 1899, in which he glorifies colonialism as a humanistic mission; Kipling, *Rudyard Kipling's Verse*, 323–24.

262. Füredi, *Colonial Wars*, 143; Townshend, *Britain's Civil Wars*, 35.

263. W. H. Ingrams, "The Problem of Nationalism in the Colonies," July 1952, TNA, CO 936/217/4/5.

264. Both states had shaped the Geneva Conventions and signed them in 1949; France ratified the Geneva Conventions on 28 June 1951, but Great Britain did not ratify the new provisions on international humanitarian law until 23 September 1957. See ICRC, *Annual Report, 1957*, 65.

265. See Veuthey, *Guérilla et droit humanitaire*, 46–48; Ramadhani, *Guerilla Warfare and International Humanitarian Law*, 52–61; Oppermann, "Anwendbarkeit der Genfer Abkommen"; Schmitt, *Theorie des Partisanen*, 29–33; Wilson, *International Law and the Use of Force*, 42–45; Dworkin, "Laws of War." On this topic see also my article: Klose, "Colonial Testing Ground."

266. Pictet, *Geneva Convention*, 32.

267. Article 3 of the Geneva Conventions in ICRC, *Geneva Conventions*, 24.

268. Oppermann, "Anwendbarkeit der Genfer Abkommen," 51–59; Wilson, "Humanitarian Protection," 37–38; Mameri, "L'application du droit de la guerre," 10; Best, *War and Law*, 177.

269. Pictet, *Geneva Convention*, 36.

270. Füredi, *Colonial Wars*, 192.

271. Minutes to T. K. Lloyd, 12 July 1954, in TNA, CO 822/774.

272. Anderson, *Histories of the Hanged*, 238.

273. Pervillé, "Guerre étrangère et guerre civile," 171–72; Talbott, *War Without a Name*, 51.

274. See law no. 99-882 of 18 October 1999, *Journal Officiel, Lois et Décrets*, 20 October 1999, 15647.

275. Mitterrand quoted in Stora, *La gangrène et l'oubli*, 15: "Nous éviterons tout ce qui pourrait apparaître comme une sorte d'état de guerre, nous ne le voulons pas."

276. On this point, see Stora, *La gangrène et l'oubli*, 13.

277. On the criminalization of irregular troops, see also Schmitt, *Theorie des Partisanen*, 35–36.

278. Stoneham, *Out of Barbarism*, 115; Edgerton, *Mau Mau*, 112; French, *British Way in Counter-Insurgency*, 60–62.

279. Governor Baring to the CO, confidential telegram, 25 July 1953, in TNA, CO 822/441; this disproves the argument put forth by Caroline Elkins, *Britain's Gulag*, 97, that the British colonial government treated Mau Mau detainees as prisoners of war.

280. For example, see Ruark, *Something of Value*; Carey, *Crisis in Kenya*, 11–14; Stoneham, *Out of Barbarism*, 113–15.

281. Stora, *La gangrène et l'oubli*, 20.

282. Pervillé, "Guerre étrangère et guerre civile," 172.

283. Leulliette, *St. Michael and the Dragon*, 3. The published account by the French paratrooper Leulliette of his wartime experiences in Algeria was censored in France because it contained several highly controversial details.

284. For the Algerian War, see especially Milleron, "L'action psychologique et la déshumanisation."

285. Baldwin, *Mau Mau Man-Hunt*, 16.

286. Edgerton, *Mau Mau*, 151; Elkins, *Britain's Gulag*, 49; Stoneham, *Out of Barbarism*, 128–29; French, *British Way in Counter-Insurgency*, 72.

287. Baldwin, *Mau Mau Man-Hunt*, 17.

288. Roy, *War in Algeria*, 15; Münchhausen, "Ziele und Widerstände," 57.

289. Horne, *Savage War*, 54.

290. Leulliette, *St. Michael and the Dragon*, 236–37.

291. Keen, *Gesichter des Bösen*, 9, 20–21.

292. Buijtenhuijs, *Essays on Mau Mau*, 105–6; Edgerton, *Mau Mau*, 125.

293. Wilkinson, "Mau Mau Movement."

294. Itote, *Mau Mau General*, 129.

295. Edgerton, *Mau Mau*, 126.

296. "Rules of Conduct in the Forest," in Itote, *Mau Mau General*, 285–91.

297. Kariuki, *Mau Mau Detainee*, 67, 75; Edgerton, *Mau Mau*, 193.

298. See Josiah Mwangi Karinbi (Kariuki) to the ICRC, 14 February 1960, ACICR, B AG 225 108-001.

299. FLN to the ICRC, 23 February 1956, ACICR, B AG 200 008-001.

300. Fraleigh, "Algerian Revolution," 194.

301. Instructions from the CCE to the ALN commanders, in Benatia, *Les actions humanitaires*, 241–42.

302. Lieutenant Colonel Goubard, "Résonance à l'intérieur de l'opération, adhésion aux

Conventions de Genève lancée par l'organisation extérieure," 24 September 1960, SHAT, 1H 1755/D1.

303. FLN resolution, 11 December 1956, in Benatia, *Les actions humanitaires*, 260.

304. Statutes of the Croissant-Rouge Algérien, 8 January 1957, in Benatia, *Les actions humanitaires*, 251–59.

305. See "Situation du CICR vis-à-vis du Gouvernement provisoire de la République Algérienne," 8 June 1959, ACICR, D EUR France1-0932; ICRC report "Le CICR et les événements d'Afrique du Nord," June 1957, ACICR, B AG 210 008-003.02, 3; Ben Ahmed, "Pierre Gaillard," 21. The CRA was officially recognized by the ICRC on 4 July 1963, only after Algerian independence.

306. French government circular memos "Activité du représentant du Croissant Rouge Algérien en Suisse," 30 August 1957; "Le Croissant Rouge Algerien intermediate entre les pays communistes et la rébellion," 10 January 1958; and "Aide Etrangère au Croissant Rouge Algérien," 11 July 1959, SHAT, 1H 1755/D1.

307. Excerpt from the Abbas declaration, 26 September 1958, ACICR, D EUR France1-0932.

308. GPRA memorandum, 24 November 1958, in Benatia, *Les actions humanitaires*, 313–20.

309. See "Communiqué du GPRA: Ratification des Conventions," 12 April 1960, ACICR, D EUR France 1-932; Ferhat Abbas to the ICRC, 11 June 1960, ACICR, B AG 202 008-007.1.

310. "Instruments d'adhesion de la République algérienne aux Conventions de Genève du 12 août 1949," in Bedjaoui, *Révolution algérienne*, 201; Veuthey, *Guérilla et droit humanitaire*, 49; Wilson, *International Law and the Use of Force*, 51.

311. Algerian Office, *White Paper*.

312. Ibid., 5; see also Bedjaoui, *Révolution algérienne*, 57.

313. Algerian Office, *White Paper*, 26–55.

314. Ibid., 56–58.

315. See Branche, "Entre droit humanitaire et intérêts politiques," 113–14.

316. Bedjaoui, "Révolution algérienne et le droit international humanitaire," 24.

317. Bedjaoui, *Révolution algérienne*, 217; Algerian Office, *White Paper*, 17; Benatia, *Les actions humanitaires*, 118.

318. ICRC delegate Hoffmann to the ICRC, note no. 7, "Concerne: Assistance aux prisonniers français," 7 August 1957, ACICR, B AG 210 008-001.

319. ICRC, *ICRC and the Algerian Conflict*, 9–10; on the question of prisoner releases, see also Comité International de la Croix-Rouge, "Résumé chronologique sur la question des prisonniers français du Front de Libération Nationale," October 1957, ACICR, B AG 210 008-003.02.

320. A synopsis of these prisoner releases to the ICRC is found in Bugnion, *Protection of War Victims*, 551.

321. See "FLN délégation du Maroc, Compte-rendu concernant la cérémonie de remise des prisonniers, 8 December 1958," in Benatia, *Les actions humanitaires*, 278–79.

322. See Algerian Office, "Treatment of Prisoners of War," SHAT, 1H 1751/D1; Algerian Office, *White Paper*, 15–17.

323. Fraleigh, "Algerian Revolution," 198.

324. Hutchinson, *Revolutionary Terrorism*, 93.

325. Belkherroubi, *Naissance et reconnaissance*, 96, 150; Branche, "Entre droit humanitaire et intérêts politiques," 124; Wilson, *International Law and the Use of Force*, 153–54.

326. P. Gaillard to ICRC delegate C. Vautier, 13 December 1954, ACICR, B AG 209 008-001.

327. ICRC paper "Concerne: Troubles intérieurs," 31 December 1954, ACICR, D EUR France1-0370.

328. ICRC, *Annual Report, 1957*, 34; Willemin and Heacock, *International Committee of the Red Cross*, 188–92.

329. "Report of the Commission of Experts for the Examination of the Question of Assistance to Political Detainees," in ICRC, *Report on the Work of the International Committee of the Red Cross*, 84–91.

330. Report of the Commission d'experts chargée d'examiner la question de l'application des principes humanitaires en cas de troubles intérieurs, 8 October 1955, ACICR, D EUR France1-0376; ICRC, *Annual Report, 1955*, 75–80.

331. Paul Rueger to ICRC President Léopold Boissier, 10 October 1955, ICRC, *Procès-verbaux des séances du comité, 1948–59*, 175–76.

332. FO to the CO, 16 February 1956, and CO to the FO, 5 June 1956, TNA, CO 936/391.

333. CO to the FO, 5 June 1956, TNA, CO 936/391.

334. ICRC, *Annual Report, 1957*, 34–35.

335. "Notes pour le Comité," 6 April 1954 and 8 June 1955, ACICR, B AG 200 108-001 and 225 108-001.

336. Kenya Committee to the ICRC, 17 March 1954, ACICR, B AG 200 108-001.

337. Senn to the ICRC, 29 June 1955, and 24 October 1955, ACICR, B AG 200 108-001.

338. Ibid., 26 March 1956.

339. "Note au CICR," 19 November 1954, ACICR, B AG 200 108-00.

340. Lady Limerick to ICRC President Boissier, 9 August 1955, ACICR, B AG 225 108-001.

341. Lady Limerick to the CO, 11 January 1957, TNA, CO 822/1258. When dealing with the ICRC, the BRC remained adamant about this point until the end of the emergency in Kenya; see Lady Limerick to ICRC President Boissier, 24 August 1959, ACICR, B AG 225 108-001. On the position held by the British government, see ICRC to H. Junod, 30 June 1959, ACICR, B AG 225 108-001; "Britain Has Barred Red Cross in Kenya," *Reynolds News*, 16 December 1956.

342. ICRC President Boissier to Lady Limerick, 12 August 1955, ACICR, B AG 225 108-001.

343. ICRC President Boissier to British Colonial Minister Lennox-Boyd, 27 December 1956, ACICR, B AG 225 108-001.

344. Press release no. 577b, 18 February 1957, in ICRC, *Collection des communiqués de presse*, nos. 562–635; "Une mission du CICR en route pour le Kenia," *Revue Internationale de la Croix-Rouge* 39, no. 459 (March 1957): 170.

345. "Une mission du CICR au Kenia," *Revue Internationale de la Croix-Rouge* 39, no. 461 (May 1957); ICRC, *Annual Report, 1957*, 39–40.

346. "Rapport sur une mission spéciale du CICR au Kenya," ACICR, B AG 225 108-002.

347. General Report on the Mission of the International Committee of the Red Cross, TNA, CO 822/1258.

348. See also "Rapport du Dr. Gailland sur la mission qu'il a effectuée avec H. P. Junod au Kénya," 26 April 1957, ICRC, *Procès-verbaux*, 48–53.

349. Baring to Colonial Secretary Lennox-Boyd, 25 June 1957, TNA, CO 822/1251.

350. Gavaghan, *Of Lions and Dung Beetles*, 235.

351. Baring to CO, telegram, 5 July 1957, TNA, CO 822/1251.

352. Junod to the ICRC, 29 July 1957, ACICR, B AG 225 108-001.

353. On the murder of prisoners in Hola Camp, see Edgerton, *Mau Mau*, 195–200; Anderson, *Histories of the Hanged*, 326–27; Elkins, *Britain's Gulag*, 344–53. For the reaction of the public see: Andrew Thompson, *Empire Strikes Back?* 212–13.

354. ICRC to the CO, 11 March 1959, TNA, CO 822/1258.

355. CO to Baring, 31 March 1959, TNA, CO 822/1249.

356. Baring to Lennox-Boyd, 29 April 1959, TNA, CO 822/1269.

357. Press release no. 682c, 12 June 1959, in ICRC, *Collection des communiqués de presse*, nos. 636–749; "Mission du CICR au Kenya," *Revue Internationale de la Croix-Rouge*, no. 487 (July 1959): 343; ICRC, *Annual Report, 1959*, 13–14.

358. ICRC vice president Marcel Junod was a cousin of H. P. Junod.

359. "Note à l'attention de M. R. Gallopin" [Roger Eduoard Gallopin, *ICRC Executive Director*], 28 August 1959, ACICR, B AG 225 108-001.

360. Marcel Junod, "Missions à Londres des Drs. Junod et Rubli 6–8 août 1959: Concerne Mission du Dr. Rubli au Kenya," 13 August 1959, ACICR, B AG 225 108-001.

361. Record of a meeting with Dr. Rubli and Dr. Marcel Junod of the International Committee of the Red Cross, 7 August 1959, TNA, CO 822/1258; see also Second Mission of the International Committee of the Red Cross to Kenya, June–July 1959, report communicated to the British government, ACICR, B AG 225 108-001, 5–6.

362. Marcel Junod, "Missions à Londres," ACICR, B AG 225 108-001.

363. Rapport du Dr. Junod sur sa mission à Londres, 13 August 1959, ACICR, B AG 225 108-001.

364. Goldsworthy, *Colonial Issues in British Politics*, 362–63; Edgerton, *Mau Mau*, 201; Anderson, *Histories of the Hanged*, 330; Elkins, *Britain's Gulag*, 353.

365. "Note au CICR," 8 November 1954, ACICR, B AG 200 008-001.

366. William H. Michel, "Entretien avec M. Pierre Mendès-France, Président du Conseil, le 31 janvier 1955," ACICR, D EUR France1-0370.

367. Mendès-France to Michel, 2 February 1955, ACICR, D EUR France1-0370.

368. *Revue Internationale de la Croix-Rouge* 39, no. 439 (July 1955): 454.

369. On the extensive activities of the ICRC during the Algerian War, see ICRC, *ICRC and the Algerian Conflict*.

370. Ibid., 12–14, 21–22; *Revue Internationale de la Croix-Rouge* 39, no. 466 (October 1957): 551–53, and vol. 40, no. 470 (February 1958): 85–86; ICRC, *Annual Report, 1957*, 27–33; press release no. 634c, 12 December 1957, in ICRC, *Collection des communiqués de presse*, vol. 8; press release no. 686c, 7 October 1959, in ICRC, *Collection des communiqués de presse*, vol. 9.

371. Report on a meeting of a ICRC delegation with the CRF president on 25 February 1958; CRF to the ICRC, 14 April 1958; P. Gaillard, "Action de la Croix-Rouge Française en Algérie," 9 June 1958; P. Gaillard to ICRC delegate H. Michel, 21 January 1959, all in ACICR, D EUR France1-0928.

372. P. Gaillard, "Aide aux populations regroupées en Algérie," 17 September 1959, ACICR, D EUR France1-0928.

373. ICRC to French Prime Minister Faure, 23 May 1955, ACICR, B AG 225 008-004.01.

374. ICRC, *ICRC and the Algerian Conflict*, 5–6.

375. Ibid., 4–5.

376. Bedjaoui, *Révolution algérienne*, 213–19; Pinto, "Application des conventions de Genève."

377. ICRC to the French government, 28 May 1958, ACICR, B AG 210 008-003.01.

378. Belkherroubi, *Naissance et reconnaissance*, 51–52; Fraleigh, "Algerian Revolution," 195–96.

379. MAE to the ICRC, 30 July 1958, ACICR, B AG 202 008-008.

380. P. Gaillard to M. le Président, 12 December 1959, ACICR, B AG 225 008-011, 6–7.

381. General Salan, memorandum, 24 November 1957, ACICR, B AG 225 008-009.01; ICRC Delegate Gailland in Algeria to the ICRC, note "Situation des prisonniers 'rebelles' capturés les armes à la main," 20 December 1957, ACICR, B AG 210 008-001.

382. General Salan, memorandum, 19 March 1958, SHAT, 1H 1100/1; Veuthey, *Guérilla et droit humanitaire*, 228.

383. Salan memo, 19 March 1958, SHAT, 1H 1100/1.

384. Branche, "Entre droit humanitaire et intérêts politiques," 107.

385. French foreign ministry to the ICRC, 27 February 1961, ACICR, B AG 202 008-007.02; Règlement du régime intérieur dans les centres militaires d'internés (CMI), 17 April 1961, SHAT, 1H 2019/D2, 2.

386. Report by C. Pilloud on the meeting with Guy Mollet, 28 August 1956, ACICR, B AG 200 008-002; report by P. Gaillard on the meeting with Guy Mollet, 15 November 1956, ACICR, B AG 225 008-002.

387. "Rapport sur les visites effectuées lors de la deuxième mission du Comité International de la Croix-Rouge," May–June 1956, ACICR, B AG 225 008-004.02, pp. 7, 15.

388. Algerian governor General Robert Lacoste to Guy Mollet, 20 August 1956, and report by W. Michel on the meeting with cabinet secretary M. Noel, 6 September 1956, both in ACICR, B AG 225 008-004.02.

389. On this point, see Mission du Comité International de la Croix-Rouge en Algérie, Octobre–Novembre 1956, Rapport communiqué au Gouvernement français, ACICR, B AG 225 008-004.03, 3, 10; Rapports sur les visites effectuées lors de la quatrième mission du CICR en Algérie, May–June 1957, ACICR, B AG 225 008-004.02, 4; Rapports sur les visites effectuées lors de la septième mission du CICR en Algérie, October–November 1959, ACICR, B AG 225 008-013, 5; Rapports sur les visites effectuées lors de la huitième mission du CICR en Algérie, January–February 1961, ACICR, B AG 225 008-023, 6, 9.

390. Paul-Albert Fevrier, report to the ICRC, 17 April 1960, ACICR, D EUR France1-0438.

391. General Hubert to the Commanders of the Army Corp Algiers, 7 October 1958, SHAT, 1H 2573/D1.

392. General Staff, memorandum, November 1961, SHAT, 1H 1493/1.

393. Rapport sur les visites effectuées lors de la deuxième mission du Comité International de la Croix-Rouge, — May–June 1956, ACICR, B AG 225 008-004.02, 14.

394. Mission du Comité International de la Croix-Rouge en Algérie, Octobre–Novembre 1956, Rapport communiqué au Gouvernement français, ACICR, B AG 225 008-004.03, 8–9.

395. Rapports sur les visites effectuées lors de la quatrième mission du CICR en Algérie, May–June 1957, ACICR, B AG 225 008-004.02, 6.

396. Rapports sur les visites effectuées lors de la cinquième mission du CICR en Algérie, November 1957–February 1958, ACICR, B AG 225 008-005, 6.

397. On this point, see Rapports sur les visites effectuées lors de la septième mission du CICR en Algérie, October–November 1959, ACICR, B AG 225 008-013, 5; Rapports sur les visites effectuées lors de la neuvième mission du CICR en Algérie, November–December 1961, ACICR, B AG 225 008-022, 4; ICRC President L. Boissier to French Foreign Minister M. Couve de Murville, 6 February 1962, ACICR, B AG 225 008-033.01.

398. P. Gaillard to M. le Président, 12 December 1959, ACICR, B AG 225 008-011, 12–14.

399. Laurent Vust, report to the ICRC, 22 May 1960, ACICR, B AG 225 008-015.05.

400. "Le rapport de la Croix-Rouge Internationale sur les camps d'internement d'Algérie," Le Monde, 5 January 1960.

401. Among other things, the FLN and the anticolonial bloc used the published ICRC report to express massive criticism of France at the United Nations in New York; see "The Report of the International Committee of the Red Cross on Torture and Inhuman Treatment of Algerians Held in French Prisons and Camps," Algerian Office, January 1960, CAOM, 81 F529; the UN delegates from Afghanistan, Burma, Ceylon, Ghana, Guinea, India, Indonesia, Iran, Iraq, Yemen, Jordan, Lebanon, Libya, Morocco, Nepal, Pakistan, Saudi Arabia, Sudan, Tunisia, and the United Arab Republic to the UN Secretary-General, 10 February 1960, MAE, NUOI carton 1067.

402. ICRC, ICRC and the Algerian Conflict, 3.

403. Branche, "Entre droit humanitaire et intérêts politiques," 116–18.

404. "The ICRC in Algeria: Human Fellowship Against Hatred," notice to the national Red Cross societies, 7 October 1960, ACICR, B AG 202 008-001.

Chapter 5. Unleashing of Colonial Violence

Note to epigraph: From Sartre's preface to Albert Memmi's book *The Colonizer and the Colonized*, published in 1957, quoted in Sartre, "Albert Memmi's *The Colonizer*," in Sartre, *Colonialism and Neocolonialism*, 53.

1. See McCormack, "Evolution of an International Criminal Law Regime," 55–63; Clark, "Nuremberg and Tokyo"; Neier, "War and War Crimes," 1–7; Ball, *Prosecuting War Crimes*, 35–93; Best, *War and Law*, 180–206.

2. Each of the four conventions contains its own article on these "grave breaches"; see ICRC, *Geneva Conventions*, 43 (Convention for the Amelioration of the Condition of the Wounded and Sick in Armed Forces in the Field, Art. 50), 69 (Convention for the Amelioration of the Condition of Wounded, Sick, and Shipwrecked Members of Armed Forces at Sea, Art. 51), 131 (Convention Relative to the Treatment of Prisoners of War, Art. 130), 211 (Convention Relative to the Protection of Civilian Persons in Time of War, Art. 147).

3. The Rome Statute of the International Criminal Court, 17 July 1998, also generally bases its definition of war crimes on this. See Article 8 of the Rome Statute of the International Criminal Court, in Roberts and Guelff, *Documents on the Laws of War*, 675–80.

4. Article 33 of the Geneva Convention Relative to the Protection of Civilian Persons in Time of War, in ICRC, *Geneva Conventions*, 166.

5. For the development and content of the codified Nuremberg principles, see United Nations, *Yearbook of the International Law Commission, 1950*, 2:182–95.

6. Ibid., 194–95.

7. This also holds true for the warfare of the Netherlands in the Dutch East Indies; see Van Doorn, "Use of Violence."

8. In this context, Jacques van Doorn and Willem Hendrix speak of "functional violence"; see Van Doorn and Hendrix, *Process of Decolonisation*, 18–24.

9. On the aspect of counter-terrorism and the use of massive violence see: French, *British Way in Counter-Insurgency*, 105–12; Bennett, "Mau Mau Emergency," 143–63; Bennett, "Other Side of the COIN," 638–64.

10. Mazower, *Dark Continent*, 176.

11. Richard A. Frost, "Some Thoughts on the Present Troubles in Kenya," report to the British Council in London, 15 April 1953, TNA, BW 15/2, 2.

12. Rawcliffe, *Struggle for Kenya*, 66–68; Edgerton, *Mau Mau*, 155; Peter Evans, *Law and Disorder*, 81; Clayton, *Counter-Insurgency*, 1; David Anderson, "Surrogates of the State," 161.

13. Rawcliffe, *Struggle for Kenya*, 68.

14. Emergency regulation "Collective Punishment," 23 November 1952, in Colony and Protectorate of Kenya, *Official Gazette Supplement*, no. 61, 25 November 1952, 591–95.

15. For example, see Baring to CO, telegram, 3 December 1952, TNA, CO 822/501; Jock Scott Intelligence Summary, 29 January 1953, 6 February 1953, 19 February 1953, TNA, WO 276/378; "Communal Punishments Will Stay," *Daily Chronicle*, 9 October 1953.

16. Colony Emergency Council, minutes, no. 235, "Collective Punishment Emergency Regulations 4A and 4D," 5 October 1953, TNA, WO 276/413.

17. N. F. Harris, "Memorandum for the Operations Committee Concerning Economic Sanctions on Kikuyu, Embu and Meru," 9 October 1953, TNA, WO 276/413.

18. "Situation Appreciation Week Ending the 4th December 1952," report by Police Commissioner O'Rorke, TNA, WO 276/378.

19. Jock Scott Intelligence Summary, 13 February 1953, TNA, WO 276/378.

20. Justice Minister Whyatt to Governor Baring, "Note on Collective Punishment," 6 December 1954, Papers on the Rule of Law, John Whyatt, RH, Mss.Afr.s.1694.

21. Memoirs of Jon Wainwright, RH, Mss.Brit.Emp.s.548, 45.

22. Don Barnett, *Urban Guerrilla*, 16.

23. Emergency regulation "Prohibited Areas," 29 October 1952, in Colony and Protectorate of Kenya, *Official Gazette Extraordinary*, Nairobi, 30 October 1952, 526–27.

24. Baring to CO, telegram, "Shooting Without Challenge in Prohibited Areas," 11 April 1953, TNA, CO 822/440.

25. "Sentries Orders and Order to Fire," Headquarters Thirty-ninth Infantry Brigade, 20 April 1953, TNA, WO 32/21721.

26. Commander in Chief Hinde, Emergency Directive No. 4, "Prohibited Areas," 30 April 1953, TNA, WO 276/510.

27. Edgerton, *Mau Mau*, 152, 167; Evans, *Law and Disorder*, 183.

28. Brockway to Colonial Minister Lyttelton, 30 April and 28 October 1953, TNA, CO 822/489.

29. Evans, *Law and Disorder*, 212; Rawcliffe, *Struggle for Kenya*, 70; Barnett, *Urban Guerrilla*, 62; Maloba, *Mau Mau and Kenya*, 93.

30. CO to Deputy Governor Crawford, 24 November 1953, TNA, CO 822/489.

31. Boer settler quoted in Friedberg, *Mau Mau Terror*, 12.

32. Emergency directive no. 5, "Role of RAF Aircraft," 3 May 1953, and Annexure no. 4, "The Use and Value of Heavy Bombing," both in TNA, WO 276/233.

33. See the reports "Size of the Royal Air Force in Kenya," June 1954; "The Future Conduct of Air Operation," 5 October 1954; and "Appreciation by the Commander-in-Chief of the Operational Situation in June 1955," 11 June 1955, all in TNA, AIR 23/8617.

34. Attacks such as carpet bombings, in which several clearly distinct military targets are treated as a single target, are considered "indiscriminate attacks." In international law, this practice was first prohibited by the first Protocol Additional to the Geneva Conventions of 8 June 1977, Article 85. See ICRC, *Protocols Additional to the Geneva Conventions*, 63–64.

35. Colonial Minister Lyttelton, "Air Operations in Kenya," secret memorandum to the government cabinet, 24 May 1954, TNA, PREM 11/696.

36. U.S. Embassy in London to the State Department, confidential telegram, 12 September 1955, NARA, RG 59.2, 745R.00/9-1255.

37. Rawcliffe, *Struggle for Kenya*, 69.

38. Dudley Thompson, *From Kingston to Kenya*, 102; Buijtenhuijs, *Le mouvement "Mau Mau,"* 366; Mockaitis, *British Counterinsurgency*, 50.

39. *Semper Fidelis*, 349–55.

40. Ibid., 351; Windeatt, "The Mau Mau Emergency Kenya. The Devonshire Regiment 1953–1955," Papers of Lieutenant Colonel J. K. Windeatt, IWM, 90/20/1, 25.

41. *Semper Fidelis*, 355.

42. Edgerton, *Mau Mau*, 166–67; Baldwin, *Mau Mau Man-Hunt*, 143; David Anderson, *Histories of the Hanged*, 258. This practice was not a British "invention" but had already been used systematically in the nineteenth century during the Belgian colonial rule of the Congo. The chopped-off hands served as proof of death, which is why there existed the office of "keeper of the hands" in several military units. See Hochschild, *King Leopold's Ghost*, 165–66.

43. Hewitt, *Kenya Cowboy*, 12.

44. Ibid., 13.

45. Situation Report of the High Command, July 1953, TNA, WO 276/452; Kenya Intelligence Committee, "Casualty Statistics," circular memo, 20 July 1953, TNA, WO 276/460.

46. High Command, "Reporting of Casualties," circular memo, 5 August 1953, TNA, WO 276/196.

47. See Appendix A, "Security Forces, Civilian and Mau Mau Casualty Reports to Be Included in Joint Sitreps," 5 August 1953, TNA, WO 276/196.

48. "Report and Findings of the Commission of Inquiry," 31 December 1953, TNA, WO 32/21722.

49. Ibid., 9–10.

50. Erskine to WO, 12 December 1953, TNA, WO 32/21722.

51. Special order, "Action to Be Taken as the Result of Court of Inquiry," issued by General Erskine, January 1954, TNA, WO 32/21722.

52. General Erskine, "McLean Court of Inquiry," report, 1 January 1954, TNA, WO 32/21722.

53. Promoted in 1953 to the rank of sergeant on the merits of his service, Idi Amin had risen by 1959 to warrant officer, the highest rank for a black African in the British colonial troops at the time. Amin, who staged a putsch in 1971 that made him Uganda's head of state, became the symbol of the African tyrant due to his cruelty. His eight-year dictatorship cost an estimated five hundred thousand victims.

54. Brigadier Percy W. P. Green, former commandant of the Fourth Uganda Battalion of the KAR, interview with Dr. William Beaver as part of the Oxford Development Records Project "The Role of British Forces in Africa," 25 October 1979, Papers of Brigadier Percy W. P. Green, RH, Mss.Afr.s.1715 (118) Box 5, 7.

55. For example, see Baldwin, *Mau Mau Man-Hunt*, 78, 132, 157, 173–74, 214–15.

56. Ibid., 90, 108.

57. Hewitt, *Kenya Cowboy*, 204.

58. Ibid., 98, 102.

59. Ibid., 200.

60. Ibid., 187–88.

61. Gikoyo, *We Fought for Freedom*, 143–44.

62. Edgerton, *Mau Mau*, 170.

63. Commander in Chief Cherrière to General Allard, 14 May 1955, quoted in Horne, *Savage War*, 114.

64. Commander in Chief Lorillot, "Instruction sur l'action de commandement à exercer en cas de dommages graves commis au cours des operations," top-secret circular memo to all commanders, 7 November 1955, SHAT, 1H 1240/D1.

65. Commander in Chief Lorillot, "Dommages aux biens en cours d'opération," circular memo to all commanders, 9 December 1955, SHAT, 1H 1240/D1.

66. Governor General Soustelle, "Attitude à observer à l'égard des populations Musulmanes dans la lutte contre le terrorisme," circular memo, 22 November 1955, SHAT, 1H 1240/D1.

67. Ibid.

68. Heymann, *Libertés publiques*, 155, 202; Branche, *La torture*, 42–51.

69. Keramane, *La pacification*, 8; Barrat and Barrat, *Livre blanc*, 119; Horne, *Savage War*, 115.

70. The village of Oradour-sur-Glane was completely destroyed and all of its inhabitants murdered on 10 June 1944 by units of the Waffen-SS and the German Wehrmacht as retaliation for actions by the French resistance. For this reason the name symbolizes the policy of brutal repression during the German occupation, and the place is today a memorial to the French resistance.

71. French conscript quoted in Vidal-Naquet, *Les crimes de l'armée française*, 6.

72. R. F. G. Sarell, British counsul general in Algiers, confidential report to the FO, 18 October 1957, TNA, FO 371/125945.

73. Diary entry of the soldier Stanislas Hutin, 25 March 1956, in Vidal-Naquet, *Les crimes de l'armée française*, 53.

74. Barrat and Barrat, *Livre blanc*, 188, 262; Branche, *La torture*, 290–99; Leulliette, *St. Michael and the Dragon*, 128–30; see especially Branche, "Des viols pendant la guerre d'Algérie."

75. Branche, "Folter und andere Rechtsverletzungen," 164–65.

76. Quote from the notes "Scènes de l'activité d'un commando de chasse, 1959–1961" by the soldier Benoît Rey, in Vidal-Naquet, *Les crimes de l'armée française*, 112.

77. Roy, *War in Algeria*, 50.

78. From the notes "En 'pacifiant' l'Algérie: 1955" by the soldier Jean-Luc Tahon, in Vidal-Naquet, *Les crimes de l'armée française*, 25.

79. See SHAT, 1H 2033/D1, "Répartition du Territoire du point de vue du contrôle des persones et des biens," from Commander in Chief Lorillot to the division commanders, 30 March 1956; and "Définition des zones suivant leur règlementation," from the governor general to the prefects of the Algerian departments, 21 April 1956.

80. SHAT, 1H 2033/D1, memos "Zone Interdite," 20 August 1956, and "Tirs en zone interdite," 3 September 1956 .

81. "Mémento sur la conduite à tenir vis-à-vis des rebelles ou suspects de rébellion," High Command, 30 April 1956, SHAT, 1H 1942/D2, 2; "Mémento à l'usage des chefs des petites unités concernant certains aspects de la recherche et de la capture des hors-la-loi," High Command, May 1957, SHAT, 1H 2577, 2.

82. Branche, "Folter und andere Rechtsverletzungen," 162.

83. From the notes "La mort d'une petite fille: 1956" by the soldier Noel Favrelière, in Vidal-Naquet, *Les crimes de l'armée française*, 55.

84. Barrat and Barrat, *Livre blanc*, 183–88, 195–99, 203–14; on the execution of civilians, see also "Mémoire sur les méthodes répressives en Algérie" from the Union Démocratique du Manifeste Algérien to the French defense ministery, 15 July 1955, CAOM, 81 F909, 1–3.

85. Report from Jacques Vergès, Maurice Courrégé, and Michel Zavrian to the ICRC president, 12 March 1960, ACICR, B AG 225 078-007.

86. Branche, *La torture*, 74–76; Mollenhauer, "Frankreichs Krieg in Algerien," 343–44.

87. Branche, *La torture*, 73; Talbott, *War Without a Name*, 92; Elsenhans, *Algerienkrieg*, 459–60.

88. Statement by a French soldier from 1958, quoted in Münchhausen, *Kolonialismus und Demokratie*, 230.

89. The notes "Un an dans les Aurès, 1956–1957" of the soldier Jacques Pucheu, in Vidal-Naquet, *Les crimes de l'armée française*, 64.

90. General Salan, memo, 19 March 1958, SHAT, 1H 1100/1.

91. "Exécutions sommaires de prisonniers en Algérie" from the ICRC to its delegate in Paris, William H. Michel, 2 June 1960, ACICR, B AG 225 008-015.05.

92. "Situation dans le département de Titeri," report by ICRC delegate Vust, 22 May 1960, ACICR, B AG 225 008-015.05.

93. Ibid.

94. "Declaration (IV, 2) Concerning Asphyxiating Gases," in Roberts and Guelff, *Documents on the Laws of War*, 60–61.

95. "Geneva Protocol for the Prohibition of the Use in War of Asphyxiating, Poisonous, or Other Gases, and of Bacteriological Methods of Warfare," in Roberts and Guelff, *Documents on the Laws of War*, 158–59.

96. See Joseph Burns Kelly, "Gas Warfare in International Law"; Best, *War and Law*, 54, 296.

97. Veuthey, *Guérilla et droit humanitaire*, 83–84.

98. See Harris and Paxman, *Higher Form of Killing*, 43–44.

99. See Kunz and Müller, *Giftgas gegen Abd el Krim*; Mücke, "Agonie einer Kolonialmacht," 264–65.

100. See Mattioli, "Entgrenzte Kriegsgewalt"; Mattioli, *Experimentierfeld der Gewalt*, 88–89, 104–10; Gartz, *Chemische Kampfstoffe*, 57–58.

101. Portugal in particular deployed large amounts of chemical weapons during its decolonization wars in Angola, Guinea, and Mozambique; see Gartz, *Chemische Kampfstoffe*, 108–9.

102. "Fiche au sujet de la requisition générale du Gouverneur Général Leonard en date du 4 novembre 1954," SHAT, 1H 2033/D1.

103. For a long time and especially during the Vietnam War, the use of napalm was the subject of heated debate and an extremely controversial topic in international law. However, incendiary weapons were not officially prohibited until 1980 with the UN Convention on Prohibitions or Restriction on the Use of Certain Conventional Weapons Which May Be Deemed to Be Excessively Injurious or to Have Indiscriminate Effects. See "Protocol on Prohibitions or Restrictions on the Use of Incendiary Weapons (1980 Protocol III)," in Roberts and Guelff, *Documents on the Laws of War*, 533–34; Best, *War and Law*, 296–99.

104. "Protestation du Croissant-Rouge Algérien concernant l'usage du napalm," 26 September 1960, ACICR, B AG 202 008-009.

105. CRA delegate Ben Yakhlef to the ICRC delegate C. Vautier, 21 May 1960; ICRC delegate for Morocco C. Vautier to the ICRC, 25 May 1960, both at ACICR, D EUR France1-0438.

106. P. Gaillard, "Usage du napalm en Algérie," note to the ICRC leadership, 30 May 1960, ACICR, B AG 202 008-009.

107. William Michel, ICRC delegate, Paris, "Entretien avec M. Langlais au Quai d'Orsay, le 24 novembre 1958 à 17h," protocol, ACICR, B AG 202 008-009, 1.

108. For example, see SHAT, 1H 2786/D4, combat orders "Débroussaillage de terrain par incendie" to Colonel Commandant de SMBAT/3/OPE, 8 July 1960; "Débroussaillage de terrain par incendie" to Colonel Commandant de SMBAT/3/OPE, 9 July 1960; and "En vue préparation missions aériennes de débroussaillage de terrain par incendie," 19 July 1960.

109. For example, see SHAT, 1H 2786/D4, combat order "Traitement par engins incendiaires d'aviation de certaines zones du Quartier de Fondouk" to Colonel Commandant de SMBAT/3/OPE, 5 July 1960.

110. SHAT, 1H 2786/D4, Chef d'Escadron Lajarriette, Commandant provisoirement le I/405, "Compte-rendu concernant résultat bombardement et largage bidons spéciaux," 28 June 1960.

111. See SHAT, 1H 2051/D2, reports of Lieutenant Colonel Legrand, "Expérimentation des fougasses," 1 June 1958, and "Expérimentation des fougasses," 14 June 1958; General Langlet, "Expérimentation de fougasses à l'essence gélifiée," 26 June 1958; and Commandant le Génie de la 2ème DIM et ZEC, 3 bureau, "Mines au Napalm: Dispositif Millet," 8 February 1961.

112. Secrétaire d'Etat aux Forces Armées "Terre" to the French High Command in Algeria, "Création d'une unité Armes Spéciales en 10ème Région Militaire," 20 December 1956, SHAT, 1H 1342/D7.

113. Defense Ministry to the French High Command in Algeria, "Création d'un Groupe Armes Spéciales pour les expérimentations nucléaires," 24 November 1958, SHAT, 1H 1342/D7.

114. This deployment of certain hormones was intended to cause uncontrolled plant growth that would eventually cause the plants to grow themselves "to death"; see Gartz, *Chemische Kampfstoffe*, 102.

115. Secret reports, SHAT, 1H 2051/D2: "Rapport sur l'emploi des armes spéciales en Xe Région des Etat-Major, 3e Bureau Antenne Armes Spéciales," 8 September 1956, 8; and Général Commandant des Armes Spéciales, "Rapport sur l'activité du commandement des armes spéciales en 10ème Région Militaire pendant la période de avril 1956 à avril 1957," 15 June 1957, 6.

116. Général Commandant des Armes Spéciales, "Rapport sur l'activité du commandement

des armes spéciales en 10ème Région Militaire pendant la période de avril 1956 à avril 1957," 15 June 1957, 7–8, 10.

117. Lieutenant-Colonel Brunet, commandant le Génie de la ZNA, "Note provisoire relative à la mise en oeuvre et à l'emploi de la Section Grottes," 1956, SHAT, 1H 2786/D4.

118. Colonel G. de Boissieu, chief of general staff, "Instruction sur l'emploi des Sections de Grottes en Algérie," 31 December 1959, SHAT, 1H 1925/D1, 6.

119. On the various special weapons, see secret reports, SHAT, 1H 2051/D2: "Rapport sur l'emploi des armes spéciales en Xe Région" from the État-major, 3e Bureau Antenne Armes Spéciales, 8 September 1956, 3, 6; Général Commandant des Armes Spéciales, "Rapport sur l'activité du commandement des armes spéciales en 10ème Région Militaire pendant la période d'avril 1956 à avril 1957," 15 June 1957, 4–6; and 411ᵉ RAA Batterie Armes Spéciales, "Rapport concernant le traitement des grottes et objectifs souterrains en 10e Région Militaire," 22 November 1958, 6–8.

120. "Protection des Sections Grottes contre l'oxyde de carbonne" from the High Command to the regional commanders, 31 March 1961, SHAT, 1H 2051/D2.

121. On the impact of irritant gases, see Gartz, *Chemische Kampfstoffe*, 101–2.

122. See Colonel Pinsard, "Note relative à l'emploi du génie dans les opérations de neutralisation de grottes," 12 January 1957, SHAT, 1H 3980/D2; General Salan, secret report "Utilisation des Armes Spéciales pour le maintien de l'ordre en Algérie," 30 November 1958, SHAT, 1H 2051/D2.

123. CRA to the ICRC, 6 May 1959; and GPRA communiqué, 12 May 1959, both in ACICR, B AG 202 008-011.

124. Abbas to the president of the ICRC, telegram, 15 May 1959, ACICR, B AG 202 008-011.

125. French Foreign Ministry to the ICRC delegate Michel, 23 May 1959, ACICR, B AG 202 008-011.

126. "Dementi de l'État-Major d'Algérie," 6 May 1959; and French defense ministry statement "Le massacre de Mac-Mahon était en réalité une libération," 13 May 1959, both in ACICR, B AG 202 008-011.

127. For example, see Commandant, Secteur d'Aumale mission report, "Neutralisation de grottes par impregnation," 22 May 1960, SHAT, 1H 2786/D4; "Fiche d'infection" of the Batterie Armes Spéciales du 411e RAA, 2ème Section, 27 September 1960, SHAT, 1H 3591/D2; Commandant, Secteur d'Ain Beida, mission report, "Infection de grottes," 30 October 1961, SHAT, 1H 3591/D2; Chef d'Escadron Carrion, Commandant Pvt. le 1/50ᵉ RA et le Quartier du Rocher Noir, report, "Recensement des sites souterrains," 10 December 1961, SHAT, 1H 2786/D4.

128. Colonel Pinsard, Commandant Pvt. la 5e DB et le Secteur Nord de la ZOT, to Général Commandant la Zone Opérationnelle de Tlemcen, secret note, "Neutralisation des grottes," 3 January 1957, SHAT, 1H 3980/D2.

129. See Stucki and Smith, "Colonial Development of Concentration Camps."

130. On Weyler's reconcentration policy, see Stucki, *Aufstand und Zwangsumsiedlung*; Kotek and Rigoulot, *Jahrhundert der Lager*, 45–55; Foner, *Spanish-Cuban-American War*, 110–18.

131. Foner, *Spanish-Cuban-American War*, 248–53; Kotek and Rigoulot, *Jahrhundert der Lager*, 54–55.

132. Richard E. Welch, "American Atrocities in the Philippines"; Schumacher, "Kolonialkrieg der USA auf den Philippinen"; Kaminski, *Konzentrationslager*, 35; Tenenbaum, *Race and Reich*, 162.

133. On Weyler as a role model for the British methods, see Hobhouse, *Brunt of War*, 28.

134. On British warfare and concentration camps during the Boer War, see Hobhouse, *Zustände in den südafrikanischen Konzentrationslagern*; Arthur Clive Martin, *Concentration Camps, 1900–1902*; Spies, *Methods of Barbarism*; Pretorius, *Scorched Earth*; Kotek and Rigoulot, *Jahrhundert der Lager*, 56–73; Pakenham, *Boer War*, 522–24, 533–49; Scholtz, *Why the Boers Lost the War*, 75–76, 122–23; Eberspächer, "Burenkrieg."

135. Marx, "Kriegsgefangene im Burenkrieg," 274–76.

136. Bridgman and Worley, "Genocide of the Herero"; Gewald, "Kaiserreich und Herero."

137. On the German concentration camps in German Southwest Africa, see Zimmerer, *Deutsche Herrschaft über Afrikaner*, 42–55; Zimmerer, "Kriegsgefangene im Kolonialkrieg"; Zimmerer, "Krieg, KZ und Völkermord"; Zeller, "Geschichte des Konzentrationslagers in Swakopmund"; Kotek and Rigoulot, *Jahrhundert der Lager*, 74–86.

138. This complete toll of victims is based on the numbers reported by the German security forces for the period between October 1904 and March 1907. See Zimmerer, "Krieg, KZ und Völkermord," 58.

139. Erichsen, "Zwangsarbeit im Konzentrationslager."

140. On this point, see R. Marston, "Resettlement as a Counterrevolutionary Technique," in which Major Marston used the case studies of Malaya, Vietnam, Algeria, Mozambique, and Rhodesia to show how well established the internment and resettlement strategy was in post-1945 colonial conflicts; for a more recent study, see especially Gerlach, "Sustainable Violence." and French, *British Way in Counter-Insurgency*, 116-123.

141. Cornaton, *Camps de regroupement*, 33.

142. Agamben, *Homo sacer*, 175–77.

143. Ibid., 178–79.

144. "No one shall be subjected to arbitrary arrest, detention or exile," Article 9 of the UN Universal Declaration of Human Rights, in Ishay, *Human Rights Reader*, 494.

145. "Everyone has the right to liberty and security of person," Article 5 of the ECHR, in Ishay, *Human Rights Reader*, 501.

146. "In time of war or other public emergency threatening the life of the nation any High Contracting Party may take measures derogating from its obligation under this Convention," Article 15 of the ECHR, in Ishay, *Human Rights Reader*, 503.

147. Lyttelton, top-secret memorandum "Detention of Supporters of Mau Mau," 8 February 1954, TNA, PREM 11/696.

148. See the quote by Churchill from 1943, in Simpson, *Detention Without Trial*, 391.

149. British Defense Ministry, "Memorandum on Detention Camps Established Under the Emergency Regulations 1952," 12 June 1959, ACICR, B AG 225 108-004.

150. Elkins, *Britain's Gulag*, 56–61; Evans, *Law and Disorder*, 159.

151. For examples of classification reports, see Mau Mau Classification Reports, 1953–56, RH, Mss.Afr.s.1534.

152. On the British detention practice, see the press release "Progress Report on the Rehabilitation of Mau Mau in Detention Camps," 16 April 1955, TNA, CO 822/794; Elkins, "Detention," 199; Edgerton, *Mau Mau*, 178.

153. FO circular memo, 30 April 1954, TNA, DO 35/5352; Governor of Kenya to Secretary of State for the Colonies, secret telegram, 13 May 1954, TNA, DO 35/5352.

154. Governor of Kenya to Secretary of State for the Colonies, telegram, 27 January 1954, TNA, PREM 11/696.

155. Secretary of State for the Colonies to Governor of Kenya, telegram, 5 February 1954, TNA, CAB 129/65.

156. "Detention Camps," secret report, 11 March 1959, TNA, CO 822/1249.

157. Anderson, *Histories of the Hanged*, 313.

158. Elkins, "Detention," 205.

159. For a good graphic depiction of the British camp system, see the chart by Caroline Elkins, in Elkins, *Britain's Gulag*, 369.

160. The places discussed were particularly remote, uninhabited islands, such as the former

quarantine island Kamaran in the Red Sea; see secret notes titled "Exile Camps for Mau Mau Terrorists," from Baring to the CO, 11 December 1954, and from the CO to Baring, 3 February 1955, TNA, CO 822/803.

161. Report of the Fifth Meeting of the Reconstruction Committee, 22 January 1954; and Terms of Reference for the Rehabilitation Advisory Committee, both in TNA, CO 822/803.

162. On the British "rehabilitation program," see Baring to Lennox-Boyd, confidential note, 27 September 1955; and press release, "Kenya Government's Rehabilitation Programme," 20 October 1955, both in TNA, CO 822/794.

163. Elspeth Huxley, "Kenya's Pipeline to Freedom."

164. Rehabilitation Progress Report 1955, TNA, CO 822/794; "Kikuyu Area Overcrowded," *Daily Telegraph*, 21 February 1957.

165. Richard Woodley quoted in Edgerton, *Mau Mau*, 180.

166. Leigh, *Shadow of the Mau Mau*, 200.

167. Ibid., 202.

168. Both newspaper articles referred to the description of prison conditions found in a prisoner's letter that managed to get smuggled out of the detention camp Lokitaung. "Kenya Prison Like Hell," *Daily Worker*, 8 December 1958; "From the Gates of Hell Jail," *Daily Herald*, 8 December 1958.

169. See especially Wanjau, *Mau Mau Author in Detention*; Muchai, *Hardcore*; Otieno, *Mau Mau's Daughter*, 77–85; Likimani, *Passbook Number F 47927*; Ndoria, *War in the Forest*; Kariuki, *Mau Mau Detainee*; Gikoyo, *We Fought for Freedom*.

170. Clough, *Mau Mau Memoirs*, 205.

171. Wanjau, *Mau Mau Author in Detention*, 29; Ndoria, *War in the Forest*, 14.

172. Baldwin, *Mau Mau Man-Hunt*, 183.

173. H. G. Waters, Public Health Report Manyani Camp, 9 May 1954, TNA, CO 822/801.

174. H. Scott, report, "Typhoid Outbreak at Manyani," 14 September 1954, TNA, CO 822/801/35; Situation Reports, "Mackinnon Road and Manyani Camps," 8 October 1954, and "Manyani and Mackinnon Road Special Camps," 15 January 1955, TNA, WO 276/428.

175. Anderson, *Histories of the Hanged*, 319.

176. See Enslin, "Health, Violence and Rehabilitation."

177. Elkins, *Britain's Gulag*, 227.

178. Ibid., 209–10; Wanjau, *Mau Mau Author in Detention*, 42, 47, 66, 124.

179. Petition by prisoners in Camp Lokitaung, 3 September 1958, TNA, CO 822/1701; Wanjau, *Mau Mau Author in Detention*, 70–72.

180. Barnett, *Urban Guerrilla*, 79.

181. On the special role of the International Labor Organization in the process of decolonization, see especially Maul, *Human Rights, Development, and Decolonization*.

182. CO to Baring, confidential telegram, 12 March 1953, TNA, CO 822/728. In hindsight, these concerns proved to be unfounded. The British government could invoke its own emergency laws, which is why forced labor in the Kenyan camps was not criticized even once by the ILO or the UN Ad Hoc Committee on Forced Labor during the entire emergency. See CO to the FO, 2 April 1954, TNA, FO 371/112516; FO report, "ECOSOC XVII-Forced Labour," 5 April 1954, on the occasion of the interministerial meeting on 2 April 1954, TNA, FO 371/112516; CO to the Trade Union Congress, 15 January 1960, TNA, CO 859/1230.

183. Gikoyo, *We Fought for Freedom*, 220.

184. Ndoria, *War in the Forest*, 119–20.

185. Elkins, *Britain's Gulag*, 187–88.

186. Baring to the CO, telegram, 22 November 1954, TNA, CO 859/560.

187. Defense Ministry, "Corporal Punishment" memos, 7 April 1955 and 31 May 1955, TNA, CO 859/560; Peter Evans, "Flogging in Kenya."

188. Kariuki, *Mau Mau Detainee*, 75–77, 90–91.

189. Wanjau, *Mau Mau Author in Detention*, 56–58.

190. Fletcher, *Truth About Kenya*.

191. Meldon to Lennox-Boyd, 4 February 1959, TNA, CO 822/1237.

192. Wanstall, "I Saw Men Tortured"; Philip Meldon's eyewitness account, "My Two Years in Kenya," and Meldon to Lennox-Boyd, 18 October 1957, both in TNA, CO 822/1237.

193. Affidavit by Victor Charles Shuter, in the matter of the Mau Mau detention camps in Kenya, 10 January 1959, TNA, CO 822/1271.

194. Ibid., 8.

195. Statement by Captain Ernest Law, TNA, CO 822/1270.

196. Affidavits by Anthony Julian Stuart Williams-Meyrick, 9 February 1959, and Leonard Bird, 11 February 1959, TNA, CO 822/1276.

197. For example, see the transcript of a petition from prisoners at Mariira Camp, in a telegram from Baring to the CO, 4 July 1958, TNA, CO 822/1705, which reports two cases of death and several of abuse; and a petition to the Labour MP Barbara Castle, 12 June 1959, TNA, CO 822/1277, in which the cases of abused prisoners are listed individually and mention is made of 999 deaths just in Embakasi Camp.

198. Wanjau, *Mau Mau Author in Detention*, 80–81, 184, 195; Gikoyo, *We Fought for Freedom*, 218, 225.

199. Kenyan attorney general Griffith-Jones, "Dilution Detention Camps—Use of Force in Enforcing Discipline," June 1957, TNA, CO 822/1251.

200. See Government of the UK, *Documents Relating to the Death of Eleven Mau Mau Detainees at Hola Camp in Kenya*; Government of the UK, *Record of Proceedings and Evidence in the Enquiry into the Deaths of Eleven Mau Mau Detainees at Hola Camp in Kenya*; Government of the UK, *Further Documents Relating to the Death of Eleven Mau Mau Detainees at Hola Camp in Kenya*.

201. Secret cabinet paper, "Kenya: Hola Detention Camp," 10 June 1959, TNA, CAB 130/164.

202. R. D. Fairn, "Report of the Committee on Emergency Detention Camps," July 1959, TNA, CO 822/1275, 13, 18.

203. Anderson, *Histories of the Hanged*, 294; Elkins, *Britain's Gulag*, 234–35; Elkins, "Detention," 206–7; Edgerton, *Mau Mau*, 92–93; Buijtenhuijs, *Le mouvement "Mau Mau,"* 218; Newsinger, "Revolt and Repression in Kenya," 175–76.

204. General Erskine, secret planning paper "Operations in 1955," TNA, WO 216/879.

205. Sorrenson, *Land Reform in the Kikuyu Country*, 110–11.

206. CO report "Rehabilitation Programmes in Kenya," July 1954, TNA, CO 822/794.

207. M. Shannon, "Social Revolution in Kikuyuland: Rehabilitation and Welfare Work in Kenya's New Village Communities, September–October 1955," copy, ACICR, B AG 200 108-001.

208. Interview with Ruth Ndegwa, 22 March 1999, quoted in Elkins, *Britain's Gulag*, 238–40.

209. Barnett and Njama, *Mau Mau from Within*, 211.

210. Price, "With the Security Forces in Kenya."

211. Baring to Lennox-Boyd, telegrams, 24 August 1955 and 29 September 1955, TNA, DO 35/5354.

212. "Intensification of Effort Against Mau Mau," District Commissioner's Office, Embu, secret planning paper, 27 May 1955, TNA, WO 276/457.

213. Elkins, *Britain's Gulag*, 244; see also Anderson, "Surrogates of the State," 169–73; Branch, *Defeating Mau Mau*, 107–16.

214. On the excess of violence used by the Home Guard, see the numerous reports by contemporaries in Elkins, *Britain's Gulag*, 244–59; Elkins, "Detention," 215–16.

215. "Intensification of Effort Against Mau Mau," TNA, WO 276/457.

216. Barnett and Njama, *Mau Mau from Within*, 332.

217. Likimani, *Passbook Number F 47927*, 60–74.

218. Fletcher, *Truth About Kenya*, 7–8; see also "45 Deaths in Kiambu Village," *East African Standard*, 17 November 1955.

219. Interview with Wandia wa Muriithi, 22 March 1999, quoted in Elkins, *Britain's Gulag*, 259.

220. Gikoyo, *We Fought for Freedom*, 227–28.

221. Barnett and Njama, *Mau Mau from Within*, 426.

222. Exact figures on the number of victims of villagization are not to be found. However, Robert Edgerton assumes that it was several tens of thousands, while the contemporaries in Caroline Elkins's work also report massive numbers of deaths; see Edgerton, *Mau Mau*, 93; Elkins, *Britain's Gulag*, 264.

223. Münchhausen, *Kolonialismus und Demokratie*, 152–53.

224. Law no. 55-385 of 3 April 1955, *Journal Officiel, Lois et Décrets*, 7 April 1955, 3479. For an overview of the various detention regulations, see also "Instruction sur le régime des détentions administratives dans les Départements Algériens," 9 December 1960, CAOM, 81 F925.

225. P. Gaillard, "Note pour le Comité aggravation et extension des troubles intérieurs en Algérie," 25 May 1955, ACICR, B AG 200 008-001; "Les camps de concentration Algériens," *France Observateur*, 16 June 1955.

226. For an overview of the very bifurcated network of camps, see the French army's camp map, 14 September 1960, SHAT, 1H 1492/D1.

227. Vergès, Zavrian, and Courrégé, *Les disparus*, 94.

228. Ibid., 96–97, 105.

229. Decree by Lacoste, 11 April 1957, SHAT, 1H 2576/2.

230. Military cabinet to Commander in Chief Salan, confidential note, 15 June 1957, SHAT, 1H 2019/D2.

231. Elsenhans, *Algerienkrieg*, 438; Branche, *La torture*, 121. The full extent of the detention measures and the entire number of people arrested cannot be clearly reconstructed because of the decentralized operations in the various military sectors.

232. Lacoste, circular memo, 23 August 1956, ACICR, B AG 225 008-003.

233. See General Salan, "Centres d'éducation et de rééducation," secret memo, 6 March 1958, and secret instructions from General Dulac, including a detailed "reeducation program," 20 May 1958, both in SHAT, 1H 1492/D1.

234. Report of the Service Central des Centres d'Hébergement to the Governor General, 17 August 1956, ACICR, B AG 225 008-002.

235. Eyewitness report of an escaped detainee from Djorf Camp, in Keramane, *La pacification*, 54–55.

236. Djorf Camp commandant to the governor general, 1956, in Barrat and Barrat, *Livre blanc*, 43.

237. Physician association of Bône to the ICRC president, 27 September 1961, ACICR, B AG 225-008-032.

238. "Rapport d'information sur les missions effectuées dans les établissements pénitentiaires et lieux d'internement: Mission exécutée en Algérie du 12 au 18 octobre 1961," CAOM, 81 F937, 13–16, 20.

239. In particular, the report of the second ICRC mission spoke of overall very primitive prison conditions in the camps inspected from May to June 1956, and the reports of the following missions continued to present proposals for improvement to the French authorities, even though the missions did find progress had been made. See Rapport sur les visites effectuées lors de la deuxième mission du Comité International de la Croix-Rouge, May-June 1956, ACICR, B AG 225 008-004.02, 7–8; Mission du Comité International de la Croix-Rouge en Algérie, October–November 1956: Rapport communiqué au Gouvernement français," ACICR, B AG 225 008-004.03, 3–4; Rapports sur les visites effectuées lors de la quatrième mission du CICR en Algérie, May-June 1957, ACICR, B AG 225 008-004.02, 4; Rapports sur les visites effectuées lors de la septième mission du CICR en Algérie, Octobre-Novembre 1959, ACICR, B AG 225 008-013, 5; Rapports sur les visites effectuées lors de la huitième mission du CICR en Algérie, January–February 1961, ACICR, B AG 225 008-023, 9.

240. Petition by internees at Arcole Camp to the Algerian governor general and the French prime minister, 2 April 1957, in Keramane, La pacification, 45–48.

241. For example, see the letter of protest from eleven lawyers to the French president, 11 October 1955, in Barrat and Barrat, Livre blanc, 109–11.

242. Eyewitness account by internee Nadji Abbas Turqui from Paul-Cazelles Camp, in Keramane, La pacification, 76; on Paul-Cazelles Camp, see also "Camp d'internement de Paul-Cazelles: Récit d'un Algérien qui y a fait un séjour de plusieurs semaines," report, CAOM, 19 PA Carton 9, Dossier 118.

243. See the report "Témoignages sur un centre de torture: La Cité Améziane à Constantine," 29 October 1959, ACICR, B AG 225 008-014.01; "La ferme Améziane, centre de torture à Constantine," Vérité-Liberté 9 (May 1961): 8; Einaudi, La ferme Améziane.

244. Barrat and Barrat, Livre blanc, 22–25.

245. See particularly the reports of the third, fourth, and fifth ICRC missions: "Mission du Comité International de la Croix-Rouge en Algérie, octobre–novembre 1956: Rapport communiqué au Gouvernement français," ACICR, B AG 225 008-004.03, 8–9; "Rapports sur les visites effectuées lors de la quatrième mission du CICR en Algérie," May-June 1957, ACICR, B AG 225 008-004.02, 6; "Rapports sur les visites effectuées lors de la cinquième mission du CICR en Algérie," November 1957–February 1958, ACICR, B AG 225 008-005, 6.

246. Lawyers Maurice Courrégé, Jacques Vergès, and Michel Zavrian to the ICRC president, 28 October 1959, ACICR, B AG 225-008-014.01.

247. Lawyers Maurice Courrégé, Yves Mathieu, Gaston Amblard, Henri Coupon, and André Bessou to the ICRC president, 1 October 1961, ACICR, B AG 225-008-024.01.

248. See General Boyer-Vidal, "Rapport de visite du secteur d'Orléansville," 27 February 1960, SHAT, 1H 2573/D1; Boyer-Vidal, "Rapport de visite du secteur du Telagh," 31 March 1960, SHAT, 1H 1100/D3; Boyer-Vidal, "Rapport de visite du secteur d'Oran," 11 April 1960, SHAT, 1H 1100/D3.

249. Paul-Albert Fevrier to the ICRC, report, 17 April 1960, ACICR, D EUR France1-0438, 9–15.

250. Ibid., 16.

251. For the definition and reasons for regroupement, see Governor General Paul Delouvrier, "Note d'information sur les regroupements de population," 25 July 1959, CAOM, 81 F107, 1–2.

252. Hogard, "Le soldat dans la guerre révolutionnaire."

253. See Cornaton, Camps de regroupement, 125, for a map outlining the resettlement operations.

254. Ibid., 120–24.

255. Ibid., 63–65.

256. Thénault, "Rappels historiques," 232.

257. For the sizes of the *zones interdites*, see SHAT, 1H 1933/D3.

258. See "Algérie: un million de personnes déplacées," *France Observateur*, 16 April 1959; "Un million d'Algériens derrière les barbelés," *L'Humanité*, 17 April 1959; "Un million d'Algériens menacés de famine," *L'Humanité*, 18 April 1959; "Un rapport révèle la situation souvent tragique d'un million d'Algériens regroupés," *Le Monde*, 18 April 1959; "Un million d'hommes, de femmes et d'enfants sont menacés de famine estime un rapport officiel," *La Croix*, 20 April 1959; "Dans les camps d'Algérie les milliers d'enfants meurent," *Libération*, 21 April 1959.

259. Rocard, "Note sur les centres de regroupement, 17 February 1959," in Rocard, *Rapport sur les camps de regroupement*, 103-53.

260. Directive from Delouvrier to army commanders, 31 March 1959, CAOM, 81 F107.

261. Directive from Delouvrier to army commanders and civilian authorities, 24 April 1959, CAOM, 81 F107.

262. Governor General Paul Delouvrier, "Note d'information sur les regroupements de population," 25 July 1959, CAOM, 81 F107, 6.

263. Inspection Générale des Regroupements report, "Les mille villages," April 1960, CAOM, 81 F444.

264. Directive from Delouvrier to army commanders and civilian authorities, 25 May 1961, SHAT, 1H 2030/D1.

265. Commander J. Florentin, "Des Regroupements de Population en Algérie," secret report, 11 December 1960, SHAT, 1H 2030/D1, 38.

266. Planning paper "Regroupement" by the commander in chief of the French Algerian army, 1 March 1960, and commander in chief General Crepin's directive to the regional commanders, "Regroupement de populations—Mille villages," 1 June 1960, both in SHAT, 1H 2030/D1.

267. General Parlange's report "Contribution de l'inspection générale des regroupements au rapport d'information générale," 13 August 1960, CAOM, 81 F444.

268. See secret protocol of the meeting between leading representatives of civilian and military offices, 1 June 1960, CAOM, 14 CAB 177, 6-7; General Parlange's directive "Campaigne d'information sur les regroupements et nouveaux villages," 4 July 1960, CAOM, 81 F444.

269. Information brochure, "Parrainage par la colonie française du Portugal du village d'Qued el Haad," CAOM, 14 CAB 177.

270. Anonymous, *Algérie: Naissance de mille villages*; even though the brochure does not indicate a publisher, it was published at the behest of French authorities.

271. Moreover, this summation of success also claimed that 2,664 new school classes for 125,000 Algerian pupils, 566 youth centers, and 835 hospitals had been set up; see ibid., 76.

272. Planhol, *Nouveaux Villages Algérois*.

273. Ibid., 106.

274. Thénault, "Rappels historiques," 236-37.

275. See the eyewitness account of February 1958 on the creation of "prohibited zones" in the north of the department Constantine, in Keramane, *La pacification*, 243-46.

276. Cornaton, *Camps de regroupement*, 80-83.

277. Benzinz, *Le camp*, 13.

278. Rocard, Note sur les centres de regroupement, 17 February 1959, in Rocard, *Rapport sur les camps de regroupement*, 126-27.

279. Ibid., 153.

280. Jean Rodhain, "Les réfugiés en Algérie: Résultats d'une enquête sur place 19 mars–2 avril 1959," CAOM, 81 F107, 7.

281. Cornaton, *Camps de regroupement*, 96.

282. Ibid., 97.

283. Fanon, *Aspekte der Algerischen Revolution*, 81–82.

284. See Rocard, Note sur les centres de regroupement, 17 February 1959, in Rocard, *Rapport sur les camps de regroupement*, 127-32; Cornaton, *Camps de regroupement*, 93-5.

285. Bourdieu and Sayad, *Déracinement*, 48.

286. Ibid., 77; Rocard, Note sur les centres de regroupement, 17 February 1959, in Rocard, *Rapport sur les camps de regroupement*, 132.

287. Bourdieu and Sayad, *Déracinement*, 29–31.

288. Cornaton, *Camps de regroupement*, 99–102.

289. Rocard, Note sur les centres de regroupement, 17 February 1959, in Rocard, *Rapport sur les camps de regroupement*, 136; Elsenhans, *Algerienkrieg*, 444–45.

290. Kotek and Rigoulot, *Jahrhundert der Lager*, 553; Thénault, "Rappels historiques," 233.

291. Fanon, *Aspekte der Algerischen Revolution*, 14.

292. According to the official figures of the UNHCR, 110,245 Algerian refugees were in Morocco and 151,903 in Tunisia in December 1959; see UNHCR, *State of the World's Refugees*, 41. On the refugee problem in Morocco and Tunisia, see especially "Rapport concernant les réfugiés algériens en territoire tunisien" by the ICRC delegate Colladon, 17 December 1957, and the ICRC report "Relief Action of the International Committee of the Red Cross on Behalf of Algerian Refugees in Morocco," March 1958, both in ACICR, D EUR France1-0924; MAE, "Note sur les réfugiés algériens au Maroc" and "Note sur les réfugiés algériens en Tunisie," 5 September 1958, MAE, NUOI Carton 560; UNHCR, *L'opération de secours aux réfugiés*; UNHCR, "Joint Operation with League of Red Cross Societies."

293. Victor Hugo quoted in Peters, *Folter*, 25.

294. Ibid., 125–27.

295. Mellor, *La torture*, 117, 161–63.

296. Del Vecchio, *Déclaration des droits de l'homme*, 40.

297. Reemtsma, "Neues Jahrhundert der Folter," 27; Vidal-Naquet, *La torture dans la république*, 14–19; Peters, *Folter*, 177–83; Branche, *La torture*, 28–31; Benot, "Décolonisation de l'Afrique française," 524–25; Benot, *Massacres coloniaux*, 165–69.

298. Excerpts from the "Report of the Commission for the Investigation of Alleged Cases of Torture in the Madras Presidency" (Madras, 1855), in Peters, *Folter*, 179; on torture in colonial India, see also Ruthven, *Torture*, 183–217.

299. Viollis, *Indochine SOS*; on torture and war crimes during the French war in Indochina, see Jacques Chégaray, "Les tortures en Indochine," in Vidal-Naquet, *Les crimes de l'armée française*, 17–20; Ruscio, "Interrogations sur certains pratiques."

300. Simon, *Contre la torture*, 24–40; Peters, *Folter*, 143; Reemtsma, "Semantik des Begriffs 'Folter,'" 257.

301. Mellor, *La torture*, 179–83.

302. Ibid., 193–222.

303. Article 5 in Ishay, *Human Rights Reader*, 494.

304. See Ishay, *Human Rights Reader*, 501, for Article 3 of the ECHR: "No one shall be subjected to torture or to inhuman or degrading treatment or punishment."

305. For the standpoint of the ICRC, see, among others, the report "La torture: Quelques idées en vue d'une délibération du CICR," 23 December 1959, ACICR, B AG 202 000-003.07.

306. See ICRC, *Geneva Conventions*, 27 ("Convention [I] for the Amelioration of the Condition of the Wounded and Sick in Armed Forces in the Field," Art. 12), 55–56 ("Convention [II] for the Amelioration of the Condition of Wounded, Sick and Shipwrecked Members of Armed Forces at Sea," Art. 12), and 166 ("Convention [IV] Relative to the Protection of Civilian Persons in Time of War," Art. 32).

307. Ibid., 83 ("Convention [III] Relative to the Treatment of Prisoners of War," Art. 17).

308. Peters, *Folter*, 174, 183; Kahn, *Sacred Violence*, 66.

309. Jean-Paul Sartre, "A Victory," in Sartre, *Colonialism and Neocolonialism*, 72.

310. ICRC memorandum "La Croix-Rouge s'élève contre la torture et l'abus des actes de violence," October 1962, ACICR, B AG 202 000-003.07.

311. Troops from the Netherlands also used torture as a means to gather information during their military operations in the Dutch East Indies from 1945 to 1949. See Van Doorn, "Use of Violence," 162–63.

312. See also Holland, "Dirty Wars," 41–42.

313. Pimlott, "British Experience," 22, 38; Mockaitis, *British Counterinsurgency*, 123; French, *British Way in Counter-Insurgency*, 27-33. On the crucial role of intelligence services in maintaining imperial control in the years before decolonization from 1914 to 1939 see especially: Martin Thomas, *Empires of Intelligence*.

314. J. M. Forster, Operational Research Unit Far East, *A Comparative Study of the Emergencies in Malaya and Kenya*, Report No. 1/1957, TNA, WO 291/1670, 74.

315. Baring to Colonial Minister Lyttelton, 24 November 1952, TNA, CO 822/450.

316. Mockaitis, *British Counterinsurgency*, 131; Füredi, "Decolonization Through Counterinsurgency," 157; Maloba, *Mau Mau and Kenya*, 83–84; for a closer analysis of the intelligence service system during the emergency, see Heather, "Intelligence and Counter-Intelligence in Kenya."

317. Commander in Chief Hinde, Emergency Directive No. 1, April 1953, TNA, WO 276/510, 2; top-secret report "Appreciation by the Commander-in-Chief of the Operational Situation in Kenya in June 1955," 11 June 1955, TNA, AIR 23/8617, 3.

318. Secret report "Operational Intelligence Instruction: Prisoner Interrogation," July 1953, TNA, WO 32/21721; "Prisoner Handling Procedure," October 1953, TNA, WO 276/382.

319. "Operational Intelligence Instruction," July 1953, TNA, WO 32/21721, 1.

320. Emergency directive no. 9, "Surrender Policy," 28 July 1953, TNA, CO 822/496.

321. War Council instruction no. 18, "The Treatment of Captured and Surrendered Terrorists," 30 November 1955, TNA, CO 822/776.

322. Barnett, *Urban Guerrilla*, 34, 62–63; Gikoyo, *We Fought for Freedom*, 204.

323. Inspector Tony Cross to the CID, Streatham Police Station, London, 1 March 1953, TNA, CO 822/489.

324. Inquiry report of the Streatham Police Station, 19 March 1953, TNA, CO 822/489; "Gestapo Way in Kenya," *Daily Worker*, 18 March 1953.

325. Edgerton, *Mau Mau*, 159, 176; Elkins, *Britain's Gulag*, 66.

326. Likimani, *Passbook Number F 47927*, 147.

327. Rawcliffe, *Struggle for Kenya*, 68.

328. Elkins, *Britain's Gulag*, 67.

329. Statement, "Church Missionary Society Press Conference," 9 February 1953; and telegrams from the CO to the Colonial Government in Kenya, 10 February 1953, and from Baring to the CO, 11 February 1953; all in TNA, CO 822/471.

330. Bewes to Baring, 28 January 1953, TNA, CO 822/471.

331. Archbishop of Canterbury to Colonial Minister Lyttelton, 10 February 1953, and Lyttelton to Baring, telegram, 12 February 1953, both in TNA, CO 822/471.

332. Baring to the CO, telegram, 11 February 1953, TNA, CO 822/471.

333. R. A. Wilkinson, "Finding of R. A. Wilkinson, 1st Class Magistrate in the Inquiry into the Death of Elisha or Elijah Gideon Njeru at Embu on 30th January 1953," TNA, CO 822/471.

334. Baring to the CO, telegram, 9 March 1953, TNA, CO 822/471.

335. Ibid., 5 October 1953.

336. "African's Death After Beating—Two Europeans Fined," *Times* (London), 1 October 1953.

337. Clayton, *Counter-Insurgency*, 44–45; Edgerton, *Mau Mau*, 160–61.

338. Baring to Colonial Minister Lyttelton, telegram, 5 June 1953, TNA, CO 822/489.

339. General Erskine, "Message to Be Distributed to All Officers of the Army, Police and the Security Forces," 23 June 1953, TNA, WO 276/511.

340. For an example, see "Parliamentary Question: Screening in Rift Valley Province," report by the Provincial Commissioner, Rift Valley Province, 20 November 1953, TNA, CO 822/499.

341. General Erskine, operations report, "The Kenya Emergency: June 1953–May 1955," 25 May 1955, TNA, WO 276/511, 5.

342. Baring to the CO, telegram, 17 December 1953, TNA, CO 822/697.

343. Secret report of Tanganyika's governor Edward Twining to the CO, 25 November 1953, TNA, CO 822/499.

344. Ibid., 2.

345. "Report on the Case of the Queen Versus Brian Hayward," 5 December 1953, TNA, CO 822/499.

346. "Statement by the Secretary of State for War," 30 November 1953, TNA, CAB 21/2906; Erskine to the WO, telegram, 9 December 1953, TNA, WO 32/21722. On these disciplinary measures see: Bennett, "British Army and Controlling Barbarisation," 59–80.

347. Clayton, *Counter-Insurgency*, 41; Edgerton, *Mau Mau*, 169; Anderson, *Histories of the Hanged*, 259.

348. On the colonial police in Kenya, see Throup, "Crime, Politics and the Police"; Sinclair, "'Settlers' Men or Policemen?" 166–97; Foran, *Kenya Police*.

349. Anderson, *Histories of the Hanged*, 260.

350. Secret note of the colonial government in Nairobi to the CO, 16 December 1953, TNA, CO 822/489.

351. Government of the UK, *Report to the Secretary of State for the Colonies*, 7–8.

352. Stockwell, "Policing During the Malayan Emergency," 114.

353. Young, paper for the Oxford Colonial Records Project, Papers of Sir Arthur Young, RH, Mss.Brit.Emp.s.486, File 1, 5.

354. Ibid., 18.

355. Young to Governor Baring, 22 November 1954, RH, Mss.Brit.Emp.s.486, File 1.

356. Evans, *Law and Disorder*, 270.

357. MacPherson to the Commissioner of Police, secret memorandum, 23 December 1954, Papers of Sir Arthur Young, RH, Mss.Brit.Emp.s.486, File 5.

358. K. P. Hadingham, report, "Alleged Murder by Chief Mundia—Karatina," to the Commissioner of Police, 22 November 1954, Papers of Sir Arthur Young, RH, Mss.Brit.Emp.s.486, File 5; on the British efforts to instrumentalize the Home Guards and to cover up atrocities they caused, see especially Anderson, "Surrogates of the State."

359. For the case of Chief Mundia, see also Branch, *Defeating Mau Mau*, 84–87.

360. Young's notes on "My letters to H. E.," 11–15, and Young's letter of resignation to Governor Baring, 28 December 1954, Papers of Sir Arthur Young, RH, Mss.Brit.Emp.s.486, File 5.

361. The opposing viewpoint in "Resignation of Colonel Young and Relations Between the Administration and Police," TNA, CO 822/1293.

362. Young's paper for the Oxford Colonial Records Project, Papers of Sir Arthur Young, RH, Mss.Brit.Emp.s.486, File 1, 29.

363. Baring to the CO, top-secret telegram, 17 January 1955, TNA, CO 822/775.

364. Sentence handed down by Judge A. C. Harrison against Ormonde Waters, Antony Fuller, Geoffrey Coppen, William Bosch, 1 September 1955, TNA, CO 822/1223; Fletcher, *Truth About Kenya*, 10–11.

365. Elkins, *Britain's Gulag*, 311.

366. Griffith-Jones's secret memorandum "Dilution Detention Camps—Use of Force in Enforcing Discipline," June 1957, TNA, CO 822/1251, 3.

367. Ibid., 4–5.

368. Ibid., 10.

369. BBC interview with Gavaghan on 17 November 2002, quoted in Elkins, *Britain's Gulag*, 322.

370. For example, see Baring's secret telegrams to Lennox-Boyd, 5 February 1957, TNA, CO 822/1249; and to the CO, 26 September and 7 October 1958, TNA, CO 822/1276.

371. Baring to Lennox-Boyd, secret telegram, 16 February 1957, TNA, CO 822/1249.

372. Baring to Colonial Minister Lennox-Boyd, confidential note, 25 June 1957, TNA, CO 822/1251.

373. Baring to the CO, 21 May 1957, TNA, CO 822/1249.

374. Lennox-Boyd to Baring, 3 July 1957, secret and personal telegram, TNA, CO 822/1251.

375. Telegrams of Lennox-Boyd to Baring, 16 July 1957, and Baring to Lennox-Boyd, 17 July 1957, TNA, CO 822/1251.

376. R. D. Fairn, "Report of the Committee on Emergency Detention Camps," July 1959, TNA, CO 822/1275, 13 and 18.

377. See Adass, "Police et violence coloniale."

378. Bourdet, "Votre Gestapo d'Algérie."

379. Mauriac, "La question."

380. "Le rapport de M. Roger Wuillaume, inspecteur général de l'administration," 2 March 1955, in Vidal-Naquet, *La raison d'état*, 67.

381. Ibid., 63–64.

382. Ibid., 62.

383. Ibid., 66–67.

384. Ibid., 68.

385. "Rapport de M. Mairey, directeur de la sûreté, sur le fonctionnement des forces de police en Algérie," 13 December 1955, in Vidal-Naquet, *La raison d'état*, 74.

386. Ibid., 89.

387. Maran, *Torture*, 51.

388. On the connection between French military doctrines and systematic torture, see Lazreg, *Torture and the Twilight of Empire*, 15–33; despite the broad geographic reference in the full title, this book concentrates primarily on the various aspects of torture in the Algerian War.

389. Trinquier, *Guerre moderne*, 39, 59–64.

390. Vidal-Naquet, *La torture dans la république*, 35.

391. Branche, *La torture*, 51.

392. General Salan, "Instruction sur la lutte contre la rébellion et le terrorisme," 30 April 1957, SHAT, 1H 2577, 4.

393. Ibid., 7.

394. Ibid., 13.

395. General Massu, secret instruction "La technique policière," 10 March 1959, SHAT, 1H 2577.

396. Ibid., 4.

397. Branche, *La torture*, 60.

398. Trinquier, *Guerre moderne*, 39.

399. Ibid., 42.

400. Massu, *Vraie bataille*, 167–68.

401. Branche, "Lutte contre le terrorisme urbain," 480.

402. Vittori, *On a torturé*, 87.

403. Vidal-Naquet, *La torture dans la république*, 48–49.

404. Elsenhans, *Algerienkrieg*, 463.

405. For a closer analysis of the DOP, see Branche, *La torture*, 195–211.

406. Münchhausen, *Kolonialismus und Demokratie*, 198.

407. Branche, *La torture*, 255–63.

408. Ibid., 52, 176.

409. "La torture-institution: De l'école de Philippeville aux DOP, 1958–1959; témoignage de quatre officiers," in Vidal-Naquet, *Les crimes de l'armée française*, 117–18; Keramane, *La pacification*, 103–4.

410. Vidal-Naquet, *La torture dans la république*, 45; Branche, *La torture*, 115.

411. In his war memoirs, General Paul Aussaresses describes extensively this military operation and his role as an intelligence officer, whereby he openly admits without regret to using torture and conducting mass executions; see Aussaresses, *Services spéciaux*, 95–178.

412. Sarell, British consul general in Algiers, confidential report to the FO, 9 August 1957, TNA, FO 371/125945.

413. Ibid.

414. Paul Teitgen quoted in Heymann, *Libertés publiques*, 166.

415. Vergès, Zavrian, and Courrégé, *Les disparus*, 10–55, 61–86.

416. See soldier Paul Lefebvre to French president René Coty, September 1958, CAOM, 19 PA Carton 9, Dossier 136.

417. Leulliette, *St. Michael and the Dragon*, 236–37.

418. Ibid., 242.

419. Branche, *La torture*, 146.

420. Pierre Vidal-Naquet, "Le 'Cahier vert' expliqué," in Vidal-Naquet, *Les crimes de l'armée française*, 91.

421. Lieutenant Colonel Mayer, Commandant le 1er Régiment de Chasseurs Parachutistes, "Rapport sur l'évasion de détenu Audin," 23 June 1957, CAOM, 19 PA Carton 9, Dossier 120.

422. Josette Audin to the rector of Algiers University, 10 July 1957, in CAOM, 19 PA Carton 9, Dossier 120.

423. Laurent Schwartz to Pierre Vidal-Naquet, 23 January 1958, CAOM, 19 PA Carton 9, Dossier 120.

424. Vidal-Naquet, *L'affaire Audin*.

425. Comité Maurice Audin, *Un homme a disparu*.

426. See also Ligue des droits de l'homme, "Nous accusons—: Dossier sur la torture et la répression en Algérie," CAOM, 19 PA Carton 9, Dossier 136.

427. Vidal-Naquet, *L'affaire Audin*, 9–10.

428. Alleg, *The Question*, 41.

429. Ibid., 45.

430. Ibid., 34.

431. For example, see Gilberte Alleg to the ICRC president, 30 May 1958; ICRC notes of a conversation between Gilberte Alleg and the ICRC delegate William Michel, 21 July 1958; Gilberte Alleg to the ICRC delegate William Michel, 13 September 1958, all in ACICR, B AG 225 008-007.

432. On the story of the book's origins and the impact of its publication, see Berchadsky, *"La question" d'Henri Alleg*.

433. Maran, *Torture*, 145; Liauzu and Liauzu, "Violence coloniale et guerre," 137–48.

434. "De la pacification à la répression: Le Dossier Jean Muller," *Cahiers du Témoignage Chrétien*, February 1957.

435. "Sommes-nous les 'vaincus de Hitler'?" *Le Monde*, 13 March 1957.

436. Simon, *Contre la torture*, 20–23; on the commitment of Pierre-Henri Simon to this cause, see also Lucet and Boespflug, *Pierre-Henri Simon*.

437. Simon, *Contre la torture*, 114.

438. On Teitgen's criticism, see "Une note de Paul Teitgen au président et aux membres de la Commission de Sauvegarde," 1 September 1957, in Vidal-Naquet, *La raison d'état*, 186–202.

439. Bollardière, *Bataille d'Alger*, 97.

440. Ibid., 149–50.

441. See Lefebvre, *Guy Mollet face à la torture*, 67–68.

442. "Déclaration de Guy Mollet de la Commission permanente de sauvegarde des droits et libertés individuels," 10 May 1957, CAOM, 19 PA Carton 9, Dossier 129.

443. On the Commission de sauvegarde, see especially Branche, "Commission de sauvegarde," 14–29.

444. Ibid., 18; Heymann, *Libertés publiques*, 136.

445. Final report of the Commission de sauvegarde, September 1957, CAOM, 19 PA Carton 9, Dossier 121, 28.

446. Ibid., 44.

447. Branche, "Commission de sauvegarde," 24; Vidal-Naquet, *La torture dans la république*, 82.

448. See "Rapport de Mission en Algérie de Robert Delavignette," 21 July 1957, CAOM, 19 PA Carton 9, Dossier 120.

449. Delavignette's letter of resignation, 22 September 1957, CAOM, 19 PA Carton 9, Dossier 122.

450. "Le rapport de synthèse de la Commission de sauvegarde des droits et libertés individuels," *Le Monde*, 14 December 1957.

451. Branche, "Commission de sauvegarde," 28.

452. "Aspects véritables de la rébellion algérienne: Une brochure du cabinet de M. Robert Lacoste," *Le Monde*, 14 December 1957.

453. Maran, *Torture*, 117–18.

454. Branche, *La torture*, 167, 212, 218.

455. Leulliette, *St. Michael and the Dragon*, 232.

456. Vittori, *On a torturé*, 13.

457. Branche, *La torture*, 57.

458. Horne, *Savage War*, 199–200; Talbott, *War Without a Name*, 92; Keramane, *La pacification*, 14–15; Alleg, *The Question*, 44–45.

459. Interview with General Massu in *Le Monde*, 22 June 2000.

460. General Massu quoted in Keller, *Psychologie der Folter*, 59.

461. Maran, *The Question*, 55–56.

462. Colonel Bigeard quoted in Périot, *Deuxième classe en Algérie*, 201.

463. See Belhadj et al., *La gangrène*; this book was the first report by a contemporary on torture in France during the Algerian War.

464. Vidal-Naquet, *La torture dans la république*, 101–14.

465. The involvement of Maurice Papon in crimes committed in the Algerian War came to light in 1997–98 during the course of the trial against him as the organizer of the deportation of French Jews during the Vichy period. Particular attention was paid to his role as the Paris police prefect in the murder of the more than two hundred Algerian demonstrators. See Einaudi, "Le Papon des ratonnades"; on the mass murder perpetrated by the state on 17 October 1961 in Paris, see especially Le Cour Grandmaison, *Le 17 octobre 1961*; Einaudi, *Octobre 1961*; House and MacMaster, *Paris 1961*.

466. Jean-Paul Sartre, "The Sleepwalkers," in Sartre, *Colonialism and Neocolonialism*, 132.

Chapter 6. International Discourse on Human Rights

Note to epigraph: From the opening address by Tom Mboya at the All African People's Conference 1958 in Accra, quoted in "Africa Talks: Algeria Is a Most Important Topic—Mboya," *Daily Graphic*, 10 December 1958.

1. Schmitt, *Theorie des Partisanen*, 78.
2. Münkler, *Die neuen Kriege*, 54–55.
3. See Beaufre, *Revolutionierung des Kriegsbildes*, 27–29; Hoffman, *Terrorismus*, 72–73.
4. Louis Pichon, "Caractères généraux de la guerre insurrectionnelle," July 1957, SHAT, 1H 2577, 1–2, 10; B. Miller, *World Order and Local Disorder*, 38, 61–62.
5. Don Barnett, *Urban Guerrilla*, 8; Maloba, *Mau Mau and Kenya*, 120; Carruthers, *Winning Hearts and Minds*, 142.
6. For example, see the transcript provided by the Provincial Special Branch Nyeri, dated 30 December 1955, of a letter from the Land Freedom Army to the Kenya Committee in London, 4 April 1955, TNA, WO 276/376. According to the remarks of Maina wa Kinyatti, the independence movement tried as early as October 1953 to send its "Kenya Land Freedom Army Charter" with its aims and demands to the governments of India, Egypt, the United States, and the Soviet Union, as well as to Pan-African sympathizers like George Padmore, Kwame Nkrumah, and W. E. B. Du Bois. In his source edition *Kenya's Freedom Struggle*, Kinyatti also presents a letter from Dedan Kimathi to the Soviet government asking for support for the Kenyan fight for independence; see Kinyatti, *Kenya's Freedom Struggle*, 16–17, 18–20.
7. Buijtenhuijs, *Le mouvement "Mau Mau,"* 400; Edgerton, *Mau Mau*, 105–6; Maloba, *Mau Mau and Kenya*, 113, 131.
8. Beaufre, *Revolutionierung des Kriegsbildes*, 63, 222; Edgerton, *Mau Mau*, 73.
9. British UN delegation to the FO, confidential telegram, 26 May 1953, TNA, FO 371/107109.
10. Commonwealth Relations Office to the British High Commissioner for Pakistan, confidential telegram, 27 May 1953, TNA, FO 371/107109.
11. British UN delegation to the FO, confidential telegram, 28 May 1953, TNA, FO 371/107109.
12. British UN delegation to the FO, confidential report, 28 May 1953, TNA, FO 371/107109.
13. Commonwealth Relations Office to the British High Commissioner for India and Pakistan, confidential note, 5 June 1953, TNA, FO 371/107109.
14. FO to the British UN delegation, confidential telegram, 12 June 1953, TNA, FO 371/107109; British UN delegation, confidential telegram, 25 June 1953, TNA, CO 822/448.
15. Afro-Asian states to UN secretary-general Hammarskjöld, telegram, 26 September 1959, UNOG, SO 215/1 UK, Violations and Complaints (April–November 1959).
16. For examples of petitions of private individuals, see those dated 19 October 1953, in TNA, FO 371/107139; 13 June 1958 and 21 June 1958, in UNOG, SO 215/1 UK, Violations and Complaints (June 1958–March 1959); 21 October 1959, UNOG, SO 215/1 UK, Violations and Complaints (April–November 1959); 11 November 1960, UNOG, SO 215/1 UK, Violations and Complaints (April–August 1960); and 16 March 1961, UNOG, SO 215/1 UK, Violations and Complaints (January–June 1961).
17. For example, see the petitions of an East German NGO, 8 October 1953, an Australian NGO, 14 October 1953, and a British NGO, 23 November 1953, all in TNA, FO 371/107139; and the petition of an African NGO, 21 May 1959, UNOG, SO 215/1 UK, Violations and Complaints (April 1959 to November 1959).
18. Petition of the League of Human Rights from Zanzibar to Secretary-General Hammarskjöld, 4 December 1957, TNA, FO 371/137056.

19. Ogot, "Mau Mau and Nationhood," 23.

20. "The Need for Land Is Their Problem," *Ceylon Daily News*, 7 April 1953.

21. British embassy in Cairo to the FO, confidential telegram, 27 August 1953, and note, 31 August 1953, both in TNA, FO 371/102721.

22. "References in the Cairo Press to Joseph Murumbi," report by the British embassy in Cairo, 8 October 1953, TNA, FO 371/102721; "British Complaint to Egypt: Mau Mau Emissary Received," *Times* (London), 29 August 1953.

23. Protocol of the FO on a conversation with Iverach McDonald from the London *Times* about Murumbi's liable suit threat, 2 October 1953, TNA, FO 371/102721.

24. On the Egypt's great importance as a location for East African anticolonial propaganda, see especially Brennan, "Radio Cairo."

25. British High Commissioner's Office for India to the Commonwealth Relations Office, 5 September 1953, TNA, FO 371/102721.

26. British Ambassador Hankey to the FO, confidential report, 21 September 1953, TNA, FO 371/102721.

27. Ibid.

28. FO to Ambassador Hankey, confidential note, 29 September 1953, TNA, FO 371/102721.

29. "Mr. Murumbi's Plans for Kenya: Aims Explained," *Times* (London), 26 September 1953.

30. On the Movement for Colonial Freedom, see Howe, *Anticolonialism in British Politics*, 231–67; Gupta, *Imperialism and the British Labour Movement*, 360–61, 367.

31. For more on Brockway himself, see Brockway, *Towards Tomorrow*.

32. Howe, *Anticolonialism in British Politics*, 244–45.

33. Murumbi, "Human Rights."

34. For a biography of Tom Mboya, see Goldsworthy, *Mboya*.

35. For example, see Mboya's press conference, 9 January 1956, TNA, CO 822/824.

36. Mboya, *Kenya Question*, 12.

37. Ibid., 17.

38. Ibid., 33, 36.

39. Goldsworthy, *Mboya*, 60–63; Ogot, "Mau Mau and Nationhood," 31–32.

40. Colonial attaché Williams from the British embassy in Washington, D.C., to the CO, 14 August 1956, TNA, CO 822/824.

41. CO to colonial attaché Williams, secret note, 17 August 1956; CO to Governor Baring, telegram, 14 August 1956, both in TNA, CO 822/824.

42. Interview with Mboya, 5 September 1956, TNA, CO 822/824.

43. For the criticism leveled by the Labour opposition regarding the government's policy for Kenya, see Howe, *Anticolonialism in British Politics*, 200–207.

44. For criticism of Brockway, see Brockway, *Why Mau Mau?* 9–10; Brockway, *African Journeys*, 166–88.

45. For more on Castle herself, see Castle, *Fighting All the Way*.

46. Goldsworthy, *Colonial Issues in British Politics*, 212–14; David Anderson, *Histories of the Hanged*, 309; Edgerton, *Mau Mau*, 157; Elkins, *Britain's Gulag*, 275–76.

47. "Labour to Fight Kenya Thugs," *Tribune*, 30 September 1955.

48. Castle, *Fighting All the Way*, 267–72.

49. "The Truth About the Secret Police," *Daily Mirror*, 9 December 1955.

50. "Justice in Kenya," *New Statesman and Nation*, 17 December 1955.

51. Anderson, *Histories of the Hanged*, 326; Elkins, *Britain's Gulag*, 307; Darwin, *End of Empire*, 16; Andrew Thompson, *Empire Strikes Back?* 212–13.

52. Peter Evans, "Martyrdom of Kenya I"; Peter Evans, "Martyrdom of Kenya II"; British

High Commissioner for India to the Commonwealth Relations Office, 12 September 1953, TNA, DO 35/5357.

53. See, for example, "Kill 751 Mau-Mau in 7 Weeks," *Barbados Observer*, 19 September 1953; "Children Burnt Alive, Castration, Murder, Starvation: A Mau-Mau Letter," *Union Messenger of St. Kitts*, 2 November 1953.

54. CO to the governors of the West Indian colonies, 14 August 1953, TNA, CO 1027/31.

55. For example, see press releases of the British embassy in Moscow to the FO, 31 October 1952 and 21 January 1957, TNA, CO 822/448 and 1227.

56. Cleary, "Myth of Mau Mau," 237, 240; Füredi, *Colonial Wars*, 158, 217.

57. Barnett and Njama, *Mau Mau from Within*, 9; Cleary, "Myth of Mau Mau," 244; Carruthers, *Winning Hearts and Minds*, 177–81.

58. Füredi, *Colonial Wars*, 212–13; Füredi, "Britain's Colonial Emergencies," 248; Maloba, *Mau Mau and Kenya*, 98; Carruthers, *Winning Hearts and Minds*, 156–57; Cleary, "Myth of Mau Mau," 239.

59. Maloba, *Mau Mau and Kenya*, 112.

60. CO memorandum "Public Relations: Kenya," 23 October 1952, TNA, CO 1027/40.

61. Commander in Chief Hinde, Emergency Directive No. 1, April 1953, TNA, WO 276/510, 14.

62. On the work of the African Information Service, see the CO reports "Some Notes on the Work of the African Information Service and the Press Office," 1953, and "Government Information Service: Press, Broadcasting and Films," 1954, TNA, CO 1027/40 and 54.

63. The Press Office and the African Information Service were merged at the start of 1954 into the Kenya Government Information Service.

64. On the work of the Kenya Press Office, see its report "Work of the Press Office," 9 September 1953, TNA, CO 1027/40; and the CO report "Government Information Service: Press, Broadcasting and Films," 1954, TNA, CO 1027/54.

65. CO report "Some Notes on the Work of the African Information Service and the Press Office," 1953, TNA, CO 1027/60. 11.

66. Dane Kennedy, "Colonial Myth of Mau Mau," 256; Carruthers, *Winning Hearts and Minds*, 144.

67. CO report "Some Notes on the Work of the African Information Service and the Press Office," 1953, TNA, CO, 1027/40, 11–12.

68. Police Commissioner O'Rorke, "Situation Appreciation Week Ending the 4th December 1952," TNA, WO 276/378.

69. Colonial Minister Lyttelton to Governor Baring, 10 July 1953, TNA, CO 1027/40.

70. BBC Foreign News Department to the CO, 4 August 1953, TNA, CO 1027/31.

71. CO to the Kenyan director of information, Brigadier William Gibson, 16 June 1953, TNA, CO 1027/31.

72. Ibid.

73. Gibson to the CO, 30 June 1953, TNA, CO 1027/31.

74. Lyttelton's speech before the House of Commons on 7 November 1952, quoted in the press release "Britain Reveals Plans to Beat Mau-Mau Terrorists," British Information Services, 7 November 1952, TNA, CO 822/448.

75. Carruthers, *Winning Hearts and Minds*, 165–66.

76. CO to Granville Roberts, head of the Kenya Public Relations Office, 26 June 1953, TNA, CO 1027/7.

77. Ibid.

78. CO, 18 August 1953, TNA, CO 1027/7.

79. See, for example, Wills, *Who Killed Kenya?* 29, 35, 40; Stoneham, *Out of Barbarism,* 11–12; Carey, *Crisis in Kenya,* 10, 32; Leigh, *Shadow of the Mau Mau,* 205.

80. Lonsdale, "Mau Maus of the Mind," 393.

81. WO, "Press Campaign in UK," 10 December 1953, TNA, WO 276/382.

82. See Kenyan colonial government, secret memorandum on Mau Mau atrocities and ritu-als, 12 January 1954, TNA, CO 822/800; Special Branch Headquarters, report, "The Oaths of Mau Mau," 8 September 1954, TNA, WO 276/234.

83. Kariuki, *Mau Mau Detainee,* 33.

84. Government of the UK, *Report to the Secretary of State for the Colonies,* appendix 2, "Memorandum on the Mau Mau Oath Ceremonies."

85. Carruthers, *Winning Hearts and Minds,* 159–60.

86. Ibid., 160; Lonsdale, "Mau Maus of the Mind," 399.

87. Blundell, *So Rough a Wind,* 168.

88. Maloba, *Mau Mau and Kenya,* 113.

89. Carruthers, *Winning Hearts and Minds,* 168–70; commercial motion pictures also seized upon the topic of the Kenyan conflict—such as the 1955 film *Simba,* directed by Brian Desmond Hurst and shot at original Kenyan locations—and tried with cinematic means to portray the "savagery" of the Mau Mau to a large general public in Great Britain.

90. Lonsdale, "Mau Maus of the Mind," 405.

91. CO to the FO, 6 December 1952, TNA, CO 1027/7.

92. FO to the CO, 10 December 1952, TNA, CO 1027/7.

93. FO, "Draft Circular to Selected Missions," 10 December 1952, TNA, CO 1027/7.

94. For example, see CO to the colonial government of northern Rhodesia and Nyasaland, 21 January 1953, TNA, CO 1027/7.

95. CO to Governor Baring, confidential telegram, 17 April 1953, TNA, CO 822/448.

96. Anderson, *Histories of the Hanged,* 177.

97. For the gruesome photographic material, see TNA, CO 1066/1.

98. Ibid., Photo Doc. 226/11.

99. Peter Evans, *Law and Disorder,* 174.

100. Maloba, *Mau Mau and Kenya,* 101; Barnett and Njama, *Mau Mau from Within,* 137–38; Carruthers, *Winning Hearts and Minds,* 138; Anderson, *Histories of the Hanged,* 177–78.

101. On the retaliation, see Evans, *Law and Disorder,* 170–71, 187–88.

102. Maloba, *Mau Mau and Kenya,* 109.

103. Article "Mau Mau: Nia yake ni. Kufukuza Wazungu Ama Je?" in the Swahili weekly newspaper *Tazama,* 15 April 1953, NARA, RG 59.2, 745R.00/4-2153.

104. U.S. Consul General Dorsz to the State Department, 21 April 1953, NARA, RG 59.2, 745R.00/4-2153.

105. *The Mau Mau in Kenya;* no official author is listed for this brochure, but in actuality it was the work of the Kenya Public Relations Office. Fred Majdalany also used some of this photo-graphic material as examples in his book; see Majdalany, *State of Emergency,* photos on 144–45.

106. Blundell, *So Rough a Wind,* 140.

107. Resolution of the Kenya Indian Congress, quoted in the press release of the Kenya Public Relations Office, 1 April 1953, TNA, CO 1027/31.

108. Copy of the statement by the Nigerian politician Abubakar in a secret note from the Kenyan colonial government to the CO, 6 May 1953, TNA, CO 1027/31.

109. Blundell, *So Rough a Wind,* 112-13.

110. Press Section of the Information Services Department to the Overseas Press Service of the Central Office of Information, confidential note, 4 November 1953, TNA, CO 1027/31.

111. Kenya Public Relations Office to the CO Press Section, 11 August 1953, TNA, CO 1027/7.

112. Colonial government in Nairobi to the CO, 4 December 1953, TNA, CO 822/701.

113. On the biography of Ralph Bunche, see Urquhart, *Ralph Bunche*; Henry, *Ralph Bunche*.

114. Ralph Bunche received the Nobel Peace Prize in 1950 for his successful mediation of a ceasefire between Israel and the Arab countries.

115. Lewis, "Daddy Wouldn't Buy Me a Mau Mau," 227.

116. Lyttelton, *Memoirs of Lord Chandos*, 394–95.

117. Mandela, *Long Walk to Freedom*, 259–60.

118. "Proclamation au peuple algérien, aux militants de la cause nationale," 31 October 1954, in Harbi and Meynier, *Le FLN*, 37.

119. Ibid.

120. "Programme de la Soummam," in Dalloz, *Textes*, 74.

121. Connelly, *Diplomatic Revolution*, 4.

122. Hoffman, *Terrorismus*, 77–78.

123. Alexander and Keiger, "France and the Algerian War," 18–19; Ellul, *FLN Propaganda in France*, 16; Ageron, "Guerres d'Indochine et d'Algérie," 65; Beaufre, *Revolutionierung des Kriegsbildes*, 204–5, 210–11; Heggoy, *Insurgency and Counterinsurgency*, 229, 254.

124. Confidential UN report "Note on the Military Situation in Algeria" for UN Secretary-General Hammarskjöld, 8 November 1957, UN ARMS, S-0188-0005-09, 1.

125. For example, see FLN to Indian Prime Minister Nehru, Yugoslavian Prime Minister Tito, and Egyptian President Nasser, July 1956, CAOM, 12 CAB 146.

126. See Al Dib, *Nasser et la révolution algérienne*.

127. Elsenhans, *Algerienkrieg*, 38; Fraleigh, "Algerian Revolution," 208, 219–20.

128. "Procès-verbal du Congrès de la Soummam," in Harbi and Meynier, *Le FLN*, 243; Fraleigh, "Algerian Revolution," 188–89.

129. Connelly, *Diplomatic Revolution*, 110–11.

130. "Composition du Premier GPRA," in Harbi and Meynier, *Le FLN*, 358–59.

131. Excerpt from the statement by Abbas, 26 September 1958, ACICR, D EUR France1-0932.

132. "Témoignage du Président Ferhat Abbas," in Harbi and Meynier, *Le FLN*, 361.

133. See Bedjaoui, *Révolution algérienne*, 115–24, 140.

134. On the GPRA's activities abroad, see the secret reports "La Rébellion Algérienne" by Captain Tripier, 20 July 1959, on the occasion of the "Conférence de Renseignements de Baden," CAOM, 81 F104, 11–19, and "Le FLN et l'étranger," 19 September 1960, CAOM, 81 F114.

135. Connelly, *Diplomatic Revolution*, 195; for a good overview of the worldwide presence of the GPRA, see Pervillé, *Atlas de la guerre d'Algérie*, 29.

136. "Note d'information sur l'évolution de la situation en Afrique du Nord au cours du mois de juillet 1957," Inspection des Forces Terrestres, Maritimes et Aériennes de l'Afrique du Nord, 5 August 1957, CAOM, 81 F1015, 4.

137. See especially Alwan, *Algeria Before the United Nations*; Mameri, *La "Question algérienne"*; Luard, *History of the United Nations*, 2:75–103; Vaisse, "La guerre perdue à l'ONU?"

138. See especially Martin Thomas, "France Accused."

139. Miller, *World Order and Local Disorder*, 52, 203–5.

140. UN SCOR Document S/3341, Saudi UN delegate to the President of the UN Security Council, 5 January 1955; "Arab in UN Hits Paris on Algeria," *New York Times*, 6 January 1955.

141. Press release, Saudi embassy, 20 January 1955, accompanied by a letter from the Committee for the Freedom of North Africa to President Eisenhower, CAOM, 81 F1010.

142. UN GAOR Document A/2924, letter from the UN delegates from Afghanistan, Egypt,

Burma, India, Indonesia, Iran, Iraq, Lebanon, Pakistan, Saudi Arabia, Syria, Thailand, and Yemen to the UN Secretary-General, 26 July 1955.

143. Article 2, paragraph 7, of the Charter of the United Nations in Ishay, *Human Rights Reader*, 492.

144. See "Note on the Algerian Question," French UN delegation before the UN General Assembly, September 1955, MAE, NUOI Carton 546; Alwan, *Algeria Before the United Nations*, 34; Mameri, *La "Question algérienne,"* 30–35; Fraleigh, "Algerian Revolution," 182; Thomas, "France Accused," 92.

145. On the debate about the Algerian question in the various bodies of the General Assembly in 1955, see "The Question of Algeria," United Nations, *Yearbook of the United Nations, 1955*, 65–69.

146. UN GAOR Resolution A/RES/909 (X) "Question of Algeria," 25 November 1955; French UN Ambassador Hervé Alphand to the MAE, telegram, 25 November 1955, MAE, NUOI Carton 547.

147. On the various discussions about the Algerian question in the UN bodies throughout the years, see "The Question of Algeria," in United Nations, *Yearbook of the United Nations, 1956*, 115–21; *1957*, 68–72; *1958*, 79–81; *1959*, 51–56; *1960*, 132–36; and *1961*, 97–99.

148. Alwan, *Algeria Before the United Nations*, 21–30.

149. Fraleigh, "Algerian Revolution," 226–27.

150. UN SCOR Document S/3609, letter from the UN delegates from Afghanistan, Egypt, Indonesia, Iran, Iraq, Jordan, Lebanon, Libya, Pakistan, Saudi Arabia, Syria, Thailand, and Yemen to the President of the UN Security Council, 13 June 1956.

151. UN GAOR Document A/3197, letter from the UN delegates from Afghanistan, Egypt, Burma, Ceylon, Indonesia, Iran, Iraq, Jordan, Lebanon, Libya, Pakistan, the Philippines, Saudi Arabia, Syria, Thailand, and Yemen to the UN Secretary-General, 1 October 1956.

152. "Texte integral du mémoire remis à M. Hammarskjöld, Secrétaire Général de l'ONU par les délégués permanents des Etats Arabes aux Nations Unies," June 1957, CAOM 81 F1015, 1.

153. UN SCOR Document S/4194, letter from the UN delegates from Afghanistan, Burma, Ceylon, Ghana, Guinea, Indonesia, Iran, Iraq, Jordan, Lebanon, Liberia, Libya, Malaya, Morocco, Nepal, Pakistan, Saudi Arabia, Sudan, Tunisia, the United Arab Republic, and Yemen to the President of the UN Security Council, 10 July 1959.

154. UN ECOSOCOR Document E/CN.4/SR.575, Commission on Human Rights (13th Session), "Summary Record of the Five Hundred and Seventy-Fifth Meeting," 24 April 1957, 5–11; Egon Schwelb, UN deputy director, Division of Human Rights, to Philippe de Seynes, UN undersecretary for Economic and Social Affairs, interoffice memorandum, 24 April 1957, UNOG, SO 212/2 (13th Session).

155. UN telegram from Geneva to New York, 24 April 1957, UNOG, SO 212/2 (13th Session).

156. UN GAOR Resolution A/RES/1012 (XI), "Question of Algeria," 15 February 1957.

157. UN GAOR Resolution A/RES/1184 (XII), "Question of Algeria," 10 December 1957.

158. See "Les États-Unis et le FLN," secret information notice, 25 August 1959, CAOM 81 F114; the French UN delegation's report "A.s. de l'affaire algérienne aux Nations Unies sous l'angle des relations publiques" to the MAE, 25 February 1961, MAE, NUOI Carton 1068.

159. "White Paper Submitted by the Delegation of the Front of National Liberation to the United Nations Organisation on the Franco-Algerian Conflict," 12 April 1956, MAE, NUOI Carton 548.

160. Ibid., 7.

161. Ibid., 14.

162. See the French UN delegation's report "Documents publiés par la delegation du FLN à New York" to the MAE, 25 January 1957, CAOM 81 F1013.

163. Ferhat Abbas and Yazid Mohamed to the President of the 11th UN General Assembly, February 1957, CAOM 81 F1013.

164. For example, see the Algerian Office press bulletin "The Forgotten War Continues in Algeria," 20 March 1957, CAOM 81 F527; "Memorandum FLN sur la guerre bactériologique," 2 May 1957, CAOM 81 F1013; FLN brochures *Les atrocités de l'imperialisme français en Algérie* and *Les atrocités françaises et les opérations d'extermination en Algérie*, September 1957, CAOM 81 F529; telegram on the torture of Algerian students in Paris from Abbas to UN Secretary-General Hammarskjöld, 27 December 1958, UNOG, SO 215/1 FRA, Violations and Complaints (April–December 1958); Algerian Office press bulletin "The War in Algeria: More Than 100 Killed per Day," March 1959, CAOM 81 F527; Algerian Office brochure *French Church Leaders Denounce Army's Excesses and Use of Torture in Algeria*, April 1959, CAOM 81 F529; French army pamphlet *La torture, thème de propagande du FLN*, July 1960, SHAT, 1H 1152/6.

165. FLN brochure *Genocide in Algeria*, June 1958, CAOM 81 F530; Connelly, *Diplomatic Revolution*, 90.

166. See especially the CRA's bilingual propaganda brochure *Les Réfugiés Algériens—The Algerian Refugees*, 1959, CAOM 81 F528.

167. FLN Delegate Chanderli to UN Secretary-General Hammarskjöld, "Memorandum on the Situation in Algeria," 24 April 1959, MAE, NUOI Carton 560.

168. For example, see petitions of an Indonesian women's organization, 31 July 1957, and an East German women's organization, 3 September 1957, UNOG, SO 215/1 FRA, Violations and Complaints (July 1957–February 1958); protest resolution of an Islamic congress, 26 March 1958, UNOG, SO 215/1 FRA, Violations and Complaints (March 1958); petition of an Arab law-yer association, 6 January 1959, and protest resolution of an international student conference, 3 June 1959, UNOG, SO 215/1 FRA, Violations and Complaints (January–September 1959); petitions of a Bulgarian union, 11 October 1959, and of workers from the CSSR, 24 October 1959, UNOG, SO 215/1 FRA, Violations and Complaints (October 1959–March 1960); protest telegram from a number of famous artists and writers, 29 July 1960, UNOG, SO 215/1 FRA, Violations and Complaints (April–December 1960); petitions of the Yugoslavian Student Union, 3 November 1960, and the Swiss Peace Council, 20 November 1960, UN ARMS, S-0442-0189-09; petition of a French union, 28 April 1961, UNOG, SO 215/1 FRA, Violations and Complaints (June–November 1961); U Hla Maung, representative of UN Technical Assistance Board and director of Special Fund Programmes in Iraq, to the Executive Office of the Secretary-General, memorandum "Notes of Protest," 25 November 1961, UN ARMS, S-0442-0190-01.

169. For example, see protest telegram of a humanitarian organization, 31 January 1957, and petitions of an Algerian union, 4 February 1957, an Algerian student association, 12 March 1957, and an American NGO, 26 April 1957, all in UNOG, SO 215/1 FRA, Violations and Complaints (October 1956–June 1957).

170. For example, see petition of a French journalist association, 6 August 1957, UNOG, SO 215/1 FRA, Violations and Complaints (July 1957–February 1958).

171. The trade unionist Aissat Idir was detained for three years before being brought to trial in January 1959. Following his surprising acquittal, however, Idir was kept in prison, where he was severly abused and eventually murdered by French paratroopers. The official report claimed that Idir died of injuries sustained in a suicide attempt. See FLN delegate Chanderli's memo-randum "The 'Accidental' Death of Mr. Aissat Idir" to UN Secretary-General Hammarskjöld, 31 July 1959, MAE, NUOI Carton 560; and petitions of an Algerian student association, 31 July 1959, and an Algerian union, 30 July 1959, UNOG, SO 215/1 FRA, Violations and Complaints (January–September 1959).

172. See Arnaud and Vergès, *Pour Djamila Bouhired*.

173. For example, see mass communication of an Egyptian newspaper, 2 March 1958; petition of an Egyptian writers' association, 9 March 1958; protest telegram of a Libyan government office, 11 March 1958, all in UNOG, SO 215/1 FRA, Violations and Complaints (March 1958).

174. Arab propaganda poster, CAOM, 81 F530.

175. Schwelb, UN deputy director, Division of Human Rights, to Cordier, executive assistant to the secretary-general, interoffice memorandum, 7 March 1958, UNOG, SO 215/1 FRA, Violations and Complaints (July 1957–February 1958).

176. French UN delegation to UN Secretary-General Hammarskjöld, 11 March 1958, UNOG, SO 215/1 FRA, Violations and Complaints (March 1958).

177. For example, see protest telegram from Jean-Paul Sartre, Pablo Picasso, and Simone de Beauvoir, among others, to the ICRC, 29 July 1960, ACICR, B AG 202 008-013.

178. For example, see FLN to the ICRC, 25 May 1957, ACICR, B AG 202 008-001; FLN to the ICRC, 13 March 1958, ACICR, B AG 225 008-010.02.

179. For example, see CRA to the Libyan Red Cross, 3 August 1960, ACICR, B AG 202 008-013.

180. For example, see Red Cross of the GDR to the ICRC, 15 August 1960; Hungarian Red Cross to the ICRC, 19 September 1960; Lebanese Red Cross to the ICRC, 4 October 1960; Venezuelan Red Cross to the ICRC, 11 October 1960; Iraqi Red Crescent to the ICRC, 16 October 1960, all in ACICR, B AG 202 008-013.

181. Hutchinson, *Revolutionary Terrorism*, 93.

182. On the importance and propaganda of *El Moudjahid*, see Fitte, *Spectroscopie d'une propagande révolutionnaire*; Gadant, *Islam et nationalisme*.

183. Algerian Delegation in the Far East, "The Problem of Algerian Refugees," Tokyo, July 1959, and "Les enfants meurent de faim dans les camps de regroupement" (news of Algeria), 20 January 1960, both in CAOM, 81 F530.

184. For example, see "Die Lager des langsamen Sterbens," *Freies Algerien*, no. 7 (October 1959); and FLN delegate Malek in Bonn, "Fünf Jahre Freiheitskampf in Algerien," *Freies Algerien*, nos. 8/9, (November/December 1959), both in CAOM, 81 F527.

185. FLN, *Kolonialistische Unterdrückung und Kriegsverbrechen*.

186. FLN cover letter, in ibid.

187. See MAE note "Demande d'inscription de la question algérienne à l'ordre du jour de la prochaine session de l'assemblée générale des Nations-Unies" to Governor General Lacoste, 9 October 1956, CAOM, 81 F1010.

188. See MAE, "Mémoire sur l'Algérie," 10 October 1956, MAE, NUOI Carton 550; MAE. "Note sur quelques aspects de l'incompétence de l'Assemblée Générale dans l'affaire algérienne," MAE, NUOI Carton 560.

189. The *Athos* was sailing under the Sudanese flag and was captured while cruising in the Mediterranean. The French navy had acted on the basis of intelligence information and found seventy tons of arms and ammunition on board that had been purchased with Egyptian money and loaded onto the ship in Alexandria. See Al Dib, *Nasser et la révolution algérienne*, 175–81; Horne, *Savage War*, 158.

190. UN SCOR Document S/3689, Letter of the French UN delegate, 25 October 1956.

191. See the above-mentioned "Dossier de Défense contre les attaques anti-coloniales," 1952, MAE, NUOI Carton 537.

192. For example, see the reports of the French embassies in Afghanistan and Ceylon to the MAE, 11 September 1956 and 9 October 1956, MAE, NUOI Carton 537; in all, reports were completed on Afghanistan, Egypt, Burma, Bolivia, Ceylon, Guatemala, India, Indonesia, Iran,

Iraq, Jordan, Liberia, Libya, Nepal, Pakistan, the Philippines, Saudi Arabia, Sudan, Syria, Thailand, the USSR, and Yemen.

193. MAE dossier "Défense de la France concernant les critiques sur notre administration sous les territoires non autonomes: Synthèse 1956 sur les Droits de l'Homme," 1956, MAE, NUOI Carton 537.

194. Ministry of the Interior to the MAE, "Assemblée générale des Nations Unies—Inscription à l'ordre du jour de la question algérienne," 13 August 1955, MAE, NUOI Carton 547.

195. Governor General Soustelle to the Ministry of the Interior, 25 August 1955, CAOM, 81 F1010; Ministry of the Interior to the MAE, "Inscription de la question algérienne à l'ordre du jour de l'Assemblée générale des Nations-Unies—Envoi de documentation," 5 September 1955, MAE, NUOI Carton 547.

196. Ministry of the Interior to the MAE, "Documentation confidentielle destinée à la délégation française aux Nations-Unies," 10 September 1955, MAE, NUOI Carton 547.

197. MAE to the Undersecretary for Algerian Affairs in the Ministry of the Interior, "Propagande au sujet de l'Algérie," 27 April 1956, CAOM, 81 F1013.

198. For example, see Ministry of the Interior to the MAE, "Documentation sur l'Algérie," 25 April 1956, MAE, NUOI Carton 549; Undersecretary for Algerian Affairs at the Ministry of the Interior to the Governor General in Algiers, "Documentation pour la délégation française à l'ONU," 4 July 1956, CAOM, 81 F1013; MAE, "Documentation sur l'Algérie," 10 August 1956, MAE, NUOI Carton 549; general delegate in Algiers to the MAE, 31 July 1959, CAOM, 14 CAB 65.

199. On the creation and tasks of the MLA, see "Inventaire de la Mission de liaison pour les affaires algériennes 1956–1965," MAE.

200. "Note sur la question algérienne" for the French UN delegation, 15 November 1956, MAE, NUOI Carton 550, 3; see also "Aide-Mémoire des MAE," 1957, MAE, NUOI Carton 549.

201. *Dossier Algérie*, 1956, CAOM, 81 F1014; see also *Dossier Algérie*, 1957, CAOM, 81 F1018.

202. See the rubric "Destruction" in *Dossier Algérie*, 1956, CAOM, 81 F1014, and *Dossier Algérie*, 1957, CAOM, 81 F1018.

203. See the rubric "Atrocités" in *Dossier Algérie*, 1956, CAOM, 81 F1014, and *Dossier Algérie*, 1957, CAOM, 81 F1018.

204. MAE, circular memo to all diplomatic missions, 10 December 1958, MAE, NUOI Carton 557; MLA, "Note pour Monsieur Langlais: Question algérienne aux Nations-Unies," 9 June 1959, MAE, NUOI Carton 561; General Delegation in Algiers to the Office of the Prime Minister, 13 July 1959, CAOM, 81 F115.

205. MLA report, "Action d'information sur l'Algérie," 27 May 1959, and General Delegation in Algiers, "Note d'information sur les regroupements de population," 26 July 1959, both in MAE, NUOI Carton 561; General Parlange's report, "Campagne d'information sur les regroupements et nouveaux villages," 4 July 1960, CAOM, 81 F444.

206. Telegrams from the French UN delegation to the MAE, 20 February 1958, and the MAE to the French UN delegation, 4 March 1958, both in MAE, NUOI Carton 557; Commander in Chief Challe's secret instruction to the regional commanders, "Suppression des zones interdites," 23 July 1959, SHAT, 1H 2033/D2.

207. "Discours de M. Lacoste devant la presse diplomatique, le 6 décembre 1956," CAOM, 81 F1012, 1.

208. For example, see Roger Vaurs to the MAE, "Filme sur l'Algérie: Programme 1960," 16 December 1959, CAOM, 81 F360.

209. Connelly, *Diplomatic Revolution*, 127–28.

210. See the report "Réunion interministerielle pour l'information de l'opinion publique étrangère sur les problèmes algériens," 19 May 1957, SHAT, 1H 2468/D3.

211. See especially the MAE's top-secret circular memo to all diplomatic missions with the "Instruction: Lutte contre les activités du FLN à l'étranger," 3 April 1959, MAE, NUOI Carton 562.

212. It was also part of the diplomatic offensive to invite chosen foreign diplomats and journalists on informational trips to Algeria, in order to demonstrate to them the French position in practice. For example, see memorandums of the Cabinet Militaire du Ministre de l'Algérie, "Visite en Algérie des diplomates étrangers," 11 October 1957, and "Voyage d'information en Algérie de diplomates étrangers," 28 November 1957 and 10 January 1958, all in CAOM, 12 CAB 170; MAE to the French UN delegation in New York, "Voyage en Algérie de personnalités étrangères," 19 November 1957, MAE, NUOI Carton 553.

213. See CAOM, 12 CAB 161, for a copy of the brochure *L'Algérie d'aujourd'hui*, a million of which were printed in June 1956.

214. CAOM, 12 CAB 161, for a copy of the brochure *Notions essentielles sur l'Algérie*, a million of which were printed in June 1956.

215. For example, see the brochure *Algérie, ici vivent côte à côte 9 500 000 Français*, CAOM, 12 CAB 161; see also the propaganda poster of the French army with the title "L'école communale enseigne que tous les hommes sont frères," 9 February 1957, SHAT, 1H 2493/D2.

216. See especially the brochures *Les grands secteurs de l'agriculture algérienne*, *Le commerce algérien*, and *L'industrie algérienne*, CAOM, 12 CAB 161.

217. See Service de l'Information du Cabinet du Ministre résidant en Algérie, *Programme et action du Gouvernement en Algérie: Mesures de pacification et réformes*, August 1956, and the brochures *L'Algérie, problème crucial à régler rapidement* and *15 mois d'action en Algérie*, all in CAOM, 12 CAB 161.

218. "Nouvelle affirmation de la politique française en Algérie: Une interview de M. Guy Mollet," 29 November 1956, *Connaissance de l'Algérie* 27 (1 December 1956).

219. Simone Buisson, *La bataille pour le plein développement de l'Algérie*, October 1960, brochure in CAOM, 81 F102.

220. *Algérie—quelques aspects des problèmes économiques et sociaux*, brochure in CAOM, 12 CAB 161.

221. For example, see the brochures *La Rébellion se désagrège: L'Algérie nouvelle se construit*, 1957, SHAT, 1H 1118/D3; and *L'Algérie vivra française*, SHAT, 1H 2473/D2.

222. See especially the French brochures *Témoignages—Transférés contre leur gré en Tunisie par les rebelles, les habitants d'une mechta, proche de la frontière à s'évader...*, November 1957, ACICR, D EUR France1-0924; and *Comment le FLN fabrique les réfugiés algériens en Tunisie*, 1958, CAOM 12 CAB 234.

223. For example, see Undersecretary for Algerian Affairs in the Ministry of the Interior to the Governor General in Algiers, "Documentation pour la délégation française à l'ONU—Attentats contre les femmes et les enfants," 26 July 1956, CAOM, 81 F1013; see also General Inspector of the French Army, General Callies, to the French High Command in Algiers, "Contre propagande en Métropole et à l'Etranger," 10 April 1957; Commander in Chief Salan to the General Inspector of the French Army, "Contre propagande en Métropole et à l'Etranger," 21 May 1957; and High Command in Algiers, "Exactions rebelles sur les femmes et les enfants," 27 December 1959, all in SHAT, 1H 2584/D1.

224. La Société d'Editions et de Régie, *Documents sur les crimes et attentats commis en Algérie par les terroristes*. Like many others, this publication was translated into English and Spanish for better distribution internationally. See Governor General in Algiers to the MAE, "Diffusion des *Documents sur les crimes et attentats commis en Algérie par les terroristes*," 5 April 1956, MAE, NUOI Carton 549.

225. La Société d'Editions et de Régie, *Documents sur les crimes et attentats commis en Algérie par les terroristes*, 6.

226. Ministère de l'Algérie, *Aspects véritables de la rébellion algérienne*.

227. Ibid., 74–75.

228. Ibid., 157.

229. Lagrot and Greco, "Les mutilations faciales."

230. See "Destinataires des tires à part de l'article du Dr. Lagrot," including a list of "Organisations Médicales Internationales," August 1956, CAOM, 12 CAB 161.

231. "Les mutilations criminelles en Algérie," special issue, *Algérie Médicale*.

232. Lombard, "La Clinique chirurgicale infantile et d'orthopédie," in ibid., 47–53.

233. Fourrier et al., "Aspects particuliers à la criminalité algérienne," in "Les mutilations criminelles en Algérie," 5–19.

234. On the massacre of Melouza, see especially Stora, "La gauche et les minorités anticolonialistes."

235. During the course of the Algerian War, a bloody "civil war" broke out between the Mouvement National Algérien (MNA), founded by Messali Hadj in December 1954, and the Liberation Front, in which the FLN was able to assert with great brutality its claim to be the sole representative of the Algerian national movement. See Stora, *La gangrène et l'oubli*, 138–44; Valette, *Guerre d'Algérie des messalistes*.

236. See propaganda poster "Melouza, Nouvelle Oradour," SHAT, 1H 2461/D2.

237. *Melouza et Wagram accusent . . . L'opinion mondiale juge les sanglants, libérateurs' de Melouza et de Wagram*, August 1957, copy of the brochure in CAOM, 12 CAB 161. Lidice is a Czech village northwest of Prague. The original village was completely destroyed by German forces on 10 June 1942 in reprisal for the assassination of Reich Protector Reinhard Heydrich. All men over sixteen years of age were executed on the spot, the women and children were sent to concentration camps. Most of the children were murdered at the Chełmno concentration camp.

238. "Texte du telegramme au sujet du massacre de Melouza envoyé par Mohammed Yazid à M. Hammarskjöld," 3 June 1957, and "Déclaration remise le 12 juin aux correspondants de la presse française par Mohammed Yazid," both in MAE, NUOI Carton 552; "Le FLN cherche à exploiter le drame de Melouza pour internationaliser le problème," *Le Monde*, 4 June 1957.

239. MAE report, "Schéma d'un plan d'action en prévision du prochain débat sur l'Algérie aux Nations-Unies," 5 June 1959, MAE, NUOI Carton 561; French UN ambassador in Geneva to the MAE, "Propagande FLN dans les milieux de l'ONU," 27 October 1960, MAE, NUOI Carton 1067.

240. Dupuy, "Présence de la France à l'ONU," 56; Plantey, "De Gaulle et l'ONU," 101–3; Couve de Murville, "La France et l'ONU," 113; Urquhart, "Un regard extérieur," 119.

241. In 1958, 1959, 1960, and 1961, the French UN delegation boycotted the UN debates on the Algerian question; see "The Question of Algeria," in United Nations, *Yearbook of the United Nations, 1958*, 79; *1959*, 52; *1960*, 132; *1961*, 97.

242. Elsenhans, *Algerienkrieg*, 80.

243. UN GAOR Resolution A/RES/1573 (XV), "Question of Algeria," 19 December 1960.

244. UN GAOR Resolution A/RES/1724 (XVI), "Question of Algeria," 20 December 1961.

245. Secret circular memo, 25102/2/49, 28 March 1949, TNA, DO 35/3776.

246. See the detailed account "The First Cyprus Case," in Simpson, *Human Rights*, 924–89; Parkinson, *Bills of Rights and Decolonization*, 34–35.

247. UN GAOR Document A/3616, Greek UN delegation to the UN secretary-general, 15 July 1957; Luard, *History of the United Nations*, 2:161–74; Johnson, "Britain and the Cyprus Problem," 113–30.

248. UN GAOR Document A/3616/Add.1, letter with explanatory memorandum from the Greek UN delegation to the UN secretary-general, 13 September 1957, 3–4.

249. Martin Thomas, *French North African Crisis*, 139-42.

250. French embassy in London to the MAE, telegram, 1 October 1955, MAE, NUOI Carton 546.

251. FO report, "French North Africa," 24 July 1956, TNA, FO 371/124445.

252. FO confidential report, 17 September 1956, TNA, FO 371/119381.

253. MAE to the French embassies in London, Ankara, and Athens, note, "La question de Chypre devant les Nations Unies," 4 March 1957, MAE, NUOI Carton 117; French ambassador in London, report, "Conversations franco-anglaises du 17 septembre 1957: Chypre et l'Algérie," 18 September 1957, MAE, Secrétariat général, Série "entretiens et messages," Carton 4.

254. Harold Beeley of the British UN delegation to the FO, secret note, 8 July 1959, TNA, FO 371/138622.

255. CO, secret circular memo, "Anglo-French Colonial Relations," 15 May 1952, TNA, DO 35/3842.

256. FO paper, "Political Discussions with Other Colonial Powers," 4 March 1957; and FO to the CO, 12 March 1957, both in TNA, FO 371/125312.

257. On the colonial talks, see "Conversations Anglo-Franco-Belges sur les questions coloniales aux Nations Unies (Bruxelles, 30 juin et 1er juillet 1955)" and "Entretiens tripartis Franco-Anglo-Belges sur les question coloniales (Londres, 1–2 octobre 1956)," both in MAE, NUOI Carton 483; FO confidential report, "Quadripartite Talks (with French, Belgians and Portugese: Paris, July 1st–5th 1957)," TNA, FO 371/125313.

258. Opitz, *Menschenrechte*, 69–74.

259. UN GAOR Resolution A/RES/2200 A (XXI), "International Covenant on Civil and Political Rights" and "International Covenant on Economic, Social, and Cultural Rights," 16 December 1966; on the content of both human rights covenants, see Ishay, *Human Rights Reader*, 507–19.

260. FO cabinet paper, "The United Nations Draft Covenants on Human Rights," 4 March 1952, TNA, LO 2/667.

261. UN GAOR Resolution A/RES/545 (VI), "Inclusion in the International Covenant or Covenants on Human Rights of an Article Relating to the Right of People to Self-Determination," 5 February 1952.

262. See FO to the British UN delegation, confidential note, 10 March 1955; CO to the FO, confidential note, 22 September 1955; and British UN delegation, confidential strategy paper, "United Kingdom Delegation to the United Nations," 28 September 1955, all in TNA, FO 371/117561; see also CO report, "United Nations Interest in Self-Determination," 22 July 1958, TNA, CO 936/399.

263. British UN delegation, confidential strategy paper, "United Kingdom Delegation to the United Nations," 3 October 1955, TNA, DO 35/10604.

264. FO report, "Human Rights: A General Guide," 29 November 1963, TNA, FO 371/172743; Parkinson, *Bills of Rights and Decolonization*, 26.

265. United Nations Department of Public Information, *United Nations Work for Human Rights*, 8, 10–11; see also Burke, *Decolonization*, 35–50.

266. French UN delegation to the MAE, "Commission des droits de l'homme: Droit des peuples à disposer d'eux-mêmes," 18 February 1955; and British embassy in Paris to the MAE, "Proposals of the Human Rights Commission on Self-Determination," 14 March 1955, both in MAE, NUOI Carton 386.

267. French UN delegation to the MAE, "Assemblée générale, Xe session, 3ème commission, Point 28: Pactes internationaux relatifs aux droits de l'homme," 17 October 1955, MAE, NUOI Carton 386; MAE note, "Projets de Pactes des droits de l'homme," 10 January 1956, MAE, NUOI Carton 384, 3.

268. MAE memorandum, "La délégation française à la Commission des droits de l'homme: Son rôle dans l'élaboration des projets de Pactes relatifs aux droits de l'homme," 1955, MAE, NUOI Carton 384, 3.

269. Note, "Conversations quadripartites de Lisbonne sur les problèmes d'outre-mer (28–30 juillet 1958)," MAE, NUOI Carton 483, 7.

270. "A Bill to Make Provision for the Establishment of Human Rights Commissions in the British Non-Self-Governing Colonies and Protectorates," submitted by Benn, 10 December 1957, TNA, CO 859/1342.

271. Benn to the UN Secretary-General Hammarskjöld, 11 February 1958, UNOG, SO 221/9 (1-3-5).

272. UN Undersecretary Hill to Benn, 13 March 1958, UNOG, SO 221/9 (1-3-5).

273. Benn to UN Undersecretary Hill, 21 March 1958, UNOG, SO 221/9 (1-3-5).

274. In 1960, the following nations joined the United Nations: Benin, Burkina Faso, Ivory Coast, Gabon, Cameroon, Congo, the Democratic Republic of the Congo, Madagascar, Mali, Niger, Nigeria, Senegal, Somalia, Togo, Chad, and the Central African Republic.

275. Lauren, *Evolution of International Human Rights*, 251; Low, *Eclipse of Empire*, 215–25.

276. Emerson, *Self-Determination Revisited*, 2, 11–18; Singh, *India and Afro-Asian Independence*, 48; Luard, *History of the United Nations*, 2:516–18; Lauren, *Power and Prejudice*, 232–33; Lauren, *Evolution of International Human Rights*, 252; Mazower, *No Enchanted Palace*, 188–89.

277. CO, secret paper, 29 September 1960, TNA, CO 936/678.

278. General Smuts quoted in Tinker, *Race*, 111.

279. Luard, *History of the United Nations*, 2:180–83.

280. UN GAOR Document A/4501, Soviet Premier Khrushchev to the United Nations, 23 September 1960; UN GAOR Document A/4502, Soviet UN delegation, draft, "Declaration on the Granting of Independence to Colonial Countries and Peoples," 23 September 1960. On the course of the entire debate before the UN General Assembly, see "Declaration on Granting Independence to Colonial Countries and Peoples," in United Nations, *Yearbook of the United Nations, 1960*, 44–50.

281. Mezerik, *Colonialism and the United Nations*, 6–8; Schümperli, *Die Vereinten Nationen und Dekolonisation*, 69; Gorman, *Great Debates at the United Nations*, 151–52; Whelan, *Indivisible Human Rights*, 141–42.

282. Mezerik, *Colonialism and the United Nations*, 9.

283. Schümperli, *Die Vereinten Nationen und Dekolonisation*, 73; El-Ayouty, *United Nations and Decolonization*, 209; Burke, *Decolonization*, 50–56.

284. UN GAOR Resolution A/RES/1514 (XV), "Declaration on the Granting of Independence to Colonial Countries and Peoples," 14 December 1960.

285. Luard, *History of the United Nations*, 2:186.

286. UN GAOR Resolution A/RES/1514 (XV), "Declaration on the Granting of Independence to Colonial Countries and Peoples," 14 December 1960.

287. UN GAOR Document A/4889, Soviet foreign minister, memorandum, "The Situation with Regard to Implementation of the Declaration on the Granting of Independence to Colonial Countries and Peoples," 26 September 1961. On the course of the entire debate before the UN General Assembly, see "The Situation with Regard to Implementation of Declaration on Granting Independence to Colonial Countries and Peoples," in United Nations, *Yearbook of the United Nations, 1961*, 44–57.

288. UN GAOR Document A/L.355, draft resolution by the Soviet UN delegation, 9 October 1961.

289. UN GAOR Resolution A/RES/1654 (XVI), "The Situation with Regard to the

Implementation of the Declaration on the Granting of Independence to Colonial Countries and Peoples," 27 November 1961.

290. The official name of the committee was Special Committee on the Situation with Regard to the Implementation of the Declaration on the Granting of Independence to Colonial Countries and Peoples; for its tasks and function, see United Nations Office of Public Information, *The Special Committee of 24 on Decolonization*; Hanstein, *Einfluß der Vereinten Nationen*, 16–17; Luard, *History of the United Nations*, 2:187–95.

291. Lauren, *Power and Prejudice*, 246–48.

292. The Antiracism Convention had been preceded in 1963 by the UN Declaration on the Elimination of All Forms of Racial Discrimination. UN GAOR Resolution A/RES/1904 (XVIII), "Declaration on the Elimination of All Forms of Racial Discrimination," 20 November 1963; on the convention, see UN GAOR Resolution A/RES/2106 A (XX), "International Convention on the Elimination of All Forms of Racial Discrimination," 21 December 1965; see also Burke, *Decolonization*, 70–75; Normand and Zaidi, *Human Rights at the UN*, 260–69.

293. MAE, "Décolonisation," 16 July 1962, MAE, NUOI Carton 1069.

294. Ibid.; MAE note "Décolonisation," MAE, 18 June 1962, MAE, NUOI Carton 1069.

295. MAE note "Participation de la France au Comité des 17 pour la décolonisation," 19 December 1961, MAE, NUOI Carton 1069.

296. British UN delegation to the CO, 18 January 1961, TNA, CO 936/679; see also British UN delegation to the FO, confidential report, 2 June 1961, TNA, DO 181/84.

297. FO strategy paper "United Kingdom Policy on Colonial Matters in the United Nations," 20 February 1961, TNA, FO 371/160903.

298. CO secret note, 19 December 1961, TNA, CO 936/679.

299. Ibid.

300. CO strategy paper, "Colonial Questions at the United Nations," 27 December 1961, TNA, CO 936/679.

301. Burke, *Decolonization*, 78–80.

302. See also the critical newspaper article by Bourdet, "France qui donna les droits de l'homme."

303. "Note relative à la ratification éventuelle de la Convention Européenne de Sauvegarde des Droits de l'Homme et des libertés fondamentales," 28 August 1961, CAOM, 81 F1023.

304. Note pour le Conseil des Ministres du 13 juin 1962, "Projet de loi autorisant la ratification de la Convention de Sauvegarde des Droits de l'Homme et des Libertés Fondamentales," CAOM, 81 F1023.

305. Hessel, "Un rôle essentiel," 253–60; Dupuy, "Présence de la France à l'ONU," 58–60.

306. Notification by the European Council, "Her Majesty's Government extend the European Convention on Human Rights to forty-two territories for whose international relations it is responsible," 23 October 1953, TNA, DO 35/7008.

307. CO, "Human Rights Provisions in Colonial Constitutions," 26 September 1962, TNA, CO 1032/283. The great influence of the former colonial powers on the postcolonial constitutions of the new independent states, including the constitutional guarantees of basic rights, is shown in the studies by Charles Parkinson, on Great Britain in particular, and by Julian Go, on the former colonial powers in general. Especially the ECHR served many African states as a model for embedding basic rights in their new constitutions. See Parkinson, *Bills of Rights and Decolonization*, particularly on Kenya, 216–25; Go, "Modeling States and Sovereignty," particularly on the basic rights, 124–31.

308. British UN delegation to the FO, confidential note, 23 March 1965, TNA, FO 371/183642.

309. Commonwealth Office, "Human Rights Policy at the United Nations," 31 May 1965, TNA, FO 371/183665.

310. See recommendations of the FO Working Group on Human Rights, "Possible United Kingdom Initiatives in the Human Rights Field," 1965; FO Steering Committee on International Organisations, strategy paper, "United Nations High Commissioner for Human Rights," 1965; and FO protocol for the Commonwealth Office, "United Nations High Commissioner for Human Rights," 18 June 1965, all in TNA, DO 181/147.

311. CO circular memo, "European Human Rights Convention," 24 January 1966, TNA, CO 936/948; see also Schmid, *Rang und Geltung der Europäischen Konvention*, 53; Geoffrey Marston, "United Kingdom's Part," 825.

312. FO to the British UN delegation, confidential note, "Policy Towards United Nations Human Rights Activities," 22 April 1966; and Commonwealth Relations Office, confidential circular memo, "Human Rights Policies at the United Nations," 28 April 1966, both in TNA, DO 181/147.

313. See British UN delegation to the FO, confidential note, 6 January 1960, TNA, FO 371/153569; CO to the FO, secret note, "Article 2 (7) and the South African Issue," 5 May 1960, TNA, FO 371/153572; FO confidential report, "The United Kingdom Attitude on Article 2 (7) of the United Nations Charter," 4 July 1960, TNA, CO 936/678.

314. On the course of the entire debate before the UN General Assembly, see "International Covenants on Human Rights," in United Nations, *Yearbook of the United Nations, 1966*, 406–33.

315. For the identical Article 1 of both of the 1966 International Covenants on Human Rights, see Ishay, *Human Rights Reader*, 507, 513.

Chapter 7. Conclusion

Note to epigraph: Jean-Paul Sartre, "Preface," in Sartre, *Colonialism and Neocolonialism*, xlviii–xlix.

1. Andrew Thompson, *Empire Strikes Back?* 234–38; Aldrich, "Colonial Past and the Postcolonial Present," 334–356.

2. Dowden, "State of Shame"; Vasagar, "Lest We Forget."

3. Law no. 2005-158 of 23 February 2005, *Journal Officiel, Lois et Décrets*, 24 February 2005, 3128–30.

4. On the debate over the controversial law, see especially Liauzu, "Une loi contre l'histoire," 28; Liauzu and Manceron, *La colonisation, la loi et l'histoire*. Under enormous pressure from French historians, other intellectuals, and diplomatic protests, the French government saw itself forced to revoke the controversial passage in the law in February 2006. See Decree no. 2006-160 of 15 February 2006, *Journal Officiel, Lois et Décrets*, 16 February 2006, 2369.

5. For example, see Ruscio, *Décolonisation tragique*; Clayton, *Wars of French Decolonization*.

6. For example, see Benot, *Massacres coloniaux*; Vidal-Naquet, *Les crimes de l'armée française*; Ferro, *Livre noir*; Elkins, *Britain's Gulag*.

7. The first approaches toward a comparative study of decolonization wars are, as mentioned earlier, smaller contributions like Van Doorn and Hendrix, *Process of Decolonisation*, and the section entitled "Guerres de décolonisations compares," in Ageron and Michel, *L'ère des décolonisations*, 9–204.

8. Hargreaves, *Decolonization*, 107–8; Darwin, *Britain and Decolonization*, 139; Darwin, *End of Empire*, 117; Low, *Eclipse of Empire*, 173–76; Reinhard, *Europäische Expansion*, 4:136; Eckert, *Kolonialismus*, 90.

9. On the special colonial situation in the settler colonies, see especially Elkins and Pedersen, *Settler Colonialism*; Dane Kennedy, *Islands of White*.

10. See particularly Amiri, *Bataille de France*.

11. The terms "electricity," "the bathtub," and "the bottleneck" refer to the methods of torture widely used in the colonies with electricity, water, and the insertion of bottlenecks in the bodily orifices of the victims; Césaire, *Discourse on Colonialism*, 70.

12. Ibid., 73.

13. Ibid., 75.

14. For an example from Great Britain, see the tribute to Commander in Chief Erskine in the report "McLean Court of Inquiry," General Erskine, 1 January 1954, TNA, WO 32/21722. An example in France is the tribute to President de Gaulle in "Hommage du Général de Gaulle à l'armée," 23 November 1961, in Vidal-Naquet, *Les crimes de l'armée française*, 170.

15. On the specific uniqueness of the system of absolute power found in the National Socialist concentration camp, see Sofsky, *Ordnung des Terrors*.

16. Jean-Paul Sartre, "A Victory," in Sartre, *Colonialism and Neocolonialism*, 68.

17. Connelly, *Diplomatic Revolution*.

18. Greenspan, "International Law and Its Protection."

19. Baxter, "Human Rights in War."

20. UN GAOR Resolution A/RES/2444 (XXIII), "Declaration on Respect for Human Rights in Armed Conflict," 19 December 1968.

21. On the process of drafting the additional protocols, see especially Baxter, "Humanitarian Law or Humanitarian Politics?"; Best, *Humanity in Warfare*, 315–29.

22. ICRC, *Protocols Additional to the Geneva Conventions of 12 August 1949*.

23. Ibid., 4.

24. The argument that human rights emerged seemingly from nowhere and overnight in the 1970s is put forth particularly by Moyn, *Last Utopia*, 3, and Eckel, "Human Rights and Decolonization," 130.

25. For the importance of human rights within the framework of the Helsinki Accords, see especially Daniel Thomas, *Helsinki Effect*.

Bibliography

Unedited Sources

Archives du Comité International de la Croix-Rouge, Geneva, Switzerland (ACICR)

Archives générales, 1951–1965 (B AG)

B AG 200: Renseignements sur l'évolution et les causes d'un conflit; rapports des délégués sur la situation politique générale.

B AG 202: Application et violations du droit international humanitaire; plaintes.

B AG 209: Divers concernant les renseignements d'ordre politique, social et économique.

B AG 210: Généralités concernant les prisonniers de guerre; rapports de visites de camps.

B AG 225: Détenus politiques et détenus de sécurité.

Délégation de Paris, 1928–1968 (D EUR France1)

D EUR France1-0370: Troubles Afrique du Nord, correspondance Michel/Mendès-France "confidentiel."

D EUR France1-0376: Application des principes humanitaires en cas de troubles intérieurs, réunion à Genève.

D EUR France1-0438: Torture en Algérie (napalm, CTT Colbert, témoignages) 24 January-7 June 1960.

D EUR France1-0924: Réfugiés algériens en Tunisie et au Maroc, secours, rapatriements.

D EUR France1-0928: Secours population regroupée en Algérie (CR française).

D EUR France1-0932: Algérie, Conventions art. 3, communications aux partis au conflit.

Centre des archives d'outre-mer, Aix-en-Provence, France (CAOM)

État des Fonds, Archives Privées, Papiers d'Agents (PA)

19 PA: Papiers de Robert Delavignette.

État des Fonds, Fonds Ministériels, Deuxième Empire Colonial, Ministère d'État Chargé des Affaires Algériennes (81 F 1–2415)

81 F63–172: Ministres, secrétaires d'état, et secrétaires généraux chargés des affaires algériennes: cabinet et services rattachés: cabinet.

81 F244–591: Ministère d'État chargé des affaires algériennes: Service des affaires politiques et de l'information: Service de presse et d'information.

81 F592–1052: Ministère d'État chargé des affaires algériennes: Service des affaires politiques et de l'information: Bureau politique.

Fonds Territoriaux Algérie, Gouvernement Général de l'Algérie, Cabinet Civil des Gouverneurs Généraux (CAB)

3 CAB: Cabinet Georges le Beau.
4 CAB: Cabinet Jean Abrial.
12 CAB: Cabinet Robert Lacoste.
14 CAB: Cabinet Paul Delouvrier.

Imperial War Museum, Department of Documents, London, Great Britain (IWM)

90/20/1: Papers of Lieutenant Colonel J. K. Windeatt.

Ministère des Affaires Étrangères, Archives des Affaires Étrangères, Paris, France (MAE)

Secrétaires d'état et ministres délégués, missions interministérielles

MLA: Mission de liaison pour les Affaires algériennes (1956–1965).

Secrétariat général

Série "entretiens et messages."

Représentations de la France dans les organisations et les commissions internationales

NUOI: Nations Unies et Organisations Internationales (1945–1959).

National Archives and Records Administration, College Park, Maryland, U.S. (NARA)

RG 59: General Records of the Department of State, 1756–1993

RG 59.2: Central Files of the Department of State, 1778–1963, Decimal Files.
RG 59.3: Records of Organizational Units, 1756–1992, Lot Files.

RG 472 A1 474 Box 99

Melnik, Constantin. "The French Campaign Against the FLN." RAND Corporation memorandum 5449 prepared for the Office of the Assistant Secretary of Defense, International Security Affairs, September 1967.
Tanham, George K. "Doctrine and Tactics of Revolutionary Warfare: The Viet Minh in Indochina." RAND Corporation research memorandum 2395, 20 September 1959.

RG 472 A1 474 Box 107

Elg, Poul. "Lessons from the Sar in Indochina." 31 May 1955.

The National Archives of the UK: Kew, Great Britain (TNA)

Air Ministry (AIR): Records Created or Inherited by the Air Ministry, the Royal Air Force, and Related Bodies

AIR 23: Air Ministry and Ministry of Defence: Royal Air Force overseas commands, reports, and correspondence.

British Council: Records of the British Council (BW)

BW 15/2: British Council: Policy (confidential papers).

Cabinet Office: Record of the Cabinet Office (CAB)

CAB 21: Cabinet Office and predecessors: Registered Files.
CAB 87: War Cabinet and Cabinet: Committees on Reconstruction, Supply and other matters: Minutes and Papers.
CAB 129: Cabinet: Memoranda.
CAB 130: Cabinet: Miscellaneous Committees: Minutes and Papers.

Colonial Office: Records of the Colonial Office, Commonwealth and Foreign and Commonwealth Offices, Empire Marketing Board, and Related Bodies (CO)

CO 323: Colonies, general, original correspondence.
CO 537: Colonial Office and predecessors, confidential general and confidential original correspondence.
CO 822: Colonial Office, East Africa, original correspondence.
CO 847: Colonial Office, Africa, original correspondence.
CO 852: Colonial Office, Economic General Department and predecessors, registered files.
CO 859: Colonial Office, Social Services Department and successors, registered files.
CO 875: Colonial Office, Public Relations Department, later Information Department, registered files.
CO 936: Colonial Office and Commonwealth Office, International and General Department and predecessors, original correspondence.
CO 1027: Colonial Office, Information Department, registered files.
CO 1032: Colonial Office and Commonwealth Office, Defence and General Department and successors, registered files, general colonial policy.
CO 1066: Colonial Office, Kenya Information Service, photographs.

Ministry of Defence: Records of the Ministry of Defence (DEFE)

DEFE 11: Ministry of Defence, Chiefs of Staff Committee, registered files.

Dominions Office: Records Created or Inherited by the Dominions Office, and of the Commonwealth Relations and Foreign and Commonwealth Offices (DO)

DO 35: Dominions Office and Commonwealth Relations Office, original correspondence.
DO 181: Commonwealth Relations Office and Commonwealth Office, United Nations Department and successors, registered file.

Foreign Office: Records Created and Inherited by the Foreign Office (FO)

FO 369: Foreign Office, Consular Department, general correspondence from 1906.
FO 371: Foreign Office, Political Departments, general correspondence, 1906–1966.
FO 930: Ministry of Information and Foreign Office, foreign publicity files.
FO 1110: Foreign Office and Foreign and Commonwealth Office, Information Research Department, general correspondence.

Law Officers Department: Record Created or Inherited by the Law Officers' Department (LO)

LO 2: Law Officers' Department, registered files.

Prime Minister's Office: Records of the Prime Minister's Office (PREM)

Prime Minister's Office, correspondence and papers, 1951–1964.

War Office: Records Created or Inherited by the War Office, Armed Forces, Judge Advocate General, and Related Bodies (WO)

WO 32: War Office and Successors, registered files.
WO 216: War Office, Office of the Chief of the Imperial General Staff, papers.
WO 276: War Office, East Africa Command, papers.
WO 291: Ministry of Supply and War Office, Military Operational Research Unit, Successors and Related Bodies, reports and papers.

Rhodes House Library, Oxford, Great Britain (RH)

Mss.Afr.s.1534: Mau Mau Classification Reports, 1953–56.
Mss.Afr.s.1580: Papers of Major General Sir Robert Hide.
Mss.Afr.s.1694: Papers on the Rule of Law, John Whyatt.
Mss.Afr.s.1715: Papers of Brigadier Percy W. P. Green.
Mss.Afr.s.1770: Papers of Thomas Askwith.
Mss.Brit.Emp.s.486: Papers of Sir Arthur Young.
Mss.Brit.Emp.s.548: Memoirs of Jon Wainwright.

Service Historique de l'Armée de Terre, Vincennes, France (SHAT)

Série H: Outre-mer de 1830 à 1973

Sous-série 1H: Algérie: La Xe région militaire et la guerre d'Algérie, 1945–1967 (1H 1091– 4881)
Sous-série 10H: Indochine: La guerre d'Indochine, 1946–1956 (10H 86–5975)

Série P: 1940–1946: Fonds confiés au département interarmées, ministériel et interministériel (DIMI)
Sous-série 11P: Divisions et brigades.

Série R: Cabinet du ministre de la défense et organismes rattachés, fonds confiés au département interarmées, ministériel et interministériel (DIMI)
Sous-série 1R: Cabinet du ministre de la défense.

United Nations Archives and Records Management Section, New York (UN ARMS)

Departmental Archives Group (DAG)

DAG-18/1.1.0: Department of Social Affairs, Office of the Assistant Secretary General, Registry Files, Human Rights Commissions and Human Rights Division.

Reports and Surveys—Records (S-0188)

S-0188-0005-09: Political and Security Council Affairs Reports (Protitch Reports), Algeria.

Political and Security Matters (S-0442)

S-0442-0189-09: International Incidents and Disputes, Algeria, Public Interest and Disputes, A/INF List GA 15th, PO 230 (PI) A/INF List GA 15th.
S-0442-0190-01: International Incidents and Disputes, Algeria, Public Interest and Opinion, A/INF List, 16th Session, PO 230 ALGE (PI) A/INF 16th.

United Nations Organization Geneva, Registry, Records and Archives Unit, Geneva, Switzerland (UNOG)

Human Rights (2nd Series), 1956–1974 (SO)

SO 212/2: Sessions of Commission on Human Rights, 13th–26th Session.
SO 215/1 FRA: Violations and Complaints Regarding Human Rights—France.
SO 215/1 UK: Violations and Complaints Regarding Human Rights—United Kingdom.

SO 221/9 (1-3-5): International Covenants on Human Rights, Comments and Suggestions, NGOs.

Edited Sources

Publications of British Government Offices
Publications of Her Majesty's Stationery Office (HMSO) in London

Corfield, F. D. *Historical Survey of the Origins and Growth of Mau Mau.* Cmd. 1030. London, 1960.
United Kingdom. Parliament. *Memorandum Relating to Indians in Kenya.* Cmd. 1922. London, 1923.
———. *Report of the Kenya Land Commission.* Cmd. 4556. London, 1934.
———. *Report to the Secretary of State for the Colonies by the Parliamentary Delegation to Kenya, 1954.* Cmd. 9081. London, January 1954.
———. *Documents Relating to the Death of Eleven Mau Mau Detainees at Hola Camp in Kenya.* Cmd. 778. London, 1959.
———. *Record of Proceedings and Evidence in the Enquiry into the Deaths of Eleven Mau Mau Detainees at Hola Camp in Kenya.* Cmd. 795. London, 1959.
———. *Further Documents Relating to the Death of Eleven Mau Mau Detainees at Hola Camp in Kenya.* Cmd. 816. London, 1959.

Publications of the Government Printing Office in Nairobi

Colony and Protectorate of Kenya. *Post-War Employment Committee Report.* Nairobi, 1943.
———. *Official Gazette Extraordinary,* Nairobi, 30 October 1952.
———. *Official Gazette Supplement,* no. 61, Nairobi, 25 November 1952.
———. *Emergency Regulations Made Under the Emergency Powers Order in Council, 1939.* Nairobi, 1954.
East Africa Command. *A Handbook on Anti-Mau Mau Operations.* Nairobi, 1954.

Publications of the Government Printing Office in Singapore

HQ Malaya Command Kuala Lumpur. *The Conduct of Anti-Terrorist Operations in Malaya.* Singapore, 1954.

Publications of the French Government
Journal Officiel de la République Française

Journal Officiel. Assemblée Consultative Provisoire. Débats, 1945–1946.
Journal Officiel, Assemblée Nationale, Débats, 12 November 1954.
Journal Officiel, Lois et Décrets, 21 September 1947.
———, 7 April 1955.
———, 17 March 1956.
———, 19 March 1956.
———, 13 May 1956.
———, 17 May 1958.
———, 23 April 1961.
———, 23 March 1962.
———, 5 January 1979.
———, 5 December 1979.

————, 20 October 1999.
————, 24 February 2005.

Publications of the International Committee of the Red Cross (ICRC)

Individual Publications

International Committee of the Red Cross, ed. *Report on the Work of the International Committee of the Red Cross (January 1 to December 31, 1953)*. Geneva, 1954.
————. *The ICRC and the Algerian Conflict*. Geneva, 1962.
————. *Protocols Additional to the Geneva Conventions of 12 August 1949*. Geneva, 1996.
————. *The Geneva Conventions of August 12, 1949*. Geneva, n.d.

Annual Reports

International Committee of the Red Cross, ed. *Annual Report, 1955*. Geneva, 1956.
————. *Annual Report, 1957*. Geneva. 1958.
————. *Annual Report, 1959*. Geneva, 1960.

Press Communiqués

International Committee of the Red Cross, ed. *Collection of the Communiqués de Presse* 8, nos. 562–635 (1957), and 9, nos. 636–749 (1958–1961).

Protocol Series

International Committee of the Red Cross, ed. Procès-Verbaux des Séances du Comité 1948–59.

Revue Internationale de la Croix-Rouge

Revue Internationale de la Croix-Rouge, no. 334, October 1946.
————, no. 439, July 1955.
————, no. 459, March 1957.
————, no. 461, May 1957.
————, no. 466, October 1957.
————, no. 470, February 1958.
————, no. 487, July 1959.

Publications of the United Nations

Individual Publications

United Nations. *Yearbook of the International Law Commission, 1950*. Vol. 2. New York, 1957.
United Nations Department of Public Information, ed. *United Nations Work for Human Rights*, New York, 1957.
United Nations Office of Public Information, ed. *The Special Committee of 24 on Decolonization: What It Is, What It Does, How It Works*. Background papers. New York, 1975.

Official Records

United Nations, ed. General Assembly, Official Records, 1946–1966 (UN GAOR).
————. ECOSOC, Official Records, 1945–1957 (UN ECOSOCOR).
————. Security Council, Official Records, 1955–1959 (UN SCOR).

Yearbook of the United Nations

United Nations, ed. *Yearbook of the United Nations, 1955*. New York, 1956.
————. *Yearbook of the United Nations, 1956*. New York, 1957.

————. *Yearbook of the United Nations, 1957.* New York, 1958.
————. *Yearbook of the United Nations, 1958.* New York, 1959.
————. *Yearbook of the United Nations, 1959.* New York, 1960.
————. *Yearbook of the United Nations, 1960.* New York, 1961.
————. *Yearbook of the United Nations, 1961.* New York, 1962.
————. *Yearbook of the United Nations, 1966.* New York, 1967.

Collections of Source Material

Barrat, Denise, and Robert Barrat, eds. *Algérie, 1956: Livre blanc sur la répression.* La Tours d'Aigues, 2001.
Bontinck, François, ed. *Aux origines de l'État indépendant du Congo: Documents tirés d'archives américaines.* Louvain, 1966.
Dalloz, Jacques, ed. *Textes sur la décolonisation.* Paris, 1989.
Elsenhans, Hartmut, ed. *Materialien zum Algerienkrieg, 1954–1962.* Berlin, 1974.
Faivre, Maurice, ed. *Les archives inédites de la politique algérienne, 1958–1962.* Paris, 2000.
Harbi, Mohammed, ed. *Les archives de la révolution algérienne.* Paris, 1981.
Harbi, Mohammed, and Gilbert Meynier, eds. *Le FLN: Documents et histoire, 1954–1962.* Paris, 2004.
Ho Chi Minh. *On Revolution: Selected Writings, 1920–66.* Ed. Bernard B. Fall. London, 1967.
Hyam, Ronald, ed. *The Labour Government and the End of Empire, 1945–1951.* Part 1, *High Policy and Administration.* British Documents on the End of Empire. series A, vol. 2. London, 1992.
Ishay, Micheline R., ed. *The Human Rights Reader: Major Political Essays, Speeches, and Documents from the Bible to the Present.* New York, 2007.
James, Robert Rhodes, ed. *Winston S. Churchill: His Complete Speeches, 1897–1963.* Vol. 6. New York, 1974.
Jauffret, Jean-Charles, ed. *La guerre d'Algérie par les documents, L'avertissement 10 février 1943–9 mars 1946.* Vincennes, 1990.
Lauterpacht, Elihu, ed. *International Law: Being the Collected Papers of Hersch Lauterpacht.* Vol. 3. Cambridge, 1977.
Roberts, Adam, and Richard Guelff, eds. *Documents on the Laws of War.* Oxford, 2000.
Rosenman, Samuel I., ed. *The Public Papers and Addresses of Franklin D. Roosevelt.* 13 vols. New York, 1938–1950.
U.S. Department of State, ed. *Foreign Relations of the United States [FRUS].* Diplomatic Papers, 1942. Vol. 1, General; the British Commonwealth; the Far East. Washington D.C., 1960.
————. *FRUS.* Diplomatic Papers, 1942. Vol. 4, The Near East and Africa. Washington D.C., 1963.
————. *FRUS.* Diplomatic Papers, 1943. Vol. 4, The Near East and Africa. Washington D.C., 1964.
Vidal-Naquet, Pierre, ed. *La raison d'état: Textes publiés par le Comité Maurice Audin.* Paris, 1962.
————. *Les crimes de l'armée française: Algérie, 1954–1962.* Paris, 2001.
Woodward, Llewellyn, ed. *British Foreign Policy in the Second World War.* Vol. 5. London, 1976.

Books and Articles

Abou-Khamseen, Manssour Ahmad. "The First French-Algerian War (1830–1848): A Reappraisal of the French Colonial Venture and the Algerian Resistance." Ph.D. diss., University of California, Berkeley, 1983.

Acland, R. *The Forward March*. London, 1941.

Adas, Michael. "Contested Hegemony: The Great War and the Afro-Asian Assault on the Civilizing Mission." In Christopher Lee, ed., *Making a World After Empire: The Bandung Moment and Its Political Afterlives*, 69–106. Athens, Ohio, 2010.

Adass, Olivier. "Quand l'Algérie française avait cent ans: Police et violence coloniale." In Claude Liauzu, ed., *Violence et colonisation: Pour en finir avec les guerres de mémoires*, 149–53. Paris, 2003.

Afshari, Reza. "On Historiography of Human Rights: Reflections on Paul Gordon Lauren's *The Evolution of International Human Rights: Visions Seen*." *Human Rights Quarterly* 29, no. 1 (February 2007): 1–67.

Agamben, Giorgio. *Homo sacer: Die Souveränität der Macht und das nackte Leben*. Frankfurt am Main, 2002.

———. *State of Exception*. Chicago, 2005.

Ageron, Charles-Robert. "Ferhat Abbas et l'évolution politique de l'Algérie musulmane pendant la deuxième guerre mondiale." *Revue Histoire Maghrébine* 4 (July 1975): 125–44.

———. *Histoire de l'Algérie contemporaine*. Paris, 1980.

———. "La survivance d'un mythe: La puissance par l'empire colonial (1944–1947)." *Revue française d'histoire d'outre-mer* 72 (1985): 387–403.

———. *La décolonisation française*. Paris, 1994.

———. "Les guerres d'Indochine et d'Algérie au miroir de 'la guerre révolutionnaire.'" In Charles-Robert Ageron and Marc Michel, eds., *L'ère des décolonisations: Actes du Colloque d'Aix-en-Provence*, 47–66. Paris, 1995.

———. "L'insurrection du 20 août 1955 dans le Nord-Constantinois: De la résistance armée à la guerre du peuple." In Charles-Robert Ageron, ed., *La guerre d'Algérie et les Algériens 1954-1962*, 27–50. Paris, 1997.

———, ed. *Les chemins de la décolonisation de l'empire français*. Paris, 1986.

Ageron, Charles-Robert, and Marc Michel, eds. *L'ère des décolonisations: Actes du Colloque d'Aix-en-Provence*. Paris, 1995.

Aggoun, Nacéra. "Psychological Propaganda During the Algerian War." In Martin S. Alexander, Martin Evans, and J. F. V. Keiger, eds., *The Algerian War and the French Army, 1954–62: Experiences, Images, Testimonies*, 193–99. Basingstoke, 2002.

Agi, Marc. *René Cassin, Prix Nobel de la paix, 1887–1976: Père de la Déclaration universelle des droits de l'homme*. Paris, 1998.

Alam, S. M. Shamsul. *Rethinking Mau Mau in Colonial Kenya*. New York, 2007.

Albertini, Rudolf von. *Dekolonisation: Die Diskussion über Zukunft und Verwaltung der Kolonien, 1919-1960*. Cologne, 1966.

Al Dib, Mohamed Fathi. *Abdel Nasser et la révolution algérienne*. Paris, 1985.

Aldrich, Robert. *Greater France: A History of French Overseas Expansion*. New York, 1996.

———. "Conclusion: The Colonial Past and the Postcolonial Present." In Martin Thomas, ed., *The French Colonial Mind. Volume Two, Violence, Military Encounters, and Colonialism*, 334–356. Lincoln, Neb., 2011.

Alexander, Martin S. "Les évaluations militaires britanniques des capacités de l'armée française en Algérie (1955–1958)." In Jean-Charles Jauffret and Maurice Vaisse, eds., *Militaires et guérilla dans la guerre d'Algérie*, 49–58. Montpellier, 2001.

Alexander, Martin S., Martin Evans, and J. F. V. Keiger, eds. *The Algerian War and the French Army, 1954–62: Experiences, Images, Testimonies*. Basingstoke, 2002.

———. "Colonial Minds Confounded: French Colonial Troops in the Battle of France, 1940." In Martin Thomas, ed., *The French Colonial Mind. Volume Two, Violence, Military Encounters, and Colonialism*, 248–282. Lincoln, Neb., 2011.

Alexander, Martin S., and J. F. V. Keiger. "France and the Algerian War, 1954–62: Strategy, Operations and Diplomacy." *Journal of Strategic Studies* 25, no. 2 (June 2002): 1–32.

Algerian Office, ed. *White Paper on the Application of the Geneva Conventions of 1949 to the French-Algerian Conflict.* New York, 1960.

Algérie Médicale. *Les mutilations criminelles en Algérie.* Vol. 61, 1957.

Alleg, Henri. *The Question.* London, 1958.

———, ed. *La guerre d'Algérie: De l'Algérie des origines à l'insurrection.* Vol. 1. Paris, 1981.

Alston, Philip. "The Commission on Human Rights." In Philip Alston, ed., *The United Nations and Human Rights: A Critical Appraisal,* 127–95. Oxford, 1992.

Alwan, Mohamed. *Algeria Before the United Nations.* New York, 1959.

Ambler, John Steward. *The French Army in Politics, 1945–1962.* Columbus, Ohio, 1966.

Amiri, Linda. *La Bataille de France: La guerre d'Algérie en métropole.* Paris, 2004.

Ampiah, Kweku. *The Political and Moral Imperatives of the Bandung Conference of 1955: The Reactions of the US, UK and Japan.* Folkestone, UK, 2007.

Anderson, Carol. *Eyes Off the Prize: The United Nations and the African American Struggle for Human Rights, 1944–1955.* Cambridge, 2006.

Anderson, David. "Policing and Communal Conflict: The Cyprus Emergency, 1954–60." In Robert Holland, ed., *Emergencies and Disorder in the European Empires After 1945,* 177–207. London, 1994.

———. "Master and Servant in Colonial Kenya, 1895–1939." *Journal of African History* 41 (2000): 459–85.

———. *Histories of the Hanged: The Dirty War in Kenya and the End of Empire.* London, 2005.

———. "Kenya, 1950s: An Uncanny Foretaste of the Iraq War." *Sunday Times* (London), 2 January 2005.

———. "Surrogates of the State: Colloboration and Atrocity in Kenya's Mau Mau War." In George Kassimeris, ed., *The Barbarization of Warfare,* 159–74. New York, 2006.

———. "Britain's Dark Secrets in Kenya." *Times* (London), 7 April 2011.

———. "It's Not Just Kenya: Squaring Up to the Seamier Side of Empire Is Long Overdue." *Guardian* (London), 25 July 2011.

———. "Mau Mau in the High Court and the 'Lost' British Empire Archives: Colonial Conspiracy, or Bureaucratic Bungle?" *Journal of Imperial and Commonwealth History* 39, no. 5 (December 2011): 699–716.

Anderson, David, and David Killingray, eds. *Policing and Decolonisation: Politics, Nationalism and the Police, 1917–65.* Manchester, 1992.

Anderson, David, and David Throup. "Africans and Agricultural Production in Colonial Kenya: The Myth of the War as a Watershed." *Journal of African History* 26 (1985): 327–45.

Ansprenger, Franz. *Auflösung der Kolonialreiche.* Munich, 1981.

Arnaud, Georges, and Jacques Vergès. *Pour Djamila Bouhired.* Paris, 1957.

Arnold, Theodor. *La guerre révolutionnaire.* Pfaffenhofen, 1961.

Arnold-Forster, William. *Charters of the Peace: A Commentary on the Atlantic Charter and the Declaration of Moscow, Cairo and Teheran.* London, 1944.

Arquilla, John. "9/11: Yesterday and Tomorrow; How We Could Lose the War on Terror." *San Francisco Chronicle,* 7 September 2003.

Atieno Odhiambo, E. S., and John Lonsdale, eds. *Mau Mau and Nationhood: Arms, Authority and Narration.* Oxford, 2003.

Aussaresses, Paul. *Services spéciaux: Algérie, 1955–1957.* Paris, 2001.

Austin, Dennis. "The British Point of No Return." In Prosser Gifford and William Roger Louis, eds., *The Transfer of Power in Africa: Decolonization, 1940–1960,* 225–47. New Haven, Conn., 1982.

Azikiwe, Nnamdi. *The Atlantic Charter and British West Africa*. Lagos, 1943.

Badjadja, Abdelkrim. "Panorama des archives de l'Algérie moderne et contemporaine." In Mohammed Harbi and Benjamin Stora, eds., *La guerre d'Algérie, 1954–2004: La fin de l'amnésie*, 631–82. Paris, 2004.

Baier, Lothar. "Gefangen in Algier: Am 19. März 1962 ging der Algerienkrieg zu Ende—die Erinnerung an dessen Schrecken bewegt Frankreich bis heute." *Die Zeit*, 14 March 2002.

Baldwin, William W. *Mau Mau Man-Hunt: The Adventures of the Only American Who Has Fought the Terrorists in Kenya*. New York, 1957.

Ball, Howard. *Prosecuting War Crimes and Genocide: The Twentieth-Century Experience*. Lawrence, Kan., 1999.

Ballreich, Hans. "Das Staatsnotrecht in Frankreich." In Hans Ballreich, Karl Doehring, Günter Jaenicke, et al., eds., *Das Staatsnotrecht in Belgien, Frankreich, Großbritannien, Italien, den Niederlanden, der Schweiz und den Vereinigten Staaten von Amerika*, 30–59. Cologne, 1955.

Barbados Observer. "Kill 751 Mau-Mau in 7 Weeks." 19 September 1953.

Barkan, Elazar. *Völker klagen an: Eine neue internationale Moral*. Düsseldorf, 2002.

Barnett, Don, ed. *The Urban Guerrilla: The Story of Mohamed Mathu*. Richmond, B.C., 1974.

Barnett, Donald, and Karari Njama. *Mau Mau from Within: Autobiography and Analysis of Kenya's Peasant Revolt*. London, 1966.

Barnett, Michael. *Empire of Humanity: A History of Humanitarianism*. Ithaca, N.Y., 2011.

Baussant, Michèle. *Les pieds-noirs*. Paris, 2002.

Baxter, Richard R. "Humanitarian Law or Humanitarian Politics? The 1974 Diplomatic Conference on Humanitarian Law." *Harvard International Law Journal* 16, no. 1 (1975): 1–26.

———. "Human Rights in War." *Bulletin of the American Academy of Arts and Sciences* 31, no. 2 (November 1977): 4–13.

Bayly, Christopher, and Tim Harper. *Forgotton Wars: Freedom and Revolution in Southeast Asia*. Cambridge, Mass., 2007.

Beauflis, Thomas. "Le colonialisme aux Indes néerlandaises." In Marc Ferro, ed., *Le livre noir du colonialisme, XVIe–XXIe siècle: De l'extermination à la repentance*, 235–65. Paris, 2003.

Beaufre, André. *Die Revolutionierung des Kriegsbildes: Neue Formen der Gewaltanwendung*. Stuttgart, 1975.

Beaugé, Florence. "Torturée par l'armée française en Algérie, 'Lila' recherche l'homme qui l'a sauvée." *Le Monde*, 20 June 2000.

———. "Général Jacques Massu: 'La torture faisait partie d'une certaine ambiance. On aurait pu faire les choses différemment.'" *Le Monde*, 22 June 2000.

———. "Général Paul Aussaresses: 'Je me suis résolu à la torture. . . . J'ai moi-même procédé à des exécutions sommaires. . . .'" *Le Monde*, 23 November 2000.

Beaumont, Roger. "Small Wars: Definitions and Dimensions." *Annals of the American Academy of Political and Social Science* 541 (September 1995): 20–35.

Beckett, Ian. *Modern Insurgencies and Counter-Insurgencies: Guerrillas and Their Opponents Since 1750*. London, 2001.

———, ed. *The Roots of Counter-Insurgency: Armies and Guerrilla Warfare, 1900–1945*. London, 1988.

Beckett, Ian, and John Pimlott, eds. *Armed Forces and Modern Counter-Insurgency*. New York, 1985.

Bedjaoui, Mohammed. *La révolution algérienne et le droit*. Brussels, 1961.

———. "La révolution algérienne et le droit international humanitaire." *L'Humanitaire Maghreb* 5, no. 5 (June 2003): 24–25.

Belhadj, Abdelkader, Bachir Bonnaza, et al. *La gangrène*. Paris, 1959.

Belkherroubi, Abdelmadjid. *La naissance et la reconnaissance de la République algérienne.* Brussels, 1972.

Ben Ahmed, Mohamed. "Pierre Gaillard: Un humanitaire dans la guerre d'Algérie." *L'Humanitaire Maghreb* 5 (June 2003): 18–21.

Benatia, Farouk. *Les actions humanitaires pendant la lutte de liberation.* Algiers, 1997.

Benenson, Peter. "Introduction." In John Calder, ed., *Gangrene,* 7–39. London, 1959.

Bennett, Huw. "The British Army and Controlling Barbarisation During the Kenya Emergency." In George Kassimeris, ed., *The Warriors's Dishonour: Barbarity, Morality and Torture in Mordern Warfare,* 59–80. Aldershot, 2006.

———. "The Mau Mau Emergency as Part of the British Army's Post-War Counter-Insurgency Experience." *Defense and Security Analysis* 23, no. 2 (June 2007): 143–163.

———. "The Other Side of the COIN: Minimum and Exemplary Force in British Army Counter-insurgency in Kenya." *Small Wars and Insurgencies,* 18, no. 4 (2007): 638–664.

———. "Minimum Force in British Counterinsurgency." *Small Wars and Insurgencies,* 21, no. 3 (2010): 459–475.

———. "Soldiers in the Court Room: The British Army's Part in the Kenya Emergency under the Legal Spotlight." *Journal of Imperial and Commonwealth History* 39, no. 5 (December 2011): 717–30.

Benot, Yves. *Massacres coloniaux, 1944–1950: La IVe République et la mise au pas des colonies françaises.* Paris, 2001.

———. "La décolonisation de l'Afrique française, 1943–1962." In Marc Ferro, ed., *Le livre noir du colonialisme, XVIe–XXIe siècle: De l'extermination à la repentance,* 517–56. Paris, 2003.

Benson, Wilfrid. "International Organization and Non-Self-Governing Territories." *Journal of Negro Education* 15, no. 3 (Summer 1946): 303–9.

Benzinz, Abdelhamid. *Le camp.* Paris, 1962.

Berchadsky, Alexis. *"La question" d'Henri Alleg: Un livre-événement dans la France en guerre d'Algérie.* Paris, 1994.

Berghahn, Volker. *Europa im Zeitalter der Weltkriege: Die Entfesselung und Entgrenzung der Gewalt.* Frankfurt am Main, 2002.

Berman, Bruce. *Control and Crisis in Colonial Kenya: The Dialectic of Domination.* London, 1990.

———. "Bureaucracy and Incumbent Violence: Colonial Administration and the Origins of the Mau Mau Emergency." In Bruce Berman and John Lonsdale, eds., *Unhappy Valley: Conflict in Kenya and Africa,* 227–64. London, 1992.

Bernard, Philippe. "Torture en Algérie: Deux généraux français affrontent leur mémoire." *Le Monde,* 23 November 2000.

Bessis, Juliette. "L'opposition France–États-Unis au Maghreb de la deuxième guerre mondiale jusqu'à l'indépendance des protectorats, 1941–1956." In Charles-Robert Ageron, ed., *Les chemins de la décolonisation de l'empire colonial français,* 341–56. Paris, 1986.

Best, Geoffrey. *Humanity in Warfare: The Modern History of the International Law of Armed Conflicts.* New York, 1980.

———. "Making the Geneva Conventions of 1949: The View from Whitehall." In Christophe Swinarski, ed., *Studies and Essays on International Humanitarian Law and Red Cross Principles in Honour of Jean Pictet,* 5–15. Geneva, 1984.

———. *War and Law Since 1945.* Oxford, 1994.

Betts, Raymond F. *France and Decolonization, 1900–1960.* New York, 1991.

———. *Decolonization.* London, 1998.

Birmingham, David. *The Decolonization of Africa.* London, 1995.

Blacker, John. "The Demography of Mau Mau: Fertility and Mortality in Kenya in the 1950s; a Demographer's Viewpoint." *African Affairs* 106, no. 423 (April 2007): 205–27.

Blet, Henri. *France d'outre mer: L'oeuvre coloniale de la troisième république.* Grenoble, 1950.

Blévis, Laure. "Droit colonial algérien de la citoyenneté: Conciliation illusoire entre des principes républicains et une logique d'occupation coloniale (1865–1947)." In Daniel Lefeuvre, ed., *La guerre d'Algérie au miroir des décolonisations françaises: Actes du colloque en l'honneur de Charles-Robert Ageron, Sorbonne, novembre 2000,* 87–103. Paris, 2000.

Blundell, Michael. *So Rough a Wind: Kenya Memoirs.* London, 1964.

Boiteau, Pierre. "Moramanga, l'Oradour malgache." *La Nouvelle Critique,* January 1954.

Bollardière, Jacques Pâris de. *Bataille d'Alger, bataille de l'homme.* Paris, 1972.

Bonnafous, Robert. *Les prisonniers français dans les camps Viêt-Minh, 1945–1954.* Montpellier, 1985.

Borgwardt, Elizabeth. *A New Deal for the World: America's Vision for Human Rights.* Cambridge, Mass., 2005.

Bourdet, Claude. "Votre Gestapo d'Algérie." *France Observateur,* 13 January 1955.

———. "La France qui donna les droits de l'homme à l'Europe." *France Observateur,* 9 August 1959.

Bourdieu, Pierre, and Abdelmalek Sayad. *Le déracinement: La crise de l'agriculture traditionnelle en Algérie.* Paris, 1964.

Bowcott, Owen. "Mau Mau Torture Claim Kenyans Win Right to Sue British Government." *Guardian,* 21 July 2011.

Branch, Daniel. *Defeating Mau Mau, Creating Kenya: Counterinsurgency, Civil War, and Decolonization.* Cambridge, 2009.

Branche, Raphaëlle. "Entre droit humanitaire et intérêts politiques: Les missions algériennes du CICR." *Revue historique* 301/1, no. 609 (January–March 1999): 101–25.

———. "La Commission de sauvegarde pendant la Guerre d'Algérie: Chronique d'un échec annoncé." *Vingtième Siècle: Revue d'histoire* 61(January–March 1999): 14–29.

———. "La lutte contre le terrorisme urbain." In Jean-Charles Jauffret and Maurice Vaisse, eds., *Militaires et guérilla dans la guerre d'Algérie,* 469–87. Montpellier, 2001.

———. *La torture et l'armée pendant la guerre d'Algérie, 1954–1962.* Paris, 2001.

———. "Des viols pendant la guerre d'Algérie." *Vingtième Siècle: Revue d'histoire* 75 (July–September 2002): 123–32.

———. "Folter und andere Rechtsverletzungen durch die französische Armee während des Algerienkrieges." In Adam Jones, ed., *Völkermord, Kriegsverbrechen und der Westen,* 156–69. Berlin, 2005.

———. *La guerre d'Algérie: Une histoire apaisée?* Paris, 2005.

Brehl, Medarus. "'Ich denke, die haben Ihnen zum Tode verholfen': Koloniale Gewalt in kollektiver Rede." In Mihran Dabag, Horst Gründer, and Uwe-K. Ketelsen, eds., *Kolonialismus: Kolonialdiskurs und Genozid,* 185–215. Munich, 2004.

Brennan, James R. "Radio Cairo and the Decolonization of East Africa, 1953–64." In Christopher Lee, ed., *Making a World After Empire: The Bandung Moment and Its Political Afterlives,* 173–95. Athens, Ohio, 2010.

Bridgman, Jon, and Leslie J. Worley. "Genocide of the Herero." In Samuel Totten, William S. Parsons, and Israel W. Charny, eds., *Century of Genocide: Eyewitness Accounts and Critical Views,* 3–40. New York, 1997.

Brockway, Fenner. *Why Mau Mau? An Analysis and a Remedy.* London, 1953.

———. *African Journeys.* London, 1955.

———. *Towards Tomorrow: The Autobiography of Fenner Brockway.* London, 1977.

Brötel, Dieter. "Dekolonisierung des französischen Empire in Indochina: Metropolitane, periphere und internationale Faktoren." In Wolfgang J. Mommsen, ed., *Das Ende der Ko-lonialreiche: Dekolonisation und die Politik der Großmächte*, 89–118. Frankfurt am Main, 1990.

Brower, Benjamin Claude. *A Desert Named Peace: The Violence of France's Empire in the Algerian Sahara, 1844–1902*. New York, 2009.

Brunn, Gerhard. *Die Europäische Einigung von 1945 bis heute*. Stuttgart, 2002.

Buchanan, Tom. "Human Rights, the Memory of War and the Making of a 'European' Identity, 1945–75." In Martin Conway and Klaus Kiran Patel, eds., *Europeanization in the Twentieth Century*, 157–71. Basingstoke, 2010.

Buck, Pearl S. *American Unity and Asia*. New York, 1942.

Bugeaud, Thomas-Robert. *L'Algérie: Des moyens de conserver et d'utiliser cette conquête*. Paris, 1842.

Bugnion, François. "The Geneva Convention of 12 August 1949: From the 1949 Diplomatic Conference to the Dawn of the New Millennium." *International Affairs* 76, no. 1 (January 2000): 41–45.

———. *The International Committee of the Red Cross and the Protection of War Victims*. Oxford, 2003.

Bührer, Tanja, Christian Stachelbeck, and Dierk Walter, eds. *Imperialkriege von 1500 bis heute: Strukturen, Akteure, Lernprozesse*. Paderborn, 2011.

Buijtenhuijs, Robert. *Le mouvement "Mau Mau": Une révolte paysanne et anti-coloniale en Af-rique noire*. Paris, 1971.

———. *Essays on Mau Mau: Contributions to Mau Mau Historiography*. Leiden, 1982.

Bunting, Madeleine. "Is This Our Hola Camp?" *Guardian*, 15 March 2004.

Burgers, Jan. "The Road to San Francisco: The Revival of the Human Rights Idea in the Twenti-eth Century." *Human Rights Quarterly* 14 (1992): 447–77.

Burke, Roland. *Decolonization and the Evolution of International Human Rights*. Philadelphia, 2010.

Busch, Peter. "Killing the Vietcong: The British Advisory Mission and the Strategic Hamlet Pro-gramme." *Journal of Strategic Studies* 25, no. 1 (March 2002): 135–62.

Bush, Barbara. *Imperialism, Race, and Resistance: Africa and Britain, 1919–1945*. London, 1999.

Cahiers du Témoignage Chrétien. "De la pacification à la répression: Le Dossier Jean Muller," February 1957.

Calder, John, ed. *Gangrene*. London, 1959.

Callwell, Charles. *Small Wars: Their Principles and Practice*. London, 1906.

Campbell, Colm. *Emergency Law in Ireland, 1918–1925*. Oxford, 1994.

Camus, Albert. *Actuelles III: Chronique algérienne, 1939–1958*. Paris, 1958.

Canosa, Raúl Izquierdo. *La reconcentración, 1896–1897*. Havana, 1997.

Carey, Walter. *Crisis in Kenya: Christian Common Sense on Mau Mau and the Colour-Bar*. Lon-don, 1953.

Carruthers, Susan L. *Winning Hearts and Minds: British Governments, the Media and Colonial Counter-Insurgency, 1944–1960*. London, 1995.

Carson, J. B. *The Life-Story of a Kenya Chief: The Life of Chief Kasina Ndoo*. London, 1958.

Casciani, Dominic. "British Mau Mau Abuse Papers Revealed." BBC News, 12 April 2011, http://www.bbc.co.uk/news/uk-13044974.

———. "Mau Mau Kenyans Allowed to Sue UK Government." BBC News, 21 July 2011, http://www.bbc.co.uk/news/uk-14232049.

Cassin, René. *La pensée et l'action*. Paris, 1972.

Castle, Barbara. *Fighting All the Way*. London, 1993.

Cecil, Paul F. *Herbicidal Warfare: The Ranch Hand Project in Vietnam*. New York, 1986.

Césaire, Aimé. *Discourse on Colonialism.* New York, 2000.

Ceylon Daily News. "The Need for Land Is Their Problem, a Kenyan Explains." 7 April 1953.

Charters, David. "From Palestine to Northern Ireland: British Adaptation to Low-Intensity Operations." In David Charters and Maurice Tugwell, eds., *Armies in Low-Intensity Conflict: A Comparative Analysis*, 169–249. London, 1989.

Chassin, Lionel-Martin. "Le rôle idéologique de l'armée." *Revue Militaire d'Information*, 10 October 1954, 10–25.

Chenevix Trench, Charles. *Men Who Ruled Kenya: The Kenya Administration, 1892–1963.* London, 1993.

Chikh, Slimane. *L'Algérie en armes ou le temps des certitudes.* Paris, 1981.

Chowdhury, Roy Subrata. *Rule of Law in a State of Emergency: The Paris Minimum Standards of Human Rights in a State of Emergency.* New York, 1989.

Clark, Roger S. "Nuremberg and Tokyo in Contemporary Perspective." In Timothy L. H. McCormack and Gerry J. Simpson, eds., *The Law of War Crimes: National and International Approaches*, 171–87. The Hague, 1997.

Clayton, Anthony. *Counter-Insurgency in Kenya: A Study of Military Operations Against Mau Mau.* Nairobi, 1976.

———. *France, Soldiers, and Africa.* London, 1988.

———. "Emergency in Morocco, 1950–56." In Robert Holland, ed., *Emergencies and Disorder in the European Empires After 1945*, 129–47. London, 1994.

———. *The Wars of French Decolonization.* London, 1994.

———. *Frontiersmen: Warfare in Africa Since 1950.* London, 1999.

Clayton, Anthony, and Donald C. Savage. *Government and Labour in Kenya, 1895–1963.* London, 1974.

Cleary, A. S. "The Myth of Mau Mau in Its International Context." *African Affairs* 89, no. 335 (April 1990): 227–45.

Clough, Marshall. *Mau Mau Memoirs: History, Memory, and Politics.* Boulder, Colo., 1998.

Clutterbuck, Richard. *The Long, Long War: Counterinsurgency in Malaya and Vietnam.* New York, 1966.

Cmiel, Kenneth. "The Recent History of Human Rights." *American Historical Review* 109, no. 1 (February 2004): 117–35.

———. "Human Rights, Freedom of Information, and the Origins of Third-World Solidarity." In Mark Philip Bradley and Patrice Petro, eds., *Truth Claims: Representation and Human Rights*, 107–30. New Brunswick, N.J., 2002.

Coates, John. *Suppressing Insurgency: An Analysis of the Malayan Emergency, 1948–1952.* Boulder, Colo., 1992.

Cobain, Ian, and Peter Walker. "Secret Memo Gave Guidelines on Abuse of Mau Mau in 1950s." *Guardian*, 11 April 2011.

Cohen, William B. "The Algerian War, the French State and Official Memory." *Historical Reflections* 28, no. 2 (Summer 2002): 219–39.

Cointet, Michèle. *De Gaulle et l'Algérie française, 1958–1962.* Paris, 1995.

Cole, Joshua. "Intimate Acts and Unspeakable Relations: Remembering Torture and the War for Algerian Independence." In Alec G. Hargreaves, ed., *Memory, Empire and Postcolonialism: Legacies of French Colonialism*, 125–41. Lanham, Md., 2005.

Comité Maurice Audin, ed. *Un homme a disparu.* Paris, n.d.

Commission to Study the Organization of Peace. "International Safeguard of Human Rights." Part 3 of *Fourth Report.* New York, 1944.

Committee on Africa, the War, and Peace Aims, ed. *The Atlantic Charter and Africa from an American Standpoint.* New York, 1942.

Conklin, Alice L. "Colonialism and Human Rights: A Contradiction in Terms? The Cases of France and West Africa, 1895–1914." *American Historical Review* 103, no. 2 (April 1998): 419–42.

———. *A Mission to Civilize: The Republican Idea of Empire in France and West Africa, 1895–1930*. Stanford, Calif., 2000.

Connaissance de l'Algérie. "Nouvelle affirmation de la politique française en Algérie: Une interview de M. Guy Mollet." 1 December 1956.

Connelly, Matthew. *A Diplomatic Revolution: Algeria's Fight for Independence and the Origins of the Post-Cold War Era*. Oxford, 2002.

Conrad, Joseph. *Heart of Darkness*. Harmondsworth, Middlesex, 1981.

Constantine, Stephen. *The Making of British Colonial Development Policy, 1914–1940*. London, 1984.

Cook, Stephen. "Whitehall Put in the Dock over Kenyan Hangings." *Guardian*, 1 December 1999.

Cooper, Frederick. "Conflict and Connection: Rethinking Colonial African History." *American Historical Review* 99, no. 5 (December 1994): 1516–45.

———. *Decolonization and African Society: The Labor Question in French and British Africa*. Cambridge, 1996.

———. *From Slaves to Squatters: Plantation Labor and Agriculture in Zanzibar and Coastal Kenya, 1890–1925*. Portsmouth, N.H., 1997.

Cooper, John. *Raphael Lemkin and the Struggle for the Genocide Convention*. Basingstoke, 2008.

Cornaton, Michel. *Les camps de regroupement de la guerre d'Algérie*. Paris, 1998.

Couve de Murville, Maurice. "La France et l'ONU entre 1958 à 1969." In André Lewin, ed., *La France et l'ONU depuis 1945*, 113–16. Condé-sur-Noireau, 1995.

Cranworth, Lord. *A Colony in the Making; or, Sport and Profit in British East Africa*. London, 1912.

Crawshaw, Nancy. *The Cyprus Revolt: An Account of the Struggle for Union with Greece*. London, 1978.

Crilly, Rob. "Mau Mau Veterans to Sue Britain over 'Torture.'" *Times* (London), 6 October 2006.

Crockatt, Richard. *The Fifty Years War: The United States and the Soviet Union in World Politics, 1941–1991*. London, 1995.

Crowder, Michael. "The Second World War: Prelude to Decolonisation in Africa." In Michael Crowder, ed., *The Cambridge History of Africa*, vol. 8, *c. 1940–c. 1975*, 8–51. Cambridge, 1984.

Curtis, Mark. "The Colonial Precedent." *Guardian*, 26 October 2004.

Daase, Christopher. *Kleine Kriege—Große Wirkung: Wie unkonventionelle Kriegsführung die internationale Politik verändert*. Baden-Baden, 1999.

Dabag, Mihran, Horst Gründer, and Uwe-K. Ketelsen, eds. *Kolonialismus: Kolonialdiskurs und Genozid*. Munich, 2004.

Dahm, Bernhard. "Der Dekolonisationsprozeß Indonesiens: Endogene und exogene Faktoren." In Wolfgang J. Mommsen, ed., *Das Ende der Kolonialreiche: Dekolonisation und die Politik der Großmächte*, 67–88. Frankfurt am Main, 1990.

Daily Chronicle. "Communal Punishments Will Stay." 9 October 1953.

Daily Graphic. "Africa Talks: Algeria Is a Most Important Topic—Mboya." 10 December 1958.

Daily Herald. "Hitler's Way Is Not Our Way, Templer." 20 April 1952.

———. "From the Gates of Hell Jail." 8 December 1958.

Daily Mail. "Mau Mau Shoot Africa's Churchill." 8 October 1952.

Daily Mirror. "The Truth About the Secret Police." 9 December 1955.

Daily Telegraph. "Kikuyu Area Overcrowded: Return of Mau Mau Detainees." 21 February 1957.

Daily Worker. "Gestapo Way in Kenya." 18 March 1953.

———. "Kenya Prison Like Hell." 8 December 1958.

Dalloz, Jacques. *The War in Indo-China, 1945–1954.* Dublin, 1990.

Daniel, Jean. *De Gaulle et l'Algérie.* Paris, 1986.

Dard, O., and D. Lefeuvre, eds. *L'Europe face à son passé colonial.* Paris, 2008.

Darwin, John. *Britain and Decolonization: The Retreat from Empire in the Post-War World.* New York, 1988.

———. *The End of Empire: The Historical Debate.* Oxford, 1991.

———. "The Central African Emergency, 1959." In Robert Holland, ed., *Emergencies and Disorder in the European Empires After 1945,* 217–34. London, 1994.

De Gaulle, Charles. *Mémoires de guerre.* Vol. 3, *Le salut, 1944–1946.* Paris, 1959.

De Lattre de Tassigny, Jean. *History of the First French Army.* London, 1952.

———. *Reconquérir: Écrits, 1944–1945.* Paris, 1985.

Del Vecchio, Giorgio. *La déclaration des droits de l'homme et du citoyen dans la Révolution française.* Rome, 1968.

Delmas, Claude. *La guerre révolutionnaire.* Paris, 1972.

Delpard, Raphael. *L'histoire des Pieds-Noirs d'Algérie.* Neuilly-sur-Seine, 2002.

Dennis, Peter. *Troubled Days of Peace: Mountbatten and South East Asia Command, 1945–46.* New York, 1987.

Déroulède, Arnaud. *OAS: Étude d'une organisation clandestine.* Hélette, 1997.

Descombin, Henry. *Guerre d'Algérie, 1959–60: Le Cinquième Bureau, ou "Le théorème du poisson."* Paris, 1994.

Devillers, Philippe. "Indochine, Indonésie: Deux décolonisations manquées." In Charles-Robert Ageron and Marc Michel, eds., *L'ère des décolonisations: Actes du Colloque d'Aix-en-Provence,* 67–83. Paris, 1995.

Dewar, Michael. *Brush Fire Wars: Minor Campaigns of the British Army Since 1945.* London, 1984.

Diner, Dan. *Das Jahrhundert verstehen: Eine universalhistorische Deutung.* Munich, 2000.

Divine, Robert. *Second Chance: The Triumph of Internationalism in America During World War II.* New York, 1967.

Dowden, Richard. "State of Shame." *Guardian,* 5 February 2005.

Dubow, Saul. "Smuts, the United Nations and the Rhetoric of Race and Rights." *Journal of Contemporary History* 43 (2008): 45–74.

Dülffer, Jost. "Chances and Limits of Armament Control, 1898–1914." In Holger Afflerbach and David Stevenson, eds., *An Improbable War: The Outbreak of World War I and the European Politcal Culture Before 1914,* 95–112. New York, 2007.

Dumett, Raymond E. "Africa's Strategic Minerals During the Second World War." *Journal of African History* 26 (1985): 381–408.

Dupuy, Jean-René. "La présence de la France à l'ONU." In André Lewin, ed., *La France et l'ONU depuis 1945,* 53–62. Condé-sur-Noireau, 1995.

Durand, André. *History of the International Committee of the Red Cross: From Sarajevo to Hiroshima.* Geneva, 1984.

Durmelat, Sylvie. "Revisiting Ghosts: Louisette Ighilahriz and the Remembering of Torture." In Alec G. Hargreaves, ed., *Memory, Empire and Postcolonialism: Legacies of French Colonialism,* 142–59. Lanham, Md., 2005.

Dworkin, Anthony. "The Laws of War in the Age of Asymmetric Conflict." In George Kassimeris, ed., *The Barbarization of Warfare,* 220–37. New York, 2006.

East African Standard. "Deaths in Kiambu Village." 17 November 1955.

Easterbrook, David L. "Kenyan Askari in World War II and Their Demobilization with Special Reference to Machakos District." In David L. Easterbrook and Bismark Myrick, eds., *Three Aspects of Crisis in Colonial Kenya*, 27–58. New York, 1975.

Easton, Stewart C. *The Rise and Fall of Western Colonialism*. New York, 1964.

Eberspächer, Cord. "'Albion zal hier ditmaal zijn Moskou vinden!' Der Burenkrieg (1899–1902)." In Thoralf Klein and Frank Schumacher, eds., *Kolonialkriege: Militärische Gewalt im Zeichen des Imperialismus*, 182–207. Hamburg, 2006.

Echenberg, Myron. "Tragedy at Thiaroye: The Senegalese Soldiers' Uprising of 1944." In R. Cohen, J. Copans, and P. Gutkind, eds., *Labor History in Africa*, 109-28. Beverly Hills, Calif., 1978.

——. "Morts pour la France: The African Soldiers in France During the Second World War." *Journal of African History* 26 (1985): 363–80.

Eckel, Jan. "Utopie der Moral, Kalkül der Macht: Menschenrechte in der globalen Politik seit 1945." *Archiv für Sozialgeschichte* 49 (2009): 437–84.

——. "Human Rights and Decolonization: New Perspectives and Open Questions." *Humanity* 1, no. 1 (Fall 2010): 111–35.

Eckert, Andreas. *Kolonialismus*. Frankfurt am Main, 2006.

——. "Predigt der Gewalt? Betrachtung zu Frantz Fanons Klassiker der Dekolonisation." *Zeithistorische Forschungen/Studies in Contemporary History*, online edition 3, no. 1 (2006).

——. "Colonialism in the European Memory." In http://www.eurotopics.net/en/home/presseschau/archiv/magazin/geschichte-verteilerseite-neu/europaeische_nationalges chichten_2008_05/apuz_eckert_kolonialismus/.

——. "African Nationalists and Human Rights, 1940s–1970s." In Stefan-Ludwig Hoffmann, ed., *Human Rights in the Twentieth Century*, 290–94. Cambridge, 2011.

Edgerton, Robert B. *Mau Mau: An African Crucible*. New York, 1989.

Einaudi, Jean-Luc. *La ferme Améziane: Enquête sur un centre de torture pendant la guerre d'Algérie*. Paris, 1991.

——. "Le Papon des ratonnades." *L'Express*, 2 October 1997.

——. *Octobre 1961 un massacre à Paris*. Paris, 2001.

El-Ayouty, Yassin. *The United Nations and Decolonization: The Role of Afro-Asia*. The Hague, 1971.

Electors' Union. *The Kenya Plan*. Nairobi, 1949.

Elkins, Caroline. "Detention, Rehabilitation and the Destruction of Kikuyu Society." In E. S. Atieno Odhiambo and John Lonsdale, eds., *Mau Mau and Nationhood: Arms, Authority and Narration*, 191–226. Oxford, 2003.

——. *Britain's Gulag: The Brutal End of Empire in Kenya*. London, 2005.

——. *Imperial Reckoning: The Untold Story of Britain's Gulag in Kenya*. New York, 2005.

——. "Race, Citizenship, and Governance: Settler Tyranny and the End of Empire." In Caroline Elkins and Susan Pedersen, eds., *Settler Colonialism in the Twentieth Century: Projects, Practices, Legacies*, 203–22. New York, 2005.

——. "Alchemy of Evidence: Mau Mau, the British Empire, and the High Court of Justice." *Journal of Imperial and Commonwealth History* 39, no. 5 (December 2011): 731–48.

Elkins, Caroline, and Susan Pedersen, eds. *Settler Colonialism in the Twentieth Century: Projects, Practices, Legacies*. New York, 2005.

Ellul, Jacques. *FLN Propaganda in France During the Algerian War*. Ottawa, 1982.

Elsenhans, Hartmut. *Frankreichs Algerienkrieg, 1954–1962, Entkolonialisierungsversuch einer kapitalistischen Metropole: Zum Zusammenbruch der Kolonialreiche*. Munich, 1974.

Emerson, Rupert. *Self-Determination Revisited in the Era of Decolonization*. Occasional Papers in International Affairs 9, Harvard University Center for International Affairs, (December 1964): 1-64.

Enslin, Ian. "Health, Violence and Rehabilitation: Conditions in Detention Camps in Kenya, 1952-60." M.A. thesis, Birkbeck College, London, 1996.

Erichsen, Caspar W. "Zwangsarbeit im Konzentrationslager auf der Haifischinsel." In Jürgen Zimmerer and Joachim Zeller, eds., *Völkermord in Deutsch-Südwestafrika: Der Kolonialkrieg (1904–1908) in Namibia und seine Folgen*, 80–85. Berlin, 2003.

Esedebe, Olisanwuche P. *Pan-Africanism: The Idea and the Movement, 1776–1963*. Washington, D.C., 1982.

Evans, Martin. "The Harkis: The Experience and Memory of France's Muslim Auxiliaries." In Martin S. Alexander, Martin Evans, and J. F. V. Keiger, eds., *The Algerian War and the French Army, 1954–62: Experiences, Images, Testimonies*, 117–33. Basingstoke, 2002.

Evans, Peter, "The Martyrdom of Kenya I: Concentration Camps." *Times of India*, 14 July 1953.

———. "The Martyrdom of Kenya II: Trigger-Happy Settlers." *Times of India*, 18 July 1953.

———. "Flogging in Kenya." *Tribune*, 29 October 1954.

———. *Law and Disorder; or, Scenes of Life in Kenya*. London, 1956.

Evans, Tony. *U.S. Hegemony and the Project of Universal Human Rights*. Basingstoke, 1996.

Fairbairn, Geoffrey. *Revolutionary Warfare and Communist Strategy: The Threat to South-East Asia*. London, 1968.

Faivre, Maurice. *Les combattants musulmans de la guerre d'Algérie: Des soldats sacrifiés*. Paris, 1995.

Faligot, Roger. *Britain's Military Strategy in Ireland: The Kitson Experiment*. London, 1983.

Fall, Bernard B. *Dschungelkrieg: Revolutionskämpfe in Südostasien, Indochina, Laos, Vietnam*. Neckargemünd, 1965.

Fanon, Frantz. *Aspekte der Algerischen Revolution*. Frankfurt am Main, 1969.

———. *The Wretched of the Earth*. Harmondsworth, Middlesex, 1970.

Featherstone, Donald. *Colonial Small Wars, 1837–1901*. Devon, 1973.

Ferro, Marc. "La conquête de l'Algérie." In Marc Ferro, ed., *Le livre noir du colonialisme, XVIe–XXIe siècle: De l'extermination à la repentance*, 490–501. Paris, 2003.

———, ed. *Le livre noir du colonialisme, XVIe–XXIe siècle: De l'extermination à la repentance*. Paris, 2003.

Fieldhouse, David. "Decolonization, Development and Dependence: A Survey of Changing Attitudes." In Prosser Gifford and William Roger Louis, eds., *The Transfer of Power in Africa: Decolonization, 1940–1960*, 483–514. New Haven, Conn., 1982.

Fitte, Albert. *Spectroscopie d'une propagande révolutionnaire: "El Moudjahid" des temps de guerre, juin 1956–mars 1962*. Montpellier, 1973.

Fitzpatrick, Joan. *Human Rights in Crisis: The International System for Protecting Rights During States of Emergency*. Philadelphia, 1994.

Fletcher, Eileen. *Truth About Kenya: An Eye Witness Account*. London, 1956.

Folz, Hans-Ernst. *Staatsnotstand und Notstandsrecht*. Cologne, 1962.

Foner, Philip S. *The Spanish-Cuban-American War and the Birth of American Imperialism, 1895–1902*. Vol. 1. New York, 1972.

Foran, Robert W. *The Kenya Police, 1887–1960*. London, 1962.

Forsythe, David P. "Human Rights and the International Committee of the Red Cross." *Human Rights Quarterly* 12, no. 2 (May 1990): 265–89.

Fraleigh, Arnold. "The Algerian Revolution as a Case Study in International Law." In Richard A. Falk, ed., *The International Law of Civil War*, 179–243. Baltimore, 1971.

France Observateur. "Les camps de concentration Algériens." 16 June 1955.

———. "Algérie: Un million de personnes déplacées." 16 April 1959.

Frémeaux, Jacques. "Guerre d'Algérie et conquête de l'Algérie." In Daniel Lefeuvre, ed., *La guerre d'Algérie au miroir des décolonisations françaises: Actes du colloque en l'honneur de Charles-Robert Ageron, Sorbonne, novembre 2000*, 195–214. Paris, 2000.

———. *La France et l'Algérie en guerre, 1830–1870, 1954–1962*. Paris, 2002.

———. "The Sahara and the Algerian War." In Martin S. Alexander, Martin Evans, and J. F. V. Keiger, eds., *The Algerian War and the French Army, 1954–62: Experiences, Images, Testimonies*, 76–87. Basingstoke, 2002.

French, David. *The British Way in Counter-Insurgency, 1945–1967*. Oxford, 2012.

Frey, Marc. "Das Ende eines Kolonialreiches: Dien Bien Phu, 13. März bis 7. Mai 1954." In Stig Förster, ed., *Schlachten der Weltgeschichte: Von Salamis bis Sinai*, 358–73. Munich, 2001.

———. "Drei Wege zur Unabhängigkeit: Die Dekolonisierung in Indochina, Indonesien und Malaya nach 1945." *Vierteljahrshefte für Zeitgeschichte* 50, no. 3 (2002): 399–433.

———. *Dekolonisierung in Südostasien: Die Vereinigten Staaten und die Auflösung der europäischen Kolonialreiche*. Munich, 2006.

Friedberg, Daniel. "The Mau Mau Terror." *New Republic*, 19 October 1953.

Front de Libération Nationale, ed. *Kolonialistische Unterdrückung und Kriegsverbrechen: Der Premier Nehru sagte "In Algerien sind die Dinge schlimmer als in Ungarn."* N.p., 1957.

Frost, Richard. *Race Against Time: Human Relations and Politics in Kenya Before Independence*. London, 1978.

Füredi, Frank. "The African Crowd in Nairobi: Popular Movements and Elite Politics." *Journal of African History* 14 (1973): 275–90.

———. "Britain's Colonial Emergencies and the Invisible Nationalists." *Journal of Historical Sociology* 2, no. 3 (1989): 240–64.

———. *The Mau Mau War in Perspective*. London, 1989.

———. "Kenya: Decolonization Through Counterinsurgency." In Anthony Gorst, Lewis Johnman, and W. Scott Lucas, eds., *Contemporary British History, 1931–1961: Politics and Limits of Policy*, 141–68. London, 1991.

———. *Colonial Wars and the Politics of Third World Nationalism*. London, 1994.

———. "Creating a Breathing Space: The Political Management of Colonial Emergencies." In Robert Holland, ed., *Emergencies and Disorder in the European Empires After 1945*, 89–106. London, 1994.

———. *The New Ideology of Imperialism: Renewing the Moral Imperative*. London, 1994.

———. *The Silent War: Imperialism and the Changing Perception of Race*. New Brunswick, N.J., 1998.

———. "The Demobilized African Soldier and the Blow to White Prestige." In David Killingray and David Omissi, eds., *Guardians of Empire: The Armed Forces of the Colonial Powers, 1700–1964*, 179–97. Manchester, 1999.

Gadant, Monique. *Islam et nationalisme en Algérie d'après "El Moudjahid" organe central du FLN de 1956 à 1962*. Paris, 1988.

Gallagher, John. *The Decline, Revival and Fall of the British Empire*. Cambridge, 1982.

Gallois, William. "Dahra and the History of Violence in Early Colonial Algeria." In Martin Thomas, ed., *The French Colonial Mind. Volume Two, Violence, Military Encounters, and Colonialism*, 3–25. Lincoln, Neb., 2011.

Gartz, Jochen. *Chemische Kampfstoffe: Der Tod kam aus Deutschland*. Löhrbach, 2003.

Gary, Joyce. *The Case for African Freedom and Other Writings*. London, 1944.

Gavaghan, Terence. *Of Lions and Dung Beetles*. Ilfracombe, UK, 1999.

Geiss, Imanuel. *Panafrikanismus: Zur Geschichte der Dekolonisation*. Frankfurt am Main, 1968.

Gerlach, Christian. "Sustainable Violence: Mass Resettlement, Strategic Villages, and Militias in

Anti-Guerrilla Warfare." In Richard Bessel and Claudia B. Haake, eds., *Removing Peoples: Forced Removal in the Modern World*, 361–93. Oxford, 2009.

Gerth, Karl-Heinz. *Der Staatsnotstand im französischen Recht*. Mainz, 1968.

Gewald, Jan-Bart. "Das deutsche Kaiserreich und die Herero des südlichen Afrikas: Der Völkermord und die Entschädigungsfrage." In Adam Jones, ed., *Völkermord, Kriegsverbrechen und der Westen*, 69–90. Berlin, 2005.

Giap, Vo Nguyen. *People's War, People's Army*. New York, 1962.

Gietz, Axel. *Die neue Alte Welt: Roosevelt, Churchill und die europäische Nachkriegsordnung*. Munich, 1986.

Gifford, Prosser, and William Rogers Louis, eds. *The Transfer of Power in Africa: Decolonization, 1940–1960*. New Haven, Conn., 1982.

Gikoyo, Gucu G. *We Fought for Freedom*. Nairobi, 1979.

Girardet, Raoul. *La crise militaire française, 1945–1962: Aspects sociologiques et idéologiques*. Paris, 1964.

——. *L'idée coloniale en France*. Paris, 1972.

Girault, Arthur. *Principes de colonisation et de législation coloniale*. Vol. 1. Paris, 1921.

Glendon, Mary Ann. *A World Made New: Eleanor Roosevelt and the Universal Declaration of Human Rights*. New York, 2001.

——. "The Forgotten Crucible: The Latin American Influence on the Universal Human Rights Idea." *Harvard Human Rights Journal* 16 (2003): 27–39.

Go, Julian. "Modeling States and Sovereignty: Postcolonial Constitutions in Asia and Africa." In Christopher Lee, ed., *Making a World After Empire: The Bandung Moment and Its Political Afterlives*, 107–39. Athens, Ohio, 2010.

Goldsworthy, David. *Colonial Issues in British Politics, 1945–1961*. Oxford, 1971.

——. *Tom Mboya: The Man Kenya Wanted to Forget*. Nairobi, 1982.

Gordon, David F. *Decolonization and the State of Kenya*. Boulder, Colo., 1986.

Gorman, Robert F. *Great Debates at the United Nations: An Encyclopedia of Fifty Key Issues, 1945–2000*. Westport, Conn., 2001.

Goudail, Agnès. "Les sources françaises de la guerre d'Algérie." In Daniel Lefeuvre, ed., *La guerre d'Algérie au miroir des décolonisations françaises: Actes du colloque en l'honneur de Charles-Robert Ageron, Sorbonne, novembre 2000*, 19–40. Paris, 2000.

Gough, David. "Mau Mau Will Sue Britain for Human Rights Abuses." *Guardian*, 29 April 1999.

Gourevitch, Philip. "Winning and Losing." *New Yorker*, 22 December 2003.

Greenspan, Morris. "International Law and Its Protection for Participants in Unconventional Warfare." *Annals of the American Academy of Political and Social Science* 341 (May 1962): 30–41.

Grimal, Henri. *Decolonization: The British, French, Dutch, and Belgian Empires, 1919–1963*. London, 1978.

Groen, Petra M. H. "Militant Response: The Dutch Use of Military Force and the Decolonization of the Dutch East Indies." In Robert Holland, ed., *Emergencies and Disorder in the European Empires After 1945*, 30–44. London, 1994.

Grosser, Alfred. *Ermordung der Menschheit: Der Genozid im Gedächtnis der Völker*. Munich, 1990.

Grundlingh, Louis. "The Recruitment of South African Blacks for Participation in the Second World War." In David Killingray and Richard Rathbone, eds., *Africa and the Second World War*, 181–203. New York, 1986.

Guelton, Frédéric. "The French Army 'Centre for Training and Preparation in Counter-Guerrilla Warfare' (CIPCG) at Arzew." In Martin Alexander and J. F. V. Keiger, eds., "France and the Algerian War, 1954–62: Strategy, Operations and Diplomacy," special issue of *Journal of Strategic Studies* 25, no. 2 (June 2002): 35–53.

Gupta, Partha Sarathi. *Imperialism and the British Labour Movement, 1914–1964*. London, 1975.

Gwynn, Charles. *Imperial Policing*. London, 1934.

Haffner, Sebastian. "Der neue Krieg." In Mao Zedong, *Theorie des Guerillakrieges, oder Strategie der Dritten Welt*, 5–34. Reinbek, 1966.

Hamoumou, Mohand. "L'histoire des harkis et français musulmans: La fin d'un tabou?" In Mohammed Harbi and Benjamin Stora, eds., *La guerre d'Algérie, 1954–2004: La fin de l'amnésie*, 317–44. Paris, 2004.

Hanrahan, Gene Z. *The Communist Struggle in Malaya*. Kuala Lumpur, 1971.

Hanstein, Rudolf von. *Der Einfluß der Vereinten Nationen auf die Sonderorganisationen—Anspruch und Wirklichkeit: Eine Untersuchung am Beispiel der Auseinandersetzungen im Hinblick auf die Dekolonisierung*. Frankfurt am Main, 1988.

Harbi, Mohammed. "Bauern und Revolution." In Bassam Tibi, ed., *Die arabische Linke*, 123–37. Frankfurt am Main, 1969.

———. *Aux origines du FLN: La scission du PPA–MTLD*. Paris, 1975.

———. *La guerre commence en Algérie*. Brussels, 1984.

———. "L'Algérie en perspectives." In Mohammed Harbi and Benjamin Stora, eds., *La guerre d'Algérie, 1954–2004: La fin de l'amnésie*, 27–45. Paris, 2004.

Harbi, Mohammed, and Benjamin Stora, eds. *La guerre d'Algérie, 1954–2004: La fin de l'amnésie*. Paris, 2004.

Hargreaves, John D. *Decolonization in Africa*. London, 1994.

Harris, Robert, and Jeremy Paxman. *A Higher Form of Killing: The Secret History of Chemical and Biological Warfare*. London, 2002.

Hashem, Zaki. *The United Nations*. Cairo, 1951.

Headrick, Rita. *African Soldiers in World War II*. Chicago, 1976.

Heather, Randall W. "Intelligence and Counter-Intelligence in Kenya During the Mau Mau Emergency." Ph.D. diss., University of Cambridge, 1994.

Heggoy, Alf Andrew. *Insurgency and Counterinsurgency in Algeria*. Bloomington, Ind., 1972.

Heideking, Jürgen. "Amerikanische Geheimdienste und Widerstandsbewegungen im Zweiten Weltkrieg." In Gerhard Schulz, ed., *Partisanen und Volkskrieg: Zur Revolutionierung des Krieges im 20. Jahrhundert*, 147–77. Göttingen, 1985.

Heinlein, Frank. *British Government Policy and Decolonisation, 1945–1963: Scrutinising the Official Mind*. London, 2002.

Hénard, Jacqueline. "Erinnerung ohne Reue: Massenmord und Folter—die späte Debatte über die Verbrechen im Algerienkrieg spaltet Frankreich." *Die Zeit*, 14 December 2000.

Henderson, Ian. *The Hunt for Kimathi*. London, 1958.

Henry, Charles P. *Ralph Bunche, Model Negro or American Other?* New York, 1999.

Hessel, Stéphane. "Un rôle essentiel dans la promotion et la protection des droits de l'homme." In André Lewin, ed., *La France et l'ONU depuis 1945*, 253–68. Condé-sur-Noireau, 1995.

Hewitt, Peter. *Kenya Cowboy: A Police Officer's Account of the Mau Mau Emergency*. London, 1999.

Heymann, Arlette. *Les libertés publiques et la guerre d'Algérie*. Paris, 1972.

Hilderbrand, Robert C. *Dumbarton Oaks: The Origins of the United Nations and the Search for Postwar Security*. Chapel Hill, N.C., 1990.

Hinden, R. "A Colonial Charter." *New Statesman and Nation*, 21 November 1942.

Hindlip, Lord. *British East Africa*. London, 1905.

Hirschfeld, Gerhard. "Kriegsverbrechen in der niederländischen Kolonialzeit: Indonesien 1945–1949." In Wolfram Wette and Gerd R. Ueberschär, eds., *Kriegsverbrechen im 20. Jahrhundert*, 447–60. Darmstadt, 2001.

Hobhouse, Emily. *Die Zustände in den südafrikanischen Konzentrationslagern*. Berlin, 1901.

————. *The Brunt of War and Where It Fell*. London, 1902.

Hobsbawm, Eric. *The Age of Extremes: A History of the World, 1914–1991*. New York, 1996.

Hochschild, Adam. *King Leopold's Ghost: A Story of Greed, Terror, and Heroism in Colonial Africa*. Boston, 1998.

Hoffman, Bruce. *Terrorismus, der unerklärte Krieg: Neue Gefahren politischer Gewalt*. Frankfurt am Main, 2001.

Hoffmann, Stefan-Ludwig. "Introduction: Genealogies of Human Rights." In Stefan-Ludwig Hoffmann, ed., *Human Rights in the Twentieth Century*, 1–26. Cambridge, 2011.

————, ed. *Human Rights in the Twentieth Century*. Cambridge, 2011.

Hogard, Jacques. "Guerre révolutionnaire et pacification." *Revue Militaire d'Information*, January 1957, 11–13.

————. "L'armée française devant la guerre révolutionnaire." *Revue de Défense Nationale*, February 1957, 77–89.

————. "Le soldat dans la guerre révolutionnaire." *Revue de Défense Nationale*, February 1957, 211–26.

————. "Stratégie et tactique dans la guerre révolutionnaire." *Revue Militaire d'Information*, June 1958, 20–35.

————. "Cette guerre de notre temps." *Revue de Défense Nationale*, August–September 1958, 1304–19.

Holborn, Louise W., ed. *War and Peace Aims of the United Nations*. 2 vols. Boston, 1943–1948.

Holbrook, Wendell P. "Oral History and the Nascent Historiography for West Africa and World War II: A Focus on Ghana." *International Journal of Oral History* 3 (1982): 149–66.

————. "British Propaganda and the Mobilization of the Gold Coast War Effort, 1939–1945." *Journal of African History* 26 (1985): 347–61.

Holcombe, A. N. *Dependent Areas in the Post-War World*. N.p., 1942.

Holland, Robert. *European Decolonization, 1918–1981: An Introductory Survey*. Basingstoke, 1985.

————. "Never, Never Land: British Colonial Policy and the Roots of Violence in Cyprus, 1950–54." In Robert Holland, ed., *Emergencies and Disorder in the European Empires After 1945*, 148–76. London, 1994.

————. "Dirty Wars: Algeria and Cyprus Compared, 1954–1962." In Charles-Robert Ageron and Marc Michel, eds., *L'ère des décolonisations: Actes du Colloque d'Aix-en-Provence*, 37–46. Paris, 1995.

————. *Britain and the Revolt in Cyprus*. Oxford, 1998.

————, ed. *Emergencies and Disorder in the European Empires After 1945*. London, 1994.

Holmes, Hugh. *One Man in His Time*. Worcester, n.d.

Hoopes, Townsend, and Douglas Brinkley. *FDR and the Creation of the U.N.* New Haven, Conn., 1997.

Horne, Alistair. *A Savage War of Peace: Algeria, 1954–1962*. New York, 1987.

Hosmer, Stephen T., and Sibylle O. Crane. *Counterinsurgency: A Symposium, April 16–20, 1962*. Santa Monica, Calif., 1962.

House, Jim, and Neil MacMaster. *Paris 1961: Algerians, State Terror, and Memory*. Oxford, 2006.

Howe, Stephen. *Anticolonialism in British Politics: The Left and the End of Empire, 1918–1964*. Oxford, 1993.

————. "Colonising and Exterminating? Memories of Imperial Violence in Britain and France," *Histoire @ Politique: Politique, culture, société* 11 (May–August 2010). http://www.histoire-politique.fr/documents/11/pistes/pdf/HP11_Howe_pdf_260510.pdf.

————. "Flakking the Mau Mau Catchers." *Journal of Imperial and Commonwealth History* 39, no. 5 (December 2011): 695–97.

Humphrey, John P. *Human Rights and the United Nations: A Great Adventure*. New York, 1984.

———. *No Distant Millennium: The International Law of Human Rights*. Paris, 1989.

Hunt, Lynn. *Inventing Human Rights: A History*. London, 2008.

Hunter, Stephen. "The Pentagon's Lessons from Reel Life: 'Battle of Algiers' Resonates in Baghdad." *Washington Post*, 4 September 2003.

Hussain, Nasser. *The Jurisprudence of Emergency: Colonialism and the Rule of Law*. Ann Arbor, Mich., 2006.

Hutchinson, Martha Crenshaw. *Revolutionary Terrorism: The FLN in Algeria, 1954–1962*. Stanford, Calif., 1978.

Huxley, Elspeth. *White Man's Country: Lord Delamere and the Making of Kenya*. London, 1935.

———. "Kenya's Pipeline to Freedom." *Daily Telegraph*, 7 December 1956.

Huxley, Julian S. "Colonies in a Changing World." *Political Quarterly* (October–December 1942): 384–99.

Ibhawoh, Bonny. *Imperialism and Human Rights: Colonial Discourse of Rights and Liberties in African History*. Albany, N.Y., 2007.

Ignatieff, Michael. "Human Rights as Politics." In Amy Gutmann, ed., *Human Rights as Politics and Idolatry*, 3–52. Princeton, N.J., 2001.

International Committee of the Red Cross, ed. *The Geneva Conventions of August 12, 1949*. Geneva, n.d.

Iriye, Akira. *Global Community: The Role of International Organizations in the Making of the Contemporary World*. Berkeley, Calif., 2004.

Itote, Warihiu. *Mau Mau General*. Nairobi, 1967.

———. *Mau Mau in Action*. Nairobi, 1985.

Jackson, Kennell, Jr. "'Impossible to Ignore Their Greatness': Survival Craft in the Mau Mau Forest Movement." In E. S. Atieno Odhiambo and John Lonsdale, eds., *Mau Mau and Nationhood: Arms, Authority and Narration*, 176–90. Oxford, 2003.

Jaenicke, Günther. "Das Staatsnotrecht in Großbritannien." In Hans Ballreich, Karl Doehring, Günther Jaenicke, et al., eds., *Das Staatsnotrecht in Belgien, Frankreich, Großbritannien, Italien, den Niederlanden, der Schweiz und den Vereinigten Staaten von Amerika*, 60–106. Cologne, 1955.

James, Lawrence. *Imperial Rearguard: Wars of Empire, 1919–85*. London, 1988.

Jauffret, Jean-Charles. "The Origins of the Algerian War: The Reaction of France and Its Army to the Two Emergencies of 8 May 1945 and 1 November 1954." In Robert Holland, ed., *Emergencies and Disorder in the European Empires After 1945*, 17–29. London, 1994.

———. "The War Culture of French Combatants in the Algerian Conflict." In Martin S. Alexander, Martin Evans, and J. F. V. Keiger, eds., *The Algerian War and the French Army, 1954–62: Experiences, Images, Testimonies*, 101–16. Basingstoke, 2002.

———. "Le mouvement des rappelés en 1955–1956." In Mohammed Harbi and Benjamin Stora, eds., *La guerre d'Algérie, 1954–2004: La fin de l'amnésie*, 133–60. Paris, 2004.

Jauffret, Jean-Charles, and Maurice Vaisse, eds. *Militaires et guérilla dans la guerre d'Algérie*. Montpellier, 2001.

Johannès, Franck. "Le général Aussaresses a été condamné à 7500 euros d'amende pour 'apologie de crimes de guerre.'" *Le Monde*, 27 January 2002.

Johnsen, Julia E., ed. *The "Eight Points" of Post-War World Reorganization*. New York, 1942.

Johnson, Glenn M., and Janusz Symonides. *The Universal Declaration of Human Rights: A History of Its Creation and Implementation, 1948–1998*. Paris, 1998.

Johnson, Edward. "Britain and the Cyprus Problem at the United Nations, 1954–1958." In Kent Fedorowich and Martin Thomas, eds. *International Diplomacy and Colonial Retreat*, 113–130. London, 2001.

Jones, Adam, ed. *Völkermord, Kriegsverbrechen und der Westen*. Berlin, 2005.

Jones, Timothy Llewellyn. *The Development of British Counterinsurgency Policies and Doctrine, 1945–52*. London, 1991.

Julien, Charles-André. *Et la Tunisie devint indépendante (1951–1957)*. Paris, 1985.

Jureidini, Paul A. *Case Studies in Insurgency and Revolutionary Warfare: Algeria, 1954–1962*. Washington, D.C., 1963.

Kaggia, Bildad. *Roots of Freedom, 1921–1963: The Autobiography of Bildad Kaggia*. Nairobi, 1975.

Kahin, George McTurnan. *The Asian-African Conference: Bandung, Indonesia, April 1955*. Ithaca, N.Y., 1955.

Kahler, Miles. *Decolonization in Britain and France: The Domestic Consequences of International Relations*. Princeton, N.J., 1984.

Kahn, Paul W. *Sacred Violence: Torture, Terror, and Sovereignty*. Ann Arbor, Mich., 2011.

Kaminski, Andrzej J. *Konzentrationslager 1896 bis heute: Eine Analyse*. Stuttgart, 1982.

Kanogo, Tabitha. *Squatters and the Roots of Mau Mau, 1905–63*. London, 1987.

Kariuki, Josiah Mwangi. *Mau Mau Detainee: The Account by a Kenyan African of His Experience in Detention Camps, 1953–1960*. Nairobi, 1975.

Kauffer, Rémi. *OAS: Histoire d'une guerre franco-française*. Paris, 2002.

Kaufmann, Michael T. "What Does Pentagon See in the 'Battle of Algiers'?" *New York Times*, 7 September 2003.

Keen, Sam. *Gesichter des Bösen: Über die Entstehung unserer Feindbilder*. Munich, 1986.

Keller, Gustav. *Die Psychologie der Folter*. Frankfurt am Main, 1981.

Kelly, George Armstrong. *Lost Soldiers: The French Army and Empire in Crisis, 1947–1962*. Cambridge, Mass., 1965.

Kelly, Joseph Burns. "Gas Warfare in International Law." *Military Law Review*, July 1960, 1–67.

Kenber, Billy. "Colonial Files: Mau Mau Camps Saw 'Unspeakable Acts.'" *Times* (London), 7 April 2011.

Kennedy, Dane. *Islands of White: Settler Society and Culture in Kenya and Southern Rhodesia, 1890–1939*. Durham, N.C., 1987.

———. "Constructing the Colonial Myth of Mau Mau." *International Journal of African Historical Studies* 25, no. 2 (1990): 241–60.

Kennedy, Paul. *The Parliament of Man: The Past, Present, and Future of the United Nations*. New York, 2007.

Kenyatta, Jomo. *Facing Mount Kenya: The Tribal Life of the Gikuyu*. London, 1938.

———. *Kenya: Land of Conflict*. International African Service Bureau 3. Manchester, 1945.

Keramane, Hafid. *La pacification: Livre noir de six années de guerre en Algérie*. Lausanne, 1960.

Kershaw, Greet. *Mau Mau from Below*. Oxford, 1997.

Kersten, Albert E. "International Intervention in the Decolonization of Indonesia, 1945–1962." In Charles-Robert Ageron and Marc Michel, eds., *L'ère des décolonisations: Actes du Colloque d'Aix-en-Provence*, 269–80. Paris, 1995.

Khenouf, Mohamed, and Michael Brett. "Algerian Nationalism and the Allied Military Strategy and Propaganda During the Second World War: The Background to Sétif." In David Killingray and Richard Rathbone, eds., *Africa and the Second World War*, 258–74. New York, 1986.

Kiernan, V. G. *From Conquest to Collapse: European Empires from 1815 to 1960*. New York, 1982.

Killingray, David. "Soldiers, Ex-Servicemen, and Politics in the Gold Coast, 1939–50." *Journal of Modern African Studies* 21 (1983): 523–34.

———. "Labour Mobilisation in British Colonial Africa for the War Effort, 1939–46." In David Killingray and Richard Rathbone, eds., *Africa and the Second World War*, 68–96. New York, 1986.

Killingray, David, and Richard Rathbone, eds. *Africa and the Second World War*. New York, 1986.

Kimball, Warren F. "The Atlantic Charter: 'With All Deliberate Speed.'" In Douglas Brinkley and David R. Facey-Crowther, eds., *The Atlantic Charter*, 83–114. New York, 1994.

Kinyatti, Maina wa, ed. *Kenya's Freedom Struggle: The Dedan Kimathi Papers*. London, 1987.

Kipling, Rudyard. *Rudyard Kipling's Verse: Definitive Edition*. London, 1949.

Kitson, Frank. *Gangs and Counter-Gangs*. London, 1960.

———. *Im Vorfeld des Krieges: Abwehr von Subversion und Aufruhr*. Stuttgart, 1974.

Kitz, Heinz-Eberhard. *Die Notstandsklausel des Artikel 15 der Europäischen Menschenrechtskonvention*. Berlin, 1982.

Klein, Thoralf, and Frank Schumacher, eds. *Kolonialkriege: Militärische Gewalt im Zeichen des Imperialismus*. Hamburg, 2006.

Klose, Fabian. " 'Source of Embarrassment'. Human Rights, State of Emergency, and the Wars of Decolonization." In Stefan-Ludwig Hoffmann, ed., *Human Rights in the Twentieth Century*, 237–57. Cambridge, 2011.

———. "The Colonial Testing Ground: The International Committee of the Red Cross and the Violent End of Empire." *Humanity* 2, no. 1 (Spring 2011): 107–126.

Knigge, Volkhard, and Norbert Frei, eds. *Verbrechen erinnern: Die Auseinandersetzung mit Holocaust und Völkermord*. Bonn, 2005.

Knipping, Franz. "Militärische Konzeptionen der französischen Résistance im Zweiten Weltkrieg." In Gerhard Schulz, ed., *Partisanen und Volkskrieg: Zur Revolutionierung des Krieges im 20. Jahrhundert*, 125–46. Göttingen, 1985.

Koerner, Francis. "Le mouvement nationaliste algérien (novembre 1942–mai 1945)." *Revue d'Histoire de la Deuxième Guerre Mondiale* 93 (1974): 45–64.

———. *Madagascar: Colonisation française et nationalisme malgache*. Paris, 1994.

Köppen, Manuel. "Im Krieg mit dem Fremden: Barbarentum und Kulturkampf." In Alexander Honold and Oliver Simons, eds., *Kolonialismus als Kultur: Literatur, Medien, Wissenschaft in der deutschen Gründerzeit des Fremden*, 263–87. Tübingen, 2002.

Korey, William. *NGOs and the Universal Declaration of Human Rights: "A Curious Grapevine."* New York, 1998.

Kotek, Joel, and Pierre Rigoulot. *Das Jahrhundert der Lager: Gefangenschaft, Zwangsarbeit, Vernichtung*. Berlin, 2001.

Kraemer, Joseph S. "Revolutionary Guerrilla Warfare and the Decolonization Movement." *Polity* 4, no. 2 (1971): 137–58.

Kunz, Rudibert, and Rolf-Dieter Müller. *Giftgas gegen Abd el Krim: Deutschland, Spanien und der Gaskrieg in Spanisch-Marokko, 1922–1927*. Freiburg, 1990.

Lacheraf, Mostapha. "Le patriotisme rural en Algérie." *Esprit* 23 (January–June 1955): 376–91.

———. *Algérie: Nation et sociéte*. Paris, 1965.

Lacheroy, Charles. "Scenario-type de guerre révolutionnaire." *Revue des Forces Terrestres*, October 1956, 25–29.

La conférence africaine française, Brazzaville, 30 janvier 1944–8 février 1944. Algiers, 1944.

La Croix. "Un million d'hommes, de femmes et d'enfants sont menacés de famine estime un rapport officiel." 20 April 1959.

"La ferme Améziane, centre de torture à Constantine." *Vérité-Liberté* 9 (May 1961).

Lagrot, F., and J. Greco. "Les mutilations faciales au cours du terrorisme en Algérie et leur reparation." *La Presse Médicale*, 27 June 1956, 1193–98.

"La guerre révolutionnaire." Special issue, *Revue Militaire d'Information*, February–March 1957.

Lapping, Brian. *End of Empire*. London, 1985.

Laqueur, Walter. *Guerrilla Warfare: A Historical and Critical Study*. New Brunswick, N.J., 1998.

Lauren, Paul Gordon. *Power and Prejudice: The Politics and Diplomacy of Racial Discrimination*. Boulder, Colo., 1996.

——. *The Evolution of International Human Rights: Visions Seen.* Philadelphia, 1998.
Lauterpacht, Hersch. *International Law and Human Rights.* New York, 1968.
Lazreg, Marnia. *Torture and the Twilight of Empire: From Algiers to Baghdad.* Princeton, N.J., 2008.
Leakey, L. S. B. *Defeating Mau Mau.* London, 1977.
Le Cour Grandmaison, Olivier. *Coloniser, exterminer: Sur la guerre et l'État colonial.* Paris, 2005.
——. *De l'indigénat: Anatomie d'un "monstre" juridique; le droit coloniale en Algérie et dans l'Empire français.* Paris, 2010.
——, ed. *Le 17 octobre 1961: Un crime d'État à Paris.* Paris, 2001.
Lee, Christopher, ed. *Making a World After Empire: The Bandung Moment and Its Political Afterlives.* Athens, Ohio, 2010.
Lee, J. M. "Forward Thinking and the War: The Colonial Office During the 1940s." *Journal of Imperial and Commonwealth History* 6, no. 1 (1977): 64–79.
Lefebvre, Denis. *Guy Mollet face à la torture en Algérie, 1956–57.* Paris, 2001.
Lefeuvre, Daniel. "Le coût de la guerre d'Algérie." In Daniel Lefeuvre, ed., *La guerre d'Algérie au miroir des décolonisations françaises: Actes du colloque en l'honneur de Charles-Robert Ageron, Sorbonne, novembre 2000,* 501–14. Paris, 2000.
——. "Les pieds-noirs." In Mohammed Harbi and Benjamin Stora, eds., *La guerre d'Algérie, 1954–2004: La fin de l'amnésie,* 267–86. Paris, 2004.
Leigh, Ione. *In the Shadow of the Mau Mau.* London, 1954.
Lemalet, Martine. *Lettres d'Algérie, 1954–1962: La guerre des appelés, la mémoire d'une génération.* Paris, 1992.
Lemesle, Raymond-Martin. *La conférence de Brazzaville de 1944, contexte et repères: Cinquantenaire des prémices de la décolonisation.* Paris, 1994.
Lemkin, Raphael. *Axis Rule in Occupied Europe: Laws of Occupation, Analysis of Government, Proposals for Redress.* Washington, D.C., 1944.
"Les mutilations criminelles en Algérie." Special issue, *Algérie Médicale* 61 (1957).
Le Tourneau, Roger. *Évolution politique de l'Afrique du Nord musulmane, 1920–1961.* Paris, 1962.
Leulliette, Pierre. *St. Michael and the Dragon: A Paratrooper in the Algerian War.* London, 1964.
Lewin, André, ed. *La France et l'ONU depuis 1945.* Condé-sur-Noireau, 1995.
Lewis, Joanna. *Empire State-Building: War and Welfare in Kenya, 1925–52.* Oxford, 2000.
——. "Daddy Wouldn't Buy Me a Mau Mau: The British Popular Press and the Demoralization of Empire." In E. S. Atieno Odhiambo and John Lonsdale, eds., *Mau Mau and Nationhood: Arms, Authority and Narration,* 227–50. Oxford, 2003.
L'Humanité. "Un million d'Algériens derrière les barbelés." 17 April 1959.
——. "Un million d'Algériens menacés de famine." 18 April 1959.
——. "Bordeaux 1942–Paris 1961: Massacres à répétition." 6 February 1999.
Liauzu, Claude. "Une loi contre l'histoire." *Le Monde diplomatique,* April 2005.
——, ed. *Violence et colonisation: Pour en finir avec les guerres de mémoires.* Paris, 2003.
Liauzu, Claude, and Josette Liauzu. "Violence coloniale et guerre d'Algérie." In Claude Liauzu, ed., *Violence et colonisation: Pour en finir avec les guerres de mémoires,* 119–48. Paris, 2003.
Liauzu, Claude, and Gilles Manceron, eds. *La colonisation, la loi et l'histoire.* Paris, 2006.
Libération. "Dans les camps d'Algérie les milliers d'enfants meurent." 21 April 1959.
Likimani, Muthoni. *Passbook Number F 47927: Women and Mau Mau in Kenya.* Basingstoke, 1985.
Lippmann, Walter. "The Post-Singapore War in the East." *Washington Post,* 21 February 1942.
Logan, Rayford W. "Dumbarton Oaks Proposals Ignore Colonial Problem." *Chicago Defender,* 9 December 1944.
Lonsdale, John. "The Depression and the Second World War in the Transformation of Kenya."

In David Killingray and Richard Rathbone, eds., *Africa and the Second World War*, 97–142. New York, 1986.

———. "Mau Maus of the Mind: Making Mau Mau and Remaking Kenya." *Journal of African History* 31, no. 3 (1990): 393–421.

———. "The Conquest State of Kenya, 1895–1905." In John Lonsdale and Bruce Berman, eds., *Unhappy Valley: Conflict in Kenya and Africa*, 13–44. London, 1992.

Louis, William Roger. *Imperialism at Bay: The United States and the Decolonization of the British Empire, 1941–1945*. Oxford, 1977.

Louis, William Roger, and Ronald Robinson. "The United States and the Liquidation of British Empire in Tropical Africa, 1941–1951." In Prosser Gifford and William Roger Louis, eds., *The Transfer of Power in Africa: Decolonization, 1940–1960*, 31–55. New Haven, Conn., 1982.

Low, D. A. *Eclipse of Empire*. Cambridge, 1991.

Luard, Evan. *A History of the United Nations*. Vol. 1, *The Years of Western Domination, 1945–1955*. New York, 1982.

———. *A History of the United Nations*. Vol. 2, *The Age of Decolonization, 1955–1965*. Basingstoke, 1989.

Lucet, Jacotte, and Thérèse Boespflug, eds. *Pierre-Henri Simon: Actes du colloque tenu à Rome le 12 décembre 1996*. Paris, 1999.

Lyttelton, Oliver. *The Memoirs of Lord Chandos*. London, 1962.

Macey, David. *Frantz Fanon: A Biography*. New York, 2001.

Macintyre, Ben. "Fifty Years Later: Britain's Kenya Cover-up Revealed." *Times* (London), 5 April 2011.

Macintyre, Ben, and Billy Kenber. "Brutal Beatings and the 'Roasting Alive' of a Suspect: What Secret Mau Mau Files Reveal." *Times* (London), 13 April 2011.

MacKay, R. W. G. *Peace Aims and the New Order*. London, 1941.

MacMaster, Neil. "The Torture Controversy (1998–2002): Towards a 'New History' of the Algerian War." *Modern and Contemporary France* 10, no. 4 (2002): 449–59.

Macmillan, Harold. *The Blast of War, 1939–1945*. London, 1967.

Madsen, Makael Rask. "France, the UK, and the 'Boomerang' of the Internationalisation of Human Rights (1945–2000)." In Simon Halliday and Patrick Schmidt, eds., *Human Rights Brought Home: Socio-Legal Perspectives on Human Rights in the National Context*, 57–86. Oxford, 2004.

———. "'Legal Diplomacy': Law, Politics and the Genesis of Postwar European Human Rights." In Stefan-Ludwig Hoffmann, ed., *Human Rights in the Twentieth Century*, 62–81. Cambridge, 2011.

Majdalany, Fred. *State of Emergency: The Full Story of Mau Mau*. London, 1962.

Maloba, Wunyabari O. *Mau Mau and Kenya: An Analysis of a Peasant Revolt*. Bloomington, Ind., 1993.

Mameri, Khalfa. *Les Nations Unies face à la "Question algérienne" (1954–1962)*. Algiers, 1969.

———. "L'application du droit de la guerre et des principes humanitaires dans les opérations de guérilla." Report presented at the conference "Droit humanitaire et conflits armés," Brussels, 28–30 January 1970.

Manchester Guardian. "Templer Rehabilitation Plan in Use in Kenya: Reforming Mau Mau Terrorists." 25 July 1953.

Mandela, Nelson. *Long Walk to Freedom*. Boston, 1994.

Mandouze, André. "Impossibilités algériennes ou le mythe des trois départements." *Esprit*, 15 (July 1947): 10–30.

Manela, Erez. *The Wilsonian Moment: Self-Determination and the International Origins of Anticolonial Nationalism*. Oxford, 2007.

Mann, Gregory. *Native Sons: West African Veterans and France in the Twentieth Century*. Durham, N.C., 2006.

Mann, Michael. "Das Gewaltdispositiv des modernen Kolonialismus." In Mihran Dabag, Horst Gründer, and Uwe-K. Ketelsen, eds., *Kolonialismus: Kolonialdiskurs und Genozid*, 111–35. Munich, 2004.

Mao Zedong. *Theorie des Guerillakrieges, oder Strategie der Dritten Welt*. Reinbek, 1966.

Maran, Rita. *Torture: The Role of Ideology in the French-Algerian War*. New York, 1989.

Marill, Jean-Marc. "L'Héritage Indochinois: Adaptation de l'armée française en Algérie (1954–1956)." *Revue Historique des Armées* 2 (1992): 26–32.

Marks, Stephen. "Principles and Norms of Human Rights Applicable in Emergency Situations: Underdevelopment, Catastrophes and Armed Conflict." In Karel Vasak, ed., *The International Dimension of Human Rights*, 1:175–212. Paris, 1982.

Marshall, Bruce D. "Free France in Africa: Gaullism and Colonialism." In Prosser Gifford and William Roger Louis, eds., *France and Britain in Africa: Imperial Rivalry and Colonial Rule*, 713–48. New Haven, Conn., 1971.

Marston, Geoffrey. "The United Kingdom's Part in the Preparation of the European Convention on Human Rights, 1950." *International and Comparative Law Quarterly* 42, no. 4 (October 1993): 796–826.

Marston, R. "Resettlement as a Counterrevolutionary Technique." *Journal of the Royal United Services Institute for Defence Studies* 124, no. 4 (4 December 1979): 46–50.

Martel, Pierre-Albin. "Le calme est revenu dans l'Algérois et en Oranie." *Le Monde*, 3 November 1954.

Martin, Arthur Clive. *The Concentration Camps, 1900–1902: Facts, Figures and Fables*. Cape Town, 1958.

Martin, Michel L. "From Algiers to N'Djamena: France's Adaptation to Low-Intensity Wars, 1830–1987." In David Charters and Maurice Tugwell, eds., *Armies in Low-Intensity Conflict: A Comparative Analysis*, 77–138. London, 1989.

Marx, Christoph. "'Die im Dunkeln sieht man nicht': Kriegsgefangene im Burenkrieg, 1899–1902." In Rüdiger Overmans, ed., *In der Hand des Feindes: Kriegsgefangenschaft von der Antike bis zum Zweiten Weltkrieg*, 255–76. Cologne, 1999.

Massu, Jacques. *La vraie bataille d'Alger*. Paris, 1971.

Mathias, Grégor. *Les SAS, une institution ambiguë, entre idéal et réalité*. Paris, 1998.

Mattioli, Aram. "Entgrenzte Kriegsgewalt: Der italienische Giftgaseinsatz in Abessinien, 1935–1936." *Vierteljahrshefte für Zeitgeschichte* 51, no. 3 (2003): 311–37.

———. *Experimentierfeld der Gewalt: Der Abessinienkrieg und seine internationale Bedeutung, 1935–1941*. Zurich, 2005.

Maul, Daniel. *Human Rights, Development and Decolonization: The International Labour Organization, 1940–70*. Basingstoke, 2012.

The Mau Mau in Kenya. Foreword by Granville Roberts. London, 1954.

Mauriac, François. "La question." *L'Express*, 15 February 1955.

Mazower, Mark. *Dark Continent: Europe's Twentieth Century*. New York, 1999.

———. "The Strange Triumph of Human Rights, 1933–1950." *Historical Journal* 47, no. 2 (June 2004): 379–98.

———. *Hitler's Empire: How the Nazis Ruled Europe*. New York, 2008.

———. *No Enchanted Palace: The End of Empire and the Ideological Origins of the United Nations*. Princeton, N.J., 2008.

———. "The End of Civilization and the Rise of Human Rights: The Mid-Twentieth-Century Disjuncture." In Stefan-Ludwig Hoffmann, ed., *Human Rights in the Twentieth Century*, 29–44. Cambridge, 2011.

Mboya, Tom. *The Kenya Question: An African Answer*. London, 1956.

McCormack, Timothy L. H. "From Sun Tzu to the Sixth Committee: The Evolution of an International Criminal Law Regime." In Timothy L. H. McCormack and Gerry J. Simpson, eds., *The Law of War Crimes: National and International Approaches*, 43–58. The Hague, 1997.

McCuen, John J. *The Art of Counter-Revolutionary War: The Strategy of Counter-Insurgency*. London, 1966.

McGhie, John. "British Brutality in Mau Mau Conflict." *Guardian*, 9 November 2002.

———. "Police Investigate Alleged British War Crimes in Kenya." *Guardian*, 14 May 2003.

McGreal, Chris. "Mau Mau Veterans to Sue Britain over Torture and Killings." *Guardian*, 5 October 2006.

———. "Shameful Legacy." *Guardian*, 13 October 2006.

———. "Torture and Killing in Kenya—Britain's Double Standard." *Guardian*, 8 April 2011.

McIntyre, David W. *Commonwealth of Nations: Origins and Impact*. London, 1977.

———. *British Decolonization, 1946–1997: When, Why and How Did the British Empire Fall?* Basingstoke, 1998.

McLaine, Ian. *Ministry of Morale: Home Front and the Ministry of Information in World War II*. London, 1979.

McMahon, Robert J. *Colonialism and Cold War: The United States and the Struggle for Indonesian Independence, 1945–49*. Ithaca, N.Y., 1981.

Meinertzhagen, Richard. *Kenya Diary, 1902–1906*. Edinburgh, 1957.

Mellor, Alec. *La torture: Son histoire, son abolition, sa réapparition au XXe siècle*. Paris, 1949.

Memmi, Albert. *The Colonizer and the Colonized*. Boston, 1991.

Metzger, Chantal. *L'empire colonial français dans la stratégie du Troisième Reich (1936–1945)*. Vol. 1. Paris, 2002.

Mezerik, A. G., ed. *Colonialism and the United Nations*. International Review Service 10, no. 83. New York, 1964.

Miller, B. *World Order and Local Disorder: The United Nations and Internal Conflicts*. Princeton, N.J., 1967.

Miller, Harry. *Jungle War in Malaya: The Campaign Against Communism, 1948–60*. London, 1972.

Milleron, Christine. "L'action psychologique et la déshumanisation de l'adversaire." In Claude Liauzu, ed., *Violence et colonisation: Pour en finir avec les guerres de mémoires*, 155–73. Paris, 2003.

Ministère de l'Algérie, ed. *Aspects véritables de la rébellion algérienne*. N.p., n.d.

Ministry of Information and Broadcasting, ed. *Government of India Press, Asian-African Conference*. New Delhi, 1955.

Mitchell, Philip. *African Afterthoughts*. London, 1954.

Mockaitis, Thomas. *British Counterinsurgency, 1919–1960*. New York, 1990.

Mollenhauer, Daniel. "Die vielen Gesichter der pacification: Frankreichs Krieg in Algerien (1954–1962)." In Thoralf Klein and Frank Schumacher, eds., *Kolonialkriege: Militärische Gewalt im Zeichen des Imperialismus*, 329–66. Hamburg, 2006.

Mommsen, Wolfgang J., ed. *Das Ende der Kolonialreiche: Dekolonisation und die Politik der Großmächte*. Frankfurt am Main, 1990.

Le Monde. "La stratégie révolutionnaire du Viêt-Minh." 3 August 1954.

———. "Sommes-nous les 'vaincus de Hitler'?" 13 March 1957.

———. "Le FLN cherche à exploiter le drame de Melouza pour internationaliser le problème." 4 June 1957.

———. "Aspects véritables de la rébellion algérienne: Une brochure du cabinet de M. Robert Lacoste." 14 December 1957.

———. "Le rapport de synthèse de la Commission de sauvegarde des droits et libertés individuels." 14 December 1957.

———. "Les principes de l'action psychologique et de la 'guerre subversive' décrits par deux de leurs practiciens." 10 July 1958.

———. "Un rapport révèle la situation souvent tragique d'un million d'Algériens regroupés." 18 April 1959.

———. "Le rapport de la Croix-Rouge Internationale sur les camps d'internement d'Algérie." 5 January 1960.

———. "Torture en Algérie: L'aveu des généraux." 23 November 2000.

———. "Le tortionnaire et le terroriste." 27 January 2002.

———. Interview with General Massu. 22 June 2002.

Morgan, D. J. *The Official History of Colonial Development: The Origins of British Aid Policy, 1924–45*. London, 1980.

Morsink, Johannes. *The Universal Declaration of Human Rights: Origins, Drafting, and Intent*. Philadelphia, 1999.

Mosley, Paul. *The Settler Economies: Studies in the Economic History of Kenya and Southern Rhodesia, 1900–1963*. Cambridge, 1983.

Moyn, Samuel. *The Last Utopia: Human Rights in History*. Cambridge, Mass., 2010.

Muchai, Karigo. *The Hardcore*. Richmond, B.C., 1973.

Mücke, Ulrich. "Agonie einer Kolonialmacht, Spaniens Krieg in Marokko (1921–1927)." In Thoralf Klein and Frank Schumacher, eds. *Kolonialkriege: Militärische Gewalt im Zeichen des Imperialismus*, 248–71. Hamburg, 2006.

Münchhausen, Thankmar von. "Ziele und Widerstände der französischen Algerienpolitik von 1945–58." Ph.D. diss., University of Heidelberg, 1962.

———. *Kolonialismus und Demokratie: Die französische Algerienpolitik von 1954–1962*. Munich, 1977.

Münkler, Herfried. *Die neuen Kriege*. Reinbek, 2002.

———. *Imperien: Die Logik der Weltherrschaft*. Bonn, 2005.

Muriuki, Godfrey. *A History of the Kikuyu, 1500–1900*. Nairobi, 1974.

Murphy, Robert David. *Diplomat unter Kriegern: Zwei Jahrzehnte Weltpolitik in besonderer Mission*. Berlin, 1966.

Murumbi, Joseph. "Human Rights: Let's Make Them Real." *Tribune*, 8 June 1956.

Myrdal, Gunnar. *An American Dilemma: The Negro Problem and Modern Democracy*. Vol. 2. New York, 1944.

Naroun, Amar. *Ferhat Abbas; ou, Les chemins de la souveraineté*. Paris, 1961.

Navarre, Henri. *Agonie de l'Indochine, 1953–1954*. Paris, 1956.

Ndoria, Peter N. *War in the Forest: The Personal Story of J. Kiboi Muriithi as Told to Peter N. Ndoria*. Nairobi, 1971.

Neier, Aryen. "War and War Crimes: A Brief History." In Omer Bartov, Anita Grossmann, and Mary Nolan, eds., *Crimes of War: Guilt and Denial in the Twentieth Century*, 1–7. New York, 2002.

Newsinger, John. "Revolt and Repression in Kenya: The 'Mau Mau' Rebellion, 1952–1960." *Science and Society* 45, no. 2 (1981): 159–85.

———. *British Counterinsurgency: From Palestine to Northern Ireland*. Basingstoke, 2002.

New Statesman and Nation. "Justice in Kenya." 17 December 1955.

New York Times. "Arab in UN Hits Paris on Algeria." 6 January 1955.

Nkrumah, Kwame [Francis Nwia-kofi]. "Education and Nationalism in Africa." *Educational Outlook*, November 1943, 32–40.

———. *Towards Colonial Freedom: Africa in the Struggle Against World Imperialism*. London, 1973.

Normand, Roger, and Sarah Zaidi. *Human Rights at the UN: The Political History of Universal Justice.* Bloomington, Ind., 2008.

Notter, Harley. *Postwar Foreign Policy Preparation, 1939–1945.* Washington, D.C., 1975.

Ochieng', W. R., and E. S. Atieno-Odhiambo. "Prologue: On Decolonization." In B. A. Ogot and W. R. Ochieng', eds., *Decolonization and Independence in Kenya, 1940–93*, xi–xviii. Nairobi, 1995.

Ogot, Bethwell A. "The Decisive Years, 1956–63." In B. A. Ogot and W. R. Ochieng', eds., *Decolonization and Independence in Kenya, 1940–93*, 48–79. Nairobi, 1995.

———. "Mau Mau and Nationhood: The Untold Story." In E. S. Atieno Odhiambo and John Lonsdale, eds., *Mau Mau and Nationhood: Arms, Authority and Narration*, 8–36. Oxford, 2003.

———. "Britain's Gulag." *Journal of African History* 46, no. 3 (2005): 493–505.

Ogot, B. A., and W. R. Ochieng', eds. *Decolonization and Independence in Kenya, 1940–93.* Nairobi, 1995.

Omouri, Noara. "Les sections administratives spécialisées et les sciences sociales." In Jean-Charles Jauffret and Maurice Vaisse, eds., *Militaires et guérilla dans la guerre d'Algérie*, 383–97. Montpellier, 2001.

Opitz, Peter J. *Menschenrechte und Internationaler Menschenrechtsschutz im 20. Jahrhundert.* Munich, 2002.

Oppermann, Thomas. *Die algerische Frage.* Stuttgart, 1959.

———. "Die Anwendbarkeit der Genfer Abkommen zum Schutze der Kriegsopfer im Algerien-Konflikt." *Archiv des Völkerrechts* 9, no. 1 (January 1961): 47–59.

Oráa, Jamie. *Human Rights in States of Emergency in International Law.* Oxford, 1992.

Osborne, M. E. *Strategic Hamlets in South-Vietnam: A Survey and a Comparison.* New York, 1965.

Osterhammel, Jürgen. "Spätkolonialismus und Dekolonisation." *Neue Politische Literatur* 44 (1992): 404–426.

———. *Kolonialismus: Geschichte, Formen, Folgen.* Munich, 1995.

———. *Colonialism: A Theoretical Overview.* 2nd ed. Princeton, N.J., 2005.

Otieno, Wambiu Waiyaki. *Mau Mau's Daughter: A Life History.* Boulder, Colo., 1998.

Ovendale, Ritchie. "Macmillan and the Wind of Change in Africa, 1957–1960." *Historical Journal* 38, no. 2 (1995): 455–77.

Overmans, Rüdiger, ed. *In der Hand des Feindes: Kriegsgefangenschaft von der Antike bis zum Zweiten Weltkrieg.* Cologne, 1999.

Padmore, George. *Pan-Africanism or Communism.* New York, 1956.

Paget, Julian. *Counter-Insurgency Campaigning.* London, 1967.

Pahlavi, Pierre Cyrill. *La guerre révolutionnaire de l'armée française en Algérie, 1954–1961: Entre esprit de conquête et conquête des esprits.* Paris, 2004.

Pakenham, Thomas. *The Boer War.* London, 1979.

Pan-Africa. "Kenya To-day, Equality Is Our Slogan." June 1947.

Paret, Peter. *French Revolutionary Warfare from Indochina to Algeria: The Analysis of a Political and Military Doctrine.* New York, 1964.

Parkinson, Charles O. H. *Bills of Rights and Decolonization: The Emergence of Domestic Human Rights Instruments in Britain's Overseas Territories.* Oxford, 2007.

Parsons, Timothy H. *The African Rank-and-File: Social Implications of Colonial Military Service in the King's African Rifles, 1902–1964.* Portsmouth, N.H., 1999.

Pellissier, Pierre. *La bataille d'Alger.* Paris, 1995.

Périot, Gérard. *Deuxième classe en Algérie.* Paris, 1962.

Person, Yves. "French West Africa and Decolonization." In Prosser Gifford and William Roger

Louis, eds., *The Transfer of Power in Africa: Decolonization, 1940–1960*, 141–72. New Haven, Conn., 1982.

Pervillé, Guy. "Guerre étrangère et guerre civile en Algérie, 1954–1962." *Relations internationales* 14 (1978): 171–96.

———. *De l'Empire français à la décolonisation*. Paris, 1991.

———. "Décolonisation 'à l'algerienne' et 'à la rhodésienne' en Afrique du Nord et en Afrique australe." In Charles-Robert Ageron and Marc Michel, eds., *L'ère des décolonisations: Actes du Colloque d'Aix-en-Provence*, 26–37. Paris, 1995.

———. *Pour une histoire de la guerre d'Algérie, 1954–1962*. Paris, 2002.

———. *Atlas de la guerre d'Algérie: De la conquête à l'indépendance*. Paris, 2003.

———. "La guerre d'Algérie: Combien de morts?" In Mohammed Harbi and Benjamin Stora, eds., *La guerre d'Algérie, 1954–2004: La fin de l'amnésie*, 477–94. Paris, 2004.

Peters, Edward. *Folter: Die Geschichte der peinlichen Befragung*. Hamburg, 1991.

Peterson, Derek. "Writing in Revolution: Independent School and Mau Mau in Nyeri." In E. S. Atieno Odhiambo and John Lonsdale, eds., *Mau Mau and Nationhood: Arms, Authority and Narration*, 76–96. Oxford, 2003.

Peterson, Gregory D. *French Experience in Algeria, 1954–1962: Blueprint for U.S. Operations in Iraq*. Fort Leavenworth, Kans., 2004.

Pictet, Jean S. "The New Geneva Conventions for the Protection of War Victims." *American Journal of International Law* 45, no. 3 (July 1951): 462–68.

———, ed. *Geneva Convention Relative to the Protection of Civilian Persons in Time of War: Commentary*. Vol. 4 of *The Geneva Conventions of 12 August 1949: Commentary*. Geneva, 1958.

Pimlott, John. "The British Army: The Dhofar Campaign, 1970–1975." In Ian Beckett and John Pimlott, eds. *Armed Forces and Modern Counter-Insurgency*, 16–45. New York, 1985.

———. "The French Army: From Indochina to Chad, 1946–1984." In Ian Beckett and John Pimlott, eds. *Armed Forces and Modern Counter-Insurgency*, 46–76. New York, 1985.

———. "The British Experience." In Ian Beckett, ed., *The Roots of Counter-Insurgency: Armies and Guerrilla Warfare, 1900–1945*, 17–39. London, 1988.

Pinto, Roger. "Pour l'application des conventions de Genève en Algérie." *Le Monde*, 6 July 1958.

Planchais, Jean. *Le malaise de l'armée*. Paris, 1958.

Planche, Jean-Louis. "La répression civile du soulèvement nord-constantinois, mai–juin 1945." In Daniel Lefeuvre, ed., *La guerre d'Algérie au miroir des décolonisations françaises: Actes du colloque en l'honneur de Charles-Robert Ageron, Sorbonne, novembre 2000*, 111–28. Paris, 2000.

Planhol, Xavier de. *Nouveaux villages algérois: Atlas blidéen, Chenoua, Mitidja occidentale*. Paris, 1961.

Plantey, Alain. "Le Général de Gaulle et l'ONU." In André Lewin, ed., *La France et l'ONU depuis 1945*, 95–112. Condé-sur-Noireau, 1995.

Plummer, Brenda Gayle. *Rising Wind: Black Americans and U.S. Foreign Affairs, 1935–1960*. Chapel Hill, N.C., 1996.

Polk, William R. *Violent Politics: A History of Insurgency, Terrorism and Guerrilla War from the American Revolution to Iraq*. New York, 2007.

Pratt, Cranford. "Colonial Governments and the Transfer of Power in East Africa." In Prosser Gifford and William Roger Louis, eds., *The Transfer of Power in Africa: Decolonization, 1940–1960*, 249–81. New Haven, Conn., 1982.

Preston, Peter. "Our Guantánamo." *Observer*, 16 January 2005.

Pretorius, Fransjohan, ed. *Scorched Earth*. Cape Town, 2001.

Price, Philips. "With the Security Forces in Kenya: In the Heart of Kikuyu Country." *Manchester Guardian*, 6 December 1954.

Prochaska, David. *Making Algeria French: Colonialism in Bône, 1870–1920*. Cambridge, 1990.

Prost, Antoine. "The Algerian War in French Collective Memory." In Jay Winter and Emmanuel Sivan, eds., *War and Remembrance in the Twentieth Century*, 161–76. Cambridge, 1999.

Raben, Remco. "Koloniale Vergangenheit und postkoloniale Moral in den Niederlanden." In Volkhard Knigge and Norbert Frei, eds., *Verbrechen erinnern: Die Auseinandersetzung mit Holocaust und Völkermord*, 90–110. Bonn, 2005.

Ramadhani, Augustino S. L. *Guerilla Warfare in Wars of National Liberation and International Humanitarian Law*. Dar es Salaam, 1981.

Rawcliffe, D. H. *The Struggle for Kenya*. London, 1954.

Recham, Belkacem. *Les musulmans algériens dans l'armée française, 1919–1945*. Paris, 1996.

Redfield, Robert. "The Ethnological Problem." In George de Huszar, ed., *New Perspectives on Peace*, 60–81. Chicago, 1944.

Reemtsma, Jan Philipp. "Der Herr schätzt den Menschen als solchen: Ein neues Jahrhundert der Folter." In Jan Philipp Reemtsma, ed., *Folter: Zur Analyse eines Herrschaftsmittels*, 25–36. Hamburg, 1991.

———. "Zur politischen Semantik des Begriffs 'Folter.'" In Jan Philipp Reemtsma, ed., *Folter: Zur Analyse eines Herrschaftsmittels*, 239–63. Hamburg, 1991.

Reid, Anthony. *The Indonesian National Revolution, 1945–1950*. Hawthorn, 1974.

Reinhard, Wolfgang. *Geschichte der europäischen Expansion*. 4 vols. Stuttgart, 1983–1990.

Reynolds News. "Britain Has Barred Red Cross in Kenya." 16 December 1956.

Rioux, Jean-Pierre, ed. *La guerre d'Algérie et les Français*. Paris, 1990.

Roberts-Wray, K. *Commonwealth and Colonial Law*. London, 1966.

Rocard, Michel. *Rapport sur les camps de regroupement et autres textes sur la guerre d'Algérie*. Paris, 2003.

Roosevelt, Elliott. *As He Saw It*. New York, 1946.

Rosberg, Carl, and John Nottingham. *The Myth of Mau Mau: Nationalism in Kenya*. New York, 1966.

Rothermund, Dietmar. *Delhi, 15 August 1947: Das Ende kolonialer Herrschaft*. Munich, 1998.

Roux, Michel. *Les harkis ou les oubliés de l'histoire, 1954–1991*. Paris, 1991.

Roy, Jules. *Schicksal Algerien*. Hamburg, 1961.

———. *The War in Algeria*. New York, 1961.

Ruark, Robert. *Something of Value*. London, 1955.

Ruedy, John. *Land Policy in Colonial Algeria*. Los Angeles, 1967.

Ruscio, Alain. *La décolonisation tragique, 1945–1962*. Paris, 1987.

———. "Interrogations sur certains pratiques de l'armée française en Indochine, 1945–54." In Claude Liauzu, ed., *Violence et colonisation: Pour en finir avec les guerres de mémoires*, 85–106. Paris, 2003.

Ruthven, Malise. *Torture: The Grand Conspiracy*. London, 1978.

Sabben-Clare, E. E. "African Troops in Asia." *African Affairs* 44 (October 1945): 151–57.

Sarrazin, François [Vincent Monteil, pseud.]. "L'Algérie, pays sans loi." *Esprit* 23, nos. 230–31 (September–October 1955): 1620–30.

———. "L'Afrique du Nord et notre destin." *Esprit* 23, no. 232 (November 1955): 1649–66.

Sartre, Jean-Paul. *Colonialism and Neocolonialism*. London, 2001.

Savarèse, Eric. *L'invention des Pieds-Noirs*. Paris, 2002.

Schabas, William A. *Genocide in International Law: The Crimes of Crimes*. Cambridge, 2000.

Schmid, Bernhard. *Rang und Geltung der Europäischen Konvention zum Schutze der Menschenrechte und Grundfreiheiten vom 3. November 1950 in den Vertragsstaaten*. Basel, 1984.

Schmitt, Carl. *Die Diktatur: Von den Anfängen des modernen Souveränitätsgedankens bis zum proletarischen Klassenkampf*. Munich, 1928.

————. *Theorie des Partisanen: Zwischenbemerkungen zum Begriff des Politischen*. Berlin, 1963.

Schoen, Paul. "Bulletin politique mensuel, août 1955: La flambée du 20 août." In Maurice Faivre, ed., *Les archives inédites de la politique algérienne, 1958–1962*, 370–71. Paris, 2000.

Scholtz, Leopold. *Why the Boers Lost the War*. Basingstoke, 2005.

Scholze, Udo. "Vor 30 Jahren: In Evian beginnt Algeriens Unabhängigkeit; Frankreichs Algerienkrieg und sein Umgang mit dieser Geschichte." *Dokumente: Zeitschrift für den deutsch-französischen Dialog* 48, no. 1 (1992): 43–47.

Schulz, Gerhard. "Zur englischen Planung des Partisanenkriegs am Vorabend des Zweiten Weltkrieges." *Vierteljahrshefte für Zeitgeschichte* 30, no. 3 (1982): 322–58.

————. "Die Irregulären: Guerilla, Partisanen und die Wandlung des Krieges seit dem 18. Jahrhundert." In Gerhard Schulz, ed., *Partisanen und Volkskrieg: Zur Revolutionierung des Krieges im 20. Jahrhundert*, 9–35. Göttingen, 1985.

Schumacher, Frank. "'Niederbrennen, plündern und töten sollt ihr': Der Kolonialkrieg der USA auf den Philippinen (1899–1913)." In Thoralf Klein and Frank Schumacher, eds., *Kolonialkriege: Militärische Gewalt im Zeichen des Imperialismus*, 109–44. Hamburg, 2006.

Schümperli, Walter. *Die Vereinten Nationen und die Dekolonisation*. Bern, 1970.

Schwarzenberger, Georg. "The Protection of Human Rights in British State Practice." *Review of Politics* 10 (April 1948): 174–89.

Semper Fidelis: Journal of the Devonshire Regiment [Eleventh Regiment of Foot]. Vol. 1, no. 8 (November 1953).

Shepard, Todd. *The Invention of Decolonization: The Algerian War and the Remaking of France*. Ithaca, N.Y., 2006.

Shipway, Martin. "Creating an Emergency: Metropolitan Constraints on French Colonial Policy and Its Breakdown in Indo-China, 1945–47." In Robert Holland, ed., *Emergencies and Disorder in the European Empires After 1945*, 1–16. London, 1994.

Shiroya, Okete J. E. "The Impact of World War II on Kenya: The Role of Ex-Servicemen in Kenya Nationalism." Ph.D. diss., Michigan State University, 1968.

Short, Anthony. *The Communist Insurrection in Malaya, 1948–1960*. London, 1975.

Sigg, Bernard W. *Le silence et la honte: Névroses de la guerre d'Algérie*. Paris, 1989.

Simon, Pierre-Henri. *Contre la torture*. Paris, 1957.

Simpson, Brian A. W. *In the Highest Degree Odious: Detention Without Trial in Wartime Britain*. Oxford, 1992.

————. *Human Rights and the End of Empire: Britain and the Genesis of the European Convention*. Oxford, 2004.

Sinclair, Georgina S. "'Settlers' Men' or Policemen? The Ambiguities of 'Colonial' Policing, 1945–1980." Ph.D. diss., University of Reading, 2002.

Singh, Lalita Prasad. *India and Afro-Asian Independence: Liberation Diplomacy in the United Nations*. New Delhi, 1993.

Sithole, Ndabaningi. *African Nationalism*. London, 1959.

Sluga, Glenda. "René Cassin: *Les droits de l'homme* and the Universality of Human Rights, 1945–1966." In Stefan-Ludwig Hoffmann, ed., *Human Rights in the Twentieth Century*, 107–24. Cambridge, 2011.

Smith, Charles. "Communal Conflict and Insurrection in Palestine, 1936–48." In David M. Anderson and David Killingray, eds., *Policing and Decolonisation: Politics, Nationalism and the Police, 1917–65*, 62–83. Manchester, 1992.

Smith, Tony. "Patterns in the Transfer of Power: A Comparative Study of French and British Decolonization." In Prosser Gifford and William Roger Louis, eds., *The Transfer of Power in Africa: Decolonization, 1940–1960*, 87–115. New Haven, Conn., 1982.

Smyth, Rosaleen. "Britain's African Colonies and British Propaganda During the Second World War." *Journal of Imperial and Commonwealth History* 13 (1985): 65–82.

Société d'Editions et de Régie, ed. *Documents sur les crimes et attentats commis en Algérie par les terroristes*. Algiers, 1956.

Sofsky, Wolfgang. *Die Ordnung des Terrors: Das Konzentrationslager*. Frankfurt am Main, 1993.

Sorrenson, Maurice Peter Keith. *Land Reform in the Kikuyu Country*. Nairobi, 1967.

———. *Origins of European Settlement in Kenya*. Nairobi, 1968.

Souyris, André. "Les conditions de la parade et de la riposte à la guerre révolutionnaire." *Revue Militaire d'Information*, February–March 1957, 89–109.

Speitkamp, Winfried. "Spätkolonialer Krieg und Erinnerungspolitik: Mau Mau in Kenia." In Helmut Berding, Klaus Heller, and Winfried Speitkamp, eds., *Krieg und Erinnerung: Fallstudien zum 19. und 20. Jahrhundert*, 193–222. Göttingen, 2000.

Spiers, Edward M. "The Use of the Dum Dum Bullet in Colonial Warfare." *Journal of Imperial and Commonwealth History* 4, no. 1 (1975): 3–14.

Spies, Stephanus B. *Methods of Barbarism? Roberts and Kitchener and Civilians in the Boer Republics, January 1900–May 1902*. Johannesburg, 2001.

Springhall, John. *Decolonization Since 1945*. Basingstoke, 2001.

Stewart, Graham. "Lessons for the US from Our Colonial History." *Times* (London), 25 February 2006.

Stockwell, A. J. "British Imperial Policy and Decolonization in Malaya, 1942–52." *Journal of Imperial and Commonwealth History* 13, no. 1 (October 1984): 68–87.

———. "Policing During the Malayan Emergency, 1948–60: Communism, Communalism and Decolonisation." In David M. Anderson and David Killingray, eds., *Policing and Decolonisation: Politics, Nationalism and the Police, 1917–65*, 105–26. Manchester, 1992.

———. "'A Widespread and Long-Concocted Plot to Overthrow Government in Malaya?' The Origins of the Malayan Emergency." In Robert Holland, ed., *Emergencies and Disorder in the European Empires After 1945*, 66–88. London, 1994.

Stone, Julius. *The Atlantic Charter: New Worlds for Old*. Sydney, 1943.

Stoneham, C. T. *Mau Mau*. London, 1953.

———. *Out of Barbarism*. London, 1955.

Stora, Benjamin. *Les sources du nationalisme algérien: Parcours idéologiques; origines des acteurs*. Paris, 1989.

———. "La gauche et les minorités anticolonialistes devant les divisions du nationalisme algérien." In Jean-Pierre Rioux, ed., *La guerre d'Algérie et les Français*, 63–78. Paris, 1990.

———. *La gangrène et l'oubli: La mémoire de la guerre d'Algérie*. Paris, 1998.

———. "Der Algerienkrieg im Gedächtnis Frankreichs." In Volkhard Knigge and Norbert Frei, eds., *Verbrechen erinnern: Die Auseinandersetzung mit Holocaust und Völkermord*, 75–89. Bonn, 2005.

———. "The 'Southern' World of the Pieds Noirs: References to and Representations of Europeans in Colonial Algeria." In Caroline Elkins and Susan Pedersen, eds., *Settler Colonialism in the Twentieth Century: Projects, Practices, Legacies*, 225–41. New York, 2005.

Stronski, Stanislaw. *The Atlantic Charter*. Bombay, 1945.

Stubbs, Richard. *Hearts and Minds in Guerrilla Warfare: The Malayan Emergency, 1948–1960*. Singapore, 1989.

Stuchtey, Benedikt. *Die europäische Expansion und ihre Feinde: Kolonialismuskritik vom 18. bis in das 20. Jahrhundert*. Munich, 2010.

Stucki, Andreas. *Aufstand und Zwangsumsiedlung: Die kubanischen Unabhängigkeitskriege 1868–1898*. Hamburg, 2012.

Stucki, Andreas, and Iain R. Smith. "The Colonial Development of Concentration Camps (1868–1902)." *Journal of Imperial and Commonwealth History* 39, no. 3 (2011): 417–37.

Suret-Canale, Jean. "From Colonization to Independence in French Tropical Africa: The Economic Background." In Prosser Gifford and William Roger Louis, eds., *The Transfer of Power in Africa: Decolonization, 1940–1960*, 445–81. New Haven, Conn., 1982.

Svensson-McCarthy, Anna-Lena. *The International Law of Human Rights and States of Exception.* The Hague, 1998.

Tabet, Radjouane Ainad. *Le 8 mai 1945 en Algérie.* Algiers, 1985.

Tabili, Laura. *"We Ask for British Justice": Workers and Racial Difference in Late Imperial Britain.* Ithaca, N.Y., 1994.

Taithe, Bertrand. *The Killer Trail: A Colonial Scandal in the Heart of Africa.* Oxford, 2009.

Talbott, John. *The War Without a Name: France in Algeria, 1954–1962.* New York, 1980.

Tan, Seng, and Amitav Acharya, eds. *Bandung Revisited: The Legacy of the 1955 Asian-African Conference for International Order.* Singapore, 2008.

Tenenbaum, Joseph. *Race and Reich: The Story of an Epoch.* New York, 1956.

Thénault, Sylvie. "D'Indochine en Algérie: Le rééducation des prisonniers dans les camps de detention." In Daniel Lefeuvre, ed., *La guerre d'Algérie au miroir des décolonisations françaises: Actes du colloque en l'honneur de Charles-Robert Ageron, Sorbonne, novembre 2000*, 235–49. Paris, 2000.

———. "Rappels historiques sur les camps de regroupement de la guerre d'Algérie." In Michel Rocard, ed., *Rapport sur les camps de regroupement et autres textes sur la guerre d'Algérie*, 227–38. Paris, 2003.

———. *Une drôle de justice: Les magistrates dans la guerre d'Algérie.* Paris, 2004.

Thomas, Daniel C. *The Helsinki Effect: International Norms, Human Rights, and the Demise of Communism.* Princeton, N.J., 2001.

Thomas, Martin. *The French Empire at War, 1940–1945,* Manchester, 1998.

———. *The French North African Crisis. Colonial Breakdown and Anglo-French Relations, 1945–62,* Basingstoke, 2000.

———. "France Accused: French North Africa Before the United Nations, 1952–1962." *Contemporary European History* 10 (March 2001): 91–121.

———. *Empires of Intelligence. Security Services and Colonial Disorder after 1914,* Berkeley, 2008.

———, ed. *The French Colonial Mind. Volume Two, Violence, Military Encounters, and Colonialism.* Lincoln, Neb., 2011.

———. "Colonial Minds and Colonial Violence: The Setif Uprising and the Savage Economics of Colonialism." In *The French Colonial Mind*, 140–173.

———. *Violence and Colonial Disorder. Police, Workers and Protest in the European Colonial Empires, 1918–1940.* Cambridge, 2012.

Thomas, Martin, Bob Moore, and L. J. Butler. *Crises of Empire. Decolonization and Europe's Imperial States, 1918–1975,* London, 2008.

Thompson, Andrew. *The Empire Strikes Back? The Impact of Imperialism on Britain from the Mid-Nineteenth Century,* Harlow, 2005.

Thompson, Dudley. *From Kingston to Kenya: The Making of a Pan-Africanist Lawyer.* Dover, Mass., 1993.

Thompson, Robert. *Revolutionary War in World Strategy, 1945–1969.* London, 1970.

———. *Defeating Communist Insurgency: Experiences from Malaya and Vietnam.* London, 1972.

Thomson, H. C. *Rhodesia and Its Government.* London, 1898.

Throup, David W. *Economic and Social Origins of Mau Mau, 1945–53.* London, 1987.

———. "Crime, Politics and the Police in Colonial Kenya, 1939–63." In David M. Anderson and David Killingray, eds., *Policing and Decolonisation: Politics, Nationalism and the Police, 1917–65*, 127–57. Manchester, 1992.

Tibi, Bassam. "Nationsbildung in den Kolonien als Prozess einer auf Gewalt basierenden Dekolonisation." In Bassam Tibi, ed., *Nationalismus in der Dritten Welt*, 38–44. Frankfurt am Main, 1971.

———. "Der Dekolonisationsprozeß Algeriens: Vom revolutionären Befreiungskrieg zum Militärregime." In Bassam Tibi and Gerhard Grohs, eds., *Zur Soziologie der Dekolonisation in Afrika*, 13–79. Frankfurt am Main, 1973.

Tillion, Germaine. *L'Algérie en 1957*. Paris, 1957.

Times (London). "British Complaint to Egypt: Mau Mau Emissary Received." 29 August 1953.

———. "Mr. Murumbi's Plans for Kenya: Aims Explained." 26 September 1953.

———. "African's Death After Beating—Two Europeans Fined." 1 October 1953.

Tinker, Hugh. *Race, Conflict and the International Order: From Empire to United Nations*. London, 1977.

———. *Men Who Overturned Empires: Fighters, Dreamers and Schemers*. Madison, Wis., 1987.

Toase, Francis. "The French Experience." In Ian Beckett, ed., *The Roots of Counter-Insurgency: Armies and Guerrilla Warfare, 1900–1945*, 40–59. London, 1988.

Tolley, Howard. *The UN Commission on Human Rights*. Boulder, Colo., 1987.

Tostain, France. "The Popular Front and the Blum-Violette Plan." In Tony Chafer and Amanda Sackur, eds., *French Colonial Empire and the Popular Front: Hope and Disillusion*, 218–29. Basingstoke, 1999.

Townshend, Charles. *The British Campaign in Ireland, 1919–1921: The Development of Political and Military Policies*. Oxford, 1975.

———. "Martial Law: Legal and Administrative Problems of Civil Emergency in Britain and the Empire, 1800–1940." *Historical Journal* 25, no. 1 (1982): 167–95.

———. *Britain's Civil Wars: Counterinsurgency in the Twentieth Century*. London, 1986.

Tribune. "Labour to Fight Kenya Thugs." 30 September 1955.

Trinquier, Roger. *La guerre moderne*. Paris, 1961.

Tronchon, Jacques. *L'insurrection malgache de 1947: Essai d'interprétation historique*. Paris, 1986.

Truman, Harry S. *Memoirs: Years of Decision*. Vol. 1. New York, 1955.

Union Messenger of St. Kitts. "Children Burnt Alive, Castration, Murder, Starvation: A Mau-Mau Letter." 2 November 1953.

United Nations High Commissioner for Refugees (UNHCR), ed. *L'opération de secours aux réfugiés au Maroc et en Tunisie*. Geneva, 1961.

———. "A Joint Operation with League of Red Cross Societies in North Africa." In UNHCR, ed., *Meeting a Challenge*, 40–45. Geneva, 1961.

———. *The State of the World's Refugees: Fifty Years of Humanitarian Action*. Oxford, 2000.

Urquhart, Brian. *Decolonization and World Peace*. Austin, Tex., 1989.

———. *Ralph Bunche: An American Life*. New York, 1993.

———. "Un regard extérieur sur 50 ans de présence française." In André Lewin, ed., *La France et l'ONU depuis 1945*, 117–22. Condé-sur-Noireau, 1995.

Vaisse, Maurice. "La guerre perdue à l'ONU?" In Jean-Pierre Rioux, ed., *La guerre d'Algérie et les Français*, 451–62. Paris, 1990.

Valette, Jacques. *La Guerre d'Algérie des messalistes, 1954–1962*. Paris, 2001.

Vandervort, Bruce. *Wars of Imperial Conquest in Africa, 1830–1914*. Bloomington, Ind., 1998.

Van Doorn, Jacques. "Use of Violence in Counter Insurgency: The Indonesian Scene, 1945–49." In Jacques van Doorn, ed., *The Soldier and Social Change*, 133–77. Beverly Hills, Calif., 1975.

———, ed. *The Soldier and Social Change: Comparative Studies in the History and Sociology of the Military*. Beverly Hills, Calif., 1975.

Van Doorn, Jacques, and Willam J. Hendrix. *Ontsporing van geweld: Over het Nederlands-Indisch-Indonesisch conflict*. Rotterdam, 1970.

———. *The Process of Decolonisation, 1945–1975: The Military Experience in Comparative Perspective*. Rotterdam, 1987.

Van Walraven, Klaas, and Jon Abbink. "Rethinking Resistance in African History." In Klaas van Walraven, Jon Abbink, and Mirjam de Bruijn, eds., *Rethinking Resistance: Revolt and Violence in African History*, 1–25. Leiden, 2003.

Vasagar, Jeevan. "Lest We Forget." *Guardian*, 7 March 2005.

Vasak, Karel. "The Council of Europe." In Karel Vasak, ed., *The International Dimension of Human Rights*, 2:457–542. Paris, 1982.

Veracini, Lorenzo. *Settler Colonialism: A Theoretical Overview*. Basingstoke, 2010.

Vergès, Jacques, Michel Zavrian, and Maurice Courrégé. *Les disparus: Le cahier vert*. Lausanne, 1959.

———. *Le droit et la colère*. Paris, 1960.

Vernet, Jacques. "Les barrages pendant la guerre d'Algérie." In Jean-Charles Jauffret and Maurice Vaisse, eds., *Militaires et guérilla dans la guerre d'Algérie*, 253–68. Montpellier, 2001.

Veuthey, Michel. *Guérilla et droit humanitaire*. Geneva, 1976.

Vidal-Naquet, Pierre. *L'affaire Audin*. Paris, 1958.

———. *La torture dans la république: Essai d'histoire et de politique contemporaines (1954–1962)*. Paris, 1998.

Viollis, Andrée. *Indochine SOS*. Paris, 1935.

Vittori, Jean-Pierre. *Nous, les appelés d'Algérie*. Paris, 1983.

———. *On a torturé en Algérie*. Paris, 2000.

Von Eschen, Penny M. *Race Against Empire: Black Americans and Anticolonialism, 1937–1957*. Ithaca, N.Y., 1997.

Wall, Irwin M. *France, the United States and the Algerian War*. Berkeley, Calif., 2001.

Walter, Dierk. "Warum Kolonialkrieg?" In Thoralf Klein and Frank Schumacher, eds., *Kolonialkriege: Militärische Gewalt im Zeichen des Imperialismus*, 14–43. Hamburg, 2006.

Waltz, Susan. "Universalizing Human Rights: The Role of Small States in the Construction of the Universal Declaration of Human Rights." *Human Rights Quarterly* 23, no. 1 (February 2001): 44–72.

———. "Reclaiming and Rebuilding the History of the Universal Declaration of Human Rights." *Third World Quarterly* 23, no. 3 (June 2002): 433–48.

Wanjau, Gakaara wa. *Mau Mau Author in Detention: An Author's Detention Diary*. Nairobi, 1988.

Wanstall, Kenneth. "I Saw Men Tortured. Ex-Major: It Happened in Kenya." *Reynolds News*, 13 January 1957.

Weigert, Stephen L. *Traditional Religion and Guerrilla Warfare in Modern Africa*. London, 1996.

Welch, Cheryl B. "Colonial Violence and the Rhetoric of Evasion: Tocqueville on Algeria." *Political Theory* 31, no. 2 (April 2003): 235–64.

Welch, Richard E., Jr. "American Atrocities in the Philippines: The Indictment and the Response." *Pacific Historical Review* 43, no. 2 (1974): 233–53.

Wells, Herbert G. *The Rights of Man, or What Are We Fighting For?* Harmondsworth, 1940.

———. *The New World Order: Whether It Is Attainable, How It Can Be Attained, and What Sort of World a World at Peace Will Have to Be*. Westport, Conn., 1974.

Wesseling, Henk L., and J. A. de Moor, eds. *Imperialism and War: Essays on Colonial Wars in Asia and Africa*. Leiden, 1989.

Westcott, Nicholas. "The Impact of the Second World War on Tanganyika, 1939–49." In David Killingray and Richard Rathbone, eds., *Africa and the Second World War*, 143–59. New York, 1986.

Whelan, Daniel J. *Indivisible Human Rights: A History*. Philadelphia, 2010.

Whitaker, Daniel. "History Lessons from the 'Splendid Little War.'" *Observer*, 17 December 2006.

Wilkinson, J. "The Mau Mau Movement: Some General and Medical Aspects." *East African Medical Journal*, 31 July 1954, 309–11.

Willemin, Georges, and Roger Heacock. *The International Committee of the Red Cross*. Boston, 1984.

Willkie, Wendell L. *One World*. New York, 1943.

Wills, Colin. *Who Killed Kenya?* London, 1953.

Wilson, Heather A. "Humanitarian Protection in Wars of National Liberation." *Arms Control* 8, no. 1 (May 1987): 36–48.

———. *International Law and the Use of Force by National Liberation Movements*. Oxford, 1988.

Windrow, Martin. *The Last Valley: Dien Bien Phu and the French Defeat in Indochina*. Cambridge, Mass., 2006.

Woyke, Wichard, ed. *Handwörterbuch der Internationalen Politik*. Bonn, 1998.

Young, Crawford. *The African Colonial State in Comparative Perspectives*. New Haven, Conn., 1994.

Younge, Gary. "Cruel and Usual." *Guardian*, 1 March 2005.

Zeller, Joachim. "'Ombepera i koza—Die Kälte tötet mich': Zur Geschichte des Konzentrationslagers in Swakopmund (1904–1908)." In Joachim Zeller and Jürgen Zimmerer, eds., *Völkermord in Deutsch-Südwestafrika: Der Kolonialkrieg (1904–1908) in Namibia und seine Folgen*, 64–79. Berlin, 2003.

Zervoudakis, Alexander J. "From Indochina to Algeria: Counter-Insurgency Lessons." In Martin S. Alexander, Martin Evans, and J. F. V. Keiger, eds., *The Algerian War and the French Army, 1954–62: Experiences, Images, Testimonies*, 43–60. Basingstoke, 2002.

Zimmerer, Jürgen. "Kriegsgefangene im Kolonialkrieg: Der Krieg gegen die Herero und Nama in Deutsch-Südwestafrika (1904–1907)." In Rüdiger Overmans, ed., *In der Hand des Feindes: Kriegsgefangenschaft von der Antike bis zum Zweiten Weltkrieg*, 277–94. Cologne, 1999.

———. *Deutsche Herrschaft über Afrikaner: Staatlicher Machtanspruch und Wirklichkeit im kolonialen Namibia*. Hamburg, 2001.

———. "Krieg, KZ und Völkermord in Südwestafrika: Der erste deutsche Genozid." In Jürgen Zimmerer and Joachim Zeller, eds., *Völkermord in Deutsch-Südwestafrika: Der Kolonialkrieg (1904–1908) in Namibia und seine Folgen*, 45–63. Berlin, 2003.

Films

Hurst, Brian Desmond, director. *Simba*. Great Britain, 1955.

Pontecorvo, Gillo, director. *La battaglia di Algeri*. Italy, 1966.

Index

Acknowledgments

My attention was first directed to the topic of human rights and colonial violence during a visit to Saint-Étienne, when various publications on the use of systematic torture by the French army during the Algerian War sparked intense debates throughout France. In connection with a seminar by Martin H. Geyer on the history of human rights and the origins of the United Nations, my ideas gradually came into focus. The project eventually led to research not only in France and Great Britain, but also in Switzerland and the United States.

I would first like to thank the staffs of the various institutions that I consulted, such as the library and archives of the United Nations in Geneva, the library and archives of the International Committee of the Red Cross in Geneva, the National Archives and the Library of Congress in Washington, D.C., the New York Public Library, the Schomburg Center for Research in Black Culture, the UN archives in New York, the Centre des archives d'outremer in Aix-en-Provence, the Service Historique de l'Armée de Terre in Château de Vincennes, the archives of the French foreign ministry on the Quai d'Orsay, the Bibliothèque National and the Bibliothèque de l'Institute du monde arabe in Paris, the National Archives in Kew, the British Library and the Imperial War Museum in London, the Rhodes House Library in Oxford, the German Historical Institutes in London and Paris, the Bavarian State Library in Munich, as well as the interlibrary loan office of the Ludwig Maximilian University library, Munich. I wish to express my special gratitude to Esther Trippel-Ngai at the UN archives in Geneva and to Maria Ize-Charrin and Carla Edelenbos at the UN Human Rights Commission, whose efforts enabled me to obtain access to hitherto unpublished and confidential files of the Human Rights Commission.

The many archival visits and subsequent findings would not have been possible without the financial support of various institutions. My special thanks goes to the Friedrich Ebert Foundation, which made my research possible by supporting this project with a three-year grant. I am also very grateful to the German Academic Exchange Service (DAAD) for financing my trips to Switzerland and the United States, just as I am to the German Historical Institutes in London and Paris for the research grants given me during my stay in Great Britain and France, respectively. In connection with the German publication of the book, I would like to thank the GHI London for giving me the opportunity to publish the original German version of this book as part of the institute's publication series and for the good collaboration with the staff members responsible for this project, Jane Rafferty and Markus Mößlang, and with Vera Babilon from Oldenbourg Verlag.

The English translation of my book was made possible with a prize awarded through the program Geisteswissenschafen International, sponsored by the Fritz Thyssen Foundation, VG Wort, the Börsenverein des Deutschen Buchhandels, and the German Federal Foreign Office, for which I am sincerely grateful. It has turned out to be my exceptionally good fortune to be included in the publication program of the University of Pennsylvania Press and thereby to work with Peter Agree. I also want to express my appreciation to Dona Geyer, whose translation brings my book to English-language readers. Both are to be very sincerely thanked for all their efforts in connection with this project.

A number of other individuals have helped me in various phases of researching and writing this study. In this context, I extend my sincere thanks to my colleagues and friends Volker Barth, Daniel Maul, Tobias Winstel, Daniela Steffgen, and Tobias Grill for their many helpful suggestions and for the time and energy they spent in reading various versions of the manuscript. I also received valuable scholarly advice, particularly in connection with this publication, from Eric D. Weitz, Hans Günter Hockerts, Peter J. Opitz, Samuel Moyn, and Raphaëlle Branche for which I am exceedingly grateful. In this regard I would particularly like to mention Martin H. Geyer. Both this book and its author are greatly indebted to him for his encouraging receptiveness to various ideas, his innovative insights as expressed in numerous conversations, and the many other ways he demonstrated his support.

My circle of supporters has not been limited to just the academic environment. The strongest pillars of support were, first and foremost, my family. I would especially like to thank my uncle Sepp Brandl, who endured with great fortitude the hours spent correcting my manuscript, and my grandparents Maria and Josef Brandl, who have been a great influence on my life. In conclusion, my final expression of gratitude is directed to the two strongest supporters of my work, my parents Marianne and Waldemar Klose. They followed my project from the beginning with great interest, gave me the encouragement I needed during difficult phases, and always backed me. For this and an infinitude of other reasons, I dedicate this book to them with gratitude and devotion.